THE **MKTG** SOLU

Print + Online

MKTG¹¹ delivers all the key terms and core concepts for the **Principles of Marketing** course.

MKTG Online provides the complete narrative from the printed text with additional interactive media and the unique functionality of **StudyBits**—all available on nearly any device!

What is a StudyBit™? Created through a deep investigation of students' challenges and workflows, the StudyBit™ functionality of **MKTG Online** enables students of different generations and learning styles to study more effectively by allowing them to learn their way. Here's how they work:

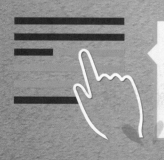

COLLECT WHAT'S IMPORTANT
Create StudyBits as you highlight text, images or take notes!

WEAK
FAIR
STRONG
UNASSIGNED

RATE AND ORGANIZE STUDYBITS
Rate your understanding and use the color-coding to quickly organize your study time and personalize your flashcards and quizzes.

StudyBit™

CORRECT
INCORRECT
INCORRECT
INCORRECT

TRACK/MONITOR PROGRESS
Use Concept Tracker to decide how you'll spend study time and study YOUR way!

85%

PERSONALIZE QUIZZES
Filter by your StudyBits to personalize quizzes or just take chapter quizzes off-the-shelf.

MKTG11
**Charles W. Lamb, Joseph F. Hair, Jr.,
Carl McDaniel**

Senior Vice President, General Manager:
  Balraj Kalsi

Product Manager: Laura Redden

Content/Media Developer: Colin Grover

Product Assistant: Eli Lewis

Marketing Manager: Katie Jergens

Digital Marketing Manager: Chris Walz

Sr. Content Project Manager: Martha Conway

Manufacturing Planner: Ron Montgomery

Sr. Art Director: Bethany Casey

Text Designer: Trish & Ted Knapke: Ke Design

Cover Designer: Lisa Kuhn: Curio Press/Trish &
  Ted Knapke: Ke Design

Cover Images: Vending Machine:
  © arsa35/iStock/Thinkstock; Tennis Shoes:
  © RubberBall Productions/Brand X Pictures/
  Getty Images

Back Cover and Special Page Images:
  Computer and tablet illustration:
  iStockphoto.com/furtaev; Smart Phone
  illustration: iStockphoto.com/dashadima;
  Feedback image: Rawpixel.com/
  Shutterstock.com

Design element: Box of words: StudioM1/
  Thinkstock

Intellectual Property Analyst: Diane Garrity

Intellectual Property Project Manager:
  Erika Mugavin

Production Service: MPS Limited

For product information and technology assistance, contact us at
Cengage Learning Customer & Sales Support, 1-800-354-9706

For permission to use material from this text or product,
submit all requests online at **www.cengage.com/permissions**
Further permissions questions can be emailed to
permissionrequest@cengage.com

Library of Congress Control Number: 2016953544

Student Edition ISBN: 978-1-337-11683-1

Student Edition with Online ISBN: 978-1-337-11680-0

Cengage Learning
20 Channel Center Street
Boston, MA 02210
USA

Cengage Learning is a leading provider of customized learning solutions with employees residing in nearly 40 different countries and sales in more than 125 countries around the world. Find your local representative at **www.cengage.com**

Cengage Learning products are represented in Canada by Nelson Education, Ltd.

To learn more about Cengage Learning Solutions, visit **www.cengage.com**

Purchase any of our products at your local college store or at our preferred online store **www.cengagebrain.com**

Printed in the United States of America
Print Number: 03   Print Year: 2017

LAMB / HAIR / McDANIEL

MKTG 11 BRIEF CONTENTS

Vending Machine: arsa35/iStock/Thinkstock; Tennis Shoes: RubberBall Productions/Brand X Pictures/Getty Images

CONTENTS

Part 1
THE WORLD OF MARKETING

Part 2
ANALYZING MARKET OPPORTUNITIES

Watcharapol Amprasert/Shutterstock.com

Part 3
PRODUCT DECISIONS

misuma/Shutterstock.com

Part 4
DISTRIBUTION DECISIONS

Alexander Kirch/Shutterstock.com

Part 5
PROMOTION AND COMMUNICATION STRATEGIES

Part 6
PRICING DECISIONS

JaysonPhotography/Shutterstock.com

MKTG
ONLINE
STUDY YOUR WAY
WITH STUDYBITS!

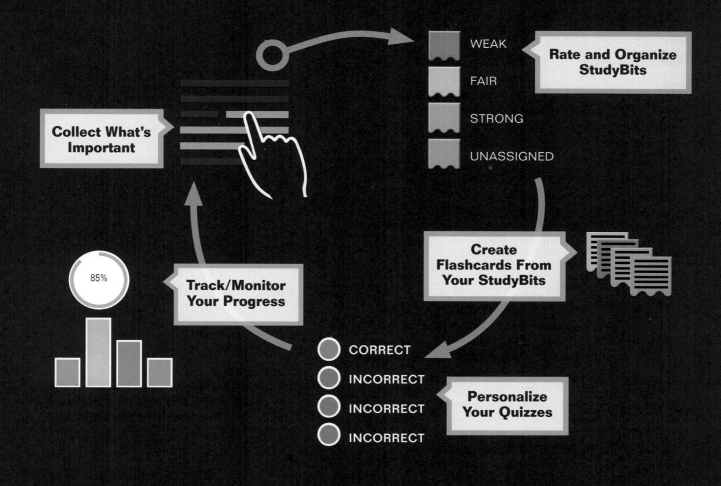

Rate and Organize StudyBits

WEAK

FAIR

STRONG

UNASSIGNED

Collect What's Important

Create Flashcards From Your StudyBits

Track/Monitor Your Progress

85%

CORRECT

INCORRECT

INCORRECT

INCORRECT

Personalize Your Quizzes

4LTR PRESS

1 | An Overview of Marketing

LEARNING OUTCOMES

After studying this chapter, you will be able to…

1-1 Define the term *marketing*

1-2 Describe four marketing management philosophies

1-3 Discuss the differences between sales and market orientations

1-4 Describe several reasons for studying marketing

After you finish this chapter go to **PAGE 13** for **STUDY TOOLS**

1-1 WHAT IS MARKETING?

What does the term *marketing* mean to you? Many people think *marketing* means personal selling. Others think it means advertising. Still others believe marketing has to do with making products available in stores, arranging displays, and maintaining inventories of products for future sales. Actually, marketing includes all of these activities and more.

Marketing has two facets. First, it is a philosophy, an attitude, a perspective, or a management orientation that stresses customer satisfaction. Second, marketing is an organization function and a set of processes used to implement this philosophy.

The American Marketing Association (AMA)'s definition of marketing focuses on the second facet. According to the AMA, **marketing** is the activity, set of institutions, and processes for creating, communicating, delivering, and exchanging offerings that have value for customers, clients, partners, and society at large.[1]

> **marketing** the activity, set of institutions, and processes for creating, communicating, delivering, and exchanging offerings that have value for customers, clients, partners, and society at large

Marketing involves more than just activities performed by a group of people in a defined area or department. In the often-quoted words of David Packard, co-founder of Hewlett-Packard, "Marketing is too important to be left only to the marketing department." Marketing entails processes that focus on delivering value and benefits to customers, not just selling goods, services, and/or ideas. It uses communication, distribution, and pricing strategies to provide customers and other stakeholders with the goods, services, ideas, values, and benefits they desire when and where they want them. It involves building long-term, mutually rewarding relationships when these benefit all parties concerned. Marketing also entails an understanding that organizations have many connected stakeholder "partners,"

including employees, suppliers, stockholders, distributors, and others.

Research shows that companies that consistently reward employees with incentives and recognition are those that perform best, while disgruntled, disengaged workers cost the U.S. economy upward of $350 billion a year in lost productivity.[2] In 2016, Google captured the number one position in *Fortune*'s "100 Best Companies to Work For" for the fifth year in a row. The company pays 100 percent of employees' health care premiums, offers paid sabbaticals, and provides bocce courts, a bowling alley, and twenty-five cafés—all for free. Google also recently increased its parental leave benefits. New parents (including dads, domestic partners, adoptive parents, and surrogate parents) now receive up to twelve weeks of fully paid baby bonding time. Google also provides $500 of "Baby Bonding Bucks" for every new parent to use during the first three months of his or her child's life.[3]

One desired outcome of marketing is an **exchange**—people giving up something in order to receive something else they would rather have. Normally, we think of money as the medium of exchange. We "give up" money to "get" the goods and services we want. Exchange does not require money, however. Two (or more) people may barter or trade such items as baseball cards or oil paintings.

> ## "Marketing is too important to be left only to the marketing department."
>
> —DAVID PACKARD, COFOUNDER OF HEWLETT-PACKARD

An exchange can take place only if the following five conditions exist:

1. There must be at least two parties.
2. Each party has something that might be of value to the other party.
3. Each party is capable of communication and delivery.
4. Each party is free to accept or reject the exchange offer.
5. Each party believes it is appropriate or desirable to deal with the other party.[4]

exchange people giving up something in order to receive something else they would rather have

Google offers many amenities to its employees, part of the reason *Fortune* ranked it as the best company to work for from 2012 to 2016

on the internal capabilities of the firm rather than on the desires and needs of the marketplace. A production orientation means that management assesses its resources and asks these questions: "What can we do best?" "What can our engineers design?" "What is easy to produce, given our equipment?" In the case of a service organization, managers ask, "What services are most convenient for the firm to offer?" and "Where do our talents lie?" The furniture industry is infamous for its disregard of customers and for its slow cycle times. For example, most traditional furniture stores (think Ashley or Haverty's) carry the same styles and varieties of furniture that they have carried for many years. They always produce and stock sofas, coffee tables, arm chairs, and end tables for the living room. Master bedroom suites always include at least a queen- or king-sized bed, two dressers, and two side tables. Regardless of what customers may actually be looking for, this is what they will find at these stores—and they have been so long-lived because what they produce has matched up with customer expectations. This has always been a production-oriented industry.

There is nothing wrong with assessing a firm's capabilities; in fact, such assessments are major considerations in strategic marketing planning (see Chapter 2). A production orientation falls short because it does not consider whether the goods and services that the firm produces most efficiently also meet the needs of the marketplace. Sometimes what a firm can best produce is exactly what the market wants. Apple has a history of production orientation, creating computers, operating systems, and other gadgetry because it can and hoping to sell the result. Some items have found a waiting market (early computers, iPod, iPhone). Other products, like the Newton, one of the first versions of a personal digital assistant (PDA), were simply flops.

In some situations, as when competition is weak or demand exceeds supply, a production-oriented firm can survive and even prosper. More often, however, firms that succeed in competitive markets have a clear understanding that they must first determine what customers want and then produce it, rather than focus on what company management thinks should be produced and hope that the product is something customers want.

Exchange will not necessarily take place even if all these conditions exist, but they must exist for exchange to be possible. For example, suppose you place an advertisement in your local newspaper stating that your used automobile is for sale at a certain price. Several people may call you to ask about the car, some may test-drive it, and one or more may even make you an offer. All five conditions that are necessary for an exchange to occur exist in this scenario. But unless you reach an agreement with a buyer and actually sell the car, an exchange will not take place.

Notice that marketing can occur even if an exchange does not occur. In the example just discussed, you would have engaged in marketing by advertising in the local newspaper even if no one bought your used automobile.

1-2 MARKETING MANAGEMENT PHILOSOPHIES

Four competing philosophies strongly influence an organization's marketing processes. These philosophies are commonly referred to as production, sales, market, and societal marketing orientations.

1-2a Production Orientation

A **production orientation** is a philosophy that focuses

1-2b Sales Orientation

A **sales orientation** is based on the belief that people will buy more goods and services if aggressive sales

techniques are used and that high sales result in high profits. Not only are sales to the final buyer emphasized, but intermediaries are also encouraged to push manufacturers' products more aggressively. To sales-oriented firms, marketing means selling things and collecting money.

The fundamental problem with a sales orientation, as with a production orientation, is a lack of understanding of the needs and wants of the marketplace. Sales-oriented companies often find that, despite the quality of their sales force, they cannot convince people to buy goods or services that are neither wanted nor needed.

1-2c Market Orientation

The **marketing concept** is a simple and intuitively appealing philosophy that articulates a market orientation. It states that the social and economic justification for an organization's existence is the satisfaction of customer wants and needs while meeting organizational objectives. What a business thinks it produces is not of primary importance to its success. Instead, what customers think they are buying—the perceived value—defines a business. The marketing concept includes the following:

- Focusing on customer wants and needs so that the organization can distinguish its product(s) from competitors' offerings
- Integrating all the organization's activities, including production, to satisfy customer wants
- Achieving long-term goals for the organization by satisfying customer wants and needs legally and responsibly

The recipe for success is to develop a thorough understanding of your customers and your competition, your distinctive capabilities that enable your company to execute plans on the basis of this customer understanding, and how to deliver the desired experience using and integrating all of the resources of the firm. For example, Kellogg's recently introduced Open for Breakfast, a forum the company uses to connect with consumers about what they are eating for breakfast. The program is also used to share stories about the foods the company makes and its pledge to care for the environment.[6]

Firms that adopt and implement the marketing concept are said to be **market oriented**, meaning they assume that a sale does not depend on an aggressive sales force but rather on a customer's decision to purchase a product. Achieving a market orientation involves obtaining information about customers, competitors, and markets; examining the information from a total business perspective; determining how to deliver superior customer value; and implementing actions to provide value to customers.

Some firms are known for delivering superior customer value and satisfaction. For example, in 2015, J.D. Power and Associates ranked Jaguar highest in customer satisfaction with dealer service among luxury automotive brands, while Buick ranked highest among mass-market brands.[7] Rankings such as these, as well as word-of-mouth from satisfied customers, drive additional sales for these automotive companies.

Understanding your competitive arena and competitors' strengths and weaknesses is a critical component of a market orientation. This includes assessing what existing or potential competitors intend to do tomorrow and

marketing concept the idea that the social and economic justification for an organization's existence is the satisfaction of customer wants and needs while meeting organizational objectives

market orientation a philosophy that assumes that a sale does not depend on an aggressive sales force but rather on a customer's decision to purchase a product; it is synonymous with the marketing concept

what they are doing today. For example, BlackBerry (formerly Research in Motion) failed to realize it was competing against computer companies as well as telecom companies, and its wireless handsets were quickly eclipsed by offerings from Google, Samsung, and Apple. Had BlackBerry been a market-oriented company, its management might have better understood the changes taking place in the market, seen the competitive threat, and developed strategies to counter the threat. Instead, it reentered the market after a five-year slump with the wholly redesigned BlackBerry 10 operating system and sleek new flagship phones. These new products were fairly well received, but they failed to push BlackBerry back into the smartphone spotlight. By contrast, American Express's success has rested largely on the company's ability to focus on customers and adapt to their changing needs over the past 160 years.[8]

LunaseeStudios/Shutterstock.com

the ozone layer, fuel shortages, pollution, and health issues have caused consumers and legislators to become more aware of the need for companies and consumers to adopt measures that conserve resources and cause less damage to the environment.

A recent Nielsen study found that 55 percent of online consumers across 60 countries support socially/environmentally responsible companies and would pay more for their products. Respondents from Latin American, Asian-Pacific, and Middle Eastern/African areas were willing to pay more than other groups for environmentally friendly products. The key to consumer purchasing lies beyond labels proclaiming sustainability, natural ingredients, or "being green." Customers want sustainable products that perform better than their unsustainable counterparts.[9] Unilever, whose brands include Dove, Lipton, Hellmann's, and Ben & Jerry's, is one company that puts sustainability at the core of its business. It has promised both to cut its environmental footprint in half and to source all its agricultural products in ways that do not degrade the earth by 2020. The company also promotes the well-being of one billion people by producing foods with less salt and fat and has developed campaigns advocating hand washing and teeth brushing.[10]

1-2d Societal Marketing Orientation

The **societal marketing orientation** extends the marketing concept by acknowledging that some products that customers want may not really be in their best interests or the best interests of society as a whole. This philosophy states that an organization exists not only to satisfy customer wants and needs and to meet organizational objectives but also to preserve or enhance individuals' and society's long-term best interests. Marketing products and containers that are less toxic than normal, are more durable, contain reusable materials, or are made of recyclable materials is consistent with a societal marketing orientation. The AMA's definition of marketing recognizes the importance of a societal marketing orientation by including "society at large" as one of the constituencies for which marketing seeks to provide value.

Although the societal marketing concept has been discussed for more than thirty years, it did not receive widespread support until the early 2000s. Concerns such as climate change, the depleting of

1-2e Who Is in Charge?

The Internet and the widespread use of social media have accelerated the shift in power from manufacturers and retailers to consumers and business users. This shift began when customers began using books, electronics, and the Internet to access information, goods, and services. Customers use their widespread knowledge to shop smarter, leading executives such as former Procter & Gamble CEO A. G. Laffey to conclude that "the customer is boss."[11] Founder of Walmart and Sam's Club Sam Walton echoed this sentiment when he reportedly once said, "There is only one boss. The customer. And he can fire everybody in the company from the chairman on down, simply by spending his money somewhere else."[12] The following quotation, attributed to everyone from L.L.Bean founder Leon Leonwood Bean to Mahatma Gandhi, has been a guiding business principle for more than seventy years: "A customer is the most important visitor on our premises. He is not dependent on us. We are dependent on him. He is not an interruption in our work. He is the purpose of it.

societal marketing orientation the idea that an organization exists not only to satisfy customer wants and needs and to meet organizational objectives but also to preserve or enhance individuals' and society's long-term best interests

He is not an outsider in our business. He is part of it. We are not doing him a favor by serving him. He is doing us a favor by giving us an opportunity to do so."[13] And as Internet use and mobile devices become increasingly pervasive, that control will continue to grow. This means that companies must create strategy from the outside in by offering distinct and compelling customer value.[14] This can be accomplished only by carefully studying customers and using deep market insights to inform and guide companies' outside-in view.[15]

1-3 DIFFERENCES BETWEEN SALES AND MARKET ORIENTATIONS

The differences between sales and market orientations are substantial. The two orientations can be compared in terms of five characteristics: the organization's focus, the firm's business, those to whom the product is directed, the firm's primary goal, and the tools used to achieve the organization's goals.

1-3a The Organization's Focus

Personnel in sales-oriented firms tend to be inward looking, focusing on selling what the organization makes rather than making what the market wants. Many of the historic sources of competitive advantage—technology, innovation, economies of scale—allowed companies to focus their efforts internally and prosper. Today, many successful firms derive their competitive advantage from

Northfoto/Shutterstock.com

Shake Shack appeals to higher-income customers with high-quality products and superior customer service.

an external, market-oriented focus. A market orientation has helped companies such as Zappos.com and Bob's Red Mill Natural Foods outperform their competitors. These companies put customers at the center of their business in ways most companies do poorly or not at all.

CUSTOMER VALUE The relationship between benefits and the sacrifice necessary to obtain those benefits is known as **customer value**. Customer value is not simply a matter of high quality. A high-quality product that is available only at a high price will not be perceived as a good value, nor will bare-bones service or low-quality goods selling for a low price. Price is a component of value (a $4,000 handbag is perceived as being more luxurious and of higher quality than one selling for $100), but low price is not the same as good value. Instead, customers value goods and services that are of the quality they expect and that are sold at prices they are willing to pay.

Value can be used to sell a Mercedes-Benz as well as a Tyson frozen chicken dinner. In other words, value is something that shoppers of all markets and at all income levels look for. Lower-income consumers are price sensitive, but they will pay for products if they deliver a benefit that is worth the money.[16] Conversely, higher-income customers may value—and be willing to pay for—high-quality products and superior customer service. Shake Shack is a fast-casual burger restaurant that targets people who care about how their food tastes and where it comes from. The company sells its burgers for higher-than-average prices, but it uses humanely raised, antibiotic- and hormone-free meat that is ground fresh from full muscle cuts instead of scraps. This meat is shipped fresh—not frozen—to all of Shake Shack's locations. Further, the company pledges not to use genetically modified organisms (GMOs) in its hamburger buns. Shake Shack's superior service, which founder Danny Meyer calls "enlightened hospitality," places a major emphasis on the happiness of its employees and customers. This service philosophy is based on the belief that white-tablecloth service is not just for expensive restaurants.[17]

CUSTOMER SATISFACTION The customers' evaluation of a good or service in terms of whether that good or service has met their needs and expectations is called **customer satisfaction**. Failure to meet needs and expectations results in dissatisfaction with the good or service. Some companies, in their passion to drive down costs, have

customer value the relationship between benefits and the sacrifice necessary to obtain those benefits

customer satisfaction customers' evaluation of a good or service in terms of whether it has met their needs and expectations

damaged their relationships with customers. Bank of America, Comcast, Dish Network, and AT&T are examples of companies where executives lost track of the delicate balance between efficiency and service.[18] Firms that have a reputation for delivering high levels of customer satisfaction do things differently from their competitors. Top management is obsessed with customer satisfaction, and employees throughout the organization understand the link between their job and satisfied customers.

The culture of the organization is to focus on delighting customers rather than on selling products.

Coming back from customer dissatisfaction can be tough, but there are some key ways that companies begin to improve customer satisfaction. Forrester Research discovered that when companies experience gains in the firm's Customer Experience Index (CxPi), they have implemented one of two major changes. Aetna, a major health insurance provider, executed the first type of

MARKETERS INTERESTED IN CUSTOMER VALUE . . .

▶ **Offer products that perform:** This is the bare minimum requirement. After grappling with the problems associated with its Vista operating system, Microsoft listened to its customers and made drastic changes for Windows 7, which received greatly improved reviews. Microsoft's subsequent release, Windows 8, performed even better than Windows 7, but consumers were much slower to embrace the operating system's incremental improvements.

▶ **Earn trust:** A stable base of loyal customers can help a firm grow and prosper. To attract customers, online eyewear company Coastal.com offers a First Pair Free program, whereby new customers receive their first pair of prescription eyeglass for free. Moreover, Coastal.com offers 366-day returns and encourages its staff members to do whatever it takes to ensure that customers are delighted by a smooth and stress-free experience. Coastal.com's dedication to earning customers' trust is evident—in 2013, the company received the STELLA Service elite seal for excellence in outstanding customer service.[19]

▶ **Avoid unrealistic pricing:** E-marketers are leveraging Internet technology to redefine how prices are set and negotiated. With lower costs, e-marketers can often offer lower prices than their brick-and-mortar counterparts. The enormous popularity of auction sites such as eBay and the customer-bid model used by Priceline and uBid.com illustrates that online customers are interested in bargain prices. In fact, as smartphone usage grows, brick-and-mortar stores are up against customers who compare prices using their smartphones and purchase items for less online while standing in the store.

▶ **Give the buyer facts:** Today's sophisticated consumer wants informative advertising and knowledgeable salespeople. It is becoming very difficult for business marketers to differentiate themselves from competitors. Rather than trying to sell products, salespeople need to find out what the customer needs, which is usually a combination of friendliness, understanding, fairness, control, options, and

Northfoto/Shutterstock.com

information.[20] In other words, salespeople need to start with the needs of the customer and work toward the solution.

▶ **Offer organization-wide commitment to great service:** Upscale fashion retailer Nordstrom is widely known for its commitment to superior service. The two overarching tenets that drive Nordstrom's legendary service are attention to detail and empowering employees. Attention to detail is demonstrated through activities such as walking customers to items they can't find instead of simply pointing them in the right direction and answering the department phone after no more than two rings. The company empowers employees by allowing them to rely on their good judgment rather than on a manager or a binder full of rules. Nordstrom employees at the store level are encouraged to build and cultivate personal relationships with their customers and to take care of them as they see fit.[21]

▶ **Co-create:** Some companies and products allow customers to help create their own experience. For example, Case-Mate, a firm that makes form-fitting cases for cell phones, laptops, and other personal devices, allows customers to design their own cases by uploading their own photos. Customers who do not have designs of their own can manipulate art from designers using the "design with" feature at case-mate.com. Either way, customers produce completely unique covers for their devices.

change—changing its decentralized, part-time customer service group into a full-time, centralized customer service team. Aetna's CxPi score rose six points in one year. Office Depot executed the second type of change—addressing customer "pain points" and making sure that what customers need is always available to them. By streamlining its supply chain and adding more stylish office products, Office Depot satisfied business customers and female shoppers, increasing its CxPi by nine points.[22]

BUILDING RELATIONSHIPS Attracting new customers to a business is only the beginning. The best companies view new-customer attraction as the launching point for developing and enhancing a long-term relationship. Companies can expand market share in three ways: attracting new customers, increasing business with existing customers, and retaining current customers. Building relationships with existing customers directly addresses two of the three possibilities and indirectly addresses the other.

Relationship marketing is a strategy that focuses on keeping and improving relationships with current customers. It assumes that many consumers and business customers prefer to have an ongoing relationship with one organization rather than switch continually among providers in their search for value. Chicago-based software company Baseline decided to focus its marketing budget on helping current customers get more out of the software they already have rather than targeting new customers. The company would rather expand current customers' awareness of what is possible with its products than focus on short term sales.[23] This long-term focus on customer needs is a hallmark of relationship marketing.

Most successful relationship marketing strategies depend on customer-oriented personnel, effective training programs, employees with the authority to make decisions and solve problems, and teamwork.

Customer-Oriented Personnel For an organization to be focused on building relationships with customers, employees' attitudes and actions must be customer oriented. An employee may be the only contact a particular customer has with the firm. In that customer's eyes, the employee *is* the firm. Any person, department, or division that is not customer oriented weakens the positive image of the entire organization. For example, a potential customer who is greeted discourteously may well assume that the employee's attitude represents the whole firm.

Customer-oriented personnel come from an organizational culture that supports its people. Marriott, a multi-billion dollar worldwide hotel chain, believes that treating employees well contributes to good customer service. The company has been among Fortune's "100 Best Companies

In 2015, *Fast Company* named Starbucks' Howard Schultz as he top customer-focused CEO in the United States. Schultz has taken several steps to improve the customer experience at Starbucks, such as installing espresso machines with lower profiles so that baristas can look customers in the eyes while making drinks.

to Work For" every year since the magazine introduced the list in 1998. For example, during the recent recession, Marriott ensured that all of its employees kept their benefits despite shorter shifts. For its focus on customer satisfaction, Marriott received the number three ranking on MSN.com's 2014 Customer Service Hall of Fame.[24]

Some companies, such as Coca-Cola, Delta Air Lines, Hershey, Kellogg, Nautilus, and Sears, have appointed chief customer officers (CCOs). These customer advocates provide an executive voice for customers and report directly to the CEO. Their responsibilities include ensuring that the company maintains a customer-centric culture and that all company employees remain focused on delivering customer value.

The Role of Training Leading marketers recognize the role of employee training in customer service and relationship building. Sales staff at the Container Store receive more than 240 hours of training and generous benefits compared to an industry average of 8 hours of training and modest benefits.

relationship marketing a strategy that focuses on keeping and improving relationships with current customers

Empowerment In addition to training, many market-oriented firms are giving employees more authority to solve customer problems on the spot. The term used to describe this delegation of authority is **empowerment**. Employees develop ownership attitudes when they are treated like part-owners of the business and are expected to act the part. These employees manage themselves, are more likely to work hard, account for their own performance and that of the company, and take prudent risks to build a stronger business and sustain the company's success. In order to empower its workers, the Ritz-Carlton chain of luxury hotels developed a set of twelve "Service Values" guidelines. These brief, easy-to-understand guidelines include statements such as "I am empowered to create unique, memorable and personal experiences for our guests" and "I own and immediately resolve guest problems." The twelve Service Values are printed on cards distributed to employees, and each day a particular value is discussed at length in Ritz-Carlton team meetings. Employees talk about what the value means to them and offer examples of how the value can be put into practice that day.[25]

Teamwork Many organizations that are frequently noted for delivering superior customer value and providing high levels of customer satisfaction, such as Southwest Airlines and Walt Disney World, assign employees to teams and teach them team-building skills. **Teamwork** entails collaborative efforts of people to accomplish common objectives. Job performance, company performance, product value, and customer satisfaction all improve when people in the same department or work group begin supporting and assisting each other and emphasize cooperation instead of competition. Performance is also enhanced when cross-functional teams align their jobs with customer needs. For example, if a team of telecommunications service representatives is working to improve interaction with customers, back-office people such as computer technicians or training personnel can become

empowerment delegation of authority to solve customers' problems quickly—usually by the first person the customer notifies regarding a problem

teamwork collaborative efforts of people to accomplish common objectives

part of the team, with the ultimate goal of delivering superior customer value and satisfaction.

1-3b The Firm's Business

A sales-oriented firm defines its business (or mission) in terms of goods and services. A market-oriented firm defines its business in terms of the benefits its customers seek. People who spend their money, time, and energy expect to receive benefits, not just goods and services. This distinction has enormous implications. For example, Microsoft's original mission was "A computer on every desk and in every home," which is product centered. Its current, benefit-oriented mission is "To empower every person and every organization on the planet to achieve more."[26] Answering the question "What is this firm's business?" in terms of the benefits customers seek, instead of goods and services, offers at least three important advantages:

- It ensures that the firm keeps focusing on customers and avoids becoming preoccupied with goods, services, or the organization's internal needs.

- It encourages innovation and creativity by reminding people that there are many ways to satisfy customer wants.

- It stimulates an awareness of changes in customer desires and preferences so that product offerings are more likely to remain relevant.

Because of the limited way it defines its business, a sales-oriented firm often misses opportunities to serve customers whose wants can be met through a wide range of product offerings instead of through specific products. For example, in 1989, 220-year-old Britannica had estimated revenues of $650 million and a worldwide sales force of 7,500. Just five years later, after three consecutive years of losses, the sales force had collapsed to as few as 280 representatives. How did this respected company sink so low? Britannica managers saw that competitors were beginning to use CD-ROMs to store huge masses of information but chose to ignore the

An emphasis on cooperation over competition can help a company's performance improve. That is why many companies have moved to using teams to get jobs done.

Rawpixel/Shutterstock.com

new computer technology as well as an offer to team up with Microsoft. In 2012, the company announced that it would stop printing its namesake books and instead focus on selling its reference works to subscribers through its website and apps for tablets and smartphones.[27]

Having a market orientation and a focus on customer wants does not mean offering customers everything they want. It is not possible, for example, to profitably manufacture and market automobile tires that will last for 100,000 miles for twenty-five dollars. Furthermore, customers' preferences must be mediated by sound professional judgment as to how to deliver the benefits they seek. Consumers have a limited set of experiences. They are unlikely to request anything beyond those experiences because they are not aware of benefits they may gain from other potential offerings. For example, before the Internet, many people thought that shopping for some products was boring and time-consuming but could not express their need for electronic shopping.

1-3c Those to Whom the Product Is Directed

A sales-oriented organization targets its products at "everybody" or "the average customer." A market-oriented organization aims at specific groups of people. The fallacy of developing products directed at the average user is that relatively few average users actually exist. Typically, populations are characterized by diversity. An average is simply a midpoint in some set of characteristics. Because most potential customers are not "average," they are not likely to be attracted to an average product marketed to the average customer. Consider the market for shampoo as one simple example. There are shampoos for oily hair, dry hair, and dandruff. Some shampoos remove the gray or color hair. Special shampoos are marketed for infants and elderly people. There are even shampoos for people with average or normal hair (whatever that is), but this is a fairly small portion of the total market for shampoo.

A market-oriented organization recognizes that different customer groups want different features or benefits. It may therefore need to develop different goods, services, and promotional appeals. A market-oriented organization carefully analyzes the market and divides it into groups of people who are fairly similar in terms of selected characteristics. Then the organization develops marketing programs that will bring about mutually satisfying exchanges with one or more of those groups. For example, Toyota developed a series of tongue-in-cheek videos and interactive web pages featuring comedian Michael Showalter to advertise the 2013 Yaris subcompact sedan. Toyota used absurdist humor and an ironic slogan ("It's a car!") to appeal to Internet-savvy teens and young adults—a prime market for inexpensive subcompact cars.[28]

CUSTOMER RELATIONSHIP MANAGEMENT Beyond knowing to whom they are directing their products or services, companies must also develop a deeper understanding of their customers. One way of doing this is through *customer relationship management.* **Customer relationship management (CRM)** is a company-wide business strategy designed to optimize profitability, revenue, and customer satisfaction by focusing on highly defined and precise customer groups. This is accomplished by organizing the company around customer segments, establishing and tracking customer interactions with the company, fostering customer-satisfying behaviors, and linking all processes of the company from its customers through its suppliers. The difference between CRM and traditional mass marketing can be compared to shooting a rifle versus a shotgun. Instead of scattering messages far and wide across the spectrum of mass media (the shotgun approach), CRM marketers now are homing in on ways to effectively communicate with each customer (the rifle approach).

Companies that adopt CRM systems are almost always market oriented, customizing product and service offerings based on data generated through interactions between the customer and the company. This strategy transcends all functional areas of the business, producing an internal system where all of the company's decisions and actions are a direct result of customer information. We will examine specific applications of CRM in several chapters throughout this book.

The emergence of **on-demand marketing** is taking CRM to a new level. As technology evolves and becomes more sophisticated, consumer expectations of their decision- and buying-related experiences have risen. Consumers (1) want to interact anywhere, anytime; (2) want to do new things with varied kinds of information in ways that create value; (3) expect data stored about them to be targeted specifically to their needs or to personalize their experiences; and (4) expect all interactions with a company to be easy. In response to these expectations, companies are developing new ways to integrate and personalize each stage of a customer's decision journey, which in turn should increase relationship-related behaviors. On-demand marketing delivers relevant experiences throughout the

customer relationship management (CRM) a company-wide business strategy designed to optimize profitability, revenue, and customer satisfaction by focusing on highly defined and precise customer groups

on-demand marketing delivering relevant experiences, integrated across both physical and virtual environments, throughout the consumer's decision and buying process

consumer's decision and buying process that are integrated across both physical and virtual environments. Trends such as the growth of mobile connectivity, better-designed websites, inexpensive communication through technology, and advances in handling big data have allowed companies to start designing on-demand marketing programs that appeal to consumers. For on-demand marketing to be successful, companies must deliver high-quality experiences across all touch points with the customer, including sales, service, product use, and marketing.

An example of on-demand marketing is Commonwealth Bank of Australia's new smartphone app that integrates and personalizes the house hunting experience. A prospective homebuyer starts by taking a picture of a house he or she likes. Using special software and location-based technology, the app finds the house and provides the list price and other information, connects with the buyer's financial data, and determines whether the buyer can be preapproved for a mortgage. This fast series of interactions decreases the hassle of searching real-estate agents' sites for a house and then connecting with agents, banks, and/or mortgage brokers—a process that traditionally takes up to a week.[29]

1-3d The Firm's Primary Goal

A sales-oriented organization seeks to achieve profitability through sales volume and tries to convince potential customers to buy, even if the seller knows that the customer and product are mismatched. Sales-oriented organizations place a higher premium on making a sale than on developing a long-term relationship with a customer. In contrast, the ultimate goal of most market-oriented organizations is to make a profit by creating customer value, providing customer satisfaction, and building long-term relationships with customers. The exception is so-called nonprofit organizations that exist to achieve goals other than profits. Nonprofit organizations can and should adopt a market orientation. Nonprofit organization marketing is explored further in Chapter 12.

1-3e Tools the Organization Uses to Achieve Its Goals

Sales-oriented organizations seek to generate sales volume through intensive promotional activities, mainly personal selling and advertising. In contrast, market-oriented organizations recognize that promotion decisions are only one of four basic marketing mix decisions that must be made: product decisions, place (or distribution) decisions, promotion decisions, and pricing decisions. A market-oriented organization recognizes that each of these four

Blend Images/Shutterstock.com

Using the correct tools for the job will help an organization achieve its goals. Marketing tools for success are covered throughout this book.

components is important. Furthermore, market-oriented organizations recognize that marketing is not just a responsibility of the marketing department. Interfunctional coordination means that skills and resources throughout the organization are needed to create, communicate, and deliver superior customer service and value.

1-3f A Word of Caution

This comparison of sales and market orientations is not meant to belittle the role of promotion, especially personal selling, in the marketing mix. Promotion is the means by which organizations communicate with present and prospective customers about the merits and characteristics of their organization and products. Effective promotion is an essential part of effective marketing. Salespeople who work for market-oriented organizations are generally perceived by their customers to be problem solvers and important links to supply sources and new products. Chapter 18 examines the nature of personal selling in more detail.

1-4 WHY STUDY MARKETING?

Now that you understand the meaning of the term *marketing*, why it is important to adopt a marketing orientation, and how organizations implement this philosophy, you may be asking, "What's in it for me?" or "Why should I study marketing?" These are important questions whether you are majoring in a business field other than marketing (such as accounting, finance, or management information systems) or a nonbusiness field (such as journalism, education, or agriculture). There are several important reasons to study marketing: Marketing plays an important role in society, marketing is important to businesses, marketing offers outstanding career opportunities, and marketing affects your life every day.

1-4a Marketing Plays an Important Role in Society

The total population of the United States exceeds 320 million people.[30] Think about how many transactions are needed each day to feed, clothe, and shelter a population of this size. The number is huge. And yet it all works quite well, partly because the well-developed U.S. economic system efficiently distributes the output of farms and factories. A typical U.S. family, for example, consumes two and a half tons of food a year.[31] Marketing makes food available when we want it, in desired quantities, at accessible locations, and in sanitary and convenient packages and forms (such as instant and frozen foods).

1-4b Marketing Is Important to Businesses

The fundamental objectives of most businesses are survival, profits, and growth. Marketing contributes directly to achieving these objectives. Marketing includes the following activities, which are vital to business organizations: assessing the wants and satisfactions of present and potential customers, designing and managing product offerings, determining prices and pricing policies, developing distribution strategies, and communicating with present and potential customers.

All businesspeople, regardless of specialization or area of responsibility, need to be familiar with the terminology and fundamentals of accounting, finance, management, and marketing. People in all business areas need to be able to communicate with specialists in other areas. Furthermore, marketing is not just a job done by people in a marketing department. Marketing is a part of the job of everyone in the organization. Therefore, a basic understanding of marketing is important to all businesspeople.

1-4c Marketing Offers Outstanding Career Opportunities

Between one-fourth and one-third of the entire civilian workforce in the United States performs marketing activities. Marketing offers great career opportunities in such areas as professional selling, marketing research, advertising, retail buying, distribution management, product management, product development, and wholesaling. Marketing career opportunities also exist in a variety of nonbusiness organizations, including hospitals, museums, universities, the armed forces, and various government and social service agencies.

1-4d Marketing in Everyday Life

Marketing plays a major role in your everyday life. You participate in the marketing process as a consumer of goods and services. About half of every dollar you spend pays for marketing costs, such as marketing research, product development, packaging, transportation, storage, advertising, and sales expenses. By developing a better understanding of marketing, you will become a better-informed consumer. You will better understand the buying process and be able to negotiate more effectively with sellers. Moreover, you will be better prepared to demand satisfaction when the goods and services you buy do not meet the standards promised by the manufacturer or the marketer.

STUDY TOOLS 1

LOCATED AT BACK OF THE TEXTBOOK
☐ Rip out Chapter Review Card

LOCATED AT WWW.CENGAGEBRAIN.COM
☐ Review Key Terms Flashcards and create your own
☐ Track your knowledge and understanding of key concepts in marketing
☐ Complete practice and graded quizzes to prepare for tests
☐ Complete interactive content within the MKTG Online experience
☐ View the chapter highlight boxes within the MKTG Online experience

2 | Strategic Planning for Competitive Advantage

LEARNING OUTCOMES

After studying this chapter, you will be able to…

2-1 Understand the importance of strategic planning

2-2 Define strategic business units (SBUs)

2-3 Identify strategic alternatives and know a basic outline for a marketing plan

2-4 Develop an appropriate business mission statement

2-5 Describe the components of a situation analysis

2-6 Identify sources of competitive advantage

2-7 Explain the criteria for stating good marketing objectives

2-8 Discuss target market strategies

2-9 Describe the elements of the marketing mix

2-10 Explain why implementation, evaluation, and control of the marketing plan are necessary

2-11 Identify several techniques that help make strategic planning effective

After you finish this chapter go to **PAGE 29** for **STUDY TOOLS**

2-1 THE NATURE OF STRATEGIC PLANNING

Strategic planning is the managerial process of creating and maintaining a fit between the organization's objectives and resources and the evolving market opportunities. The goal of strategic planning is long-run profitability and growth. Thus, strategic decisions require long-term commitments of resources.

A strategic error can threaten a firm's survival. On the other hand, a good strategic plan can help protect and grow the firm's resources. For instance, if the March of Dimes had decided to focus only on fighting polio, the organization would no longer exist because polio is widely viewed as a conquered disease. The March of Dimes survived by making the strategic decision to switch to fighting birth defects.

Strategic marketing management addresses two questions: (1) What is the organization's main activity at a particular time? (2) How will it reach its goals? Here are some examples of strategic decisions:

- In an effort to halt decreasing sales and compete with other fast food and fast causal chains, McDonald's has unveiled plans to allow customers to customize their orders for the first time. This offering, called Create a Taste, lets customers use their tablet computers to choose toppings for their sandwiches.[1]

- In 2016, Walmart decided to close its small-format Walmart Express locations. These stores were designed to target geographical areas that its larger stores could not, such as urban centers. Profitability proved a challenge at these locations because they

> **strategic planning** the managerial process of creating and maintaining a fit between the organization's objectives and resources and the evolving market opportunities

were not big enough to sell higher-margin products like appliances and apparel.[2]

- Following founder Howard Schultz's vision of maintaining an entrepreneurial approach to strategy, Starbucks recently opened the Starbucks Reserve Roastery and Tasting Room in Seattle to appeal to upscale coffee lovers. The company also has plans to expand its food and beverage menu.[3]

All these decisions have affected or will affect each organization's long-run course, its allocation of resources, and ultimately its financial success. In contrast, an operating decision, such as changing the package design for Post Grape-Nuts cereal or altering the sweetness of a Kraft salad dressing, probably will not have a big impact on the long-run profitability of the company.

2-2 STRATEGIC BUSINESS UNITS

Large companies may manage a number of very different businesses, called strategic business units (SBUs). Each SBU has its own rate of return on investment, growth potential, and associated

> "There are a lot of great ideas that have come and gone in [the digital advertising] industry. Im-plementation many times is more important than the actual idea."
>
> —DAVID MOORE, CEO OF 24/7 REAL MEDIA

risks, and requires its own strategies and funding. When properly created, an SBU has the following characteristics:

- A distinct mission and a specific target market
- Control over its resources
- Its own competitors

strategic business unit (SBU) a subgroup of a single business or collection of related businesses within the larger organization

- A single business or a collection of related businesses
- Plans independent of the other SBUs in the total organization.

In theory, an SBU should have its own resources for handling basic business functions: accounting, engineering, manufacturing, and marketing. In practice, however, because of company tradition, management philosophy, and production and distribution economies, SBUs sometimes share manufacturing facilities, distribution channels, and even top managers.

EXHIBIT 2.1	ANSOFF'S OPPORTUNITY MATRIX	
	Present Product	**New Product**
Present Market	*Market Penetration* Starbucks sells more coffee to customers who register their reloadable Starbucks cards.	*Product Development* Starbucks develops powdered instant coffee called Via.
New Market	*Market Development* Starbucks opens stores in Brazil and Chile.	*Diversification* Starbucks launches Hear Music and buys Ethos Water.

2-3 STRATEGIC ALTERNATIVES

There are several tools available that a company, or SBU, can use to manage the strategic direction of its portfolio of businesses. Three of the most commonly used tools are Ansoff's strategic opportunity matrix, the Boston Consulting Group model, and the General Electric model. Selecting which strategic alternative to pursue depends on which of two philosophies a company maintains about when to expect profits—right away or after increasing market share. In the long run, market share and profitability are compatible goals. For example, Amazon lost hundreds of millions of dollars its first few years, and the company posted quarterly net losses as recently as 2013. Amazon's primary goal is market share—not profit. It sacrifices short-term profit for long-term market share, and thus larger long-term profits.[4]

2-3a Ansoff's Strategic Opportunity Matrix

One method for developing alternatives is Ansoff's strategic opportunity matrix (see Exhibit 2.1), which matches products with markets. Firms can explore these four options:

market penetration
a marketing strategy that tries to increase market share among existing customers

market development
a marketing strategy that entails attracting new customers to existing products

product development
a marketing strategy that entails the creation of new products for present markets

- **Market penetration:** A firm using the **market penetration** alternative would try to increase market share among existing customers. Fast-food giant McDonald's introduced all day Breakfast in 2015 in an attempt to

Television personality Brody Jenner serves up some Egg McMuffins at the 2016 Daytona 500 in honor of McDonald's new all day Breakfast.

encourage its breakfast-loving customers to visit the restaurant more often.[5]

- **Market development:** **Market development** means attracting new customers to existing products. Ideally, new uses for old products stimulate additional sales among existing customers while also bringing in new buyers. McDonald's, for example, has opened restaurants in Russia, China, and Italy and is eagerly expanding into Eastern European countries. In the nonprofit arena, the growing emphasis on continuing education and executive development by colleges and universities is a market development strategy.

- **Product development:** A **product development** strategy entails the creation of new products for present markets. In 2016, Abbott Laboratories introduced a new line of healthy snacks called Curate Bars to complement its Ensure and Glucerna meal-replacement lines and its Similac infant formula line. These bars feature unique flavors, rich textures, and healthy ingredients to appeal to the growing health-conscious market.[6]

Gerardo Mora/Getty Images

- **Diversification:** Diversification is a strategy of increasing sales by introducing new products into new markets. For example, Harley-Davidson recently launched two new motorcycle models made specifically for women after the company saw a 30 percent increase in sales to female riders over the last decade. The new bikes are sleeker than men's bikes and have smaller hand grips, lower seats, and different foot peg positions to appeal to female riders.[7] A diversification strategy can be risky when a firm is entering unfamiliar markets. However, it can be very profitable when a firm is entering markets with little or no competition.

2-3b The Innovation Matrix

Critics of Ansoff's matrix mention that the matrix does not reflect the reality of how businesses grow—that modern businesses plan growth in a more fluid manner based on current capabilities rather than the clear-cut sectors outlined by the opportunity matrix. To reflect this, Bansi Nagji and Geoff Tuff, global innovation managers at Monitor Group, have recently developed a system that enables a company to see exactly what types of assets need to be developed and what types of markets are possible to grow into (or create) based on the company's core capabilities, as shown in Exhibit 2.2.

EXHIBIT 2.2   INNOVATION MATRIX

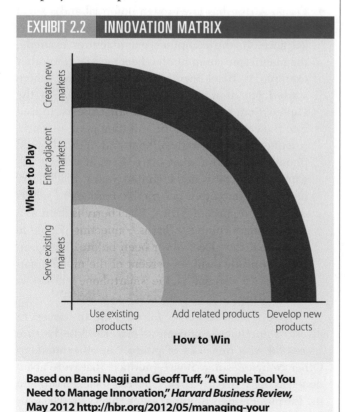

Based on Bansi Nagji and Geoff Tuff, "A Simple Tool You Need to Manage Innovation," *Harvard Business Review*, May 2012 http://hbr.org/2012/05/managing-your-innovation-portfolio/ar/1 (accessed June 1, 2012).

The layout of the innovation matrix demonstrates that as a company moves away from its core capabilities (the lower left) it traverses a range of change and innovation rather than choosing one of the four sectors in Ansoff's matrix. These ranges are broken down into three levels:

1. **Core Innovation:** Represented by the yellow circle in Exhibit 2.2, these decisions implement changes that use existing assets to provide added convenience to existing customers and potentially entice customers from other brands. Packaging changes, such as Tide's laundry detergent pods, fall into this category.

2. **Adjacent Innovation:** Represented by the orange arc in Exhibit 2.2, these decisions are designed to take company strengths into new markets. This space uses existing abilities in new ways. For example, Botox, the popular cosmetic drug, was originally developed to treat intestinal problems and to treat crossed eyes. Leveraging the drug into cosmetic medicine has dramatically increased the market for Botox.

3. **Transformational Innovation:** Represented by the red arc in Exhibit 2.2, these decisions result in brand-new markets, products, and often new businesses. The company must rely on new, unfamiliar assets to develop the type of breakthrough decisions that fall in this category. The wearable, remote-controlled GoPro documentary video camera is a prime example of developing an immature market with a brand-new experience.[8]

2-3c The Boston Consulting Group Model

Management must find a balance among the SBUs that yields the overall organization's desired growth and profits with an acceptable level of risk. Some SBUs generate large amounts of cash, and others need cash to foster growth. The challenge is to balance the organization's portfolio of SBUs for the best long-term performance.

To determine the future cash contributions and cash requirements expected for each SBU, managers can use the Boston Consulting Group's portfolio matrix. The **portfolio matrix** classifies each SBU by its present or forecast growth and market share. The underlying assumption is that market share and profitability are strongly linked. The measure of market share used in the portfolio approach is *relative market share*, the ratio between the company's share and the share of the largest competitor.

diversification a strategy of increasing sales by introducing new products into new markets

portfolio matrix a tool for allocating resources among products or strategic business units on the basis of relative market share and market growth rate

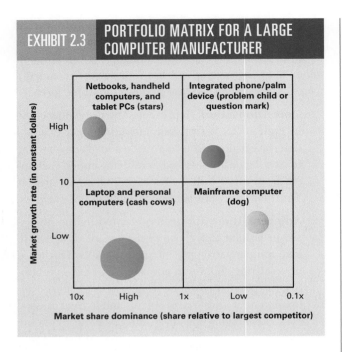

EXHIBIT 2.3 — PORTFOLIO MATRIX FOR A LARGE COMPUTER MANUFACTURER

Netbooks, handheld computers, and tablet PCs (stars)

Integrated phone/palm device (problem child or question mark)

Laptop and personal computers (cash cows)

Mainframe computer (dog)

Market growth rate (in constant dollars)

High

10

Low

10x   High   1x   Low   0.1x

Market share dominance (share relative to largest competitor)

For example, if a firm has a 50 percent share and the competitor has five percent, the ratio is 10 to 1. If a firm has a 10 percent market share and the largest competitor has 20 percent, the ratio is 0.5 to 1.

Exhibit 2.3 is a hypothetical portfolio matrix for a computer manufacturer. The size of the circle in each cell of the matrix represents dollar sales of the SBU relative to dollar sales of the company's other SBUs. The portfolio matrix breaks SBUs into four categories:

- **Stars:** A **star** is a fast-growing market leader. For example, the iPad is one of Apple's stars. Star SBUs usually have large profits but need lots of cash to finance rapid growth. The best marketing tactic is to protect existing market share by reinvesting earnings in product improvement, better distribution, more promotion, and production efficiency. Management must capture new users as they enter the market.

- **Cash cows:** A **cash cow** is an SBU that generates more cash than it needs to maintain its market share. It is in a low-growth market, but the product has a dominant market share. Personal computers and laptops are categorized as cash cows in

Exhibit 2.3. The basic strategy for a cash cow is to maintain market dominance by being the price leader and making technological improvements in the product. Managers should resist pressure to extend the basic line unless they can dramatically increase demand. Instead, they should allocate excess cash to the product categories where growth prospects are the greatest. For example, Heinz has two cash cows: ketchup and Weight Watchers frozen dinners.

- **Problem children:** A **problem child**, also called a **question mark**, shows rapid growth but poor profit margins. It has a low market share in a high-growth industry. Problem children need a great deal of cash. Without cash support, they eventually become dogs. The strategy options are to invest heavily to gain better market share, acquire competitors to get the necessary market share, or drop the SBU. Sometimes a firm can reposition the products of the SBU to move them into the star category. Elixir guitar strings, made by W. L. Gore & Associates, maker of Gore-Tex and Glide floss, were originally tested and marketed to Walt Disney theme parks to control puppets. After trial and failure, Gore repositioned and marketed heavily to musicians, who have loved the strings ever since.

- **Dogs:** A **dog** has low growth potential and a small market share. Most dogs eventually leave the marketplace. In the computer manufacturer example, the mainframe computer has become a dog. Another example is BlackBerry's smartphone line, which started out as a star for its manufacturer in the United States. Over time, the BlackBerry moved into the cash cow category, and then more recently, to a question mark, as the iPhone and Android-based phones captured market share. Even if it never regains its star status in the United States, BlackBerry has moved into other geographic markets to sell its devices. In parts of Africa, Blackberry is seen as a revolutionary company that is connecting people in a way that they have never been before. The company currently owns 48 percent of the mobile market and 70 percent of the smartphone market in South Africa.[9]

While typical strategies for dogs are to harvest or divest, sometimes companies—like BlackBerry—are successful with this class of product in other markets. Other companies may revive products that were abandoned as dogs. In early 2014, Church's Chicken brought its Purple Pepper dipping sauce back to the market using a "Back by Popular Demand" promotional campaign.[10]

star in the portfolio matrix, a business unit that is a fast-growing market leader

cash cow in the portfolio matrix, a business unit that generates more cash than it needs to maintain its market share

problem child (question mark) in the portfolio matrix, a business unit that shows rapid growth but poor profit margins

dog in the portfolio matrix, a business unit that has low growth potential and a small market share

Kevin Mazur/Getty Images

Despite a popular co-branding venture with media juggernaut Oprah Winfrey, Starbucks began shuttering its Teavana Tea Bars in 2016.

After classifying the company's SBUs in the matrix, the next step is to allocate future resources for each. The four basic strategies are to:

- **Build:** If an organization has an SBU that it believes has the potential to be a star (probably a problem child at present), building would be an appropriate goal. The organization may decide to give up short-term profits and use its financial resources to achieve this goal. Apple postponed further work on the iPad to pursue the iPhone. The wait paid off when Apple was able to repurpose much of the iOS software and the iPhone's App Store for the iPad, making development less expensive and getting the product into the marketplace more quickly.[11]

- **Hold:** If an SBU is a very successful cash cow, a key goal would surely be to hold or preserve market share so that the organization can take advantage of the very positive cash flow. Fashion-based reality series *Project Runway* is a cash cow for the Lifetime cable television channel and parent companies Hearst and Disney. New seasons and spin-off editions such as *Project Runway: Under the Gunn* are expected for years to come.[12]

- **Harvest:** This strategy is appropriate for all SBUs except those classified as stars. The basic goal is to increase the short-term cash return without too much concern for the long-run impact. It is especially worthwhile when more cash is needed from a cash cow with long-run prospects that are unfavorable because of a low market growth rate. For instance, Lever Brothers has been harvesting Lifebuoy soap for a number of years with little promotional backing.

- **Divest:** Getting rid of SBUs with low shares of low-growth markets is often appropriate. Problem children and dogs are most suitable for this strategy. Starbucks, for example, is in the process of closing the unprofitable Teavana Tea Bars it acquired in 2012.[13]

2-3d The General Electric Model

The third model for selecting strategic alternatives was originally developed by General Electric (GE). The dimensions used in this model—market attractiveness and company strength—are richer and more complex than those used in the Boston Consulting Group model, but are harder to quantify.

Exhibit 2.4 presents the GE model. The horizontal axis, Business Position, refers to how well positioned the organization is to take advantage of market opportunities. Business position answers questions such as: Does the firm have the technology it needs to effectively penetrate the market? Are its financial resources adequate? Can manufacturing costs be held down below those of the competition? Can the firm cope with change? The vertical axis measures the attractiveness of a market, which is expressed both quantitatively and qualitatively. Some attributes of an attractive market are high profitability, rapid growth, a lack of government regulation, consumer insensitivity to a price increase, a lack of competition, and availability of technology. The grid is divided into three overall attractiveness zones for each dimension: high, medium, and low.

Those SBUs (or markets) that have low overall attractiveness (indicated by the red cells in Exhibit 2.4) should be avoided if the organization is not already serving them. If the firm is in these markets, it should either

EXHIBIT 2.4	GENERAL ELECTRIC MODEL		
Market Attractiveness High	CAUTIOUSLY INVEST	INVEST/GROW	INVEST/GROW
Medium	HARVEST/DIVEST	CAUTIOUSLY INVEST	INVEST/GROW
Low	HARVEST/DIVEST	HARVEST/DIVEST	CAUTIOUSLY INVEST
	Low	Medium	High
	Business Position		

harvest or divest those SBUs. The organization should selectively maintain markets with medium attractiveness (indicated by the yellow cells in Exhibit 2.4). If attractiveness begins to slip, then the organization should withdraw from the market.

Conditions that are highly attractive—a thriving market plus a strong business position (the green cells in Exhibit 2.4)—are the best candidates for investment. For example, when Beats Electronics launched a new line of over-the-ear headphones in 2008, the consumer headphone market was strong but steady, led by inexpensive, inconspicuous earbuds. Four years later, the heavily branded and premium-priced Beats by Dr. Dre—helmed by legendary hip-hop producer Dr. Dre—captured 40 percent of all U.S. headphone sales, fueling market growth from $1.8 billion in 2011 to $2.4 billion in 2012.[14]

2-3e The Marketing Plan

Based on the company's or SBU's overall strategy, marketing managers can create a marketing plan for individual products, brands, lines, or customer groups. **Planning** is the process of anticipating future events and determining strategies to achieve organizational objectives in the future. **Marketing planning** involves designing activities relating to marketing objectives and the changing marketing environment. Marketing planning is the basis for all marketing strategies and decisions. Issues such as product lines, distribution channels, marketing communications, and pricing are all delineated in the **marketing plan**. The marketing plan is a written document that acts as a guidebook of marketing activities for the marketing manager. In this chapter, you will learn the importance of writing a marketing plan and the types of information contained in a marketing plan.

2-3f Why Write a Marketing Plan?

By specifying objectives and defining the actions required to attain them, you can provide in a marketing plan the basis by which actual and expected performance can be compared. Marketing can be one of the most expensive and complicated business activities, but it is also one of the most important. The written marketing plan provides clearly stated activities that help employees and managers understand and work toward common goals.

Writing a marketing plan allows you to examine the marketing environment in conjunction with the inner workings of the business. Once the marketing plan is written, it serves as a reference point for the success of future activities. Finally, the marketing plan allows the marketing manager to enter the marketplace with an awareness of possibilities and problems.

2-3g Marketing Plan Elements

Marketing plans can be presented in many different ways. Most businesses need a written marketing plan because a marketing plan is large and can be complex. The details about tasks and activity assignments may be lost if communicated orally. Regardless of the way a marketing plan is presented, some elements are common to all marketing plans. Exhibit 2.5 shows these elements, which include defining the business mission, performing a situation analysis, defining objectives, delineating a target market, and establishing components of the marketing mix. Other elements that may be included in a plan are budgets, implementation timetables, required marketing research efforts, or elements of advanced strategic planning.

2-3h Writing the Marketing Plan

The creation and implementation of a complete marketing plan will allow the organization to achieve marketing objectives and succeed. However, the marketing plan is only as good as the information it contains and the effort, creativity, and thought that went into its creation. Having a good marketing information system and a wealth of competitive intelligence (covered in Chapter 9) is critical to a thorough and accurate situation analysis. The role of managerial intuition is also important in the creation and selection of marketing strategies. Managers must weigh any information against its accuracy and their own judgment when making a marketing decision.

Note that the overall structure of the marketing plan (Exhibit 2.5) should not be viewed as a series of sequential planning steps. Many of the marketing plan elements are decided simultaneously and in conjunction with one another. Further, every marketing plan has different content, depending on the organization, its mission, objectives, targets, and marketing mix components. There is not one single correct format for a marketing plan. Many organizations have their own distinctive format or terminology for creating a marketing

planning the process of anticipating future events and determining strategies to achieve organizational objectives in the future

marketing planning designing activities relating to marketing objectives and the changing marketing environment

marketing plan a written document that acts as a guidebook of marketing activities for the marketing manager

EXHIBIT 2.5   ELEMENTS OF A MARKETING PLAN

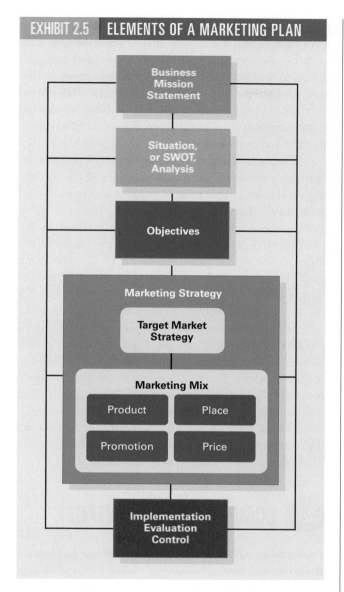

Business
Mission
Statement

Situation,
or SWOT,
Analysis

Objectives

Marketing Strategy

Target Market
Strategy

Marketing Mix

| Product | Place |
| Promotion | Price |

Implementation
Evaluation
Control

Care must be taken when stating a business mission. Companies like Procter and Gamble have earned the right to be broad in their mission's wording.

plan. Every marketing plan should be unique to the firm for which it was created. Remember, however, that although the format and order of presentation should be flexible, the same types of questions and topic areas should be covered in any marketing plan.

 2-4 ## DEFINING THE BUSINESS MISSION

The foundation of any marketing plan is the firm's mission statement, which answers the question "What business are we in?" The way a firm defines its business mission profoundly affects the firm's long-run resource allocation, profitability, and survival. The mission statement is based on a careful analysis of benefits sought by present and potential customers and an analysis of existing and anticipated environmental conditions.

The firm's mission statement establishes boundaries for all subsequent decisions, objectives, and strategies.

A mission statement should focus on the market or markets the organization is attempting to serve rather than on the good or service offered. Otherwise, a new technology may quickly make the good or service obsolete and the mission statement irrelevant to company functions. Business mission statements that are stated too narrowly suffer from **marketing myopia**—defining a business in terms of goods and services rather than in terms of the benefits customers seek. In this context, *myopia* means narrow, short-term thinking. For example, Frito-Lay defines its mission as being in the snack-food business rather than in the corn chip business. The mission of sports teams is not just to play games but also to serve the interests of the fans.

Alternatively, business missions may be stated too broadly. "To provide products of superior quality and value that improve the lives of the world's consumers" is probably too broad a mission statement for any firm except Procter & Gamble. Care must be taken when stating what business a firm is in. For example, the mission of Ben & Jerry's centers on three important aspects of its ice cream business: (1) Product: "To make, distribute and sell the finest quality all natural ice cream and euphoric concoctions with a continued commitment to incorporating

mission statement a statement of the firm's business based on a careful analysis of benefits sought by present and potential customers and an analysis of existing and anticipated environmental conditions

marketing myopia defining a business in terms of goods and services rather than in terms of the benefits customers seek

Bryan Busovicki/Shutterstock.com

wholesome, natural ingredients and promoting business practices that respect the Earth and the Environment"; (2) Economic: "To operate the Company on a sustainable financial basis of profitable growth, increasing value for our stakeholders and expanding opportunities for development and career growth for our employees"; and (3) Social: "To operate the Company in a way that actively recognizes the central role that business plays in society by initiating innovative ways to improve the quality of life locally, nationally, and internationally."[15] By correctly stating the business mission in terms of the benefits that customers seek, the foundation for the marketing plan is set. Many companies are focusing on designing more appropriate mission statements because these statements are frequently displayed on the companies' websites.

2-5 CONDUCTING A SITUATION ANALYSIS

Marketers must understand the current and potential environment in which the product or service will be marketed. A situation analysis is sometimes referred to as a **SWOT analysis**—that is, the firm should identify its internal strengths (**S**) and weaknesses (**W**) and also examine external opportunities (**O**) and threats (**T**).

When examining internal strengths and weaknesses, the marketing manager should focus on organizational resources such as production costs, marketing skills, financial resources, company or brand image, employee capabilities, and available technology. For example, when Dell's stock fell sharply throughout the mid-2010s, management needed to examine strengths and weaknesses in the company and its competition. Dell had a $6 billion server business (strength), but the shrinking PC market accounted for a significant 24 percent of sales (weakness). Competitors like IBM and Hewlett-Packard (HP) were moving heavily into software and consulting, so to avoid them, Dell moved into the enterprise IT and services market. The shift was not enough to offset poor sales in other areas, however, and in 2013, the company entered buyout talks with private investors such as Blackstone and company founder Michael S. Dell. Dell ultimately went private and continues to sell computers, software, and related services.[16] Another issue to consider in this section of the marketing plan is the historical background of the firm— its sales and profit history.

When examining external opportunities and threats, marketing managers must analyze aspects of the marketing environment. This process is called **environmental scanning**—the collection and interpretation of information about forces, events, and relationships in the external environment that may affect the future of the organization or the implementation of the marketing plan. Environmental scanning helps identify market opportunities and threats and provides guidelines for the design of marketing strategy. Increasing competition from overseas firms and the fast growth of digital technology essentially ended Kodak's consumer film business. After emerging from bankruptcy, Kodak has repositioned the firm as a smaller, business-to-business company that offers commercial printing and digital imaging services.[17] The six most often studied macroenvironmental forces are social, demographic, economic, technological, political and legal, and competitive. These forces are examined in detail in Chapter 4.

2-6 COMPETITIVE ADVANTAGE

Performing a SWOT analysis allows firms to identify their **competitive advantage.** A competitive advantage is a set of unique features of a company and its products that are perceived by the target market as significant and superior to those of the competition. It is the factor or factors that cause customers to patronize a firm and not the competition. There are three types of competitive advantage: cost, product/service differentiation, and niche.

2-6a Cost Competitive Advantage

Cost leadership can result from obtaining inexpensive raw materials, creating an efficient scale of plant operations, designing products for ease of manufacture, controlling overhead costs, and avoiding marginal customers. Southwest Airlines has been successful at bringing down airfares through its short route point-to-point business model, no-frills service, single flight strategy, and highly productive employees.[18] Having a **cost competitive advantage** means being the low-cost competitor in an industry while

SWOT analysis identifying internal strengths (S) and weaknesses (W) and also examining external opportunities (O) and threats (T)

environmental scanning collection and interpretation of information about forces, events, and relationships in the external environment that may affect the future of the organization or the implementation of the marketing plan

competitive advantage a set of unique features of a company and its products that are perceived by the target market as significant and superior to those of the competition

cost competitive advantage being the low-cost competitor in an industry while maintaining satisfactory profit margins

maintaining satisfactory profit margins. Costs can be reduced in a variety of ways:

- **Experience curves:** Experience curves tell us that costs decline at a predictable rate as experience with a product increases. The experience curve effect encompasses a broad range of manufacturing, marketing, and administrative costs. Experience curves reflect learning by doing, technological advances, and economies of scale. Firms like Boeing use historical experience curves as a basis for predicting and setting prices. Experience curves allow management to forecast costs and set prices based on anticipated costs as opposed to current costs.

- **Efficient labor:** Labor costs can be an important component of total costs in low-skill, labor-intensive industries such as product assembly and apparel manufacturing. Many U.S. publishers and software developers send data entry, design, and formatting tasks to India, where skilled engineers are available at lower overall cost.

- **No-frills goods and services:** Marketers can lower costs by removing frills and options from a product or service. Southwest Airlines, for example, offers low fares but no seat assignments or meals. Low costs give Southwest a higher load factor and greater economies of scale, which, in turn, mean lower prices.

- **Government subsidies:** Governments can provide grants and interest-free loans to target industries. Such government assistance enabled Japanese semiconductor manufacturers to become global leaders.

- **Product design:** Cutting-edge design technology can help offset high labor costs. BMW is a world leader in designing cars for ease of manufacture and assembly. Reverse engineering—the process of disassembling a product piece by piece to learn its components and obtain clues as to the manufacturing process—can also mean savings. Reverse engineering a low-cost competitor's product can save research and design costs. The car industry often uses reverse engineering.

- **Reengineering:** Reengineering entails fundamental rethinking and redesign of business processes to achieve dramatic improvements in critical measures of performance. It often involves reorganizing functional departments such as sales, engineering, and production into cross-disciplinary teams.

Ivan Cholakov/Shutterstock.com

- **Production innovations:** Production innovations such as new technology and simplified production techniques help lower the average cost of production. Technologies such as computer-aided design (CAD) and computer-aided manufacturing (CAM) and increasingly sophisticated robots help companies such as Boeing, Ford, and General Electric reduce their manufacturing costs.

- **New methods of service delivery:** Medical expenses have been substantially lowered by the use of outpatient surgery and walk-in clinics. Online-only magazines deliver great savings, and even some print magazines are exploring ways to go online to save material and shipping costs.

2-6b Product/Service Differentiation Competitive Advantage

Because cost competitive advantages are subject to continual erosion, product/service differentiation tends to provide a longer-lasting competitive advantage. The durability of this strategy tends to make it more attractive to many top managers. A **product/service differentiation competitive advantage** exists when a firm provides something that is unique and valuable to buyers beyond simply offering a lower price than that of the competition. Examples include brand names (Lexus), a strong dealer network (Caterpillar for construction work), product reliability (Maytag appliances), image (Neiman Marcus in retailing), or service (Zappos). Uniqlo, a fast-fashion retailer with 840 stores in

experience curves curves that show costs declining at a predictable rate as experience with a product increases

product/service differentiation competitive advantage the provision of something that is unique and valuable to buyers beyond simply offering a lower price than that of the competition

Japan and 1,170 stores outside Japan, is among the top five global clothing retailers. The company provides high-quality casual wear at reasonable prices. It differentiates itself from the competition in several ways. First, it develops and brands innovative fabrics like HeatTech, which turns moisture into heat and has air pockets in the fabric to retain that heat. HeatTech is thin and comfortable, and enables stylish designs different from the standard apparel made for warmth. Second, Uniqlo emphasizes the in-store experience, which involves carefully hiring, training, and managing all touchpoints with the customer. Every morning, for example, Uniqlo employees practice interacting with shoppers. Finally, the company has a recycling effort that moves millions of articles of discarded Uniqlo clothing to needy people around the world.[19]

2-6c Niche Competitive Advantage

A **niche competitive advantage** seeks to target and effectively serve a single segment of the market (see Chapter 8). For small companies with limited resources that potentially face giant competitors, niche targeting may be the only viable option. A market segment that has good growth potential but is not crucial to the success of major competitors is a good candidate for developing a niche strategy.

Many companies using a niche strategy serve only a limited geographic market. Stew Leonard's is an extremely successful but small grocery store chain found only in Connecticut and New York. Blue Bell Ice cream is available in only about 26 percent of the nation's supermarkets, but it ranks as one of the top three best-selling ice creams in the country.[20]

The Chef's Garden, a 225-acre Ohio farm, specializes in growing and shipping rare artisan vegetables directly to its customers. Chefs from all over the world call to order or request a unique item, which is grown and shipped by the Chef's Garden. The farm provides personal services and specialized premium vegetables that aren't available anywhere else and relies on its customers to supply it with ideas for what they would like to be able to offer in their restaurants. The excellent service and feeling of contribution keep chefs coming back.[21]

niche competitive advantage the advantage achieved when a firm seeks to target and effectively serve a small segment of the market

sustainable competitive advantage an advantage that cannot be copied by the competition

2-6d Building Sustainable Competitive Advantage

The key to having a competitive advantage is the ability

Customers have a loyalty to Caterpillar due to its strong network of dealerships.

to sustain that advantage. A **sustainable competitive advantage** is one that cannot be copied by the competition. For example, Amazon is the undisputed leader of online retailing. The company has achieved sustainable competitive advantage through its ability to offer the lowest prices, the widest variety of products, and a well-developed, efficient delivery network. In addition, Amazon has a massive number of users with credit cards on file, making the purchase process quick and easy for customers.[22] In contrast, when Datril was introduced into the pain-reliever market, it was touted as being exactly like Tylenol, only cheaper. Tylenol responded by lowering its price, thus destroying Datril's competitive advantage and ability to remain on the market. In this case, low price was not a sustainable competitive advantage. Without a competitive advantage, target customers do not perceive any reason to patronize an organization instead of its competitors.

The notion of competitive advantage means that a successful firm will stake out a position unique in some manner from its rivals. Imitation by competitors indicates a lack of competitive advantage and almost ensures mediocre performance. Moreover, competitors rarely stand still, so it is not surprising that imitation causes managers to feel trapped in a seemingly endless game of catch-up. They are regularly surprised by the new accomplishments of their rivals.

Rather than copy competitors, companies need to build their own competitive advantages. The sources of tomorrow's competitive advantages are the skills and assets of the organization. Assets include patents, copyrights, locations, equipment, and technology that are superior

AP Images/Mark Lennihan

Speedy low-cost shipping has long been a competitive advantage for Amazon. While drone delivery may be a ways off, the company currently offers free same-day delivery for Amazon Prime members in more than two dozen markets as well as two-hour delivery on Amazon Prime Now orders.

MARKETING OBJECTIVES SHOULD BE...

▶ **Realistic:** Managers should develop objectives that have a chance of being met. For example, it may be unrealistic for start-up firms or new products to command dominant market share, given other competitors in the marketplace.

▶ **Measurable:** Managers need to be able to quantitatively measure whether or not an objective has been met. For example, it would be difficult to determine success for an objective that states, "To increase sales of cat food." If the company sells one percent more cat food, does that mean the objective was met? Instead, a specific number should be stated, "To increase sales of Purina brand cat food from $300 million to $345 million."

▶ **Time specific:** By what time should the objective be met? "To increase sales of Purina brand cat food between January 1, 2017 and December 31, 2017."

▶ **Compared to a benchmark:** If the objective is to increase sales by 15 percent, it is important to know the baseline against which the objective will be measured. Will it be current sales? Last year's sales? For example, "To increase sales of Purina brand cat food by 15 percent over 2016 sales of $300 million."

to those of the competition. Skills are functions such as customer service and promotion that the firm performs better than its competitors. Marketing managers should continually focus the firm's skills and assets on sustaining and creating competitive advantages.

Remember, a sustainable competitive advantage is a function of the speed with which competitors can imitate a leading company's strategy and plans. Imitation requires a competitor to identify the leader's competitive advantage, determine how it is achieved, and then learn how to duplicate it.

2-7 SETTING MARKETING PLAN OBJECTIVES

Before the details of a marketing plan can be developed, objectives for the plan must be stated. Without objectives, there is no basis for measuring the success of marketing plan activities.

A **marketing objective** is a statement of what is to be accomplished through marketing activities.

A strong marketing objective for Purina might be: "To increase sales of Purina brand cat food between January 1, 2017 and December 31, 2017 by 15 percent, compared to 2016 sales of $300 million."

Objectives must be consistent with and indicate the priorities of the organization. Specifically, objectives flow

from the business mission statement to the rest of the marketing plan.

Carefully specified objectives serve several functions. First, they communicate marketing management philosophies and provide direction for lower-level marketing managers so that marketing efforts are integrated and pointed in a consistent direction. Objectives also serve as motivators by creating something for employees to strive for. When objectives are attainable and challenging, they motivate those charged with achieving the objectives. Additionally, the process of writing specific objectives forces executives to clarify their thinking. Finally, objectives form a basis for control: the effectiveness of a plan can be gauged in light of the stated objectives.

2-8 DESCRIBING THE TARGET MARKET

Marketing strategy in-volves the activities of se-lecting and describing

marketing objective a statement of what is to be accomplished through marketing activities

marketing strategy the activities of selecting and describing one or more target markets and developing and maintaining a marketing mix that will produce mutually satisfying exchanges with target markets

one or more target markets and developing and maintaining a marketing mix that will produce mutually satisfying exchanges with target markets.

2-8a Target Market Strategy

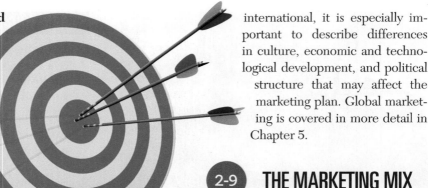

Style-photography/Shutterstock.com

A market segment is a group of individuals or organizations who share one or more characteristics. They therefore may have relatively similar product needs. For example, parents of newborn babies need formula, diapers, and special foods.

The target market strategy identifies the market segment or segments on which to focus. This process begins with a **market opportunity analysis (MOA)**—the description and estimation of the size and sales potential of market segments that are of interest to the firm and the assessment of key competitors in these market segments. After the firm describes the market segments, it may target one or more of them. There are three general strategies for selecting target markets.

Target markets can be selected by appealing to the entire market with one marketing mix, concentrating on one segment, or appealing to multiple market segments using multiple marketing mixes. The characteristics, advantages, and disadvantages of each strategic option are examined in Chapter 8. Target markets could be eighteen- to twenty-five-year-old females who are interested in fashion (*Vogue* magazine), people concerned about sugar and calories in their soft drinks (Diet Pepsi), or parents without the time to potty train their children (Booty Camp classes where kids are potty trained).

Any market segment that is targeted must be fully described. Demographics, psychographics, and buyer behavior should be assessed. Buyer behavior is covered in Chapters 6 and 7. If segments are differentiated by ethnicity, multicultural aspects of the marketing mix should be examined. If the target market is international, it is especially important to describe differences in culture, economic and technological development, and political structure that may affect the marketing plan. Global marketing is covered in more detail in Chapter 5.

2-9 THE MARKETING MIX

The term **marketing mix** refers to a unique blend of product, place (distribution), promotion, and pricing strategies (often referred to as the **four Ps**) designed to produce mutually satisfying exchanges with a target market. The marketing manager can control each component of the marketing mix, but the strategies for all four components must be blended to achieve optimal results. Any marketing mix is only as good as its weakest component. For example, the first pump toothpastes were distributed over cosmetics counters and failed. Not until pump toothpastes were distributed the same way as tube toothpastes did the products succeed. The best promotion and the lowest price cannot save a poor product. Similarly, excellent products with poor placing, pricing, or promotion will likely fail.

Successful marketing mixes have been carefully designed to satisfy target markets. At first glance, McDonald's and Wendy's may appear to have roughly identical marketing mixes because they are both in the fast-food hamburger business. However, McDonald's has been most successful at targeting parents with young children for lunchtime meals, whereas Wendy's targets the adult crowd for lunches and dinner. McDonald's has playgrounds, Ronald McDonald the clown, and children's Happy Meals. Wendy's has salad bars, carpeted restaurants, and no playgrounds.

Variations in marketing mixes do not occur by chance. Astute marketing managers devise marketing strategies to gain advantages over competitors and best serve the needs and wants of a particular target market segment. By manipulating elements of the marketing mix, marketing managers can fine-tune the customer offering and achieve competitive success.

2-9a Product Strategies

Of the four Ps, the marketing mix typically starts with the product. The heart of the marketing mix, the starting point, is the product offering and product strategy. It is hard to design a place strategy, decide on a promotion campaign, or set a price without knowing the product to be marketed.

market opportunity analysis (MOA) the description and estimation of the size and sales potential of market segments that are of interest to the firm and the assessment of key competitors in these market segments

marketing mix (four Ps) a unique blend of product, place (distribution), promotion, and pricing strategies designed to produce mutually satisfying exchanges with a target market

The product includes not only the physical unit but also its package, warranty, after-sale service, brand name, company image, value, and many other factors. A Godiva chocolate has many product elements: the chocolate itself, a fancy gold wrapper, a customer satisfaction guarantee, and the prestige of the Godiva brand name. We buy things not only for what they do (benefits) but also for what they mean to us (status, quality, or reputation).

Products can be tangible goods such as computers, ideas like those offered by a consultant, or services such as medical care. Products should also offer customer value. Product decisions are covered in Chapters 10 and 11, and services marketing is detailed in Chapter 12.

2-9b Place (Distribution) Strategies

Place, or distribution, strategies are concerned with making products available when and where customers want them. Would you rather buy a kiwi fruit at the 24-hour grocery store within walking distance or fly to Australia to pick your own? A part of this P—place— is physical distribution, which involves all the business activities concerned with storing and transporting raw materials or finished products. The goal is to make sure products arrive in usable condition at designated places when needed. Place strategies are covered in Chapters 13 and 14.

2-9c Promotion Strategies

Promotion includes advertising, public relations, sales promotion, and personal selling. Promotion's role in the marketing mix is to bring about mutually satisfying exchanges with target markets by informing, educating, persuading, and reminding them of the benefits of an organization or a product. A good promotion strategy, like using a beloved cartoon character such as Sponge-Bob SquarePants to sell gummy snacks, can dramatically increase sales. Each element of this P—promotion—is coordinated and managed with the others to create a promotional blend or mix. These integrated marketing communications activities are described in Chapters 16, 17, and 18. Technology-driven and social media aspects of promotional marketing are covered in Chapter 19.

2-9d Pricing Strategies

Price is what a buyer must give up in order to obtain a product. It is often the most flexible of the four Ps— the quickest element to change. Marketers can raise or lower prices more frequently and easily than they can change other marketing mix variables. Price is an important competitive weapon and is very important to the organization because price multiplied by the number of units sold equals total revenue for the firm. Pricing decisions are covered in Chapters 20 and 21.

2-10 FOLLOWING UP ON THE MARKETING PLAN

One of the keys to success overlooked by many businesses is to actively follow up on the marketing plan. The time spent researching, developing, and writing a useful and accurate marketing plan goes to waste if the plan is not used by the organization. One of the best ways to get the most out of a marketing plan is to correctly implement it. Once the first steps to implementation are taken, evaluation and control will help guide the organization to success as laid out by the marketing plan.

2-10a Implementation

Implementation is the process that turns a marketing plan into action assignments and ensures that these assignments are executed in a way that accomplishes the plan's objectives. Implementation activities may involve detailed job assignments, activity descriptions, time lines, budgets, and lots of communication. Implementation requires delegating authority and responsibility, determining a time frame for completing tasks, and allocating resources. Sometimes a strategic plan also requires task force management. A *task force* is a tightly organized unit under the direction of a manager who, usually, has broad authority. A task force is established to accomplish a single goal or mission and thus works against a deadline.

Implementing a plan has another dimension: gaining acceptance. New plans mean change, and change creates resistance. One reason people resist change is that they fear they will lose something. For example, when new-product research is taken away from marketing research and given to a new-product department, the director of marketing research will naturally resist this loss of part of his or her domain. Misunderstanding and lack of trust also create opposition to change, but effective communication through open discussion and teamwork can be one way of overcoming resistance to change.

Although implementation is essentially "doing what you said you were going to do," many organizations repeatedly experience failures in strategy implementation. Brilliant marketing plans are doomed to fail if they are not properly implemented. These detailed communications may or may not be part of the written marketing plan. If they are not part of the plan, they should be specified elsewhere as soon as the plan has been communicated. Strong, forward-thinking leadership can overcome resistance to change, even in large, highly integrated companies where change seems very unlikely.

2-10b Evaluation and Control

After a marketing plan is implemented, it should be evaluated. **Evaluation** entails gauging the extent to which marketing objectives have been achieved during the specified time period. Four common reasons for failing to achieve a marketing objective are unrealistic marketing objectives, inappropriate marketing strategies in the plan, poor implementation, and changes in the environment after the objective was specified and the strategy was implemented.

Once a plan is chosen and implemented, its effectiveness must be monitored. **Control** provides the mechanisms for evaluating marketing results in light of the plan's objectives and for correcting actions that do not help the organization reach those objectives within budget guidelines. Firms need to establish formal and informal control programs to make the entire operation more efficient.

Perhaps the broadest control device available to marketing managers is the **marketing audit**—a thorough, systematic, periodic evaluation of the objectives, strategies, structure, and performance of the marketing organization. A marketing audit helps management allocate marketing resources efficiently.

Although the main purpose of the marketing audit is to develop a full profile of the organization's marketing effort and to provide a basis for developing and revising the marketing plan, it is also an excellent way to improve communication and raise the level of marketing consciousness within the organization. It is a useful vehicle for selling the philosophy and techniques of strategic marketing to other members of the organization.

2-10c Post-audit Tasks

After the audit has been completed, three tasks remain. First, the audit should profile existing weaknesses and inhibiting factors, as well as the firm's strengths and the new opportunities available to it. Recommendations have to be judged and prioritized so that those with the potential to contribute most to improved marketing performance can be implemented first. The usefulness of the data also depends on the auditor's skill in interpreting and presenting the data so decision makers can quickly grasp the major points.

The second task is to ensure that the role of the audit has been clearly communicated. It is unlikely that the suggestions will require radical change in the way

implementation the process that turns a marketing plan into action assignments and ensures that these assignments are executed in a way that accomplishes the plan's objectives

evaluation gauging the extent to which the marketing objectives have been achieved during the specified time period

control provides the mechanisms for evaluating marketing results in light of the plan's objectives and for correcting actions that do not help the organization reach those objectives within budget guidelines

marketing audit a thorough, systematic, periodic evaluation of the objectives, strategies, structure, and performance of the marketing organization

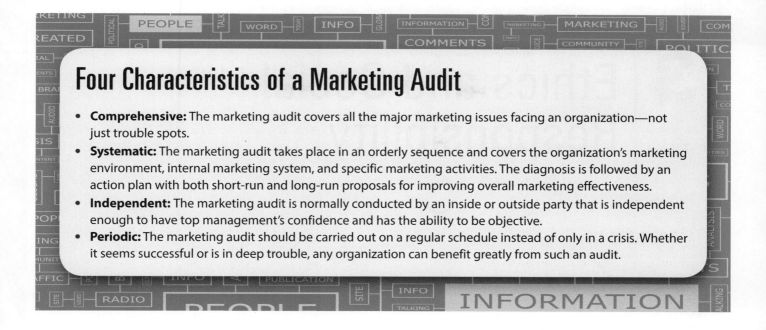

Four Characteristics of a Marketing Audit

- **Comprehensive:** The marketing audit covers all the major marketing issues facing an organization—not just trouble spots.
- **Systematic:** The marketing audit takes place in an orderly sequence and covers the organization's marketing environment, internal marketing system, and specific marketing activities. The diagnosis is followed by an action plan with both short-run and long-run proposals for improving overall marketing effectiveness.
- **Independent:** The marketing audit is normally conducted by an inside or outside party that is independent enough to have top management's confidence and has the ability to be objective.
- **Periodic:** The marketing audit should be carried out on a regular schedule instead of only in a crisis. Whether it seems successful or is in deep trouble, any organization can benefit greatly from such an audit.

the firm operates. The audit's main role is to address the question "Where are we now?" and to suggest ways to improve what the firm already does.

The final post-audit task is to make someone accountable for implementing recommendations. All too often, reports are presented, applauded, and filed away to gather dust. The person made accountable should be someone who is committed to the project and who has the managerial power to make things happen.

 2-11 **EFFECTIVE STRATEGIC PLANNING**

Effective strategic planning requires continual attention, creativity, and management commitment. Strategic planning should not be an annual exercise in which managers go through the motions and forget about strategic planning until the next year. It should be an ongoing process because the environment is continually changing and the firm's resources and capabilities are continually evolving.

Sound strategic planning is based on creativity. Managers should challenge assumptions about the firm and the environment and establish new strategies. For example, major oil companies developed the concept of the gasoline service station in an age when cars needed frequent and rather elaborate servicing. These major companies held on to the full-service approach, but independents were quick to respond to new realities and moved to lower-cost self-service and convenience store operations. Major companies took several decades to catch up.

Perhaps the most critical element in successful strategic planning is top management's support and participation. Google, for example, strongly supports educational and leadership programs for employees, as well as opportunities to address management with ideas and concerns.[24]

STUDY TOOLS **2**

LOCATED AT BACK OF THE TEXTBOOK
- ☐ Rip out Chapter Review Card

LOCATED AT WWW.CENGAGEBRAIN.COM
- ☐ Review Key Terms Flashcards and create your own
- ☐ Track your knowledge and understanding of key concepts in marketing
- ☐ Complete practice and graded quizzes to prepare for tests
- ☐ Complete interactive content within the MKTG Online experience
- ☐ View the chapter highlight boxes within the MKTG Online experience

3 | Ethics and Social Responsibility

LEARNING OUTCOMES

After studying this chapter, you will be able to...

- **3-1** Explain the determinants of a civil society
- **3-2** Explain the concept of ethical behavior
- **3-3** Describe ethical behavior in business
- **3-4** Discuss corporate social responsibility
- **3-5** Describe the arguments for and against society responsibility
- **3-6** Explain cause-related marketing

After you finish this chapter go to **PAGE 46** for **STUDY TOOLS**

3-1 DETERMINANTS OF A CIVIL SOCIETY

Have you ever stopped to think about the social glue that binds society together? That is, what factors keep people and organizations from running amok and doing harm, and what factors create order in a society like ours? The answer lies in **social control**, defined as any means used to maintain behavioral norms and regulate conflict.[1] **Behavioral norms** are standards of proper or acceptable behavior. Social control is part of your life at every level, from your family, to your local community, to the nation, to the global civilization. Several modes of social control are important to marketing:

1. **Ethics:** **Ethics** are the moral principles or values that generally govern the conduct of an individual or a group. Ethical rules and guidelines, along with customs and traditions, provide principles of right action.

2. **Laws:** Often, ethical rules and guidelines are codified into law. Laws created by governments are then enforced by governmental authority. This is how the dictum "Thou shall not steal" has become part of formal law throughout the land. Law, however, is not a

perfect mechanism for ensuring good corporate and employee behavior. This is because laws often address the lowest common denominator of socially acceptable behavior. In other words, just because something is legal does not mean that it is ethical. For example, Log Cabin All Natural Table Syrup has no artificial flavors or colors, nor does it contain preservatives or high-fructose corn syrup. It is sold in a traditional jug similar to those used by many Vermont maple sugar

Rawpixel.com/Shutterstock.com

makers, complete with a picture of a snow-covered log cabin on the label, evoking the woods of the Green Mountain State. However, while Log Cabin All Natural Table Syrup may indeed be "natural" and "authentic," as the jug suggests, it isn't maple syrup. The top ingredients are brown rice syrup, water, and sugar.[2] Log Cabin does not explicitly state that the product contains real maple syrup, but the packaging certainly suggests it. Is this ethical? What's your opinion?

3. **Formal and Informal Groups:** Businesses, professional organizations (such as the American Marketing Association and the American Medical Association), and clubs (such as Shriners and Ducks Unlimited) all have codes of conduct. These codes prescribe acceptable and desired behaviors of their members.

4. **Self-regulation:** Self-regulation involves the voluntary acceptance of standards established by nongovernmental entities, such as the American Association of Advertising Agencies (AAAA) or the National Association of Manufacturers. The AAAA has a self-regulation arm that deals with deceptive advertising. Other associations have regulations relating to child labor, environmental issues, conservation, and a host of other issues.

5. **The Media:** In an open, democratic society, the media play a key role in informing the public about the actions of individuals and organizations—both good and bad. The Children's Online Privacy Protection Act (COPPA) requires website operators to obtain verifiable consent from parents before collecting personal information about children under age thirteen. Yelp paid a $450,000 fine for collecting information on children under thirteen.[3] More than 40 million students rely on Google Apps for Education. This suite of educational apps complies with the U.S. Family Educational Rights and Privacy Act (FERPA)—a fact that Google states explicitly in its contracts with schools. Google also requires that schools using Google Apps for Education obtain parental consent before students can use the apps. This conforms to COPPA requirements.[4]

6. **An Active Civil Society:** An informed and engaged society can help mold individual and corporate

social control any means used to maintain behavioral norms and regulate conflict

behavioral norms standards of proper or acceptable behavior. Several modes of social control are important to marketing

ethics the moral principles or values that generally govern the conduct of an individual or a group

behavior. The last state in the union to get a Walmart store was Vermont. Citizen campaigns against the big-box retailer were deciding factors in management's decision to avoid the state. Fifty-two percent of consumers say that they would stop buying a company's products if the company was acting unethically.[5] One-third of the U.S. baby boomers (persons born between 1946 and 1964) make an effort to buy from "good" companies, such as those that take an active role in their communities.[6]

All six of the preceding factors—individually and in combination—are critical to achieving a socially coherent, vibrant, civilized society. These six factors (the social glue) are more important today than ever before due to the increasing complexity of the global economy and the melding of customs and traditions within societies.

3-2 THE CONCEPT OF ETHICAL BEHAVIOR

It has been said that ethics is something everyone likes to talk about but nobody can define. Others have suggested that defining ethics is like trying to nail Jell-O to a wall. You begin to think that you understand it, but that is when it starts squirting out between your fingers.

Simply put, ethics can be viewed as the standard of behavior by which conduct is judged. Standards that are legal may not always be ethical, and vice versa. Laws are the values and standards enforceable by the courts. Ethics, then, consists of personal moral principles. For example, there is no legal statute that makes it a crime for someone to "cut in line." Yet, if someone does not want to wait in line and cuts to the front, it often makes others very angry.

If you have ever resented a line-cutter, then you understand ethics and have applied ethical standards in life. Waiting your turn in line is a social expectation that exists because lines ensure order and allocate the space and time needed to complete transactions. Waiting your turn is an expected but unwritten behavior that plays a critical role in an orderly society.

So it is with ethics. Ethics consists of those unwritten rules we have developed for our interactions with one another. These unwritten rules govern us when we are sharing resources or honoring contracts. "Waiting your turn" is a higher standard than the laws that are passed to maintain order. Those laws apply when physical force or threats are used to push to the front of the line. Assault, battery, and threats are forms of criminal conduct for which the offender can be prosecuted. But the law does not apply to the stealthy line-cutter who simply sneaks to the front, perhaps using a friend and a conversation as a decoy. No laws are broken, but the notions of fairness and justice are offended by one individual putting himself or herself above others and taking advantage of others' time and position.

Ethical questions range from practical, narrowly defined issues, such as a businessperson's obligation to be honest with customers, to broader social and philosophical questions, such as whether a company is responsible for preserving the environment and protecting employee rights. Many ethical dilemmas develop from conflicts between the differing interests of company owners and their workers, customers, and surrounding community. Managers must balance the ideal against the practical—that is, the need to produce a reasonable profit for the company's shareholders against honesty in business practices and concern for environmental and social issues.

3-2a Ethical Theories

People usually base their individual choice of ethical theory on their life experiences. The following are some of the ethical theories that apply to marketing.[7]

DEONTOLOGY The **deontological theory** states that people should adhere to their obligations and duties when analyzing an ethical dilemma. This means that a person will follow his or her obligations to another individual or society because upholding one's duty is what is considered ethically correct. For instance, a deontologist will always keep his promises to a friend and will follow the law. A person who follows this theory will produce very consistent decisions because they will be based on the individual's set duties.

Note that deontological theory is not necessarily concerned with the welfare of others. For example, suppose a salesperson has decided that it is her ethical duty (and very practical) to always be on time to meetings with clients. Today she is running late. How is she supposed to drive? Is the deontologist

Sideways Design/Shutterstock.com

PLEASE Take A Number

A84

deontological theory ethical theory that states that people should adhere to their obligations and duties when analyzing an ethical dilemma

supposed to speed, breaking the law to uphold her duty to society, or is the deontologist supposed to arrive at her meeting late, breaking her duty to be on time? This scenario of conflicting obligations does not lead us to a clear, ethically correct resolution, nor does it protect the welfare of others from the deontologist's decision.

UTILITARIANISM The **utilitarian ethical theory** is founded on the ability to predict the consequences of an action. To a utilitarian, the choice that yields the greatest benefit to the most people is the choice that is ethically correct. One benefit of this ethical theory is that the utilitarian can compare similar predicted solutions and use a point system to determine which choice is more beneficial for more people. This point system provides a logical and rational argument for each decision and allows a person to use it on a case-by-case context.

There are two types of utilitarianism: act utilitarianism and rule utilitarianism. *Act utilitarianism* adheres exactly to the definition of utilitarianism as just described. In act utilitarianism, a person performs the acts that benefit the most people, regardless of personal feelings or societal constraints such as laws. *Rule utilitarianism*, however, takes into account the law and is concerned with fairness. A rule utilitarian seeks to benefit the most people but through the fairest and most just means available. Therefore, added benefits of rule utilitarianism are that it values justice and doing good at the same time.

As is true of all ethical theories, however, both act and rule utilitarianism contain numerous flaws. Inherent in both are the flaws associated with predicting the future. Did President Obama's cancellation of the Keystone Pipeline help the most people, or did it not? The issue is very complex, involving environmentalists on one side and oil companies on the other. The environmentalists believed that the pipeline would have done irreversible damage to local ecosystems, while the companies believed that it would have provided jobs, a boost to the economy, and long-term energy independence. Although people can use their life experiences to attempt to predict outcomes, no human being can be certain that his predictions will be true. This uncertainty can lead to unexpected results, making the utilitarian look unethical as time passes because his choice did not benefit the most people as he predicted.

Another assumption that a utilitarian must make is that he has the ability to compare the various types of consequences against each other on a similar scale.

However, comparing material gains such as money against intangible gains such as happiness is impossible because their qualities differ so greatly.

CASUIST The **casuist ethical theory** compares a current ethical dilemma with examples of similar ethical dilemmas and their outcomes. This allows one to determine the severity of the situation and to create the best possible solution according to others' experiences. Usually, one will find examples that represent the extremes of the situation so that a compromise can be reached that will include the wisdom gained from the previous situations.

One drawback to this ethical theory is that there may not be a set of similar examples for a given ethical dilemma. Perhaps that which is controversial and ethically questionable is new and unexpected. Along the same line of thinking, this theory assumes that the results of the current ethical dilemma will be similar to results in the examples. This may not be necessarily true and would greatly hinder the effectiveness of applying this ethical theory.

MORAL RELATIVISM **Moral relativism** is a belief in time-and-place ethics, that is, the truth of a moral judgment is relative to the judging person or group. According to a moral relativist, for example, arson is not always wrong—if you live in a neighborhood where drug dealers are operating a crystal meth lab or crack house, committing arson by burning down the meth lab may be ethically justified. If you are a parent and your child is starving, stealing a loaf of bread is ethically correct. The proper resolution to ethical dilemmas is based upon weighing the competing factors at the moment and then making a determination to take the lesser of the evils as the resolution. Moral relativists do not believe in absolute rules. Their beliefs center on the pressure of the moment and whether the pressure justifies the action taken.

VIRTUE ETHICS Aristotle and Plato taught that solving ethical dilemmas requires training—that individuals solve ethical dilemmas when they develop and nurture a set of virtues. A **virtue** is a character trait valued as being good. Aristotle taught

utilitarian ethical theory ethical theory that is founded on the ability to predict the consequences of an action

casuist ethical theory ethical theory that compares a current ethical dilemma with examples of similar ethical dilemmas and their outcomes

moral relativism an ethical theory of time-and-place ethics; that is, the belief that ethical truths depend on the individuals and groups holding them

virtue a character trait valued as being good

the importance of cultivating virtue in his students and then having them solve ethical dilemmas using those virtues once they had become an integral part of his students' being through their virtue training.

Some modern philosophers have embraced this notion of virtue and have developed lists of what constitutes a virtuous businessperson. Some common virtues for business people are self-discipline, friendliness, caring, courage, compassion, trust, responsibility, honesty, determination, enthusiasm, and humility. You may see other lists of virtues that are longer or shorter, but here is a good start for core business virtues.

3-3 ETHICAL BEHAVIOR IN BUSINESS

Depending upon which, if any, ethical theory a businessperson has accepted and uses in his or her daily conduct, the action taken may vary. For example, faced with bribing a foreign official to get a critically needed contract or shutting down a factory and laying off a thousand workers, a person following a deontology strategy would not pay the bribe. Why? A deontologist always follows the law. However, a moral relativist would probably pay the bribe.

While the boundaries of what is legal and what is not are often fairly clear (for example, do not run a red light, do not steal money from a bank, and do not kill anyone), the boundaries of ethical decision making are predicated on which ethical theory one is following. The law typically relies on juries to determine if an act is legal or illegal. Society determines whether an action is ethical or unethical. Recently, Volkswagen was caught acting in a manner that was both illegal and unethical. The issue began when California and federal officials asked Volkswagen why certain vehicles were passing emissions tests in labs but polluting more on the road. That question led to a battery of tests that exposed more discrepancies, and after a series of agitated meetings, Volkswagen admitted that it had been using secret technology to circumvent emissions tests. U.S. authorities alleged that Volkswagen had installed software on 500,000 cars sold in the United States that made them appear to run cleaner than they actually did on the road.[8] Analysts estimate that this software was also installed on an additional 10.5 million vehicles worldwide. When driven in the "normal" mode, affected cars can emit nitrogen oxide (linked to lung cancer) at levels up to 40 times higher than the

CEO of Volkswagen Group of America Michael Horn testifies during a House Energy and Commerce Oversight and Investigations Subcommittee hearing titled "Volkswagen's Emissions Cheating Allegations: Initial Questions" on October 8, 2015.

federal limit.[9] In early 2016, Volkswagen was ordered not to sell any new diesels. Additional certified pre-owned diesels were also placed under stop-sale orders.[10]

Morals are the rules people develop as a result of cultural values and norms. Culture is a socializing force that dictates what is right and wrong. Moral standards may also reflect the laws and regulations that affect social and economic behavior. Thus, morals can be considered a foundation of ethical behavior.

Morals are usually characterized as good or bad. "Good" and "bad" have many different connotations. One such connotation is "effective" and "ineffective." A good salesperson makes or exceeds the assigned quota. If the salesperson sells a new computer system or HDTV to a disadvantaged consumer—knowing full well that the person cannot keep up the monthly payments—is that still a good salesperson? What if the sale enables the salesperson to exceed his or her quota?

"Good" and "bad" can also refer to "conforming" and "deviant" behaviors. A doctor who runs large ads offering discounts on open-heart surgery would be considered bad, or unprofessional, because he or she is not conforming to the norms of the medical profession. "Good" and "bad" also express the distinction between law-abiding and criminal behavior. And finally, different religions define "good" and "bad" in markedly different ways. A Muslim who eats pork would be considered bad by other Muslims, for example. Religion is just one of the many factors that affect a businessperson's ethics.

morals the rules people develop as a result of cultural values and norms

3-3a Morality and Business Ethics

Today's business ethics actually consist of a subset of major life values learned since birth. The values businesspeople use to make decisions have been acquired through family, educational, and religious institutions.

Ethical values are situation specific and time oriented. Everyone must have an ethical base that applies to conduct in the business world and in personal life. One approach to developing a personal set of ethics is to examine the consequences of a particular act. Who is helped or hurt? How long do the consequences last? What actions produce the greatest good for the greatest number of people? A second approach stresses the importance of rules. Rules come in the form of customs, laws, professional standards, and common sense. "Always treat others as you would like to be treated" is an example of a rule.

A third approach to personal ethics emphasizes the development of moral character within individuals. In this approach, ethical development is thought to consist of three levels.[11]

- *Preconventional morality*, the most basic level, is childlike. It is calculating, self-centered, and even selfish, based on what will be immediately punished or rewarded. Fortunately, most businesspeople have progressed beyond the self-centered and manipulative actions of preconventional morality.

- *Conventional morality* moves from an egocentric viewpoint toward the expectations of society. Loyalty and obedience to the organization (or society) become paramount. A marketing decision maker operating at this level of moral development would be concerned only with whether a proposed action is legal and how it will be viewed by others.

- *Postconventional morality* represents the morality of the mature adult. At this level, people are less concerned about how others might see them and more concerned about how they see and judge themselves over the long run. A marketing decision maker who has attained a postconventional level of morality might ask, "Even though it is legal and will increase company profits, is it right in the long run? Might it do more harm than good in the end?"

3-3b Ethical Decision Making

Ethical questions rarely have cut-and-dried answers. Studies show that the following factors tend to influence ethical decision making and judgments:[12]

- **Extent of ethical problems within the organization:** Marketing professionals who perceive fewer ethical problems in their organizations tend to disapprove more strongly of "unethical" or questionable practices than those who perceive more ethical problems. Apparently, the healthier the ethical environment, the more likely it is that marketers will take a strong stand against questionable practices.

- **Top management's actions on ethics:** Top managers can influence the behavior of marketing professionals by encouraging ethical behavior and discouraging unethical behavior. Researchers found that when top managers develop a strong ethical culture, there is reduced pressure to perform unethical acts, fewer unethical acts are performed, and unethical behavior is reported more frequently.[13]

- **Potential magnitude of the consequences:** The greater the harm done to victims, the more likely that marketing professionals will recognize a problem as unethical.

- **Social consensus:** The greater the degree of agreement among managerial peers that an action is harmful, the more likely that marketers will recognize a problem as unethical. Research has found that a strong ethical culture among coworkers decreases observations of ethical misconduct. In companies with strong ethical cultures, 9 percent of employees observed misconduct, compared with 31 percent in companies with weaker cultures.[14]

- **Probability of a harmful outcome:** The greater the likelihood that an action will result in a harmful outcome, the more likely that marketers will recognize a problem as unethical.

- **Length of time between the decision and the onset of consequences:** The shorter the length of time between the action and the onset of negative consequences, the more likely that marketers will perceive a problem as unethical.

- **Number of people to be affected:** The greater the number of persons affected by a negative outcome, the more likely that marketers will recognize a problem as unethical.

As you can see, many factors determine the nature of an ethical decision. In October 2014, drugstore chain CVS ceased all sales of cigarettes and other tobacco products, becoming the first national pharmacy to do so.

CVS President and CEO Larry Merlo said that the decision better aligned the company with its purpose of improving customer health, and that it was simply the right thing to do.[15] Which of the above factors do you think contributed to CVS' decision?

In this February 2014 photo, cigarettes and other tobacco products can be seen on sale behind the counter at a New York City CVS location. As of October 1, 2014, CVS became the first chain of national pharmacies to remove cigarettes from its shelves.

3-3c **Ethical Guidelines and Training**

In recent years, many organizations have become more interested in ethical issues. One sign of this interest is the increase in the number of large companies that appoint ethics officers—from virtually none several years ago to over 40 percent of large corporations today.[16] In addition, many companies of various sizes have developed a **code of ethics** as a guideline to help marketing managers and other employees make better decisions. Creating ethics guidelines has several advantages:

- A code of ethics helps employees identify what their firm recognizes as acceptable business practices.

- A code of ethics can be an effective internal control of behavior, which is more desirable than external controls such as government regulation.

- A written code helps employees avoid confusion when determining whether their decisions are ethical.

- The process of formulating the code of ethics facilitates discussion among employees about what is right and wrong and ultimately leads to better decisions.

code of ethics a guideline to help marketing managers and other employees make better decisions

Foreign Corrupt Practices Act (FCPA) a law that prohibits U.S. corporations from making illegal payments to public officials of foreign governments to obtain business rights or to enhance their business dealings in those countries

Ethics training is an effective way to help employees put good ethics into practice. The Ethics Resource Center's National Business Ethics Survey (NBES) found that 81 percent of companies provide ethics training. Only 33 percent of workers observed misconduct in large companies with effective ethics and compliance programs (E&C). Compare this to a misconduct rate of 51 percent among all large companies and 62 percent among large companies that do not have effective E&C programs. Pressure for workers to compromise standards was just 3 percent among big companies with effective E&C programs, versus 23 percent among those without an effective program.[17] Still, simply giving employees a long list of *dos* and *don'ts* does not really help employees navigate the gray areas or adapt to a changing world market. In Carson City, Nevada, all governmental lobbyists are required to attend a course on ethics and policy before they can meet with lawmakers. The training outlines exactly how and when lobbyists are allowed to interact with lawmakers and how to report any money they spend. A clear understanding of ethical expectations is essential to an industry like lobbying, where illicit—often illegal—actions are taken to promote individual causes.

THE MOST ETHICAL COMPANIES Each year, *Ethisphere* magazine (targeted toward top management and focused on ethical leadership) examines more than 5,000 companies in thirty separate industries, seeking the world's most ethical companies. It then lists the top 100. The magazine uses a rigorous format to identify true ethical leadership. A few of the selected winners are shown in Exhibit 3.1.

3-3d **Ethics in Other Countries**

Studies suggest that ethical beliefs vary little from culture to culture. Certain practices, however, such as the use of illegal payments and bribes, are far more acceptable in some places than in others, though enforced laws are increasingly making the practice less accepted. One such law, the **Foreign Corrupt Practices Act (FCPA)**, was enacted because Congress was concerned about U.S. corporations' use of illegal payments and bribes in international business dealings. This act prohibits U.S. corporations from making illegal payments to public officials of foreign governments to obtain business rights or to enhance their business dealings in those countries. The act has been criticized for putting U.S. businesses at a

COSTCO's Code of Ethics

One of America's most admired companies is Costco. The firm's mission is "To continually provide our members with quality goods and services at the lowest possible prices." To achieve this mission, Costco conducts its business using the following code of ethics.

I. Obey the Law

The law is irrefutable. Absent a moral imperative to challenge a law, we must conduct our business in total compliance with the laws of every community where we do business.

II. Take Care of Our Members

Costco membership is open to business owners, as well as individuals. Our members are our reason for being - the key to our success. If we don't keep our members happy, little else that we do will make a difference. There are plenty of shopping alternatives for our members and if they fail to show up, we cannot survive. Our members have extended a trust to Costco by virtue of paying a fee to shop with us. We will succeed only if we do not violate the trust they have extended to us, and that trust extends to every area of our business. To continue to earn their trust, we pledge to:

- Provide top-quality products at the best prices in the market.
- Provide high quality, safe and wholesome food products by requiring that both vendors and employees be in compliance with the highest food safety standards in the industry.
- Provide our members with a 100% satisfaction guaranteed warranty on every product and service we sell, including their membership fee.
- Assure our members that every product we sell is authentic in make and in representation of performance.
- Make our shopping environment a pleasant experience by making our members feel welcome as our guests.
- Provide products to our members that will be ecologically sensitive.
- Provide our members with the best customer service in the retail industry.
- Give back to our communities through employee volunteerism and employee and corporate contributions to United Way and Children's Hospitals.

III. Take Care of Our Employees

Our employees are our most important asset. We believe we have the very best employees in the warehouse club industry, and we are committed to providing them with rewarding challenges and ample opportunities for personal and career growth. We pledge to provide our employees with:

- Competitive wages
- Great benefits
- A safe and healthy work environment
- Challenging and fun work
- An atmosphere free from harassment or discrimination
- An Open Door Policy that allows access to ascending levels of management to resolve issues
- Opportunities to give back to their communities through volunteerism and fund-raising.

IV. Respect Our Suppliers

Our suppliers are our partners in business and for us to prosper as a company, they must prosper with us. To that end, we strive to:

- Treat all suppliers and their representatives as you would expect to be treated if visiting their place of business.
- Honor all commitments.
- Protect all suppliers' property assigned to Costco as though it were our own.
- Not accept gratuities of any kind from a supplier.
- Avoid actual or apparent conflicts of interest, including creating a business in competition with the Company or working for or on behalf of another employers in competition with the Company.

These guidelines are exactly that – guidelines – some common sense rules for the conduct of our business. At the core of our philosophy as a company is the

(Continued)

implicit understanding that all of us, employees and management alike, must conduct ourselves in an honest and ethical manner every day. In fact, dishonest conduct will not be tolerated. To do any less would be unfair to the overwhelming majority of our employees who support and respect Costco's commitment to ethical business conduct. If you are ever in doubt as to what course of action to take on a business matter that is open to varying ethical interpretation, TAKE THE HIGH ROAD AND DO WHAT IS RIGHT.

If we follow the four principles of our Code of Ethics throughout our organization, then we will achieve our fifth principle and ultimate goal, which is to:

V. Reward Our Shareholders

Source: Excerpted from Costco Code of Ethics, 2016.

competitive disadvantage. Many contend that bribery is an unpleasant but necessary part of international business, especially in countries such as China, where business gift giving is widely accepted and expected. But, as prosecutions under the FCPA have increased worldwide, some countries are implementing their own anti-bribery laws. For example, even though China is among the three countries with the most international corruption cases prosecuted under the FCPA, the country is working to develop its own anti-bribery laws. President Xi Jinping has vigorously attacked corruption and bribery in the Communist party, and has swept tens of thousands out of office. Many have been sent to prison.[18]

3-4 CORPORATE SOCIAL RESPONSIBILITY

Corporate social responsibility (CSR) is a business's concern for society's welfare. This concern is demonstrated by managers who consider both the long-range best interests of the company and the company's relationship to the society within which it operates.

3-4a Stakeholders and Social Responsibility

An important aspect of social responsibility is stakeholder theory. Stakeholder theory says that social responsibility is paying attention to the interest of every affected stakeholder in every aspect of a firm's operation. The stakeholders in a typical corporation are shown in Exhibit 3.2.

- *Employees* have their jobs and incomes at stake.

corporate social responsibility (CSR) a business's concern for society's welfare

stakeholder theory ethical theory stating that social responsibility is paying attention to the interest of every affected stakeholder in every aspect of a firm's operation

EXHIBIT 3.1	SELECTED WINNERS OF THE WORLD'S MOST ETHICAL COMPANIES	
Company	**Industry**
Rockwell Collins	Aerospace and Defense
H&M Hennes & Mauritz	Apparel
Levi Strauss & Co.	Apparel
Cummins, Inc.	Automotive
Ford Motor Company	Autos
MasterCard	Payment Services
Dun & Bradstreet	Business Services
Manpower Group	Business Services
Dell Inc.	Computer Hardware
Intel Corporation	Computer Hardware
Wipro Limited	Computer Services
Holland American Line	Leisure and Recreation
Microsoft	Computer Software
Symantec	Computer Software
Henkel AG & Co.	Consumer Products
Aflac	Insurance
Waste Management	Environmental Services
Starbucks	Food and Beverage
PepsiCo	Food and Beverage
L'OREAL	Health and Beauty
Cleveland Clinic	Healthcare Services
3M Company	Industrial Manufacturing
Deere & Company	Industrial Manufacturing
General Electric	Industrial Manufacturing
Marks and Spencer	Retail
UPS	Logistics and Transportation

Source: "2016 World's Most Ethical Companies," Ethisphere, http://ethisphere.com (Accessed March 18, 2016).

If the firm moves or closes, employees often face a severe hardship. In return for their labor, employees expect wages, benefits, and meaningful work. In return for their loyalty, workers expect the company to carry them through difficult times.

EXHIBIT 3.2 | STAKEHOLDERS IN A TYPICAL CORPORATION

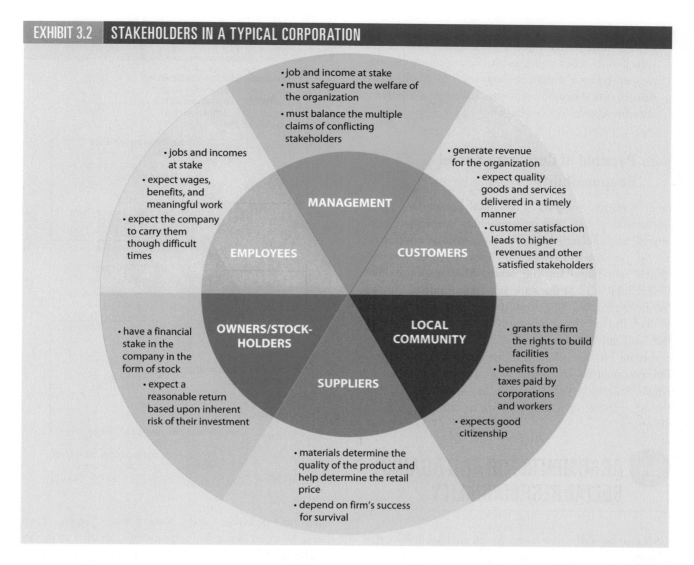

- *Management* plays a special role, as they also have a stake in the corporation. Like employees, managers have their jobs and incomes at stake. On the other hand, management must safeguard the welfare of the organization. Sometimes this means balancing the multiple claims of conflicting stakeholders. For example, stockholders want a higher return on investment and perhaps lower costs by moving factories overseas. This naturally conflicts with the interests of employees, the local community, and perhaps suppliers.

- *Customers* generate the revenue for the organization. In exchange, they expect high-quality goods and services delivered in a timely manner. Customer satisfaction leads to higher revenues and the ability to enhance the satisfaction of other stakeholders.

- *The local community*, through its government, grants the firm the right to build facilities. In turn, the community benefits directly from local taxes paid by the corporation and indirectly by property and sales taxes paid by the workers. The firm is expected to be a good citizen by paying a fair wage, not polluting the environment, and so forth.

- *Suppliers* are vital to the success of the firm. For example, if a critical part is not available for an assembly line, then production grinds to a halt. The materials supplied determine the quality of the product produced and create a cost floor, which helps determine the retail price. In turn, the firm is the customer of the supplier and is therefore vital to the success and survival of the supplier. A supplier that fails to deliver quality products can create numerous problems for a firm. For example, Burger King stopped buying beef from an Irish supplier whose patties were found to contain traces of horse meat in Britain and Ireland.[19]

- *Owners* have a financial stake in the form of stock in a corporation. They expect a reasonable return based upon the amount of inherent risk on their investment.

Sometimes managers and employees receive a portion of their compensation in company stock. When Apple launched its initial public stock offering, 30 Apple employees became instant millionaires.[20] Similarly, more than 10,000 Microsoft employees have become millionaires from their stock holdings.[21]

3-4b Pyramid of Corporate Social Responsibility

One theorist suggests that total corporate social responsibility has four components: economic, legal, ethical, and philanthropic. The **pyramid of corporate social responsibility** portrays economic performance as the foundation for the other three responsibilities (see Exhibit 3.3). At the same time that it pursues profits (economic responsibility), however, a business is expected to obey the law (legal responsibility); to do what is right, just, and fair (ethical responsibilities); and to be a good corporate citizen (philanthropic responsibility). These four components are distinct but together constitute the whole. Still, if the company does not make a profit, then the other three responsibilities are moot.

3-5 ARGUMENTS FOR AND AGAINST SOCIAL RESPONSIBILITY

CSR can be a divisive issue. Some analysts believe that a business should focus on making a profit and leave social and environmental problems to nonprofit organizations and government. Economist Milton Friedman believed that the free market, not companies, should decide what is best for the world.[22] Friedman argued that when business executives spend more money than necessary—to purchase delivery vehicles with hybrid engines, pay higher wages in developing countries, or even donate company funds to charity—they are spending shareholders' money to further their own agendas. It would be better to pay dividends and let the shareholders give the money away if they choose.

On the other hand, CSR has an increasing number of supporters based on several compelling factors. One is that it is simply the right thing to do. Some societal problems,

pyramid of corporate social responsibility a model that suggests corporate social responsibility is composed of economic, legal, ethical, and philanthropic responsibilities and that a firm's economic performance supports the entire structure

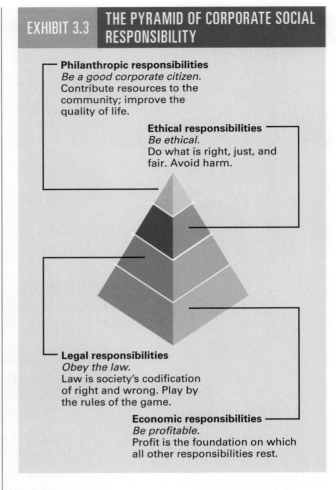

EXHIBIT 3.3 THE PYRAMID OF CORPORATE SOCIAL RESPONSIBILITY

Philanthropic responsibilities
Be a good corporate citizen.
Contribute resources to the community; improve the quality of life.

Ethical responsibilities
Be ethical.
Do what is right, just, and fair. Avoid harm.

Legal responsibilities
Obey the law.
Law is society's codification of right and wrong. Play by the rules of the game.

Economic responsibilities
Be profitable.
Profit is the foundation on which all other responsibilities rest.

such as pollution and poverty-level wages, have been brought about by corporations' actions; it is the responsibility of business to right these wrongs. Businesses also have the resources, so businesses should be given the chance to solve social problems. For example, businesses can provide a fair work environment, safe products, and informative advertising.

Recent research has found that being socially responsible and training front line employees about social responsibility can have a positive impact on the firm. In a business-to-business environment, researchers found that social responsibility activities can raise customer trust and identification with the firm. These factors, in turn, build customer loyalty, which often leads to higher profits.[23]

If a customer has a bad experience with a firm, an active social responsibility program can dampen negative word-of-mouth and social media comments.[24] Even corporations convicted of illegal acts can benefit from being socially responsible. The average fine levied against a firm convicted of bribery under the

This reusable tumbler was purchased from a Starbucks location in the Chelsea neighborhood of New York City. Consumers have long criticized Starbucks' use of disposable containers, so the introduction of the reusable cup benefited both the company and its customers.

PepsiCo sustainability initiatives delivered more than $375 million in estimated cost savings between 2010 and 2016.

Foreign Corrupt Practices Act is 40 percent lower if the firm has a comprehensive social responsibility program.[25]

Another, more pragmatic, reason for being socially responsible is that if businesses do not act responsibly, then government will create new regulations and perhaps levy fines against them.

Finally, social responsibility can produce a direct profit. Smart companies can prosper and build value by tackling social problems. Starbucks rolled out a reusable plastic tumbler that customers could buy for $1 instead of using a disposable cardboard cup for each coffee they buy. Not only does the reusable tumbler reduce energy use, landfill waste, and litter, it saves Starbucks the cost of the disposable cups and encourages customers to buy their daily cup of coffee from the company. Recently, Starbucks introduced a $30 double-walled tumbler made from recycled materials. Customers who brought the tumbler back to the store for refills received free coffee for a month.[26]

3-5a Growth of Social Responsibility

The social responsibility of businesses is growing around the world. Companies around the globe are coming under increasing pressure from governments, advocacy groups, investors, prospective employees, current employees, and consumers to make their organizations more socially responsible. In turn, firms are seeing social responsibility as an opportunity. A recent global survey from the Nielsen Company, one of the world's largest marketing research firms, found that 55 percent of respondents around the world were willing to pay extra for products and services from companies providing positive social and environmental impact (see Exhibit 3.4).[27] More than half of the survey participants had bought at least one product or service in the past six months from a socially responsible company.[28]

UNITED NATIONS GLOBAL COMPACT One way that U.S. firms can do more is by joining the United Nations Global Compact (UNGC). The UNGC, the world's largest global corporate citizenship initiative, has seen its ranks swell over the past few years. In 2001—the first full year after its launch—just sixty-seven companies joined, agreeing to abide by ten principles (see "The Ten Principles of the United Nations Global Compact"). In 2016, there were more than 8000 business participants.[29]

3-5b Becoming a B Corp

Smaller companies that wish to join the social responsibility and sustainability movement are turning to the B Corp movement.[30] To become a B Corp Certified company, a firm must score at least 80 points on a 200-point assessment. Criteria include things like fair compensation for workers, how much waste the

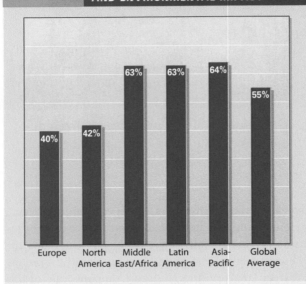

EXHIBIT 3.4 PERCENT OF RESPONDENTS WILLING TO PAY EXTRA FOR PRODUCTS AND SERVICES FROM COMPANIES COMMITTED TO POSITIVE SOCIAL AND ENVIRONMENTAL IMPACT

Europe	North America	Middle East/Africa	Latin America	Asia-Pacific	Global Average
40%	42%	63%	63%	64%	55%

Source: "It Pays to Be Green: Corporate Social Responsibility Meets the Bottom Line," *Nielsen*, June 17, 2014, www.nielsen.com/us/en/insights/news/2014/it-pays-to-be-green-corporate-social-responsibility-meets-the-bottom-line.html (Accessed November 3, 2015).

THE TEN PRINCIPLES OF THE UNITED NATIONS GLOBAL COMPACT

Human Rights

▶ **Principle 1:** Businesses should support and respect the protection of internationally proclaimed human rights.

▶ **Principle 2:** Businesses should make sure that they are not complicit in human rights abuses.

Labor

▶ **Principle 3:** Businesses should uphold the freedom of association and the effective recognition of the right to collective bargaining.

▶ **Principle 4:** Businesses should uphold the elimination of all forms of forced and compulsory labor.

▶ **Principle 5:** Businesses should uphold the effective abolition of child labor.

▶ **Principle 6:** Businesses should uphold the elimination of discrimination in respect of employment and occupation.

Environment

▶ **Principle 7:** Businesses should support a precautionary approach to environmental challenges.

▶ **Principle 8:** Businesses should undertake initiatives to promote greater environmental responsibility.

▶ **Principle 9:** Businesses should encourage the development and diffusion of environmentally friendly technologies.

Anti-Corruption

▶ **Principle 10:** Businesses should work against corruption in all its forms, including extortion and bribery

Source: https://www.unglobalcompact.org/AboutThe GC/TheTenPrinciples/index.html

company produces, and the company's work with local businesses. Firms such as Patagonia, Ben & Jerry's, online crafts marketplace Etsy, and Danone have qualified. New Seasons Market, a 13-store grocery chain in Oregon, stamps the B Corp logo on all of its grocery bags and gives employees B Corp badges to wear. The logo helps attract socially-minded shoppers and helps in recruiting new workers.

Four-hundred and fifty new B Corps were certified in 2015. More than 11,000 companies are now using the B Impact Assessment, which measures a firm's social and environmental impact.[31] You can review this assessment at: http://bimpactassessment.net.

SUSTAINABILITY A significant part of the B Impact Assessment is measuring a firm's **sustainability**. Sustainability is the idea that socially responsible companies will outperform their peers by focusing on the world's social, economic, and environmental problems. Sustainable

> **sustainability** the idea that socially responsible companies will outperform their peers by focusing on the world's social problems and viewing them as opportunities to build profits and help the world at the same time

companies view these problems as opportunities to build profits and help the world at the same time. Environmental sustainability is concerned with the physical environment. Environmentally sustainable companies believe that threats to the environment should be minimized or eliminated. For example, developing long-term sources of clean water improves health and preserves local ecosystems while creating a competitive advantage. Social sustainability means developing processes and structures that not only meet the needs of a current community, but benefit future generations as well. Building schools and providing means for children to attend those schools is an example of creating social sustainability. In a business context, economic sustainability is the efficient use of assets so that a company can continue operating profitably over time. A company cannot be socially or environmentally responsible if it goes out of business.

3-5c Green Marketing

An outgrowth of the social responsibility and sustainability movements is green marketing. **Green marketing** is the development and marketing of products designed to minimize negative effects on the physical environment or to improve the environment. One approach that firms use to indicate that they are part of the green movement is to use third-party eco-logos. Examples include the chasing-arrows recycling logo (the product is either recyclable or contains recycled materials); the Energy Star logo (the product is energy efficient); and Certified Organic (the U.S. Department of Agriculture created standards relative to soil quality, animal raising practices, pest and weed control, and the use of additives). These logos can enhance a product's sales and profitability.

Nearly four in 10 Americans (about 93 million people) say that they are dedicated to buying green products and services. Green purchasing is driven by young adults (age 18 to 34) and Hispanics; about half of the respondents in these groups report that they regularly seek out green products. Young adults are also more likely to be interested in a company's green practices and to avoid companies with poor environmental records.[32]

When a firm is accused of an act that is perceived as not environmentally friendly, it can create a significant amount of negative publicity. *The Wall Street Journal* recently ran a story about consumer products manufacturer the Honest Company, which was co-founded by actor Jessica Alba. The Honest Company advertises products that are safer and more ecologically friendly than those made by other brands—but this may not actually be the case. *The Wall Street Journal* found that a shampoo made by The Honest Company contained cleaning agent sodium lauryl sulfate (SLS) despite claims to the contrary:

The Jessica Alba co-founded Honest Company faced public scrutiny for manufacturing products that did not fit the company's safe and ecologically-friendly messaging.

Helga Esteb/Shutterstock.com

The company lists SLS first in the "Honestly free of" label of verboten ingredients it puts on bottles of its laundry detergent, one of Honest's first and most popular products.

But two independent lab tests commissioned by *The Wall Street Journal* determined Honest's liquid laundry detergent contains SLS.

"Our findings support that there is a significant amount of sodium lauryl sulfate" in Honest's detergent, said Barbara Pavan, a chemist at one of the labs, Impact Analytical. Another lab, Chemir, a division of EAG Inc., said its test for SLS found about the same concentration as Tide, which is made by P&G. "It was not a trace amount," said Matthew Hynes, a chemist at Chemir who conducted the test.

"We do not make our products with sodium lauryl sulfate," said Kevin Ewell, the company's research and development manager.

Honest said its manufacturing partners and suppliers have provided assurances that its products don't contain SLS beyond possible trace amounts. Honest provided the Journal with a document it said was from its detergent manufacturer, Earth Friendly Products LLC, that stated there was zero "SLS content" in the product. Earth Friendly in turn said the document came from its own chemical supplier, a company called Trichromatic West Inc., which it relied on to test and certify that there was no SLS.

Trichromatic told the Journal the certificate wasn't based on any testing and there was a "misunderstanding" with the detergent maker. It said the "SLS content" was listed as zero because it didn't add any SLS to the material it provided to Earth Friendly and "there would be no reason to test specifically for SLS".[33]

According to USA TODAY, the Honest

> **green marketing** the development and marketing of products designed to minimize negative effects on the physical environment or to improve the environment

Company released a statement disputing the *Wall Street Journal's* claims:

"Despite providing the *Wall Street Journal* with substantial evidence to the contrary, they falsely claimed our laundry detergent contains Sodium Lauryl Sulfate (SLS). To set the record straight, we use Sodium Coco Sulfate (SCS) in our brand's laundry detergent because it is a gentler alternative that is less irritating and safer to use. Rigorous testing and analysis both by our internal research and development teams as well as further testing by external partners have confirmed this fact."

Honest called the *Wall Street Journal's* reporting "reckless" and said it "substituted junk science for credible journalism. We stand behind our laundry detergent and take very seriously the responsibility we have to our consumers to create safe and effective products."

In response, the *Wall Street Journal* said, "The *Journal's* report is accurate, fair and meets the *Journal"s* established and trusted high standards, including giving the Honest Company numerous opportunities to respond to our findings. We took great care in preparing this story, relying on two tests with two different labs and numerous experts during an extensive and lengthy investigation."[34]

3-5d Leaders in Social Responsibility

Global leaders in social responsibility include Dow Chemical, which created an advanced purification process that converts human sewage into potable water, and Unilever, whose Lifebuoy soap brand launched "Global Hand Washing Day."[35] This public service campaign,targeted at children in developing countries, was recognized in 53 countries, and two videos about the importance of hand washing were viewed more than 30 million times.[36] Social responsibility is not limited to corporate giants like Dow and Unilever, however. M-Kopa Solar, a Kenyan company, sells solar power to people with incomes of less than $2 a day. The innovative energy company charges $35 up front and then 45 cents per day for a year. After that, the system is the customer's to keep. M-Kopa's solar-based energy is designed to replace Kerosene lamps, which emit an acrid smoke that irritates eyes and throats and slowly turns walls and ceilings black.[37]

Two names at the top of many social responsibility lists are Patagonia and Tom's Shoes. Patagonia, a private outdoor clothing manufacturer was founded by Yvon Chouinard, but is now headed by Rose Marcario.

Patagonia's decision to Responsible Economy is so strong that the company advises customers not to buy its products if they don't absolutely need to.

Marcario worked in high tech and for a private equity company before landing at Patagonia. After arriving in 2008, one of her first acts was to switch the company's mailing packages to recyclable bags. On Black Friday of that year, the company ran one of its most famous ads, titled, "Don't Buy This Jacket." As part of its Worn

Wear program, Patagonia employees 45 full-time repair technicians in Reno, Nevada. The company sends a biodiesel truck around the country to repair Patagonia clothing.

It's not always easy to think about profits and social responsibility at the same time, and Marcario is often tested. All Patagonia employees are encouraged to engage with their communities, either by volunteering, marching for a cause, or hosting a meeting at the store (after hours). Activism is so ingrained in the company culture that it hosts an annual conference, called Tools for Grassroots Activists, that brings together instigators of all types, including many who work at Patagonia.[38] Though a noble effort, this initiative met some resistance in Japan, Patagonia's second-largest market after the United States. The problem, Marcario reported, was that what seemed like a gentle nudge in one culture was interpreted as mandatory in another. A number of Japanese stores had recently hosted civil-disobedience and nonviolence training before a protest at a nearby dam, and some employees felt like they were expected to get arrested to prove their loyalty to the company cause.[39]

Blake Mycoskie founded TOMS Shoes more than a decade ago. A shoe manufacturer with social responsibility coded into its DNA, TOMS donates a pair of shoes to the world's poorest people for every pair sold to customers in the developed world. TOMS has expanded its mission since its founding, and is now funding sight-saving surgeries, helping to ensure safe drinking water, and creating jobs in poor communities like Port-au-Prince, Haiti. Mycoskie sold half of his company in 2015, which netted him $200 million after taxes.[40] Mycoskie used half of that money to launch TOMS Social Entrepreneurship Fund, an investment fund for small, purpose-driven companies. TOMS Social Entrepreneurship Fund has already made 16 investments ranging from $25,000 to $1 million. Some of the firms it supports are very small, such as ArtLifting, which sells artworks created by homeless and disabled people.[41]

Dick's Sporting Goods CEO Ed Stack (right) presents Superbowl-winning football coach Jon Gruden with the company's first-ever Sports Matter Impact Award at a Dick's Sporting Goods Foundation panel discussion on April 19, 2016. The award was accompanied by a $25,000 donation for Gruden to give to a youth sports program of his choosing.

efforts of a for-profit firm and a nonprofit organization for mutual benefit. The for-profit firm hopes to generate extra sales, and the nonprofit in turn hopes to receive money, goods, and/or services. Any marketing effort that targets social or other charitable causes can be referred to as cause-related marketing. Cause marketing differs from corporate giving (philanthropy), as the latter generally involves a specific donation that is tax deductible, whereas cause marketing is a marketing relationship not based on a straight donation.

Cause-related marketing is very popular and is estimated to generate about $7 billion a year in revenue.[42] It creates good public relations for the firm and will often stimulate sales of the brand. Nevertheless, the huge growth of cause-related marketing can lead to *consumer cause fatigue*. Researchers have found that businesses need to guard against being perceived as exploiting a cause simply to sell more of a product.[43]

Examples of cause-related marketing used by large companies are abundant. Clothing retailer H&M ran a promotion during the 2014 back-to-school sales period that promised that

 CAUSE-RELATED MARKETING

A sometimes controversial subset of social responsibility is cause-related marketing. Sometimes referred to as simply "cause marketing," it is the cooperative

> **cause-related marketing**
> the cooperative marketing efforts between a for-profit firm and a nonprofit organization

for every denim item purchased, the company would donate a new denim item to someone in need. The promotion was called "Wear Denim, Share Denim." Similarly, Starbucks recently launched "suspended coffee," a program where when customers bought coffee, they could support a fund that gives free coffee to people who cannot afford to pay. Quaker Oats recently created a contest called "Quaker Chewy for Charity." Every time a customer uploaded a photo or drawing of a customized lunch bag to Quaker's special Facebook app, could the company pledged to "show some lunch bag love" and send a 10 pound food donation to Food Banks Canada.[44]

Billions of dollars have been cut from youth sports programs in recent years. Sixty percent of children in the United States must now pay a fee to play a sport, and if they cannot pay, then they cannot play. Dick's Sporting Goods and the Dick's Sporting Goods Foundation recently announced a $25-million multi-year commitment to support youth athletic programs, including donations to and sponsorships of local sports teams. The Dick's Sporting Goods Foundation simultaneously launched a Sports Matter initiative to accomplish two major goals: first, to raise awareness about the issue of underfunded youth athletics, and second, to create a crowd-funding platform through which youth sports teams could raise money. Teams chosen to participate in the initiative were to received a matching grant from the foundation.

The results were convincing: 184 teams representing 35 states and 35 unique sports joined the initiative, raising more than $2 million in donations during the five-week fundraising campaign. With the addition of Dick's Sporting Goods Foundation's matching grants, that total rose to more than $4.6 million. Through this initiative, Dick's was able to support thousands of young athletes and raise awareness about the financial challenges affecting youth sports programs across the country.[45]

Cause-related marketing does not always target the firm's customers. When Hewlett-Packard's HP Foundation sought to launch an initiative to engage its 300,000 worldwide employees, it turned to Kiva, the world's first personal micro-lending marketplace. The two organizations joined forces to create Matter to a Million, a program that offered each HP employee $25 toward funding a Kiva micro-loan for an entrepreneur in a developing country.

Employees responded enthusiastically. In just nine days, they loaned more than $1 million using the $25 Kiva gift cards. Within six months, that number had risen to $4.2 million. Less than one year from the program's launch, HP employees had loaned upward of $6 million to aspiring businesspeople in need. HP incentivized employee participation by not only making it easy to redeem their $25 credits, but by offering an additional $25 Kiva credit if employees made their loans within 48 hours of the program's launch. This initiative had a redemption rate of nearly 70 percent.[46]

STUDY TOOLS 3

LOCATED AT BACK OF THE TEXTBOOK

- [ ] Rip out Chapter Review Card

LOCATED AT WWW.CENGAGEBRAIN.COM

- [ ] Review Key Terms Flashcards and create your own
- [ ] Track your knowledge and understanding of key concepts in marketing
- [ ] Complete practice and graded quizzes to prepare for tests
- [ ] Complete interactive content within the MKTG Online experience
- [ ] View the chapter highlight boxes within the MKTG Online experience

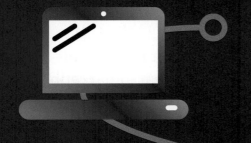

4 | The Marketing Environment

LEARNING OUTCOMES

After studying this chapter, you will be able to…

4-1 Discuss the external environment of marketing and explain how it affects a firm

4-2 Describe the social factors that affect marketing

4-3 Explain the importance to marketing managers of current demographic trends

4-4 Explain the importance to marketing managers of growing ethnic markets

4-5 Identify consumer and marketer reactions to the state of the economy

4-6 Identify the impact of technology on a firm

4-7 Discuss the political and legal environment of marketing

4-8 Explain the basics of foreign and domestic competition

After finishing this chapter go to **PAGE 67** for **STUDY TOOLS**

4-1 THE EXTERNAL MARKETING ENVIRONMENT

Perhaps the most important decisions a marketing manager must make relate to the creation of the marketing mix. Recall from Chapters 1 and 2 that a marketing mix is the unique combination of product, place (distribution), promotion, and price strategies. The marketing mix is, of course, under the firm's control and is designed to appeal to a specific group of potential buyers, or target market. A target market is a group of people or organizations for which an organization designs, implements, and maintains a marketing mix intended to meet the needs of that group, resulting in mutually satisfying exchanges.

Managers must alter the marketing mix because of changes in the environment in which consumers live, work, and make purchasing decisions. Also, as markets mature, some new consumers become part of the target market; others drop out. Those who remain may have different tastes, needs, incomes, lifestyles, and buying habits than the original target consumers. Technology, and the resulting change in buying habits, meant that consumers no longer have those "Kodak Moments" when taking pictures of a birthday party or an exceptional sunset. Digital photography has sent 35-millimeter film the way of the horse and buggy. Unfortunately, shifting technology ultimately led to the bankruptcy of Eastman Kodak.

Although managers can control the marketing mix, they cannot control elements in the external

target market a group of people or organizations for which an organization designs, implements, and maintains a marketing mix intended to meet the need of that group, resulting in mutually satisfying exchanges

environment that continually mold and reshape the target market. Controllable and uncontrollable variables affect the target market, whether it consists of consumers or business purchasers. The uncontrollable elements in the center of the environment continually evolve and create changes in the target market. Think, for example, about how social media have changed your world. In contrast, managers can shape and reshape the marketing mix to influence the target market. That is, managers react to changes in the external environment and attempt to create a more effective marketing mix.

4-1a Understanding the External Environment

Unless marketing managers understand the external environment, the firm cannot intelligently plan for the future. Thus, many organizations assemble a team of specialists to continually collect and evaluate environmental information, a process called *environmental scanning*. The goal in gathering the environmental data is to identify future market opportunities and threats.

UNDERSTAND CURRENT CUSTOMERS You must first understand how customers buy, why they buy, what they buy, and when they buy. A major California supermarket chain recently found that 28 percent of its customers were Asian American, and that Asian American loyalty to the chain was average at best. To better understand the Asian American grocery store shopper, the chain launched a second study. It found that Asian Americans spend 70 percent more than average on skin care preparations products, 25 percent more on fragrances, 15 percent more on hair care, 12 percent more on soap and bath products, and 7 percent more on cosmetics.[1]

Millennial Asian American women not only care deeply about their own appearances, they also shop for the men in their households. They purchase men's toiletries 9 percent more frequently than do non-Asian American female heads of households, and they spend 20 percent more on average.

In light of these findings, the supermarket chain is considering offering free cosmetic consultations and free store-label product samples to increase trust and willingness to try new items. The chain also is planning to change the packaging of its store brands to project a more upscale and high-quality image.

UNDERSTAND HOW CONSUMER DECISIONS ARE MADE Consumers don't simply go into the first store they see and buy the first item they see. They research, waffle between products, and sometimes, decide not to buy altogether. Mobile shopping is one factor that has had a significant impact on the consumer decision-making process. In the United States, 90 percent of people keep their mobile phones within reach at all times.[2] Knowing this, many retailers have worked to make shopping easier—from anywhere.

Amazon's 1-Click Ordering allows users to completely bypass the checkout process after setting default shipping and payment options. This is not only convenient, but it also reduces the time that a customer has to back out of the order. Target recently partnered with Curbside, an app that allows mobile shoppers to buy items online and then drive to a store for immediate curbside delivery. The total pickup time is usually less than 30 seconds, so a busy mom can plan dinner on her phone, pick up the groceries, and drive home without ever setting foot inside the store.[3]

More than 85 percent of mobile time is spent in apps, and 80 percent of app time is spent exclusively in an individual's top three apps.[4] Retailers like Amazon and Target know that they must create stellar app experiences if they want to keep coming out on the right side of consumer decisions. For a broader discussion of how consumers make decisions, see Chapter 6.

IDENTIFY THE MOST VALUABLE CUSTOMERS AND UNDERSTAND THEIR NEEDS Often, 20 percent of a firm's customers produce eighty percent of the firm's revenue. An organization must understand what drives that loyalty and then take steps to ensure that those drivers are maintained and enhanced. Airlines use loyalty programs to satisfy and retain their best customers. For example, persons who fly more than 100,000 miles a year on American Airlines are called Executive Platinum members. They are granted priority boarding and seating, free domestic upgrades, no fees for checked luggage, coupons for international upgrades, and other benefits.

UNDERSTAND THE COMPETITION Successful firms know their competitors and attempt to forecast those competitors' future moves. Competitors threaten a firm's

Despite being one of America's largest sporting goods chains, Sports Authority filed for bankruptcy in 2016 amidst pressure from Dick's Sporting Goods.

Northfoto/Shutterstock.com

market share, its profitability and its very existence. Competitors that crop up because of new technologies can create a challenging competitive environment for traditional old-line firms. Uber and Lyft, for example, have made life difficult for traditional taxi cab companies. Unhappy with the lack of regulation facing these app-driven ride-sharing services, cab drivers in Paris and London recently went on strike, closing down these major cities' central business districts. The Yellow Cab Company was forced to file for bankruptcy in San Francisco after Uber and Lyft literally drove it out of the market.[5] This story is not uncommon. Increased competition from American Furniture Warehouse, Living Spaces, and Conn's sent The Room Store into bankruptcy in December 2015.[6] With 463 stores, Sports Authority was one of America's largest sporting goods chains. However, the company filed for bankruptcy in 2016 amidst pressure from Dick's Sporting Goods, which offered better in-store merchandise presentation, more modern technology, and shop-in-shops for fast-growing brands like Nike and Under Armour.[7]

4-2 SOCIAL FACTORS

Social change is perhaps the most difficult external variable for marketing managers to forecast, influence, or integrate into marketing plans. Social factors include our attitudes, values, and lifestyles. Social factors influence the products people buy; the prices paid for products; the effectiveness of specific promotions; and how, where, and when people expect to purchase products.

4-2a American Values

A *value* is a strongly held and enduring belief. America's core values strongly influence attitudes and lifestyles:

- **Self-sufficiency:** Every person should stand on his or her own two feet.

- **Upward mobility:** Success would come to anyone who got an education, worked hard, and played by the rules.

- **Work ethic:** Hard work, dedication to family, and frugality were moral and right.

- **Equality:** No one should expect to be treated differently from anybody else.

- **Individualism:** Each person is unique and special.

- **Achievement orientation:** Emphasis on getting things done by setting goals, planning, and measuring results.

These core values still hold for a majority of Americans today. A person's values are key determinants of what is important and not important, what actions to take or not to take, and how one behaves in social situations.

People typically form values through interaction with family, friends, and other influencers such as teachers, religious leaders, and politicians. The changing environment can also play a key role in shaping one's values.

Values influence our buying habits. Today's consumers are demanding, inquisitive, and discriminating. No longer willing to tolerate products that break down, they are insisting on high-quality goods that save time, energy, and often calories. U.S. consumers rank the characteristics of product quality as (1) reliability, (2) durability, (3) easy maintenance, (4) ease of use, (5) a trusted brand name, and (6) a low price. Shoppers are also concerned about nutrition and want to know what is in their food; many have environmental concerns as well.

4-2b The Growth of Component Lifestyles

People in the United States today are piecing together **component lifestyles**. A lifestyle is a mode of living; it is the way people decide to live their lives. With component lifestyles, people are choosing products and services that meet diverse needs and interests rather than conforming to traditional stereotypes.

In the past, a person's profession—for instance, banker—defined his or her lifestyle. Today, a person can be a banker and also a gourmet, fitness enthusiast,

dedicated single parent, and Internet guru. Each of these lifestyles is associated with different goods and services and represents a different target audience. Component lifestyles increase the complexity of consumers' buying habits. Each consumer's unique lifestyle can require a different marketing mix.

4-2c How Social Media Have Changed Our Behavior

In 2016, nearly half of the world's population—3 billion people—were on the Internet. Beyond accessing the Internet via computer, tablet, or smartphone, today there is much talk about the Internet of Things. In 2008, the number of "things" (clothing, thermostats, washing machines, fitness trackers, and lightbulbs, for example) connected to the Internet exceeded the number of people on earth. By 2020 there will be 50 billion connected tools, devices, and even cattle.[8] Yes, Dutch startup Sparked is developing a wireless sensor for cattle. When one is sick or pregnant, the sensor sends a message to the farmer. Similarly, Corventis makes a wireless cardiac monitor that doctors can use to monitor people for health risks in real time. And this is just the beginning—the Internet of Things has the potential to change life as we know it in nearly every area of life.

Social media are making profound changes in the way we obtain and consume information—consumers are interacting; sharing beliefs, values, ideas, and interests; and, of course, making purchases at a dizzying rate. These media have even played a major role in the beginnings of revolutions!

What exactly are social media? They are web-based and mobile technologies that allow the creation and exchange of user-generated content. Social media encompasses a wide variety of content formats—you have most likely used sites such as Facebook, YouTube, Twitter, Tumblr, Instagram, and Pinterest, each of which serves a different function (see Chapter 18). These media have changed the way we communicate, keep track of others, browse for products and services, and make purchases. Social networking is part of regular life for people of all ages. Of the 3 billion Internet users, 2 billion use social media. Slightly more women than men use social media. At 89 percent, the heaviest users by age are 18- to 29-year-olds. Usage rates are lower among older age groups.[9]

More than one minute out of every five spent on the Internet worldwide is dedicated to social networking. Facebook, Instagram,

component lifestyles the practice of choosing goods and services that meet one's diverse needs and interests rather than conforming to a single, traditional lifestyle

Pinterest, LinkedIn, and Twitter are the most-used social networking sites worldwide. Facebook, by far, is the world's most popular, with more than 1.4 billion users. Sixty-six percent of Millennials around the world use Facebook.[10] A recent survey of persons using the Internet in America found:

- Multi-platform use is on the rise. Fifty-two percent of online adults now use two or more social media sites.
- For the first time, more than half of all online adults 65 and older (56 percent) use Facebook. This represents 31 percent of all seniors.
- For the first time, roughly half of Internet-using young adults ages 18 through 29 (53 percent) use Instagram.
- Women dominate Pinterest. Forty-two percent of online women now use the platform, compared with 13 percent of online men.[11]

New York marketing research firm Crowdtap recently found that of the people who were either looking to purchase a vehicle in the next year or had purchased a vehicle in the previous year, 80 percent were more likely to turn to their social networks than to car salespeople for car-buying advice. Sixty-eight percent even said that they had purchased a car they found on social media. Almost all of the respondents (95 percent) reported that they would talk about car models they liked on social media. The most influential car recommendations came from friends or family (36 percent), followed by online review sites (19 percent), and social media (16 percent).[12]

HOW FIRMS USE SOCIAL MEDIA Social networking has changed the game when it comes to opinion sharing. Now, consumers can reach many people at once with their views—and can respond to brands and events in real time. In turn, marketers can use social media to engage customers in their products and services. Marketers have learned that social media are not like network television, where a message is pushed out to a mass audience. Instead, social media enable firms to create conversations with customers and establish meaningful connections. In other words, social media marketing can humanize brands. Marketers for brands like Absolut Vodka and Hellman's Mayonnaise post custom videos about their products to Facebook and then invite feedback. Clearly it's a winning strategy—Facebook now attracts over a billion video views per day.

With nine out of ten large and medium-sized U.S. companies now active on social networks, firms are scrambling to build effective social marketing programs. Nearly 80 percent of these companies now have dedicated social media teams to create persuasive marketing

Selena Gomez models some Adidas NEO shoes at a news conference for the new initiative.

Helga Esteb/Shutterstock.com

campaigns and stay on top of emerging social media trends. One such trend is for companies to use their own employees for social media promotions. Recent research has found that business news and new product information is much more effective when shared by employees on social media than by an anonymous corporate source.[13]

Another trend is the increased sophistication of social media promotion. In contrast to old-fashioned banner ads, the new generation of native social media advertisements—sponsored posts on Facebook and promoted tweets on Twitter, for example—look and act a lot like normal updates from friends and followers. They're also able to be targeted with increasing precision. Social media advertisers are now able to drill down not just by age and gender, but by interests, location, company affiliation, and role. This way, the ads a person sees are more likely to be ones that her or she actually may want to see.[14]

Many firms are now successfully using social media to drive sales. When fast-food chain Wendy's released the Pretzel Bacon Cheeseburger, it quickly became the chain's most successful product launch ever. Fans tweeted about their love for the new burger, and Wendy's turned the tweets (misspellings and all) into a series of silly love song music videos (including one staring Nick Lachey). In addition to being reported on all of the major news channels, the videos received 7.5 million Facebook views.[15]

When Adidas decided to launch the Adidas NEO collection, the brand recruited singer and actress Selena Gomez—along with her 30 million-plus Twitter followers. Gomez shared pictures of herself wearing her favorite Adidas items on social media, then called upon her fans to get involved in the campaign in exchange for autographed items. Her most popular Adidas NEO tweet generated more than 17,000 retweets.[16]

A number of firms use social media to build goodwill for their products instead of trying to stimulate immediate sales. Travel bag manufacturer eBags knows that its customers are savvy travelers, so its Facebook page keeps customers coming back with tips to make traveling even easier. eBags regularly offers useful content on its page about packing, travel hygiene, and other travel related tips.[17]

 4-3 # DEMOGRAPHIC FACTORS

Another uncontrollable variable in the external environment—also extremely important to marketing managers—is demography, the study of people's vital statistics, such as age, race and ethnicity, and location. Demographics are significant because the basis for any market is people. Demographic characteristics are strongly related to consumer buying behavior in the marketplace.

4-3a Population

People are directly or indirectly the basis of all markets, making population the most basic statistic in marketing. There are more than seven billion people alive today. China has the largest population with 1.38 billion persons; India is second with 1.32 billion.[18] The U.S. population is slightly over 318 million. Older Americans have moved to retirement communities like the Villages in Central Florida. This area is the nation's fastest growing metropolitan area. Midland and Odessa, in western Texas, are the second and third fastest growing areas in the country. Both cities have seen an employment boom in recent years amid new techniques to extract oil and natural gas. This growth may slow or stop in coming years as global oil prices tumbled.

Rural areas away from the oil fields, meanwhile, posted their first-ever net loss of population in 2012. The populations of the U.S. rural regions—from the Great Plains to the Mississippi delta to rural New England—are aging. These populations are not receiving many young transplants to replace those who die or migrate to urban areas. In many parts of the country, multigenerational households are increasingly common.

Multi-generational families often contain unmarried young adults. By the middle of the twenty-first century, it is forecasted that 29 percent of the population will be single and living in either a single adult or multi-generational household.[19] This doesn't necessarily mean that Americans are opting for lifelong singlehood, however. A closer look at the statistics show that young people are simply marrying at later ages. In 1970, most American women (86 percent) were married by the time they were 25 to 29 years old. According to projections, more than 80 percent won't be married until age 35 to 39 by 2030.[20] Ultimately, most people want a partner and not to be alone—just not as soon as they did before.

In South Korea, single households make up roughly the same percentage as in the United States. Marketers have responded by creating new single-serve meal offerings, but singles themselves want more. The Zipbob app enables single people to find others with similar interests with whom they can share a meal. The app connects groups of single people who are looking for togetherness, not solitude.[21]

Population is a broad statistic that is most useful to marketers when broken into smaller, more specific increments. For example, age groups present opportunities to focus on a section of the population and offer opportunities for marketers. These groups are called tweens, teens, Millennials (or Generation Y), Generation X, and baby boomers. Each cohort has its own needs, values, and consumption patterns.

TWEENS America's tweens (ages 8 to 12) are a population of more than twenty million. With access to information, opinions, and sophistication well beyond their years (and purchasing power to match), these young consumers are directly or indirectly responsible for sales of over $180 billion annually. Tweens themselves spend about $51 billion per year, and the remainder is spent by parents and family members for them.[22]

With such spending power, this age group is very attractive to many markets. One of the fastest growing tween markets is mobile games and other advertising- and microtransaction-based smartphone apps. In the United States, nearly 78 percent of tweens own a mobile phone

> **demography** the study of people's vital statistics, such as age, race and ethnicity, and location

and almost half (47 percent) have smartphones.[23] Thirty-four percent of tweens spend two hours or less with screen media (smartphones, laptops, TV) every day. On the other hand, 11 percent spend more than 8 hours a day using screen media![24]

Tweens live in a period of transition. They are bridging being a kid and being a teenager. They still not only look back at the safe world of childhood, but also look forward to the unknown but exciting world ahead. A researcher recently described seven developmental needs of tweens:

- Physical activity
- A sense of accomplishment and achievement
- Self-definition
- Creative expression
- Positive social interaction
- Structure and clear limits
- Meaningful participation.[25]

With so many needs, marketers have targeted a broad array of products and services at tweens. These include a tween chef cook-off, Pottery Barn Kids products, nail art kits, a variety of smartphones, a mountaineering club, PBS Kids Digital, Digital Kids Media, 360Kid, and the list goes on.

TEENS There are approximately 25 million teenagers in the United States, and they spend approximately 72 hours per week tuned in electronically to television, the Internet, music, video games, and cell phones. About 95 percent of U.S. teens use the Internet. Of those online, approximately 90 percent use social media. They still prefer face-to-face communication to communicating electronically, however. Twenty-five percent of teens claim that social networking makes them less shy. Teens also note that networking enables them to keep in touch with friends that they can't see on a regular basis (89 percent); helps them get to know other students better (69 percent); and enables them to connect with people who share common interests (55 percent).[26]

On a given day, teens spend about nine hours using media (digital, radio, TV) for entertainment. That's more time than they spend sleeping, and more time than they spend with their parents and educators.[27] This may seem impossible, but

Approximately 90 percent of teenagers that use the Internet, also use some form of social media.

many of those hours are spent multitasking (such as doing homework and using social media at the same time). Seventy-five percent of teens listen to music while doing homework.[28] Sixty-two percent of teen boys enjoy playing video games "a lot" versus 20 percent of teen girls, whereas 44 percent of teen girls say they enjoy social media "a lot" versus 20 percent of boys.[29] Overall, however, the "most favorite" activities among teens are still music and TV.

In many households, teens are now passing technology down to their parents, not the other way around. Researchers have found that teens are commonly the ones telling their parents to buy smartphones and tablets and are often the driving force behind their families' technology upgrades.[30]

Teens command an immense amount of buying power. Worldwide, they spend approximately $980 billion every year.[31] In the United States, $256 billion is spent on products for teens (whether bought *for* or *by* the teens themselves).[32] Although much of that money comes from parents, teens make many shopping decisions. When buying for themselves, approximately 55 percent of teens wait for items to go on sale. Most teens would rather buy a physical object than an intangible one. According to a Packaged Facts study, 75 percent would rather have a new pair of shoes than 50 new MP3 downloads, and 63 percent would choose a new pair of jeans over concert tickets.[33]

MILLENNIALS Millennials, or **Generation Y**, are people born between 1979 and 1994. Initially, Millennials were a smaller cohort than baby boomers. However, due to

Millennials people born between 1979 and 1994

immigration and the aging of the boomer generation, the seventy-seven million Gen Yers in the United States passed the boomers in total population in 2010. Millennials are now the largest group in America's workforce, making up 37 percent of all workers. Baby boomers currently account for 34 percent of the workforce—a number that is declining rapidly as more and more boomers enter retirement.[34]

Millennials are currently in two different stages of the life cycle. The youngest members of Gen Y, born in 1994, are just entering young adulthood. In contrast, the oldest Gen Yers, born in 1979, turned 38 years old in 2017. They have started their careers, and many have become parents for the first time, leading to dramatic lifestyle changes. In the United States, Millennials gave birth to 85 percent of all babies born in 2015.[35] They care for their babies rather than go out, and they spend money on baby products. Gen Yers already spend more than $200 billion annually; over their lifetimes, they will likely spend about $10 trillion.[36]

The oldest Millennials are now beginning to move up the managerial ranks and will soon enter their 20 years of peak earning power. Yet both younger and older Millennials tend to look at unemployment a bit differently than do older generations. Gen Yers are more idealistic and eager to please, and they want to do their jobs well. Yet staying at one company for a life-long career is not high on the list. Some employers believe that early adulthood for these workers is more like "extended adolescence."[37] One researcher estimates that the average Millennial will hold 15 to 16 jobs during his or her career.[38] This turnover is costing employers billions. The same study claims that Gen Yers lack support at work in areas of mentorship, purpose, and self-expression. Unhappy younger Millennials are quick to change jobs. The average job tenure of workers age 20 to 24 is now less than 16 months.[39]

Some companies, such as auditing firm Ernst & Young and consumer products giant Philips, have begun hosting mentorship mixers to foster the development of relationships between younger and older colleagues. IBM, Coca-Cola, and Visa have relaxed their dress codes and convened councils of Millennial employees to discuss everything from marketing strategies to workplace policies.[40] Advertising and marketing firm Grey Global Group has begun seating assistant account executives—all a year or two out of college—in areas called "base camp." The idea is to give these Gen Yers a place to build strong ties and show each other the ropes without bothering older colleagues. The base camp has one senior vice president who sits in the area and acts as a mentor and counselor.[41]

Millennials as consumers have been raised from childhood to adulthood in the digital world. This has impacted what they buy, how they buy, and how they use the products and services they buy. Among recent findings are:

- Ninety-two percent use a smartphone or tablet while watching TV, and 47 percent use their devices to access content related to what they are currently watching.

- Seventy-one percent would rather buy than rent a car. Fifty-nine percent would rather rent than buy a house. Sixty-one percent admit that they can't afford a house.

- Thirty-three percent rely mostly on blogs before they make a purchase.

- Sixty-two percent say that if a brand engages with them on social networks, they are more likely to become loyal customers.[42]

GENERATION X Generation X—people born between 1965 and 1978—consists of 65 million U.S. consumers. They range in age from 39 to 52 years old. It was the first generation of latchkey children—products of dual-career households or, in roughly half of the cases, of divorced or separated parents. Gen Xers often spent more time without adult support and guidance than any other age cohort. This experience made them independent, resilient, and adaptable.

Gen Xers are in their primary earning years and have acquired a disproportionate amount of spending power relative to the size of their group. They have an estimated 31 percent of total income dollars.[43] Gen Xers have higher average incomes than their Millennial and baby boomer counterparts. Higher incomes have contributed to Gen Xers' optimistic outlook on the future. Two-thirds are either "satisfied" or "very satisfied" with their lives, yet they are also concerned about crime, climate change, and their health.[44]

Saving money is a major priority for Gen Xers, who tend to be frugal and seek value when making purchases. About half note that providing for their children's college expenses is a major goal. They also want to become financially independent, buy or upgrade a home, and provide an estate for their heirs. Sixty-six percent plan to keep working during their normal retirement years because they haven't yet reached their financial goals.[45]

About 40 percent have a parent or family member living with them, and many support aging parents in other ways.[46] They place a high value on education and knowledge and tend to do a significant amount of research before making a major purchase.

> **Generation X** people born between 1965 and 1978

Marketers need to provide a lot of accurate information about their products—particularly why their goods or services are a great value.

Gen Xers have spent about 30 years in the digital revolution and are not stopping now. Eighty-four percent bought a smartphone in the last two years and 71 percent bought a new tablet.[47] Sixty percent use a smartphone every day while 67 percent use a laptop or PC every day.[48] Gen Xers tend to go online to shop, bank, research products, find the best deals, and read the news. Personalized ads boost brand favorability and purchase intent with Gen Xers more than with any other generational group.[49]

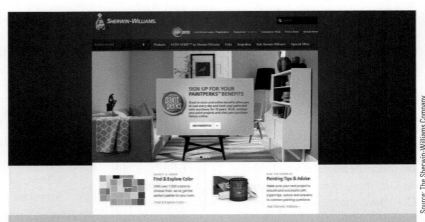

Sherwin Williams redesigned its paint cans with a fresh, clean look and larger type fonts in order to effectively target baby boomers.

BABY BOOMERS There are approximately 75 million **baby boomers** (persons born between 1946 and 1964) in the United States. With average life expectancy at an all-time high of 77.4 years, more and more Americans over fifty consider middle age a new start on life. The size of the baby boom cohort group has been decreasing in size since 2012. The pace of this decline will accelerate as the baby boomers grow older. When the first baby boomers turned 65 in 2011, there were 77 million of them. In 2030, when the baby boomers will be between 66 and 84 years old, that number is projected to drop to 60 million.[50]

While baby boomers' current incomes are relatively low because many have retired, they accumulated a substantial amount of wealth over their working years. Baby boomers outspend other generations by an estimated $400 billion a year on consumer goods and services. Boomers outspend other cohorts in categories such as gifts, personal care products, medical care, food away from home, and entertainment.

Boomers have long been a tempting target market because of their sheer numbers. Cadillac sales should have skyrocketed in the 1980s and 1990s because boomers were reaching luxury car age, life stage, and income level. Cadillac was a preferred brand of the Silent Generation (those born between 1923 and 1945), but it was failing to connect with boomers. Research showed that boomers viewed Cadillac as their father's car. To combat this image, Cadillac developed a generational marketing strategy starting with its product development and extending into its promotional communication.

baby boomers people born between 1946 and 1964

In 2003, Cadillac unveiled the CTS, a mid-sized luxury sedan heralded as the "first modern Cadillac" and designed to compete with brands such as Audi, BMW and Mercedes-Benz. Rather than showing a stately, boxy car pulling up to a country club, Cadillac's television sports featured the sleek CTS coasting down dusty roads with Led Zeppelin raging in the background. After 20 years of stagnation, Cadillac sales shot up 16 percent in one year because of the CTS.[51]

Like other cohort groups, boomers believe that price and quality are very important when making purchase decisions. Baby boomers tend to be influenced more by traditional advertising, sales reps, and word-of-mouth recommendations than other groups. Yet they are also very active in seeking product information online. Boomers tend to use laptops and tablets more than smartphones when conducting product research. While boomers make fewer product purchases online than do some other cohorts, the same is not true for services. Boomers now make most of their travel purchases online.

Marketers targeting baby boomers must avoid the perception that boomers are old. Words such as "senior," "elderly," and "aged" can quickly drive away potential customers. Boomers today are active and feel entitled to enjoy the good life. It is best to target boomers based upon their lifestyles, purchase behaviors, and core values, such as healthy eating, exercise, and family. Simplifying instructions for product assembly and use makes life easier for boomers. Enlarging font size may enable boomers to avoid reaching for their reading glasses. Realizing that holding up a heavy paint can and reaching for your glasses at the same time can be tough, Sherwin Williams completely redesigned its can with a clean, crisp look and large fonts.

4-4 GROWING ETHNIC MARKETS

The American demographic profile is rapidly changing as racial and ethnic groups continue to grow. The minority population today is about 118 million. By 2050, around one in three U.S. residents will be Hispanic. The United States will flip completely to a majority-minority makeup in 2041, meaning that whites of European ancestry will make up less than 50 percent of the population. Already, minorities make up about half of all Americans under the age of five.[52] As the demographic environment of America evolves, so too must the marketing mix change to reach growing target markets.

4-4a Marketing to Hispanic Americans

With a population of 50 million, Hispanics make up the largest U.S. minority.[53] The term *Hispanic* encompasses people of many different backgrounds. Nearly 60 percent of Hispanic Americans are of Mexican descent. Puerto Ricans, the next largest group, make up just under ten percent of Hispanics. Other groups, including Central Americans, Dominicans, South Americans, and Cubans, each account for less than five percent of all Hispanics. Yet racial lines are blurring. A quarter of Hispanic marriages now involve a non-Hispanic partner.[54]

Hispanics make up the largest group to use mobile devices for any type of transaction, from banking to watching movies.[55] Companies like Metro PCS, Boost Mobile and Verizon have substantially increased their marketing budgets targeted toward Hispanics. Research showed that 49 percent of Hispanics planned to change their smartphones in 2016.[56] This is not surprising, as 42 percent of the Hispanic population are Millennials.[57]

Hispanic Millennials still embrace parts of their original culture, mostly in the areas of family, music and food. Yet they also look forward to being successful in business and perhaps owning their own company. Hispanic Millennials tend to be more open-minded about relationships than their parents. Yet they willingly accept future family obligations and the difficulties of supporting parents and grandparents.[58]

Hispanic Millennials in the United States are particularly prone to taking a bilingual, bicultural approach to their media consumption. Forty percent of Hispanic Millennials consume an equal amount of Spanish and English media.[59] Spending on Hispanic media now tops $5.7 billion in the United States.[60] The leading advertisers targeting Hispanics are Procter & Gamble, AT&T, and L'Oreal. The 2014 World Cup was very popular in the Hispanic market, and Kraft Foods targeted Hispanics with its "Flavor of the Championship" campaign. Throughout this campaign, Kraft used social media to suggest appropriate recipes for World Cup viewing parties. Hispanics spend most of their leisure time at home viewing media. Hispanic Millennials often utilize online video streaming services in addition to broadcast television for content consumption. Nielsen Research states that "Latinos stream 6 hours and 15 minutes of online video per month, 60 percent more than non-Hispanic users."[61] To remain relevant and win U.S. Hispanics' viewership, marketers have begun putting more emphasis on video content specifically designed for and targeted at Hispanics.

4-4b Marketing to African Americans

There are approximately 44 million African Americans (14 percent of the country's population). They are young—53 percent are under the age of 35—giving them a strong influence on the latest trends, especially in regards to music and pop culture. Higher academic achievement has translated into increases in

Hispanics make up the largest group using mobile devices today. Hispanic millennials often utilize online video streaming services like Netflix and Hulu in addition to broadcast television.

Rido/Shutterstock.com

household income; 44 percent of all African American households now earn $50,000 or more and 23 percent earn more than $75,000. Higher household incomes, coupled with an overall population growth, are driving the substantial purchasing power of the African American consumer upwards. Total purchasing power is expected to reach $1.3 trillion within a few years.[62]

Anchored by a rich heritage, African Americans believe in strong cultural connections. Forty percent expect brands to support social causes, and there is a general expectation that brands reflect their values.[63] As consumers, African Americans' buying patterns focus on family and cooking ingredients tied to cultural traditions. African Americans are voracious radio listeners—91 percent tune in and listen for more than 15 hours every week.[64] African Americans are also heavy users of technology, and eighty-three percent own a smartphone. Seventy-nine percent of African American women agree that pursuing good health is important. In the last five years, there has been a 40 percent increase in shopping at health food stores (like Whole Foods, Trader Joe's, and Fresh Market) among African Americans age 18 to 54 with annual incomes greater than $50,000.[65]

When Fox introduced hip-hop soap opera *Empire*, it became an instant hit. The program connected powerfully with African American viewers, who make up 61 percent of the show's audience. *Empire's* initial success resulted from a month-long marketing campaign that played up the family drama and musical aspects of the show, targeting African Americans. The campaign ran across numerous mediums, including print, radio, traditional online, social media, streaming music, and television. Since *Empire* is about the music industry, the music used to promote the show had to be chosen carefully. Fox ultimately settled on a mixture of popular artists (including Kanye West) and original music from the show. On Black Friday 2014, Fox distributed gold *Empire* tote bags at ten malls across the country. They even targeted 450 barbershops and hair salons with promotional items, commissioned a custom *Empire*-themed Adidas shoe, and created custom-made jewelry that tied into the show.[66]

African Americans tend to be loyal to both brands and stores; they spend 18 percent more than the general population on store brands. They are also more likely to patronize convenience, drug stores, and dollar stores than other groups. Relative to other cohorts, they spend more on groceries and hair care products.[67] Featuring nonwhite Americans has become a cornerstone of Cheerios' promotional strategy. A recent Honey Nut Cheerios commercial features musician Usher and Buzz Bee dancing and discussing heart health while Usher's song "She Came to Give It to You" plays in the background. Usher was chosen for the spot because of his broad appeal—he has more than 50.5 million Facebook fans.[68]

4-4c Marketing to Asian Americans

The Asian American population reached 19 million in 2017. U.S. births have been the primary driving force behind the increase in the Hispanic and African American populations. By contrast, Asian American population growth has been fueled primarily by immigration. Sixty-six percent of Asian Americans were foreign-born.[69] California and Hawaii are home to the largest Asian American populations. Asian Americans, who still represent only 6 percent of the U.S. population, have the highest average family income of all groups. At $67,000, it exceeds the average U.S. household income by roughly $15,000.[70] Forty-nine percent of Asian Americans have a bachelor's degree compared to 28 percent of the general population.[71] Because Asian Americans are younger (the average age is 34), better educated, and have higher incomes than average, they are sometimes called a "marketer's dream." Asian Americans are heavy users of technology. Moreover, they are early adopters of the latest digital gadgets. They visit computer and consumer electronics websites 36 percent more often and spend 72 percent more time at these sites than the total. They download more information and entertainment from mobile and use social media more than any other ethnic segment.[72] Because of their high level of education, Asian Americans are thriving in America's technology sector.

Although Asian Americans embrace the values of the larger U.S. population, they also hold on to the cultural values of their particular subgroup. Consider language: many Asian Americans, particularly Koreans and Chinese, speak their native tongue at home (though Filipinos are far less likely to do so). Cultural values are also apparent in the ways different groups make big-ticket purchases. In Japanese American homes, husbands alone make large purchase decisions nearly half the time; wives decide only about six percent of the time. In Filipino families, however, wives make these decisions a little more often than their husbands do, although, by far, most decisions are made by husbands and wives jointly or with the input of other family members.

Only a small percentage of Asian Americans (14 percent) describe themselves as "American." Nineteen percent say they are "Asian" or "Asian American," and 62 percent mention their country of origin. About half claim that they speak English "very well."[73] Eighty-two percent of Asian Americans say that they are "overall happier with life" compared to 75 percent among the general public.[74]

Asian Americans are 31 percent more likely to buy organic foods and 23 percent more likely than the general consumer to evaluate the nutrition of the products they buy. Eighty-eight percent of Asian-Americans own credit cards compared to 66 percent of the U.S. population.[75]

Asian Americans like to shop at stores owned and managed by other Asian Americans. Small businesses such as flower shops, grocery stores, and appliance stores are often best equipped to offer the products that Asian Americans want. For example, at first glance, the Hannam Chain supermarket in Los Angeles's Koreatown seems like any other grocery store. But next to the Kraft American singles and the State Fair corn dogs are jars of whole cabbage kimchi. A snack bar in another part of the store cooks up aromatic mung cakes, and an entire aisle is devoted to dried seafood.

Asian Americans are 31 percent more likely to buy organic foods and 23 percent more likely than the general consumers to evaluate the nutrition of the products they buy.

VectorLifestylepic/Shutterstock.com

leaving the labor market, the share of households with zero earners jumped from 20 percent to 25 percent over the same time period. The unemployment rate was 4.9 percent in mid-2016, which is the lowest it had been in seven years. Scars from the Great Recession continue to affect the United States as 2.6 million people continue to suffer from long-term unemployment (defined as not having a job for 27 weeks or longer).[78]

Education is the primary determinant of a person's earning potential. For example, just 1 percent of workers with only a high school education earn over $100,000 annually. By comparison, 13 percent of college-educated workers earn six figures or more. People with a bachelor's degree take home an average of 38 percent more than those with just a high school diploma. Over a lifetime, an individual with a bachelor's degree will earn more than twice as much total income as a nondegree holder.[79]

In recent years, stores that cater to lower-income consumers—like Family Dollar and Dollar General—have done well. Procter & Gamble (P&G) has found that its typical middle-class customers are increasingly unwilling to spend their money on household staples with extra features, such as Tide with bleach. Many customers have switched to cheaper brands, while P&G brands like Bounce fabric softener and Bounty paper towels suffered. To regain market share, P&G has launched its bargain-priced Gain dish soap. The firm has also reduced some package sizes of Tide in order to sell them at Walmart for less than ten dollars.

ECONOMIC FACTORS

In addition to social and demographic factors, marketing managers must understand and react to the economic environment. The three economic areas of greatest concern to most marketers are consumers' incomes, inflation, and recession.

4-5a Consumers' Incomes

As disposable (or after-tax) incomes rise, more families and individuals can afford the "good life." In recent years, however, average U.S. incomes have actually fallen. The annual median household income in the United States in 2016 was approximately $57,000, though the median household income varies widely from state to state.[76] This means half of all U.S. households earned less, and the other half earned more. The real (adjusted for inflation) median household income has fallen since 2009. This is due partly to a drop in the number of households with two or more wage earners from 44 percent in 2009 to around 39 percent in 2016.[77] Also, because baby boomers are retiring at increasing rates and subsequently

4-5b Purchasing Power

Even when incomes rise, a higher standard of living does not necessarily result. Increased standards of living are a function of purchasing power. **Purchasing power** is measured by comparing income to the relative cost of a standard set of goods and services in different geographic areas, usually referred to as the *cost of living*. Another way to

> **purchasing power** a comparison of income versus the relative cost of a standard set of goods and services in different geographic areas

think of purchasing power is income minus the cost of living (i.e., expenses). In general, a cost of living index takes into account housing, food and groceries, transportation, utilities, health care, and miscellaneous expenses such as clothing, services, and entertainment. Home-Fair.com's salary calculator uses these metrics when it determines that the cost of living in New York City is almost three times the cost of living in Youngstown, Ohio. This means that a worker living in New York City must earn nearly $279,500 to have the same standard of living as someone making $100,000 in Youngstown.

When income is high relative to the cost of living, people have more discretionary income. That means they have more money to spend on nonessential items (in other words, on wants rather than needs). This information is important to marketers for obvious reasons. Consumers with high purchasing power can afford to spend more money without jeopardizing their budget for necessities like food, housing, and utilities. They also have the ability to purchase higher-priced necessities—for example, a more expensive car, a home in a more expensive neighborhood, or a designer handbag versus a purse from a discount store.

4-5c Inflation

Inflation is a measure of the decrease in the value of money, generally expressed as the percentage reduction in value since the previous year, which is the rate of inflation. Thus, in simple terms, an inflation rate of five percent means you will need 5 percent more units of money than you would have needed last year to buy the same basket of products. If inflation is 5 percent, you can expect that, on average, prices have risen by about 5 percent since the previous year. Of course, if pay raises are matching the rate of inflation, then employees will be no worse off in terms of the immediate purchasing power of their salaries.

In times of low inflation, businesses seeking to increase their profit margins can do so only by increasing their efficiency. If they significantly increase prices, no one will purchase their goods or services. The Great Recession brought inflation rates to almost zero. In January 2016, the inflation rate was 1.4 percent.[80] By contrast, Venezuela had the highest inflation rate in 2015 at 159 percent.[81]

In creating marketing strategies to cope with inflation, managers must realize that, regardless of what happens to the seller's cost, the buyer is not going to pay more for a product than the subjective value he or she places on it. No matter how compelling the justification might be for a 10 percent price increase, marketers must always examine its impact on demand. Many marketers try to hold prices level for as long as is practical.

iStockphoto.com/igroup

4-5d Recession

A **recession** is a period of economic activity characterized by negative growth. More precisely, a recession is defined as occurring when the gross domestic product falls for two consecutive quarters. Gross domestic product is the total market value of all final goods and services produced during a period of time. The official beginning of the Great Recession of 2008–2009 was December 2007. While the causes of the recession are very complex, this one began with the collapse of inflated housing prices. Those high prices led people to take out mortgages they could not afford from banks that should have known the money would not be repaid. By 2008, the recession had spread around the globe. A slow economic recovery began in July 2009 and continues to this day.

4-6 TECHNOLOGY AND INNOVATION

Technological success is based upon innovation, and innovation requires imagination and risk taking. Bringing new technology to the marketplace requires a corporate structure and management actions that will lead to success. Great corporate leaders must embed innovation into the lifeblood of the company. Managers should hire employees with a tolerance for risk. Then, workers must be told not to fear innovation failure. Not everything works the first time. Some of the greatest innovations in recent years, such as 3-D printing, hydraulic fracturing, quantum computing, and autonomous vehicles, all had setbacks before a successful product was created.

Shell, one of the world's largest oil producers, has created the Idea Factory, a technology-forward

inflation a measure of the decrease in the value of money, expressed as the percentage reduction in value since the previous year

recession a period of economic activity characterized by negative growth, which reduces demand for goods and services

development platform consisting of four pillars. These are:

- **Game Changer:** This program works at the early or "blue sky" stage of innovation. If a start-up proves its concept, and it aligns with Shell's goals and passes a rigorous approval process, it qualifies for funding and technological help from Shell's engineers.
- **Shell Technology Ventures:** Shell's venture capital arm funds start-ups and entrepreneurs.
- **Shell Tech Works:** This program looks for technology created in other industries but that addresses areas that also apply to Shell.
- **Universities:** Shell collaborates with universities from around the world to complement its internal research and development department.

Some of the innovations that have come from Shell's Idea Factory include visualization tools to print 3-D pictures of rock and oil formations, solar power technologies that assist oil recovery, space robots, and the world's largest floating structure—a floating liquefaction plant for natural gas.[82] A recent trend in stimulating innovation is the founding of a startup incubator (or accelerator). Here, companies provide mentoring, office space, and in many cases, funding to startups that are developing products and services that relate to the companies' areas of interest. Tech giants like Alphabet, Intel, and Microsoft have internal incubators. Other companies follow an external model whereby the startup operates independently but is guided by the brand's marketing and R&D teams.[83]

4-6a Research

The United States, historically, has excelled at both basic and applied research. **Basic research** (or *pure research*) attempts to expand the frontiers of knowledge but is not aimed at a specific, pragmatic problem. Basic research aims to confirm an existing theory or to learn more about a concept or phenomenon. For example, basic research might focus on high-energy physics. **Applied research**, in contrast, attempts to develop new or improved products. The United States has dramatically improved its track record in applied research. For example, the United States leads the world in applying basic research to aircraft design and propulsion systems. Many companies, particularly small and medium-sized firms, cannot afford the luxury of basic research. The difficulty of earning a profit from basic research discoveries has led a whole generation of management to cut spending on basic research.[84] This is unfortunate, because U.S. government expenditures on basic research as a percentage of gross domestic product have been declining for fifty years.[85]

The two industries where companies continue to spend a large share of their budgets on basic research are information technology and pharmaceuticals.

4-6b Stimulating Innovation

Companies attempting to innovate often limit their searches to areas they are already familiar with. This can help lead to incremental progress but rarely leads to a dramatic breakthrough. Companies are now using several approaches such as Shell's Idea Factory to keep innovation strong. These include:

- **Building scenarios:** Some firms use teams of writers to imagine detailed opportunities and threats for their companies, partners, and collaborators in future markets. Ikea, famous for selling inexpensive assemble-it-yourself furniture, recently launched the Concept Kitchen 2025 initiative to explore how technology and furniture might be combined to better suit our everyday needs. One result of Concept Kitchen 2025 was the Table for Living, which uses an overhead camera to record the ingredients on the table's surface. The camera sends the images to special software on your home PC for analysis. After sifting through a database of recipes, the software sends recipes that use the ingredients on your table to an overhead projector, displaying them directly on the table's surface. Ikea's goal is to mass-produce this and other smart furniture without making it more expensive than conventional options. The company is considering adding other helpful technologies such as induction coils to heat the food and perhaps even a charging dock for a smartphone.[86]
- **Enlisting the Web:** A few companies have created websites that act as literal marketplaces of ideas where innovators can go to look for help with scientific and business challenges.
- **Talking to early adopters:** Early adopters tend to be innovators themselves. They are risk takers and look for new things or wish for something better to help in daily tasks at home and work.
- **Using marketing research:** Firms find out what customers like and dislike about their products and competitors' products.
- **Creating an innovative environment:** Companies let employees know that they have the "freedom to fail." They create intranets to encourage sharing ideas. Most

basic research pure research that aims to confirm an existing theory or to learn more about a concept or phenomenon

applied research research that attempts to develop new or improved products

importantly, top management must lead by example to create an atmosphere where innovation is encouraged and rewarded.

- **Catering to entrepreneurs:** Policies that reserve blocks of time for scientists or engineers to explore their own ideas have worked well at some companies. At 3M, scientists can spend fifteen percent of their time on projects they dream up themselves—a freedom that led to the development of the yellow Post-It note. Google is well known in the tech industry for its "20% time" policy, which grants employees a day a week to follow their entrepreneurial passions.[87]

Although developing new technology internally is a key to creating and maintaining a long-term competitive advantage, external technology is also important to managers for two reasons. First, by acquiring the technology, the firm may be able to operate more efficiently or create a better product. Second, a new technology may render existing products obsolete.

Radio frequency identification (RFID) chips were supposed to be a game changer for inventory tracking. Walmart tried using them, but was less than satisfied. JC Penney found that the chips interfered with existing anti-theft sensors. The company removed the anti-theft sensors, and shoplifting surged. Zara, a fashion chain that operates in 88 countries, claims to have learned from others' mistakes and is using RFID chips in a new way. A Zara employee suggested putting the RFID chips inside items' security tags. The security tag's plastic case protects the chip, preventing interference and allowing for reuse.

Before the new tags, taking inventory took 40 employees about five hours to complete. Now, ten employees walking down store aisles while waving pistol-like scanners can finish in half the time.[88] Each time a garment is sold, data from its chip prompts the stockroom to send out an identical item. Previously, store employees using paper sales reports restocked shelves a few times a day. If a customer can't find an item, a salesperson can point an iPod camera at a similar item's bar code and, using data gathered by the chips, see whether the

leedsn/Shutterstock.com

desired item is available in the store, at a nearby Zara store, or online.[89]

THE RELATIONSHIP BETWEEN INNOVATION AND EMPLOYMENT Eighty-four percent of executives believe that innovation is very important for their growth strategies, but this doesn't always translate into good news for workers.[90] Tom Kalil, Deputy Director of The White House Office of Science and Technology Policy, says, "We don't want to compete on the basis of price and wages. We want to be competing on the basis of generating new products and services that the rest of the world can't yet make."[91] Tesla, for its part, is innovating across the entire business model. Innovation is evident not just in Tesla's cars, but also in the super-charger network that charges these cars in minutes instead of hours and the way owners can upgrade their cars from standard to self-driving simply by downloading a software upgrade.

Though it is not always apparent, there is a direct link between innovation and employment. Since the first Industrial Revolution, innovation has tended to result in unskilled workers and outdated jobs being replaced with more skilled workers and higher-paying jobs. Tesla currently has around 14,000 employees, while Ford has almost 200,000. Tesla is a smaller company in general, but it is also more nimble and innovative, allowing it to do more with far fewer employees.[92] To put it another way, consider the impact that iTunes had on the music industry. This single piece of innovative software disrupted existing processes, services, systems, technology, marketing strategies, cost structure, management, and business models. The same can be said for Amazon and Netflix. Did net employment go up? When is the last time you bought a CD at a record shop or visited a video rental store?

One area where scientists are beginning to worry about innovation and employment is in the area of robotics. To date, robots that can think like humans are still mostly at the conceptual stage. However, IBM supercomputer Watson handily beat two accomplished contestants on the game show Jeopardy, and in 2016, Google AI AlphaGo won several matches against the world champion of Go. MIT economist Erik Brynjolfsson has long dismissed the notion that automation will eventually eliminate jobs that require thinking, judgment, and dexterity. However, recent advances in driverless cars and computers than can interpret facial expressions have him rethinking his position.[93] Robots can recommend stock portfolios depending on your investment needs, operate entire train systems, conduct legal research, generate online advertising, translate conversations, author news stories, tend gardens, and more.

Many skeptics now admit that some jobs will indeed be replaced with other, higher-paying jobs, but jobs that need a human touch simply cannot be replaced. A barista making a shot of espresso can deal with a leaky cup or a customer asking for a shot of milk. A conscientious cab driver can alert passengers that they are about to leave a phone or package behind. A good bartender knows when to tell a joke or lend a sympathetic ear. These specialized tasks all require a human consciousness . . . for now. Unquestionably, America must innovate to remain a leader in the world marketplace. Hopefully, better paying and more interesting jobs will be there to fill the gaps as it does.

 ## 4-7 POLITICAL AND LEGAL FACTORS

Business needs government regulation to protect innovators of new technology, the interests of society in general, one business from another, and consumers. In turn, government needs business because the marketplace generates taxes that support public efforts to educate our youth, pave our roads, protect our shores, and the like.

Every aspect of the marketing mix is subject to laws and restrictions. It is the duty of marketing managers or their legal assistants to understand these laws and conform to them, because failure to comply with regulations can have major consequences for a firm. Sometimes just sensing trends and taking corrective action before a government agency acts can help avoid regulation.

4-7a Federal Legislation

Federal laws that affect marketing fall into several categories of regulatory activity: competitive environment, pricing, advertising and promotion, and consumer privacy. The key pieces of legislation in these areas are summarized in Exhibit 4.1. The primary federal laws that protect consumers are shown in Exhibit 4.2. The Patient Protection and Affordable Care Act, commonly called Obamacare, has had a significant impact on marketing. A few key provisions of the Act are that:

- Large employers must offer coverage to full-time workers.
- Workers cannot be denied coverage.
- A person cannot be dropped when he or she is sick.
- A worker cannot be denied coverage for a preexisting condition.
- Young adults can stay on their parents' plans until age 26.[94]

EXHIBIT 4.1	PRIMARY U.S. LAWS THAT AFFECT MARKETING
Legislation	**Impact on Marketing**
Sherman Act of 1890	Makes trusts and conspiracies in restraint of trade illegal; makes monopolies and attempts to monopolize misdemeanors.
Clayton Act of 1914	Outlaws discrimination in prices to different buyers; prohibits tying contracts (which require the buyer of one product to also buy another item in the line); makes illegal the combining of two or more competing corporations by pooling ownership of stock.
Federal Trade Commission Act of 1914	Created the Federal Trade Commission to deal with antitrust matters; outlaws unfair methods of competition.
Robinson-Patman Act of 1936	Prohibits charging different prices to different buyers of merchandise of like grade and quantity; requires sellers to make any supplementary services or allowances available to all purchasers on a proportionately equal basis.
Wheeler-Lea Amendments to FTC Act of 1938	Broadens the Federal Trade Commission's power to prohibit practices that might injure the public without affecting competition; outlaws false and deceptive advertising.
Lanham Act of 1946	Establishes protection for trademarks.
Celler-Kefauver Antimerger Act of 1950	Strengthens the Clayton Act to prevent corporate acquisitions that reduce competition.
Hart-Scott-Rodino Act of 1976	Requires large companies to notify the government of their intent to merge.
Foreign Corrupt Practices Act of 1977	Prohibits bribery of foreign officials to obtain business.

EXHIBIT 4.2   PRIMARY U.S. LAWS PROTECTING CONSUMERS

Legislation	Impact on Marketing
Federal Food and Drug Act of 1906	Prohibits adulteration and misbranding of foods and drugs involved in interstate commerce; strengthened by the Food, Drug, and Cosmetic Act (1938) and the Kefauver-Harris Drug Amendment (1962).
Federal Hazardous Substances Act of 1960	Requires warning labels on hazardous household chemicals.
Kefauver-Harris Drug Amendment of 1962	Requires that manufacturers conduct tests to prove drug effectiveness and safety.
Consumer Credit Protection Act of 1968	Requires that lenders fully disclose true interest rates and all other charges to credit customers for loans and installment purchases.
Child Protection and Toy Safety Act of 1969	Prevents marketing of products so dangerous that adequate safety warnings cannot be given.
Public Health Smoking Act of 1970	Prohibits cigarette advertising on television and radio and revises the health hazard warning on cigarette packages.
Poison Prevention Labeling Act of 1970	Requires safety packaging for products that may be harmful to children.
National Environmental Policy Act of 1970	Established the Environmental Protection Agency to deal with various types of pollution and organizations that create pollution.
Public Health Cigarette Smoking Act of 1971	Prohibits tobacco advertising on radio and television.
Consumer Product Safety Act of 1972	Created the Consumer Product Safety Commission, which has authority to specify safety standards for most products.
Child Protection Act of 1990	Regulates the number of minutes of advertising on children's television.
Children's Online Privacy Protection Act of 1998	Empowers the FTC to set rules regarding how and when marketers must obtain parental permission before asking children marketing research questions.
Aviation Security Act of 2001	Requires airlines to take extra security measures to protect passengers, including the installation of stronger cockpit doors, improved baggage screening, and increased security training for airport personnel.
Homeland Security Act of 2002	Protects consumers against terrorist acts; created the Department of Homeland Security.
Do Not Call Law of 2003	Protects consumers against unwanted telemarketing calls.
CAN-SPAM Act of 2003	Protects consumers against unwanted e-mail, or spam.
Credit Card Act of 2009	Provides many credit card protections.
Restoring American Financial Stability Act of 2010	Created the Consumer Financial Protection Bureau to protect consumers against unfair, abusive, and deceptive financial practices.
Patient Protection and Affordable Care Act	Overhauled the U.S. healthcare system; mandated and subsidized health insurance for individuals.

In 2010, Congress passed the Restoring American Financial Stability Act, which brought sweeping changes to bank and financial market regulations. The legislation created the Consumer Financial Protection Bureau (CFPB) to oversee checking accounts, private student loans, mortgages, and other financial products. The agency deals with unfair, abusive, and deceptive practices. Some groups have expressed concerns that the CFPB is assembling massive databases on credit cards, credit monitoring, debt cancellation products, auto loans, and payday loans. CFPB officials claim that they need the information to make effective rules and enforce those policies. One way or another, the CFPB has certainly had a significant impact on several United States businesses—the agency has recovered more than $4.6 billion from financial services firms in the name of wronged consumers.[95] The most common violations include unfair billing, illegal fees and kickbacks, deception, and discrimination.

4-7b State and Local Laws

Legislation that affects marketing varies state by state. Oregon, for example, limits utility advertising to 0.5 percent of the company's net income. California has forced industry to improve consumer products and has enacted legislation to lower the energy consumption of refrigerators, freezers, and air conditioners. Several states, including California and North Carolina, are considering levying a tax on all in-state commercial advertising.

Many states and cities are attempting to fight obesity by regulating fast-food chains and other restaurants. For example, California and New York have passed a law banning trans fats in restaurants and bakeries, New York City chain restaurants must now display calorie counts on menus, and Boston has banned trans fats in restaurants. New York City enacted a law prohibiting restaurants from selling soft drinks larger than 16 ounces, but the ban was overturned a day before it was to go into effect.

4-7c Regulatory Agencies

Although some state regulatory bodies actively pursue violators of their marketing statutes, federal regulators generally have the greatest clout. The Consumer Product Safety Commission, the Federal Trade Commission, and the Food and Drug Administration are the three federal agencies most directly and actively involved in marketing affairs. These agencies, plus others, are discussed throughout the book, but a brief introduction is in order at this point.

CONSUMER PRODUCT SAFETY COMMISSION The sole purpose of the Consumer Product Safety Commission (CPSC) is to protect the health and safety of consumers in and around their homes. The CPSC has the power to set mandatory safety standards for almost all products consumers use (about 15,000 items) and can fine offending firms up to $500,000 and sentence their officers to up to a year in prison. It can also ban dangerous products from the marketplace. The CPSC oversees about 400 recalls per year. In 2008, Congress passed the Consumer Product Safety Improvement Act. The law is aimed primarily at children's products, which are defined as those used by individuals 12 years old or younger. The law addresses items such as cribs, electronics and video games, school supplies, science kits, toys, and pacifiers. The law requires mandatory testing and labeling and increases fines and prison time for violators.

FOOD AND DRUG ADMINISTRATION The Food and Drug Administration (FDA), another powerful agency, is charged with enforcing regulations against selling and distributing adulterated, misbranded, or hazardous food and drug products. In 2009, the Tobacco Control Act was passed. This act gave the FDA authority to regulate tobacco products, with a special emphasis on preventing their use by children and young people and reducing the impact of tobacco on public health. Another recent FDA action is the "Bad Ad" program. It is geared toward health care providers to help them recognize misleading prescription drug promotions and gives them an easy way to report the activity to the FDA.

FEDERAL TRADE COMMISSION The Federal Trade Commission (FTC) is empowered to prevent persons or corporations from using unfair methods of competition in commerce. The FTC consists of five members, each holding office for seven years. Over the years, Congress has greatly expanded the powers of the FTC. Its responsibilities have grown so large that the FTC has created several bureaus to better organize its operations. One of the most important is the Bureau of Competition, which promotes and protects competition.

The Bureau of Competition:

- reviews mergers and acquisitions, and challenges those that would likely lead to higher prices, fewer choices, or less innovation;

- seeks out and challenges anti-competitive conduct in the marketplace, including monopolization and agreements between competitors;

- promotes competition in industries where consumer impact is high, such as health care, real estate, oil and gas, technology, and consumer goods; and

- provides information and holds conferences and workshops for consumers, businesses, and policy makers on competition issues for market analysis.

The FTC's Bureau of Consumer Protection works for the consumer to prevent fraud, deception, and unfair business practices in the marketplace. The Bureau of Consumer Protection claims that it:

- enhances consumer confidence by enforcing federal laws that protect consumers;

- empowers consumers with free information to help them exercise their rights and to spot and avoid fraud and deception; and

- wants to hear from consumers who want to get information or file a complaint about fraud or identity theft.[96]

Another important FTC bureau is the Bureau of Economics. It provides economic analysis and support to antitrust and consumer protection investigations. Many consumer protection issues today involve the Internet.

4-7d Consumer Privacy

The popularity of the Internet for targeted advertising, for collecting consumer data, and as a repository for sensitive consumer data has alarmed privacy-minded consumers. In 2003, the U.S. Congress passed the CAN-SPAM Act in an attempt to regulate unsolicited e-mail advertising. The act prohibits commercial e-mailers from using false addresses and presenting false or misleading information, among other restrictions.

Consumer Product Safety Commission (CPSC) a federal agency established to protect the health and safety of consumers in and around their homes

Food and Drug Administration (FDA) a federal agency charged with enforcing regulations against selling and distributing adulterated, misbranded, or hazardous food and drug products

Federal Trade Commission (FTC) a federal agency empowered to prevent persons or corporations from using unfair methods of competition in commerce

Internet users who once felt fairly anonymous when using the Web are now disturbed by the amount of information marketers collect about them and their children as they visit various sites in cyberspace. The FTC, with jurisdiction under the Children's Online Privacy Protection Act, requires websites operators to post a privacy policy on their home page and a link to the policy on every page where personal information is collected.

Despite federal efforts, online tracking has become widespread and pervasive. A vast amount of personal data is collected through application software, commonly called *apps*. For example, some widely used apps on Facebook gather volumes of information when they are downloaded. A Wall Street Journal analysis of the 100 most popular Facebook apps found that some seek e-mail addresses, current locations, and even sexual preferences. Information is collected not only from app users but also from their Facebook friends.

Successful tracking has created a $170 billion online-advertising business that is growing rapidly. There are more than 300 companies collecting data about users.[97] More than half the time, data collectors piggyback on each other. When a user visits a website that has a code for one type of tracking technology, the data collection triggers other tracking technologies that are not embedded on the site. Piggybacking means that websites really do not know how much data are being gathered about their users.

Acxiom uses more than 23,000 computer servers to collect, collate, and analyze consumer data. The firm has created the world's largest consumer database—the servers process more than fifty trillion data transactions a year. The database contains information on over 500 million consumers worldwide, with about 1,500 data points per person.[98] Acxiom customers include firms like E°Trade, Ford, Wells Fargo, Macy's, and many other major firms seeking consumer insights. Acxiom integrates online, mobile, and offline data to create in-depth consumer behavior portraits. The firm's proprietary software, PersonicX, assigns consumers to one of 70 detailed socioeconomic clusters. For example, the "savvy single" cluster includes mobile, upper-middle-class singles who do their banking online, attend pro sports events, are sensitive to prices, and respond to free-shipping offers.[99]

Many consumers don't want to be part of huge databases—they want their privacy back. Ninety-three percent of adults say that controlling *who* can get information about them is important. Ninety percent say that controlling *what* information is collected about them is important.[100]

In 2016, the Federal Communications Commission (FCC) announced new rules to improve consumer privacy online. These rules will shield millions of consumers from unwanted use of their information by Internet service providers like Comcast and Time Warner. (Popular Web platforms like Alphabet's Google and Facebook are not affected by the FCC rules, as they are regulated by the Federal Trade Commission.)[101]

A major privacy dispute erupted between Apple and the FBI after investigators recovered the iPhone of Syed Rizwan Farook, who had recently opened fire on a holiday office party in San Bernardino, killing 14 and injuring 22. Investigators couldn't unlock the iPhone because of a security feature that locks the phone down after more than 10 attempts are made to guess the device's passcode.

The Justice Department got a court order compelling Apple to help them bypass the passcode security features, but Apple fought the order, setting the stage for a court fight on privacy. As the two sides geared up for that fight, FBI officials announced that they had exhausted all possible avenues of unlocking the phone before obtaining the court order against Apple.

In the public and legal debate that followed, the FBI argued that the law doesn't support a company making phones that are "warrant proof"—unable to be opened even with a signed order from a judge. Apple replied that it was fighting the order because doing what the FBI wanted would create a new security vulnerability for untold millions of iPhone users.

In spring 2016, the FBI announced that it had opened the phone without Apple's help. Opening the phone ended the legal showdown, but the basic question of whether the government can force technology companies to help it access customers' data remains.[102]

 ## 4-8 COMPETITIVE FACTORS

The competitive environment encompasses the number of competitors a firm must face, the relative size of the competitors, and the degree of interdependence within the industry. Management has little control over the competitive environment confronting a firm.

4-8a Competition for Market Share and Profits

As U.S. population growth slows, global competition increases, costs rise, and available resources tighten,

A vending machine is a perfect example of competition for market share. Several brands are competing for the business of the person who has the munchies.

Lissandra Melo/Shutterstock.com

found Amazon to have one of the best reputations in America. Amazon's success, spurred by extremely competitive prices, hurt Sears, JCPenney, Borders, and Best Buy, and even contributed to Circuit City's going out of business. At first glance, Alphabet's Google and Amazon don't seem to be competitors. Google is a search engine that sells ads and Amazon is a retailer that sells and delivers goods. However, Google is slowly getting into the market for on-demand goods and has launched a same-day delivery service called Google Express in several major markets. Google doesn't own massive warehouses like Amazon, but works with local retailers like Walgreens and Walmart. Conversely, people don't tend to think of Amazon as search engine, but if someone is looking for something to buy, she is probably looking on Amazon. Forty-five percent of people looking for something to buy start on Amazon.[104] Both companies already compete fiercely in the media streaming industry. Is this the beginning of the clash of the titans? Only time will tell.

4-8b Global Competition

Boeing is a very savvy international business competitor. Now Airbus, Boeing's primary competitor, is going to start assembling planes in the United States. Many foreign competitors also consider the United States to be a ripe target market. Thus, a U.S. marketing manager can no longer focus only on domestic competitors. In automobiles, textiles, watches, televisions, steel, and many other areas, foreign competition has been strong. In the past, foreign firms penetrated U.S. markets by concentrating on price, but the emphasis has switched to product quality. Nestlé, Sony, and Rolls-Royce are noted for quality, not cheap prices. Global competition is discussed in much more detail in Chapter 5.

firms find that they must work harder to maintain their profits and market share, regardless of the form of the competitive market. Sometimes technology advances can usher in a whole new set of competitors that can change a firm's business model. For example, one of the United States' most competitive companies is Amazon. The firm has more than 245 million customers that rely on Amazon for everything from flat screen televisions to dog food.[103] Several polls have

STUDY TOOLS 4

LOCATED AT BACK OF THE TEXTBOOK
☐ Rip out Chapter Review Card

LOCATED AT WWW.CENGAGEBRAIN.COM
☐ Review Key Terms Flashcards and create your own
☐ Track your knowledge and understanding of key concepts in marketing
☐ Complete practice and graded quizzes to prepare for tests
☐ Complete interactive content within the MKTG Online experience
☐ View the chapter highlight boxes within the MKTG Online experience

5 | Developing a Global Vision

LEARNING OUTCOMES

After studying this chapter, you will be able to...

5-1 Discuss the importance of global marketing

5-2 Discuss the impact of multinational firms on the world economy

5-3 Describe the external environment facing global marketers

5-4 Identify the various ways of entering the global marketplace

5-5 List the basic elements involved in developing a global marketing mix

5-6 Discover how the Internet is affecting global marketing

After finishing this chapter go to **PAGE 91** for **STUDY TOOLS**

5-1 REWARDS OF GLOBAL MARKETING AND THE SHIFTING GLOBAL BUSINESS LANDSCAPE

Today, global revolutions are underway in many areas of our lives: management, politics, communications, and technology. The word *global* has assumed a new meaning, referring to a boundless mobility and competition in social, business, and intellectual arenas. Global marketing—marketing that targets markets throughout the world—has become an imperative for business.

U.S. managers must develop a global vision not only to recognize and react to international marketing opportunities but also to remain competitive at home. Often a U.S. firm's toughest domestic competition comes from foreign companies. Consider the impact of Toyota and Honda on Ford and General Motors, for example. Moreover, a global vision enables a manager to understand that customer and distribution networks operate worldwide, blurring geographic and political barriers and making them increasingly irrelevant to business decisions. In summary, having a global vision means recognizing and reacting to international marketing opportunities, using effective global marketing strategies, and being aware of threats from foreign competitors in all markets.

World trade climbed from $200 billion in 1991 to more than $18 trillion in merchandise exports alone in 2016. Weaker demand in China and a number of emerging markets caused the value of goods crossing

global marketing marketing that targets markets throughout the world

global vision recognizing and reacting to international marketing opportunities, using effective global marketing strategies, and being aware of threats from foreign competitors in all markets

international borders to fall 13 percent in 2015. This marked the first global trade contraction since 2009. Trade was projected to grow in 2016, but at a rate of less than 3 percent.[1] These low and negative growth rates indicate that marketers are facing many challenges to their customary practices. Product development costs are rising, the life of products is getting shorter, and new technology is spreading around the world faster than ever. But marketing winners relish the pace of change instead of fear it.

Adopting a global vision can be very lucrative for a company. It is no accident that firms like Apple, Nestle, IBM, and Procter & Gamble are among the largest and most successful multinational firms in the world. Each has a global vision that managers understand and follow.

The foundation of a successful global vision is a corporate structure that provides a continual flow of fresh ideas. One firm that has such a structure is Otis Elevator Company. Otis is the world's largest manufacturer of people moving products, including elevators, escalators, and moving walkways. The firm employs more than 64,000 people around the world and offers products in more than 200 countries. Manufacturing is done in North America, South America, Europe, and Asia. Engineering

and test centers are located in the United States, Austria, Brazil, China, Czech Republic, France, Germany, India, Italy, Japan, Korea, and Spain. Having input from engineers around the world enables Otis to maintain its position as the world leader in people moving design. Otis's new Skyrise elevator can move at speeds of up to 5000 feet per minute!

Of course, global marketing is not a one-way street whereby only U.S. companies sell their wares and services throughout the world. Foreign competition in the domestic market was once relatively rare but now is found in almost every industry. In fact, in many industries, U.S. businesses have lost significant market share to imported products. In electronics, cameras, automobiles, fine china, tractors, leather goods, and a host of other consumer and industrial products, U.S. companies have struggled at home to maintain their market shares against foreign competitors.

5-1a Importance of Global Marketing to the United States

Many countries depend more on international commerce than the United States does. For example, France, the United Kingdom, and Germany derive 28, 30, and

Although some countries depend more on international commerce than the United States does, the impact of international business on the U.S. economy is still impressive:

- Jobs supported by exports pay, on average, eighteen percent more than other jobs do.[2]
- More than 11 million Americans hold jobs that are supported by exports.[3]
- Every U.S. state has realized net employment gains directly attributed to foreign trade.
- The United States exports more than $2.3 trillion in goods and services each year.[4]

46 percent of their respective **gross domestic products (GDP)** from world trade—considerably more than the United States' 14 percent.[5] Gross domestic product is the total market value of all final goods and services produced in a country for a given time period (usually a year or a quarter of a year). *Final* in this sense refers to final products that are sold, not to intermediate products used in the assembly of a final product. For example, if the value of a brake (an intermediate product) and that of a car (the final product) were both counted, the brake would be counted twice. Therefore, GDP counts only final goods and services in its valuation of a country's production.

The main types of goods that the United States exports are automobiles, agricultural goods, machines, airplanes, computers, chemicals, and petroleum products. One-half of all wheat, rice, and soybeans grown in the United States is exported, as is four-fifths of all cotton.[6] Services that the United States exports are primarily educational, financial, legal, licensing-, and travel-related. Since 1980, U.S. services exports have grown more than 700 percent.[7] When a foreign tourist visits the United States, all the money she spends while stateside is counted as a travel-related export. Why is this? Because she is buying a service product (travel) and is simply coming to the United States to pick it up!

Traditionally, only very large multinational companies have seriously attempted to compete worldwide. However, more and more small and medium sized companies have begun pursuing international markets, and some are even beginning to play a critical role in driving export growth. Today, a record 304,000 small and medium size firms export goods from the United States. The U.S.

Ford manufactures the Fiesta in several countries, but no Fiestas are being built in the United States.

Ed Aldridge/Shutterstock.com

government is working with these firms to expand small business trade. The Export–Import bank of the United States, for example, helps thousands of small businesses obtain financing to expand their export sales. In 2015, the Export-Import Bank authorized $17 billion to support 109,000 U.S. jobs.[8]

In addition, the Small Business Administration provided $18 million in support for small businesses that exported or desired to start exporting. This support included participation in foreign trade missions and market sales trips, aid in designing international marketing strategies, export trade show exhibits, and training.[9]

JOB OUTSOURCING AND INSHORING The notion of **outsourcing** (sending U.S. jobs abroad) has been highly controversial for several decades. Many executives have said that it leads to corporate growth, efficiency, productivity, and revenue growth. Most companies see cost savings as a key driver in outsourcing. But outsourcing also has its negative side. For instance, Detroit has suffered

gross domestic product (GDP) the total market value of all final goods and services produced in a country for a given time period

outsourcing sending U.S. jobs abroad

Imports Can Help Too

Many people view exports as generally good for the United States and view imports as generally harmful to the United States. Indeed, waves upon waves of U.S. factories have had to close over the years because they could not compete with low-cost imports. China is widely known as the largest supplier of imports to the United States. Some claim that Chinese goods are so cheap because Chinese manufacturers pay their employees inhumane wages. Although China's wages are still relatively low, they have doubled since 2008. Further, nearly half of the United States' non-oil imports come from developed, high-wage countries like France, Germany, Ireland, and Switzerland. These countries all have higher average wages than does the United States, so low wages (and low prices) are only one factor driving the popularity of imports.[10]

While some employers can't compete with lower-cost imports, many U.S. workers actually owe their jobs to imports. Transportation workers move goods around the country. Workers for manufacturers, wholesalers, and retailers research and place orders with foreign suppliers for products ranging from paper boxes to computer servers.

More than 60 percent of U.S. imports are raw materials, components, and machinery used to make goods or grow crops.[11] American manufacturers use these imported inputs when locally produced substitutes are either not available or too expensive. Imported inputs thus keep American manufacturing competitive—both locally and globally.

International trade gives U.S. consumers access to a wider variety of goods at lower prices, thus raising real wages and allowing families to buy more even if their incomes stagnate. This is especially important for middle-class consumers who spend a large share of their disposable incomes on heavily traded food and clothing items. Compared to a world with no trade, median-income consumers gain an estimated 29 percent of their purchasing power from trade.[12]

as many factories in the auto industry have been shut down and relocated around the world. Ford manufactures the Fiesta compact sedan in several countries around the world—including Mexico—but no Fiestas are being built in the United States.

Recently, some companies have begun to suspect that outsourcing's negatives outweigh its positives. Improperly designed parts and products have caused production delays, and rising wages in the developing world have rendered American rates more competitive. Increased fuel and transportation costs associated with long-distance shipping, coupled with falling U.S. energy costs, have given impetus to inshoring, returning production jobs to the United States. Rapid consumer product innovation has led to the need to keep product designers, marketing researchers, logistics experts, and manufacturers in close proximity so that they can work quickly as a team. Thus, shrinking development and manufacturing timelines have further contributed to inshoring.

Walmart is also aiding the cause by promising to stock more "Made in the USA" goods. The firm plans to buy $50 billion of such goods as a start. This decision has already caused a ripple of effects. Redman & Associates, which manufactures battery-powered children's cars in China, recently announced a new factory in Rogers, Arkansas—not too far from Walmart's Bentonville, Arkansas headquarters.[13]

BENEFITS OF GLOBALIZATION Traditional economic theory says that globalization relies on competition to drive down prices and increase product and service quality. Business goes to the countries that operate most efficiently and/or have the technology to produce what is needed. In summary, globalization expands economic freedom, spurs competition, and raises the productivity and living standards of people in countries that open themselves to the global marketplace. For less developed countries, globalization also offers access to foreign capital, global export markets, and advanced technology while breaking the monopoly of inefficient and protected domestic producers. Faster

inshoring returning production jobs to the United States growth, in turn, reduces poverty, encourages democratization, and promotes higher labor and environmental standards. Though government officials in developing countries may face more difficult choices as a result of globalization, their citizens enjoy greater individual freedom. In this sense, globalization acts as a check on governmental power by making it more difficult for governments to abuse the freedom and property of their citizens.

Globalization deserves credit for helping lift many millions out of poverty and for improving standards of living of low-wage families. In developing countries around the world, globalization has created a vibrant middle class that has elevated the standard of living for hundreds of millions of people.

COSTS OF GLOBALIZATION A key tenet of globalization is free trade—that is, trade among nations without barriers or restrictions. Basic economic theory tells us that if nations specialize in producing what they produce best and engage in trade with each other, then all countries will be better off. In practice, however, global trade creates clear winners and losers.

Countries restrict trade and create barriers for a number of reasons (many of which are discussed later in the chapter). If a country can boost exports and limit imports, then more jobs are created and there is less competition for local businesses. A recent MIT study concluded that from 1999 to 2011, imports from China into the United States killed approximately 2.4 million U.S. jobs.[14] (Granted, some of these job losses resulted from rapid changes in technology and the growing use of robots. Even if China disappeared tomorrow, far fewer jobs would return to American shores than originally left.)

Globalization's impact on jobs would not have been so bad if workers had found jobs in other industries or cities—but many didn't. Many laid-off factory workers are still living off unemployment benefits a decade later. While most Americans continue to believe in free trade (58 percent see it as an opportunity), the question of how to handle these job losses remains. Trade adjustment assistance—payments made to workers who have lost their jobs to foreign competition—now costs more than $600 million annually.[15] So when you buy an imported sofa from China, keep in mind that thousands of unemployed Tennessee residents now receive trade adjustment assistance because of the state's heavy dependence on furniture manufacturing.[16]

multinational corporation
a company that is heavily engaged in international trade, beyond exporting and importing

MULTINATIONAL FIRMS

The United States has a number of large companies that are global marketers. Many of them have been very successful. A company that is heavily engaged in international trade, beyond exporting and importing, is called a **multinational corporation**. A multinational corporation moves resources, goods, services, and skills across national boundaries without regard to the country in which its headquarters is located.

Multinationals often develop their global business in stages. In the first stage, companies operate in one country and sell into others. Second-stage multinationals set up foreign subsidiaries to handle sales in one country. In the third stage, multinationals operate an entire line of business in another country. The fourth stage has evolved primarily due to the Internet and involves mostly high-tech companies. For these firms, the executive suite is virtual. Their top executives and core corporate functions are in different countries, wherever the firms can gain a competitive edge through the availability of talent or capital, low costs, or proximity to their most important customers.

A multinational company may have several worldwide headquarters, depending on where certain markets or technologies are located. Britain's APV, a maker of food-processing equipment, has a different headquarters for each of its worldwide businesses.

Many U.S.-based multinationals earn a large percentage of their total revenue abroad. Caterpillar, the construction-equipment company, receives 67 percent of its revenue from overseas markets, and General Electric earns 54 percent of its revenue abroad. Other large American exporters include General Motors, Ford, Hewlett-Packard, IBM, and Boeing.

5-2a Are Multinationals Beneficial?

Although multinationals comprise far less than 1 percent of U.S. companies, they account for about 20 percent of all private jobs, 25 percent of all private wages, half of total exports of goods, and a remarkable $680 billion in research and development (R&D) spending.[17] For decades, U.S. multinationals have driven an outsized share of U.S. productivity growth, the foundation of rising standards of living for everyone. Current leaders in global innovation include Apple, Alphabet, Amazon, and Gilead.

The role of multinational corporations in developing nations is a subject of controversy. The ability of multinationals to tap financial, physical, and human resources from all over the world and combine them economically and profitably can benefit any country.

They also often possess and can transfer the most up-to-date technology. Critics, however, claim that often the wrong kind of technology is transferred to developing nations. Usually, it is **capital intensive** (requiring a greater expenditure for equipment than for labor) and thus does not substantially increase employment. A "modern sector" then emerges in the nation, employing a small proportion of the labor force with relatively high productivity and income levels and with increasingly capital-intensive technologies. In addition, multinationals sometimes push for very quick production turn-around times, which has led to long hours and dangerous working conditions. In 2013, a Bangladesh garment factory collapsed and more than 1,100 people died as they rushed to meet production quotas for firms such as Benetton and Marks & Spencer. Other critics say that the firms take more wealth out of developing nations than they bring in, thus widening the gap between rich and poor nations. The petroleum industry in particular has been heavily criticized in the past for its actions in some developing countries.

To counter such criticism, more and more multinationals are taking a proactive role in being good global citizens. Sometimes companies are spurred to action by government regulation; in other cases, multinationals are attempting to protect their good brand names. Some companies, such as Apple, Walmart, Calvin Klein, and Tommy Hilfiger, have begun conducting factory inspections to protect the health and safety of their workers. Coca-Cola has trained a half million women in 44 countries to become small-scale businesspeople. Coca-Cola has nurtured female owners of "sari-sari" convenience stores in the Philippines, farmers growing mangos in Kenya, and poor villagers building tiny recycling operations out of discarded bottles from trash heaps in Mexico.

5-2b Global Marketing Standardization

Traditionally, marketing-oriented multinational corporations have operated somewhat differently in each country. They use a strategy of providing different product features, packaging, advertising, and so on. However, Ted Levitt, a former Harvard professor, has described a trend toward what he refers to as "global marketing," with a slightly different meaning.[18] He contends that communication and technology have made the world smaller so that almost all consumers everywhere want all the things they have heard about, seen, or experienced. Thus, he sees the emergence of global markets for standardized consumer products on a huge scale, as opposed to segmented foreign markets with different products. In this book, *global marketing* is defined as individuals

Coca-Cola has made an effort to provide opportunities for over half a million women in 44 countries.

and organizations using a global vision to effectively market goods and services across national boundaries. To make the distinction, we can refer to Levitt's notion as **global marketing standardization**.

Global marketing standardization presumes that the markets throughout the world are becoming more alike. Firms practicing global marketing standardization produce "globally standardized products" to be sold the same way all over the world. Most smartphones and tablets, for example, are standardized globally except for the languages displayed. These devices allow the user to switch easily from one language to another. Uniform production should enable companies to lower production and marketing costs and increase profits. Levitt has cited Coca-Cola, Colgate-Palmolive, and McDonald's as successful global marketers. His critics point out, however, that the success of these three companies is really based on variation, not on offering the same product everywhere. McDonald's, for example, changes its salad dressings and provides self-serve espresso for French tastes. It sells bulgogi burgers in South Korea and falafel burgers in Egypt. Further, the fact that Coca-Cola and Colgate-Palmolive sell some of their products in more than 160 countries does not signify that they have adopted a high degree of standardization for all their products globally. Only three Coca-Cola brands are standardized, and one of them, Sprite, has a different formulation in Japan.

Companies with separate subsidiaries in other countries can be said to operate using a multidomestic

capital intensive using more capital than labor in the production process

global marketing standardization production of uniform products that can be sold the same way all over the world

strategy. A **multidomestic strategy** occurs when multinational firms enable individual subsidiaries to compete independently in domestic markets. Simply put, multidomestic strategy is how multinational firms use strategic business units (see Chapter 2). Colgate-Palmolive uses both strategies: Axion paste dishwashing detergent, for example, was formulated for developing countries, and La Croix Plus detergent was custom made for the French market.

Nevertheless, some multinational corporations are moving beyond multidomestic strategies toward a degree of global marketing standardization. Colgate toothpaste and Nike shoes are marketed the same ways globally, using global marketing standardization.

Source: Taobao.com

With a keen understanding of Chinese culture, Taobao proved to be stiff competition for eBay in China

5-3 EXTERNAL ENVIRONMENT FACED BY GLOBAL MARKETERS

A global marketer or a firm considering global marketing must consider the external environment. Many of the same environmental factors that operate in the domestic market also exist internationally. These factors include culture, economic development, the global economy, political structure and actions, demographic makeup, and natural resources.

5-3a Culture

Central to any society is the common set of values shared by its citizens that determines what is socially acceptable. Culture underlies the family, the educational system, religion, and the social class system. The network of social organizations generates overlapping roles and status positions. These values and roles have a tremendous effect on people's preferences and thus on marketers' options. A company that does not understand a country's culture is doomed to failure in that country. Cultural blunders lead to misunderstandings and often perceptions of rudeness or even incompetence. For example, when people in India shake hands, they sometimes do so rather limply. This is not a sign of weakness or disinterest; instead, a soft handshake conveys respect. Avoiding eye contact is also a sign of deference in India.

When eBay entered China in 2001, it did quite well because it had no competition. But when the Chinese competitor Taobao launched, eBay quickly lost ground. Its market share dropped from eighty percent to 7 percent in just five years. If you looked at eBay's site in China, you would recognize it—it looks very similar to eBay's U.S. site. This failure to adapt to Chinese culture led to eBay's decline: Americans do not want celebrity gossip or social interaction when they shop online, but the Chinese do.

Taobao is more than a one-stop shop for online shoppers—it is a social forum as well. The site features pictures and descriptions—very long descriptions—of products, but shoppers can also chat online about current trends, share shopping tips, and catch up on celebrity news at Taobao. Chinese shoppers are more inclined to follow fashion trends than American shoppers are, so Taobao lists trends in order of popularity, unlike eBay. Finally, when eBay entered China, it did not allow direct communication between buyers and sellers. As in the United States, all communication was handled by eBay's messaging system. This system was not well received in China because Chinese are much less likely than Americans to buy from strangers. Chinese Internet users expect websites to be much denser than many Western Internet users are used to. That is, Chinese websites tend to have more links, many more images, and longer page lengths than Western websites do. Eye-grabbing animations and floating images are common on Chinese sites. A page with less text, fewer embedded links, and nice imagery might be called "well-designed" by Western Internet users but "boring" by Chinese ones.

multidomestic strategy
when multinational firms enable individual subsidiaries to compete independently in domestic markets

Language is another important aspect of culture that can create problems for marketers. Marketers must take care in translating product names, slogans, instructions, and promotional messages so as not to convey the wrong meaning. Koreans pronounce the name of auto manufacturer Hyundai as "hi-yun-day." In United States advertisements, the company name is pronounced "hun-day," like "Sunday." More significantly, the name of baby food manufacturer Gerber is French for vomiting! Free translation software, such as babelfish.com or Google Translate, allows users to input text in one language and output in another language. But marketers must take care using the software, as it can have unintended results—the best being unintelligible, the worst being insulting.

Each country has its own customs and traditions that determine business practices and influence negotiations with foreign customers. In many countries, personal relationships are more important than financial considerations. For instance, skipping social engagements in Mexico may lead to lost sales. Negotiations in Japan often include long evenings of dining, drinking, and entertaining, and only after a close personal relationship has been formed do business negotiations begin.

Making successful sales presentations abroad requires a thorough understanding of the country's culture. Germans, for example, do not like risk and need strong reassurance. A successful presentation to a German client will emphasize three points: the bottom-line benefits of the product or service, that there will be strong service support, and that the product is guaranteed. In southern Europe, it is an insult to show a price list. Without negotiating, you will not close the sale. The English want plenty of documentation for product claims and are less likely to simply accept the word of the sales representative. Scandinavian and Dutch companies are more likely to approach business transactions as Americans do than are companies in any other country.

5-3b Economic Factors

A second major factor in the external environment facing the global marketer is the level of economic development in the countries where it operates. In general, complex and sophisticated industries are found in developed countries, and more basic industries are found in less developed nations. Average family incomes are higher in the more developed countries compared to the less developed countries. Larger incomes mean greater purchasing power and demand, not only for consumer goods and services, but also for the machinery and workers required to produce consumer goods.

According to the World Bank, the average *gross national income (GNI)* per capita for the world is $10,858.[19] GNI is a country's GDP (defined earlier) together with its income received from other countries (mainly interest and dividends) less similar payments made to other countries. The United States' GNI per capita is $55,200, but it is not the world's highest. That honor goes to Bermuda at $106,140. Of course, there are many very poor countries: Rwanda, $700; Afghanistan, $680; Ethiopia, $550; Guinea, $470; and Democratic Republic of Congo, $380.[20] GNI per capita is one measure of the ability of a country's citizens to buy various goods and services. A marketer with a global vision can use these data to aid in measuring market potential in countries around the globe.

Not only is per capita income a consideration when going abroad, but so is the cost of doing business in a country. Although it is not the same as the cost of doing business, the most expensive places in the world to live are Singapore, Hong Kong, Zurich, Geneva, Paris, and London.[21]

THE BALANCE OF TRADE AND THE BALANCE OF PAYMENTS The more U.S. firms that export their wares, the better the country's **balance of trade**—the difference between the value of a country's exports and the value of its imports over a given period. A country that exports more goods or services than it imports is said to have a favorable balance of trade; a country that imports more than it exports is said to have an unfavorable balance of trade. In other words, when imports exceed exports, more money flows out of the country than flows into it.

The United States has trade surpluses with Hong Kong, the Netherlands, the United Arab Emirates, and Australia, but it has substantial trade deficits with China, Japan, Germany, and Mexico.[22] Indeed, although U.S. exports have been doing well, the country imports more than it exports. The United States' balance of trade deficit was $47.06 billion in 2016, marking the fortieth straight year of trade deficit. As long as the United States continues to buy more goods than it sells abroad, it will have a deficit and an unfavorable balance of trade.[23]

The difference between a country's total payments to other countries and its total receipts from other countries is its **balance of payments**. This figure includes the balance of imports and exports (the balance of trade), long-term investments in overseas plants and equipment, government loans to and from other countries, gifts and foreign aid, military expenditures made in other countries, and money deposits in and withdrawals from foreign banks.

balance of trade the difference between the value of a country's exports and the value of its imports over a given period

balance of payments the difference between a country's total payments to other countries and its total receipts from other countries

The United States had a favorable balance of payments from about 1900 until 1971. Since then, the country's overall payments have exceeded its receipts—due largely to the United States' military presence abroad.

5-3c The Global Economy

A global marketer today must be fully aware of the intertwined nature of the global economy. In the past, the size of the U.S. economy was so large that global markets tended to move up or down depending on its health. It was said, "If America sneezes, then the rest of the world catches a cold." This is still true today, but less so than in the past. Slow growth in America—and even slower growth in China, Europe and Japan—have hampered global economic progress. Even China's astronomical growth rate is much lower today than in recent years. Unfortunately, politics is playing an increasingly important role in the development of the BRICS countries (Brazil, Russia, India, China, and South Africa). Brazil is rife with political scandal, and due to antiquated labor laws, overly generous government pensions, traditional work customs (women retire at age 50 and men at 55), the country is experiencing its worst recession in 25 years. Russia's economy is held back by economic sanctions and the country's over-dependence on energy exports amidst plummeting energy prices. Despite China's slowed growth rate, it is now the world's second largest economy behind the United States.[24] The number of millionaires in the Asia-Pacific region is greater than the number of millionaires in the United States and Canada combined. For its part, South Africa is working hard to raise its electric generating capacity—a factor that has hindered productivity in the past and has dissuaded some multinationals from investing in the country.[25]

Perhaps the brightest light among the BRICS is India, which expects its economy to grow around 8 percent in 2017. India is less dependent on exports than are the other BRICS countries, making it less vulnerable to slowing economics worldwide. Lower energy prices have helped India as well, as it is a major energy importer. Most importantly, Prime Minister Narendra Modi is opening India up to private investment like never before.[26] This move is poised to spur major economic growth over the next five years.

5-3d Political Structure and Actions

Political structure is a fourth important variable facing global marketers. Government policies run the gamut from no private ownership and minimal individual freedom to little central government and maximum personal freedom. As rights of private property increase, government-owned industries and centralized planning tend to decrease. But a political environment is rarely at one extreme or the other. India, for instance, is a republic with elements of socialism, monopoly capitalism, and competitive capitalism in its political ideology.

Regulation gives businesses the framework they need to grow and prosper. For example, a well-designed land administration system can provide reliable data on the ownership of property and the protection of property rights.

Regulation can also produce fairer outcomes when one business or position is much more powerful than another. In a country with no labor laws, an employer might force employees to work 14 hour days or longer, for little pay, and under dangerous working conditions.

On the other hand, regulation can overburden businesses and make it virtually impossible for them operate. In Equatorial Guinea, it takes 18 procedures and 135 days to start a new business.[27] It is no surprise, then, that multinationals shy away from this country. If resolving a commercial dispute takes too much time (1,402 days in Guatemala), potential clients and suppliers might be hesitant to do business with companies based in that country.

According to the World Bank Group, the easiest places to do business are Singapore, New Zealand, Denmark, South Korea, Hong Kong, the United Kingdom, the United States, Sweden, Norway, and Finland. The hardest places to do business are Eritrea, Libya, South Sudan, Venezuela, and the Central African Republic.[28]

It is not uncommon for international politics to affect business laws. China has investigated dozens of America's largest multinationals—companies structured to compete with other corporations, not governments. Among the investigated companies, Google left China after enduring cyber-attacks and governmental pressure to release user information. Apple CEO Tim Cook expressed "sincere apologies" in the wake of Beijing's media campaign against the company. Adobe shut down both its China headquarters and ended its research and development in the country. Not all of China's oversight is excessive, however. Walmart was fined $9.8 million for misleading pricing, selling poor quality products, and selling donkey meat that turned out to be fox. But Walmart is also doing something rare for a Western company: telling the Chinese government that it needs to clean up its *own* act.

In the United States and most other countries, manufacturers rather than retailers are responsible for ensuring product quality. In China, however, retailers are accountable. In 2014, Walmart executives met with China's Food and Drug Administration and urged officials to step up their inspections of food purveyors. Walmart later reported that it ended relationships with 300 suppliers in 2014 because they didn't pass the retailer's testing and safety standards. Those 300 suppliers had paperwork proving that they passed muster with local food watchdogs, however. Clearly, international business can be a proxy for political jousting when governments enter the mix.[29]

Russia has also directly attacked American companies in the wake of political disagreement. In 2014, Russia seized the Crimean peninsula, leading to an onslaught of sanctions from the European Union (EU), the United States, and others. Russia fought back, banning these countries from selling billions of dollars worth of fruits, vegetables, fish, and meat to Russians. Russia then went after McDonald's, closing down a number of restaurants for "sanitary conditions."

These restaurants have since reopened and McDonald's is, once again, expanding in Russia. The firm has developed more local suppliers and now receives 85 percent of its supplies from companies inside Russia. This helps smooth out losses from currency swings and sidesteps Russia's ban on food imports. McDonald's has opened 120 new restaurants since the government's shutdown.[30]

French auto manufacturer Renault took a controlling interest in Russian auto producer AvtoVAZ after investing $2.3 billion in the company. To turn the perennial money-loser around, Renault brought in seasoned executive Bo Andersson as President. Andersson laid off thousands, stopped kickbacks, and renegotiated supplier contracts. His actions created so much discontent that word reached Russia's political elite. Andersson was soon after let go—a none-too-subtle reminder that Russia continues to mix politics and business. According to a Russian spokesperson, Andersson mishandled layoffs and shouldn't have taken business away from local suppliers.[31]

LEGAL CONSIDERATIONS As you can see, legal considerations are often intertwined with the political environment. In France, nationalistic sentiments led to a law that requires pop music stations to play at least forty percent of their songs in French (even though French teenagers love American and English rock and roll).

Many legal structures are designed to either encourage or limit trade. Recent trends have leaned toward the latter; between 2008 and 2016, more than 3,500 protectionist measures were introduced around the world.[32] Nevertheless, the most common legal structures affecting trade are:

- **Tariff:** a tax levied on the goods entering a country. Because a tariff is a tax, it will either reduce the profits of the firms paying the tariff or raise prices to buyers, or both. Normally, a tariff raises prices of the imported goods and makes it easier for domestic firms to compete. In general, the U.S. economy is open to imports. America has tariffs on 1,000 product categories, but at a relatively low rate of 1.4 percent. Exceptions to this are footwear and apparel, which carry a rate that is ten percent higher. Globally, tariffs on manufactured goods continue to fall. In 1990, the average tariff rate in developing and industrialized countries was 24 percent. Today, that rate is less than 8 percent.[33]

- **Quota** a limit on the amount of a specific product that can enter a country. Several U.S. companies have sought quotas as a means of protection from foreign competition. The United States, for example, has a quota on raw cane sugar.

- **Boycott:** the exclusion of all products from certain countries or companies. Governments use boycotts to exclude companies from countries with which they have a political dispute. Several Arab nations have boycotted products made in Israel.

- **Exchange control:** a law compelling a company earning foreign exchange (money) from its exports to sell it to a control agency, usually a central bank. A company wishing to buy goods abroad must first obtain a foreign currency exchange from the control agency. For example, if Ford has a plant in Venezuela that makes F-150 pickup trucks and then exports them to other South American countries, the money made on those sales is foreign currency. These funds have to be sold to a control agency in Venezuela. When Ford needs to buy, say, brakes for the F-150 from Mexico, it goes to the control agency to get the funds. Some countries with foreign exchange controls are Argentina, Brazil, China, Iceland, India, North Korea, Russia, and Venezuela.

- **Market grouping (also known as a common trade alliance):** occurs when several countries agree to work together to form a common trade area that enhances trade opportunities. The best-known market grouping is the EU, which will be discussed later in this chapter.

Robinimages2013/Shutterstock.com

- **Trade agreement:** an agreement to stimulate international trade. Not all government efforts are meant to stifle imports or investment by foreign corporations. The largest Latin American trade agreement is Mercosur, which includes Argentina, Bolivia, Brazil, Chile, Colombia, Ecuador, Paraguay, Peru, Uruguay, and Venezuela. The elimination of most tariffs among the trading partners has resulted in trade revenues of more than $16 billion annually. The economic boom created by Mercosur will undoubtedly cause other nations to seek trade agreements on their own or to enter Mercosur.

THE URUGUAY ROUND, THE FAILED DOHA ROUND, AND BILATERAL AGREEMENTS The Uruguay Round is a trade agreement that has dramatically lowered trade barriers worldwide. Adopted in 1994, the agreement has been signed by 162 nations. It is the most ambitious global trade agreement ever negotiated. The agreement has reduced tariffs by one-third worldwide—a move that has raised global income by over $235 billion annually.[34] Perhaps most notable is the recognition of new global realities. For the first time, a trade agreement covers services, intellectual property rights, and trade-related investment measures such as exchange controls.

The Uruguay Round made several major changes in world trading practices:

- **Entertainment, pharmaceuticals, integrated circuits, and software:** The rules protect patents, copyrights, and trademarks for twenty years. Computer programs receive 50 years of protection, and semiconductor chips receive 10 years of protection. But many developing nations were given a decade to phase in patent protection for drugs. Also France, which limits the number of U.S. movies and television shows that can be shown, refused to liberalize market access for the U.S. entertainment industry.

- **Financial, legal, and accounting services:** Services came under international trading rules for the first time, creating a vast opportunity for these competitive U.S. industries. Now, it is easier for managers and key personnel to be admitted to a country. Licensing standards for professionals, such as doctors, cannot discriminate against foreign applicants. That is, foreign applicants cannot be held to higher standards than domestic practitioners.

- **Agriculture:** Europe is gradually reducing farm subsidies, opening new opportunities for such U.S. farm exports as wheat and corn. Japan and Korea are beginning to import rice. But U.S. growers of sugar and citrus fruit have had their subsidies trimmed.

- **Textiles and apparel:** Strict quotas limiting imports from developing countries are being phased out, causing further job losses in the U.S. clothing trade. But retailers are the big winners, because past quotas have added $15 billion a year to clothing prices.

- **A new trade organization:** The World Trade Organization (WTO) replaced the old General Agreement on Tariffs and Trade (GATT), which was created in 1948. The WTO eliminated the extensive loopholes of which GATT members took advantage. Today, all WTO members must fully comply with all agreements under the Uruguay Round. The WTO also has an effective dispute settlement procedure with strict time limits to resolve disputes. More than 500 disputes have been brought before the WTO since its inception. Recently, the United States filed a dispute against China for providing subsidies for exporters. The United States accused China of providing almost $1 billion in illegal subsidies between 2015 and 2016.[35]

The latest round of WTO trade talks began in Doha, Qatar, in 2001. For the most part, the periodic meetings of WTO members under the Doha Round have been very contentious. One of the most contentious goals of the round was for the major developing countries (BRICS) to lower tariffs on industrial goods in exchange for European and American tariff and subsidy cuts on farm products. Concerned that lowering tariffs would result in an economically damaging influx of foreign cotton, sugar, and rice, China and India demanded a safeguard clause that would allow them to raise tariffs on those crops if imports surged. At a 2015 meeting of the WTO, trade ministers from more than 160 countries failed to agree that they should keep the negotiations going. After 14 years of talks, members of the WTO effectively ended the Doha round of negotiations. It became clear in recent years that the talks, which were originally supposed to conclude in 2005, were paralyzed because neither developed economies (like the United States and the European Union) nor developing countries (like China and India) were willing to make fundamental concessions.

Mercosur the largest Latin American trade agreement; includes Argentina, Bolivia, Brazil, Chile, Colombia, Ecuador, Paraguay, Peru, Uruguay, and Venezuela

Uruguay Round a trade agreement to dramatically lower trade barriers worldwide; created the World Trade Organization

World Trade Organization (WTO) a trade organization that replaced the old General Agreement on Tariffs and Trade (GATT)

General Agreement on Tariffs and Trade (GATT) a trade agreement that contained loopholes enabling countries to avoid trade-barrier reduction agreements

At the start of the Doha round, American and European officials committed to producing a trade agreement that would promote development in poorer countries without requiring them to reduce import barriers to the same extent as industrialized nations. As developing countries—particularly China and India—began exporting far more than they were importing, wealthier countries started demanding that they agree to lower import barriers and cut subsidies to their farmers. China and India refused, insisting that the member states stick to the original paramaters.[36]

The lack of progress surrounding the Doha Round led several other coalitions to form and negotiate alternative free-trade alliances. The Transatlantic Trade and Investment Partnership, which saw negotiations begin in 2013, is a proposed partnership between the United States and the European Union. The agreement would be a major benefit to Europe because of the continent's continued economic weakness. Ten million European jobs depend upon American exports, but this agreement's negotiations have stalled over how trade disputes should be settled. In most trade agreements, disputes are settled through arbitration. This lets companies bypass host-country courts, which can be biased in favor of their home governments' positions. The United States favors the arbitration process, but the European Union wants to replace it with a different system.[37]

After five years and 19 formal rounds of review, the Trans-Pacific Partnership (TPP) was finalized on October 5, 2015. (As of this writing, the TPP must still be approved by Congress.) The biggest regional trade agreement in history, the TPP would create new trade rules among 12 participating countries: Australia, Brunei, Chile, Malaysia, New Zealand, Peru, Singapore, Vietnam, the United States, Japan, Mexico, and Canada. The TPP cuts tariffs for industries such as cars and agriculture, but its main concern is the removal of non-tariff barriers like overly complicated custom procedures, buy-domestic rules for government agencies, and barriers to trade in services.

The TPP is particularly timely as recent technologies have made international trade in telecommunications, finance, education, and health care a reality. For example, a hospital in America might outsource patient monitoring to nurses in Malaysia, diagnostics to technicians in Japan, and consultations to doctors in Canada.

From left, Chile President Michelle Bachelet, Colombia President Juan Manuel Santos, Mexico President Enrique Pena Nieto, and Peru President Ollanta Humala speak on a panel during the 2015 Business Summit of the Pacific Alliance.

AP Images/Rodrigo Abd

This service trade benefiting all four countries would be made easier by the TPP.[38]

Another agreement, the Pacific Alliance, was signed in 2012 by Colombia, Chile, Peru, and Mexico to create a single region for the free movement of goods, services, investment, capital, and people. Implementation of the Pacific Alliance began in 2014 with the goal of abolishing tariffs on 92 percent of merchandise trade as soon as possible, with the remainder being eliminated by 2020. Costa Rica was recently accepted as a fifth member of the Alliance, which now boasts a market of 210 million people.[39]

This agreement has gotten the attention of a number of countries around the world. Thirty-four nations from six continents now act as observers at Alliance meetings, and several Asian countries have already asked to be admitted as full members.[40] This interest derives from Alliance members' commitment to free markets, free trade, and democracy—which cannot be said of some South American countries (including Brazil, Argentina, and Venezuela). Observer nations are also attracted to the Pacific Alliance because of market size; the Alliance already accounts for half of all South American exports.[41]

NORTH AMERICAN FREE TRADE AGREEMENT At the time it was instituted, the **North American Free Trade Agreement (NAFTA)** created the

> **North American Free Trade Agreement (NAFTA)** an agreement between Canada, the United States, and Mexico that created the world's then-largest free trade zone

world's largest free trade zone. Ratified by the U.S. Congress in 1993, the agreement includes Canada, the United States, and Mexico, with a combined population of 450 million. Agricultural goods, manufactured products, and raw materials now flow freely across borders, boosting economic growth, profits, and jobs for all three countries.[42] Since NAFTA's implementation in 1994, trade with Canada and Mexico has quadrupled to $1.14 trillion. These countries now buy about one-third of U.S. merchandise exports, which have ballooned from $142 billion to $515 billion.[43] The Act supports 14 million U.S. jobs.

While the quantitative benefits of NAFTA are obvious, the real question is whether the alliance has brought *prosperity* to all three countries. Cheaper imports generally lower the cost of living. This disproportionately benefits low-income people because they spend a greater percentage of their money on goods than do people with higher incomes. On the other hand, NAFTA has resulted in many low-skilled and assembly line jobs moving from the United States to Mexico. Until 2008, the A.O. Smith Electric motor factory employed 1,100 people in Scottsville, Kentucky. A.O. Smith moved its production to Mexico to take advantage of low-cost labor—a transition facilitated by the passage of NAFTA.

The Economic Policy Institute, a think tank critical of free-trade agreements, estimates that NAFTA has cost the United States 850,000 jobs.[44] Other nonpartisan groups have pointed out that economies are extremely complex systems, and that different conclusions can be reached based upon the factors considered and the assumptions made. China joining the WTO and the United States establishing normal trade relationships with China have themselves resulted in huge changes to American imports, exports, and employment. Some economists believe that these shifts, not NAFTA, have the greatest effect on the U.S. economy.[45]

Still other economists believe that NAFTA has increased prosperity, and that the Detroit auto industry might no longer exist without it. Inexpensive labor in Mexico can perform basic tasks like assembly, but higher-paid automotive engineers, planners, and designers all work in America. The Honda CR-V is assembled in El Salto, Mexico, but it uses an American-made motor and transmission. Roughly 70 percent of its content is either American- or Canadian-made.[46]

Dominican Republic–Central America Free Trade Agreement (CAFTA-DR)
a trade agreement instituted in 2005 that includes Costa Rica, the Dominican Republic, El Salvador, Guatemala, Honduras, Nicaragua, and the United States

European Union (EU)
a free trade zone encompassing 28 European countries

DOMINICAN REPUBLIC–CENTRAL AMERICA FREE TRADE AGREEMENT The Dominican Republic–Central America Free Trade Agreement (CAFTA-DR) was instituted in 2005. Because it joined after the original agreement was signed, the Dominican Republic was amended to the original agreement title (Central America Free Trade Agreement, or CAFTA). Besides the United States and the Dominican Republic, the agreement includes Costa Rica, El Salvador, Guatemala, Honduras, and Nicaragua.

As of 2015, all consumer and industrial goods exported to CAFTA-DR countries are no longer subject to tariffs. Tariffs on agricultural goods will be phased out by 2020. The agreement also covers intellectual property rights, transparency, electronic commerce, and telecommunications. The CAFTA-DR countries comprise the 14th largest U.S. export market in the world. Today, the U.S. exports more than $30 billion in goods to the five Central American countries and Dominican Republic.[47]

EUROPEAN UNION The European Union (EU) is one of the world's most important free trade zones and now encompasses most of Europe. Actually much more than a free trade zone, it is also a political and economic community. As a free trade zone, however, the EU guarantees the freedom of movement of people, goods, services, and capital between member states. It also maintains a common trade policy with outside nations and a regional development policy. The EU represents member nations in the WTO. Recently, the EU also began venturing into foreign policy as well, getting involved in issues such as Iran's refining of uranium.

The EU currently has twenty-eight member states: Austria, Belgium, Bulgaria, Croatia, Cyprus, the Czech Republic, Denmark, Estonia, Finland, France, Germany, Greece, Hungary, Ireland, Italy, Latvia, Lithuania, Luxembourg, Malta, the Netherlands, Poland, Portugal, Romania, Slovakia, Slovenia, Spain, Sweden, and the United Kingdom. In summer 2016, the United Kingdom voted to leave the European Union. Exit polls showed that the British people wanted their government to control its own political and economic future. As of press time, no action has been taken by the British or the EU.

The EU is the largest economy in the world (with the United States and China very close behind). The EU is also a huge market, with a population of nearly 510 million and a GDP of $18,399 billion.[48] The United States and the EU have the largest bilateral trade and investment relationship in world history. Together, they account for almost half of the entire world GDP and nearly one-third of world trade flows. U.S. and EU companies have invested trillions of dollars in each other's economies, contributing to significant job growth on both sides of the Atlantic. The relationship between these two economic superpowers has also shaped the global economy as a whole—the United States and the EU are primary trade partners for almost every other country in the world.

The EU is a very attractive market for multinational firms. But the EU presents marketing challenges because, even with standardized regulations, marketers will not be able to produce a single European product for a generic European consumer. With more than 14 different languages and individual national customs, Europe will always be far more diverse than the United States. Thus, product differences will continue to be necessary. Atag Holdings NV, a diversified Dutch company whose main business is kitchen appliances, was confident it could cater to both the "potato" and "spaghetti" belts—marketers' terms for consumer preferences in northern and southern Europe. But Atag quickly discovered that preferences vary much more than that. Ovens, burner shape and size, knob and clock placement, temperature range, and colors vary greatly from country to country. Although Atag's kitchenware unit has lifted foreign sales to 25 percent of its total from 4 percent in the mid-1990s, it now believes that its diversified products and speed in delivering them—rather than the magic bullet of a Europroduct—will keep it competitive.

A serious issue facing many multinational firms operating in the EU today is data privacy. The European Commission, composed of one member from each EU country, proposes legislation, and along with the European Court of Justice, enforces the EU's laws. In October 2015, on the advice of the European Commission, the European Court of Justice voided the EU's Safe Harbor agreement, which allowed foreign companies to store Europeans' personal data on American servers. The agreement had been extremely useful to large Internet companies like Facebook and smaller firms that, for example, outsourced payroll and other computer services to American companies. The problem with Safe Harbor was that it rested on the assumption that America protected privacy to European standards.[49] A new agreement called Privacy Shield was created by American and European negotiators in early 2016. This agreement assures that Europeans' data will be shielded from American surveillance agencies, such as the National Security Agency, and will be enforced by the U.S. Federal Trade Commission. A European company or individual who experiences a breach in privacy can file a complaint directly to an ombudsman at the U.S. State Department.

Individual EU member countries can also fine companies over data privacy issues. France recently threatened to fine Facebook if it didn't change the way it collected and used information about Internet users. Five other European countries have also launched probes against Facebook for privacy violations.[50] Fearing fines of its own, Microsoft decided to offer European customers the option of storing their cloud data in Germany.[51]

THE WORLD BANK, THE INTERNATIONAL MONETARY FUND, AND THE G-20 Two international financial organizations are instrumental in fostering global trade. The World Bank offers low-interest loans to developing nations. Originally, the purpose of the loans was to help these nations build infrastructure such as roads, power plants, schools, drainage projects, and hospitals. Now the World Bank offers loans to help developing nations relieve their debt burdens. To receive the loans, countries must pledge to lower trade barriers and aid private enterprise. In addition to making loans, the World Bank is a major source of advice and information for developing nations. The International Monetary Fund (IMF) was founded in 1945, one year after the creation of the World Bank, to promote trade through financial cooperation and eliminate trade barriers in the process. The IMF makes short-term loans to member nations that are unable to meet their budgetary expenses. It operates as a lender of last resort for troubled nations, such as Greece. In exchange for these emergency loans, IMF lenders frequently extract significant commitments from the borrowing nations to address the problems that led to the crises. These steps may include curtailing imports or even devaluing the currency. Greece, working with both the IMF and the EU, has raised taxes to unprecedented levels, cut government spending (including pensions), and implemented labor reforms such as reducing minimum wage as part of its austerity measures to receive loans from the IMF and the European Union. In summer 2016, Greece received an additional 86 billion euros and further forgiveness of existing debt. The objective of these actions was to put Greece on a path of sustainable growth. The IMF's generosity is not infinite, however. The organization recently suspended loans to Mozambique after it determined the African country had violated terms of its IMF agreement by failing to disclose more than $1 billion in other loans.[52]

> **World Bank** an international bank that offers low-interest loans, advice, and information to developing nations

> **International Monetary Fund (IMF)** an international organization that acts as a lender of last resort, providing loans to troubled nations, and also works to promote trade through financial cooperation

The **Group of Twenty (G-20)** finance ministers and central bank governors was established in 1999 to bring together industrialized and developing economies to discuss key issues in the global economy. The G-20 is a forum for international economic development that promotes discussion between industrial and emerging-market countries on key issues related to global economic stability. By contributing to the strengthening of the international financial system and providing opportunities for discussion on national policies, international cooperation, and international financial institutions, the G-20 helps support growth and development across the globe. The members of the G-20 are shown in Exhibit 5.1.

In 2016, the G-20 sharpened its focus on countries that serve as tax shelters and those that haven't agreed to new international standards on tax transparency and information sharing. The G-20 even declared that it would enforce "punitive sanctions" against uncooperative tax shelter countries. The G-20 also recommitted itself to fostering global economic growth in 2016.[53]

5-3e Demographic Makeup

Two primary determinants of any consumer market are wealth and population. The global urban population has grown by an average of 65 million people every year over the past three decades—the equivalent of adding seven Chicagos a year.[54]

China, India, and Indonesia are three of the most densely populated nations in the world. But that fact alone is not particularly useful to marketers. They also need to know whether the population is mostly urban or rural, because marketers may not have easy access to rural consumers. Belgium, for example, with about ninety percent of the population living in urban settings, is a more attractive market.

Over the past quarter-century, world economic growth has lifted 1.25 billion people out of poverty. In 1990, 37 percent of the world's population was in extreme poverty, defined by the World Bank as living on less than $1.90 a day. Today, the bank estimates that 9.6 percent of the world lives in this destitute state— a marked improvement.[55] The increased consumption that helped pull so many people out of poverty was spurred largely by massive population growth. Between 2015 and 2030,

Group of Twenty (G-20) a forum for international economic development that promotes discussion between industrial and emerging-market countries on key issues related to global economic stability

EXHIBIT 5.1 MEMBERS OF THE G-20

Argentina	European Union	Italy	South Africa
Australia	France	Japan	Republic of Korea
Brazil	Germany	Mexico	Turkey
Canada	India	Russia	United Kingdom
China	Indonesia	Saudi Arabia	United States

however, 75 percent of global consumption growth will be driven by individuals spending more. Three groups will generate about half the world's consumption growth: the retiring and elderly in developed countries, China's working age population, and North America's working age population.[56]

Many older adults in developed nations have saved sufficiently for retirement. In the United States, two-thirds of all new cars are sold to consumers over the age of 50.[57] The elderly also spend more per person than younger people do because of their increasing health care needs. By 2030, this group will grow by 20 percent (an additional 100 million people) and per capita consumption is expected to more than double.

By 2030, China's working-age population will account for 12 cents of every dollar spent in cities worldwide. This group has the very real potential to reshape global consumption, just as America's baby boomers— the richest generation in history—did in their prime years.[58]

North America's working age population will increase per capita consumption by a modest 24 percent between 2015 to 2030. Many younger consumers are both poorer and more cost-conscious than the previous generations. Interestingly, well-to-do young adults are much better off than their poorer cohorts. In 2016, the average net worth of the top 20 percent of young-adult households was eight times that of the bottom 80 percent—twice what it was in 2000.[59]

Even though the retiring and elderly are an important part of consumption growth, they present challenges as well. Most notably, the world's population is getting older. While aging has been evident in developed economies for some time—Japan and Russia have seen their populations age for several years running— the demographic deficit is now spreading to China and will soon reach Latin America. The European Commission predicts that by 2060, Germany's population will shrink by one-fifth and the number of working age Germans will fall from 54 million in 2010 to 36 million in 2060. China's labor force peaked in 2012. Thailand's fertility rate has fallen from 5 in the 1970s to 1.4 today.

Thirty years ago, only a small share of the global population lived in countries with fertility rates substantially below those needed to replace each generation—2.1 children per woman. By 2013, about 60 percent of the world's population lived in countries with fertility rates below the replacement rate.[60] For the first time in human history, increasing aging rates could cause the planet's population to plateau in most of the world. A smaller workforce will place a greater emphasis on productivity for driving growth, and caring for large numbers of elderly people will put severe pressure on government finances.[61]

5-3f Natural Resources

A final factor in the external environment that has become more evident in recent years is the distribution of natural resources.

Steep declines in the price of oil in 2014 and 2016 had a very negative impact on America's oil producers—particularly shale oil companies. Falling prices proved an economic boon to American consumers, however. Thanks to oil dropping to below $50 a barrel, the typical American household saved about $800 in 2016. People who depend upon home heating oil also saved around $800.

Fresh water makes up just 2.5 percent of the total volume of the world's water. Given that almost 70 percent of this fresh water exists in the form of ice and permanent snow cover, and that there are 7.3 billion people on the planet, demand for water could soon exceed supply.[62] The United Nations predicts that by 2025, 1.8 billion people will be living in a country with an absolute water scarcity.[63] This will impact agriculture, the location of production facilities, demand for water conservation products, and many other goods and services.

Some natural resources are already found in just a few select countries. This enables these countries to restrict supply, and therefore, inflate prices. Two rare earth elements, scandium and terbium, are used in everything from the powerful magnets located in wind turbines to the electronic circuits in smartphones. Although they are not as rare as the name suggests, 97 percent of the world's supply of these materials comes from China. Similarly, plants cannot grow without phosphorous, a key ingredient in fertilizer. Phosphate rock is found in only a handful of countries, including the United States, Morocco, and China.

Natural resources can have a major impact on international marketing. Warm climate and lack of water mean that many of Africa's countries will remain importers of foodstuffs. The United States, on the other hand, must rely on Africa for many precious metals. Vast

The distribution of natural resources has become a major issue in the external environment in the last decade.

Kokhanchikov/Shutterstock.com

differences in the locations and quantities available of natural resources create international dependencies, huge shifts of wealth, inflation and recession, export opportunities for countries with abundant resources, and even a stimulus for military intervention.

GLOBAL MARKETING BY THE INDIVIDUAL FIRM

A company should consider entering the global marketplace only after its management has a solid grasp of the global environment.

Companies decide to "go global" for a number of reasons. Perhaps the most important is to earn additional profits. Managers may believe that international sales will result in higher profit margins or more added-on profits. A second stimulus is that a firm may have a unique product or technological advantage not available to other international competitors. Such advantages should result in major business successes abroad. In other situations, management may have exclusive market information about foreign customers, marketplaces, or market situations not known to others. While exclusivity can provide an initial motivation for international marketing, managers must realize that competitors can be expected to catch up with the firm's information advantage. Finally, saturated domestic markets, excess capacity, and potential for economies of scale can also be motivators to go global. Economies of scale mean that average per-unit production costs fall as output is increased.

Many firms form multinational partnerships—called strategic alliances—to assist them in penetrating global markets; strategic alliances are examined in Chapter 7. Five other methods of entering the global marketplace are, in order of risk from least to most, exporting, licensing and franchising, contract manufacturing, joint venture, and direct investment (see Exhibit 5.2).

5-4a Exporting

When a company decides to enter the global market, exporting is usually the least complicated and least risky alternative. **Exporting** is selling domestically produced products to buyers in other countries. A company can sell directly to foreign importers or buyers. China is currently the world's largest exporter, but the United States and Germany are not far behind.

Over 7 million U.S. jobs are supported by manufactured exports. Only about one percent of U.S. companies export, and most of those (58 percent) export to just one country. Small and medium-sized companies account for 98 percent of U.S. exporters but represent less than a third of the value of U.S. exported products.[64]

The U.S. Commercial Services, part of the U.S. Department of Commerce, helps U.S. businesses export goods and services to markets worldwide. This organization has offices in 14 countries and stations employees in U.S. embassies in nine additional markets. Among its various duties, the Commercial Services holds conferences around the United States to explain the benefits, types, and avenues of exporting. For example, one conference held in Fort Lauderdale, Florida in the summer of 2016 focused on exporting opportunities in Central and South America.

The Services also provides marketing research information and conducts trade shows featuring U.S. products and services in countries around the world. Potential exporters can also join trade missions, whereby U.S. companies in specific industries travel together as a delegation, attend market briefings, participate in site visits and networking receptions, and have one-on-one matchmaking appointments with potential buyers. Some recent Services trade missions explored health care technology in Saudi Arabia and Kuwait, renewable energy in Mexico, and U.S. franchises in Turkey.[65]

Instead of selling directly to foreign buyers, a company may decide to sell to intermediaries located in its domestic market. The most common intermediary is the export merchant, also known as a **buyer for export**, which is usually treated like a domestic customer by the domestic manufacturer. The buyer for export assumes all risks and sells internationally for its own account. The domestic firm is involved only to the extent that its products are bought in foreign markets.

A second type of intermediary is the **export broker**, who plays the traditional broker's role by bringing buyer and seller together. The manufacturer still retains title and assumes all the risks. Export brokers operate primarily in agricultural products and raw materials.

Export agents, a third type of intermediary, are foreign sales agents/distributors who live in the foreign country and perform the same functions as domestic manufacturers' agents, helping with international financing, shipping, and so on. The U.S. Department of Commerce has an agent/distributor service that helps about 5,000 U.S. companies each year find an agent or distributor in virtually any country of the world. A second category of agents resides in the manufacturer's country but represents foreign buyers. This type of agent acts as a hired purchasing agent for foreign customers operating in the exporter's home market.

exporting selling domestically produced products to buyers in other countries

buyer for export an intermediary in the global market that assumes all ownership risks and sells globally for its own account

export broker an intermediary who plays the traditional broker's role by bringing buyer and seller together

export agent an intermediary who acts like a manufacturer's agent for the exporter; the export agent lives in the foreign market

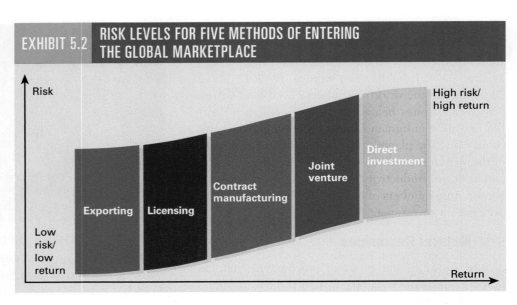

EXHIBIT 5.2 RISK LEVELS FOR FIVE METHODS OF ENTERING THE GLOBAL MARKETPLACE

Risk — Low risk/low return — High risk/high return — Return

Exporting — Licensing — Contract manufacturing — Joint venture — Direct investment

5-4b Licensing and Franchising

Another effective way for a firm to move into the global arena with relatively little risk is to sell a license to manufacture its product to someone in a foreign country. Licensing is the legal process whereby a licensor allows another firm to use its manufacturing process, trademarks, patents, trade secrets, or other proprietary knowledge. The licensee, in turn, pays the licensor a royalty or fee agreed on by both parties.

A licensor must make sure it can exercise sufficient control over the licensee's activities to ensure proper quality, pricing, distribution, and so on. Licensing may also create a new competitor in the long run, if the licensee decides to void the license agreement. International law is often ineffective in stopping such actions. Two common ways of maintaining effective control over licensees are shipping one or more critical components from the United States and locally registering patents and trademarks to the U.S. firm, not to the licensee. Garment companies maintain control by delivering only so many labels per day; they also supply their own fabric, collect the scraps, and do accurate unit counts.

Franchising is a form of licensing that has grown rapidly in recent years. More than 400 U.S. franchisors operate more than 40,000 outlets in foreign countries, and more than half of all international franchises are for fast-food restaurants and business services. Why are fast-food franchises so popular? They offer consistency. Whether they're in Alabama or Alaska, McDonald's customers can expect the same Big Mac and fries. In international markets, however, chains often have to adapt to local tastes and cultures. In Europe, for example, drinking an espresso coffee is the norm after lunch. In order to avoid standing in line twice or drinking a cold espresso after a burger and fries, McDonald's customers in much of Europe are given a token with their meal. They simply put the token in a self-serve machine, and out comes a steaming espresso.

Sometimes a franchise has to change its recipes to adapt to local cultures. In Japan, one popular Pizza Hut pie is topped with prawn, squid, tuna, mayonnaise, broccoli, onions, and tomato sauce. Another mixes teriyaki chicken with corn, seaweed, and mayonnaise. In South Korea, customers can get their pizza crusts stuffed with sweet potato mousse. In the Middle East, an adventurous customer can order his or her pizza with cheeseburgers embedded into the crust. Both McDonald's and Burger King have introduced all-black burgers in Japan. Americans may mistake them for a meal left on the grill too long—the buns, cheese, and sauce are pitch black—but they've actually been colored by squid ink.[66]

5-4c Contract Manufacturing

Firms that do not want to become involved in licensing or to become heavily involved in global marketing may engage in contract manufacturing, which is private label manufacturing by a foreign company. The foreign company produces a certain volume of products to specification, with the domestic firm's brand name on the goods. The domestic company usually handles the marketing. Thus, the domestic firm can broaden its global marketing base without investing in overseas plants and equipment. After establishing a solid base, the domestic firm may switch to a joint venture or direct investment.

5-4d Joint Venture

Joint ventures are somewhat similar to licensing agreements. In an international joint venture, the domestic firm buys part of a foreign company or joins with a foreign company to create a new entity. Thanks to a joint venture between General Electric (GE) and CFM International, workers assemble the best-selling aircraft engine in history in a huge factory just south of Paris. The engine's core, consisting of the combustion chamber and related elements, is produced in a GE factory near Cincinnati, Ohio and shipped to France. Once the core arrives in France, engineers and technicians in blue overalls carefully marry the core to French-made turbo fans, turbines, and compressors. Combined, these parts form jet engines weighing two and a half tons each. Every month, about 65 of these engines are tested and shipped out.[67]

Not all international joint ventures involve a foreign corporation, however. In 2016, manufacturer of mobile phone microchips Qualcomm announced a

licensing the legal process whereby a licensor allows another firm to use its manufacturing process, trademarks, patents, trade secrets, or other proprietary knowledge

contract manufacturing private label manufacturing by a foreign company

joint venture when a domestic firm buys part of a foreign company or joins with a foreign company to create a new entity

joint venture with the government of China's Guizhou province. This joint venture was launched to produce both standard Qualcomm service chips and a slightly modified chip to meet the needs of the Chinese cloud computing market.[68]

While potentially very lucrative, joint ventures can also be very risky. Many fail. Sometimes joint venture partners simply cannot agree on management strategies and policies. Often, joint ventures are the only way a government will allow a foreign company to enter its country. Joint ventures enable the local firm or government to acquire managerial skills and new technology.

5-4e Direct Investment

Active ownership of a foreign company or of overseas manufacturing or marketing facilities is called **direct foreign investment**. Direct foreign investment by U.S. firms is currently about $245 billion annually.[69] Direct investors have either a controlling interest or a large minority interest in the firm. Thus, they have the greatest potential reward and the greatest potential risk.

A firm may make a direct foreign investment by acquiring an interest in an existing company or by building new facilities. It might do so because it has trouble transferring some resource to a foreign operation or getting that resource locally. One important resource is personnel, especially managers. If the local labor market is tight, the firm may buy an entire foreign firm and retain all its employees instead of paying higher salaries than competitors.

The United States is a popular place for direct investment by international companies. Foreign direct investment in the United States accounts for approximately $2.9 trillion.[70] The United States continues to receive more foreign investment flows than any country in the world. The United Kingdom is home to the largest investors in the United States, followed by Japan, the Netherlands, Canada, and Luxembourg. U.S. affiliates of foreign firms employ more than 5.8 million people in the United States. These companies spend more than $50 billion on U.S. research and development and export over $345 billion worth of goods manufactured in the United States.[71]

5-5 THE GLOBAL MARKETING MIX

direct foreign investment
active ownership of a foreign company or of overseas manufacturing or marketing facilities

To succeed, firms seeking to enter into foreign trade must still adhere to the principles of the **marketing mix.** Information gathered on foreign markets through research is the basis for the four Ps of global marketing strategy: product, place (distribution), promotion, and price. Marketing managers who understand the advantages and disadvantages of different ways of entering the global market and the effect of the external environment on the firm's marketing mix have a better chance of reaching their goals.

The first step in creating a marketing mix is developing a thorough understanding of the global target market. Often this knowledge can be obtained through the same types of marketing research used in the domestic market (see Chapter 9). However, global marketing research is conducted in vastly different environments. Conducting a survey can be difficult in developing countries where telephone ownership is growing but is not always common and mail delivery is slow or sporadic. Drawing samples based on known population parameters is often difficult because of the lack of data. In some cities in Africa, Asia, Mexico, and South America, street maps are unavailable, streets are unidentified, and houses are unnumbered. Moreover, the questions a marketer can ask may differ in other cultures. In some cultures, people tend to be more private than in the United States and will not respond to personal questions on surveys. For instance, in France, questions about one's age and income are considered especially rude.

5-5a Product Decisions

With the proper information, a good marketing mix can be developed. One important decision is whether to alter the product or the promotion for the global marketplace. Other options are to radically change the product or to adjust either the promotional message or the product to suit local conditions.

ONE PRODUCT, ONE MESSAGE The strategy of global marketing standardization, which was discussed earlier, means developing a single product for all markets and promoting it the same way all over the world. For instance, Procter & Gamble (P&G) uses the same product and promotional themes for Head & Shoulders in China as it does in the United States. The advertising draws attention to a person's dandruff problem, which stands out in a nation of black-haired people. Head & Shoulders is now the best-selling shampoo in China despite costing over 300 percent more than local brands. P&G markets its rich portfolio of personal-care, beauty, grooming, health, and fabric products in more than 180 countries. The firm has 20 brands that sell more than $1 billion annually around the world. Some brands, such as Duracell batteries, are heavily standardized. P&G has moved away from standardization for other brands, however. Its Axe line of male grooming products uses a constantly running sociological study in order to keep its video ads up to date with the latest trends among young men. Axe's promotion, bottle size, and pricing also change according to which country is being targeted.[72]

Apple is often thought of as leader in global marketing standardization, but even Apple takes local markets into account. For example, although iPhones look and operate the same everywhere, their power cords, pricing, and wireless carrier specifics differ. Apple follows a strict customer service protocol in its stores around the world, but this protocol is always tailored to local cultures. Once a location for a store is selected, Apple executives make certain that the store design has an inviting appeal and that it fits into the surrounding architecture. Apple's localized e-commerce websites follow a standardized design, yet the content is always translated into the local language and checked by native speakers to make certain that nothing is lost in translation.

Global marketing standardization can sometimes backfire. Unchanged products may fail simply because of cultural factors. Any type of war game tends to do very poorly in Germany, even though Germany is by far the world's biggest game-playing nation. A successful game in Germany is highly detailed and has a thick rulebook. In Russia, Campbell's Soups failed because housewives prefer to make soup from scratch.

Sometimes the desire for absolute standardization must give way to practical considerations and local market dynamics. For example, because of the negative connotations of the word *diet* among European females, the European version of Diet Coke is Coca-Cola Light. Even if the brand name differs by market—as with Lay's potato chips, which are called Sabritas in Mexico—a strong visual relationship may be created by uniform application of the brandmark and graphic elements on packaging.

PRODUCT INVENTION In the context of global marketing, product invention can be taken to mean either creating a new product for a market or drastically changing an existing product. For example, more than 100 unique Pringles potato chip flavors have been invented for international markets. Prawn Cocktail (the United Kingdom), Seaweed (Japan), Blueberry (China), Cinnamon Sweet Potato (France), and Bangkok Grilled Chicken Wing (Thailand) are some of the many Pringles flavors available outside the United States. Chinese consumers found Oreo cookies "too sweet," while Indian consumers said that they were "too bitter." In response, Kraft changed the recipe in each country and created a new Green Tea Oreo flavor for China.

PRODUCT ADAPTATION Another alternative for global marketers is to alter a basic product to meet local conditions. In India, Starbucks sells a tandoori paneer roll. KFC makes a "paneer zinger." Burger King sells its classic Whopper hamburger alongside a cheese-based Paneer King burger. This is largely how international food brands court India's 1.25 billion consumers—by playing to local tastes. But Domino's is doing more than simply creating new products in its attempt to woo Indian customers. It has reimagined everything about itself, from changing the flour it uses to maintaining a delicate balance between local tastes and Western influence. This dedication to adaptation has made Domino's India's largest international foreign-food chain; the company currently has 806 stores across 170 cities—more than twice as many as McDonald's.[73]

Pizza dough and toppings have much in common with Indian roti (flat bread) and subji (vegetables). Pizza also carries two important keystones of local Indian culture—shared plates and food that can be eaten with your hands. After eight months of research, Domino's introduced a small pizza called "Pizza Mania." It sells for 60 cents, is made in 2.5 minutes, and takes just six minutes to bake. The company also created a "cheese burst" (topped with chicken, salami, and classic Indian spices) and the "Taco Indiana" dish inspired by northern India's kebabs and parathas. In southern India, where pizza is less popular, research led to a spicy raw banana pizza.[74]

5-5b Promotion Adaptation

Another global marketing strategy is to maintain the same basic product but alter the promotional strategy. For example, bicycles are mainly pleasure vehicles in the United States, but in many parts of the world, they are a family's main mode of transportation. Thus, promotion in these countries should stress durability and efficiency. In contrast, U.S. advertising may emphasize escaping and having fun.

Language barriers, translation problems, and cultural differences have generated numerous headaches for international marketing managers. For example, a toothpaste claiming to give users white teeth was especially inappropriate in many areas of Southeast Asia, where the well-to-do chew betel nuts and black teeth are a sign of higher social status.

In markets where milk consumption is low, cereal manufacturer Kellogg found that it needed to communicate how to eat cold cereal. To solve this problem, Kellogg launched a series of advertisements explaining the need for adequate amounts of milk on cold cereal. Kellogg similarly stumbled when it launched Corn Flakes in rural African areas. Many consumers had grown up eating Mielie Meal, a ground maize porridge, and they initially thought that they should use hot water to prepare Corn Flakes like they did with Mielie Meal. Kellogg ran ads promoting how to use milk with cold cereal and also introduced a porridge product to meet the needs of consumers wanting a hot breakfast item.[75]

Unilever's Lifebuoy hand soap virtually disappeared from the American market 50 years ago, but it is alive and well internationally. Lifebuoy dominates the market in India and is a leading seller in several emerging markets. With its new "Help a Child Reach 5," campaign, Lifebuoy pledged to help save lives by spreading the importance of good handwashing habits around the world. This campaign is driven by two staggering figures. First, 2 million children fail to reach their fifth birthday every year because of illnesses like diarrhea and pneumonia. Second, washing one's hands with soap at key occasions can reduce diarrhea by 45 percent and pneumonia by 23 percent, substantially reducing infant deaths worldwide.[76]

5-5c Place (Distribution)

Solving promotional and product problems does not guarantee global marketing success. The product must still get adequate distribution. For example, Europeans do not play sports as much as Americans do, so they do not visit sporting-goods stores as often. Realizing this, Reebok started selling its shoes in about 800 traditional shoe stores in France. In just one year, the company doubled its French sales.

Taiwanese convenience stores are quite different from what is found in the United States. Beyond the staple snacks, they provide an array of services including dry cleaning, train and concert ticket reservations, traffic fine and utility payment, hot sit-down meals, mail drop-off, and book pickup. They also deliver everything from refrigerators to multicourse banquets. As you might expect, heavy convenience store patronage is the norm in Taiwan.

McDonald's recently unveiled plans to expand its Chinese locations from 2,200 to 3,500 over the next five years. As it decides where to place these 1,300 new stores, McDonald's needs to consider a number of key factors. For one, McDonald's must find reliable suppliers that can deliver salad makings, buns, potatoes, and a host of other items in a timely manner. Moreover, the quality must be consistent. In 2014, a problem with a supplier left several Chinese McDonald's restaurants without chicken or hamburgers.[77] Contrary to the franchise model seen

exchange rate the price of one country's currency in terms of another country's currency

in the United States, McDonald's owned and operated all of its restaurants in China until the mid-2000s. This is a costly strategy, but the firm felt it was important for orderly growth and to ensure quality. Today, McDonald's hopes to cut costs in its international markets by franchising 95 percent of its outlets worldwide.[78]

Finding the right franchisee to operate a McDonald's or a foreign distributor to sell a small manufacturer's product can be quite difficult. As a function of the U.S. Department of Commerce, the U.S. Export Assistance Center offers a Gold Key matchmaking service to do just that. For smaller companies, this service can help locate overseas representatives or distributors. For bigger companies like McDonald's, it screens potential partners that meet the firm's criteria. The firm can then send a representative to the target country to interview the prescreened partners. To further screen foreign partners, many U.S. firms turn to World-Check, a database of high-risk individuals and companies from around the globe. This database can uncover hidden risks in potential business relationships.[79]

5-5d Pricing

Once marketing managers have determined a global product and promotion strategy, they can select the remainder of the marketing mix. Pricing presents some unique problems in the global sphere. Exporters must not only cover their production costs but also consider transportation costs, insurance, taxes, and tariffs. When deciding on a final price, marketers must also determine how much customers are willing to spend on a particular product. Marketers also need to ensure that their foreign buyers will pay the price. Because developing nations lack mass purchasing power, selling to them often poses special pricing problems. Sometimes a product can be simplified in order to lower the price. A firm must not assume low-income countries are willing to accept lower quality, however. L'Oréal was unsuccessful selling cheap shampoo in India, so the company targets the rising class. It now sells a $17 Paris face powder and a $25 Vichy sunscreen. Both products are very popular.

EXCHANGE RATES The exchange rate is the price of one country's currency in terms of another country's currency. If a country's currency *appreciates*, less of that country's currency is needed to buy another country's currency. If a country's currency *depreciates*, more of that currency will be needed to buy another country's currency.

How do appreciation and depreciation affect the prices of a country's goods? If, say, the U.S. dollar depreciates relative to the Japanese yen, U.S. residents will need to pay more dollars to buy Japanese goods. On April 29, 2016, $1.00 was worth ¥106.71. At this exchange rate, a U.S. resident would pay $18,742 for a ¥2 million Toyota automobile (2 million divided by 106.71 = 18,742). If the dollar depreciates to $1.00 being worth ¥95, then the same vehicle will cost the U.S. resident $21,053 (2 million divided by 95 = 21,053).

As the dollar depreciates, the prices of Japanese goods rise for U.S. residents, so they buy fewer Japanese goods—thus, U.S. imports may decline. At the same time, as the dollar depreciates relative to the yen, the yen appreciates relative to the dollar. This means prices of U.S. goods fall for the Japanese, so they buy more U.S. goods—and U.S. exports rise.

Currency markets operate under a system of **floating exchange rates**. Prices of different currencies "float" up and down based on the demand for and the supply of each currency. Global currency traders create the supply of and demand for a particular country's currency based on that country's investment, trade potential, and economic strength. Government actions can also impact exchange rates. Sanctions imposed against Russia for invading Crimea and engaging in the Ukrainian border conflict caused the Russian ruble to plunge in value.

Theoretically, exchange rates should adjust over time so that one dollar buys the same amount everywhere. However, because so many factors can influence exchange rates, currencies sometimes become overvalued or undervalued. Every year, The *Economist* magazine analyzes the cost of a Big Mac around the world to create a somewhat tongue-in-cheek index of currency valuations. In other words, *The Economist* converts the cost of a Big Mac from local currencies to U.S. dollars using current exchange rates and sees how they compare. On January 6, 2016, the cost of a U.S. Big Mac was $4.93, whereas the equivalent dollar

cost in Switzerland was $6.44. Thus, the Swiss franc is overvalued relative to the dollar. The price of a Big Mac in Japan was $3.12; in Mexico, $2.81; in India, $1.90; and in Russia, $1.53.[80] All of these currencies were undervalued relative to the dollar.

DUMPING **Dumping** is the sale of an exported product at a price lower than that charged for the same or a like product in the "home" market of the exporter. This practice is regarded as a form of price discrimination that can potentially harm the importing nation's competing industries. Dumping may occur as a result of exporter business strategies that include (1) trying to increase an overseas market share, (2) temporarily distributing products in overseas markets to offset slack demand in the home market, (3) lowering unit costs by exploiting large-scale production, and (4) attempting to maintain stable prices during periods of exchange rate fluctuations.

Historically, the dumping of goods has presented serious problems in international trade. As a result, dumping has led to significant disagreements among countries and diverse views about its harmfulness. Some trade economists view dumping as harmful only when it involves the use of "predatory" practices that intentionally try to eliminate competition and gain monopoly power in a market. They believe that predatory dumping rarely occurs and that anti-dumping rules are a protectionist tool whose cost to consumers and import-using industries exceeds the benefits to the industries receiving protection.

Over the past decade, the United States International Trade Commission declared anti-dumping duties in more than 80 investigations of foreign companies.[81] While most cases were brought against Chinese companies, firms from more than 25 different countries faced anti-dumping duties. The products involved ranged from washing machines from Korea and Mexico to steel pressure pipes from Malaysia, Thailand, and Vietnam. Five new cases were filed between January and May 2016 on products such as raw pistachios from Iran and frozen shrimp from Brazil, China, India, Thailand, and Vietnam.[82]

floating exchange rates a system in which prices of different currencies move up and down based on the demand for and the supply of each currency

dumping the sale of an exported product at a price lower than that charged for the same or a like product in the "home" market of the exporter

OtnaYdur/Shutterstock.com

After the incredible success of Earth Hour 2016, the WWF announced that the 2017 Earth Hour global campaign would be held on March 25, 2017.

COUNTERTRADE Global trade does not always involve cash. Countertrade is a fast-growing way to conduct global business. In **countertrade**, all or part of the payment for goods or services is in the form of other goods or services. Countertrade is thus a form of barter (swapping goods for goods), an age-old practice whose origins have been traced back to cave dwellers. The U.S. Department of Commerce says that roughly thirty percent of all global trade is countertrade.[83] In fact, both India and China have made billion-dollar government purchasing lists, with most of the goods to be paid for by countertrade.

One common type of countertrade is straight barter. The Malaysian government purchased 20 diesel-electric locomotives from General Electric in exchange for a supply of 200,000 metric tons of palm oil. Sometimes, countertrades involve both cash and goods. General Motors sold locomotive and diesel engines to Yugoslavia in exchange for $4 million and Yugoslavian cutting tools.[84] Another form of countertrade is the compensation agreement. Typically, a company provides technology and equipment for a plant in a developing nation and agrees to take full or partial payment in goods produced by that plant. For example, General Tire Company supplied equipment and know-how for a Romanian truck tire plant. In turn, General Tire sold the tires it received from the plant

countertrade a form of trade in which all or part of the payment for goods or services is in the form of other goods or services

in the United States under the Victoria brand name. Both sides benefit even though they do not use cash.

5-6 THE IMPACT OF THE INTERNET

In many respects, going global is easier than it has ever been before. Opening an e-commerce site on the Internet immediately puts a company in the international marketplace. Sophisticated language translation software can make any site accessible to people around the world. Global shippers such as UPS, FedEx, and DHL help solve international e-commerce distribution complexities. E4X Inc. offers software to ease currency conversions by allowing customers to pay in the currency of their choice. E4X collects the payment from the customer and then pays the site in U.S. dollars. Nevertheless, the promise of "borderless commerce" and the global "Internet economy" are still being restrained by the old brick-and-mortar rules, regulations, and habits. For example, Lands' End is not allowed to mention its unconditional refund policy on its e-commerce site in Germany because German retailers, which normally do not allow returns after 14 days, sued and won a court ruling blocking mention of it.

5-6a Social Media in Global Marketing

Because Facebook, YouTube, Twitter, Pinterest, and other social media are popular around the world, firms both large and small have embraced social media marketing. Independent room and property rental service Airbnb relies heavily on social media marketing. In one recent campaign, Airbnb asked people to perform random acts of hospitality for strangers and then post videos or photos with the them using the hashtag #OneLessStranger. Within less than three weeks, more than 3 million people around the world were engaging with, creating content for, or talking about the campaign.[85]

In 2008, the World Wildlife Foundation (WWF) created a global digital campaign called Earth Hour. Participants in the annual event turn off their lights for one hour to demonstrate how easy it is to battle climate change. In 2016, the WWF recently took the campaign to Norway, which has extreme daylight hours in different seasons. To promote the campaign, the organization placed a Blackout Banner across Norway's top social media sites. With a single tap of the banner, the user's screen went black. Finger swiping the black screen slowly revealed the Earth Hour countdown. The promotion attracted nearly a million viewers.[86]

Managers of global social media campaigns must always be aware of the cultures of the countries in which they operate. Global energy drink giant Red Bull sparked a major spat with Kenyans after it posted a video that seemed to imply that Kenyans were backward to Facebook. The video clip featured South African motorcycle rider Brian Capper, who started the video off by expressing his shock at how many people spoke English in Nairobi. "I've been blown away with the amount of people that speak English. I had absolutely no idea what to expect from that point of view; just about everybody I spoke to spoke English, which was really surprising for me," said the rider. "They are unbelievably knowledgeable ... they know what's going on with the rest of the world."[87] Capper's comments did not go down well with many, as Red Bull's Facebook page quickly filled with angry comments such as:

> "Seems like a nice guy and cool video, but seriously, what era is he and the Red Bull crew living in!

Surprised about the English and saying 3rd world country, eyes need to be open to Kenya! And the dude is from SA as well, so should really know better."

> "Don't you just love the ignorance of these people! Surprised that Kenyans speak English? We speak better English than you dude. All in all, great biking skills! Now go back to school."[88]

These reactions are reminiscent of a similar outcry after Korean Air termed Kenyans "primitive" in an online advertising campaign about the company's direct flights to Nairobi. The advertisement read in part: "Fly to Nairobi with Korean Air and enjoy the grand African savanna, the safari tour, and the indigenous people full of primitive energy." The words 'primitive energy' annoyed many Kenyans, who forced the airline to retract the ad and issue an apology on social media.[89]

STUDY TOOLS 5

LOCATED AT BACK OF THE TEXTBOOK

☐ Rip out Chapter Review Card

LOCATED AT WWW.CENGAGEBRAIN.COM

☐ Review Key Terms Flashcards and create your own

☐ Track your knowledge and understanding of key concepts in marketing

☐ Complete practice and graded quizzes to prepare for tests

☐ Complete interactive content within the MKTG Online experience

☐ View the chapter highlight boxes within the MKTG Online experience

6 | Consumer Decision Making

LEARNING OUTCOMES

After studying this chapter, you will be able to...

6-1 Explain why marketing managers should understand consumer behavior

6-2 Analyze the components of the consumer decision-making process

6-3 Explain the consumer's postpurchase evaluation process

6-4 Identify the types of consumer buying decisions and discuss the significance of consumer involvement

6-5 Describe how some marketers are reconceptualizing the consumer decision-making process.

6-6 Identify and understand the cultural factors that affect consumer buying decisions

6-7 Identify and understand the social factors that affect consumer buying decisions

6-8 Identify and understand the individual factors that affect consumer buying decisions

6-9 Identify and understand the psychological factors that affect consumer buying decisions

After finishing this chapter go to **PAGE 119** for **STUDY TOOLS**

6-1 THE IMPORTANCE OF UNDERSTANDING CONSUMER BEHAVIOR

Consumers' product and service preferences are constantly changing. Marketing managers must understand these desires in order to create a proper marketing mix for a well-defined market. So it is critical that marketing managers have a thorough knowledge of consumer behavior. Consumer behavior describes how consumers make purchase decisions and how they use and dispose of the purchased goods or services. The study of consumer behavior also includes factors that influence purchase decisions and product use.

consumer behavior
processes a consumer uses to make purchase decisions, as well as to use and dispose of purchased goods or services; also includes factors that influence purchase decisions and product use

Understanding how consumers make purchase decisions can help marketing managers in several ways. For example, if the product development manager for Trek bicycles learns through research that a more comfortable seat is a key attribute for purchasers of mountain bikes, Trek can redesign the seat to meet that criterion. If the firm cannot change the design in the short run, it can use promotion in an effort to change consumers' decision-making criteria. Trek, for example, could promote the ultra-light weight, durability, and performance of its current mountain bikes.

Watcharapol Amprasert/Shutterstock.com

Buying a mountain bike, or anything else, is all about value. **Value** is a personal assessment of the net worth one obtains from making a purchase. To put it another way, value is what you get minus what you give up. When you buy something, you hope to get benefits like relief from hunger, durability, convenience, prestige, affection, happiness, a sense of belonging...the list goes on. In order to receive these benefits, you must give something up. You may sacrifice money, self-image, time, convenience, effort, opportunity, or a combination thereof. Value can also mean an enduring belief shared by a society that a specific mode of conduct is personally or socially preferable to another mode of conduct. This definition of "value" will be discussed later in the chapter.

Purchases are made based upon **perceived value**, which is what you *expect* to get. The actual value may be more or less than you expected. Recently, one of your authors bought a well-known brand of coffee maker with a thermal carafe. He likes to drink coffee all morning, but found that traditional coffee makers' heating elements tended to turn the coffee bitter and thick-tasting after a few hours. The thermal carafe has no such heating element, so the coffee stays fresh. That is, if the coffee actually makes it into the carafe. The carafe lid has a valve that lets the coffee drip into the carafe basin. However, the valve tends to stick, and after about a week of use, the valve stuck during a fill-up and coffee went all over the kitchen counter. No value there! (For the curious, the author has moved on to a new traditional-style coffee maker.)

The value received from a purchase can be broken down into two categories. **Utilitarian value** is derived from a product or service that helps the consumer solve problems and accomplish tasks. Buying a washing machine and dryer gives you a convenient means of cleaning your clothes. Buying a new pair of eyeglasses lets you better view the computer screen. Utilitarian value, then, is a means to an end. Value is provided because the purchase allows something good to happen.

value a personal assessment of the net worth one obtains from making a purchase, or the enduring belief that a specific mode of conduct is personally or socially preferable to another mode of conduct

perceived value the value a consumer *expects* to obtain from a purchase

utilitarian value a value derived from a product or service that helps the consumer solve problems and accomplish tasks

The second form of value is **hedonic value**. Hedonic value is an end in itself rather than as a means to an end. The purchase tends to give us good feelings, happiness, and satisfaction. The value is provided entirely through the experience and emotions associated with consumption, not because another end is accomplished. Taking a ski vacation or a trip to the beach gives us hedonic value. Spending a day in a spa is a source of hedonic value. A coffee maker provides utilitarian value, but the coffee itself provides hedonic value.

Utilitarian and hedonic values are not mutually exclusive. In some cases, the purchase experience can give you both hedonic and utilitarian value. Morton's The Steakhouse is considered to be one of the top steak restaurant chains in the United States. Going to a Morton's and enjoying the atmosphere and a fine steak will give you hedonic value. At the same time, it satisfies your hunger pangs and thus provides utilitarian value. Some of the best consumer experiences are high in both utilitarian and hedonic value.[1]

Acquiring value comes from making a purchase. How does one go about making the decision to buy? We will explore this topic next.

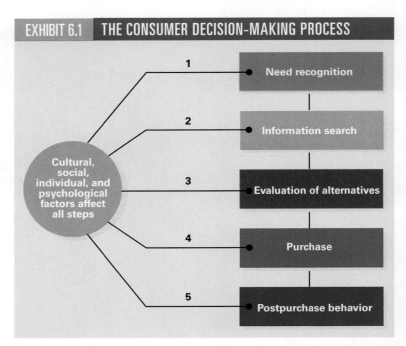

EXHIBIT 6.1   THE CONSUMER DECISION-MAKING PROCESS

6-2 THE TRADITIONAL CONSUMER DECISION-MAKING PROCESS

When buying products, particularly new or expensive items, consumers generally follow the **consumer decision-making process** shown in Exhibit 6.1: (1) need recognition, (2) information search, (3) evaluation of alternatives, (4) purchase, and (5) postpurchase behavior. These five steps represent the traditional buying process, which can be used as a guide for studying how consumers make decisions. It is important to note, though, that consumers' decisions do not always proceed in order through all of these steps. In fact, the consumer may end the process at any time or may not even make a purchase. Note too that technology is changing how people make decisions. A new conceptualization of the buying process is discussed later in the chapter. We begin, however, by examining the traditional purchase process in greater detail.

6-2a Need Recognition

The first stage in the consumer decision-making process is need recognition. **Need recognition** is the result of an imbalance between actual and desired states. The imbalance arouses and activates the consumer decision-making process. A **want** is the recognition of an unfulfilled need and a product that will satisfy it. For example, have you ever gotten blisters from an old running shoe and realized you needed new shoes? Or maybe you have seen a new sports car drive down the street and wanted to buy it. Wants can be viewed in terms of four goals: economizing, sustaining, treating, and rewarding.[2] The specific goal that a consumer is trying to fulfill influences how he or she allocates money, time, and effort. Consider a coffee drinker who has just run out of coffee at home. If she wanted to satisfy an economizing goal, she might purchase one of three brands she uses frequently because it is the one that is currently on sale. If, however, she wanted to satisfy a sustaining goal, she would be more likely to purchase her favorite brand because she prefers the taste over the other two brands she sometimes buys. If she wanted to satisfy a treating goal, she might buy a cup of coffee at Starbucks. Finally, if she wanted to satisfy a rewarding goal, she might opt to order a latte while reading her favorite book at a trendy new cafe.

hedonic value a value that acts as an end in itself rather than as a means to an end

consumer decision-making process a five-step process used by consumers when buying goods or services

need recognition result of an imbalance between actual and desired states

want recognition of an unfulfilled need and a product that will satisfy it

Source: Fitbit, Inc.

> A want can be for a specific product, or it can be for a certain attribute or feature of a product.

may purchase the Orbit, for example, because the band pairs with the Runtastic app to display information about recent runs right on the wearer's wrist.

6-2b Information Search

After recognizing a need or want, consumers search for information about the various alternatives available to satisfy it. For example, you know you are interested in seeing a movie, but you are not sure what to see. So you visit the Rotten Tomatoes website to see what is getting great reviews by both critics and your peers on Facebook. This is a type of information search, which can occur internally, externally, or both. In an **internal information search**, the person recalls information stored in the memory. This stored information stems largely from previous experience with a product. For example, while traveling with your family, you may choose to stay at a hotel you have stayed in before because you remember that the hotel had clean rooms and friendly service.

In contrast, an **external information search** seeks information in the outside environment. There are two basic types of external information sources: nonmarketing-controlled and marketing-controlled. A **nonmarketing-controlled information source** is a product information source that is not associated with marketers promoting a product. These information sources include personal experiences (trying or observing a new product), personal sources (family, friends, acquaintances, and coworkers who may recommend a product or service), and public sources (such as Rotten Tomatoes, *Consumer Reports*, and other rating organizations that comment on products and services). Once you have read reviews on Rotten Tomatoes to decide which movie to see (public source), you may search your memory for positive theater experiences to determine where you will go (personal experience). Or you might rely on a friend's recommendation to try

Need recognition is triggered when a consumer is exposed to either an internal or an external **stimulus**, which is any unit of input affecting one or more of the five senses: sight, smell, taste, touch, and hearing. *Internal stimuli* are occurrences you experience, such as hunger or thirst. For example, you may hear your stomach growl and then realize you are hungry. *External stimuli* are influences from an outside source. In today's digital age, stimuli can come from a multitude of sources. Perhaps it was a YouTube video that created a purchase desire. Perhaps it was a Google search on a smartphone or an interactive advertisement playing on a large touch-enabled screen. Or perhaps it was a friend's video posted on Facebook using a new GoPro camera.

The imbalance between actual and desired states is sometimes referred to as the *want–got gap*. That is, there is a difference between what a customer has and what he or she would like to have. This gap does not always trigger consumer action. The gap must be large enough to drive the consumer to do something. Just because your stomach growls once does not mean that you necessarily will stop what you are doing and go eat.

A marketing manager's objective is to get consumers to recognize this want–got gap. Advertising, sales promotion, and social media often provide this stimulus. Surveying buyer preferences provides marketers with information about consumer needs and wants that can be used to tailor products and services. Marketing managers can create wants on the part of the consumer. An ad promoting a healthy, active lifestyle and the fun of fitness tracking may inspire you to purchase a wearable fitness tracker like a Fitbit Charge HR or a Runtastic Orbit. A want can be for a specific product, or it can be for a certain attribute or feature of a product. A runner

---

stimulus any unit of input affecting one or more of the five senses: sight, smell, taste, touch, hearing

internal information search the process of recalling past information stored in the memory

external information search the process of seeking information in the outside environment

nonmarketing-controlled information source a product information source that is not associated with advertising or promotion

out a new theater (personal source). Marketers gather information on how these information sources work and use it to attract customers. For example, car manufacturers know that younger customers are likely to get information from friends and family, so they try to develop enthusiasm for their products via word of mouth and social media.

Living in the digital age has changed the way consumers get nonmarketing-controlled information. It can be from blogs, Amazon, social media, web forums, or consumer opinion sites such as www.consumerreview.com, www.tripadvisor.com, or www.epinions.com. Eighty percent of U.S. consumers research electronics, computers, and media online before making an in-store purchase, and a quarter of shoppers utilize at least four sources for product information. To give you an idea of the number of searches this implies, Google averages more than 100 billion searches a month.[3] This number is only going to expand.

The Internet has changed the quality of information available to make purchase decisions. In the past, consumers used quality proxies to help determine what to buy. A proxy could be a brand name ("it is made by Sony so it must be good"), price ("higher price meant higher quality"), or origin ("made in the USA is better"). Today, consumers can appraise a product based upon how it is evaluated by others. If you are looking for a hotel in New York City, for example, you can easily view a ranking of all New York hotels based upon thousands of reviews on website like TripAdvisor. This provides much better information than simply relying on a brand name (such as Hilton) because you have the direct experience of others to guide you. A word of caution, however: researchers using data from a large private label retailer's website found that approximately 5 percent of product reviews were submitted by people with no record of ever having purchased the products they were reviewing.[4] Expedia avoids this problem by only allowing customers who have purchased a service (such as a flight, car, or hotel room) to write a review. Similarly, Amazon identifies whether a review matches a confirmed transaction.

Social media are playing an ever-increasing role in consumer information search. Eighty-one percent of respondents to a recent survey reported that social media posts made by family and friends directly impacted their purchase decisions. Seventy-eight percent reported that posts made by companies influenced their buying decisions.[5]

Although the use of a mobile device to make purchases is rising, consumers primarily use their smartphones and tablets to research products before buying. One survey found that 70 percent of respondents planned to research products on their mobile devices and then purchased them in-store.[6] In-store research and price comparisons conducted on mobile devices while shopping have become standard practice for many consumers.

Not every information search is about comparing Product or Service Firm A with Product or Service Firm B. Yet, the online search can still influence purchase patterns. For example, a shopper may browse recipe website or watch cooking demonstration videos before deciding on a dinner party menu. This research helps the shopper decide which ingredients to purchase at the supermarket.

A **marketing-controlled information source** is biased toward a specific product because it originates with marketers promoting that product. Marketing-controlled information sources include mass media advertising (radio, newspaper, television, and magazine advertising), sales promotion (contests, displays, premiums, and so forth), salespeople, product labels and packaging, and digital media. In 2016, the Web influenced more than half of all retail transactions, representing sales of almost $2 trillion.[7] Research shows that developing a social media community with a dedicated fan base, such as an active Facebook page, significantly strengthens customer relationships with a company and brand. Moreover, it has a positive impact on revenue and profits.[8]

The Internet has changed the quality of information available to make purchase decisions.

Source: TripAdvisor

marketing-controlled information source a product information source that originates with marketers promoting the product

The extent to which an individual conducts an external search depends on his or her perceived risk, knowledge, prior experience, and level of interest in the good or service. Generally, as the perceived risk of the purchase increases, the consumer enlarges the search and considers more alternative brands. For example, suppose that you want to purchase a surround-sound system for your home entertainment system. The decision is relatively risky because of the expense and technical nature of the surround-sound system, so you are motivated to search for information about models, prices, options, compatibility with existing entertainment products, and capabilities. You may decide to compare attributes of many speaker systems because the value of the time expended finding the "right" stereo will be less than the cost of buying the wrong system.

A consumer's knowledge about the product or service will also affect the extent of an external information search. A consumer who is knowledgeable and well informed about a potential purchase is less likely to search for additional information. In addition, the more knowledgeable consumers are, the more efficiently they will conduct the search process, thereby requiring less time to search. For example, many consumers know that Spirit Airlines and other discount airlines have much lower fares, so they generally use the discounters and do not even check fares at other carriers.

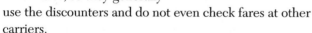

Radu Bercan/Shutterstock.com

The extent of a consumer's external search is also affected by confidence in one's decision-making ability. A confident consumer not only has sufficient stored information about the product but also feels self-assured about making the right decision. People lacking this confidence will continue an information search even when they know a great deal about the product. Consumers with prior experience in buying a certain product will have less perceived risk than inexperienced consumers. Therefore, they will spend less time searching and limit the number of products they consider.

A third factor influencing the external information search is product experience. Consumers who have had a positive experience with a product are more likely to limit their search to items related to the positive experience. For example, when flying, consumers are likely to choose airlines with which they have had positive experiences, such as consistent on-time arrivals, and avoid airlines with which they have had a negative experience, such as lost luggage.

Finally, the extent of the search is positively related to the amount of interest a consumer has in a product. A consumer who is more interested in a product will spend more time searching for information and alternatives. For example, suppose you are a dedicated runner who reads jogging and fitness magazines and catalogs. In searching for a new pair of running shoes, you may enjoy reading about the new brands available and spend more time and effort than other buyers in deciding on the right shoe.

The consumer's information search should yield a group of brands, sometimes called the buyer's **evoked set** (or **consideration set**), which are the consumer's most preferred alternatives. From this set, the buyer will further evaluate the alternatives and make a choice. Consumers do not consider all brands available in a product category, but they do seriously consider a much smaller set. For example, from the many brands of pizza available, consumers are likely to consider only the alternatives that fit their price range, location, take-out/delivery needs, and taste preferences. Having too many choices can, in fact, confuse consumers and cause them to delay the decision to buy, or in some instances, cause them not to buy at all.

6-2c Evaluation of Alternatives and Purchase

After getting information and constructing an evoked set of alternative products, the consumer is ready to make a decision. A consumer will use the information stored in memory and obtained from outside sources to develop a set of criteria. Recent research has shown that exposure to certain cues in your everyday environment can affect decision criteria and purchase. For example, when NASA landed the *Pathfinder* spacecraft on Mars, it captured media attention worldwide. The candy maker Mars also

evoked set (consideration set) a group of brands resulting from an information search from which a buyer can choose

noted a rather unusual increase in sales. Although the Mars bar takes its name from the company's founder and not the planet, consumers apparently responded to news about the planet Mars by purchasing more Mars bars.

The environment, internal information, and external information help consumers evaluate and compare alternatives. One way to begin narrowing the number of choices in the evoked set is to pick a product attribute and then exclude all products in the set that do not have that attribute. For example, assume Jane and Jill, both college sophomores, are looking for their first apartment. They need a two-bedroom apartment, reasonably priced and located near campus. They want the apartment to have a swimming pool, washer and dryer, and covered parking. Jane and Jill begin their search with all fifty apartments in the area and systematically eliminate complexes that lack the features they need. Hence, they may reduce their list to ten apartments that possess all of the desired attributes. Now, they can use cutoffs to further narrow their choices. Cutoffs are either minimum or maximum levels of an attribute that an alternative must pass to be considered. Suppose Jane and Jill set a maximum of $1,000 per month for rent. Then all apartments with rent higher than $1,000 will be eliminated, further reducing the list of apartments from ten to eight. A final way to narrow the choices is to rank the attributes under consideration in order of importance and evaluate the products based on how well each performs on the most important attributes. To reach a final decision on one of the remaining eight apartments, Jane and Jill may decide proximity to campus is the most important attribute. As a result, they will choose to rent the apartment closest to campus.

If new brands are added to an evoked set, the consumer's evaluation of the existing brands in that set changes. As a result, certain brands in the original set may become more desirable. Suppose Jane and Jill find two apartments located an equal distance from campus, one priced at $800 and the other at $750. Faced with this choice, they may decide that the $800 apartment is too expensive given that a comparable apartment is cheaper. If they add a $900 apartment to the list, however, then they may perceive the $800 apartment as more reasonable and decide to rent it.

The purchase decision process described above is a piecemeal process. That is, the evaluation is made by examining alternative advantages and disadvantages along important product attributes. A different way consumers can evaluate a product is according to a categorization process. The evaluation of an alternative depends upon the particular category to which it is assigned. Categories can be very general (motorized forms of transportation), or

they can be very specific (Harley-Davidson motorcycles). Typically, these categories are associated with some degree of liking or disliking. To the extent that the product can be assigned membership in a particular category, it will receive an evaluation similar to that attached to the category. If you go to the grocery store and see a new organic food on the shelf, you may evaluate it on your liking and opinions of organic food.

So, when consumers rely on a categorization process, a product's evaluation depends on the particular category to which it is perceived as belonging. Given this, companies need to understand whether consumers are using categories that evoke the desired evaluations. Indeed, how a product is categorized can strongly influence consumer demand. For example, what products come to mind when you think about the "morning beverages" category? To the soft drink industry's dismay, far too few consumers include sodas in this category. Several attempts have been made at getting soft drinks on the breakfast table, but with little success.

Brand extensions, in which a well-known and respected brand name from one product category is extended into other product categories, is one way companies employ categorization to their advantage. Brand extensions are a common business practice. For example, mixed martial arts promotional organization Ultimate Fighting Championship (UFC) has built its brand on pay-per-view events, cable and network television broadcasts, and merchandising. The UFC launched a 24-hour full-service gym in Long Island, New York. In addition to martial arts–themed activities, the UFC Gym features standard fitness equipment, a café, and signature classes like Hot Hula and Hi-Octane Conditioning.

Another factor that can influence the evaluation process is exposure to the price of the product or service. Suppose you walk into a department store and see a display of sweaters that catches your eye. When you walk over to the display, you look at a tag on a sweater to find a price of $49.99. Suppose instead you walk into the store and see a rack of clothes labeled with a large $49.99 sign. With this price in mind, you browse through the options and find a sweater that fits your tastes. Researchers have found that when consumers see the product cue first (scenario one), evaluation is strongly related to the product's attractiveness or desirability. When the first cue is the price (scenario two), evaluation is related more to the product's value.[9]

TO BUY OR NOT TO BUY Ultimately, the consumer has to decide whether to buy or not buy. Specifically, consumers must decide:

1. Whether to buy

2. When to buy

3. What to buy (product type and brand)

4. Where to buy (type of retailer, specific retailer, online or in store)

5. How to pay

PLANNED VERSUS IMPULSE PURCHASE Complex and expensive items are typically purchased only after the consumer has collected a large amount of information. People rarely buy a new home on impulse. Often, consumers will make a *partially planned purchase* when they know the product category they want to buy (shirts, pants, reading lamp, car floor mats) but wait until they get to the store or go online to choose a specific style or brand. Finally, there is the *unplanned purchase*, which people buy on impulse. Research has found that 75 percent of adults in the United States have made an impulse purchase. We often think of impulse purchasing as buying inexpensive items at the grocery store checkout. This, however, is not always the case. In the survey above, 16 percent said that they spent $500 to $1,000 on impulse purchases while 10 percent spent more than $1,000.[10] According to new research, the percentage of people who make impulse purchases varies by product category:

- Apparel: 19 percent

- Gift cards: 44 percent

- Home decor: 40 percent

- Beauty products: 38 percent

- Home improvement: 35 percent[11]

A purchase may be in a planned category (for example, soup), but decisions regarding the brand (Campbell's), package (can), and type (tomato) are all made on impulse. Researchers using in-store video cameras observed that when shoppers make impulse buys, they tend to touch and examine the item more, stand further from the shelf, and are less likely to refer to their shopping lists, coupons, or in-store circulars.[12]

PSYCHOLOGICAL OWNERSHIP Consumers sometimes develop feelings of ownership without even owning the good, service, or brand.[13] For example, think about how you feel when you choose a seat on the first day of class. Then, when you come to class on the second day,

The UFC Gym extends the Ultimate Fighting Championship's combative nature and gritty aesthetic into a new product category.

Source: UFC Gym

where do you usually sit? How do you feel if someone else is sitting in your seat? This feeling of "It's mine!" is called psychological, or perceived, ownership. Psychological ownership is important to marketers because when consumers feel a sense of ownership of a product, they are willing to pay more for it and are more likely to tell other consumers about it.[14] Consumers develop this kind of relationship with a product when they are able to control it, when they invest themselves in it, or when they come to know it intimately. Researchers have found that simply touching a product or imagining owning it enhances feelings of psychological ownership. When customers of Threadless T-Shirts were given the opportunity to vote on upcoming shirt designs, their willingness to pay more for the shirts increased because they felt a greater sense of ownership of them. Even liking a Facebook post can feel like a vote of confidence for a product and can enhance customers' feelings of ownership.[15] Clearly, psychological ownership can have a significant influence on consumer behavior. Marketing managers need to be aware of it when developing their marketing strategies.

6-3 POSTPURCHASE BEHAVIOR

When buying products, consumers expect certain outcomes from the purchase. How well these expectations are met determines whether the consumer is satisfied or dissatisfied with the purchase. For example, if a person bids on a used KitchenAid mixer from eBay and wins, she may have fairly low expectations regarding performance. If the mixer's performance turns out to be of superior quality, then the person's satisfaction will be high because her expectations were exceeded.

Conversely, if the person bids on a new Kitchen Aid mixer expecting superior quality and performance, but the mixer breaks within one month, she will be very dissatisfied because her expectations were not met. Price often influences the level of expectations for a product or service.

For the marketer, an important element of any postpurchase evaluation is reducing any lingering doubts that the decision was sound. When people recognize inconsistency between their values or opinions and their behavior, they tend to feel an inner tension called **cognitive dissonance**. For example, suppose Angelika is looking to purchase an e-reader. After evaluating her options, she has decided to purchase an iPad, even though it is much more expensive than other dedicated e-readers. Prior to choosing the iPad, Angelika may experience inner tension or anxiety because she is worried that the current top-of-the-line technology, which costs much more than the middle-of-the-line technology, will be obsolete in a couple months. That feeling of dissonance arises as her worries over obsolescence battle her practical nature, which is focused on the lower cost of a Kindle Paperwhite and its adequate—but less fancy—technology.

Consumers try to reduce dissonance by justifying their decision. They may seek new information that reinforces positive ideas about the purchase, avoid information that contradicts their decision, or revoke the original decision by returning the product. In some instances, people deliberately seek contrary information in order to refute it and reduce dissonance. Dissatisfied customers sometimes rely on word of mouth to reduce cognitive dissonance by letting friends and family know they are displeased.

Marketing managers can help reduce dissonance through effective communication with purchasers. For example, a customer service manager may slip a note inside the package congratulating the buyer on making a wise decision. Postpurchase letters sent by manufacturers and dissonance-reducing statements in instruction booklets may help customers feel at ease with their purchase. Advertising that displays the product's superiority over competing brands or guarantees can also help relieve the possible dissonance of someone who has already bought the product. Apple's Genius Bar and superior customer service will ease cognitive dissonance for purchasers of an iPad because they know that the company is there to support them.

An excellent opportunity for a company to reduce (or if handled poorly, increase) cognitive dissonance is when a customer has a question or complaint and tries to contact the company. Too many firms view their contact centers as cost centers and every contact as a problem to be minimized by making it as hard as possible to speak to a customer representative. Have you ever gone through four or five automated sequences, pushing a series of buttons, only to be told, "We are experiencing a higher than normal call volume and you can expect a lengthy delay." Not only does this raise cognitive dissonance, it can also destroy brand loyalty. Marketing-oriented companies perceive the contact center as an opportunity to engage customers and reinforce the brand promise. At these companies, there is no long menu of buttons to push. Instead, a service rep answers on the first or second ring and is empowered to solve customer problems. A recent study found that positive contact experiences resulted in consumers being 15 times more likely to say that they would definitely buy again than those with negative contact experiences. Of four different channels for a company to interact with its customers, telephone was most effective. Eighty-six percent of respondents said that speaking on the phone with a service rep enabled them to resolve their issues. Chat earned a 70 percent success rate, e-mail 44 percent, and Facebook 27 percent.[16]

 TYPES OF CONSUMER BUYING DECISIONS AND CONSUMER INVOLVEMENT

All consumer buying decisions generally fall along a continuum of three broad categories: routine response behavior, limited decision making, and extensive decision making (see Exhibit 6.2). Goods and services in these three categories can best be described in terms of five factors:

- Level of consumer involvement
- Length of time to make a decision
- Cost of the good or service
- Degree of information search
- Number of alternatives considered

The level of consumer involvement is perhaps the most significant determinant in classifying buying decisions. **Involvement** is the amount of time and effort a buyer invests in the search, evaluation, and decision processes of consumer behavior.

cognitive dissonance inner tension that a consumer experiences after recognizing an inconsistency between behavior and values or opinions

involvement the amount of time and effort a buyer invests in the search, evaluation, and decision processes of consumer behavior

EXHIBIT 6.2 — CONTINUUM OF CONSUMER BUYING DECISIONS

	Routine	Limited	Extensive
Involvement	Low	Low to moderate	High
Time	Short	Short to moderate	Long
Cost	Low	Low to moderate	High
Information Search	Internal only	Mostly internal	Internal and external
Number of Alternatives	One	Few	Many

Frequently purchased, low-cost goods and services are generally associated with **routine response behavior**. These goods and services can also be called *low-involvement products* because consumers spend little time on search and decision before making the purchase. Usually, buyers are familiar with several different brands in the product category but stick with one brand. For example, a person may routinely buy Tropicana orange juice. Consumers engaged in routine response behavior normally do not experience need recognition until they are exposed to advertising or see the product displayed on a store shelf. Consumers buy first and evaluate later, whereas the reverse is true for extensive decision making. A consumer who has previously purchased whitening toothpaste and was satisfied with it will probably walk to the toothpaste aisle and select that same brand without spending twenty minutes examining all other alternatives.

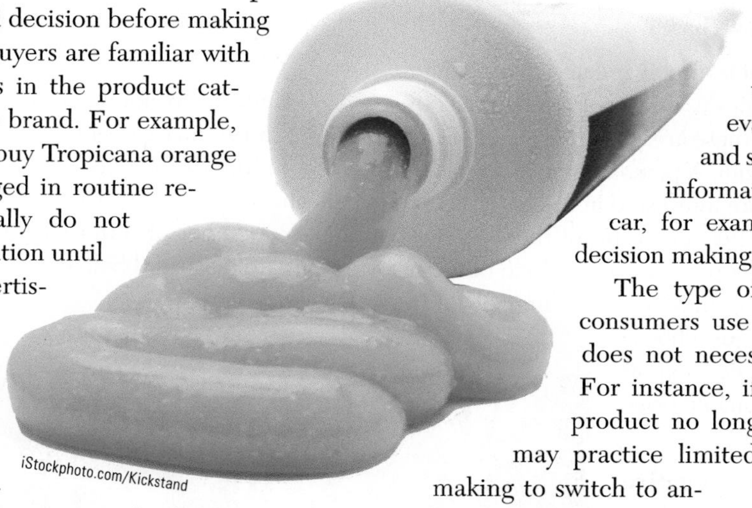

iStockphoto.com/Kickstand

Limited decision making typically occurs when a consumer has previous product experience but is unfamiliar with the current brands available. Limited decision making is also associated with lower levels of involvement (although higher than routine decisions) because consumers expend only moderate effort in searching for information or in considering various alternatives. For example, what happens if the consumer's usual brand of whitening toothpaste is sold out? Assuming that toothpaste is needed, the consumer will be forced to choose another brand. Before making a final decision, the consumer will likely evaluate several other brands based on their active ingredients, their

promotional claims, and the consumer's prior experiences.

Consumers practice **extensive decision making** when buying an unfamiliar, expensive product or an infrequently bought item. This process is the most complex type of consumer buying decision and is associated with high involvement on the part of the consumer. This process resembles the model outlined in Exhibit 6.1. These consumers want to make the right decision, so they want to know as much as they can about the product category and available brands. People usually experience the most cognitive dissonance when buying high-involvement products. Buyers use several criteria for evaluating their options and spend much time seeking information. Buying a home or a car, for example, requires extensive decision making.

The type of decision making that consumers use to purchase a product does not necessarily remain constant. For instance, if a routinely purchased product no longer satisfies, consumers may practice limited or extensive decision making to switch to another brand. And people who first use extensive decision making may then use limited or routine decision making for future purchases. For example, when a family gets a new puppy, they will spend a lot of time and energy trying out different toys to determine which one the dog prefers. Once the new owners learn that the dog prefers a bone to a ball, however, the purchase no longer requires extensive evaluation and will become routine.

routine response behavior the type of decision making exhibited by consumers buying frequently purchased, low-cost goods and services; requires little search and decision time

limited decision making the type of decision making that requires a moderate amount of time for gathering information and deliberating about an unfamiliar brand in a familiar product category

extensive decision making the most complex type of consumer decision making, used when buying an unfamiliar, expensive product or an infrequently bought item; requires use of several criteria for evaluating options and much time for seeking information

6-4a Factors Determining the Level of Consumer Involvement

The level of involvement in the purchase depends on the following factors:

- **Previous experience:** When consumers have had previous experience with a good or service, the level of involvement typically decreases. After repeated product trials, consumers learn to make quick choices. Because consumers are familiar with the product and know whether it will satisfy their needs, they become less involved in the purchase. For example, a consumer purchasing cereal has many brands to choose from—just think of any grocery store cereal aisle. If the consumer always buys the same brand because it satisfies his hunger, then he has a low level of involvement. When a consumer purchases a new category of cereal for the first time, however, it likely will be a much more involved purchase.

- **Interest:** Involvement is directly related to consumer interests, as in cars, music, movies, bicycling, or on-line games. Naturally, these areas of interest vary from one individual to another. A person highly involved in bike racing will be more interested in the type of bike she owns and will spend quite a bit of time evaluating different bikes. If a person wants a bike only for recreation, however, he may be fairly uninvolved in the purchase. He may just choose a bike from the most convenient location and in a reasonable price range.

- **Perceived risk of negative consequences:** As the perceived risk in purchasing a product increases, so does a consumer's level of involvement. The types of risks that concern consumers include financial risk, social risk, and psychological risk.

  - Financial risk is exposure to loss of wealth or purchasing power. Because high risk is associated with high-priced purchases, consumers tend to become extremely involved. Therefore, price and involvement are usually directly related: As price increases, so does the level of involvement. For example, someone who is purchasing a new car for the first time (higher perceived risk) will spend a lot of time and effort making this purchase.

  - Social risks occur when consumers buy products that can affect people's social opinions of them (for example, driving an old, beat-up car or wearing unstylish clothes).

  - Psychological risks occur if consumers believe that making the wrong decision might cause some concern or anxiety. For example, some consumers feel guilty about eating foods that are not healthy, such as regular ice cream rather than fat-free frozen yogurt.

- **Social visibility:** Involvement also increases as the social visibility of a product increases. Products often on social display include clothing (especially designer labels), jewelry, cars, and furniture. All these items make a statement about the purchaser and, therefore, carry a social risk.

High involvement means that the consumer cares about a product category or a specific good or service. The product or service is relevant and important, and means something to the buyer. High involvement can take a number of different forms. The most important types are discussed below:

Purchase involvement depends on level of interest. If this shopper is looking to use a bike as her main mode of transportation, then she is highly involved in this purchase decision.

yellowdog/Cultura RM/Alamy Stock Photo

- *Product involvement* means that a product category has high personal relevance. Product enthusiasts are consumers with high involvement in a product category. The fashion industry has a large segment of product enthusiasts. These people are seeking the latest fashion trends and want to wear the latest clothes.

- *Situational involvement* means that the circumstances of a purchase may temporarily transform a low-involvement decision into a high-involvement one. High involvement comes into play when the consumer perceives risk in a specific situation. For example, an individual might routinely buy low-priced brands of liquor and wine. When the boss visits, however, the consumer might make a high-involvement decision and buy more prestigious brands.

- *Shopping involvement* represents the personal relevance of the process of shopping. Some people enjoy the process of shopping even if they do not plan to buy anything. For others, shopping is an enjoyable social activity. Many consumers also engage in **showrooming**—examining merchandise in a physical retail location without purchasing it, and then shopping online for a better deal on the same item.

- *Enduring involvement* represents an ongoing interest in some product, such as kitchen gadgets, or activity, such as fishing. The consumer is always searching for opportunities to consume the product or participate in the activity. Enduring involvement typically gives personal gratification to consumers as they continue to learn about, shop for, and consume these goods and services. Therefore, there is often linkage between enduring involvement, shopping, and product involvement.

- *Emotional involvement* represents how emotional a consumer gets during some specific consumption activity. Emotional involvement is closely related to enduring involvement because the things that consumers care most about will eventually create high emotional involvement. Sports fans typify consumers with high emotional involvement.

6-4b Marketing Implications of Involvement

Marketing strategy varies according to the level of involvement associated with the product. For high-involvement product purchases, marketing managers have several objectives. First, promotion to the target market should be extensive and informative. A good

Tide uses bright, eye-catching packaging to draw customers to what is otherwise a low-involvement product.

ad gives consumers the information they need for making the purchase decision and specifies the benefits and unique advantages of owning the product. For example, Ford has a vehicle with many custom options that is marketed to small business owners. One example of a recent print ad shows how one entrepreneur customized his Ford Transit to help improve the efficiency of his home theater and electronics installation business. Ford highlights the fact that unique businesses need unique and customizable transportation. The Transit comes in three body lengths, each offering a unique volume and payload capacity. There are also three different roof heights to choose from, and of course, several different engines.

For low-involvement product purchases, consumers may not recognize their wants until they are in the store. Therefore, in-store promotion is an important tool when promoting low-involvement products. Marketing managers focus on package design so the product will be eye-catching and easily recognized on the shelf. Examples of products that take this approach are Campbell's soups, Tide detergent, Velveeta cheese, and Heinz ketchup. In-store displays also stimulate sales of low-involvement products. A good display can explain the product's purpose and prompt recognition of a want. Displays of snack foods in supermarkets have been known to

showrooming the practice of examining merchandise in a physical retail location without purchasing it, and then shopping online for a better deal on the same item

increase sales many times above normal. Coupons, cents-off deals, and two-for-one offers also effectively promote low-involvement items.

Researchers have found that another way to increase involvement is to offer products on a "limited availability" basis. McDonald's, for example, has regularly cycled its McRib sandwich on and off its menu for more than 30 years. Marketers can use several ways to trigger limited availability, including daily specials (for example special soup *du jour*), day of the week (for example, Sunday brunch), promotional periods (for example, item availability for a limited time only), harvest time (for example, corn in the summer), and small production runs (for example, limited edition items). Limited availability creates a "get it now or never" mentality. Researchers have found that consuming such products leads to more consumer enjoyment than if the items were always available.[17]

6-5 RECONCEPTUALIZING THE CONSUMER DECISION MAKING PROCESS

Rapid changes in digital technology have given consumers unprecedented power to express likes and dislikes, compare prices, find the best deals, sift through huge numbers of recommendations on sites like Trip Advisor and Yelp, and finally, have items delivered quickly—sometimes on the same day the order was placed. In short, the balance of power has shifted largely from the marketer to the consumer. Because of these remarkable changes, many marketers today are totally reconceptualizing the consumer decision making process.

6-5a The Consumer Decision Journey

One of the hottest phrases in marketing today is "the consumer decision journey." Exhibit 6.3 depicts this journey and explains how marketers are trying to regain control from consumers by streamlining the decision making process.

The consumer decision journey begins when an advertisement or other stimulus causes a consumer to research a number of products or services to meet his or her needs. Even at this early stage, the consumer may drop a number of items from the potential purchase set. The second phase of the journey begins when the consumer evaluates the alternatives using input from peers, reviewers, retailers, the brand itself, and competitors. At this stage, new brands may be added and options from the initial set may be dropped as the selection criteria shift. The consumer then buys (or doesn't buy) the product, and if he or she enjoys the purchase, may advocate and bond with the brand. This feedback loop of ratings, rankings, and referrals pressures brands to deliver a superior experience on an ongoing basis. Researchers have found that 60 percent of consumers of facial skin care products conduct an online search after a purchase is made.[18] This is part of developing a deeper bond with the skin care product while eliminating cognitive dissonance.

Progressive firms armed with new technologies are actively working to exert greater influence over the decision making journey. On order to minimize (or in some cases eliminate) the "consider and evaluate" phases of the consumer journey, a company must have four distinct but interconnected capabilities:

- *Automation* streamlines journey steps. One example is letting people take a picture of a check and deposit it through an app rather than depositing it in person. While process automation is highly technical, it should always be done with simple, useful, and increasingly engaging consumer-side experiences in mind.

- *Proactive personalization* uses information—either based on past interactions or collected through external sources—to instantaneously customize the customer experience. This capability ranges from a website remembering a customer's login preferences to an airline automatically adding a frequent traveler to its upgrade list.

- *Contextual interaction* uses knowledge about where a customer is in the journey to deliver them to the next set of interactions. Consider, for example, a retail website displaying the status of a recent order on its homepage. Some hotels are pushing the boundaries of contextual interaction by configuring their apps to operate like keys when guests approach their rooms.

- *Journey innovation* extends customer interactions to new sources of value, such as related products or partnered businesses. Many companies mine their data to figure out what adjacent goods or services a shopper might be interested in, then they put those products in front of the shopper in the middle of his or her journey. The best companies conduct open-ended testing

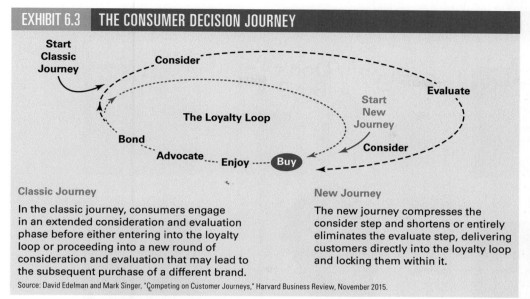

EXHIBIT 6.3   THE CONSUMER DECISION JOURNEY

Classic Journey

In the classic journey, consumers engage in an extended consideration and evaluation phase before either entering into the loyalty loop or proceeding into a new round of consideration and evaluation that may lead to the subsequent purchase of a different brand.

New Journey

The new journey compresses the consider step and shortens or entirely eliminates the evaluate step, delivering customers directly into the loyalty loop and locking them within it.

Source: David Edelman and Mark Singer, "Competing on Customer Journeys," Harvard Business Review, November 2015.

and constantly prototype new services and features to best meet customer needs in the ever-changing, digitally-connected market. For example, Delta Airline's app integrates with ride-sharing service Uber so that travelers can book cars to pick them up when they arrive at their destinations.[19]

To understand how a company can influence the consumer decision journey, consider California-based solar panel provider Sungevity. This company's "product" is a seamless, personalized customer journey built on innovative data management about the solar potential of each home. Consider the following Sungevity experience:

One of us (David) experienced the Sungevity journey firsthand. The process began when he received a mailing with the message "Open this to find out how much the Edelman family can save on energy costs with solar panels." The letter within contained a unique URL that led to a Google Earth image of David's house with solar panels superimposed on the roof. The next click led to a page with custom calculations of energy savings, developed from Sungevity's estimates of the family's energy use, the roof angle, the presence of nearby trees, and the energy-generation potential of the 23 panels the company expected the roof to hold.

Another click connected David through his desktop to a live sales rep looking at the same pages David was. The rep expertly answered his questions and instantly sent him links to videos that explained the installation process and the economics of leasing versus buying. Two days later, Sungevity e-mailed David with the names and numbers of nearby homeowners who used its system and had agreed to

serve as references. After checking these references, David returned to Sungevity's site, where a single click connected him to a rep who knew precisely where he was on the journey and had a tailored lease ready for him. The rep e-mailed it and walked David through it, and then David e-signed. When he next visited the website, the landing page had changed to track the progress of the permitting and installation, with fresh alerts arriving as the process proceeded. Now, as a Sungevity customer, David receives regular reports on his panels' energy generation and the resulting savings, along with tips on ways to conserve energy, based on his household's characteristics.

Starting with its initial outreach and continuing to the installation and ongoing management of David's panels, Sungevity customized and automated each step of the journey, making it so simple—and so compelling—for him to move from one step to the next that he never actively considered alternative providers. In essence, the company reconfigured the classic model of the consumer decision journey, immediately paring the consideration set to one brand, streamlining the evaluation phase and delivering David directly into the "loyalty loop."[20]

Another way firms are keeping customers in the loyalty loop is by using automated reordering. Express Scripts, the largest pharmacy benefit management organization in the United States, can automatically reorder customer prescriptions when it is time to refill. Customers also receive reminders that they can save money if they transfer their prescriptions to Express Scripts when they fill prescriptions at local pharmacies. Similarly, when a customer orders an e-book on Amazon, the company uses finely-tuned algorithms to suggest other books that he or she might want to read. Amazon offers automatic order scheduling on thousands of items from diapers to soft drinks. Customers can customize which items are sent, what day of the month they are sent, and how frequently they are sent. Some coffee makers,

EXHIBIT 6.4 FACTORS THAT AFFECT THE CONSUMER DECISION JOURNEY

Social Factors

Reference groups

Opinion leaders

Family

Buy?

Don't Buy?

Cultural Factors

Culture and values

Subculture

Social class

Individual Factors
Gender
Age and family
  life cycle stage
Personality,
  self-concept,
  and lifestyle

Psychological Factors
Perception
Motivation
Learning
Beliefs and
  attitudes

Consumer Decision-Making Process

Photomondo/Photodisc/Getty Images

printers, and washing machines can even use WiFi and special sensors to automatically place orders when supplies run low.

6-5b Factors Affecting Consumer Decision Making

Whether framed as the traditional consumer decision making process or the consumer decision journey, it is important to understand that consumer decision-making does not occur in a vacuum. On the contrary, underlying cultural, social, individual, and psychological factors strongly influence the decision process. These factors have an effect from the time a consumer perceives a stimulus and considers the product or service through postpurchase evaluation. Cultural factors, which include culture and values, subculture, and social class, exert a broad influence over consumer decision making. Social factors sum up the social interactions between a consumer and influential groups of people, such as reference groups, opinion leaders, and family members. Individual factors, which include gender, age, family life cycle stage, personality, self-concept, and lifestyle, are unique to each individual and play a major role in the type of products and

culture the set of values, norms, attitudes, and other meaningful symbols that shape human behavior and the artifacts, or products, of that behavior as they are transmitted from one generation to the next

services consumers want. Psychological factors determine how consumers perceive and interact with their environments and influence the ultimate decisions consumers make. They include perception, motivation, and learning. Exhibit 6.4 summarizes these influences, and the following sections cover each in more detail.

6-6 CULTURAL INFLUENCES ON CONSUMER BUYING DECISIONS

Of all the factors that affect consumer decision making, cultural factors exert the broadest and deepest influence. Marketers must understand the way people's culture and its accompanying values, as well as their subculture and social class, influence their buying behavior.

6-6a Culture and Values

Culture is the set of values, norms, attitudes, and other meaningful symbols that shape human behavior and the artifacts, or products, of that behavior as they are transmitted from one generation to the next. It is the essential character of a society that distinguishes it from other cultural groups. The underlying elements of every culture are the values, language, myths, customs, rituals, and laws that guide the behavior of the people.

Culture is pervasive. Cultural values and influences are the ocean in which individuals swim, and yet most are completely unaware that it is there. What people eat, how they dress, what they think and feel, and what language they speak are all dimensions of culture. Culture encompasses all the things consumers do without conscious choice because their culture's values, customs, and rituals are ingrained in their daily habits.

Culture is functional. Human interaction creates values and prescribes acceptable behavior for each culture. By establishing common expectations, culture gives order to society. Sometimes these expectations are enacted into laws. For example, drivers in our culture must stop at a red light. Other times these expectations are taken for granted: grocery stores and hospitals are open 24 hours, whereas banks are open only during "bankers' hours," typically nine in the morning until five in the afternoon.

Culture is learned. Consumers are not born knowing the values and norms of their society. Instead, they must learn what is acceptable from family and friends. Children learn the values that will govern their behavior from parents, teachers, and peers. As members of our society, they learn to shake hands when they greet someone, to drive on the right-hand side of the road, and to eat pizza and drink Coca-Cola.

Culture is dynamic. It adapts to changing needs and an evolving environment. The rapid growth of technology in today's world has accelerated the rate of cultural change. Our culture is beginning to tell us when it is okay to send a text message and when it is considered impolite. Assume that you are on a first date with someone in a nice, romantic restaurant and your date is talking to you about his or her favorite things to do. Pulling out your smartphone to check a text will probably lead to a very short date. Cultural norms will continue to evolve because of our need for social patterns that solve problems.

The most defining element of a culture is its values. Recall that "value" can refer to an enduring belief shared by a society that a specific mode of conduct is personally or socially preferable to another mode of conduct. People's value systems have a great effect on their consumer behavior. Consumers with similar value systems tend to react alike to prices and other marketing-related inducements. Values also correspond to consumption patterns. For example, Americans place a high value on convenience. This value has created lucrative markets for products such as breakfast bars, energy bars, and nutrition bars that allow consumers to eat on the go. Values can also influence consumers' television viewing habits or the magazines they read. For instance, people who strongly object to violence avoid crime shows and vegetarians avoid cooking magazines that feature numerous meat-based recipes.

6-6b Subculture

A culture can be divided into subcultures on the basis of demographic characteristics, geographic regions, national and ethnic background, political beliefs, and religious beliefs. A subculture is a homogeneous group of people who share elements of the overall culture as well as cultural elements unique to their own group. Within subcultures, people's attitudes, values, and purchase decisions are even more similar than they are within the broader culture. Subcultural differences may result in considerable variation within a culture in what, how, when, and where people buy goods and services.

Once marketers identify subcultures, they can design special marketing to serve their needs. The United States' growing Hispanic population has made South and Central American subcultures a prime focus for many companies, for example. Recall that marketing to Hispanics was discussed in Chapter 4.

In the United States alone, countless subcultures can be identified. Many are concentrated geographically. People who belong to the Church of Jesus Christ of Latter-Day Saints, for example, are clustered mainly in Utah; Cajuns are located in the bayou regions of southern Louisiana. Many Hispanics live in states bordering Mexico, whereas the majority of Chinese, Japanese, and Korean Americans are found on the West Coast. Other subcultures are geographically dispersed. Computer hackers, people who are hearing or visually impaired, Harley-Davidson bikers, military families, and university professors may be found throughout the country. Yet they have identifiable attitudes, values, and needs that distinguish them from the larger culture.

Today, America has a rapidly growing number of binational households. In such households, one spouse was born and raised in the United States while the other was originally from another country. This often creates cultural complexity in family purchase decision making. Researchers have found that the partner with the greatest cultural competence (knowledge of the customs of the country of residence) plays the family role

> **subculture** a homogeneous group of people who share elements of the overall culture as well as unique elements of their own group

The popularity of massive, multi-day music festivals has created an opportunity for fans of electronic dance music (EDM) to get together and create their own subculture.

of cultural bridge, arbitrator, and translator. This spouse compensates for her relative advantage in purchase decision making by giving up control in other decisions. Therefore, the immigrant spouse may gain greater influence in decisions relating to vacations, education, and food.[21]

6-6c Social Class

The United States, like other societies, has a social class system. A **social class** is a group of people who are considered nearly equal in status or community esteem, who regularly socialize among themselves both formally and informally, and who share behavioral norms.

A number of techniques have been used to measure social class, and a number of criteria have been used to define it. One view of contemporary U.S. status structure is shown in Exhibit 6.5.

As you can see from Exhibit 6.5, the upper and upper middle classes comprise the small segment of affluent and wealthy Americans. In terms of consumer buying patterns, the affluent are more likely to own their own homes and purchase new cars and trucks and are less likely to smoke. The very rich flex their financial muscles by spending more on vacation homes, jewelry, vacations and cruises, and housekeeping and gardening

social class a group of people in a society who are considered nearly equal in status or community esteem, who regularly socialize among themselves both formally and informally, and who share behavioral norms

services. The most affluent consumers are more likely to attend art auctions and galleries, dance performances, operas, the theater, museums, concerts, and sporting events. What types of things do the wealthiest of the wealthy buy? The most expensive new car in the world is the Lamborghini Veneno. It goes from 0 to 60 miles per hour in 2.8 seconds and has a top speed of 221 mph. Only three of these cars are made a year at a price of $4,500,000 each.[22] Unfortunately, if you want one, you must get on a waiting list.

The majority of Americans today define themselves as middle class, regardless of their actual income or educational attainment. This phenomenon most likely occurs because working-class Americans tend to aspire to the middle-class lifestyle, while some of those who do achieve some affluence call themselves middle-class as a matter of principle.

The working class is a distinct subset of the middle class. Interest in organized labor is one of the most common attributes among the working class. This group often rates job security as the most important reason for taking a job. The working-class person depends heavily on relatives and the community for economic and emotional support.

Lifestyle distinctions between the social classes are greater than the distinctions within a given class. The most significant difference between the classes occurs between the middle and lower classes, where there is a major shift in lifestyles. Members of the lower class have annual incomes at or below the poverty level—$11,770 for individuals and $24,250 for families of four (as defined by the federal government).[23]

Social class is typically measured as a combination of occupation, income, education, wealth, and other variables. For instance, affluent upper-class consumers are more likely to be salaried executives or self-employed professionals with at least an undergraduate degree. Working-class or middle-class consumers are more likely to be hourly service workers or blue-collar employees with only a high school education. Educational attainment, however, seems to be the most reliable indicator of a person's social and economic status. Those with college degrees or graduate degrees are more likely to fall into the upper classes, while those with some college

EXHIBIT 6.5 | U.S. SOCIAL CLASSES

Upper Classes		
Capitalist class	1%	People whose investment decisions shape the national economy; income mostly from assets, earned or inherited; university connections
Upper middle class	14%	Upper-level managers, professionals, owners of medium-sized businesses; well-to-do, stay-at-home homemakers who decline occupational work by choice; college educated; family income well above national average
Middle Classes		
Middle class	33%	Middle-level white-collar, top-level blue-collar; education past high school typical; income somewhat above national average; loss of manufacturing jobs has reduced the population of this class
Working class	32%	Middle-level blue-collar, lower-level white-collar; income below national average; largely working in skilled or semi-skilled service jobs
Lower Classes		
Working poor	11–12%	Low-paid service workers and operatives; some high school education; below mainstream in living standard; crime and hunger are daily threats
Underclass	8–9%	People who are not regularly employed and who depend primarily on the welfare system for sustenance; little schooling; living standard below poverty line

experience fall closest to traditional concepts of the middle class.

Marketers are interested in social class for two main reasons. First, social class often indicates which medium to use for promotion. Suppose an insurance company seeks to sell its policies to middle-class families. It might advertise during the local evening news because middle-class families tend to watch more television than other classes do. If the company wanted to sell more policies to upscale individuals, it might place an ad in a business publication like the *Wall Street Journal*. The Internet, long the domain of more educated and affluent families, has become an increasingly important advertising outlet for advertisers hoping to reach blue-collar workers and homemakers.

Second, knowing what products appeal to which social classes can help marketers determine where to best distribute their products. Affluent Americans, one-fifth of the U.S. population, spend more of their discretionary income on one-of-a-kind items. Because many lower-income consumers are still struggling to recover from job loss, retailers such as Walmart are selling smaller packages of items because customers do not have enough cash to buy more standard-size products.

Knowing what products appeal to which social classes can help marketers determine where to best distribute their products.

6-7 SOCIAL INFLUENCES ON CONSUMER BUYING DECISIONS

Many consumers seek out the opinions of others to reduce their search and evaluation effort or uncertainty, especially as the perceived risk of the decision increases. Consumers may also seek out others' opinions for guidance on new products or services, products with image-related attributes, or products for which attribute information is lacking or uninformative. Specifically, consumers interact socially with reference groups, opinion leaders, and family members to obtain product information and decision approval.

6-7a Reference Groups

People interact with many reference groups. A **reference group** consists of all the formal and informal groups that influence the buying behavior of an individual. Consumers may use products or brands to identify with or become a member of a group. They learn from observing how members of their reference groups consume, and they use the same criteria to make their own consumer decisions.

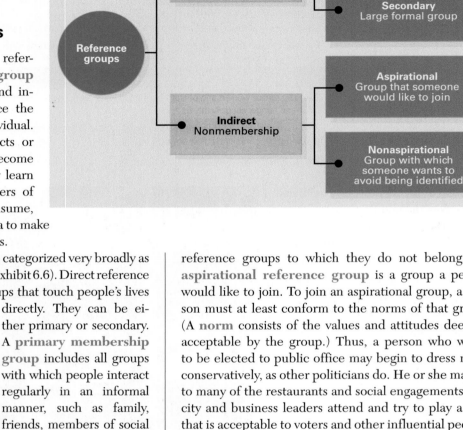

Reference groups can be categorized very broadly as either direct or indirect (see Exhibit 6.6). Direct reference groups are membership groups that touch people's lives directly. They can be either primary or secondary. A **primary membership group** includes all groups with which people interact regularly in an informal manner, such as family, friends, members of social media, such as Facebook and coworkers. Today, they may also communicate by e-mail, text messages, Facebook, Skype, or other social media as well as face-to-face. In contrast, people associate with a **secondary membership group** less consistently and more formally. These groups might include clubs, professional groups, and religious groups.

Consumers also are influenced by many indirect, nonmembership reference groups to which they do not belong. An **aspirational reference group** is a group a person would like to join. To join an aspirational group, a person must at least conform to the norms of that group. (A **norm** consists of the values and attitudes deemed acceptable by the group.) Thus, a person who wants to be elected to public office may begin to dress more conservatively, as other politicians do. He or she may go to many of the restaurants and social engagements that city and business leaders attend and try to play a role that is acceptable to voters and other influential people.

Nonaspirational reference groups, or dissociative groups, influence our behavior when we try to maintain distance from them. A consumer may avoid buying some types of clothing or cars, going to certain restaurants or stores, or even buying a home in a certain neighborhood to avoid being associated with a particular group. For middle- and upper-middle-class professionals who take an interest in Harley-Davidson motorcycles, biker gangs serve as both an aspirational and a nonaspirational reference group. Though the professionals (derisively called RUBS—rich urban bikers—by hardcore Harley enthusiasts) aspire to the freedom, community, and tough posturing of biker gangs, they do not aspire to the perpetual life on the road, crime, or violence of gangs. Thus, a professional may buy a Harley because of the gangs, but he may intentionally buy a specific model not typically associated with those gangs.

reference group all of the formal and informal groups in society that influence an individual's purchasing behavior

primary membership group a reference group with which people interact regularly in an informal, face-to-face manner, such as family, friends, and coworkers

secondary membership group a reference group with which people associate less consistently and more formally than a primary membership group, such as a club, professional group, or religious group

aspirational reference group a group that someone would like to join

norm a value or attitude deemed acceptable by a group

nonaspirational reference group a group with which an individual does not want to associate

Members of the Hells Angels biker gang protest in Oslo, Norway against police bias toward motorcycle gangs.

Reference groups are particularly powerful in influencing the clothes people wear, the cars they drive, the electronics they use, the activities they participate in, the foods they eat, and the luxury goods they purchase. In short, the activities, values, and goals of reference groups directly influence consumer behavior. For marketers, reference groups have three important implications: (1) They serve as information sources and influence perceptions; (2) they affect an individual's aspiration levels; and (3) their norms either constrain or stimulate consumer behavior.

6-7b Opinion Leaders

Reference groups and social media groups (for example, your friends on Facebook) frequently include individuals known as group leaders, or **opinion leaders**—persons who influence others. Obviously, it is important for marketing managers to persuade such people to purchase their goods or services. They are often the most influential, informed, plugged-in, and vocal members of society. Technology companies have found that teenagers, because of their willingness to experiment, are key opinion leaders for the success of new technologies.

Opinion leadership is a casual phenomenon and is usually inconspicuous, so locating opinion leaders offline can be a challenge. An opinion leader in one field, such as cooking, may not be an opinion leader in another, such as sports. In fact, it is rare to find an opinion leader who spans multiple diverse domains. Thus, marketers often try to create opinion leaders. They may use high school cheerleaders to model new fall fashions or civic leaders to promote insurance, new cars, and other merchandise. On a national level, companies sometimes use movie stars, sports figures, and other celebrities to promote products, hoping they are appropriate opinion leaders. The effectiveness of celebrity endorsements varies, though, depending largely on how credible and attractive the spokesperson is and how familiar people are with him or her. Endorsements are most likely to succeed if a reasonable association between the spokesperson and the product can be established.

Increasingly, marketers are looking to social media to find opinion leaders, but the sheer volume of posts and platforms makes determining true opinion leaders challenging. So, marketers are focusing their attention on platforms such as Facebook, Pinterest, and Tumblr because those sites better identify the social trends that are shaping consumer behavior. With their unprecedented ability to network and communicate with each other, people often rely on each other's opinions more than marketing messages when making purchase decisions. And social media are becoming a key way that people communicate their opinions.

Social media have made identification of opinion leaders easier than ever before. Klout, for example, collects data from 13 social networks and search data from Bing and Google to measure a person's influence. The firm also looks at offline data such as how often the individual is mentioned in traditional media like magazines and newspapers. Klout then tabulates a score for each person ranging from 1 to 100.

Klout's Perks program has expanded from offering certain opinion leaders coupons and product samples to helping brands send out invitations for product launches, promotional events, and concerts. The company recently launched VIP Perks, a program that tracks opinion leaders' mobile devices to tell when they enter a store or restaurant. Marketers have used the program to offer social influencers with high Klout scores seat upgrades at Cirque Du Soleil shows and access to VIP airport

opinion leader an individual who influences the opinions of others

lounges. Research has found that when social media influencers purchase a new product, they tend to share this information right away with their social networks.[24]

6-7c Family

The family is the most important social institution for many consumers, strongly influencing values, attitudes, self-concept, and buying behavior. For example, a family that strongly values good health will have a grocery list distinctly different from that of a family that views every dinner as a gourmet event. Moreover, the family is responsible for the **socialization process**, the passing down of cultural values and norms to children. Children learn by observing their parents' consumption patterns, so they tend to shop in similar patterns.

Decision-making roles among family members tend to vary significantly, depending on the type of item purchased. Family members assume a variety of roles in the purchase process. *Initiators* suggest, initiate, or plant the seed for the purchase process. The initiator can be any member of the family. For example, Sister might initiate the product search by asking for a new bicycle as a birthday present. *Influencers* are members of the family whose opinions are valued. In our example, Mom might function as a price-range watchdog, an influencer whose main role is to veto or approve price ranges. Brother may give his opinion on certain makes of bicycles. The *decision maker* is the family member who actually makes the decision to buy or not to buy. For example, Dad or Mom is likely to choose the final brand and model of bicycle to buy after seeking further information from Sister about cosmetic features such as color and then imposing additional criteria of his or her own, such as durability and safety. The *purchaser* (probably Dad or Mom) is the one who actually exchanges money for the product. Finally, the *consumer* is the actual user—in this case, Sister.

Marketers should consider family purchase situations along with the distribution of consumer and decision-maker roles among family members. Ordinarily, marketing views the individual as both decision maker and consumer. Family marketing adds several other possibilities: sometimes more than one family member or all family members are involved in the decision, sometimes only children are involved in the decision, sometimes more than one consumer is involved, and sometimes the decision maker and the consumer are different people. In most households, when parental joint decisions are being made, spouses consider

socialization process how cultural values and norms are passed down to children

By working with children to develop a drink they like, Innocent Smoothies for kids can advertise kid-friendly flavors with healthy benefits, satisfying moms and kids.

their partner's needs and perceptions to maintain decision fairness and harmony. This tends to minimize family conflict. When couples agree to narrow down their options before making a purchase, they are more likely to be satisfied with the eventual outcome and less likely to feel regret.

6-7d Individual Differences in Susceptibility to Social Influences

Social influence plays an important role in consumer behavior, but not all persons are equally influenced in their purchase decisions. Some have a strong need to build the images others have of them by buying products used by other members of their reference groups. Seeking approval of others through the "correct" product ownership is very important to these consumers. This is particularly true for conspicuous items (those that others can easily see) such as clothes, jewelry, cars, and even mobile devices. These individuals have a strong desire to avoid negative impressions in public settings. For example, wearing the wrong bathing suit at the university swimming pool would be very distressing to this type of consumer.

Consumers differ in their feelings of connectedness to other consumers. A consumer with a **separated self-schema** perceives himself as distinct and separate from others. A person with a **connected self-schema** sees himself as an integral part of a group. Research has found that individuals who feel connected respond more favorably to advertisements that promote group belonging and cohesion.

The influence of other people on how a consumer behaves is strongest when that consumer knows or feels that she is being watched. Researchers have found this to be especially true when individuals are consuming or buying personal products. Some people will not buy memberships to athletic clubs because they don't want to work out with (or even around) a group of people. They fear how they may appear to others.[25]

6-8 INDIVIDUAL INFLUENCES ON CONSUMER BUYING DECISIONS

While individuality impacts a person's susceptibility to social influences, factors such as gender, age, life cycle stage, personality, self-concept, and lifestyle also play important roles in consumer decision making. Individual characteristics are generally stable over the course of one's life. For instance, most people do not change their gender, and the act of changing personality or lifestyle requires a complete reorientation of one's life. In the case of age and life cycle stage, these changes occur gradually over time.

6-8a Gender

Physiological differences between men and women result in many different needs, such as with health and beauty products. Just as important are the distinct cultural, social, and economic roles played by men and women and the effects that these have on their decision-making processes. A recent survey found that 52 percent of women have purchased a product based upon a marketer's portrayal of women.[26] Messages and videos for companies such as Nike, Always, and Under Armour were perceived as very positive. The Dove "Real Beauty" campaign was named the number one ad of the 21st century by *Advertising Age*. Under Armour's "I Will What I

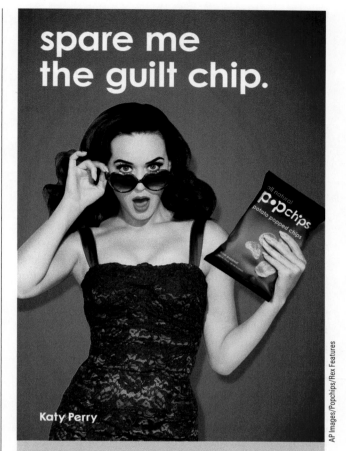

Katy Perry

AP Images/Popchips/Rex Features

What social and individual factors do you think this advertisement appeals to?

Want" ad also fared well for its portrayal of women pushing back against the idea of perfection and simply embracing themselves (see an example at www.youtube.com/watch?v=ZY0cdXr_1MA).

Trends in gender marketing are influenced by the changing roles of men and women in society. For example, men used to rely on the women in their lives to shop for them. Today, however, more men are shopping for themselves. More than seventy percent of men shop online and about 48 percent shop from mobile devices. When doing so, men use smartphones twice as often as they use tablets. Men are price-conscious, often scanning QR codes rather than typing in URLs to retrieve promotional materials, coupons, and product information. In fact, a Harris Interactive poll found that, "men have become the chief coupon-cutters of the mobile era."[27]

separated self-schema a perspective whereby a consumer sees himself or herself as distinct and separate from others

connected self-schema a perspective whereby a consumer sees himself or herself as an integral part of a group

6-8b Age and Family Life Cycle Stage

A consumer's age and family life cycle stage can have a significant impact on his or her behavior. How old a consumer is generally indicates what products he or she may be interested in purchasing. Consumer tastes in food, clothing, cars, furniture, and recreation are often age related.

Related to a person's age is his or her place in the family life cycle. As Chapter 8 explains in more detail, the *family life cycle* is an orderly series of stages through which consumers' attitudes and behavioral tendencies evolve through maturity, experience, and changing income and status. Marketers often define their target markets in terms of family life cycle, such as "young singles," "young married couples with children," and "middle-aged married couples without children." For instance, young singles spend more than average on alcoholic beverages, education, and entertainment. New parents typically increase their spending on health care, clothing, housing, and food and decrease their spending on alcohol, education, and transportation. Households with older children spend more on food, entertainment, personal care products, and education, as well as cars and gasoline. After their children leave home, spending by older couples on vehicles, women's clothing, and health care typically increases. For instance, the presence of children in the home is the most significant determinant of the type of vehicle that's driven off the new car lot. Parents are the ultimate need-driven car consumers, requiring larger cars and trucks to haul their children and all their belongings. It comes as no surprise, then, that for all households with children, SUVs rank either first or second among new-vehicle purchases, followed by minivans.

NONTRADITIONAL LIFE CYCLES Marketers should also be aware of the many nontraditional life cycle paths that are common today and provide insights into the needs and wants of such consumers as divorced parents, lifelong singles, and childless couples. Three decades ago, married couples with children under the age of 18 accounted for about half of U.S. households. Today, such families make up only 23 percent of all households, while people living alone or with nonfamily members represent more than thirty percent. Furthermore, according to the U.S. Census Bureau, the number of single-mother households grew by 25 percent over the last decade. The shift toward more single-parent households is part of a broader societal change that has put more women on the career track.

SINGLE PARENTS Careers often create a *poverty of time* for single parents. To cope with the dual demands of a career and raising children, single parents are always on the lookout for time saving products like quick-preparation foods and no-iron clothing. Rightly so, more and more marketers are catering to the single parent market. eTargetMedia maintains a list of over 9,500,000 active single parents that it rents out for both e-mail and postal advertising campaigns. The firm says that the list is ideal for offers pertaining to education, childcare, insurance, photo sharing, parenting magazines and books, camps, and children's recreation.[28]

LIFE EVENTS Another way to look at the life cycle is to look at major events in one's life over time. Life-changing events can occur at any time. A few examples are death of a spouse, moving, birth or adoption of a child, retirement, job loss, divorce, and marriage. Typically, such events are quite stressful, and consumers will often take steps to minimize that stress. Many times, life-changing events will mean new consumption patterns. For example, a recently divorced person may try to improve his or her appearance by joining a health club and dieting. Someone moving to a different city will need a new dentist, grocery store, auto service center, and doctor, among other things. Marketers realize that life events often mean a chance to gain a new customer. The Welcome Wagon offers free gifts and services for area newcomers. Lowe's sends out a discount coupon to those moving to a new community. And when you put your home on the market, you will quickly start receiving flyers from moving companies promising a great price on moving your household goods.

Age and family life cycle stage can have a significant impact on a person's behavior.

6-8c Personality, Self-Concept, and Lifestyle

Each consumer has a unique personality. **Personality** is a broad concept that can be thought of as a way of organizing and grouping how an individual typically reacts to situations. Thus, personality combines psychological makeup and environmental forces. It includes people's underlying dispositions, especially their most dominant characteristics. Although personality is one of the least useful concepts in the study of consumer behavior, some marketers believe personality influences the types and brands of products purchased. For instance, the type of car, clothes, or jewelry a consumer buys may reflect one or more personality traits.

Self-concept, or self-perception, is how consumers perceive themselves. Self-concept includes attitudes, perceptions, beliefs, and self-evaluations. Although self-concept may change, the change is often gradual. Through self-concept, people define their identity, which in turn provides for consistent and coherent behavior.

Self-concept combines the **ideal self-image** (the way an individual would like to be perceived) and the **real self-image** (how an individual actually perceives himself or herself). Generally, we try to raise our real self-image toward our ideal (or at least narrow the gap). Consumers seldom buy products that jeopardize their self-image. For example, someone who sees herself as a trendsetter would not buy clothing that does not project a contemporary image.

Human behavior depends largely on self-concept. Because consumers want to protect their identity as individuals, the products they buy, the stores they patronize, and the credit cards they carry support their self-image. No other product quite reflects a person's self-image as much as the car he or she drives. For example, many young consumers do not like family sedans like the Honda Accord or Toyota Camry and say they would buy one for their mom but not for themselves. Likewise, younger parents may avoid purchasing minivans because they do not want to sacrifice the youthful image they have of themselves just because they have new responsibilities. To combat decreasing sales, marketers of the Nissan Quest minivan decided to reposition it as something other than a "mom mobile" or "soccer mom car." They chose the ad copy "Passion built it. Passion will fill it up," followed by "What if we made a minivan that changed the way people think of minivans?"

By influencing the degree to which consumers perceive a good or service to be self-relevant, marketers can affect consumers' motivation to learn about, shop for, and buy a certain brand. Marketers also consider self-concept important because it helps explain the relationship between individuals' perceptions of themselves and their consumer behavior.

Many companies now use psychographics to better understand their market segments. For many years, marketers selling products to mothers conveniently assumed that all moms were fairly homogeneous and concerned about the same things—the health and well-being of their children—and that they could all be reached with a similar message. But recent lifestyle research has shown that there are traditional, blended, and nontraditional moms, and companies like Procter & Gamble and Pillsbury are using strategies to reach these different types of mothers. Psychographics is also effective with other market segments. Psychographics and lifestyle segmentation are discussed in more detail in Chapter 8.

6-9 PSYCHOLOGICAL INFLUENCES ON CONSUMER BUYING DECISIONS

An individual's buying decisions are further influenced by psychological factors: perception, motivation, and learning. These factors are what consumers use to interact with their world. They are the tools consumers use to recognize their feelings, gather and analyze information, formulate thoughts and opinions, and take action. Unlike the other three influences on consumer behavior, psychological influences can be affected by a person's environment because they are applied on specific occasions. For example, you will perceive different stimuli and process these stimuli in different ways depending on whether you are sitting in class concentrating on the instructor, sitting outside of class talking to friends, or sitting in your dorm room streaming a video.

6-9a Perception

The world is full of stimuli. A stimulus is any unit of input affecting one or more of the five senses: sight, smell, taste, touch, and hearing. The process by which we select, organize, and interpret these stimuli into a meaningful and coherent picture is called **perception**. In essence,

---

personality a way of organizing and grouping the consistencies of an individual's reactions to situations

self-concept how consumers perceive themselves in terms of attitudes, perceptions, beliefs, and self-evaluations

ideal self-image the way an individual would like to be perceived

real self-image the way an individual actually perceives himself or herself

perception the process by which people select, organize, and interpret stimuli into a meaningful and coherent picture

perception is how we see the world around us. We act based upon perceptions that may or may not reflect reality. Suppose you are driving to the grocery and you see a house with smoke pouring from the roof. Your perception is that the house is on fire, so you quickly stop to warn any occupants and to call 911. As you approach the house, you hear laughter coming from the back yard. As you peek around the corner, you see a family burning a big pile of leaves and the wind carrying the smoke over the roof. There is no house fire. When you get to the grocery, you see a big, beautiful ripe pineapple and immediately put it in your cart. When you get home, you cut into the pineapple—only to find that it has a rotten core and is inedible. In both cases, you acted based upon perceptions that did not reflect reality.

People cannot perceive every stimulus in their environment. Therefore, they use **selective exposure** to decide which stimuli to notice and which to ignore. A typical consumer is exposed to nearly 3,000 advertising messages a day but notices only between 11 and 20.

The familiarity of an object, contrast, movement, intensity (such as increased volume), and smell are cues that influence perception. Consumers use these cues to identify and define products and brands. Double Tree hotels always have fresh chocolate chip cookies at the reception desk and the entire area smells like just-baked cookies. For most travelers, this cues feelings of warmth and comfort. Cutting-edge consumer research has found that a cluttered, chaotic environment results in consumers spending more. Why does this occur? The perception of a cluttered environment impairs self-control. Disorganized surroundings threaten one's sense of personal control, which in turn taxes one's self-regulatory abilities.[29]

The shape of a product's packaging, such as Coca-Cola's signature contour bottle, can influence perception. Color is another cue, and it plays a key role in consumers' perceptions. Packaged foods manufacturers use color to trigger unconscious associations for grocery shoppers who typically make their shopping decisions in the blink of an eye. Think of the red and white Campbell's soup can and the green and white Green Giant frozen vegetable box, for example.

Eurobanks/iStock/Thinkstock

Two other concepts closely related to selective exposure are selective distortion and selective retention. **Selective distortion** occurs when consumers change or distort information that conflicts with their feelings or beliefs. For example, suppose a college student buys a Dell tablet. After the purchase, if the student gets new information about an alternative brand, such as an Asus Transformer, he or she may distort the information to make it more consistent with the prior view that the Dell is just as good as the Transformer, if not better. Business travelers who are Executive Platinum frequent flyers on American Airlines may distort or discount information about the quality of United Airlines' business class service. The frequent flyer may think to herself, "Yes, the service is OK but the seats are uncomfortable and the planes are always late."

Selective retention is remembering only information that supports personal feelings or beliefs. The consumer forgets all information that may be inconsistent. After reading a pamphlet that contradicts one's political beliefs, for instance, a person may forget many of the points outlined in it. Similarly, consumers may see a news report on suspected illegal practices by their favorite retail store but soon forget the reason the store was featured on the news.

Which stimuli will be perceived often depends on the individual. People can be exposed to the same stimuli under identical conditions but perceive them very differently. For example, two people viewing a television commercial may have different interpretations of the advertising message. One person may be thoroughly engrossed by the message and become highly motivated to buy the product. Thirty seconds after the ad ends, the second person may not be able to recall the content of the message or even the product advertised.

MARKETING IMPLICATIONS OF PERCEPTION

Marketers must recognize the importance of cues, or signals, in consumers' perception of products. Marketing managers first identify the important attributes, such as price or quality, that the targeted consumers want in a product and then design signals to communicate these attributes. For example, consumers will pay more for candy in expensive-looking foil packages. But shiny labels

selective exposure a process whereby a consumer notices certain stimuli and ignores others

selective distortion a process whereby a consumer changes or distorts information that conflicts with his or her feelings or beliefs

selective retention a process whereby a consumer remembers only that information that supports his or her personal beliefs

From May to November 2016, AB-Inbev changed the name of its flagship beer, Budweiser, to simply "America." Even though Budweiser is manufactured by a Belgian company, this campaign was designed to reinforce the perception that Budweiser is a classic American brand for proud Americans.

on wine bottles signify less expensive wines; dull labels indicate more expensive wines. Marketers also often use price as a signal to consumers that the product is of higher quality than competing products. Of course, brand names send signals to consumers. The brand names of Close-Up toothpaste, DieHard batteries, and Caress moisturizing soap, for example, identify important product qualities. Names chosen for search engines and sites on the Internet, such as Yahoo!, Amazon, and Bing, are intended to convey excitement and intensity and vastness.

Consumers also associate quality and reliability with certain brand names. Companies watch their brand identity closely, in large part because a strong link has been established between perceived brand value and customer loyalty. Brand names that consistently enjoy high perceived value from consumers include Google, Disney, National Geographic, Mercedes-Benz, and Fisher-Price. Naming a product after a place can also add perceived value by association. Brand names using the words Santa Fe, Dakota, or Texas convey a sense of openness, freedom, and youth, but products named after other locations might conjure up images of pollution and crime. Marketing managers are also interested in the *threshold level of perception*, the minimum difference in a stimulus that the consumer will notice. This concept is sometimes referred to as the "just-noticeable difference." For example, how much would Apple have to drop the price of its 15-inch MacBook Pro with Retina display before

consumers perceived it as a bargain—$100? $300? $500? Alternatively, how much could Hershey shrink its milk chocolate bar before consumers noticed that it was smaller, but selling for the same price?

Besides changing such stimuli as price, package size, and volume, marketers can change the product or attempt to reposition its image. But marketers must be careful when adding features. How many new services will discounter Target need to add before consumers perceive it as a full-service department store? How many sporty features will General Motors have to add to a basic two-door sedan before consumers start perceiving it as a sports car?

Marketing managers who intend to do business in global markets should be aware of how foreign consumers perceive their products. For instance, in Japan, product labels are often written in English or French, even though they may not translate into anything meaningful. Many Japanese associate foreign words on product labels with the exotic, the expensive, and high quality.

6-9b Motivation

By studying motivation, marketers can analyze the major forces influencing consumers to buy or not buy products. When you buy a product, you usually do so to fulfill some kind of need. These needs become motives when they are aroused sufficiently. For instance, suppose this morning you were so hungry before class that you needed to eat something. In response to that need, you stopped at Subway for a breakfast sandwich. In other words, you were motivated by hunger to stop at Subway. A **motive** is the driving force that causes a person to take action to satisfy specific needs.

Why are people driven by particular needs at particular times? One theory is **Maslow's hierarchy of needs**, illustrated in Exhibit 6.7, which arranges needs in ascending order of importance: physiological, safety, social, esteem, and self-actualization. As a person fulfills one need, a higher-level need becomes more important.

The most basic human needs—that is, the needs for food, water, and shelter—are *physiological*. Because they are essential to survival, these needs must be satisfied first. Ads showing a juicy hamburger or a runner gulping down Gatorade after a marathon are examples of appeals to satisfy the physiological needs of hunger and thirst.

motive a driving force that causes a person to take action to satisfy specific needs

Maslow's hierarchy of needs a method of classifying human needs and motivations into five categories in ascending order of importance: physiological, safety, social, esteem, and self-actualization

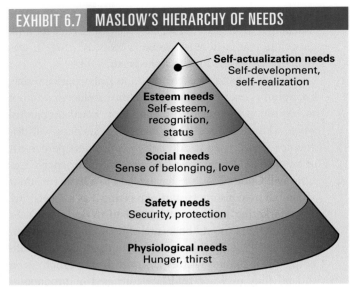

EXHIBIT 6.7 MASLOW'S HIERARCHY OF NEEDS

Self-actualization needs
Self-development, self-realization

Esteem needs
Self-esteem, recognition, status

Social needs
Sense of belonging, love

Safety needs
Security, protection

Physiological needs
Hunger, thirst

Safety needs include security and freedom from pain and discomfort. Marketers sometimes appeal to consumers' fears and anxieties about safety to sell their products. For example, aware of the aging population's health fears, the retail medical imaging centers Heart Check America and HealthScreen America advertise that they offer consumers a full body scan for early detection of health problems such as coronary disease and cancer. Some companies or industries advertise to allay consumer fears. For example, in the wake of the September 11, 2001, terrorist attacks, the airline industry found itself having to conduct an image campaign to reassure consumers about the safety of air travel.

After physiological and safety needs have been fulfilled, *social needs*—especially love and a sense of belonging—become the focus. Love includes acceptance by one's peers, as well as sex and romantic love. Marketing managers probably appeal more to this need than to any other. Ads for clothes, cosmetics, and vacation packages suggest that buying the product can bring love.

Love is acceptance without regard to one's contribution. Esteem is acceptance based on one's contribution to the group. *Self-esteem needs* include self-respect and a sense of accomplishment. Esteem needs also include prestige, fame, and recognition of one's accomplishments. Montblanc pens, Mercedes-Benz automobiles, and Neiman Marcus stores all appeal to esteem needs.

The highest human need is *self-actualization*.

learning a process that creates changes in behavior, immediate or expected, through experience and practice

It refers to finding self-fulfillment and self-expression, reaching the point in life at which "people are what they feel they should be." Maslow believed that very few people ever attain this level. Even so, advertisements may focus on this type of need. For example, American Express ads convey the message that acquiring an AmEx card is one of the highest attainments in life. The Centurion card, often called simply "the black card," requires a $5,000 initiation fee and carries an annual fee of $2,500.

6-9c Learning

Almost all consumer behavior results from **learning**, which is the process that creates changes in behavior through experience and practice. It is not possible to observe learning directly, but we can infer when it has occurred by a person's actions. For example, suppose you see an advertisement for a new and improved cold medicine. If you go to the store that day and buy that remedy, we infer that you have learned something about the cold medicine.

There are two types of learning: experiential and conceptual. *Experiential learning* occurs when an experience changes your behavior. For example, if the new cold medicine does not relieve your symptoms, you may not buy that brand again. *Conceptual learning*, which is not acquired through direct experience but based upon reasoning, is the second type of learning. Assume, for example, that you are standing at a soft drink machine and notice a new diet flavor with an artificial sweetener. Because someone has told you that diet beverages leave an aftertaste, you choose a different drink. You have learned that you would not like this new diet drink without ever trying it.

Reinforcement and repetition boost learning. Reinforcement can be positive or negative. If you see a vendor selling frozen yogurt (stimulus), buy it (response), and find the yogurt to be quite refreshing (reward), your behavior has been positively reinforced. On the other hand, if you buy a new flavor of yogurt and it does not taste good (negative reinforcement), you will not buy that flavor of yogurt again (response). Without positive or negative reinforcement, a person will not be motivated to repeat the behavior pattern or to avoid it. Thus, if a new brand evokes neutral feelings, some marketing activity, such as a price change or an increase in promotion, may be required to induce further consumption. Learning theory is helpful in reminding marketers that concrete and timely strategies are what reinforce desired consumer behavior.

Repetition is a key strategy in promotional campaigns because it can lead to increased learning. Most marketers use repetitious advertising so that consumers will learn what their unique advantage is over the competition. Generally, to heighten learning, advertising messages should be spread out over time rather than clustered together.

A related learning concept useful to marketing managers is **stimulus generalization**. In theory, stimulus generalization occurs when one response is extended to a second stimulus similar to the first. Marketers often use a successful, well-known brand name for a family of products because it gives consumers familiarity with and knowledge about each product in the family. Such brand name families spur the introduction of new products and facilitate the sale of existing items. OXO relies on consumers' familiarity with its popular kitchen and household products to sell office and medical supplies; Sony's film division relies on name recognition from its home technology, such as the PlayStation. Clorox bathroom cleaner relies on familiarity with Clorox bleach, and Dove shampoo relies on familiarity with Dove soap. Branding is examined in more detail in Chapter 10.

Dcwcreations/Shutterstock.com

Another form of stimulus generalization occurs when retailers or wholesalers design their packages to resemble well-known manufacturers' brands. Such imitation conveys the notion that the store brand is as good as the national manufacturer's brand.

The opposite of stimulus generalization is **stimulus discrimination**, which means learning to differentiate among similar products. Consumers may perceive one product as more rewarding or stimulating, even if it is virtually indistinguishable from competitors. For example, some consumers prefer Miller Lite and others prefer Bud Light.

With some types of products—such as aspirin, gasoline, bleach, and paper towels—marketers rely on promotion to point out brand differences that consumers would otherwise not recognize. This process, called *product differentiation*, is discussed in more detail in Chapter 8. Usually, product differentiation is based on superficial differences. For example, Bayer tells consumers that it is the aspirin "doctors recommend most."

stimulus generalization a form of learning that occurs when one response is extended to a second stimulus similar to the first

stimulus discrimination a learned ability to differentiate among similar products

STUDY TOOLS 6

LOCATED AT BACK OF THE TEXTBOOK

☐ Rip out Chapter Review Card

LOCATED AT WWW.CENGAGEBRAIN.COM

☐ Review Key Terms Flashcards and create your own

☐ Track your knowledge and understanding of key concepts in marketing

☐ Complete practice and graded quizzes to prepare for tests

☐ Complete interactive content within the MKTG Online experience

☐ View the chapter highlight boxes within the MKTG Online experience

7 | Business Marketing

LEARNING OUTCOMES

After studying this chapter, you will be able to…

7-1 Describe business marketing

7-2 Describe trends in B-to-B Internet marketing

7-3 Discuss the role of relationship marketing and strategic alliances in business marketing

7-4 Identify the four major categories of business market customers

7-5 Explain the North American Industry Classification System

7-6 Explain the major differences between business and consumer markets

7-7 Describe the seven types of business goods and services

7-8 Discuss the unique aspects of business buying behavior

After you finish this chapter go to **PAGE 135** for **STUDY TOOLS**

7-1 WHAT IS BUSINESS MARKETING?

Business marketing (also called industrial, business-to-business, B-to-B, or B2B marketing) is the marketing of goods and services to individuals and organizations for purposes other than personal consumption. The sale of a personal computer (PC) to your college or university is an example of business marketing. A **business product**, or **industrial product**, is used to manufacture other goods or services, to facilitate an organization's operations, or to resell to other customers. A **consumer product** is bought to satisfy an individual's personal wants or needs. The key characteristic distinguishing business products from consumer products is intended use, not physical form.

How do you distinguish between a consumer product and a business product? A product that is purchased for personal or family consumption or as a gift is a consumer good. If that same product, such as a PC or a cell phone, is bought for use in a business, it is a business product. Some common items that are sold as both consumer goods and business products are office supplies (e.g., pens, paper, and staple removers). Some items, such as forklifts, are more commonly sold as business products than as consumer goods.

business marketing (industrial, business-to-business, B-to-B, or B2B marketing) the marketing of goods and services to individuals and organizations for purposes other than personal consumption

business product (industrial product) a product used to manufacture other goods or services, to facilitate an organization's operations, or to resell to other customers

consumer product a product bought to satisfy an individual's personal wants or needs

The size of the business market in the United States and most other countries substantially exceeds that of the consumer market. In the business market, a single customer can account for a huge volume of purchases. For example, IBM's purchasing department spends more than $40 billion annually on business products. Procter & Gamble (P&G) Apple, Merck, Dell, and Kimberly-Clark each spend more than half of their annual revenue on business products.[1]

Some large firms that produce goods such as steel, computer memory chips, or production equipment market exclusively to business customers. Other firms market to both businesses and to consumers. Hewlett-Packard marketed exclusively to business customers in the past but now markets laser printers and personal computers to consumers. Sony, traditionally a consumer marketer, now sells office automation products to businesses. Kodak used to sell its cameras exclusively to consumers, but has opted to sell its commercial printing services to businesses since emerging from bankruptcy in 2013. All of these companies have had to make organizational and marketing changes to expand into the new market categories.

> The key characteristic distinguishing business products from consumer products is intended use, not physical form.

7-2 TRENDS IN B-TO-B INTERNET MARKETING

Over the past decade, marketers have become more and more sophisticated in their use of the Internet. Companies have had to transition from "We have a website because our customer does" to having a site that attracts, interests, satisfies, informs, and retains customers. B-to-B companies are increasingly leveraging the Internet as an effective sales and promotion platform (much like B-to-C companies have done for decades). B-to-B companies use the Internet in three major ways. First, they use their websites to facilitate communication and orders. Second, they use digital marketing to increase brand awareness. Third, they use digital marketing—primarily in the form of content marketing—to position their businesses as thought leaders and therefore generate sales leads. Companies selling to business buyers face the same challenges as all marketers, including determining the target market and deciding how best to reach it.

Most B-to-B companies see LinkedIn as the most beneficial platform through which to distribute content.

Every year, new applications that provide additional information about customers are developed. These applications often also lower costs, increase supply chain efficiency, or enhance customer retention, loyalty, and trust. Increasingly, business customers expect suppliers to know them personally, monitor people's movement within their company, and offer personal interaction through social media, e-mail, and personal mailers. As such, we have seen B-to-B marketers use technology like smartphones and tablets to facilitate orders and enhance customer experiences.

A few years ago, many people thought the Internet would eliminate the need for distributors. Why would customers pay a distributor's markup when they could buy directly from the manufacturer with a few mouse clicks? This has occurred less frequently than many expected because distributors often perform important functions such as providing credit, aggregating supplies from multiple sources, making deliveries, and processing returns. Many business customers, especially small firms, depend on knowledgeable distributors for information and advice that is not available to them online.

Social media usage has been the most pervasive B-to-B and B-to-C marketing trend of the past five years. Most companies use e-mail marketing, search engine optimization, paid search, and display advertising to pull customers to their websites. This field of marketing requires vigilant adjustment to keep track of new applications and platforms, as well as constant evaluation to determine whether these new avenues are beneficial to (or used by) customers. Generally, B-to-C marketers were faster to adopt social media as part of the promotional mix. B-to-B marketers did not initially see the value in these tools. However, that has changed as social media has become more popular.

Content marketing is a strategic marketing approach focused on creating and distributing valuable, relevant, and consistent content. The goal of this content is to attract and retain a clearly defined audience, and ultimately, drive profitable customer action. This strategy has played an important role for B-to-B marketers. Content marketing includes media such as videos, podcasts, webinars, blog posts, white papers, e-books, slide decks, and more. Sharing valuable insights and interesting content can position a company as a though leader in an area. A 2014 study by the Content Marketing Institute and MarketingProfs found that 86 percent of respondents use content marketing, but many struggle with developing effective content. More than 55 percent of respondents stated plans to increase their content marketing usage in 2015.[2] Most companies use content marketing to increase brand awareness and generate leads. Increasing engagement comes in at a close third. Interestingly, while most B-to-C companies favor Facebook as their primary social media platform, most B-to-B companies see LinkedIn as the most beneficial platform through which to distribute content. Regardless of the platform used, the key to social media-based content marketing for B-to-B marketers is to create compelling and useful content for customers. For example, HubSpot and Marketo develop white papers and e-books on topics such as generating leads through social media for customers and potential customers.

As they build reputations in their business areas, many marketers use social media to increase awareness and build relationships and community. Social media platforms like YouTube, LinkedIn, Twitter, and Facebook provide great conversational platforms for doing just that. While building community is important, B-to-B

Content marketing a strategic marketing approach that focuses on creating and distributing content that is valuable, relevant and consistent.

marketers are also using social media to gather leads (as you may have gathered from the HubSpot and Marketo white paper example). Other goals include product promotion, traffic building, search engine optimization (SEO), competitive intelligence and listening, customer feedback and support, and product development.

As platforms such as mobile and streaming video grow, marketers must develop new ways to measure campaign effectiveness. For example, after using social analytics to determine the most effective hashtag from its "Internet of Everything" campaign, Cisco was able to increase usage of one particularly effective hashtag by 440 percent. Global information and measurement company Nielsen recently launched Nielsen Online Campaign Ratings, a "much-anticipated advertising measurement solution."[3] According to data collected through this new platform, less than half of all online advertisement impressions reach their intended audiences. Depending on the medium used, customer targeting varies between a 30 percent and 50 percent coverage rate.[4] Some metrics that are particularly useful for increasing the success of a social media campaign are awareness, engagement, and conversion. *Awareness* is the attention that social media attracts, such as the number of followers or fans. Awareness is generally used as the first step in the marketing funnel, and social media is often paired with paid digital media like display advertising and text-based ads to increase its effectiveness. *Engagement* refers to the interactions between the brand and the audience, such as comments, retweets, shares, and searches. The purpose of engagement is to get customers to respond to brand-led posts and to start conversations themselves. *Conversions* occur when action is taken and include everything from downloading a piece of content (like a white paper) to actually making a purchase. Each of these metrics affects the return on investment.

7-3 RELATIONSHIP MARKETING AND STRATEGIC ALLIANCES

As explained in Chapter 1, relationship marketing is a strategy that entails seeking and establishing ongoing partnerships with customers. Relationship marketing has become an important business marketing strategy as customers have become more demanding and competition has become more intense. Loyal customers are also more profitable than those who are price sensitive and perceive little or no difference among brands or suppliers.

Relationship marketing is increasingly important as business suppliers use platforms like Facebook, Twitter, and other social networking sites to advertise themselves to businesses. Social networking sites encourage

The Top Social Media Tools for B-to-B Marketers

BtoB Marketing Magazine surveyed hundreds of B-to-B marketers regarding their social media usage, and while LinkedIn, Facebook, and Twitter were used by the majority of respondents, LinkedIn was the most used social media tool overall (chosen by 94 percent of respondents). Runners up were Twitter (89 percent), Facebook (77 percent), YouTube (77 percent), and Google+ (61 percent). LinkedIn is so popular because it drives more traffic and leads than other platforms for B-to-B marketers. The company has only increased its favor among B-to-B marketers by adding new B-to-B-friendly features like sponsored company updates, groups connected to topics, products and services pages, and a thought leader blogging program.[5]

B-to-B marketers have begun making use of social advertising platforms such as advertisement exchanges on LinkedIn, promoted tweets on Twitter, and pinning content on corporate Pinterest accounts. For example, building materials manufacturer FireRock pins pictures of completed renovation projects on its Pinterest boards to inspire unique design ideas among contractors and home builders alike.[6]

businesses to shop around and research options for all their needs. This means that, for many suppliers, retaining their current customers has become a primary focus, whereas acquiring new customers was the focus in the past. Maintaining a steady dialogue between the supplier and the customer is a proven way to gain repeat business.[7]

7-3a Strategic Alliances

A **strategic alliance**, sometimes called a **strategic partnership**, is a cooperative agreement between business firms. Strategic alliances can take the form of licensing or distribution agreements, joint ventures, research and development consortia, and partnerships. They may be between manufacturers, manufacturers and customers, manufacturers and suppliers, and manufacturers and channel intermediaries.

Business marketers form strategic alliances to strengthen operations and better compete. In 2015, Disney/ABC Television Group formed a strategic alliance with Internet search company Yahoo. Under the partnership, ABC entertainment programming was promoted on the Yahoo website, and in return, some of the heads of Yahoo's digital magazine were featured on *Good Morning America*, ABC's morning television show. Additionally, behind-the-scenes footage from several ABC shows was featured exclusively on Yahoo.[8]

Sometimes alliance partners are fierce competitors. Take, for example, the partnership between Amazon and Netflix. In 2014, Amazon introduced the Fire TV and the Fire TV Stick, both of which allow users to stream digital media to their home televisions. This product supports several media services, including Netflix, despite that Netflix offers competing services. Instead of trying to compete with Netflix, Amazon included its services in order to offer its customers a satisfactory product.[9]

Other alliances are formed between companies that operate in

ABC News President Ben Sherwood (left) and Yahoo Executive Vice President of Americas Ross Levinsohn recently held a joint press conference to announce that ABC News content would be featured prominently on Yahoo's front page.

completely different industries. For example, in an effort to become more committed to sustainability, manufacturer of construction equipment Caterpillar recently partnered with SunSelect Produce to construct hydroponic greenhouses.[10] SunSelect is planning to purchase land adjacent to Caterpillar so that it can use the waste products produced by Caterpillar's heat and power cogeneration facilities to power their greenhouses and produce premium vegetables in a sustainable manner.

For an alliance to succeed in the long term, it must be built on commitment and trust. **Relationship commitment** means that a firm believes an ongoing relationship with some other firm is so important that it warrants maximum efforts at maintaining it indefinitely.[11] A perceived breakdown in commitment by one of the parties often leads to a breakdown in the relationship.

Trust exists when one party has confidence in an exchange partner's reliability and integrity.[12] Some alliances fail when participants lack trust in their trading partners. Consider, for example, the failed partnership

strategic alliance (strategic partnership) a cooperative agreement between business firms

relationship commitment a firm's belief that an ongoing relationship with another firm is so important that the relationship warrants maximum efforts at maintaining it indefinitely

trust the condition that exists when one party has confidence in an exchange partner's reliability and integrity

between Phones 4U, an independent phone retailer based in the United Kingdom, and Vodaphone, a British telecommunications company. While the two companies could have created a successful partnership, Vodaphone made the decision to cut ties with Phones 4U in 2014.[13] Vodaphone claimed that Phones 4U refused to improve upon the terms of their agreement when the contract came up for renewal, but Phones 4U believed that it was misled during negotiations and that cutting ties was an unfair decision. This decision forced Phones 4U to lay off thousands of employees and left the company struggling to restructure its business.

7-3b Relationships in Other Cultures

Although the terms *relationship marketing* and *strategic alliances* are fairly new and popularized mostly by American business executives and educators, the concepts have long been familiar in other cultures. Businesses in China, Japan, Korea, Mexico, and much of Europe rely heavily on personal relationships.

In Japan, for example, exchange between firms is based on personal relationships that are developed through what is called *amae*, or indulgent dependency. *Amae* is the feeling of nurturing concern for, and dependence upon, another. Reciprocity and personal relationships contribute to *amae*. Relationships between companies can develop into a keiretsu—a network of interlocking corporate affiliates. Within a *keiretsu*, executives may sit on the boards of their customers or their suppliers. Members of a *keiretsu* trade with each other whenever possible and often engage in joint product development, finance, and marketing activity. For example, the Toyota Group *keiretsu* includes 14 core companies and another 170 that receive preferential treatment. Toyota holds an equity position in many of these 170 member firms and is represented on many of their boards of directors.

Many firms have found that the best way to compete in Asian countries is to form relationships with Asian firms. Microsoft recently partnered with several Asian companies in order to expand the availability of its products in China.[14] One such alliance was formed with 21Vianet, a Chinese Internet service provider, and Unisplendour Corporation Limited, a Chinese technology firm. Together, these companies launched a new public cloud service in China. By partnering with local firms, Microsoft became the first U.S. company to launch a public cloud in China.

Organizations like General Motors are OEMs because they buy business goods and incorporate them into the products they produce.

7-4 MAJOR CATEGORIES OF BUSINESS CUSTOMERS

The business market consists of four major categories of customers: producers, resellers, governments, and institutions.

7-4a Producers

The producer segment of the business market includes profit-oriented individuals and organizations that use purchased goods and services to produce other products, to incorporate into other products, or to facilitate the daily operations of the organization. Examples of producers include construction, manufacturing, transportation, finance, real estate, and food service firms. In the United States, there are more than thirteen million firms in the producer segment of the business market. Some of these firms are small, and others are among the world's largest businesses.

Producers are often called original equipment manufacturers, or OEMs. This term includes all individuals and organizations that buy business goods and incorporate them into the products they produce for eventual sale to other producers or to consumers. Companies such as General Motors that buy steel, paint, tires, and batteries are said to be OEMs.

> **keiretsu** a network of interlocking corporate affiliates
>
> **original equipment manufacturers (OEMs)** individuals and organizations that buy business goods and incorporate them into the products they produce for eventual sale to other producers or to consumers

7-4b Resellers

The reseller market includes retail and wholesale businesses that buy finished goods and resell them for a profit. A retailer sells mainly to final consumers; wholesalers sell mostly to retailers and other organizational customers. There are approximately 1.5 million retailers and 500,000 wholesalers operating in the United States. Consumer product firms like P&G, Kraft Foods, and Coca-Cola sell directly to large retailers and retail chains and through wholesalers to smaller retail units. Retailing is explored in detail in Chapter 14.

Business product distributors are wholesalers that buy business products and resell them to business customers. They often carry thousands of items in stock and employ sales forces to call on business customers. Businesses that wish to buy a gross of pencils or a hundred pounds of fertilizer typically purchase these items from local distributors rather than directly from manufacturers such as Empire Pencil or Dow Chemical.

7-4c Governments

A third major segment of the business market is government. Government organizations include thousands of federal, state, and local buying units. Collectively, these government units account for the greatest volume of purchases of any customer category in the United States. The federal government alone spent upwards of $3 trillion in the 2015 fiscal year.[15]

Marketing to government agencies can be an overwhelming undertaking, but companies that learn how the system works can position themselves to win lucrative contracts and build lasting, rewarding relationships.[16]

Companies like Kroger are resellers of products offered by P&G and Coca-Cola.

Marketing to government agencies traditionally has not been an activity for companies seeking quick returns. The aphorism "hurry up and wait" is often cited as a characteristic of marketing to government agencies. Contracts for government purchases are often put out for bid. Interested vendors submit bids (usually sealed) to provide specified products during a particular time. Sometimes the lowest bidder is awarded the contract. When the lowest bidder is not awarded the contract, strong evidence must be presented to justify the decision. Grounds for rejecting the lowest bid include lack of experience, inadequate financing, or poor past performance. Bidding allows all potential suppliers a fair chance at winning government contracts and helps ensure that public funds are spent wisely.

FEDERAL GOVERNMENT Name just about any good or service and chances are that someone in the federal government uses it. The U.S. federal government buys goods and services valued at more than $875 billion per year, making it the world's largest customer.[17]

Although much of the federal government's buying is centralized, no single federal agency contracts for all the government's requirements, and no single buyer in any agency purchases all that the agency needs. We can view the federal government as a combination of several large companies with overlapping responsibilities and thousands of small independent units. One popular source of information about government procurement is *FedBizOpps*. Until recently, businesses hoping to sell to the federal government found the document (previously called *Commerce Business Daily*) unorganized, and it often arrived too late to be useful. The online version (www.cbd-net.com) is timelier and allows contractors to find leads using key word searches. Other examples of publications designed to explain how to do business with the federal government include *Doing Business with the General Services Administration*, *Selling to the Military*, and *Selling to the U.S. Air Force*.

STATE, COUNTY, AND CITY GOVERNMENT Selling to states, counties, and cities can be less frustrating for both small and large vendors than selling to the federal government. Paperwork is typically simpler and more manageable than it is at the federal level. But vendors must decide which of the more than 89,000 government units are likely to buy their wares. State and local buying agencies include school districts, highway departments, government-operated hospitals, housing agencies, and many other departments and divisions.

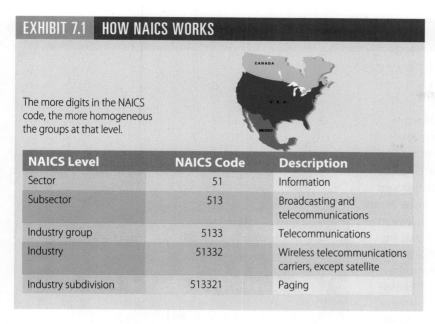

EXHIBIT 7.1 HOW NAICS WORKS

The more digits in the NAICS code, the more homogeneous the groups at that level.

NAICS Level	NAICS Code	Description
Sector	51	Information
Subsector	513	Broadcasting and telecommunications
Industry group	5133	Telecommunications
Industry	51332	Wireless telecommunications carriers, except satellite
Industry subdivision	513321	Paging

7-4d Institutions

The fourth major segment of the business market consists of institutions that seek to achieve goals other than the standard business goals of profit, market share, and return on investment. This segment includes schools, hospitals, colleges and universities, churches, labor unions, fraternal organizations, civic clubs, foundations, and other so-called nonbusiness organizations. Some institutional purchasers operate similar to governments in that the purchasing process is influenced, determined, or administered by government units. Other institutional purchasers are organized more like corporations.[18]

7-5 THE NORTH AMERICAN INDUSTRY CLASSIFICATION SYSTEM

The North American Industry Classification System (NAICS) is an industry classification system introduced in 1997 to replace the standard industrial classification system (SIC). NAICS (pronounced *nakes*) is a system for classifying North American business establishments. The system, developed jointly by the United States, Canada, and Mexico, provides a common industry classification system for the North American Free Trade Agreement (NAFTA) partners. Goods- or service-producing firms that use identical or similar production processes are grouped together.

NAICS is an extremely valuable tool for business marketers engaged in analyzing, segmenting, and targeting markets. Each classification group is relatively homogeneous in terms of raw materials required, components used, manufacturing processes employed, and problems faced. Therefore, if a supplier understands the needs and requirements of a few firms within a classification, requirements can be projected for all firms in that category. The number, size, and geographic dispersion of firms can also be identified. This information can be converted to market potential estimates, market share estimates, and sales forecasts. It can also be used for identifying potential new customers. NAICS codes can help identify firms that may be prospective users of a supplier's goods and services. The more digits in a code, the more homogeneous the group. A sample of how NAICS codes function is listed in Exhibit 7.1. For a complete listing of all NAICS codes, see www.naics.com/search.htm.

7-6 BUSINESS VERSUS CONSUMER MARKETS

The basic philosophy and practice of marketing are the same whether the customer is a business organization or a consumer. Business markets do, however, have characteristics different from consumer markets.

7-6a Demand

Consumer demand for products is quite different from demand in the business market. Unlike consumer demand, business demand is derived, inelastic, joint, and fluctuating.

DERIVED DEMAND The demand for business products is called **derived demand** because organizations buy products to be used in producing their customers' products. For instance, the demand for timber is derived from, or based upon, the demand for new construction houses. Despite emerging from the Great Recession in the early 2010s, the United States'

North American Industry Classification System (NAICS) a detailed numbering system developed by the United States, Canada, and Mexico to classify North American business establishments by their main production processes

derived demand the demand for business products

Boeing's Big Blunder

The success or failure of one bid can make the difference between prosperity and bankruptcy. By early 2013, Boeing had delivered 50 of the 848 orders placed for its new, top-of-the-line 787 Dreamliner aircraft. But when reports of onboard fires and emergency landings began to emerge, all fifty Dreamliners were grounded pending investigation of a potentially faulty lithium-ion battery. These events spelled potential disaster for Boeing. The 848 orders were placed by just 56 customers, some ordering as many as 74 units. Each Dreamliner costs approximately $225 million, so a loss of even one of the orders would be devastating. Boeing pledged to fix the problem as quickly as possible and resume production and delivery, but irreparable damage may have already been done to the company's sales and image.[19]

Crowds look on as a Boeing 787 Dreamliner taxies to the runway at the Air-Venture airshow in Oshkosh, Wisconsin.

new housing market has still not made a strong comeback. A decrease in demand for new construction houses has resulted in low timber prices, leading many South Carolinian timber producers to delay harvesting their timber.[20] Because demand is derived, business marketers must carefully monitor demand patterns and changing preferences in final consumer markets, even though their customers are not in those markets. Moreover, business marketers must carefully monitor their customers' forecasts because derived demand is based on expectations of future demand for those customers' products.

Some business marketers not only monitor final consumer demand and customer forecasts, but also try to influence final consumer demand. Aluminum producers use television and magazine advertisements to point out the convenience and recycling opportunities that aluminum offers to consumers who can choose to purchase soft drinks in either aluminum or plastic containers.

INELASTIC DEMAND The demand for many business products is inelastic with regard to price. *Inelastic demand* means that an increase or decrease in the price of the product will not significantly affect

demand for the product. This will be discussed further in Chapter 19.

The price of a product used in the production of, or as part of, a final product is often a minor portion of the final product's total price. Therefore, demand for the final consumer product is not affected. If the price of automobile paint or spark plugs rises significantly, say, 200 percent in one year, do you think the number of new automobiles sold that year will be affected? Probably not.

JOINT DEMAND Joint demand occurs when two or more items are used together in a final product. For example, a decline in the availability of memory chips will slow production of microcomputers, which will in turn reduce the demand for disk drives. Likewise, the demand for Apple operating systems exists as long as there is demand for Apple computers. Sales of the two products are directly linked.

FLUCTUATING DEMAND The demand for business products—particularly new plants and equipment—tends to be less stable than the demand for consumer products. A small increase or decrease in consumer demand can produce a much larger change in demand for the facilities and equipment needed

joint demand the demand for two or more items used together in a final product

to make the consumer product. Economists refer to this phenomenon as the **multiplier effect** (or **accelerator principle**).

Cummins Inc., a producer of heavy-duty diesel engines, uses sophisticated surface grinders to make parts. Suppose Cummins is using 20 surface grinders. Each machine lasts about 10 years. Purchases have been timed so two machines will wear out and be replaced annually. If the demand for engine parts does not change, two grinders will be bought this year. If the demand for parts declines slightly, only eighteen grinders may be needed, and Cummins will not replace the worn ones. However, suppose that next year demand returns to previous levels plus a little more. To meet the new level of demand, Cummins will need to replace the two machines that wore out in the previous year, the two that wore out in the current year, plus one or more additional machines. The multiplier effect works this way in many industries, producing highly fluctuating demand for business products.

7-6b Purchase Volume

Business customers tend to buy in large quantities. Just imagine the size of Kellogg's typical order for the wheat bran and raisins used to manufacture Raisin Bran. Or consider that in 2014, the Chicago Transit Authority (CTA) began accepting bids to fulfill a purchase order of 846 new rail cars to replace its aging fleet. The purchase budget was estimated at $2 billion—quite a bit larger than the CTA's $2.25 ride fare.[21]

7-6c Number of Customers

Business marketers usually have far fewer customers than consumer marketers. The advantage is that it is a lot easier to identify prospective buyers, monitor current customers' needs and levels of satisfaction, and personally attend to existing customers. The main disadvantage is that each customer becomes crucial—especially for those manufacturers that have only one customer. In many cases, this customer is the U.S. government.

7-6d Concentration of Customers

Manufacturing operations in the United States tend to be more geographically concentrated than consumer markets. More than half of all U.S. manufacturers concentrate the majority of their operations in the following eight states: California, New York, Ohio, Illinois, Michigan, Texas, Pennsylvania, and New Jersey.[22] Most large metropolitan areas host large numbers of business customers.

7-6e Distribution Structure

Many consumer products pass through a distribution system that includes the producer, one or more wholesalers, and a retailer. In business marketing, however, because of many of the characteristics already mentioned, channels of distribution for business marketing are typically shorter. Direct channels, where manufacturers market directly to users, are much more common. The use of direct channels has increased dramatically in the past decade with the introduction of various Internet buying and selling schemes. One such technique is called a **business-to-business online exchange**, which is an electronic trading floor that provides companies with integrated links to their customers and suppliers. The goal of B-to-B exchanges is to simplify business purchasing and to make it more efficient. Alibaba.com is a B-to-B e-commerce portal based in China that allows companies from all over the world to purchase goods and services from Chinese suppliers. Recently, the website has begun expanding to include suppliers from countries outside of China, including the United States. Alibaba.com serves buyers in more than 190 countries worldwide and has suppliers representing more than 40 major product categories. The mission of Alibaba.com is to allow suppliers to reach a global audience and to help buyers quickly find the products and services they need.[23]

7-6f Nature of Buying

Unlike consumers, business buyers usually approach purchasing rather formally. Businesses use professionally trained purchasing agents or buyers who spend their entire career purchasing a limited number of items. They get to know the items and the sellers well. Some professional purchasers earn the designation of Certified Purchasing Manager (CPM) after participating in a rigorous certification program.

7-6g Nature of Buying Influence

Typically, more people are involved in a single business purchase decision than in a consumer purchase. Experts from fields as varied as quality control, marketing, and finance, as well as professional buyers and users, may be grouped in a buying center (discussed later in this chapter).

multiplier effect (accelerator principle) phenomenon in which a small increase or decrease in consumer demand can produce a much larger change in demand for the facilities and equipment needed to make the consumer product

business-to-business online exchange an electronic trading floor that provides companies with integrated links to their customers and suppliers

7-6h Type of Negotiations

Consumers are used to negotiating price on automobiles and real estate. In most cases, however, American consumers expect sellers to set the price and other conditions of sale, such as time of delivery and credit terms. In contrast, negotiating is common in business marketing. Buyers and sellers negotiate product specifications, delivery dates, payment terms, and other pricing matters. Sometimes these negotiations occur during many meetings over several months. Final contracts are often very long and detailed.

7-6i Use of Reciprocity

Business purchasers often choose to buy from their own customers, a practice known as reciprocity. For example, General Motors buys engines for use in its automobiles and trucks from BorgWarner, which in turn buys many of the automobiles and trucks it needs from General Motors. This practice is neither unethical nor illegal unless one party coerces the other and the result is unfair competition. Reciprocity is generally considered a reasonable business practice. If all possible suppliers sell a similar product for about the same price, does it not make sense to buy from those firms that buy from you?

7-6j Use of Leasing

Consumers normally buy products rather than lease them. But businesses commonly lease expensive equipment such as computers, construction equipment and vehicles, and automobiles. Leasing allows firms to reduce capital outflow, acquire a seller's latest products, receive better services, and gain tax advantages.

The leaser, the firm providing the product, may be either the manufacturer or an independent firm. The benefits to the leaser include greater total revenue from leasing compared to selling and an opportunity to do business with customers who cannot afford to buy.

7-6k Primary Promotional Method

Business marketers tend to emphasize personal selling in their promotion efforts, especially for expensive items, custom-designed products, large-volume purchases, and situations requiring negotiations. The sale of many business products requires a great deal of personal contact. Personal selling is discussed in more detail in Chapter 17.

 ## 7-7 TYPES OF BUSINESS PRODUCTS

Business products generally fall into one of the following seven categories, depending on their use: major equipment, accessory equipment, raw materials, component parts, processed materials, supplies, and business services.

7-7a Major Equipment

Major equipment includes capital goods such as large or expensive machines, mainframe computers, blast furnaces, generators, airplanes, and buildings. (These items are also commonly called installations.) Major equipment is depreciated over time rather than charged as an expense in the year it is purchased. In addition, major equipment is often custom designed for each customer. Personal selling is an important part of the marketing strategy for major equipment because distribution channels are almost always direct from the producer to the business user.

7-7b Accessory Equipment

Accessory equipment is generally less expensive and shorter-lived than major equipment. Examples include portable drills, power tools, microcomputers, and computer software. Accessory equipment is often charged as an expense in the year it is bought rather than depreciated over its useful life. In contrast to major equipment, accessories are more often standardized and are usually bought by more customers. These customers tend to be widely dispersed. For example, all types of businesses buy microcomputers.

Local industrial distributors (wholesalers) play an important role in the marketing of accessory equipment because business buyers often purchase accessories from them. Regardless of where accessories are bought, advertising is a more vital promotional tool for accessory equipment than for major equipment.

7-7c Raw Materials

Raw materials are unprocessed extractive or agricultural products—for example, mineral ore, timber, wheat, corn, fruits, vegetables, and fish. Raw materials become part of finished products. Extensive users, such as steel or lumber mills and food canners, generally buy huge quantities of raw materials. Because there is often a large

---

reciprocity a practice whereby business purchasers choose to buy from their own customers

major equipment (installations) capital goods such as large or expensive machines, mainframe computers, blast furnaces, generators, airplanes, and buildings

accessory equipment goods, such as portable tools and office equipment, that are less expensive and shorter-lived than major equipment

raw materials unprocessed extractive or agricultural products, such as mineral ore, lumber, wheat, corn, fruits, vegetables, and fish

The market tends to set the price of raw materials, and individual producers have little pricing flexibility.

number of relatively small sellers of raw materials, none can greatly influence price or supply. Thus, the market tends to set the price of raw materials, and individual producers have little pricing flexibility. Promotion is almost always via personal selling, and distribution channels are usually direct from producer to business user.

7-7d Component Parts

Component parts are either finished items ready for assembly or products that need very little processing before becoming part of some other product. Caterpillar diesel engines are component parts used in heavy-duty trucks. Other examples include spark plugs, tires, and electric motors for automobiles. A special feature of component parts is that they can retain their identity after becoming part of the final product. For example, automobile tires are clearly recognizable as part of a car. Moreover, because component parts often wear out, they may need to be replaced several times during the life of the final product. Thus, there are two important markets for many component parts: the OEM market and the replacement market.

The availability of component parts is often a key factor in OEMs meeting their production deadlines. In 2015, Apple had to delay shipments for a highly anticipated new product, the Apple Watch, after being forced to switch suppliers for one of the watch's component parts. AAC Technologies, a Chinese components manufacturer, was originally supposed to supply the taptic engine—the component of the Apple Watch that makes it vibrate when a notification is received. AAC's parts were found to be defective, so Apple had to scramble to find a

iStockphoto.com/Mutlu Kurtbas

new supplier for the part, causing a delay in production and product shipments.[24]

The replacement market is composed of organizations and individuals buying component parts to replace worn-out parts. Because components often retain their identity in final products, users may choose to replace a component part with the same brand used by the manufacturer—for example, the same brand of automobile tires or battery. The replacement market operates differently from the OEM market, however. Whether replacement buyers are organizations or individuals, they tend to demonstrate the characteristics of consumer markets that were discussed in the previous section. Consider, for example, a replacement part for a piece of construction equipment such as a bulldozer or a crane. When a piece of equipment breaks down, it is usually important to acquire a replacement part and have it installed as soon as possible. Purchasers typically buy from local or regional dealers. Negotiations do not occur, and neither reciprocity nor leasing is usually an issue.

7-7e Processed Materials

Processed materials are products used directly in manufacturing other products. Unlike raw materials, they have had some processing. Examples include sheet metal, chemicals, specialty steel, treated lumber, corn syrup, and plastics. Unlike component parts, processed materials do not retain their identity in final products.

Timber, harvested from forests, is a raw material. Fluff pulp, a soft, white absorbent, is produced from loblolly pine timber by mills such as International Paper Co. The fluff pulp then becomes part of disposable diapers, bandages, and other sanitary products.[25]

Most processed materials are marketed to OEMs or to distributors servicing the OEM market. Processed materials are generally bought according to customer specifications or to some industry standard, as is the case with steel and plywood. Price and service are important factors in choosing a vendor.

7-7f Supplies

Supplies are consumable items that do not become part of the final product—for example, lubricants, detergents, paper towels, pencils, and paper. Supplies are normally standardized

component parts either finished items ready for assembly or products that need very little processing before becoming part of some other product

processed materials products used directly in manufacturing other products

supplies consumable items that do not become part of the final product

items that purchasing agents routinely buy. Supplies typically have relatively short lives and are inexpensive compared to other business goods. Because supplies generally fall into one of three categories—maintenance, repair, or operating supplies—this category is often referred to as MRO items. Competition in the MRO market is intense. Bic and Paper Mate, for example, battle for business purchases of inexpensive ballpoint pens.

7-7g Business Services

Business services are expense items that do not become part of a final product. Businesses often retain outside providers to perform janitorial, advertising, legal, management consulting, marketing research, maintenance, and other services. Contracting an outside provider makes sense when it costs less than hiring or assigning an employee to perform the task, when an outside provider is needed for particular expertise, or when the need is infrequent.

 ## 7-8 BUSINESS BUYING BEHAVIOR

As you probably have already concluded, business buyers behave differently from consumers. Understanding how purchase decisions are made in organizations is a first step in developing a business selling strategy. Business buying behavior has five important aspects: buying centers, evaluative criteria, buying situations, business ethics, and customer service.

7-8a Buying Centers

In many cases, more than one person is involved in a purchase decision. A salesperson must determine the buying situation and the information required from the buying organization's perspective to anticipate the size and composition of the buying center.[26]

A **buying center** includes all those people in an organization who become involved in the purchase decision. Membership and influence vary from company to company. For instance, in engineering-dominated firms like Bell Helicopter, the buying center may consist almost entirely of engineers. In marketing-oriented firms like Toyota and IBM, marketing and engineering have almost equal authority. In

business services expense items that do not become part of a final product

buying center all those people in an organization who become involved in the purchase decision

EXHIBIT 7.2 BUYING CENTER ROLES FOR COMPUTER PURCHASES

Role	Illustration
Initiator	Division general manager proposes to replace company's computer network.
Influencers/evaluators	Corporate controller's office and vice president of information services have an important say in which system and vendor the company will deal with.
Gatekeepers	Corporate departments for purchasing and information services analyze company's needs and recommend likely matches with potential vendors.
Decider	Vice president of administration, with advice from others, selects vendor the company will deal with and system it will buy.
Purchaser	Purchasing agent negotiates terms of sale.
Users	All division employees use the computers.

consumer goods firms like Clorox Corporation, product managers and other marketing decision makers may dominate the buying center. In a small manufacturing company, almost everyone may be a member.

The number of people involved in a buying center varies with the complexity and importance of a purchase decision. The average buying center includes more than one person and up to four per purchase.[27] The composition of the buying group will usually change from one purchase to another and sometimes even during various stages of the buying process. To make matters more complicated, buying centers do not appear on formal organization charts.

For example, even though a formal committee may have been set up to choose a new plant site, it is only part of the buying center. Other people, like the company president, often play informal yet powerful roles. In a lengthy decision-making process, such as finding a new plant location, some members may drop out of the buying center when they can no longer play a useful role. Others whose talents are needed then become part of the center. No formal announcement of "who is in" and "who is out" is ever made.

ROLES IN THE BUYING CENTER As in family purchasing decisions, several people may each play a role in the business purchase process:

- The *initiator* is the person who first suggests making a purchase.

- *Influencers/evaluators* are people who influence the buying decision. They often help define specifications and provide information for evaluating options. Technical personnel are especially important as influencers.

- *Gatekeepers* are group members who regulate the flow of information. Frequently, the purchasing agent views the gatekeeping role as a source of his or her power. A secretary may also act as a gatekeeper by determining which vendors get an appointment with a buyer.

- The *decider* is the person who has the formal or informal power to choose or approve the selection of the supplier or brand. In complex situations, it is often difficult to determine who makes the final decision.

- The *purchaser* is the person who actually negotiates the purchase. It could be anyone from the president of the company to the purchasing agent, depending on the importance of the decision.

- *Users* are members of the organization who will actually use the product. Users often initiate the buying process and help define product specifications.

IMPLICATIONS OF BUYING CENTERS FOR THE MARKETING MANAGER Successful vendors realize the importance of identifying who is in the decision-making unit, each member's relative influence in the buying decision, and each member's evaluative criteria. Key influencers are frequently located outside of the purchasing department. Successful selling strategies often focus on determining the most important buying influences and tailoring sales presentations to the evaluative criteria most important to these buying center members. An example illustrating the basic buying center roles is shown in Exhibit 7.2.

Marketers are often frustrated by their inability to reach c-level (chief) executives who play important roles in many buying centers. Marketers who want to build executive-level contacts must become involved in the buying process early on. This is when eighty percent of executives get involved—when major purchase decisions are being made. Executives often ensconce themselves in the buying process because they want to understand current business issues, establish project objectives, and set the overall project strategy.[28] Senior executives are typically not involved in the middle phases of the buying process but often get involved again later in the process to monitor the deal's closing. Executives look for four characteristics in sales representatives:

- The ability to marshal resources

- An understanding of the buyer's business goals

- Responsiveness to requests

- Willingness to be held accountable

Some firms have developed strategies to reach executives throughout the buying process and during non-buying phases of the relationship. For example, FedEx Corp. has initiated a marketing effort called "access" aimed at c-level executives. It includes direct mail, e-mail, and a custom magazine prepared exclusively

Some firms have developed strategies to reach "c-level" executives, with FedEx leading the way.

View Apart/Shutterstock.com

for c-level executives. It also hosts exclusive leadership events for these senior executives. Other firms have developed programs utilizing a combination of print, online, and events to reach the elusive c-level audience.[29]

7-8b Evaluative Criteria

Business buyers evaluate products and suppliers against three important criteria: quality, service, and price.

QUALITY In this case, *quality* refers to technical suitability. A superior tool can do a better job in the production process and superior packaging can increase dealer and consumer acceptance of a brand. Evaluation of quality also applies to the salesperson and the salesperson's firm. Business buyers want to deal with reputable salespeople and companies that are financially responsible. Quality improvement should be part of every organization's marketing strategy.

SERVICE Almost as much as they want satisfactory products, business buyers want satisfactory service. A purchase offers several opportunities for service. Suppose a vendor is selling heavy equipment. Prepurchase service could include a survey of the buyer's needs. After thorough analysis of the survey findings, the vendor could prepare a report and recommendations in the form of a purchasing proposal. If a purchase results, postpurchase service might consist of installing the equipment and training those who will be using it. Postsale services may also include maintenance and repairs.

Another service that business buyers seek is dependability of supply. They must be able to count on delivery of what was ordered when it is scheduled to be delivered. Buyers also welcome services that help them sell their finished products. Services of this sort are especially appropriate when the seller's product is an identifiable part of the buyer's end product.

PRICE Business buyers want to buy at low prices—at the lowest prices, under most circumstances. However, a buyer who pressures a supplier to cut prices to a point at which the supplier loses money on the sale almost forces shortcuts on quality. The buyer also may, in effect, force the supplier to quit selling to him or her. Then a new source of supply will have to be found.

7-8c Buying Situations

Often, business firms, especially manufacturers, must decide whether to make something or buy it from an outside supplier. The decision is essentially one of economics. Can an item of similar quality be bought at a lower price elsewhere? If not, is manufacturing it in-house the best use of limited company resources? For example, Briggs & Stratton Corporation, a major manufacturer of four-cycle engines, might be able to save $150,000 annually on outside purchases by spending $500,000 on the equipment needed to produce gas throttles internally. Yet Briggs & Stratton could also use that $500,000 to upgrade its carburetor assembly line, which would save $225,000 annually. If a firm does decide to buy a product instead of making it, the purchase will be a new buy, a modified rebuy, or a straight rebuy.

NEW BUY A **new buy** is a situation requiring the purchase of a product for the first time. For example, suppose a manufacturing company needs a better way to page its managers while they are working on the shop floor. Currently, each of the several managers has a distinct ring—for example, two short and one long—that sounds over the plant intercom whenever he or she is being paged by anyone in the factory. The company decides to replace its buzzer system of paging with handheld wireless radio technology that will allow managers to communicate immediately with the department initiating the page. This situation represents the greatest opportunity for new vendors. No long-term relationship has been established for this product, specifications may be somewhat fluid, and buyers are generally more open to new vendors.

If the new item is a raw material or a critical component part, the buyer cannot afford to run out of supply. The seller must be able to convince the buyer that the seller's firm can consistently deliver a high-quality product on time.

new buy a situation requiring the purchase of a product for the first time

modified rebuy a situation in which the purchaser wants some change in the original good or service

straight rebuy a situation in which the purchaser reorders the same goods or services without looking for new information or investigating other suppliers

MODIFIED REBUY A **modified rebuy** is normally less critical and less time-consuming than a new buy. In a modified rebuy situation, the purchaser wants some change in the original good or service. It may be a new color, greater tensile strength in a component part, more respondents in a marketing research study, or additional services in a janitorial contract.

Because the two parties are familiar with each other and credibility has been established, the buyer and seller can concentrate on the specifics of the modification. But in some cases, modified rebuys are open to outside bidders. The purchaser uses this strategy to ensure that the new terms are competitive. An example would be the manufacturing company buying radios with a vibrating feature for managers who have trouble hearing the ring over the factory noise. The firm may open the bidding to examine the price, quality, and service offerings of several suppliers.

STRAIGHT REBUY A **straight rebuy** is a situation vendors prefer. The purchaser is not looking for new information or other suppliers. An order is placed and the product is provided as in previous orders. Usually, a straight rebuy is routine because the terms of the purchase have been agreed to in earlier negotiations. An example would be the previously cited manufacturing company purchasing additional radios for new managers from the same supplier on a regular basis.

One common instrument used in straight rebuy situations is the purchasing contract. Purchasing contracts are used with products that are bought often and in high volume. In essence, the purchasing contract makes the buyer's decision making routine and promises the salesperson a sure sale. The advantage to the buyer is a quick, confident decision, and to the salesperson, reduced or eliminated competition. Nevertheless, suppliers must remember not to take straight rebuy relationships for granted. Retaining existing customers is much easier than attracting new ones.

7-8d Business Ethics

As we noted in Chapter 3, *ethics* refers to the moral principles or values that generally govern the conduct of an individual or a group. Ethics can also be viewed as the standard of behavior by which conduct is judged.

Although we have heard a lot about corporate misbehavior in recent years, most people, and most companies, follow ethical practices. To help achieve this, over half of all major corporations offer ethics training to employees.

rui vale sousa/Shutterstock.com

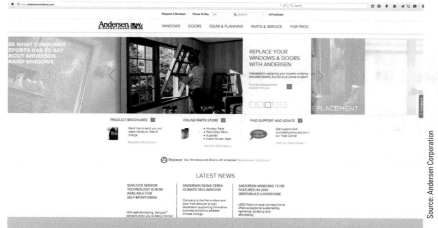

Andersen Windows and Doors assesses the loyalty of its trade customers by their willingness to carry its windows and doors.

Many companies also have codes of ethics that help guide buyers and sellers. For example, Home Depot has a clearly written code of ethics available on its corporate website that acts as an ethical guide for all its employees.

7-8e Customer Service

Business marketers are increasingly recognizing the benefits of developing a formal system to monitor customer opinions and perceptions of the quality of customer service. Companies such as FedEx, IBM, and Oracle build their strategies not only around products but also around highly developed service skills.[30] These companies understand that keeping current customers satisfied is just as important as attracting new ones, if not more so. Leading-edge firms are obsessed not only with delivering high-quality customer service but also with measuring satisfaction, loyalty, relationship quality, and other indicators of nonfinancial performance. Delivering consistent, high-quality customer service is an important basis for establishing competitive advantage and differentiating one's company from competitors. Cisco Systems uses a web-based survey to determine the presale and postsale satisfaction of customers.[31]

Most firms find it necessary to develop measures unique to their own strategies, value propositions, and target markets. For example, Andersen Windows and Doors assesses the loyalty of its trade customers by their willingness to continue carrying its windows and doors, recommend its products to colleagues and customers, increase their volume with the company, and put its products in their own homes. Basically, each firm's measures should not only ask "What are your expectations?" and "How are we doing?" but should also reflect what the firm wants its customers to do.

Some customers are more valuable than others. They may have greater value because they spend more, buy higher-margin products, have a well-known name, or have the potential of becoming a bigger customer in the future. Some companies selectively provide different levels of service to customers based on their value to the business. By giving the most valuable customers superior service, a firm is more likely to keep them happy, hopefully increasing retention of these high-value customers and maximizing the total business value they generate over time.

To achieve this goal, the firm must be able to divide customers into two or more groups based on their value. It must also create and apply policies that govern how service will be allocated among groups. Policies might establish which customers' phone calls get "fast tracked" and which customers are directed to use the Web and/or voice self-service, how specific e-mail questions are routed, and who is given access to online chat and who is not.

Providing different customers with different levels of service is a very sensitive matter. It must be handled very carefully and very discreetly to avoid offending lesser-value, but still important, customers.

8 | Segmenting and Targeting Markets

After finishing this chapter go to **PAGE 151** for **STUDY TOOLS**

8-1 MARKETS AND MARKET SEGMENTS

The term *market* means different things to different people. We are all familiar with the supermarket, stock market, labor market, fish market, and flea market. All these types of markets share several characteristics. First, they are composed of people (consumer markets) or organizations (business markets). Second, these people or organizations have wants and needs that can be satisfied by particular product categories. Third, they have the ability to buy the products they seek. Fourth, they are willing to exchange their resources, usually money or credit, for desired products. In sum, a **market** is (1) people or organizations with (2) needs or wants and with (3) the ability and (4) the willingness to buy. A group of people or an organization that lacks any one of these characteristics is not a market.

market people or organizations with needs or wants and the ability and willingness to buy

market segment a subgroup of people or organizations sharing one or more characteristics that cause them to have similar product needs

Within a market, a **market segment** is a subgroup of people or organizations sharing one or more characteristics that cause them to have similar product needs. At one extreme, we can define every person and every organization in the world as a market segment because each is unique. At the other extreme, we can define the entire consumer market as one large market segment and the business market as another large segment. All people have some similar characteristics and needs, as do all organizations.

From a marketing perspective, market segments can be described as somewhere between the two extremes. The process of dividing a market into meaningful, relatively similar, and identifiable segments, or groups, is called **market segmentation**. The purpose of market segmentation is to enable the marketer to tailor marketing mixes to meet the needs of one or more specific segments.

8-2 THE IMPORTANCE OF MARKET SEGMENTATION

Until the 1960s, few firms practiced market segmentation. When they did, it was more likely a haphazard effort than a formal marketing strategy. Before 1960, for example, the Coca-Cola Company produced only one beverage and aimed it at the entire soft drink market. Today, Coca-Cola offers more than a dozen different products to market segments based on diverse consumer preferences for flavors, calorie, and caffeine content. Coca-Cola offers traditional soft drinks, energy drinks

(including POWERade), flavored teas, fruit drinks (Minute Maid), and water (Dasani).

Market segmentation plays a key role in the marketing strategy of almost all successful organizations and is a powerful marketing tool for several reasons. Most important, nearly all markets include groups of people or organizations with different product needs and preferences. Market segmentation helps marketers define customer needs and wants more precisely. Because market segments differ in size and potential, segmentation helps decision makers to more accurately define marketing objectives and better allocate resources. In turn, performance can be better evaluated when objectives are more precise.

Jax & Bones has successfully appealed to affluent customers with high-end pet products. For example, the company produces a $200 dog bed that it sells in upscale retailers such as Bloomingdale's, Pottery Barn, and Barneys New York. The company's owner creates pet beds that reflect the latest colors, fabrics, textures, and styles. When memory foam became popular in human beds, Jax & Bones

market segmentation
the process of dividing a market into meaningful, relatively similar, and identifiable segments or groups

added memory foam to its beds. Last year, when gray, silver, and blue were popular in home design, these colors were incorporated into Jax & Bones' beds.[1]

8-3 CRITERIA FOR SUCCESSFUL SEGMENTATION

Marketers segment markets for three important reasons. First, segmentation enables marketers to identify groups of customers with similar needs and to analyze the characteristics and buying behavior of these groups. Second, segmentation provides marketers with information to help them design marketing mixes specifically matched with the characteristics and desires of one or more segments. Third, segmentation is consistent with the marketing concept of satisfying customer wants and needs while meeting the organization's objectives.

To be useful, a segmentation scheme must produce segments that meet four basic criteria:

1. **Substantiality:** A segment must be large enough to warrant developing and maintaining a special marketing mix. This criterion does not necessarily mean that a segment must have many potential customers. For example, marketers of custom-designed homes and business buildings, commercial airplanes, and large computer systems typically develop marketing programs tailored to each potential customer's needs. In most cases, however, a market segment needs many potential customers to make commercial sense. In the 1980s, home banking failed because not enough people owned personal computers. Today, a larger number of people own computers, and home banking is a thriving industry.

2. **Identifiability and measurability:** Segments must be identifiable and their size measurable. Data about the population within geographic boundaries, the number of people in various age categories, and other social and demographic characteristics are often easy to get, and they provide fairly concrete measures of segment size. Suppose that a social service agency wants to identify segments by their readiness to participate in a drug and alcohol program or in prenatal care. Unless the agency can measure how many people are willing, indifferent, or unwilling to participate, it will have trouble gauging whether there are enough people to justify setting up the service.

3. **Accessibility:** The firm must be able to reach members of targeted segments with customized marketing mixes. Some market segments are hard to reach—for example, senior citizens (especially those with reading or hearing disabilities), individuals who do not speak English, and the illiterate.

4. **Responsiveness:** Markets can be segmented using any criteria that seem logical. Unless one market segment responds to a marketing mix differently than other segments, however, that segment need not be treated separately. For instance, if all customers are equally price conscious about a product, there is no need to offer high-, medium-, and low-priced versions to different segments.

8-4 BASES FOR SEGMENTING CONSUMER MARKETS

Marketers use segmentation bases, or variables, which are characteristics of individuals, groups, or organizations, to divide a total market into segments. The choice of segmentation bases is crucial because an inappropriate segmentation strategy may lead to lost sales and missed profit opportunities. The key is to identify bases that will produce substantial, measurable, and accessible segments that exhibit different response patterns to marketing mixes.

Markets can be segmented using a single variable, such as age group, or several variables, such as age group, gender, and education. Although it is less precise, single-variable segmentation has the advantage of being simpler and easier to use than multiple-variable segmentation. The disadvantages of multiple-variable segmentation are that it is often harder to use than single-variable segmentation; usable secondary data are less likely to be available; and as the number of segmentation bases increases, the size of individual segments decreases. Nevertheless, the current trend is toward using more rather than fewer variables to segment most markets. Multiple-variable segmentation is clearly more precise than single-variable segmentation.

Consumer goods marketers commonly use one or more of the following characteristics to segment markets: geography, demographics, psychographics, benefits sought, and usage rate.

8-4a Geographic Segmentation

Geographic segmentation refers to segmenting markets by region of a country or the world, market

segmentation bases (variables) characteristics of individuals, groups, or organizations

geographic segmentation segmenting markets by region of a country or the world, market size, market density, or climate

size, market density, or climate. Market density means the number of people within a unit of land, such as a census tract. Climate is commonly used for geographic segmentation because of its dramatic impact on residents' needs and purchasing behavior. Snowblowers, water and snow skis, clothing, and air-conditioning and heating systems are products with varying appeal, depending on climate.

Consumer goods companies take a geographic approach to marketing for several reasons. First, firms continually need to find ways to grow. Target's growth strategy includes opening smaller stores in urban locations such as San Francisco, Chicago, and Washington, DC. These stores are designed to provide quick-trip shopping, customized product assortments, and services tailored to customers living in large cities.[2]

8-4b Demographic Segmentation

Marketers often segment markets on the basis of demographic information because it is widely available and often related to consumers' buying and consuming behavior. Some common bases of **demographic segmentation** are age, gender, income, ethnic background, and family life cycle.

AGE SEGMENTATION Marketers use a variety of terms to refer to different age groups. Examples include newborns, infants, young children, tweens, Millennials, Generation X, baby boomers, and seniors. Age segmentation can be an important tool, as a brief exploration of the market potential of several age segments illustrates.

Many companies have long targeted parents of babies and young children with products such as disposable diapers, baby food, and toys. Recently, other companies that have not traditionally marketed to young children are developing products and services to attract this group. For example, high-intensity fitness company CrossFit recently developed a program for kids in an attempt to tackle childhood obesity. The coaches for these group fitness classes create special workouts and games like "Hungry, Hungry Hippos" and "Farmers and Lumberjacks" to make classes fun and kid-friendly.[3]

The tween and teenage cohort following the Millennials is sometimes called Generation Z. This group accounts for 25.9 percent of the U.S. population and contributes $44 billion to the U.S. economy.[4] Born after 1995, Gen Zers are diverse, risk averse, and incredibly tech savvy. Never having known a world without the Internet, they expect everything to be instantaneous.[5] To attract Generation Z, Google is considering offering user

Meagan Tandy, star of ABC Family show Jane by Design, attends Aeropostale's sixth annual Teens for Jeans event.

s_bukley/Shutterstock.com

accounts to children under the age of 13. These accounts will include a way for parents to control account usage. Similarly, Facebook allows teens age 13 to 17 to post publicly on its site.[6] In another effort to reach tween shoppers, Aeropostale joined with the ABC Family television network to offer apparel seen on Pretty Little Liars, a television show that appeals to this demographic.[7]

The Millennial market makes up 25 percent of the adult population in the United States.[8] This group is both idealistic and pragmatic, and is the most technology-proficient generation ever. The top brand attributes important to Millennials include trustworthiness, creativity, intelligence, authenticity, and confidence.[9] Millennials are more likely than other generations to take a company's social responsibility into account before making a purchase decision.[10] Brands like TOMS Shoes and Chipotle appeal

demographic segmentation segmenting markets by age, gender, income, ethnic background, and family life cycle

to this group because they offer social value and align their brands with a higher purpose. These brands also invite participation and co-creation, both of which appeal to Millennials.[11]

Generation X is smaller than both the Millennials and the baby boomers, making up only sixteen percent of the total population. Members of Generation X are at a life stage where they are often stuck between supporting their aging parents and young children (earning Gen X the nickname "the sandwich generation"). They grew up as *latchkey kids*, meaning that they spent time alone at home while their (often divorced) parents worked long into the night. They are the best-educated generation—29 percent have earned a bachelor's degree or better. They tend to be disloyal to brands and skeptical of big business. Many of them are parents, and they make purchasing decisions with thought for and input from their families.[12] Gen Xers desire an experience, not just a product. This desire has led to an increase in offbeat events such as Vancouver, Canada's Dine Out Vancouver food festival. More than a series of tastings and tours, the multi-day festival features experiences such as a drag queen cabaret and dinner show inspired by the film *The Birdcage*, a brunch crawl, the Grape Debate (where top wine experts debate contemporary topics), and prix fixe menus at numerous restaurants throughout the city.[13]

Recall from Chapter 4 that people born between 1946 and 1964 are often called baby boomers. Boomers make up 24.7 percent of the total population and they constitute almost one-third of the adult population. They outspend the average consumer in nearly every product category, including food, household furnishings, entertainment, and personal care.[14] They are living longer, healthier, more active and connected lives, and will spend time and money doing whatever is necessary to maintain vitality as they age. This group spends more than other age brackets on dining out, housing, alcohol, and healthcare. Moreover, boomers' spending on vehicles is growing faster than any other demographic. Marketers should target boomers based on their core values, such as healthy eating and aging well. General Mills' Cheerios ads have long focused on heart health to reach boomers, for example.[15]

Consumers age 70 and older are part of the war generation and the Great Depression generation.

Mayakova/Shutterstock.com

Together, this group is often called the silent generation for its ability to quietly persevere through great hardships. The smallest generation of the last 100 years, members of The smallest generation of the last 100 years, members of this group were taught to play by the rules. They tend to be cautious and are the healthiest, most educated, and wealthiest group of elders this country has ever seen.[16] However, as consumers age, they do require some modifications in the way they live and the products they purchase. According to gerontologist Stephen Golant, for example, aging individuals may need to install "well-placed handrails or grab bars, ramps, easy-access bathrooms, easy-access kitchens, stair lifts, widened doors or hallways, and modified sink faucets or cabinets" in their homes.[17]

GENDER SEGMENTATION In the United States, women make 70 to 80 percent of purchases of consumer goods each year.[18] They are an experienced purchasing group with the responsibility of purchasing the majority of household items. They also are increasingly part of what were once considered all-male markets, such as financial markets. Women tend to view money and wealth differently than men do. They do not seek to accumulate money for the sake of accumulation, but rather associate it with security, independence, and quality of life for themselves and their families. They also tend to research investments in-depth more than men do. Thus, financial advisors need to use different strategies to appeal to women.[19] Tesla, whose initial customers were overwhelmingly male, designed its first sport utility vehicle (SUV) to appeal to women because women buy more than half of all SUVs sold in the United States. The company's designers conducted focus group research with women, most of whom drove SUVs, to learn what they liked and did not like about their vehicles.[20] Marketers of products such as clothing, cosmetics, food, personal-care items, magazines, jewelry, and gifts still commonly segment markets by gender, and many of these marketers are going after the less-traditional male market. A recent study showed that 43 percent of American men use skin care products beyond razors and shaving cream. The Ohio Valley Beard Supply Co. has built its brand on the belief that men—with or without beards—want products that not only condition hair and

According to the Ohio Valley Beard Supply Co., modern men want hygiene products that are both functional and fragrant.

soften skin, but also smell good while they do it. Among men without beards, the basic benefits of soft, smooth skin and a pleasant fragrance are still relevant.[21] Similarly, Procter & Gamble sponsored "man-aisles" in some Walmart, Target, and Walgreen's stores in the United States and Canada. These aisles group all men's products in one place and use shelf displays and small TV screens to guide men to skin-care items.[22]

INCOME SEGMENTATION Income is a popular demographic variable for segmenting markets because income level influences consumers' wants and determines their buying power. Many markets are segmented by income, including the markets for housing, clothing, automobiles, and food. Some companies have found success in marketing to the very poor. For example, people living in developing nations are emerging as reliable customers for multinational companies like Coca-Cola and McDonald's.[23] In the United States, dollar stores such as Family Dollar Stores and Dollar General have seen continual growth in recent years. These stores serve the 46.5 million Americans living below the poverty line by offering basic groceries and other necessities at deeply discounted prices.[24] On the other hand, wholesale clubs Costco and Sam's Club appeal to many income segments. High-income customers looking for luxury want products that exhibit careful craftsmanship, timeless design, prestige, and exclusivity. Luxury brands such as Chanel and Louis Vuitton do not focus on mass popularity, but instead try to set long-lasting standards of good taste.[25]

ETHNIC SEGMENTATION In the past, ethnic groups in the United States were expected to conform to a homogenized, Anglo-centric ideal. This was evident both in how mass-produced products were marketed as well as in the selective way that films, television, advertisements, and popular music portrayed America's diverse population. Until the 1970s, ethnic foods were rarely sold except in specialty stores. Increasing numbers of ethnic minorities and increased buying power have changed this. Hispanic Americans, African Americans, and Asian Americans are the three largest ethnic groups in the United States. In the American Southwest, Caucasian populations comprise less than half the population and have become the minority to other ethnic groups combined. To meet the needs and wants of expanding ethnic populations, some companies, such as McDonald's and Kmart, make products geared toward specific ethnic groups. In an effort to reach the Hispanic population, the Kellogg Company launched a digital platform called Dias Grandiosos that featured recipes, cooking tips, articles, and original content designed for Latino families.[26] Many department stores carry Fashion Fair Cosmetics, a line of beauty products created specifically for (and marketed toward) African American women.[27]

FAMILY LIFE CYCLE SEGMENTATION The demographic factors of gender, age, and income often do not sufficiently explain why consumer buying behavior varies. Frequently, consumption patterns among people of the same age and gender differ because they are in different stages of the family life cycle. The **family life cycle (FLC)** is a series of stages determined by a combination of age, marital status, and the presence or absence of children.

The life cycle stage consisting of the married-couple household used to be considered the traditional family in the United States. Today, however, married couples make up just half of households, down from 72 percent in the 1960s.[28] Single adults are increasingly in the majority on many fronts. Already, unmarried Americans make up 42 percent of the workforce, 40 percent of home buyers, and one of the most potent consumer groups on record. Exhibit 8.1 illustrates numerous FLC patterns and shows how families' needs, incomes, resources, and expenditures differ at each stage. The horizontal flow shows the traditional FLC. The lower part of the exhibit gives some of the characteristics and purchase patterns of families in each stage of the traditional life cycle. The exhibit also acknowledges that about half of all first marriages end in divorce. If young marrieds move into the young divorced

> **family life cycle (FLC)**
> a series of stages determined by a combination of age, marital status, and the presence or absence of children

EXHIBIT 8.1   FAMILY LIFE CYCLE

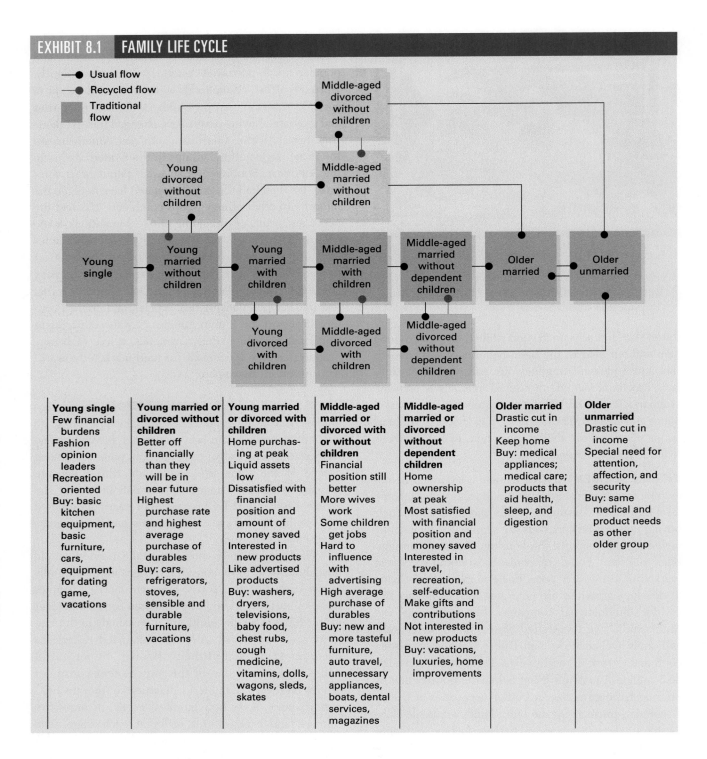

Young single	Young married or divorced without children	Young married or divorced with children	Middle-aged married or divorced with or without children	Middle-aged married or divorced without dependent children	Older married	Older unmarried
Few financial burdens	Better off financially than they will be in near future	Home purchasing at peak	Financial position still better	Home ownership at peak	Drastic cut in income	Drastic cut in income
Fashion opinion leaders	Highest purchase rate and highest average purchase of durables	Liquid assets low	More wives work	Most satisfied with financial position and money saved	Keep home	Special need for attention, affection, and security
Recreation oriented	Buy: cars, refrigerators, stoves, sensible and durable furniture, vacations	Dissatisfied with financial position and amount of money saved	Some children get jobs	Interested in travel, recreation, self-education	Buy: medical appliances; medical care; products that aid health, sleep, and digestion	Buy: same medical and product needs as other older group
Buy: basic kitchen equipment, basic furniture, cars, equipment for dating game, vacations		Interested in new products	Hard to influence with advertising	Make gifts and contributions		
		Like advertised products	High average purchase of durables	Not interested in new products		
		Buy: washers, dryers, televisions, baby food, chest rubs, cough medicine, vitamins, dolls, wagons, sleds, skates	Buy: new and more tasteful furniture, auto travel, unnecessary appliances, boats, dental services, magazines	Buy: vacations, luxuries, home improvements		

stage, their consumption patterns often revert to those of the young single stage of the cycle.

About four out of five divorced persons remarry by middle age and reenter the traditional life cycle, as indicated by the "recycled flow" in the exhibit. Consumers are especially receptive to marketing efforts at certain points in the life cycle. For example, baby boomers have increased needs for health care services, while families with babies need diapers, toys, and baby clothes.

8-4c Psychographic Segmentation

Age, gender, income, ethnicity, FLC stage, and other demographic variables are usually helpful in developing segmentation strategies, but often, they do not paint the entire picture. Demographics provide the skeleton, but psychographics add meat to the bones. **Psychographic segmentation** is market segmentation on the basis of the following psychographic segmentation variables:

- **Personality:** Personality reflects a person's traits, attitudes, and habits. Clothing is the ultimate personality descriptor. Fashionistas wear high-end, trendy clothes, and hipsters enjoy jeans and T-shirts with tennis shoes. People buy clothes that they feel represent their personalities and give others an idea of who they are.

- **Motives:** Marketers of baby products and life insurance appeal to consumers' emotional motives—namely, to care for their loved ones. Using appeals to economy, reliability, and dependability, carmakers like Subaru and Suzuki target customers with rational motives. Carmakers like Mercedes-Benz, Jaguar, and Cadillac appeal to customers with status-related motives.

- **Lifestyles:** Lifestyle segmentation divides people into groups according to the way they spend their time, the importance of the things around them, their beliefs, and socioeconomic characteristics such as income and education. For example, record stores specializing in vinyl are targeting young people who are listening to independent labels and often pride themselves on being independent of big business. LEED-certified appliances appeal to environmentally conscious "green" consumers. PepsiCo is promoting its no-calorie, sugar-free flavored water, Aquafina FlavorSplash, to consumers who are health conscious.

- **Geodemographics:** **Geodemographic segmentation** clusters potential customers into neighborhood lifestyle categories. It combines geographic, demographic, and lifestyle segmentations. Geodemographic segmentation helps marketers develop marketing programs tailored to prospective buyers who live in small geographic regions, such as neighborhoods, or who have very specific lifestyle and demographic characteristics. College students, for example, often share similar demographics and lifestyles and tend to cluster around campus. Knowing this, marketing teams for startups and tech companies

like Google often launch ambassador programs at insular college campuses. Student brand ambassadors for the Google Pizza Program bought pizza for their computer science peers during tough times and around deadlines. This helped the company create buzz and form ties with talented programmers. Through these programs, students are transformed into word-of-mouth marketers to their geodemographic peers.[29]

Psychographic variables can be used individually to segment markets or can be combined with other variables to provide more detailed descriptions of market segments. One approach is for marketers and advertisers to purchase information from a collector, such as eXelate Media, in order to reach the audience they want. eXelate, part of consumer research firm Nielsen, gathers information about web-browsing habits through cookies placed on websites. Nielsen, using eXelate, organizes groups according to this information. One group, the "young digerati," includes 25- to 45-year-olds who:

- Are tech savvy
- Are affluent
- Live in trendy condos
- Read the *Economist*
- Have an annual income of $88,000

An automaker can purchase that list and the list of people who visit car blogs and then target ads to the young digerati interested in cars.[30]

8-4d Benefit Segmentation

Benefit segmentation is the process of grouping customers into market segments according to the benefits they seek from the product. Most types of market segmentation are based on the assumption that this variable and customers' needs are related. Benefit segmentation is different because it groups potential customers on the basis of

psychographic segmentation segmenting markets on the basis of personality, motives, lifestyles, and geodemographics

geodemographic segmentation segmenting potential customers into neighborhood lifestyle categories

benefit segmentation the process of grouping customers into market segments according to the benefits they seek from the product

Kraphix/Shutterstock.com

their needs or wants rather than on some other characteristic, such as age or gender. The snack-food market, for example, can be divided into six benefit segments: nutritional snackers, weight watchers, guilty snackers, party snackers, indiscriminate snackers, and economical snackers.

Customer profiles can be developed by examining demographic information associated with people seeking certain benefits. This information can be used to match marketing strategies with selected markets. Dish Network developed Sling TV, a streaming live television service that is available on devices such as gaming consoles and mobile devices, to appeal to people who want to get away from traditional TV sets and cable boxes. The service costs $20 a month for a basic package (additional channels can be purchased), and there are no set-up fees or commitments. Sling TV emphasizes family-friendly programming, which is especially attractive to families with young children.[31]

8-4e Usage-Rate Segmentation

Usage-rate segmentation divides a market by the amount of product bought or consumed. Categories vary with the product, but they are likely to include some combination of the following: former users, potential users, first-time users, light or irregular users, medium users, and heavy users. Segmenting by usage rate enables marketers to focus their efforts on heavy users or to develop multiple marketing mixes aimed at different segments. Because heavy users often account for a sizable portion of all product sales, some marketers focus on the heavy-user segment.

The **80/20 principle** holds that 20 percent of all customers generate 80 percent of the demand. Although the percentages usually are not exact, the general idea often holds true. Multinational corporations require vast amounts of computer storage, but these giant enterprises make up just a small percentage of the data storage market. When data storage manufacturer Actifio found that eighty percent of its customers were midsize enterprises that bought computer storage in relatively modest batches of 100 terabytes (about 100,000 gigabytes), it developed the Actifio 100T, a storage appliance that allowed midsize enterprises to scale up to two petabytes (about two million gigabytes) of capacity. In this way, Actifio's 80 percent of low-demand customers could transition over time toward its 20 percent of high-demand customers.[32]

Developing customers into heavy users is the goal behind many frequency/loyalty programs like the airlines' frequent flyer programs. Most supermarkets and other retailers have also designed loyalty programs that reward the heavy-user segment with deals available only to them, such as in-store coupon dispensing systems, loyalty card programs, and special price deals on selected merchandise.

8-5 BASES FOR SEGMENTING BUSINESS MARKETS

The business market consists of four broad segments: producers, resellers, government, and institutions. (For a detailed discussion of the characteristics of these segments, see Chapter 7.) Whether marketers focus on only one or on all four of these segments, they are likely to find diversity among potential customers. Thus, further market segmentation offers just as many benefits to business marketers as it does to consumer product marketers.

8-5a Company Characteristics

Company characteristics, such as geographic location, type of company, company size, and product use, can be important segmentation variables. Some markets tend to be regional because buyers prefer to purchase from local suppliers, and distant suppliers may have difficulty competing in terms of price and service. Therefore, firms that sell to geographically concentrated industries benefit by locating close to their markets.

Segmenting by customer type allows business marketers to tailor their marketing mixes to the unique needs of particular types of organizations or industries. For example, the Amazon Webstore platform allows businesses from single-person operations to multinational corporations to operate Amazon-hosted online shops. Entrepreneurs can easily set up templatized shops featuring products that are warehoused and fulfilled by Amazon, while enterprise-level corporations like Fruit of the Loom, Spalding, and Bacardi can use the platform to manage large-scale, customized Web stores. Amazon Webstore's Web site, http://webstore.amazon.com, caters to companies' diverse needs with an array of hosting packages and information pages segmented by both business size and business type.[33]

Volume of purchase (heavy, moderate, light) is a commonly used basis for business segmentation. Another is the buying organization's size, which may affect its purchasing procedures, the types and quantities of products it needs, and its responses to different marketing mixes. Banks frequently offer different services, lines of credit, and overall attention to commercial customers based on their size. Many products, especially raw materials like steel, wood, and petroleum, have diverse applications. How customers use a product may influence the amount they buy, their buying criteria, and their selection of vendors. For example, a producer of springs may have customers who use the product in applications as diverse as making machine tools, bicycles, surgical devices, office equipment, telephones, and missile systems.

8-5b Buying Processes

Many business marketers find it helpful to segment customers and prospective customers on the basis of how they buy. For example, companies can segment some business markets by ranking key purchasing criteria, such as price, quality, technical support, and service. Atlas Overhead Door has developed a commanding position in the industrial door market by providing customized products in just 4 weeks, which is much faster than the industry average of 12 to 15 weeks. Atlas's primary market is companies with an immediate need for customized doors.

The purchasing strategies of buyers may provide useful segments. Two purchasing profiles that have been identified are satisficers and optimizers. **Satisficers** contact familiar suppliers and place the order with the first one to satisfy product and delivery requirements. **Optimizers** consider numerous suppliers (both familiar and unfamiliar), solicit bids, and study all proposals carefully before selecting one.

The personal characteristics of the buyers themselves (their demographic characteristics, decision style, tolerance for risk, confidence level, job responsibilities, and so on) influence their buying behavior and thus offer a viable basis for segmenting some business markets.

Satisficer

Piotr Marcinski/Shutterstock.com

Optimizer

dragon_fang/Shutterstock.com

1. **Select a market or product category for study:** Define the overall market or product category to be studied. It may be a market in which the firm already competes, a new but related market or product category, or a totally new market.

2. **Choose a basis or bases for segmenting the market:** This step requires managerial insight, creativity, and market knowledge. There are no scientific procedures for selecting segmentation variables. However, a successful segmentation scheme must produce segments that meet the four basic criteria discussed earlier in this chapter.

3. **Select segmentation descriptors:** After choosing one or more bases, the marketer must select the segmentation descriptors. Descriptors identify the specific segmentation variables to use. For example, if a company selects demographics as a basis of segmentation, it may use age, occupation, and income as descriptors. A company that selects usage-rate segmentation needs to decide whether to go after heavy users, nonusers, or light users.

4. **Profile and analyze segments:** The profile should include the segments' size, expected growth, purchase frequency, current brand usage, brand loyalty, and long-term sales and profit potential. This information can then be used to rank potential market segments by profit opportunity, risk, consistency with organizational mission and objectives, and other factors important to the firm.

5. **Select markets:** Selecting markets is not a part of but a natural outcome of the segmentation process. It is a major decision that influences and often directly determines the firm's marketing mix. This topic is examined in greater detail later in this chapter.

6. **Design, implement, and maintain appropriate marketing mixes:** The marketing mix has been described as product, place (distribution), promotion, and pricing strategies intended to bring about a mutually satisfying

8-6 STEPS IN SEGMENTING A MARKET

The purpose of market segmentation, in both consumer and business markets, is to identify marketing opportunities.

satisficers business customers who place an order with the first familiar supplier to satisfy product and delivery requirements

optimizers business customers who consider numerous suppliers (both familiar and unfamiliar), solicit bids, and study all proposals carefully before selecting one

Too Many Cooks

Campbell Soup Co. has classified home cooks into six distinct profile types: the passionate kitchen master, the familiar taste pleaser, the familiar taste pleaser (Mexican), the constrained wishful eater, the disciplined health manager, and the uninvolved quick fixer. The company uses these types as a foundation to develop and market new products and create recipes. For example, the passionate kitchen master loves to cook, usually has the time to do so, and knows how to make many dishes without a recipe. On the other end of the spectrum is the uninvolved quick fixer, who doesn't enjoy cooking and would be happy to snack all day. Campbell's develops unique approaches for each, as members of one market will not likely be persuaded to buy by a marketing mix targeted at the other. [34]

exchange relationship with a market. These topics are explored in detail in Chapters 10 through 20.

Markets are dynamic, so it is important that companies proactively monitor their segmentation strategies over time. Often, once customers or prospects have been assigned to a segment, marketers think their task is done. Once customers are assigned to an age segment, for example, they stay there until they reach the next age bracket or category, which could be ten years in the future. Thus, the segmentation classifications are static, but the customers and prospects are changing. Dynamic segmentation approaches adjust to fit the changes that occur in customers' lives. For example, American Eagle mainly targets 10-year-old boys and girls with its 77 kids stores. However, some segments are targeted by too many players, and choosing to enter those kinds of segments can be particularly challenging. For example, there are so many online fashion stores using flash sales to attract bargain hunters that *RetailMeNot* put together a list of nine that it thinks are worth visiting. [35]

target market a group of people or organizations for which an organization designs, implements, and maintains a marketing mix intended to meet the needs of that group, resulting in mutually satisfying exchanges

undifferentiated targeting strategy a marketing approach that views the market as one big market with no individual segments and thus uses a single marketing mix

8-7 STRATEGIES FOR SELECTING TARGET MARKETS

So far, this chapter has focused on the market segmentation process, which is only the first step in deciding whom to approach about buying a product. The next task is to choose one or more target markets. A **target market** is a group of people or organizations for which an organization designs, implements, and maintains a marketing mix intended to meet the needs of that group, resulting in mutually satisfying exchanges.

Because most markets will include customers with different characteristics, lifestyles, backgrounds, and income levels, it is unlikely that a single marketing mix will attract all segments of the market. Thus, if a marketer wishes to appeal to more than one segment of the market, it must develop different marketing mixes. The three general strategies for selecting target markets—undifferentiated, concentrated, and multisegment targeting—are illustrated in Exhibit 8.2, which also illustrates the advantages and disadvantages of each targeting strategy.

8-7a Undifferentiated Targeting

A firm using an **undifferentiated targeting strategy** essentially adopts a mass-market philosophy, viewing the market as one big market with no individual segments. The firm uses one marketing mix for the entire market. A firm that adopts an undifferentiated targeting strategy assumes that individual customers have similar needs that can be met with a common marketing mix.

The first firm in an industry sometimes uses an undifferentiated targeting strategy. With no competition, the firm may not need to tailor marketing mixes to the preferences of market segments. Henry Ford's famous comment about the Model T is a classic example of an undifferentiated targeting strategy: "They can have their car in any color they want, as long as it's black." At one time, Coca-Cola used this strategy with a single product and a single size of its familiar green bottle. Marketers of commodity products, such as flour and sugar, are also likely to use an undifferentiated targeting strategy.

One advantage of undifferentiated marketing is the potential for saving on production and marketing. Because only one item is produced, the firm should be able to achieve economies of mass production. Also, marketing costs may be lower when there is only one product to

EXHIBIT 8.2 ADVANTAGES AND DISADVANTAGES OF TARGET MARKETING STRATEGIES

Targeting Strategy	Advantages	Disadvantages
Undifferentiated Targeting	• Potential savings on production/ marketing costs	• Unimaginative product offerings • Company more susceptible to competition
Concentrated Targeting	• Concentration of resources • Can better meet the needs of a narrowly defined segment • Allows some small firms to better compete with larger firms • Strong positioning	• Segments too small or changing • Large competitors may more effectively market to niche segment
Multisegment Targeting	• Greater financial success • Economies of scale in producing/ marketing	• High costs • Cannibalization

promote and a single channel of distribution. Too often, however, an undifferentiated strategy emerges by default rather than by design, reflecting a failure to consider the advantages of a segmented approach. The result is often sterile, unimaginative product offerings that have little appeal to anyone.

Another problem associated with undifferentiated targeting is that it makes the company more susceptible to competitive inroads. Hershey lost a big share of the candy market to Mars and other candy companies before it changed to a multisegment targeting strategy. Coca-Cola forfeited its position as the leading seller of cola drinks in supermarkets to PepsiCo in the late 1950s, when Pepsi began offering several sizes of containers.

You might think a firm producing a standard product such as toilet tissue would adopt an undifferentiated strategy. However, this market has industrial segments and consumer segments. Industrial buyers want an economical, single-ply product sold in boxes of a hundred rolls (or jumbo rolls a foot in diameter to use in public restrooms). The consumer market demands a more versatile product in smaller quantities. Within the consumer market, the product is differentiated with designer print or no print, as cushioned or noncushioned, and as economy priced or luxury priced. Undifferentiated marketing can succeed in certain situations, though. A small grocery store in a small, isolated town may define all of the people who live in the town as its target market. It may offer one marketing mix and generally satisfy everyone in town. This strategy is not likely to be as effective if there are three or four grocery stores in town.

8-7b Concentrated Targeting

With a **concentrated targeting strategy**, a firm selects a market **niche** (one segment of a market) for targeting its marketing efforts. Because the firm is appealing to a single segment, it can concentrate on understanding the needs, motives, and satisfactions of that segment's members and on developing and maintaining a highly specialized marketing mix. Some firms find that concentrating resources and meeting the needs of a narrowly defined market segment is more profitable than spreading resources over several different segments.

Intelligentsia Coffee & Tea, a Chicago-based coffee roaster/retailer, targets serious coffee drinkers with hand-roasted, ground, and poured super-gourmet coffee or tea served by seriously educated baristas. The company also offers training classes for the at-home or out-of-town coffee aficionado. Starting price—$200 per class.

Small firms often adopt a concentrated targeting strategy to compete effectively with much larger firms. For example, Enterprise Rent-A-Car, number one in the car rental industry, started as a small company catering to people with cars in the shop. Some other firms use a concentrated strategy to establish a strong position in a desirable market segment. Porsche, for instance, targets an upscale automobile market through "class appeal, not mass appeal."

Concentrated targeting violates the old adage "Don't put all your eggs in one basket." If the chosen segment is too small or if it shrinks because of

concentrated targeting strategy a strategy used to select one segment of a market for targeting marketing efforts

niche one segment of a market

A bag of Intelligentsia coffee sits on a shelf before being shipped from the company's Chicago, Illinois headquarters

environmental changes, the firm may suffer negative consequences. For instance, OshKosh B'gosh was highly successful selling children's wear in the 1980s. It was so successful, however, that the children's line came to define OshKosh's image to the extent that the company could not sell clothes to anyone else. Attempts at marketing older children's clothing, women's casual clothes, and maternity wear were all abandoned. Recognizing it was in the children's wear business, the company expanded into products such as kids' shoes, children's eyewear, and plush toys.

A concentrated strategy can also be disastrous for a firm that is not successful in its narrowly defined target market. Before Procter & Gamble (P&G) introduced Head & Shoulders shampoo, several small firms were already selling antidandruff shampoos. Head & Shoulders was introduced with a large promotional campaign, and the new brand captured over half the market immediately. Within a year, several of the firms that had been concentrating on this market segment went out of business.

multisegment targeting strategy a strategy that chooses two or more well-defined market segments and develops a distinct marketing mix for each

cannibalization a situation that occurs when sales of a new product cut into sales of a firm's existing products

8-7c Multisegment Targeting

A firm that chooses to serve two or more well-defined market segments and develops a distinct marketing mix for each has a **multisegment targeting strategy**. P&G offers 18 different laundry detergents, each targeting a different segment of the market. For example, Tide is a tough, powerful cleaner, and Era is good for stain treatment and removal. Zipcar, a membership-based car sharing company that provides car rentals to its members billable by the hour or day, shifted its targeting strategy from urban centers, adding services for business and universities like the University of Minnesota, which has five Zipcar stations located around its campus. On campuses across the nation, Zipcar targeting is further subdivided into faculty/staff and student markets.[36]

Multisegment targeting offers many potential benefits to firms, including greater sales volume, higher profits, larger market share, and economies of scale in manufacturing and marketing. Yet it may also involve greater product design, production, promotion, inventory, marketing research, and management costs. Before deciding to use this strategy, firms should compare the benefits and costs of multisegment targeting to those of undifferentiated and concentrated targeting.

Another potential cost of multisegment targeting is **cannibalization**, which occurs when sales of a new product cut into sales of a firm's existing products. For example, the iPad peaked as a share of Apple's revenue in 2012 when iPhone screens were only three-and-a-half inches. Since then, however, sales of iPads have dropped at a greater rate than the tablet market average. Why? The larger-screened iPhone 6 series phones cannibalized the iPad. Customers who once supplemented their small-screened iPhones with larger iPads decided that they could do without the extra device. iPad sales could drop even further as new MacBook models compete with tablets in size and weight.[37]

8-8 CRM AS A TARGETING TOOL

Recall from Chapter 1 that CRM entails tracking interactions with customers to optimize customer satisfaction and long-term company profits. Companies that successfully implement CRM tend to customize the goods and services offered to their customers based on data generated through interactions between carefully defined groups of customers and the company. CRM can also allow marketers to target customers with extremely relevant offerings. Birchbox, a company that creates custom boxes of beauty, grooming, and lifestyle product samples, uses CRM to personalize the customer experience. Birchbox reps get to know each customer via profile information, carefully monitoring product

Zipcar representative Travis Reik explains the car sharing process to University of Mississippi junior, Abby Oliver, shortly after Ole Miss accounced a partnership with the company.

reviews, and general activity on the company's website. They then put together customized samples and editorial content that feels personal to customers. If a customer likes a sample, he can use Birchbox to buy the full product. [38]

As many firms have discovered, a detailed and segmented understanding of customers can be advantageous. There are at least four trends that will lead to the continuing growth of CRM: personalization, time savings, loyalty, and technology.

- **Personalization:** One-size-fits-all marketing is no longer relevant. Consumers want to be treated as the individuals they are, with their own unique sets of needs and wants. By its personalized nature, CRM can fulfill this desire.

- **Time savings:** Direct and personal marketing efforts will continue to grow to meet the needs of consumers who no longer have the time to spend shopping and making purchase decisions. With the personal and targeted nature of CRM, consumers can spend less time making purchase decisions and more time doing the things that are important to them.

- **Loyalty:** Consumers will be loyal only to those companies and brands that have earned their loyalty and reinforced it at every purchase occasion. CRM techniques focus on finding a firm's best customers, rewarding them for their loyalty, and thanking them for their business.

- **Technology:** Mass-media approaches will decline in importance as advances in market research and

database technology allow marketers to collect detailed information on their customers. New technology offers marketers a more cost-effective way to reach customers and enables businesses to personalize their messages. For example, My.Yahoo.com greets each user by name and offers information in which the user has expressed interest. Similarly, RedEnvelope.com helps customers keep track of special occasions and offers personalized gift recommendations. With the help of database technology, CRM can track a business's customers as individuals, even if they number in the millions.

CRM is a huge commitment and often requires a 180-degree turnaround for marketers who spent the last half of the twentieth century developing and implementing mass-marketing efforts. Although mass marketing will probably continue to be used, especially to create brand awareness or to remind consumers of a product, the advantages of CRM cannot be ignored.

8-9 POSITIONING

Marketers segment their markets and then choose which segment, or segments, to target with their marketing mix. Then, based on the target market(s), they can develop the product's **positioning**, a process that influences potential customers' overall perception of a brand, product line, or organization in general. **Position** is the place a product, brand, or group of products occupies in consumers' minds relative to competing offerings. Consumer goods marketers are particularly concerned with positioning. Coca-Cola has multiple cola brands, each positioned to target a different market. For example, Coca-Cola Zero is positioned on its bold taste and zero calories, Caffeine Free Coca-Cola is positioned as a no-caffeine alternative, and Tab is positioned as a cola drink for dieters. [39]

Positioning assumes that consumers compare products on the basis of important features. Marketing efforts that emphasize irrelevant features are therefore likely to misfire. For example, Crystal Pepsi and a clear version of Coca-Cola's Tab failed because consumers perceived the "clear" positioning as more of a marketing gimmick than a benefit.

> **positioning** developing a specific marketing mix to influence potential customers' overall perception of a brand, product line, or organization in general
>
> **position** the place a product, brand, or group of products occupies in consumers' minds relative to competing offerings

Effective positioning requires assessing the positions occupied by competing products, determining the important dimensions underlying these positions, and choosing a position in the market where the organization's marketing efforts will have the greatest impact. Casual-dining restaurant chain Ruby Tuesday recently found that what consumers remembered most about eating in a Ruby Tuesday restaurant was the Garden Bar. In response, the company decided to differentiate itself from competitors by focusing on vegetables. Today, Ruby Tuesday is positioned as a place to get a great salad with a full menu on the side. The Garden Bar offers 70 ingredients, customers can make as many trips as they want, and they can customize their salads however they like. This focus addresses a consumer trend toward eating more healthfully, and is something most competitors do not offer.[40] One positioning strategy that many firms use to distinguish their products from competitors is based on **product differentiation**. The distinctions between products can be either real or perceived. For example, Kentucky Fried Chicken differentiates itself from other fast-food fried chicken restaurants with its secret blend of eleven herbs and spices (perceived), as well as unique offerings like the Double Down, Famous Bowl, and Bucket & Bites Meal (real).[41] However, many everyday products, such as bleaches, aspirin, unleaded regular gasoline, and some soaps, are differentiated by such trivial means as brand names, packaging, color, smell, or "secret" additives. The marketer attempts to convince consumers that a particular brand is distinctive and that they should demand it.

Some firms, instead of using product differentiation, position their products as being similar to competing products or brands. Two examples of this positioning are artificial sweeteners advertised as tasting like sugar and margarine as tasting like butter.

Unique menu items help Kentucky Fried Chicken differentiate itself from other fast-food fried chicken restaurants.

stumbled in sales when it tried to attract a younger core customer. To recover, Saks invested in research to determine its core customers in its fifty-four stores across the country. The perceptual map in Exhibit 8.3 shows how Saks uses customer demographics such as spending levels and preferred styles to build a matrix that charts the best mix of clothes and accessories to stock in each store.

8-9b Positioning Bases

Firms use a variety of bases for positioning, including the following:

- **Attribute:** A product is associated with an attribute, product feature, or customer benefit. In engineering its products, Seventh Generation focuses on removing common toxins and chemicals from household products to make them safe for everyone in the household.

- **Price and quality:** This positioning base may stress high price as a signal of quality or emphasize low price as an indication of value. Neiman Marcus uses the high-price strategy; Walmart has successfully followed the low-price and value strategy. The mass merchandiser Target has developed an interesting position based on price and quality. It is an "upscale discounter," sticking to low prices but offering higher quality and design than most discount chains.

- **Use or application:** Stressing uses or applications can be an effective means of positioning a product with buyers. Danone introduced its Kahlúa liqueur using advertising to point out 228 ways to consume the product.

product differentiation a positioning strategy that some firms use to distinguish their products from those of competitors

perceptual mapping a means of displaying or graphing, in two or more dimensions, the location of products, brands, or groups of products in customers' minds

repositioning changing consumers' perceptions of a brand in relation to competing brands

8-9a Perceptual Mapping

Perceptual mapping is a means of displaying or graphing, in two or more dimensions, the location of products, brands, or groups of products in customers' minds. For example, Saks Incorporated, the department store chain,

- **Product user:** This positioning base focuses on a personality or type of user. Gap Inc. has several different brands: Gap stores offer basic casual pieces, such as jeans and T-shirts, to middle-of-the-road consumers at mid-level prices; Old Navy offers low-priced, trendy casual wear geared to youth and college-age groups; and Banana Republic is a luxury brand offering fashionable, luxurious business and casual wear to 25- to 35-year-olds.[42]

- **Product class:** The objective here is to position the product as being associated with a particular category of products—for example, positioning a margarine brand with butter. Alternatively, products can be disassociated with a category.

- **Competitor:** Positioning against competitors is part of any positioning strategy. Apple positions the iPhone as cooler and more up-to-date than Windows-based smartphones, and Samsung positions the Galaxy series as cooler and more up-to-date than the iPhone.

- **Emotion:** Positioning using emotion focuses on how the product makes customers feel. A number of companies use this approach. For example, Nike's "Just Do It" campaign did not tell consumers what "it" is, but most got the emotional message of achievement and courage. Instead of focusing its advertising on the rational attribute of knowledge, Google positioned its search engine as an enabler of customers' feelings of discovery, wisdom, and competence.[43]

8-9c Repositioning

Sometimes products or companies are repositioned in order to sustain growth in slow markets or to correct positioning mistakes. **Repositioning** is changing consumers' perceptions of a brand in relation to competing brands. For example, in its early years, the Hyundai brand was synonymous with cheap, low-quality cars. To reposition its brand, Hyundai redesigned its cars to be more contemporary-looking and started a supportive warranty program. Consumer perceptions changed because customers appreciated the new designs and were reassured of the cars' performance by the generous warranties. Today, Hyundai's brand reputation has vastly improved.[44]

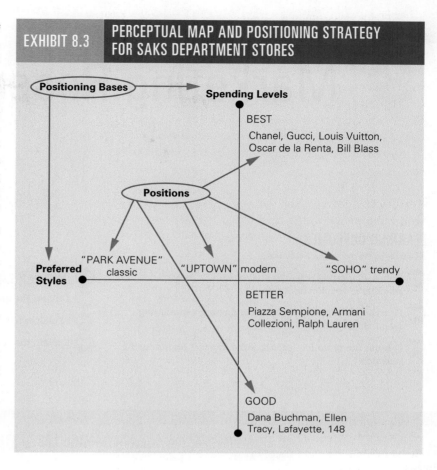

EXHIBIT 8.3   PERCEPTUAL MAP AND POSITIONING STRATEGY FOR SAKS DEPARTMENT STORES

9 | Marketing Research

LEARNING OUTCOMES

After studying this chapter, you will be able to...

9-1 Define marketing research and explain its importance to marketing decision making

9-2 Describe the steps involved in conducting a marketing research project

9-3 Discuss the profound impact of the Internet on marketing research

9-4 Describe the growing importance of mobile research

9-5 Discuss the growing importance of scanner-based research

9-6 Explain when marketing research should be conducted

9-7 Explain the concept of competitive intelligence

Andrey_Popov/Shutterstock.com

After finishing this chapter go to **PAGE 173** for **STUDY TOOLS**

9-1 THE ROLE OF MARKETING RESEARCH

Marketing research is the process of planning, collecting, and analyzing data relevant to a marketing decision. The results of this analysis are then communicated to management. Thus, marketing research is the function that links the consumer, customer, and public to the marketer through information. Marketing research plays a key role in the marketing system. It provides decision makers with data on the effectiveness of the current marketing mix and insights for necessary changes. Furthermore, marketing research is a main data source for management information systems. In other words, the findings of a marketing research project become data for management decision making.

Marketing research has three roles: descriptive, diagnostic, and predictive. Its *descriptive* role includes gathering and presenting factual statements. For example, what is the historic sales trend in the industry? What are consumers' attitudes toward a product and its advertising? Its *diagnostic* role includes explaining data, such as determining the impact on sales of a change in the design of the package. Its *predictive* function is to address "what if" questions. For example, how can the researcher use the descriptive and diagnostic research to predict the results of a planned marketing decision?

marketing research the process of planning, collecting, and analyzing data relevant to a marketing decision

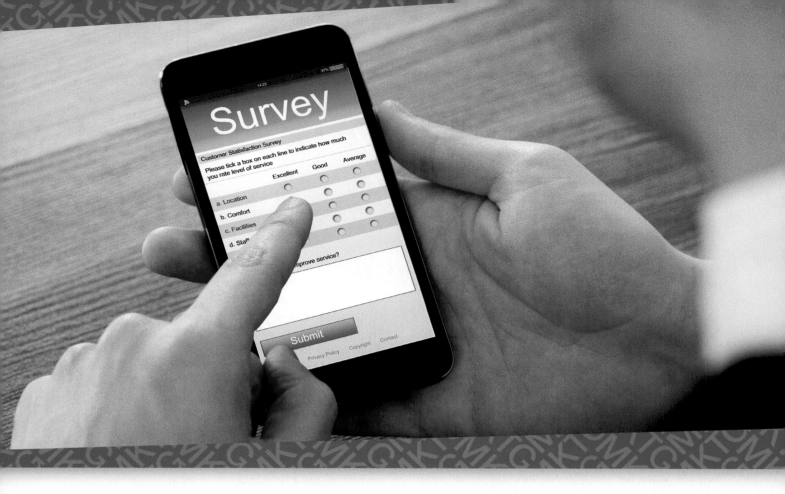

9-1a Management Uses of Marketing Research

Marketing research can help managers in several ways. First, it improves the quality of decision making, allowing marketers to explore the desirability of various alternatives before arriving at a path forward. Second, it helps managers trace problems. Was the initial decision incorrect? Did an unforeseen change in the external environment cause the plan to fail? How can the same mistake be avoided in the future? Questions like these can be answered through marketing research. Third, marketing research can help managers understand very detailed and complicated relationships. Most importantly, sound marketing research can help managers serve both current and future customers accurately and efficiently. Researchers have found that people like things that are familiar to them. In other words, if you frequently see a product's logo as a child, you are more likely to try that product as an adult. Ford is using this research to create a continuous stream of brand-loyal customers in its pipeline.

For the last several decades, Ford's advertising has focused primarily on adults, as they were the ones buying new cars. However, in an effort to build brand affinity at a young age and prepare for the future of driving, Ford has begun considering the interests of Generation Z (such as emotional bonding and high-energy social activities) when developing its marketing messaging. For example, instead of using raw power and a devil-may-care attitude to sell the Mustang sports car, a recent ad showed how the car could bring friends together, complete with shots of young people surfing, painting, and playing guitar—with the Mustang parked at the scene of each adventure.[1]

Marketing research can also help managers understand whether and when changes should be made to existing products and services. The majority of supermarket chains put four key departments at the center of each store: grocery, frozen, dairy, and alcohol. Less important departments like bakery, produce, deli, meats, and seafood typically line the perimeter of the store. Understanding consumer purchase patterns enables grocery chain marketing managers to determine whether departments should be moved and/or reorganized. Researchers have found that salty snacks are very popular among families with children: 58 percent of parents report that their kids ask them to buy salty treats. Candy is also very popular among this segment. Requests for candy peak among parents with three- to seven-year-olds (63 percent) and eight- to twelve-year-olds (65 percent) before dropping to 54 percent among the 13- to 17-year-old set. Similar patterns emerge when it comes to cookies (64 percent among parents with three- to seven-year-olds, 68 percent among those with eight- to twelve-year-olds, and 57 percent among those with 13- to 17-year-olds).[2]

Cereal sales are declining overall, but researchers have found that 90 percent of American households with kids under age 18 buy at least one box of cereal per year. Cereal buyers with kids purchase an average of nearly 28 boxes of cereal per year, compared to roughly 17 boxes among those without children.[3]

9-1b Understanding the Ever-Changing Marketplace

Marketing research helps managers understand what is going on in the marketplace and take advantage of opportunities. Now, with big data analytics (discussed later), we can understand the marketing environment like never before. Historically speaking, marketing research has been practiced for as long as marketing has existed. The early Phoenicians carried out market demand studies as they traded in the various ports of the Mediterranean Sea. Marco Polo's diary indicates he performed marketing research as he traveled to China. There is even evidence that the Spanish systematically conducted "market surveys" as they explored the New World, and there are examples of marketing research conducted during the Renaissance.

Returning to the present, one of the hottest trends in technology today is the Internet of Things (IoT). This term refers to everyday devices like refrigerators, toys, lightbulbs, and hot water heaters connecting wirelessly to a network to improve their functionality. An early leader in this market was the Nest Thermostat. Nest learns the temperatures you like throughout the week and then turns itself down when you are away. It can be controlled via an app, so you can increase or decrease the temperature while lying in bed. So what does this trend mean to manufacturers of appliances, clothing, fitness devices, and countless other items? At the end of 2015, 13 percent of consumers had an IoT device in their homes. By 2019, 69 percent plan to have at least one IoT

Constantine Pankin/Shutterstock.com

device, such as a thermostat or security system. Adoption of wearable IoT technology (such as smartwatches and fitness devices) is also expected to increase; nearly half of consumers already own or planning to purchase a device in this category by 2019.

The findings of a nationwide marketing research study indicate that consumers living in the ten largest U.S. cities are more likely than the national average to identify as early adopters. Findings varied by region, however: 74 percent of consumers living in the Northeast plan to adopt an in-home IoT device by 2019, compared to 68 percent in the Midwest and 66 percent in the Southeast. Consumers living in the Northeast are approximately 50 percent more likely than those living in the Southeast and Midwest to adopt a smart smoke detector in 2016. Fifty-eight percent of consumers living in the Northeast plan to adopt wearable technology by 2019, with the Southeast and Midwest close behind at 57 and 55 percent, respectively. Men are more likely than women to plan to purchase an in-home IoT device by 2019 (70 percent compared to 67 percent). Younger consumers are most likely to adopt connected technologies later on, while older consumers are slightly more likely to already own certain products.[4]

9-2 STEPS IN A MARKETING RESEARCH PROJECT

Virtually all firms that have adopted the marketing concept engage in some marketing research because it offers decision makers many benefits. Some companies spend millions on marketing research; others, particularly smaller firms, conduct informal, limited-scale research studies.

Whether a research project costs $200 or $2 million, the same general process should be followed. The marketing research process is a scientific approach to decision making that maximizes the chance of getting accurate and meaningful results. Exhibit 9.1 traces the seven steps in the research process, which begins with the recognition of a marketing problem or opportunity. As changes occur in the firm's external environment, marketing managers are faced with the questions "Should we change the existing marketing mix?" and, if so, "How?" Marketing research may be used to evaluate product, promotion, distribution, or pricing alternatives.

Suppose a pet food manufacturer wants to know if it is targeting the right customers in the United States. To learn more about its most likely customers, the manufacturer decides to conduct a survey among pet owners in the United States.

Sixty-two percent of Americans have at least one pet in their households. Dogs are most popular— 71 percent of pet owners have at least one dog. Forty-nine percent have one or more cats; one in ten has fish (11 percent); and less than one in ten has a bird (8 percent) or some other type of pet (9 percent). Together, these pet owners spend more than $20 billion a year in pet care. Of the more than $9 billion spent on dog food alone, $2.6 billion is spent on dog treats. Interestingly, only $476 million is spent on cat treats.[5]

This example illustrates an important point about problem/opportunity definition. The **marketing research problem** involves determining what information is needed and how that information can be obtained efficiently and effectively. The **marketing research objective**, then, is the goal statement. The marketing research objective defines the specific information needed to solve the marketing problem and provides insightful decision-making information. This requires specific pieces of information needed to solve the marketing research problem. Managers must combine this information with their own experience and other information to make proper decisions. The pet food manufacturers' marketing research problem was to gather specific information about pet owners in the United States using a national survey. The marketing research objective was to determine whether the company was targeting the right customers.

By contrast, the **management decision problem** is action oriented. Management problems tend to be much broader in scope and far more general than marketing research problems, which must be narrowly defined and specific if the research effort is to be successful. Sometimes several research studies must be conducted to solve a broad management

Yuriy Rudyy/Shutterstock.com

problem. For the pet food manufacturer, the management decision problem might be increasing the effectiveness of its marketing.

9-2a Secondary Data

A valuable tool throughout the research process, particularly in the problem/opportunity identification stage, is **secondary data**— data previously collected for any purpose other than the one at hand. Secondary information originating within the company includes the company's websites, annual reports, reports to stockholders,

marketing research problem determining what information is needed and how that information can be obtained efficiently and effectively

marketing research objective the specific information needed to solve a marketing research problem; the objective should be to provide insightful decision-making information

management decision problem a broad-based problem that uses marketing research in order for managers to take proper actions

secondary data data previously collected for any purpose other than the one at hand

blogs, product testing results perhaps made available to the news media, YouTube videos, social media posts, and house periodicals composed by the company's personnel for communication to employees, customers, or others. Often, this information is incorporated into a company's internal database.

Innumerable outside sources of secondary information also exist, some in the forms of government departments and agencies (federal, state, and local) that compile and post summaries of business data. Trade and industry associations also publish secondary data. Still more data are available in business periodicals and other news media that regularly publish studies and articles on the economy, specific industries, and even individual companies. The unpublished summarized secondary information from these sources corresponds to internal reports, memos, or special-purpose analyses with limited circulation. Competitive considerations in the organization may preclude publication of these summaries.

Secondary data save time and money if they help solve the researcher's problem. Even if the problem is not solved, secondary data have other advantages. They can aid in formulating the problem statement and suggest research methods and other types of data needed for solving the problem. In addition, secondary data can pinpoint the kinds of people to approach and their locations and serve as a basis of comparison for other data. The disadvantages of secondary data stem mainly from a mismatch between the researcher's unique problem and the purpose for which the secondary data were originally gathered, which are typically different. For example, a company wanted to determine the market potential for a fireplace log made of coal rather than compressed wood by-products. The researcher found plenty of secondary data about total wood consumed as fuel, quantities consumed in each state, and types of wood burned. Secondary data were also available about consumer attitudes and purchase patterns of wood by-product fireplace logs. The wealth of secondary data provided the researcher with many insights into the artificial log market. Yet nowhere was there any information that would tell the firm whether consumers would buy artificial logs made of coal.

The quality of secondary data may also pose a problem. Often, secondary data sources do not give detailed information that would enable a researcher to assess their quality or relevance. Whenever possible, a researcher needs to address these important questions: Who gathered the data? Why were the data obtained? What methodology was used? How were classifications (such as heavy users versus light users) developed and defined? When was the information gathered?

THE GROWING IMPORTANCE OF SOCIAL MEDIA DATA Facebook owns and controls data collected from 1.1 billion daily users and 1.55 billion monthly active users.[6] The user databases of social media sites like Twitter, Pinterest, and Facebook tell these companies' marketers a lot about who you are and what you are like, though often on an anonymous basis.

In an effort to expand its information databases even further, Facebook now combines its social data with third-party information from data brokerages like Acxiom, Datalogix, and Alliance Data Systems. Using data collected from loyalty card programs and other mechanisms, these firms aggregate information about which items and brands consumers buy. Using software that obscures identifying information (such as e-mail addresses and phone numbers), they then combine their databases with Facebook's and group users based on certain combinations of data. This data includes the websites that Facebook members visit, e-mail lists they may have signed up for, and the ways they spend money, both online and offline—among many, many other metrics.[7] General Motors uses this new type of data synthesis to target younger buyers who might be interested in its Chevrolet Sonic. Pepsi uses it to show different ads based on whether a user regularly buys Pepsi, Diet Pepsi, or is a Pepsi switcher (i.e., a person who tends to switch soda brands and is more price sensitive).

Another new Facebook tool allows advertisers to calculate their *return on investment* (total profit minus expenses divided by the investment made) on Facebook ads by tallying the actions taken by ad viewers. These actions include click-throughs, registrations, shopping cart checkouts, and other metrics. The tool also enables marketers to deliver ads to people who are most likely to make further purchases.[8]

Facebook has shifted much of its focus from tracking cookies (small files stored on users' machines that track online activity) to Facebook logins. The goal of this shift is to improve ad targeting by associating views with a person's account instead of a particular device or IP address. (A number of people might use the same computer, but each likely has his or her own Facebook account.) This move has helped Facebook ensure that the 2.5 million advertisers who buy views from specific age groups and/or genders actually reach the people they want to. According to Facebook, advertisers now

If you see these buttons, Facebook may be tracking your browsing history—whether you click on them or not.

reach their intended targets 89 percent of the time. Across Internet ad networks, the average is about 55 percent.[9]

Facebook has also begun using the like and share buttons embedded in non-Facebook websites to track peoples' browsing histories so it can more accurately and narrowly target ads. This tracking ability doesn't even require someone to click the buttons—the embedded code passively watches and records browsing behavior.[10]

THE INCREDIBLE WORLD OF BIG DATA Big data is the exponential growth in the volume, variety, and velocity of information and the development of complex new tools to analyze and create meaning from such data. In the past, the flow of data was slow, steady, and predictable. All data was quantitative (countable)—many firms collected sales numbers by store, by product line, and at most, perhaps by a few other measures. Today, data is constantly streaming in from social media, as well as other sources. Advanced big data databases allow the analysis of unstructured data such as e-mails, audio files, and YouTube videos.

In 2016, real-time advertising auctions were estimated to account for a third of the $25 billion spent on digital display advertising in the United States.[11] Big data enables these auctions to take place in mere seconds. For example, suppose a bored woman sits waiting in an airline lounge. She scrolls through her iPhone and taps on a brightly colored icon to launch a free mobile game. In the instant before the app loads, predictive analytics firm Flurry collects data about the woman: here we have a new mother, business traveler, fashion follower, in her late 20s, and somewhere near JFK airport. Flurry then holds an automated auction among potential advertisers to fill an ad space that displays while the app is loading. In a fraction of a second, the mobile ad exchange picks the highest bidder with the best-fitting parameters, and the woman's screen flashes to an ad for Maui Jim sunglasses.[12]

Big data is gathered both online and offline. Even if data are collected and entered into databases manually, big data tool sets allow companies to catalog customer attributes and analyze which characteristics they have in common. Lattice Engines, for instance, used a small amount of big data to find that a determining factor in whether a prospect was in the market for a new router from Juniper Networks was if the prospect had recently signed a lease for new office space—a non-intuitive attribute that never would have been discovered without big data analysis.[13]

Along with advanced data analysis tools came a software program called Hadoop, developed by Apache and named for a child's toy elephant. Traditionally, complex computer programs had to run on huge, expensive mainframe computers. Hadoop allows queries to be split up and run much more efficiently. Using Hadoop, different analytic tasks are distributed among numerous inexpensive computer servers, each of which solves part of the problem before reassembling the queries when the work is finished. Thus, with the aid of modern databases, software, and hardware, big data can be analyzed faster and cheaper than ever before.[14]

The ability to crunch numbers means nothing, however, if humans cannot use or even access that information. Most people cannot remember a string of numbers longer than their phone numbers. Modern databases sometimes contain billions of pieces of data, so the question quickly arose as to how big data could be presented in a meaningful way. The answer to this question is data visualization. Visualization acts as an engine for bringing patterns to light—even the subtlest of patterns woven into the largest of data sets. It also enables managers to share, describe, and explain what big data has uncovered.

> **big data** the exponential growth in the volume, variety, and velocity of information and the development of complex, new tools to analyze and create meaning from such data

Jeopardy! champions Ken Jennings (left) and Brad Rutter face off against IBM's Watson.

Specialty women's apparel retailer Chicos uses big data analytics to find key brand influencers online and to determine how brand-related conversations impact sales. Sprint's Virgin Mobile uses analytics to tailor specific phone offers to particular customer types. For example, one effort promoted higher-end contract-free smartphones to individuals who could afford the monthly contractual plan but were likely to prefer the company's prepaid option. This offer resulted in increased customer retention and higher profits for Virgin Mobile. Online automotive market Edmunds.com uses big data analytics to help auto dealers predict how long a given car will remain on their lots. This helps dealers minimize the number of days a car remains unsold. Macy's adjusts pricing in near-real time for 73 million items based on demand and inventory. Walmart uses big data, including semantic search and synonym mining, to produce relevant search results for online shoppers. Semantic search improves purchase completion by 10 to 15 percent—a figure that is worth billions to Walmart.

One fast food chain is using cameras to determine what to display on its digital drive-through menu boards. When drive-through lines are longer, the menu board features products that can be served up quickly. When lines are shorter, the menu board features higher margin items that take longer to prepare. Similarly, the Los Angeles and Santa Cruz police departments are using big data to predict where crime will occur down to 500 square feet. Los Angeles has

seen a 33 percent reduction in burglary and a 21 percent reduction in violent crime in areas where the software is being used.[15]

A major U.S. wireless carrier recently began analyzing voice conversations—a difficult source of unstructured data—between customers and call reps. The carrier wanted to discover why customers were calling into service centers after making online payments. Using big data analytics, the internal team uncovered an answer that wasn't available by other means. As it turned out, customers wanted reassurance from a call rep that their services would not be interrupted due to a late payment. With this valuable insight, the carrier enacted a plan to proactively reassure customers that their payments would assure uninterrupted service. The result was an immediate drop in calls to customer service.

With big data analytics, this carrier can "listen to customers" in a way never before possible. By integrating and analyzing data like social posts and calls verbatim, the company has greatly enriched its individual customer portraits and service efforts. The company has also gained a significant advantage over competitors because it can quickly target communications and marketing efforts based on customer segments instead of making blind guesses and hoping for the best.[16]

Big data analytics focuses not only on gathering data, but also on learning and adapting based on that data. New cognitive (learning) analytic programs like IBM's Watson develop a deep understanding of information as it is gathered. Watson has already played against two former champions on the trivia game show Jeopardy—and won! Cognitive analytics answers questions like "What does your next potential customer look like?" and "What should you say to them to deliver a delightful experience and convert them to repeat buyers?" As trends change and people's behavior changes, Watson will learn and adapt over time. And it never forgets.[17]

9-2b Planning the Research Design and Gathering Primary Data

Good secondary data and big data can help researchers conduct a thorough situation analysis. With that information, researchers can list their unanswered questions

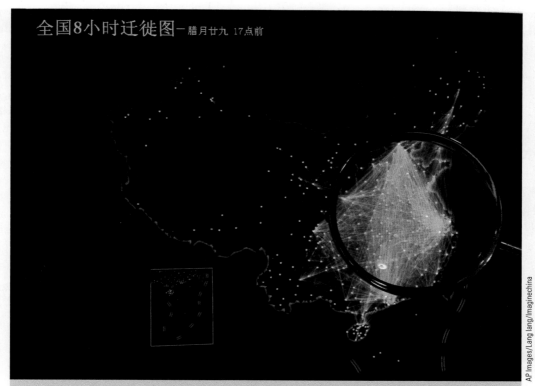

全国8小时迁徙图-腊月廿九 17点前

Baidu Migrate, a data visualization tool developed by China's largest search engine, uses smartphone data to track migration during the company's 40-day spring festival travel rush.

and rank them. Researchers must then decide the exact information required to answer the questions. The **research design** specifies which research questions must be answered, how and when the data will be gathered, and how the data will be analyzed. Typically, the project budget is finalized after the research design has been approved.

Sometimes research questions can be answered by gathering more secondary data; otherwise, primary data may be needed. **Primary data**, or information collected for the first time, are used for solving the particular problem under investigation. The main advantage of primary data is that they can answer specific research questions that secondary data cannot answer. Before training new flight attendants on passenger etiquette, airlines need to know what really irritates passengers. This primary data could help new flight attendants understand the behaviors that can quickly escalate into a problem. In a recent survey, Americans were asked to rank the most frustrating behaviors exhibited by fellow passengers. "Rear seat kickers" topped the list of most aggravating co-passengers (61 percent), followed by inattentive parents (59 percent), and passengers giving off a strong odor (50 percent). Three-quarters of Americans said that "small talk is fine" but they prefer to keep to themselves most of the flight. Sixteen percent said that they use flights as an "opportunity to meet and talk to new people"—a subgroup that 66 percent of Americans said they would "dread" sitting next to. Thirty-two percent of Americans said they would prefer to have reclining seats banned entirely or at least restricted to set times during short-haul flights, but only 31 percent of Americans refuse to recline their own seats.[18] Primary data are current, and researchers know the source. Sometimes researchers gather the data themselves rather than assign projects to outside companies. Researchers also specify the methodology of the research. Secrecy can be maintained because the information is proprietary. In contrast, much secondary data is available to all interested parties for relatively small fees or free.

research design specifies which research questions must be answered, how and when the data will be gathered, and how the data will be analyzed

primary data information that is collected for the first time; used for solving the particular problem under investigation

EXHIBIT 9.2 CHARACTERISTICS OF TRADITIONAL FORMS OF SURVEY RESEARCH

Characteristic	In-Home Personal Interviews	Mall Intercept Interviews	Central-Location Telephone Interviews	Self-Administered and One-Time Mail Surveys	Mail Panel Surveys	Executive Interviews	Focus Groups
Cost	High	Moderate	Moderate	Low	Moderate	High	Low
Time span	Moderate	Moderate	Fast	Slow	Relatively slow	Moderate	Fast
Use of interviewer probes	Yes	Yes	Yes	No	Yes	Yes	Yes
Ability to show concepts to respondent	Yes (also taste tests)	Yes (also taste tests)	No	Yes	Yes	Yes	Yes
Management control over interviewer	Low	Moderate	High	N/A	N/A	Moderate	High
General data quality	High	Moderate	High to moderate	Moderate to low	Moderate	High	Moderate
Ability to collect large amounts of data	High	Moderate	Moderate to low	Low to moderate	Moderate	Moderate	Moderate
Ability to handle complex questionnaires	High	Moderate	High, if computer aided	Low	Low	High	N/A

Gathering primary data can be expensive; costs can range from a few thousand dollars for a limited survey to several million for a nationwide study. For instance, a nationwide, 15-minute telephone interview with 1,000 adult males can cost $50,000 or more for everything, including a data analysis and report. Because primary data gathering is so expensive, many firms do not bother to conduct in-person interviews. Instead, they use the Internet. Larger companies that conduct many research projects use another cost-saving technique. They *piggyback studies*, or gather data on two different projects using one questionnaire. Nevertheless, the disadvantages of primary data gathering are usually offset by the advantages. It is often the only way of solving a research problem. And with a variety of techniques available for research—including surveys, observations, and experiments—primary research can address almost any marketing question.

SURVEY RESEARCH The most popular technique for gathering primary data is **survey research**, in which a researcher either interacts with people or posts a questionnaire

online to obtain facts, opinions, and attitudes. Exhibit 9.2 summarizes the characteristics of traditional forms of survey research.

In-Home Personal Interviews Although in-home personal interviews often provide high-quality information, they tend to be very expensive because of the interviewers' travel time and mileage costs. Therefore, they are rapidly disappearing from the American and European researchers' survey toolbox. They are, however, still popular in many less developed countries around the globe.

Mall Intercept Interviews The **mall intercept interview** is conducted in the common area of a shopping mall or in a market research office within the mall. To conduct this type of interview, the research firm rents office space in the mall or pays a significant daily fee. One drawback is that it is hard to get a representative sample of the population. One advantage is the ability of the interviewer to probe when necessary—a technique used to clarify a person's response and ask for more detailed information.

Mall intercept interviews must be brief. Only the shortest ones are conducted while respondents are standing. Often, researchers invite respondents into the office for interviews, which are still generally less than fifteen minutes long. The overall quality of mall

survey research the most popular technique for gathering primary data, in which a researcher interacts with people to obtain facts, opinions, and attitudes

mall intercept interview a survey research method that involves interviewing people in the common areas of shopping malls

intercept interviews is about the same as telephone interviews. They are often used to conduct taste tests that require respondents to sample several different products.

Marketing researchers use computer technology to speed the mall interview process. One technique is **computer-assisted personal interviewing**. The researcher conducts in-person interviews, reads questions to the respondent off a computer screen, and directly keys the respondent's answers into the computer. A second approach is **computer-assisted self-interviewing**. A mall interviewer intercepts and directs willing respondents to nearby computers. Each respondent reads questions off a computer screen and directly keys his or her answers into the computer. A third use of computer technology is fully automated self-interviewing. Respondents are guided by interviewers or independently approach a centrally located computer station or kiosk, read questions off a screen, and directly key their answers into the station's computer.

Telephone Interviews Telephone interviews cost less than personal interviews, but cost is rapidly increasing due to respondent refusals to participate. Most telephone interviewing is conducted from a specially designed phone room called a **central-location telephone (CLT) facility**.

A CLT facility has many phone lines, individual interviewing stations, headsets, and sometimes monitoring equipment. The research firm typically will interview people nationwide from a single location. The federal "Do Not Call" law does not apply to survey research.

Most CLT facilities offer computer-assisted interviewing. The interviewer reads the questions from a computer screen and enters the respondent's data directly into the computer, saving time. Hallmark Cards found that an interviewer administered a printed questionnaire for its Shoebox greeting cards in 28 minutes. The same questionnaire administered with computer assistance took only 18 minutes. The researcher can stop the survey at any point and immediately print out the survey results, allowing the research design to be refined as necessary.

MAIL SURVEYS Mail surveys have several benefits: relatively low cost, elimination of interviewers and field supervisors, centralized control, and actual or promised anonymity for respondents (which may draw more

candid responses). A disadvantage is that mail questionnaires usually produce low response rates. The resulting sample may therefore not represent the surveyed population. Another serious problem with mail surveys is that no one probes respondents to clarify or elaborate on their answers. If a respondent uses the word "convenience," there is no way to clarify exactly what he means. Convenience could refer to location, store hours, or a host of other factors.

Mail panels offer an alternative to the one-shot mail survey. A mail panel consists of a sample of households recruited to participate by mail for a given period. Panel members often receive gifts in return for their participation. Essentially, the panel is a sample used several times. In contrast to one-time mail surveys, the response rates from mail panels are high. Rates of 70 percent (of those who agree to participate) are not uncommon. One-shot mail surveys and mail panels have rapidly moved online.

Executive Interviews An **executive interview** usually involves interviewing businesspeople at their offices concerning industrial products or services, a process that is very expensive. First, individuals involved in the purchase decision for the product in question must be identified and located, which can itself be expensive and time-consuming. Once a qualified person is located, the next step is to get that person to agree to be interviewed and to set a time for the interview. Finally, an interviewer must go to the particular place at the appointed time. Long waits are frequently encountered; cancellations are not uncommon. This type of survey requires the very best interviewers because they are frequently interviewing on topics that they know very little about. Many of these interviews have also moved online.

computer-assisted personal interviewing an interviewing method in which the interviewer reads questions from a computer screen and enters the respondent's data directly into the computer

computer-assisted self-interviewing an interviewing method in which a mall interviewer intercepts and directs willing respondents to nearby computers where each respondent reads questions off a computer screen and directly keys his or her answers into the computer

central-location telephone (CLT) facility a specially designed phone room used to conduct telephone interviewing

executive interview a type of survey that usually involves interviewing business people at their offices concerning industrial products or services

Open-Ended Questions	Closed-Ended Questions	Scaled-Response Question
1. What advantages, if any, do you think ordering online offers compared to shopping at a local retail outlet? (*Probe*: What else?) 2. Why do you have one or more of your rugs or carpets professionally cleaned rather than cleaning them yourself or having someone else in the household clean them? 3. What is it about the color of the eye shadow that makes you like it the best?	**Dichotomous** 1. Did you heat the Danish product before serving It? Yes .... 1 No .... 2 2. The federal government doesn't care what people like me think. Agree .... 1 Disagree .... 2 **Multiple Choice** 1. I'd like you to think back to the last footwear of any kind that you bought. I'll read you a list of descriptions and would like for you to tell me which category they fall into. (*Read list and circle proper category.*) Dress and/or formal .... 1 Casual .... 2 Canvas/trainer /gym shoes .... 3 Specialized athletic shoes .... 4 Boots .... 5 2. In the last three months, have you used Noxzema skin cream .... (*Circle all that apply.*) As a facial wash .... 1 For moisturizing the skin .... 2 For treating blemishes .... 3 For cleansing the skin .... 4 For treating dry skin .... 5 For softening skin .... 6 For sunburn .... 7 For making the facial skin smooth 8	Now that you have used the rug cleaner, would you say that you . . . (*Circle one.*) Would definitely buy it .... 1 Would probably buy it .... 2 Might or might not buy it .... 3 Probably would not buy it .... 4 Definitely would not buy it 5

Focus Groups A **focus group** is a type of personal interviewing. Often recruited by random telephone screening, seven to ten people with certain desired characteristics form a focus group. These qualified consumers are usually offered an incentive (typically $30 to $50) to participate in a group discussion. The meeting place (sometimes resembling a living room, sometimes featuring a conference table) has audiotaping and perhaps videotaping equipment. It also likely has a viewing room with a one-way mirror so that clients (manufacturers or retailers) can watch the session. During the session, a moderator, hired by the research company, leads the group discussion. Focus groups can be used to gauge consumer response to a product or promotion and are occasionally used to brainstorm new-product ideas or to screen concepts for new products. Focus groups also represent an efficient way of learning how products are actually used in the home. Lewis Stone, former manager of Colgate-Palmolive's research and development division, says the following about focus groups:

If it weren't for focus groups, Colgate-Palmolive Co. might never know that some women squeeze their bottles of dishwashing soap, others squeeeeeze them, and still others squeeeeeeeeeze out the desired amount. Then there are the ones who use the soap 'neat.' That is, they put the product directly on a sponge or washcloth and wash the dishes under running water until the suds run out. Then they apply more detergent.

Stone was explaining how body language, exhibited during focus groups, provides insights into a product that are not apparent from reading questionnaires on habits and practices. Panelists' descriptions of how they perform tasks highlight need gaps, which can improve an existing product or demonstrate how a new product might be received.

QUESTIONNAIRE DESIGN All forms of survey research require a questionnaire. Questionnaires ensure that all respondents will be asked the same series of questions. Questionnaires include three basic types of questions: open-ended, closed-ended, and scaled-response (see Exhibit 9.3). An **open-ended question**

focus group seven to ten people who participate in a group discussion led by a moderator

open-ended question an interview question that encourages an answer phrased in the respondent's own words

encourages an answer phrased in the respondent's own words. Researchers get a rich array of information based on the respondent's frame of reference (What do you think about the new flavor?). In contrast, a **closed-ended question** asks the respondent to make a selection from a limited list of responses. Closed-ended questions can either be what marketing researchers call dichotomous (Do you like the new flavor? Yes or No.) or multiple choice. A **scaled-response question** is a closed-ended question designed to measure the intensity of a respondent's answer.

Closed-ended and scaled-response questions are easier to tabulate than open-ended questions because response choices are fixed. On the other hand, unless the researcher designs the closed-ended question very carefully, an important choice may be omitted. For example, suppose a food study asked this question: "Besides meat, which of the following items do you normally add to tacos that you prepare at home?"

Avocado	1	Olives (black/green)	6
Cheese (Monterey Jack/cheddar)	2	Onions (red/white)	7
Guacamole	3	Peppers (red/green)	8
Lettuce	4	Pimiento	9
Mexican hot sauce	5	Sour cream	0

The list seems complete, doesn't it? However, consider the following responses: "I usually add a green, avocado-tasting hot sauce," "I cut up a mixture of lettuce and spinach," "I'm a vegetarian—I don't use meat at all," and "My taco is filled only with guacamole." How would you code these replies? As you can see, the question needs an "other" category.

A good question must be clear and concise and avoid ambiguous language. The answer to the question "Do you live within ten minutes of here?" depends on the mode of transportation (maybe the person walks), driving speed, perceived time, and other factors. Language should also be clear. As such, jargon should be avoided, and wording should be geared to the target audience. A question such as "What is the level of efficacy of your preponderant dishwasher powder?" would probably be greeted by a lot of blank stares. It would be much simpler to say "Are you (1) very satisfied, (2) somewhat satisfied, or (3) not satisfied with your current brand of dishwasher powder?"

Stating the survey's purpose at the beginning of the interview may improve clarity, but it may also increase the chances of receiving biased responses.

Many times, respondents will try to provide answers that they believe are "correct" or that the interviewer wants to hear. To avoid bias at the question level, researchers should avoid leading questions and adjectives that cause respondents to think of the topic in a certain way.

Finally, to ensure clarity, the interviewer should avoid asking two questions in one—for example, "How did you like the taste and texture of the Pepperidge Farm coffee cake?" This should be divided into two questions, one concerning taste and the other texture.

OBSERVATION RESEARCH In contrast to survey research, **observation research** entails watching what people do or using machines to watch what people do. Specifically, it can be defined as the systematic process of recording the behavioral patterns of people, objects, and occurrences without questioning them. A market researcher using the observation technique witnesses and records information as events occur or compiles evidence from records of past events. Carried a step further, observation may involve watching people or phenomena and may be conducted by human observers or machines. Examples of these various observational situations are shown in Exhibit 9.4.

Some common forms of people-watching-people research are one-way mirror observations, mystery shoppers, and behavioral targeting. A one-way mirror allows the researchers to see the participants, but the participants cannot see the researchers.

Mystery Shoppers **Mystery shoppers** are researchers posing as customers who gather observational data about a store (for example, are the shelves neatly stocked?) and collect data about customer/employee interactions. The interaction is not an interview, and communication occurs only so that the mystery shopper can observe the actions and comments of the employee. Mystery shopping is, therefore, classified as an observational marketing research method even though communication is often involved. Restaurant chains like Subway use mystery shoppers to evaluate store cleanliness and quality of service.

closed-ended question an interview question that asks the respondent to make a selection from a limited list of responses

scaled-response question a closed-ended question designed to measure the intensity of a respondent's answer

observation research a research method that relies on four types of observation: people watching people, people watching an activity, machines watching people, and machines watching an activity

mystery shoppers researchers posing as customers who gather observational data about a store

EXHIBIT 9.4 OBSERVATIONAL SITUATIONS

Situation	Example
People watching people	Observers stationed in supermarkets watch consumers select frozen Mexican dinners; the purpose is to see how much comparison shopping people do at the point of purchase.
People watching an activity	An observer stationed at an intersection counts traffic moving in various directions.
Machines watching people	Movie or videotape cameras record behavior as in the people-watching-people example above.
Machines watching an activity	Traffic-counting machines monitor traffic flow.

Behavioral Targeting Behavioral targeting (BT), sometimes simply called tracking, began as a simple process by placing cookies in users' browsers or mobile apps to track which websites they visited, how long they lingered, what they searched for, and what they bought. All of this information can be tracked anonymously—a "fly on the wall" perspective. While survey research is a great way to find out the "why" and the "how," behavioral targeting lets the researcher find out the "how much," the "how often," and the "where." Also, through **social media monitoring**, using automated tools to monitor online buzz, chatter, and conversations, a researcher can learn what is being said about the brand and the competition. Tracking is the basis for input into online databases. Companies like Tapad track customers across multiple devices—personal desktop computers, laptops, smartphones, and tablets, for example. If a customer is using multiple devices at the same time, Tapad knows, and knows what she is doing on each.

behavioral targeting (BT) a form of observation marketing research that combines a consumer's online activity with psychographic and demographic profiles compiled in databases

social media monitoring the use of automated tools to monitor online buzz, chatter, and conversations

ethnographic research the study of human behavior in its natural context; involves observation of behavior and physical setting

ETHNOGRAPHIC RESEARCH Ethnographic research comes to marketing from the field of anthropology. The technique is becoming increasingly popular in marketing research. **Ethnographic research**, or the study of human behavior in its natural context, involves observation of behavior and physical setting. Ethnographers directly observe the population they are studying. As "participant observers," ethnographers can use their intimacy with the people they are studying to gain richer, deeper insights into culture and behavior—in short, what makes people do what they do?

Managers at Cambridge SoundWorks recently faced a perplexing problem. Male customers stood wide-eyed and wallets-ready when sales reps showed off the company's hi-fi "blow-your-hair-back" stereo speakers in retail outlets across the country, but sales were slumping. Why didn't such unabashed enthusiasm for the product translate into more—and bigger ticket—sales?

To find out, the Andover, Massachusetts-based stereo equipment manufacturer and retailer hired research firm Design Continuum to follow a dozen prospective customers over the course of two weeks. After the two weeks were up, the researchers concluded that the high-end speaker market suffered from something they referred to as "the spouse acceptance factor." While men adored the big black boxes, women hated their unsightly appearance. Concerned about how speakers might look in the living room, women frequently talked their husbands out of buying the cool (but hideous) stereo equipment. Even those who purchased the products had trouble showing them off. Men would attempt to display the loudspeakers as trophies in their living rooms while women would hide them behind plants, vases, and chairs. "Women would come into the store, look at the speakers, and say, 'that thing is ugly,'" said principal at Design Continuum Ellen Di Resta. "The men would lose the argument and leave the store without a stereo. The solution was to give the target market what men and women *both* wanted: a great sound system that looks like furniture so you don't have to hide it."

Armed with this knowledge, Cambridge SoundWorks unveiled a new line of spouse-friendly speakers. The furniture-like Newton Series of speakers and home theater systems comes in an array of colors and finishes. The result? The Newton Series is the fastest-growing and best-selling product line in Cambridge SoundWorks' history.[19]

VIRTUAL SHOPPING Advances in computer technology have enabled researchers to simulate an actual retail store environment on a computer screen. Depending on the type of simulation, a shopper can "pick up" a package by touching its image on the monitor and rotate it to examine all sides. Like buying on most online retailers, the shopper touches the shopping cart to add an item to the basket. During the shopping process, the computer unobtrusively records the amount of time the consumer

As consumer-grade virtual reality headsets grow in popularity, virtual shopping will likely become a reality for the average person.

spends shopping in each product category, the time the consumer spends examining each side of a product, the quantity of the product the consumer purchases, and the order in which items are purchased.

A major apparel retailer using a computer simulated environment recently found that men have trouble putting outfits together. Men also hesitate to pick up clothing items because they can't fold them back the same way. With this knowledge, the apparel chain made two major changes: it began selling items together as complete outfit solutions and folded shirts and other clothes more simply. Sales of men's clothes increased by 40 percent.[20]

Virtual shopping research is growing rapidly. According to the U.S. Department of Agriculture, approximately 50,000 new consumer packaged goods are introduced each year.[21] All are vying for very limited retail shelf space. Any process, such as virtual shopping, that can speed product development time and lower costs is always welcomed by manufacturers. Some companies outside of retail have even begun experimenting with virtual shopping and other simulated environment tools—many telecom, financial, automotive, aviation, and fast-food companies are using such tools to better serve their customers.

EXPERIMENTS An **experiment** is a method a researcher can use to gather primary data. The researcher alters one or more variables—price, package design, shelf space, advertising theme, advertising expenditures—while observing the effects of those alterations on another variable (usually sales). The best experiments are those in which all factors except one are held constant. The researcher can then observe what changes in sales, for example, result from changes in the amount of money spent on advertising.

Holding all other factors constant in the external environment is a monumental and costly, if not impossible, task. Such factors as competitors' actions, weather, and economic conditions are beyond the researcher's control. Yet market researchers have ways to account for the ever-changing external environment. Mars, the candy company, was losing sales to other candy companies. Traditional surveys showed that the shrinking candy bar was not perceived as a good value. Mars wondered whether a bigger bar sold at the same price would increase sales enough to offset the higher ingredient costs. The company designed an experiment in which the marketing mix stayed the same in different markets but the size of the candy bar varied. The substantial increase in sales of the bigger bar quickly proved that the additional costs would be more than covered by the additional revenue. Mars increased the bar size—along with its market share and profits.

9-2c Specifying the Sampling Procedures

Once the researchers decide how they will collect primary data, their next step is to select the sampling procedures they will use. A firm can seldom take a census of all possible users of a new product, nor can they all be interviewed. Therefore, a firm must select a sample of the group to be interviewed. A **sample** is a subset from a larger population.

Several questions must be answered before a sampling plan is chosen. First, the population, or **universe**, of interest must be defined. This is the group from which the sample will be drawn. It should include all the people whose opinions, behavior, preferences, attitudes, and so on, are of interest to the marketer. For example, in a study whose purpose is to determine the market for a new canned dog food, the universe might be defined to include all current buyers of canned dog food.

After the universe has been defined, the next question is whether the sample must be representative of the population. If the answer is yes, a probability sample is needed. Otherwise, a non-probability sample might be considered.

experiment a method of gathering primary data in which the researcher alters one or more variables while observing the effects of those alterations on another variable

sample a subset from a larger population

universe the population from which a sample will be drawn

SAMPLE → ← UNIVERSE

Artush/Shutterstock.com

Guy Shapira/Shutterstock.com

PROBABILITY SAMPLES A **probability sample** is a sample in which every element in the population has a known statistical likelihood of being selected. Its most desirable feature is that scientific rules can be used to ensure that the sample represents the population.

> **probability sample** a sample in which every element in the population has a known statistical likelihood of being selected
>
> **random sample** a sample arranged in such a way that every element of the population has an equal chance of being selected as part of the sample
>
> **nonprobability sample** any sample in which little or no attempt is made to get a representative cross section of the population
>
> **convenience sample** a form of nonprobability sample using respondents who are convenient or readily accessible to the researcher—for example, employees, friends, or relatives
>
> **measurement error** an error that occurs when there is a difference between the information desired by the researcher and the information provided by the measurement process
>
> **sampling error** an error that occurs when a sample somehow does not represent the target population
>
> **frame error** an error that occurs when a sample drawn from a population differs from the target population
>
> **random error** an error that occurs when the selected sample is an imperfect representation of the overall population

One type of probability sample is a **random sample**—a sample arranged in such a way that every element of the population has an equal chance of being selected as part of the sample. For example, suppose a university is interested in getting a cross section of student opinions on a proposed sports complex to be built using student activity fees. If the university can acquire an up-to-date list of all the enrolled students, it can draw a random sample by using random numbers from a table (found in most statistics books) to select students from the list. Common forms of probability and nonprobability samples are shown in Exhibit 9.5.

NONPROBABILITY SAMPLES Any sample in which little or no attempt is made to get a representative cross section of the population can be considered a **nonprobability sample**. Therefore, the probability of selection of each sampling unit is not known. A common form of a nonprobability sample is the **convenience sample**, which uses respondents who are convenient or readily accessible to the researcher—for instance, employees, friends, or relatives.

Nonprobability samples are acceptable as long as the researcher understands their nonrepresentative nature. Because of their lower cost, nonprobability samples are sometimes used in marketing research.

TYPES OF ERRORS Whenever a sample is used in marketing research, two major types of errors may occur: measurement error and sampling error. **Measurement error** occurs when there is a difference between the information desired by the researcher and the information provided by the measurement process. For example, people may tell an interviewer that they purchase Crest toothpaste when they do not. Measurement error generally tends to be larger than sampling error.

Sampling error occurs when a sample somehow does not represent the target population. Sampling error can be one of several types. Nonresponse error occurs when the sample actually interviewed differs from the sample drawn. This error happens because the original people selected to be interviewed either refused to cooperate or were inaccessible.

Frame error, another type of sampling error, arises if the sample drawn from a population differs from the target population. For instance, suppose a telephone survey is conducted to find out Chicago beer drinkers' attitudes toward Coors. If a Chicago telephone directory is used as the *frame* (the device or list from which the respondents are selected), the survey will contain a frame error. Not all Chicago beer drinkers have landline phones, and many phone numbers are unlisted. An ideal sample (in other words, a sample with no frame error) matches all important characteristics of the target population to be surveyed. Could you find a perfect frame for Chicago beer drinkers?

Random error occurs when the selected sample is an imperfect representation of the overall population.

EXHIBIT 9.5 TYPES OF SAMPLES

Probability Samples	
Simple Random Sample	Every member of the population has a known and equal chance of selection.
Stratified Sample	The population is divided into mutually exclusive groups (such as gender or age); then random samples are drawn from each group.
Cluster Sample	The population is divided into mutually exclusive groups (such as geographic areas); then a random sample of clusters is selected. The researcher then collects data from all the elements in the selected clusters or from a probability sample of elements within each selected cluster.
Systematic Sample	A list of the population is obtained—e.g., all persons with a checking account at XYZ Bank—and a skip interval is obtained by dividing the sample size by the population size. If the sample size is 100 and the bank has 1,000 customers, then the skip interval is 10. The beginning number is randomly chosen within the skip interval. If the beginning number is 8, then the skip pattern would be 8, 18, 28, ...
Nonprobability Samples	
Convenience Sample	The researcher selects the easiest population members from which to obtain information.
Judgment Sample	The researcher's selection criteria are based on personal judgment that the elements (persons) chosen will likely give accurate information.
Quota Sample	The researcher finds a prescribed number of people in several categories—e.g., owners of large dogs versus owners of small dogs. Respondents are not selected on probability sampling criteria.
Snowball Sample	Additional respondents are selected on the basis of referrals from the initial respondents. This method is used when a desired type of respondent is hard to find—e.g., persons who have taken round-the-world cruises in the last three years. This technique employs the old adage "Birds of a feather flock together."

Random error represents how accurately the chosen sample's true average (mean) value reflects the population's true average (mean) value. For example, we might take a random sample of beer drinkers in Chicago and find that 16 percent regularly drink Coors beer. The next day, we might repeat the same sampling procedure and discover that 14 percent regularly drink Coors beer. The difference is due to random error. Error is common to all surveys, yet it is often not reported or is underreported. Typically, the only error mentioned in a written report is sampling error.

9-2d Collecting the Data

Marketing research field service firms are used to collect some primary data. A **field service firm** specializes in interviewing respondents on a subcontracted basis. Many have offices, often in malls, throughout the country. A typical marketing research study involves data collection in several cities, which may require the marketer to work with a comparable number of field service firms. Besides conducting interviews, field service firms provide focus group facilities, mall intercept locations, test product storage, and kitchen facilities to prepare test food products.

9-2e Analyzing the Data

After collecting the data, the marketing researcher proceeds to the next step in the research process: data analysis. The purpose of this analysis is to interpret and draw conclusions from the mass of collected data. The marketing researcher tries to organize and analyze those data by using one or more techniques common to marketing research: one-way frequency counts, cross-tabulations, and more sophisticated statistical analysis. Of these three techniques, one-way frequency counts are the simplest. One-way frequency tables simply record the responses to a question. For example, the answers to the question "What brand of microwave popcorn do you buy most often?" would provide a one-way frequency distribution. One-way frequency tables are always done in data analysis, at least as a first step, because they provide the researcher with a general picture of the study's results. A **cross-tabulation** lets the analyst look at the responses to one question in relation to the responses to one or more other questions. For example, in Exhibit 9.6, what is the association between gender and the brand of microwave popcorn bought most frequently?

Researchers can use many other more powerful and sophisticated statistical techniques, such as hypothesis testing, measures of association, and

field service firm a firm that specializes in interviewing respondents on a subcontracted basis

cross-tabulation a method of analyzing data that lets the analyst look at the responses to one question in relation to the responses to one or more other questions

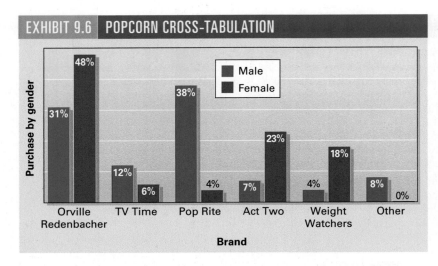

EXHIBIT 9.6 POPCORN CROSS-TABULATION

Purchase by gender

Male
Female

Orville Redenbacher: 31% / 48%
TV Time: 12% / 6%
Pop Rite: 38% / 4%
Act Two: 7% / 23%
Weight Watchers: 4% / 18%
Other: 8% / 0%

Brand

regression analysis. A description of these techniques goes beyond the scope of this book but can be found in any good marketing research textbook. The use of sophisticated statistical techniques depends on the researchers' objectives and the nature of the data gathered.

9-2f Preparing and Presenting the Report

After data analysis has been completed, the researcher must prepare the report and communicate the conclusions and recommendations to management. This is a key step in the process. If the marketing researcher wants managers to carry out the recommendations, he or she must convince them that the results are credible and justified by the data collected.

Researchers are usually required to present both written and oral reports on the project. Today, the written report is often no more than a copy of the PowerPoint slides used in the oral presentation. Both reports should be tailored to the audience. They should begin with a clear, concise statement of the research objectives, followed by a complete but brief and simple explanation of the research design or methodology employed. A summary of major findings should come next. The conclusion of the report should also present recommendations to management.

Most people who enter marketing will become research users rather than research suppliers. Thus, they must know what to notice in a report. As with many other items we purchase, quality is not always readily apparent. Nor does a high price guarantee superior quality. The basis for measuring the quality of a marketing research report is the research proposal. Did the report meet the objectives established in the proposal? Was the methodology outlined in the proposal followed? Are the conclusions based on logical deductions from the data analysis? Do the recommendations seem prudent, given the conclusions?

9-2g Following Up

The final step in the marketing research process is to follow up. The researcher should determine why management did or did not carry out the recommendations in the report. Was sufficient decision-making information included? What could have been done to make the report more useful to management? A good rapport between the product manager, or whoever authorized the project, and the market researcher is essential. Often, they must work together on many studies throughout the year.

9-3 THE PROFOUND IMPACT OF THE INTERNET ON MARKETING RESEARCH

More than 90 percent of U.S. marketing research companies conduct some form of online research. Paper questionnaires are going the way of the horse and buggy in marketing research Online survey research has replaced computer-assisted telephone interviewing as the most popular mode of data collection. The majority of online research is done through incentivized panels (discussed later in the chapter).

9-3a Advantages of Internet Surveys

The huge growth in the popularity of Internet surveys is the result of the many advantages offered by the Internet. The specific advantages of Internet surveys, which are often sent to mobile devices, are many:

- **Rapid development, real-time reporting:** Internet surveys can be broadcast to thousands of potential respondents simultaneously. Respondents complete surveys simultaneously; then results are tabulated and posted for corporate clients to view as the returns arrive. The effect: survey results can be in a client's hands in significantly less time than would be required for traditional paper surveys.

- **Dramatically reduced costs:** The Internet can cut costs by 25 to 40 percent and provide results in half the time it takes to do traditional telephone surveys. Traditional survey methods are labor-intensive efforts incurring training, telecommunications, and management costs. Electronic methods eliminate these completely. While costs for traditional survey techniques rise proportionally with the number of interviews desired, electronic solicitations can grow in volume with little increase in project costs.

- **Personalized questions and data:** Internet surveys can be highly personalized for greater relevance to each respondent's own situation, thus speeding the response process.

- **Improved respondent participation:** Internet surveys take half as much time to complete as phone interviews, can be accomplished at the respondent's convenience (for example, after work hours), and are much more stimulating and engaging. As a result, Internet surveys enjoy much higher response rates.

- **Contact with the hard-to-reach:** Certain groups—doctors, high-income professionals, top management in Global 2000 firms—are among the most surveyed on the planet and the most difficult to reach. Many of these groups are well represented online. Internet surveys provide convenient anytime/anywhere access that makes it easy for busy professionals to participate.

9-3b Uses of the Internet by Marketing Researchers

Marketing researchers use the Internet to administer surveys, conduct focus groups, and perform a variety of other types of marketing research.

METHODS OF CONDUCTING ONLINE SURVEYS
There are several basic methods for conducting online surveys: web survey systems, survey design and web hosting sites, and online panel providers.

Web Survey Systems
Web survey systems are software systems specifically designed for web questionnaire construction and delivery. They consist of an integrated questionnaire designer, web server, database, and data delivery program designed for use by nonprogrammers.

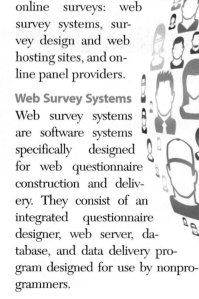

iStockphoto.com/bgblue

The web server distributes the questionnaire and files responses in a database. The user can query the server at any time via the Web for completion statistics, descriptive statistics on responses, and graphical displays of data. Some popular online survey research software packages are Sawtooth CiW, Infopoll, SurveyMonkey, and SurveyPro.

Google Consumer Surveys Google, with more than a billion unique visitors worldwide, has entered the do-it-yourself web survey arena. It does this in a rather unique manner; see www.google.com/insights/consumersurveys/home. Certain websites host premium content that usually requires a subscription or access fee. With Google Consumer Surveys, however, a visitor can gain access to the premium content by answering a couple of questions instead of paying the fee. Surveys are limited to ten questions. The first is typically a screening question such as, "Have you purchased anything online in the past ninety days?" The remaining questions are more substantive, such as "Which promotion would you be most interested in—free shipping, 15 percent off, free returns, or saving $25 on your next purchase of $150?" Basic demographic and location information are inferred from Google's big data database. Google Consumer Surveys are fast and cheap, and the Pew Research Center has found that Google's sample both conforms closely to the overall Internet population and is not biased toward heavy Internet users.[22]

Online Panel Providers Often, researchers use online panel providers for a ready-made sample population. Online panel providers such as Survey Sampling International and e-Rewards pre-recruit people who agree to participate in online market research surveys.

Some online panels are created for specific industries and may have a few thousand panel members, while the large commercial online panels have millions of people waiting to be surveyed. When people join online panels, they answer an extensive profiling questionnaire that enables the panel provider to target research efforts to panel members who meet specific criteria.

Some critics of online panels suggest that they are not representative of the target population. Others claim that offering incentives to join a panel leads to bias and misleading results. One such critic called online panels "a club of people who signed up to take point-and-click surveys for points redeemable for cash and gifts."[23] Online panel researchers contend that they use a number of interventions to detect poor quality online surveys. These include speed detection, straight-line response detection, challenge questions, IP address location checking, digital fingerprinting to identify multiple registrations, and analysis of aggregate responses.

ONLINE FOCUS GROUPS A number of research firms are currently conducting focus groups online. The process is fairly simple. The research firm builds a database of respondents via a screening questionnaire on its website. When a client comes to a firm with a need for a particular focus group, the firm goes to its database and identifies individuals who appear to qualify. It sends an e-mail to these individuals, asking them to log on to a particular site at a particular time scheduled for the group. Many times, these groups are joined by respondents on mobile devices. The firm pays them an incentive for their participation.

The firm develops a discussion guide similar to the one used for a conventional focus group, and a moderator runs the group by typing in questions online for all to see. The group operates in an environment similar to that of a chat room so that all participants see all questions and all responses. The firm captures the complete text of the focus group and makes it available for review after the group has finished.

Online focus groups also allow respondents to view things such as a concept statement, a mockup of a print ad, or a short product demonstration video. The moderator simply provides a URL for the respondents to go to in another browser window.

More advanced virtual focus group software reserves a frame (section) of the screen for stimuli to be shown. Here, the moderator has control over what is shown in the stimulus area. Many online groups are now conducted with audio and video feeds as well. One advantage of this approach is that the respondent does not have to do any work to see the stimuli. There are many other advantages of online groups:

- **Better participation rates:** Typically, online focus groups can be conducted over the course of days; once participants are recruited, they are less likely to pull out due to time conflicts.

- **Cost-effectiveness:** Face-to-face focus groups incur costs for facility rental, airfare, hotel, and food. None of these costs is incurred with online focus groups.

- **Broad geographic scope:** Time is flexible online; respondents can be gathered from all over the world.

- **Accessibility:** Online focus groups allow access to individuals who otherwise might be difficult to recruit (for example, business travelers, senior executives, mothers with infants).

WEB COMMUNITY RESEARCH A web community is a carefully selected group of consumers who agree to participate in an ongoing dialogue with a particular corporation. All community interaction takes place on a custom-designed website. During the life of the community—which may last anywhere from six months to a

Benefits of Web Community Research

The popularity and marketing power of web communities stems from several key benefits:

- Provide cost-effective, flexible research.
- Help companies create customer-focused organizations by putting employees into direct contact with consumers.
- Achieve customer-derived innovation.
- Establish brand advocates who are emotionally invested in a company's success.
- Engage customers in a space where they are comfortable, allowing clients to interact with them on a deeper level.
- Offer real-time results, enabling clients to explore ideas that normal time constraints prohibit.

year or more—community members respond to questions posed by the corporation on a regular basis. In addition to responding to the corporation's questions, community members talk to one another about topics that are of interest to them.

Hyatt used a community of travel enthusiasts from the United States, Britain, France, Australia, Chile, and Mexico to gain insights about various travel-related topics. Hyatt learned, for example, that sampling local cuisine is one of the best parts of business travelers' trips, and that women do the majority of packing for family vacations. After several travelers expressed an interest in selecting their rooms online, Hyatt launched an initiative examining what it might take to add that functionality to its system. When Procter & Gamble (P&G) was developing scents for a new product line, it asked members of its online community to record the scents that they encountered over the course of a day that made them feel good. By week's end, P&G had received images, videos, and simple text tributes to cut grass, fresh paint, Play Dough, and other aromas that revealed volumes about how scent triggers not just nostalgia, but also feelings of competence, adventurousness, comfort, and other powerful emotions.[24]

9-4 THE GROWING IMPORTANCE OF MOBILE RESEARCH

Although desktop and laptop computers are the primary devices used for completing online research, the picture is changing rapidly. Mobile survey traffic now accounts for approximately 30 percent of interview responses. Nearly one in four mobile surveys are taken outside of the home—often at work.[25]

Mobile surveys are designed to fit into the brief cracks of time that open up when a person waits for a plane, is early for an appointment, commutes to work on a train, or stands in a line. Marketers strive to engage respondents "in the moment" because mobile research provides immediate feedback when a consumer makes a decision to purchase, consumes a product, or experiences some form of promotion. As new and better apps make the survey experience easier and more intuitive, the use of mobile surveys will continue to rise. As screen size decreases, so do survey completion rates. Seventy-six percent of surveys are completed on desktop; 70 percent on tablet; and 59 percent on mobile phone.[26] New responsive design technology automatically adjusts the content and navigation of a website to fit the dimensions and resolution of any screen it is viewed on.[27]

Nearly one in four mobile surveys are taken outside of the home—often at work.

One advertiser wanted to conduct a survey on the televised advertisements that ran during the Super Bowl. The client wanted to measure real-time reactions, but most people do not sit in front of their desktop computers during the big game. They do, however, multitask using their smartphones. Respondents were recruited in advance of game day, and then during the game, surveys were pushed out in real time to collect feedback on commercials as they aired.[28]

An *ethnography shop-along* used to mean accompanying a participant on a shopping trip, but with today's mobile qualitative research tools, shop-alongs can be completely self-guided. Mondelez Canada recently set out to launch Potato Thins, a low-calorie snack food, in the United States. Potato Thins are packaged in a resealable pouch, differentiating the product and allowing customers to consume small portions of the bag at a time. Before the launch, Mondelez Canada set up a research experiment to determine which grocery store shelf location would give Potato Thins the biggest boost. The key concern for Mondelez was to learn about shoppers' logic and motivations when it comes to in-store navigation and healthy snacking. Survey participants were sent on a "snacking safari" whereby they recorded their shopping and purchase habits by taking photos on their mobile devices. Researchers found that consumers demonstrated one of two distinct behaviors when shopping for snacks—hunting or browsing.

When hunting, consumers tended to ignore signage, as they knew which aisles to head for. When browsing, participants went up and down the aisles of the store, gathering the items they needed and keeping an eye out for new items.[29]

After the shopping safari, respondents were introduced to Potato Thins. Researchers asked whether they should be placed in the chip or cracker aisle, and the majority of participants picked the cracker aisle. One participant said, "I could see them in the snack food area, close to the chips. However, I would likely miss purchasing them, as I tend to avoid going down that aisle as it's too tempting and not healthy. So I suppose that it would be better to merchandise them close to the crackers." Researchers also concluded that the bag may look out of place on the chip aisle due to its size. One participant said, "The size of the package is quite small, so if you wanted to serve these rather than regular chips you would have to purchase quite a number of packages."[30]

9-5 SCANNER-BASED RESEARCH

Scanner-based research is a system for gathering information from respondents by continuously monitoring the advertising, promotion, and pricing they are exposed to and the things they buy. Scanner-based research also entails the aggregation of scanner data from retailers, analysis, and identification of sales trends by industry, company, product line, and individual brand. The variables measured are advertising campaigns, coupons, displays, and product prices. The result is a huge database of marketing efforts and consumer behavior.

The two major scanner-based suppliers are SymphonyIRI Group Inc. and the Nielsen Company. Each has about half of the market, but SymphonyIRI is the founder of scanner-based research.[31] SymphonyIRI's **InfoScan** is, a scanner-based sales-tracking service for the consumer packaged-goods industry. Retail sales, detailed consumer purchasing information (including measurement of store loyalty and total grocery basket expenditures), and promotional activity by manufacturers and retailers are monitored and evaluated for all bar-coded products. Data are collected weekly from supermarkets, drugstores, and mass merchandisers.

Some companies have begun using neuromarketing to study microscopic changes in skin moisture, heart rate, brain waves, and other biometrics to see how consumers react to things such as package designs and ads. **Neuromarketing** is the process of researching brain patterns and measuring certain physiological responses to marketing stimuli. It is a fresh attempt to better understand consumers' responses to promotion and purchase motivations.

scanner-based research a system for gathering information from a single group of respondents by continuously monitoring the advertising, promotion, and pricing they are exposed to and the things they buy

InfoScan a scanner-based sales-tracking service for the consumer packaged-goods industry

neuromarketing a field of marketing that studies the body's responses to marketing stimuli

9-6 WHEN SHOULD MARKETING RESEARCH BE CONDUCTED?

When managers have several possible solutions to a problem, they should not instinctively call for marketing research. In fact, the first decision to make is whether to conduct marketing research at all.

Some companies have been conducting research in certain markets for many years. Such firms understand the characteristics of target customers and their likes and dislikes about existing products. Under these circumstances, further research would be repetitive and waste money. P&G, for example, has extensive knowledge of the coffee market. After it conducted initial taste tests with Folgers Instant Coffee, P&G went into national distribution without further research. Sara Lee followed the same strategy with its frozen croissants, as did Quaker Oats with Chewy Granola Bars. This tactic, however, can backfire. Marketers may think they understand a particular market thoroughly and so bypass market research for a product, only to have the product fail and be withdrawn from the market.

If information were available and free, managers would rarely refuse more, but because marketing information can require a great deal of time and expense to accumulate, they might decide to forgo additional information. Ultimately, the willingness to acquire additional decision-making information depends on managers' perceptions of its quality, price, and timing. Research should be undertaken only when the expected value of the information is greater than the cost of obtaining it.

9-6a Customer Relationship Management

Recall from the beginning of the chapter that databases and big data play a key role in marketing decision making. A key subset of data management systems is a customer relationship management (CRM) system. CRM was introduced in Chapters 1 and 8. The key to managing relationships with customers is the CRM cycle (Exhibit 9.7).

To initiate the CRM cycle, a company must *identify customer relationships with the organization*. This may simply entail learning who the customers are or where they are located, or it may require more detailed information about the products and services they are using. Next, the company must *understand the interactions with current customers*. Companies accomplish this by collecting data on all types of communications a customer has with the company.

Using this knowledge of its customers and their interactions, the company then *captures relevant customer data on interactions*. Big data analytics are used not only to enhance the collection of customer data but

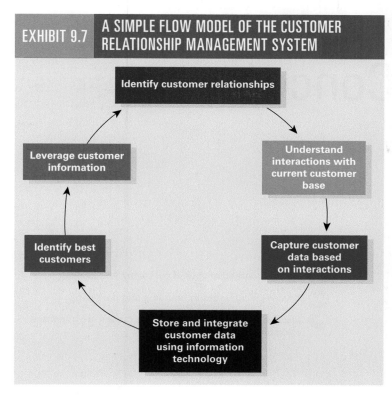

EXHIBIT 9.7 A SIMPLE FLOW MODEL OF THE CUSTOMER RELATIONSHIP MANAGEMENT SYSTEM

Identify customer relationships

Understand interactions with current customer base

Capture customer data based on interactions

Store and integrate customer data using information technology

Identify best customers

Leverage customer information

also to *store and integrate customer data* throughout the company, and ultimately, to "get to know" customers on a more personal level. Customer data are the firsthand responses that are obtained from customers through investigation or by asking direct questions.

Every customer wants to be a company's main priority. Yet not all customers are equally important in the eyes of a business. Consequently, the company must *identify its profitable and unprofitable customers.* Big data analytics compile actionable data about the purchase habits of a firm's current and potential customers. Essentially, analytics transform customer data into customer information a company can use to make managerial decisions. Big data analytics are examined in more detail in Chapter 14.

Once customer data are analyzed and transformed into usable information, the information must be *leveraged.* The CRM system sends the customer information to all areas of a business because the customer interacts with all aspects of the business. Essentially, the company is trying to enhance customer relationships by getting the right information to the right person in the right place at the right time.

9-7 COMPETITIVE INTELLIGENCE

Derived from military intelligence, competitive intelligence is an important tool for helping a firm overcome a competitor's advantage. Specifically, competitive intelligence can help identify the advantage and play a major role in determining how it was achieved. It also helps a firm identify areas where it can achieve its own competitive advantages.

Competitive intelligence (CI) helps managers assess their competitors and their vendors in order to become more efficient and effective competitors. Intelligence is analyzed information. It becomes decision-making intelligence when it has implications for the organization. For example, a primary competitor may have plans to introduce a product with performance standards equal to those of the company gathering the information but with a 15 percent cost advantage. The new product will reach the market in eight months. This intelligence has important decision-making and policy consequences for management. CI and environmental scanning (see Chapter 2) combine to create marketing intelligence.

The Internet is an important resource for gathering CI, but noncomputer sources can be equally valuable. Some examples include company salespeople, industry experts, CI consultants, government agencies, Uniform Commercial Code filings, suppliers, periodicals, the Yellow Pages, and industry trade shows.

competitive intelligence (CI) an intelligence system that helps managers assess their competition and vendors in order to become more efficient and effective competitors

STUDY TOOLS 9

LOCATED AT BACK OF THE TEXTBOOK
☐ Rip out Chapter Review Card

LOCATED AT WWW.CENGAGEBRAIN.COM
☐ Review Key Terms Flashcards and create your own
☐ Track your knowledge and understanding of key concepts in marketing
☐ Complete practice and graded quizzes to prepare for tests
☐ Complete interactive content within the MKTG Online experience
☐ View the chapter highlight boxes within the MKTG Online experience

10 | Product Concepts

LEARNING OUTCOMES

After studying this chapter, you will be able to...

10-1 Define the term *product*

10-2 Classify consumer products

10-3 Define the terms *product item*, *product line*, and *product mix*

10-4 Describe marketing uses of branding

10-5 Describe marketing uses of packaging and labeling

10-6 Discuss global issues in branding and packaging

10-7 Describe how and why product warranties are important marketing tools

misuma/Shutterstock.com

After finishing this chapter go to **PAGE 188** for **STUDY TOOLS**

10-1 WHAT IS A PRODUCT?

The product offering, the heart of an organization's marketing program, is usually the starting point in creating a marketing mix. A marketing manager cannot determine a price, design a promotion strategy, or create a distribution channel until the firm has a product to sell. Moreover, an excellent distribution channel, a persuasive promotion campaign, and a fair price have no value when the product offering is poor or inadequate.

A **product** may be defined as everything, both favorable and unfavorable, that a person receives in an exchange. A product may be a tangible good like a pair of shoes, a service like a haircut, an idea like "don't litter," or any combination of these three. Packaging, style, color, options, and size are some typical product features. Just as important are intangibles such as service, the seller's image, the manufacturer's reputation, and the way consumers believe others will view the product.

To most people, the term *product* means a tangible good. However, services and ideas are also products. (Chapter 12 focuses specifically on the unique aspects of marketing services.) The marketing process identified in Chapter 1 is the same whether the product marketed is a good, a service, an idea, or some combination of these.

10-2 TYPES OF CONSUMER PRODUCTS

Products can be classified as either business (industrial) or consumer, depending on the buyer's intentions. The key distinction between the two types

> **product** everything, both favorable and unfavorable, that a person receives in an exchange

of products is their intended use. If the intended use is a business purpose, the product is classified as a business or industrial product. As explained in Chapter 7, a business product is used to manufacture other goods or services, to facilitate an organization's operations, or to resell to other customers. A consumer product is bought to satisfy an individual's personal wants or needs. Sometimes the same item can be classified as either a business or a consumer product, depending on its intended use. Examples include lightbulbs, pencils and paper, and computers.

We need to know about product classifications because business and consumer products are marketed differently. They are marketed to different target markets and tend to use different distribution, promotion, and pricing strategies.

Chapter 7 examined seven categories of business products: major equipment, accessory equipment, component parts, processed materials, raw materials, supplies, and services. This chapter examines an effective way of categorizing consumer products. Although there are several ways to classify them, the most popular approach includes these four types: convenience products, shopping products, specialty products, and unsought

> A marketing manager cannot determine a price, design a promotion strategy, or create a distribution channel until the firm has a product to sell.

products. This approach classifies products according to how much effort is normally used to shop for them.

10-2a Convenience Products

A **convenience product** is a relatively inexpensive item that merits little shopping effort—that is, a consumer is unwilling to shop extensively for such an item. Candy, soft drinks, aspirin, small hardware items, dry cleaning, and car washes fall into the convenience product category.

convenience product
a relatively inexpensive item that merits little shopping effort

Consumers buy convenience products regularly, usually without much planning. Nevertheless, consumers do know the brand names of popular convenience products, such as Coca-Cola, Bayer aspirin, and Old Spice deodorant. Convenience products normally require wide distribution in order to sell sufficient quantities to meet profit goals. For example, the gum brand Extra is available everywhere, including Walmart, Walgreens, gas stations, newsstands, and vending machines.

10-2b Shopping Products

A **shopping product** is usually more expensive than a convenience product and is found in fewer stores. Consumers usually buy a shopping product only after comparing several brands or stores on style, practicality, price, and lifestyle compatibility. They are willing to invest some effort into this process to get the desired benefits.

There are two types of shopping products: homogeneous and heterogeneous. Consumers perceive *homogeneous* shopping products as basically similar—for example, washers, dryers, refrigerators, and televisions. With homogeneous shopping products, consumers typically look for the lowest-priced brand that has the desired features. For example, they might compare Kenmore, Whirlpool, and General Electric refrigerators.

In contrast, consumers perceive *heterogeneous* shopping products as essentially different—for example, furniture, clothing, housing, and universities. Consumers often have trouble comparing heterogeneous shopping products because the prices, quality, and features vary so much. The benefit of comparing heterogeneous shopping products is "finding the best product or brand for me"; this decision is often highly individual. For example, it would be difficult to compare a small, private college with a large, public university, or IKEA with La-Z-Boy.

10-2c Specialty Products

When consumers search extensively for a particular item and are very reluctant to accept substitutes, that item is a **specialty product**. Omega watches, Rolls-Royce automobiles, Bose speakers, Ruth's Chris Steak House, and highly

Consumers perceive houses as heterogeneous because of variety and differences.

karamysh/Shutterstock.com

specialized forms of medical care are generally considered specialty products.

Marketers of specialty products often use selective, status-conscious advertising to maintain a product's exclusive image. Distribution is often limited to one or a very few outlets in a geographic area. Brand names and quality of service are often very important.

10-2d Unsought Products

A product unknown to the potential buyer or a known product that the buyer does not actively seek is referred to as an **unsought product**. New products fall into this category until advertising and distribution increase consumer awareness of them.

Some goods are always marketed as unsought items, especially needed products we do not like to think about or care to spend money on. Insurance, burial plots, and similar items require aggressive personal selling and highly persuasive advertising. Salespeople actively seek leads to potential buyers. Because consumers usually do not seek out this type of product, the company must go directly to them through a salesperson, direct mail, or direct response advertising.

10-3 PRODUCT ITEMS, LINES, AND MIXES

Rarely does a company sell a single product. More often, it sells a variety of things. A **product item** is a specific version of a product that can be designated as a distinct offering among an organization's products. Campbell's Cream of Chicken soup is an example of a product item (see Exhibit 10.1).

shopping product a product that requires comparison shopping because it is usually more expensive than a convenience product and is found in fewer stores

specialty product a particular item for which consumers search extensively and are very reluctant to accept substitutes

unsought product a product unknown to the potential buyer or a known product that the buyer does not actively seek

product item a specific version of a product that can be designated as a distinct offering among an organization's products

EXHIBIT 10.1 CAMPBELL'S PRODUCT LINES AND PRODUCT MIX

	Soups	**Sauces**	**Frozen Entrées**	**Beverages**	**Biscuits**
Width of the Product Mix					
Depth of the Product Lines **DEPTH**	Cream of Chicken	Cheddar Cheese	Macaroni and Cheese	Tomato Juice	Arnott's:
	Cream of Mushroom	Alfredo	Golden Chicken	V-Fusion Juices	Water Cracker
	Vegetable Beef	Italian Tomato	Fricassee	V8 Splash	Butternut Snap
	Chicken Noodle	Hollandaise	Traditional Lasagna		Chocolate Ripple
	Tomato				Spicy Fruit Roll
	Bean with Bacon				Chocolate Wheaten
	Minestrone				
	Clam Chowder				
	French Onion				
	and more				

A group of closely related product items is called a **product line**. For example, the column in Exhibit 10.1 titled "Soups" represents one of Campbell's product lines. Different container sizes and shapes also distinguish items in a product line. Diet Coke, for example, is available in cans and various plastic containers. Each size and each container are separate product items.

An organization's **product mix** includes all the products it sells. All Campbell's products—soups, sauces, frozen entrées, beverages, and biscuits—constitute its product mix. Each product item in the product mix may require a separate marketing strategy.

In some cases, however, product lines and even entire product mixes share some marketing strategy components. For example, UPS promotes its various services by demonstrating its commitment to helping customers with the tagline "United Problem Solvers." Organizations derive several benefits from organizing related items into product lines:

- **Advertising economies:** Product lines provide economies of scale in advertising. Several products can be advertised under the umbrella of the line. Campbell's can talk about its soups being "M'm, M'm, Good!" and promote the entire line.

- **Package uniformity:** A product line can benefit from package uniformity. All packages in the line may have a common look and still keep their individual identities. Campbell's soup, with its recognizable red and white labels, is again a good example.

- **Standardized components:** Product lines allow firms to standardize components, thus reducing manufacturing and inventory costs. For example, General Motors uses the same parts on many automobile makes and models.

- **Efficient sales and distribution:** A product line enables sales personnel for companies like Procter & Gamble to provide a full range of choices to customers. Distributors and retailers are often more inclined to stock the company's products if it offers a full line. Transportation and warehousing costs are likely to be lower for a product line than for a collection of individual items.

- **Equivalent quality:** Purchasers usually expect and believe that all products in a line are about equal in quality. Consumers expect that all Campbell's soups and all Gillette razors will be of similar quality.

Product mix width (or breadth) refers to the number of product lines an organization offers. In Exhibit 10.1, for example, the width of Campbell's product mix is five product lines. **Product line depth** is the number of product items in a product line. As shown in Exhibit 10.1, the sauces product line consists of four product items; the frozen entrée product line includes three product items.

Firms increase the *width* of their product mix to diversify risk. To generate sales and boost profits, firms spread risk across many product lines rather than depend on only one or two. Firms also widen their product mix to capitalize on

---

product line a group of closely related product items

product mix all products that an organization sells

product mix width the number of product lines an organization offers

product line depth the number of product items in a product line

CEO of Barnes & Noble Michael Huseby introduces the Android-powered Samsung Galaxy Tab 4 Nook at a Barnes & Noble store in New York City. Barnes & Noble began selling the new high-powered e-reader to compete with tablet and laptop makers such as Microsoft and Apple.

established reputations. For example, leading fitness wear manufacturer Under Armour recently added a wearable activity tracker to its product mix. Called the HealthBox, this device analyzes sleep, daily activity, workout intensity, and weight. The company is working to widen its product mix across the industry of health and fitness.[1]

Firms increase the *depth* of their product lines to attract buyers with different preferences, to increase sales and profits by further segmenting the market, to capitalize on economies of scale in production and marketing, and to even out seasonal sales patterns.

10-3a Adjustments to Product Items, Lines, and Mixes

Over time, firms change product items, lines, and mixes to take advantage of new technical or product developments or to respond to changes in the environment. They may adjust by modifying products,

product modification
changing one or more of a product's characteristics

repositioning products, or extending or contracting product lines.

PRODUCT MODIFICATION Marketing managers must decide if and when to modify existing products. **Product modification** is a change in one or more of a product's characteristics:

- **Quality modification:** a change in a product's dependability or durability. Reducing a product's quality may let the manufacturer lower the price and appeal to target markets unable to afford the original product. Conversely, increasing quality can help the firm compete with rival firms. For example, Barnes & Noble offers a color version of its Nook that runs Android apps, allowing it to compete with tablet and laptop makers such as Microsoft and Apple. Increasing quality can also result in increased brand loyalty, greater ability to raise prices, or new opportunities for market segmentation.

- **Functional modification:** a change in a product's versatility, effectiveness, convenience, or safety.

Oil-Dri Corporation of America, a leading manufacturer of quality cat litter, recently introduced Cat's Pride Fresh & Light Ultimate Care litter. This product has a unique formula that is 50 percent lighter than other litters and features 10-day odor control, ultra-strong clumping, and dust-free scooping.[2]

- **Style modification:** an aesthetic (how the product looks) product change rather than a quality or functional change. Clothing and auto manufacturers commonly use style modifications to motivate customers to replace products before they are worn out.

Planned obsolescence is a term commonly used to describe the practice of modifying products so that those that have already been sold become obsolete before they actually need replacement. For example, products such as printers and cell phones become obsolete because technology changes so quickly.

Some argue that planned obsolescence is wasteful; some claim it is unethical. Marketers respond that consumers favor style modifications because they like changes in the appearance of goods such as clothing and cars. Marketers also contend that consumers, not manufacturers and marketers, decide when styles are obsolete.

REPOSITIONING Repositioning, as Chapter 8 explained, involves changing consumers' perceptions of a brand. SeaWorld, one of America's leading tourist attractions, received negative publicity from the documentary film *Blackfish*, which exposed how the company trained and treated orcas. As a result, the company decided to phase out orca breeding and end the stunt-based shows featuring these animals. SeaWorld repositioned its brand toward preserving and protecting sea creatures and made animal care and sensitivity to wildlife central to its mission. Now, orcas at SeaWorld are presented in naturalistic settings rather than in theatrical shows.[3] Changing demographics, declining sales, and changes in the social environment often motivate a firm to reposition an established brand. Retailer Target, for example, plans to reposition its brand toward Hispanic shoppers. The company's research showed that while only 38 percent of its shoppers said that the store was their favorite, 54 percent of Hispanic Millennials said that Target was their favorite store. Several departments, including the baby department, will be renovated to focus on marketing to Hispanic moms. Target also plans to be the first brand to launch a Spanish-language ad campaign on an English-language network.[4]

Krispy Kreme developed a line of beverages that it made available to sell in grocery, convenience, and mass merchandise stores.

PRODUCT LINE EXTENSIONS A **product line extension** occurs when a company's management decides to add products to an existing product line in order to compete more broadly in the industry. Donut maker Krispy Kreme recently launched a series of ready-to-drink iced coffees that consumers can purchase nationwide in grocery, convenience, and mass merchandise stores. The drinks are relatively inexpensive, convenient, and are offered in mocha, vanilla, and caramel flavors. The company hopes to attract more coffee drinkers, as well as retail customers, to its products.[5]

A company can add too many products, or demand can change for the type of products that were introduced over time. When this happens, a product line is overextended. Product lines can be overextended when:

- Some products in the line do not contribute to profits because of low sales or they cannibalize sales of other items in the line.

- Manufacturing or marketing resources are disproportionately allocated to slow-moving products.

- Some items in the line are obsolete because of new-product entries in the line or new products offered by competitors.

planned obsolescence the practice of modifying products so those that have already been sold become obsolete before they actually need replacement

product line extension adding additional products to an existing product line in order to compete more broadly in the industry

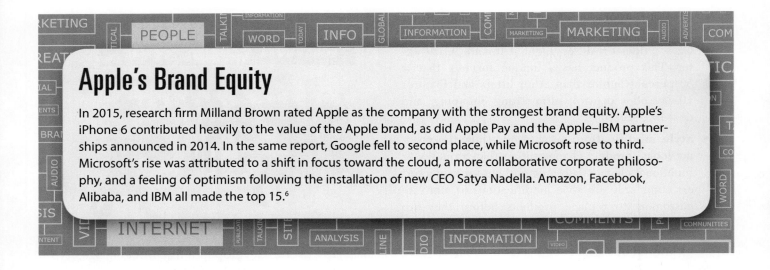

PRODUCT LINE CONTRACTION Sometimes marketers can get carried away with product extensions. (Does the world really need 31 varieties of Head & Shoulders shampoo?) Contracting product lines is a strategic way to deal with overextension. In early 2016, Toyota axed Scion, which the company had positioned as a "youth" brand. Scion helped Toyota attract younger buyers (with an average age of 36), but the company failed to clearly differentiate Scion from its other small cars. Toyota did not provide enough marketing support to generate a critical sales mass, and what marketing there was focused on fuel economy and price—not enough to give Scion a competitive differentiation, particularly as gas prices plummeted. All is not lost for fans of the Scion brand, however, as Toyota plans to incorporate several Scion models into its remaining brands.[7]

Indeed, three major benefits are likely when a firm contracts an overextended product line. First, resources become concentrated on the most important products. Second, managers no longer waste resources trying to improve the sales and profits of poorly performing products. Third, new-product items have a greater chance of being successful because more financial and human resources are available to manage them.

brand a name, term, symbol, design, or combination thereof that identifies a seller's products and differentiates them from competitors' products

brand name that part of a brand that can be spoken, including letters, words, and numbers

brand mark the elements of a brand that cannot be spoken

brand equity the value of a company or brand name

global brand a brand that obtains at least a one-third of its earnings from outside its home country, is recognizable outside its home base of customers, and has publicly available marketing and financial data

 BRANDING

10-4

The success of any business or consumer product depends in part on the target market's ability to distinguish one product from another. Branding is the main tool marketers use to distinguish their products from those of the competition.

A **brand** is a name, term, symbol, design, or combination thereof that identifies a seller's products and differentiates them from competitors' products. A **brand name** is that part of a brand that can be spoken, including letters (GM, YMCA), words (Chevrolet), and numbers (WD-40, 7-Eleven). The elements of a brand that cannot be spoken are called the **brand mark**—for example, the well-known Mercedes-Benz and Delta Air Lines symbols.

10-4a Benefits of Branding

Branding has three main purposes: product identification, repeat sales, and new-product sales. The most important purpose is *product identification*. Branding allows marketers to distinguish their products from all others. Many brand names are familiar to consumers and indicate quality.

The term **brand equity** refers to the value of a company or brand name. A brand that has high awareness, perceived quality, and brand loyalty among customers has high brand equity—a valuable asset indeed. See Exhibit 10.2 for some classic examples of companies that leverage their brand equity to the fullest.

The term **global brand** refers to a brand that obtains at least one-third of its earnings from outside its home country, is recognizable outside its home base

YUM! believes that it must adapt its restaurants to local tastes and different cultural and political climates.

EXHIBIT 10.2 | THE POWER OF BRAND EQUITY

Product Category	Dominant Brand Name
Children's Entertainment	Disney
Laundry Detergent	Tide
Tablet Computer	Apple
Toothpaste	Crest
Microprocessor	Intel
Soup	Campbell's
Bologna	Oscar Meyer
Ketchup	Heinz
Bleach	Clorox
Greeting Cards	Hallmark
Overnight Mail	FedEx
Copiers	Xerox
Gelatin	Jell-O
Hamburgers	McDonald's
Baby Lotion	Johnson & Johnson
Tissues	Kleenex
Acetaminophen	Tylenol
Coffee	Starbucks
Information Search	Google

Source: Data from Chris Moorman.

of customers, and has publicly available marketing and financial data. Yum! Brands, which owns Pizza Hut, KFC, and Taco Bell, is a good example of a company that has developed strong global brands. Yum! management believes that it must adapt its restaurants to local tastes and different cultural and political climates. In Japan, for instance, KFC sells tempura crispy strips. In northern England, KFC focuses on gravy and potatoes, and in Thailand, it offers rice with soy or sweet chili sauce.

The best generator of *repeat sales* is satisfied customers. Branding helps consumers identify products they wish to buy again and avoid those they do not. **Brand loyalty**, a consistent preference for one brand over all others, is quite high in some product categories. More than half the consumers in product categories such as cigarettes, mayonnaise, toothpaste, coffee, headache remedies, bath soap, and ketchup are loyal to one brand. Many students go to college and purchase the same brands they used at home rather than choosing by price. Brand identity is essential to developing brand loyalty.

The third main purpose of branding is to *facilitate new-product sales*. Having a well-known and respected company and brand name is extremely useful when introducing new products.

10-4b Branding Strategies

Firms face complex branding decisions. Firms may choose to follow a policy of using manufacturers' brands, private (distributor) brands, or both. In either case, they must then decide among a policy of individual branding (different brands for different products), family branding (common names for different products), or a combination of individual branding and family branding.

brand loyalty consistent preference for one brand over all others

Key Advantages of Carrying Manufacturers' Brands	Key Advantages of Carrying Private Brands
• Heavy advertising to the consumer by manufacturers such as Procter & Gamble helps develop strong consumer loyalties.	• A wholesaler or retailer can usually earn higher profits on its own brand. In addition, because the private brand is exclusive, there is less pressure to mark down the price to meet competition.
• Well-known manufacturers' brands, such as Kodak and Fisher-Price, can attract new customers and enhance the dealer's (wholesaler's or retailer's) prestige.	• A manufacturer can decide to drop a brand or a reseller at any time or even become a direct competitor to its dealers.
• Many manufacturers offer rapid delivery, enabling the dealer to carry less inventory.	• A private brand ties the customer to the wholesaler or retailer. A person who wants a DieHard battery must go to Sears.
• If a dealer happens to sell a manufacturer's brand of poor quality, the customer may simply switch brands and remain loyal to the dealer.	• Wholesalers and retailers have no control over the intensity of distribution of manufacturers' brands. Walmart store managers don't have to worry about competing with other sellers of Sam's American Choice products or Ol' Roy dog food. They know that these brands are sold only in Walmart and Sam's Club stores.

MANUFACTURERS' BRANDS VERSUS PRIVATE BRANDS The brand name of a manufacturer—such as Kodak, La-Z-Boy, and Fruit of the Loom—is called a **manufacturer's brand**. Sometimes "national brand" is used as a synonym for "manufacturer's brand." This term is not always accurate, however, because many manufacturers serve only regional markets. Using "manufacturer's brand" precisely defines the brand's owner.

A **private brand**, also known as a private label or store brand, is a brand name owned by a wholesaler or a retailer. Target's Archer Farms brand is a popular private label, for example. Private labels are increasing in popularity and price as customers develop loyalties to store brands such as Archer Farms. Private brands have seen strong growth since the start of the Great Recession in 2008, more than doubling in sales and capturing about 25 percent of all grocery store volume. Much of this growth has occurred in the dry groceries and non-foods categories because of changing shopper behavior and heavy competition.[8] Sensing these trends, Amazon recently launched private label brands in men's, women's, and children's apparel. The company now owns seven private-label fashion brands, and in 2015, sponsored New York Men's Fashion Week for the first time.[9]

Retailers love consumers' greater acceptance of private brands. Because overhead is low and there are no marketing costs, private label products bring 10 percent higher profit margins, on average, than manufacturers' brands. More than that, a trusted store brand can differentiate a chain from its competitors. Exhibit 10.3 illustrates key issues that wholesalers and retailers should consider in deciding whether to sell manufacturers' brands or private brands. Many firms offer a combination of both.

Instead of marketing private brands as cheaper and inferior to manufacturers' brands, many retailers are creating and promoting their own **captive brands**. These brands carry no evidence of the store's affiliation, are manufactured by a third party, and are sold exclusively at the chains. This strategy allows the retailer to ask a price similar or equal to manufacturers' brands, and the captive brands are typically displayed alongside mainstream products. A recent study showed that many consumers believe that store brands are equivalent to name brands in flavor, packaging, and assortment, and 37 percent of consumers prefer to buy store brands over manufacturers' brands. Interestingly, Millennial shoppers were found to be more likely than other demographic groups to buy store brand foods in general.[10] For example, Simple Truth and Simple Truth Organic are Kroger's lines of natural and organic products designed to meet consumer desire for upscale brands. In 2014, these private brands accounted for $1.2 billion in sales for Kroger.[11]

INDIVIDUAL BRANDS VERSUS FAMILY BRANDS Many companies use different brand names for different products, a practice referred to as **individual branding**. Companies use individual brands when their products vary greatly in use or performance. For instance, it would not make sense to use the same brand name for a pair of

manufacturer's brand the brand name of a manufacturer

private brand a brand name owned by a wholesaler or a retailer

captive brand a brand manufactured by a third party for an exclusive retailer, without evidence of that retailer's affiliation

individual branding using different brand names for different products

Most grocery stores sell all different types of brands side-by-side.

dress socks and a baseball bat. Procter & Gamble targets different segments of the laundry detergent market with Bold, Cheer, Dash, Dreft, Era, Gain, and Tide.

By contrast, a company that markets several different products under the same brand name is practicing **family branding**. Jack Daniel's family brand includes whiskey, coffee, barbeque sauce, heat-and-serve meat products like brisket and pulled pork, mustard, playing cards, and clothing lines.

CO-BRANDING **Co-branding** entails placing two or more brand names on a product or its package. Three common types of co-branding are ingredient branding, cooperative branding, and complementary branding. *Ingredient branding* identifies the brand of a part that makes up the product. For example, Church & Dwight co-branded an entire line of Arm & Hammer laundry detergents with OxiClean, a popular household cleaner and stain remover. OxiClean is also co-branded with Kaboom shower cleaner and Xtra detergent.[12] *Cooperative branding* occurs when two brands receiving equal treatment (in the context of an advertisement) borrow from each other's brand equity. A promotional contest jointly sponsored by Ramada Inn, American Express, and United Airlines used cooperative branding. Guests at Ramada who paid with an American Express card were automatically entered in a contest and were eligible to win more than 100 getaways for two at any Ramada in the continental United States and round-trip airfare from United. In 2014, Bruegger's Bagels and Jamba Juice announced that five co-branded and co-operated locations would be opened across

Florida. "Pairing Bruegger's Bagels with [Jamba Juice parent company] Great Service Restaurants is a fantastic match," said Paul Carolan, chief development officer for Le Duff America, which owns Bruegger's Bagels. "Great Service Restaurants shares our passion for community, quality, and providing exceptional guest experiences."[13] Finally, with complementary branding, products are advertised or marketed together to suggest usage, such as a spirits brand (Seagram's) and a compatible mixer (7Up).

Co-branding is a useful strategy when a combination of brand names enhances the prestige or perceived value of a product or when it benefits brand owners and users. Co-branding may also be used to increase a company's presence in markets where it has little room to differentiate itself or has limited market share. For example, Doc Popcorn and Dippin' Dots plan to join together to open their first co-branded store. The companies will sell sweet and savory flavors of popcorn as well as ice cream products under the same roof. This move will allow both brands to continue to grow domestically and internationally over the coming years.[14]

10-4c Trademarks

A **trademark** is the exclusive right to use a brand or part of a brand. Others are prohibited from using the brand without permission. A **service mark** performs the same function for services, such as H&R Block and Weight Watchers. Parts of a brand or other product identification may qualify for trademark protection. Some examples are:

- Sounds, such as the MGM lion's roar.
- Shapes, such as the Jeep front grille and the Coca-Cola bottle.
- Ornamental colors or designs, such as the decoration on Nike tennis shoes, the black-and-copper color combination of a Duracell battery, Levi's small tag on the left side of the

family branding marketing several different products under the same brand name

co-branding placing two or more brand names on a product or its package

trademark the exclusive right to use a brand or part of a brand

service mark a trademark for a service

Empire stars Bryshere Gray, Terrence Howard, and Trai Byers (from left) arrive at a premiere event for the hit show. In 2016, Fox won a trademark case brought against the television network by similarly named music company Empire.

rear pocket of its jeans, or the cutoff black cone on the top of Cross pens.

- Catchy phrases, such as Prudential's "Own a Piece of the Rock," Mountain Dew's "Do the Dew," and Nike's "Just Do It!"

- Abbreviations, such as Bud, Coke, or the Met.

It is important to understand that trademark rights come from use rather than registration. An intent-to-use application is filed with the U.S. Patent and Trademark Office, and a company must have a genuine intention to use the mark when it files and must actually use it within three years of the granting of the application. Trademark protection typically lasts for ten years.[15] To renew the trademark, the company must prove it is using the mark. Rights to a trademark last as long as the mark is used. Normally, if the firm does not use it for two years, the trademark is considered abandoned, and a new user can claim exclusive ownership of the mark.

The Digital Millennium Copyright Act (DMCA) explicitly applies trademark law to the digital world. This law includes financial penalties for those who violate trademarks or register an otherwise trademarked term as a domain name. The DMCA has come under some criticism for its more restrictive provisions. For example, some are concerned that this law has been abused by governments to silence political criticism on the Internet.[16]

Companies that fail to protect their trademarks face the possibility that their product names will become generic. A **generic product name** identifies a product by class or type and cannot be trademarked. Former brand names that were not sufficiently protected by their owners and were subsequently declared to be generic product names by U.S. courts include aspirin, cellophane, linoleum, thermos, kerosene, monopoly, cola, and shredded wheat.

Companies such as Rolls-Royce, Cross, Xerox, Levi Strauss, Frigidaire, and McDonald's aggressively enforce their trademarks. Rolls-Royce, Coca-Cola, and Xerox even run newspaper and magazine ads stating that their names are trademarks and should not be used as descriptive or generic terms. Television network Fox recently won a trademark victory for the name of hit show *Empire* against San Francisco-based hip-hop music company Empire. The music company offered to recall the claim—that its brand was being tarnished by the show's portrayal of a music label run by a drug dealer who liked to murder his friends—for $8 million, or for guest spots for their artists and $5 million. The judge who decided the case wrote that "'Empire' has genuine relevance to the *Empire* Series and it was not arbitrarily chosen to exploit Empire Distribution's fame."[17]

To try to stem the number of trademark infringements, violations carry steep penalties. But despite the risk of incurring a penalty, infringement lawsuits are still common. Serious conflict can occur when brand names resemble one another too closely. Fashion brand Gucci has accused Guess of trademark violations for years. In 2015, a French court ruled in Guess's favor, finding that no trademark infringement, counterfeiting, or unfair competition between the two brands occurred. The court found that Guess had diluted Gucci's logos, not copied them. An American court ruled, however, that Guess was guilty of copying four of Gucci's five trademarked logos. This example also illustrates that there is no such thing as a global trademark.[18]

generic product name identifies a product by class or type and cannot be trademarked

Companies must also contend with fake or unauthorized brands. Knockoffs of trademarked clothing lines are easy to find in cheap shops all over the world, and loose imitations are found in some reputable department stores as well. Today, whole stores are faked in China. Stores selling real iPhones and iPads in stores with sparse décor and bright lighting may seem like authentic Apple stores but are frequently imitating the real deal. Numerous fast-food restaurants have become victims of knock-off stores throughout China: Pizza Huh (Pizza Hut), Mak Dak (McDonald's), and Taco Bell Grande (Taco Bell) mimic the American chains' layouts and products. FBC, KFG, KLG, MFC, and OFC all lift Kentucky Fried Chicken's iconic logo, color scheme, and menu.[19]

In Europe, you can sue counterfeiters only if your brand, logo, or trademark is formally registered. Formal registration used to be required in each country in which a company sought protection. However, today a company can register its trademark in all European Union member countries with one application.

10-5 PACKAGING

Packages have always served a practical function— that is, they hold contents together and protect goods as they move through the distribution channel. Today, however, packaging is also a container for promoting the product and making it easier and safer to use.

10-5a Packaging Functions

The three most important functions of packaging are to contain and protect products; promote products; and facilitate the storage, use, and convenience of products. A fourth function of packaging that is becoming increasingly important is to facilitate recycling and reduce environmental damage.

CONTAINING AND PROTECTING PRODUCTS The most obvious function of packaging is to contain products that are liquid, granular, or otherwise divisible. Packaging also enables manufacturers, wholesalers, and retailers to market products in specific quantities, such as ounces.

Physical protection is another obvious function of packaging. Most products are handled several times between the time they are manufactured, harvested, or otherwise produced and the time they are consumed or used. Many products are also shipped, stored, and inspected several times between production and consumption. Some, like milk, need to be refrigerated.

Others, like beer, are sensitive to light. Still others, like medicines and bandages, need to be kept sterile. Packages protect products from breakage, evaporation, spillage, spoilage, light, heat, cold, infestation, and many other conditions.

PROMOTING PRODUCTS Packaging does more than identify the brand, list the ingredients, specify features, and give directions. A package differentiates a product from competing products and may associate a new product with a family of other products from the same manufacturer. However, some products' packaging lacks useful information. The Food and Drug Administration (FDA) is looking to remedy inconsistent and incomplete food packaging information by adding more facts to nutrition labels. These changes include listing the number of servings in each container and printing the calorie count for each serving in larger, bolder type. The FDA hopes that these changes will catch consumers' eyes and help them better manage their health.[20]

Packages use designs, colors, shapes, and materials to try to influence consumers' perceptions and buying behavior. For example, marketing research shows that health-conscious consumers are likely to think that any food is probably good for them as long as it comes in green packaging. Packaging can influence other consumer perceptions of a brand as well. In 2016, Coca-Cola introduced the Diet Coke It's Mine program, which featured millions of unique package designs for the brand. The company partnered with HP Inc. to use the innovative HP Indigo digital printing technology to design the labels. The brand first created 36 base designs inspired by the bubbles, fizz, taste, and spirit of Diet Coke. Then, using these base designs, the HP software automatically generated millions of entirely new graphics. Coca-Cola also partnered with celebrity stylist Brad Goreski to host an It's Mine pop-up fashion house experience in New York City at the start of Fashion Week. Diet Coke consumers who participate in the experience can choose label designs that they believe reflect both their individual personalities and their looks.[21]

FACILITATING STORAGE, USE, AND CONVENIENCE Wholesalers and retailers prefer packages that are easy to ship, store, and stock on shelves. They also like packages that protect products, prevent spoilage or breakage, and extend the product's shelf life.

Consumers' requirements for storage, use, and convenience cover many dimensions. Consumers are constantly seeking items that are easy to handle, open, and reclose, although some consumers want packages that are tamperproof or childproof. Research indicates that hard-to-open packages are among consumers' top complaints—especially when it comes to clamshell electronics packaging. Indeed, Quora users voted clamshell packaging "the worst piece of design ever done." There is even a Wikipedia page devoted to "wrap rage," the anger associated with trying to open clamshells and other poorly designed packages.[22] As oil prices force the cost of plastics used in packaging skyward, companies such as Amazon, Target, and Walmart are pushing suppliers to do away with excessive and infuriating packaging. Such packaging innovations as zipper tear strips, hinged lids, tab slots, screw-on tops, simple cardboard boxes, and pour spouts were introduced to solve these and other problems. Easy openings are especially important for kids and aging baby boomers.

Some firms use packaging to segment markets. For example, a C&H sugar carton with an easy-to-pour, reclosable top is targeted to consumers who do not do a lot of baking and are willing to pay at least 20 cents more for the package. Different-sized packages appeal to heavy, moderate, and light users. Campbell's soup is packaged in single-serving cans aimed at the elderly and singles market segments. Packaging convenience can increase a product's utility and, therefore, its market share and profits.

FACILITATING RECYCLING AND REDUCING ENVIRONMENTAL DAMAGE One of the most important packaging issues today is eco-consciousness, a trend that has recently been in and out of consumer and media attention. Studies conflict as to whether consumers will pay more for eco-friendly packaging, though consumers repeatedly iterate the desire to purchase such products. A recent study showed that 63 percent of U.S. consumers believe that reusable and repurposable packaging is important when choosing products. Companies have responded by looking for alternative packaging materials that are more ecologically friendly.[23]

10-5b Labeling

An integral part of any package is its label. Labeling generally takes one of two forms: persuasive or informational. **Persuasive labeling** focuses on a promotional theme or logo, and consumer information is secondary. Note that

The Disappearing Package

Some firms use innovative packaging to target environmentally concerned market segments. Package designer Aaron Mickelson's the Disappearing Package project showcased several inventive ways to make packaging more sustainable. Mickelson's designs include bar soap packaging that dissolves under shower water, trash bag packaging that doubles as a container and can be used as a trash bag itself, perforated tea bag booklets (eliminating the need for a box), and a rolled up tear-away detergent pod package with product information printed across the outside of the conjoined pods.[24]

Brand & product info are printed directly on the surface with soap-soluble ink.

Courtesy of Chapel House Photography

the standard promotional claims—such as "new," "improved," and "super"—are no longer very persuasive. Consumers have been saturated with "newness" and thus discount these claims.

Informational labeling, by contrast, is designed to help consumers make proper product selections and lower their cognitive dissonance after the purchase. Most major furniture manufacturers affix labels to their wares that explain the products' construction features, such as type of frame, number of coils, and fabric characteristics. The Nutritional Labeling and Education Act of 1990 mandated detailed nutritional information on most food packages and standards for health claims on food packaging. An important outcome of this legislation has been guidelines from the

Food and Drug Administration for using terms such as *low fat*, *light*, *reduced cholesterol*, *low sodium*, *low calorie*, *low carb*, and *fresh*. Getting the right information is very important to consumers, so some corporations are working on new technologies to help consumers shop smart. For example, micro-sensor technology can monitor a beverage's temperature and freshness, providing more information than a simple "best by" date. Sensors can also promote food safety by detecting whether packages have been tampered with. Seafood Analytics created technology to detect and flag warning signs that could lead to seafood contamination, such as improper dates for when a fish was caught, harvested, and put on ice.[25]

GREENWASHING There are numerous products in every product category that use *greenwashing* to try and sell products. Greenwashing is when a product or company attempts to give the impression of environmental friendliness whether or not it is environmentally friendly.

As consumer demand for green products appeared to escalate, green certifications proliferated. Companies could create their own certifications and logos, resulting in more than 300 possible certification labels, ranging in price from free to thousands of dollars. Consumer distrust and confusion caused the Federal Trade Commission to issue new rules. Starting in late 2011, new regulations apply to labeling products with green-certification logos. If the same company that produced the product performed the certification, that relationship must be clearly marked. This benefits organizations such as Green Seal, which uses unbiased, third-party scientists and experts to verify claims about emissions or biodegradability, and hopes to increase consumer confidence in green products.[26]

10-5c Universal Product Codes

The **universal product codes (UPCs)** that appear on most items in supermarkets and other high-volume outlets were first introduced in 1974. Because the numerical codes appear as a series of thick and thin vertical lines, they are often called *bar codes*. The lines are read by computerized optical scanners that match codes with brand names, package sizes, and prices. They also print information on cash register tapes and help retailers rapidly and accurately prepare records of customer purchases, control inventories, and track sales. The UPC system and scanners are also used in scanner-based research (see Chapter 9).

10-6 GLOBAL ISSUES IN BRANDING AND PACKAGING

When planning to enter a foreign market with an existing product, a firm has three options for handling the brand name:

- **One brand name everywhere:** This strategy is useful when the company markets mainly one product and the brand name does not have negative connotations in any local market. The Coca-Cola Company uses a one-brand-name strategy in more than 195 countries around the world. The advantages of a one-brand-name strategy are greater identification of the product from market to market and ease of coordinating promotion from market to market.

- **Adaptations and modifications:** A one-brand-name strategy is not possible when the name cannot be pronounced in the local language, when the brand name is owned by someone else, or when the brand name has a negative or vulgar connotation in the local language. The Iranian detergent Barf, for example, might encounter some problems in the U.S. market.

- **Different brand names in different markets:** Local brand names are often used when translation or pronunciation problems occur, when the marketer wants the brand to appear to be a local brand, or when regulations require localization. Unilever's Axe line of male grooming products is called Lynx in England, Ireland, Australia, and New Zealand. PepsiCo changed the name of its eponymous cola to Pecsi in Argentina to reflect the way the word is pronounced with an Argentinian accent.

In addition to global branding decisions, companies must consider global packaging needs. Three aspects of packaging that are especially important in international marketing are labeling, aesthetics, and climate considerations. The major *labeling* concern is properly translating ingredient, promotional, and instructional information on labels. Care must also be employed in meeting all local labeling requirements. Several years ago, an Italian judge ordered that all bottles of Coca-Cola be removed from retail shelves because the ingredients were not properly labeled. Labeling is also harder in countries like Belgium and Finland, which require packaging to be bilingual.

universal product codes (UPCs) a series of thick and thin vertical lines (bar codes) readable by computerized optical scanners that represent numbers used to track products

Package *aesthetics* may also require some attention. Even though simple visual elements of the brand, such as a symbol or logo, can be a standardizing element across products and countries, marketers must stay attuned to cultural traits in host countries. For example, colors may have different connotations. Red is associated with witchcraft in some countries, green may be a sign of danger, and white may be symbolic of death. Such cultural differences could necessitate a packaging change if colors are chosen for another country's interpretation. In the United States, green typically symbolizes an eco-friendly product, but that packaging could keep customers away in a country where green indicates danger. Aesthetics also influence package size. Soft drinks are not sold in six-packs in countries that lack refrigeration. In some countries, products such as detergent may be bought only in small quantities because of a lack of storage space. Other products, such as cigarettes, may be bought in small quantities, and even single units, because of the low purchasing power of buyers.

Extreme climates and long-distance shipping necessitate sturdier and more durable packages for goods sold overseas. Spillage, spoilage, and breakage are all more important concerns when products are shipped long distances or frequently handled during shipping and storage. Packages may also need to ensure a longer product life if the time between production and consumption lengthens significantly.

warranty a confirmation of the quality or performance of a good or service

express warranty a written guarantee

implied warranty an unwritten guarantee that the good or service is fit for the purpose for which it was sold

 PRODUCT WARRANTIES

Just as a package is designed to protect the product, a warranty protects the buyer and gives essential information about the product. A warranty confirms the quality or performance of a good or service. An express warranty is a written guarantee. Express warranties range from simple statements—such as "100-percent cotton" (a guarantee of quality) and "complete satisfaction guaranteed" (a statement of performance)—to extensive documents written in technical language. In contrast, an implied warranty is an unwritten guarantee that the good or service is fit for the purpose for which it was sold. All sales have an implied warranty under the Uniform Commercial Code.

Congress passed the Magnuson-Moss Warranty–Federal Trade Commission Improvement Act in 1975 to help consumers understand warranties and get action from manufacturers and dealers. A manufacturer that promises a full warranty must meet certain minimum standards, including repair "within a reasonable time and without charge" of any defects and replacement of the merchandise or a full refund if the product does not work "after a reasonable number of attempts" at repair. Any warranty that does not live up to this tough prescription must be "conspicuously" promoted as a limited warranty.

STUDY TOOLS 10

LOCATED AT BACK OF THE TEXTBOOK
☐ Rip out Chapter Review Card

LOCATED AT WWW.CENGAGEBRAIN.COM
☐ Review Key Terms Flashcards and create your own
☐ Track your knowledge and understanding of key concepts in marketing
☐ Complete practice and graded quizzes to prepare for tests
☐ Complete interactive content within the MKTG Online experience
☐ View the chapter highlight boxes within the MKTG Online experience

MKTG
ONLINE

PREPARE FOR TESTS ON THE STUDYBOARD!

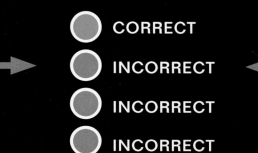

CORRECT

INCORRECT

INCORRECT

INCORRECT

Personalize Quizzes from Your StudyBits

Take Practice Quizzes by Chapter

CHAPTER QUIZZES
Chapter 1
Chapter 2
Chapter 3
Chapter 4

4LTR PRESS

Access MKTG ONLINE at www.cengagebrain.com

11 | Developing and Managing Products

Mega Pixel/Shutterstock.com

11-1 THE IMPORTANCE OF NEW PRODUCTS

New products are important to sustain growth, increase revenues and profits, and replace obsolete items. Each year *Fast Company* rates and ranks its most innovative companies, based on the ability to buck tradition in the interest of reaching more people, building a better business, and spurring mass-market appeal for unusual or highly technical products or services. In 2015, the top five companies were Warby Parker, Apple, Alibaba, Google, and Instagram.[1] All of these firms have reputations for relying heavily on technology.

11-1a Introduction of New Products

Some companies spend a considerable amount of money each year developing new products. At Pfizer, the world's largest research-based pharmaceutical company, approximately $1.2 billion is spent on research and development for every new product released.[2] Other companies with large research and development (R&D) spending include Volkswagen ($15.3 billion per year), Samsung ($14.1 billion per year), and Intel ($11.5 billion per year).[3]

Sometimes it is difficult to decide when to replace a successful product. Gillette Co. has a history of introducing new shaving systems (razors and accompanying blades) before the previous generation of products begins experiencing a sales decline. In fact, Gillette *expects* to cannibalize the sales of older models with its newer introductions. In early 2015, Apple reintroduced the MacBook line of laptops, effectively replacing the popular MacBook Air line. Apple executives agreed that the MacBook Air needed to be replaced to keep customers

satisfied, but the design of the new MacBook required complex decisions, tradeoffs, and risks. The new version features a retina display, thinner design, and a longer-lasting battery.[4] Clearly, the introduction of a new product is a monumental undertaking with a lot of open-ended questions—even for an established, multi-billion dollar company like Apple.

11-1b Categories of New Products

The term **new product** is somewhat confusing because its meaning varies widely. Actually, the term has several "correct" definitions. A product can be new to the world, to the market, to the producer or seller, or some combination of these. There are six categories of new products:

- **New-to-the-world products (also called** discontinuous innovations): These products create an entirely new market. For example, Gatorade recently announced that it is developing a microchip-fitted "smart cap" water bottle that will inform users how much they need to drink to stay properly hydrated during workouts. The bottle will communicate digitally with a sweat patch worn by the user to provide

> The average fast-moving consumer goods company introduces seventy to eighty new products per year.

the updates.[5] New-to-the-world products represent the smallest category of new products.

- **New product lines:** These products, which the firm has not previously offered, allow it to enter an established market. For example, Moleskine's first products were simple black-covered journals. Since then, the company has expanded into pens, travel bags, and even digital creative tools available on the iPhone and iPad.[6]

- Additions to existing product lines: This category includes new products that supplement

> **new product** a product new to the world, the market, the producer, the seller, or some combination of these

Musician Colin Dieden of The Mowgli's tries a quesalupa before surprising fans at Taco Bell's pre-order pick-up event on February 6, 2016.

Randy Shropshire/Getty Images

a firm's established line. Fast-food restaurant chain Taco Bell recently added the "quesalupa"—a combination of a quesadilla and a chalupa—to its menu. Leading up to the quesalupa's unveiling, Taco Bell launched an advertising campaign in early 2016 to encourage customers to pre-order a mysterious new menu item to be unveiled in a Super Bowl commercial. Customers who unknowingly pre-ordered the quesalupa were able to try it a day earlier than the masses. According to Taco Bell's chief marketing officer, Marisa Thalberg, the campaign was a success, resulting in tens of thousands of pre-orders for the new line extension item.[7]

- **Improvements or revisions of existing products:** The "new and improved" product may be significantly or only slightly changed. For example, every year Apple introduces a new version of the iPhone. Some new versions are vastly different than earlier versions, while others focus on more minimal updates. In late 2014, Apple introduced the iPhone 6, which featured a larger screen with 38 percent more pixels than the iPhone 5S and an upgraded camera that could record videos in slow motion. 2015's iPhone 6S, by contrast, added a slightly faster processor and a pressure-sensitive screen.[8]

- **Repositioned products:** These are existing products targeted at new markets or market segments, or ones repositioned to change the current market's perception of the product or company, which may be done to boost declining sales. Mercedes is repositioning

its ultra-luxurious Maybach line as a sub-brand to appeal to its most status-conscious customers. Although Mercedes is already known for luxurious vehicles, the Maybach line is intended to "set a new benchmark for exclusivity." The Mercedes-Maybach line will feature exceptionally comfortable and spacious seating and lavishly designed interiors.[9]

- **Lower-priced products:** This category refers to products that provide performance similar to competing brands at a lower price. The HP LaserJet Color MFP is a scanner, copier, printer, and fax machine combined. This new product is priced lower than many conventional color copiers and much lower than the combined price of the four items purchased separately.

11-2 THE NEW-PRODUCT DEVELOPMENT PROCESS

The management consulting firm Booz Allen Hamilton has studied the new-product development process for more than 30 years. Analyzing five major studies undertaken during this period, the firm has concluded that the companies most likely to succeed in developing and introducing new products are those that take the following actions:

- Make the long-term commitment needed to support innovation and new-product development.

- Use a company-specific approach, driven by corporate objectives and strategies, with a well-defined new-product strategy at its core.

- Capitalize on experience to achieve and maintain competitive advantage.

- Establish an environment—a management style, organizational structure, and degree of top management support—conducive to achieving company-specific new-product and corporate objectives.

Most companies follow a formal new-product development process, usually starting with a new-product strategy. Exhibit 11.1 traces the seven-step process, which is discussed in detail in this section. The exhibit is funnel-shaped to highlight the fact that each stage acts as a screen to filter out unworkable ideas.

11-2a New-Product Strategy

A **new-product strategy** links the new-product development process with the objectives of the marketing department, the business unit, and the corporation.

new-product strategy a plan that links the new-product development process with the objectives of the marketing department, the business unit, and the corporation

A new-product strategy must be compatible with these objectives, and in turn, all three of the objectives must be consistent with one another.

A new-product strategy is part of the organization's overall marketing strategy. It sharpens the focus and provides general guidelines for generating, screening, and evaluating new-product ideas. The new-product strategy specifies the roles that new products must play in the organization's overall plan and describes the characteristics of products the organization wants to offer and the markets it wants to serve.

11-2b Idea Generation

New-product ideas come from many sources, including customers, employees, distributors, competitors, R&D, consultants, and other experts.

CUSTOMERS The marketing concept suggests that customers' wants and needs should be the springboard for developing new products. Companies can derive insight from listening to Internet chatter or reading blogs, which often indicate early trends or areas consumers are interested in seeing develop or change. Another approach for generating new-product ideas is using what some companies are calling "customer innovation centers." The idea is to provide a forum for meeting with customers and directly involving them in the innovation process.

EMPLOYEES Sometimes employees know a company's products and processes better than anyone else. Many firms have formal and informal processes in place for employees to propose new product ideas. To encourage participation, some companies run contests, hold votes, and set up idea kiosks.[10]

Some companies even allow their employees time at work to try and come up with new ideas. Google encourages its engineers to spend 20 percent of their time working on innovative independent projects. This policy has led to several successful innovations, such as Gmail and Google News.[11]

EXHIBIT 11.1   NEW-PRODUCT DEVELOPMENT PROCESS

1 New-product strategy
2 Idea generation
3 Idea screening
4 Business analysis
5 Development
6 Test marketing
7 Commercialization

New product

Source: https://us.havaianas.com/

For Havianas Customers, Customization is Key

In the saturated summer sandals market, flip-flop manufacturer Havianas utilizes customization as a way to stand out. Havianas' online customization tool allows customers to combine different patterns and colors to create their own unique pairs of flip flops.[12]

Some firms reward employees for coming up with creative new ideas. In an effort to encourage risk-taking through new ideas, companies like Google have begun implementing rewards for employees who fail after taking a big risk. Some of the most innovative Google ideas (such as driverless cars and Google glass) were developed through the Google X program. In order to promote innovative thinking and eliminate the fear of coming up with bad ideas among Google X employees, the company rewards failure. According to Google X employee Astro Teller, "You must reward people for failing. If not, they won't take risks and make breakthroughs. If you don't reward failure, people will hang on to a doomed idea for fear of the consequences. That wastes time and saps an organization's spirit."[13]

DISTRIBUTORS A well-trained sales force routinely asks distributors about needs that are not being met. Because they are closer to end users, distributors are often more aware of customer needs than are manufacturers. The inspiration for Rubbermaid's Sidekick, a litter-free lunch box, came from a distributor who suggested that the company place some of its plastic containers inside a lunch box and sell the box as an alternative to plastic wrap and paper bags.

COMPETITORS No firms rely solely on internally generated ideas for new products. As discussed in Chapter 9, a big part of any organization's marketing intelligence system should be monitoring the performance of competitors' products. One purpose of competitive monitoring is to determine which, if any, of the competitors' products should be copied. There is plenty of information about competitors on the Internet. Fuld & Company is a preeminent research and consulting firm in the field of competitive intelligence. Its clients include more than half of the United States. *Fortune* 500 list and numerous international firms.[14]

RESEARCH AND DEVELOPMENT R&D is carried out in four distinct ways. You learned about basic research and applied research in Chapter 4. The other two ways are product development and product modification. **Product development** goes beyond applied research by converting applications into marketable

Jake Burton Carpenter (center) speaks at the Vermont Ski and Snowboard Museum after Governor Peter Shumlin (right of center) signed a bill declaring skiing and snowboarding as the official state sports of Vermont.

products. Product modification makes cosmetic or functional changes to existing products. Many new-product breakthroughs come from R&D activities.

Founder and CEO of Burton Snowboards Jake Burton Carpenter believes that his company has been so successful because it invests considerably more in R&D than its competitors do. "We have to continue to make the best product out there," says Carpenter. "The minute we get beat on an innovation or make a mistake on quality we lose our lead."[15] While the United States is the global leader in research and development, this lead is beginning to slip. The United States' share has grown from 25 percent to 34 percent at the same time as China's share alone has jumped more than sevenfold to 15 percent. Still, the United States spends $429 billion per year on R&D—more than twice that spent by China ($208 billion) and nearly three times that spent by Japan ($147 billion).[16]

CONSULTANTS Outside consultants are always available to examine a business and recommend product ideas. Examples include the Weston Group, Booz Allen Hamilton, and Management Decisions Inc. Traditionally, consultants determine whether a company has a balanced portfolio of products and, if not, what new-product ideas are needed to offset the imbalance. For example, Continuum is an award-winning consultancy firm that

product development
a marketing strategy that entails the creation of marketable new products; the process of converting applications for new technologies into marketable products

designs new goods and services, works on brand make-overs, and conducts consumer research. Clients include PepsiCo, Moen, American Express, Samsung, Reebok, and Sprint.[17]

OTHER EXPERTS A technique that is being used increasingly to generate new product ideas is called "crowdsourcing." General information regarding ideas being sought is provided to a wide range of potential sources such as industry experts, independent researchers, and academics. These experts then develop ideas for the company. In addition to field experts, firms such as Quirky Inc. and General Electric Company have used crowdsourcing to generate ideas from the general public and freelance inventors. Lego is using crowdsourcing to develop new ideas for its building block sets. Lego fans and enthusiasts can suggest ideas for new concepts via "Lego Ideas," a program set up by the toymaker. In order to qualify for a review by the marketing team, users must submit photos and a description of their idea to the Lego Ideas website, where other users can view and vote to support the idea. If the idea receives support from 10,000 users, it is sent to the Lego marketing team.[18] For a more thorough discussion of crowdsourcing, see Chapter 18.

Creativity is the wellspring of new-product ideas, regardless of who comes up with them. A variety of approaches and techniques have been developed to stimulate creative thinking. The two considered most useful for generating new-product ideas are brainstorming and focus group exercises. The goal of **brainstorming** is to get a group to think of unlimited ways to vary a product or solve a problem. Group members avoid criticism of an idea, no matter how ridiculous it may seem. Objective evaluation is postponed. The sheer quantity of ideas is what matters. As noted in Chapter 9, an objective of focus group interviews is to stimulate insightful comments through group interaction. In the industrial market, machine tools, keyboard designs, aircraft interiors, and backhoe accessories have evolved from focus groups.

11-2c Idea Screening

After new ideas have been generated, they pass through the first filter in the product development process. This stage, called **screening**, eliminates ideas that are inconsistent with the organization's new-product strategy or are obviously inappropriate for some other reason. The new-product committee, the new-product department, or some other formally appointed group performs the screening review.

Concept tests are often used at the screening stage to rate concept (or product) alternatives. A **concept test** evaluates a new-product idea, usually before any prototype has been created. Typically, researchers get consumer reactions to descriptions and visual representations of a proposed product. Concept tests are considered fairly good predictors of success for line extensions. They have also been relatively precise predictors of success for new products that are not copycat items, are not easily classified into existing product categories, and do not require major changes in consumer behavior—such as Betty Crocker Tuna Helper. However, concept tests are usually inaccurate in predicting the success of new products that create new consumption patterns and require major changes in consumer behavior—such as microwave ovens, digital music players, and computers.

11-2d Business Analysis

New-product ideas that survive the initial screening process move to the **business analysis** stage, where preliminary figures for demand, cost, sales, and profitability are calculated. For the first time, costs and revenues are estimated and compared. Depending on the nature of the product and the company, this process may be simple or complex.

The newness of the product, the size of the market, and the nature of the competition all affect the accuracy of revenue projections. In an established market like soft drinks, industry estimates of total market size are available. Forecasting market share for a new entry in a new, fragmented, or relatively small niche is a bigger challenge.

Analyzing overall economic trends and their impact on estimated sales is especially important in product categories that are sensitive to fluctuations in the business cycle. If consumers view the economy as uncertain and risky, they will put off buying durable goods such as major home appliances, automobiles, and homes. Likewise, business buyers postpone major equipment purchases if they expect a recession. Understanding the market potential is important because costs increase dramatically once a product idea enters the development stage.

brainstorming the process of getting a group to think of unlimited ways to vary a product or solve a problem

screening the first filter in the product development process, which eliminates ideas that are inconsistent with the organization's new-product strategy or are obviously inappropriate for some other reason

concept test a test to evaluate a new-product idea, usually before any prototype has been created

business analysis the second stage of the screening process where preliminary figures for demand, cost, sales, and profitability are calculated

11-2e Development

In the early stage of **development**, the R&D or engineering department may develop a prototype of the product. A process called 3D printing, or additive manufacturing, is sometimes used to create three-dimensional prototypes quickly and at a relatively low cost. During this stage, the firm should start sketching a marketing strategy. The marketing department should decide on the product's packaging, branding, labeling, and so forth. In addition, it should map out preliminary promotion, price, and distribution strategies. The feasibility of manufacturing the product at an acceptable cost should be thoroughly examined. The development stage can last a long time and thus be very expensive. It took ten years to develop Crest toothpaste, fifteen years to develop the Polaroid Colorpack camera and the Xerox copy machine, 18 years to develop Minute Rice, and 51 years to develop the television. Video game developer Ubisoft took more than five years to develop open-world action game Watch Dogs and more than six years to develop racing game The Crew. The time invested in development, however, can often have a tremendous payoff. Watch Dogs broke launch day sales for Ubisoft, selling more than 4 million units during its first week.[19]

The development process works best when all the involved areas (R&D, marketing, engineering,

3D Printing (or additive manufacturing) is sometimes used to create three-dimensional prototypes quickly and at a relatively low cost.

Stefano Tinti/Shutterstock.com

development the stage in the product development process in which a prototype is developed and a marketing strategy is outlined

production, and even suppliers) work together rather than sequentially, a process called **simultaneous product development**. This approach allows firms to shorten the development process and reduce costs. With simultaneous product development, all relevant functional areas and outside suppliers participate in all stages of the development process. Rather than proceeding through highly structured stages, the cross-functional team operates in unison. Involving key suppliers early in the process capitalizes on their knowledge and enables them to develop critical component parts.

The Internet is a useful tool for implementing simultaneous product development. On the Web, multiple partners from a variety of locations can meet regularly to assess new-product ideas, analyze markets and demographics, and review cost information. Ideas judged to be feasible can quickly be converted into new products. The best-managed global firms leverage their global networks by sharing best practices, knowledge, and technology.[20] Without the Internet, it would be impossible to conduct simultaneous product development from different parts of the world. Some firms use online brain trusts to solve technical problems. InnoCentive Inc. is a network of 80,000 self-selected science problem solvers in 173 countries. Its clients include NASA, *Popular Science*, and *The Economist*. When one of InnoCentive's partners selects an idea for development, it no longer tries to develop the idea from the ground up with its own resources and time. Instead, it issues a brief to its network of thinkers, researchers, technology entrepreneurs, and inventors around the world, hoping to generate dialogue, suggestions, and solutions.

Innovative firms are also gathering a variety of R&D input from customers online. Wheaties NEXT Challenge allowed customers to vote for which elite athlete would be featured on the next Wheaties cereal box by logging workouts through the MapMyFitness program. For each workout that was logged, a vote was cast for the participant's favorite Wheaties athlete. More than 71,000 people participated in the challenge.[21]

Laboratory tests are often conducted on prototype models during the development stage. User safety is an important aspect of laboratory testing, which actually subjects products to much more severe treatment than is expected by end users. The Consumer Product Safety Act of 1972 requires manufacturers to conduct a "reasonable testing program" to ensure that their products conform to established safety standards.

Many products that test well in the laboratory are also tried out in homes or businesses. Examples of product categories well suited for such use tests include human and pet food products, household cleaning products, and industrial chemicals and supplies. These products are all relatively inexpensive, and their performance characteristics are apparent to users. For example, P&G tests a variety of personal and home-care products in the community around its Cincinnati, Ohio, headquarters.

11-2f Test Marketing

After products and marketing programs have been developed, they are usually tested in the marketplace. **Test marketing** is the limited introduction of a product and a marketing program to determine the reactions of potential customers in a market situation. Test marketing allows management to evaluate alternative strategies and to assess how well the various aspects of the marketing mix fit together. Even established products are test marketed to assess new marketing strategies.

The cities chosen as test sites should reflect market conditions in the new product's projected market area. Yet no "magic city" exists that can universally represent market conditions, and a product's success in one city does not guarantee that it will be a nationwide hit. When selecting test market cities, researchers should therefore find locations where the demographics and purchasing habits mirror the overall market. The company should also have good distribution in test cities. Wendy's uses Columbus, Ohio as a test market for new burgers. Because the city has a nearly perfect cross-section of America's demographic breakdown, it is the perfect testing ground for new products. Most recently, Wendy's tested the reception of its Ciabatta Bacon Cheeseburger.[22] Moreover, test locations should be isolated from the media. If the television stations in a particular market reach a very large area outside that market, the advertising used for the test product may pull in many consumers from outside the market. The product may then appear more successful than it really is.

THE HIGH COSTS OF TEST MARKETING Test marketing frequently takes one year or longer, and costs can exceed $1 million. Some products remain in test markets even longer. In an effort to expand its

simultaneous product development a team-oriented approach to new-product development

test marketing the limited introduction of a product and a marketing program to determine the reactions of potential customers in a market situation

Wendy's uses Columbus, Ohio, as a test market for new burgers and menu items.

promotion, pricing, or advertising campaign. The purpose is to hide or distort the normal conditions that the testing firm might expect in the market.

ALTERNATIVES TO TEST MARKETING Many firms are looking for cheaper, faster, safer alternatives to traditional test marketing. In the early 1980s, Information Resources Inc. pioneered one alternative: scanner-based research (discussed in Chapter 9). A typical supermarket scanner test costs about $300,000. Another alternative to traditional test marketing is **simulated (laboratory) market testing**. Advertising and other promotional materials for several products, including the test product, are shown to members of the product's target market. These people are then taken to shop at a mock or real store, where their purchases are recorded. Shopper behavior, including repeat purchasing, is monitored to assess the product's likely performance under true market conditions. Research firms offer simulated market tests for $25,000 to $100,000, compared to $1 million or more for full-scale test marketing.

The Internet offers a fast, cost-effective way to conduct test marketing. P&G uses the Internet to assess customer demand for potential new products. Many products that are not available in grocery stores or drugstores can be sampled from P&G's website devoted to samples and coupons, www.pgeveryday.com.[24]

Despite these alternatives, most firms still consider test marketing essential for most new products. The high price of failure simply prohibits the widespread introduction of most new products without testing.

11-2g Commercialization

The final stage in the new-product development process is **commercialization**, the decision to market a product. The decision to commercialize the product sets several tasks in motion: ordering production materials and equipment, starting production, building inventories, shipping the product to field distribution points, training the sales force, announcing the new product to the trade, and advertising to potential customers.

The time from the initial commercialization decision to the product's actual introduction varies. It can range from a few weeks for simple products that use existing equipment to several years for technical products that require custom manufacturing equipment. And the total cost of development and initial introduction can be staggering.

product offerings, Starbucks launched the Dark Barrel Latte in select Ohio and Florida locations in September 2014. Some describe this new latte as having a taste similar to Guinness beer. As of this printing, the drink is yet to become more widely available.[23]

Despite the cost, many firms believe it is better to fail in a test market than in a national introduction. Because test marketing is so expensive, some companies do not test line extensions of well-known brands.

The high cost of test marketing is not just financial. One unavoidable problem is that test marketing exposes the new product and its marketing mix to competitors before its introduction. Thus, the element of surprise is lost. Competitors can also sabotage or "jam" a testing program by introducing their own sales

simulated (laboratory) market testing the presentation of advertising and other promotional materials for several products, including a test product, to members of the product's target market

commercialization the decision to market a product

11-3 WHY SOME PRODUCTS SUCCEED AND OTHERS FAIL

Despite the amount of time and money spent on developing and testing new products, a large proportion of new product introductions fail. Products fail for a number of reasons. One common reason is that they simply do not offer any discernible benefit compared to existing products. Another commonly cited factor in new-product failures is a poor match between product features and customer desires. For example, there are telephone systems on the market with more than 700 different functions, although the average user is happy with just ten functions. Other reasons for failure include overestimation of market size, incorrect targeting or positioning, a price too high or too low, inadequate distribution, poor promotion, or simply an inferior product.

Estimates of the percentages of new products that fail vary. Many estimates range as high as 80 to 90 percent.[25] Failure can be a matter of degree, however. Absolute failure occurs when a company cannot recoup its development, marketing, and production costs—the product actually loses money for the company. A relative product failure results when the product returns a profit but fails to achieve sales, profit, or market share

goals. Examples of product failures in 2014 include the Amazon Fire Phone, detergent-free laundry systems, the Nike FuelBand, and Burger King's Satisfries, a healthier alternative to regular fries.[26]

High costs and other risks of developing and testing new products do not stop many companies, such as Newell Rubbermaid, Colgate-Palmolive, Campbell Soup Company, and 3M, from aggressively developing and introducing new products. These companies depend on new products to increase revenues and profits. The most important factor in successful new-product introduction is a good match between the product and market needs—as the marketing concept would predict. Successful new products deliver a meaningful and perceivable benefit to a sizable number of people or organizations and are different in some meaningful way from their intended substitutes.

11-4 GLOBAL ISSUES IN NEW-PRODUCT DEVELOPMENT

Increasing globalization of markets and competition provides a reason for multinational firms to consider new-product development from a worldwide perspective. A firm that starts with a global strategy is better able to develop products that are marketable worldwide. In many multinational corporations, every product is developed for potential worldwide distribution, and unique market requirements are satisfied during development whenever possible.

Some global marketers design their products to meet regulations in their major markets and then, if necessary, meet smaller markets' requirements country by country. Nissan develops lead-country car models that, with minor changes, can be sold in most markets. With this approach, Nissan has been able to reduce the number of its basic models from 48 to 18. Some products, however, have little potential for global market penetration without modification. Succeeding in some countries (such as China) often requires companies to develop products that meet the unique needs of these populations. In

Augmented reality mobile game *Pokemon Go* proved massively successful thanks to its innovative technology and use of long-beloved characters. The game quickly surpassed Twitter, Tinder, and Facebook in daily active users and more than doubled Nintendo's stock price.

other cases, companies cannot sell their products at affordable prices and still make a profit in many countries.

11-5 THE SPREAD OF NEW PRODUCTS

Managers have a better chance of successfully marketing products if they understand how consumers learn about and adopt products.

11-5a Diffusion of Innovation

An **innovation** is a product perceived as new by a potential adopter. It really does not matter whether the product is "new to the world" or some other category of new product. If it is new to a potential adopter, it is an innovation in this context. **Diffusion** is the process by which the adoption of an innovation spreads. Five categories of adopters participate in the diffusion process.

INNOVATORS Innovators are the first 2.5 percent of all those who adopt the product. Innovators are eager to try new ideas and products, almost as an obsession. In addition to having higher incomes, they are more worldly and more active outside their community than noninnovators. They rely less on group norms and are more self-confident. Because they are well educated, they are more likely to get their information from scientific sources and experts. Innovators are characterized as being venturesome.

EARLY ADOPTERS Early adopters are the next 13.5 percent to adopt the product. Although early adopters are not the very first, they do adopt early in the product's life cycle. Compared to innovators, they rely much more on group norms and values. They are also more oriented to the local community, in contrast to the innovators' worldly outlook. Early adopters are more likely than innovators to be opinion leaders because of their closer affiliation with groups. Early adopters are a new product's best friends. Because viral, buzz, and word-of-mouth advertising is on

innovation a product perceived as new by a potential adopter

diffusion the process by which the adoption of an innovation spreads

the rise, marketers focus a lot of attention identifying the group that begins the viral marketing chain—the influencers. Part of the challenge is that this group of customers is distinguished not by demographics but by behavior. Influencers come from all age, gender, and income groups, and they do not use media any differently than other users who are considered followers. The characteristic influencers share is their desire to talk to others about their experiences with goods and services. A desire to earn the respect of others is a dominant characteristic among early adopters.

EARLY MAJORITY The next 34 percent to adopt are called the early majority. The early majority weighs the pros and cons before adopting a new product. They are likely to collect more information and evaluate more brands than early adopters, thereby extending the adoption process. They rely on the group for information but are unlikely to be opinion leaders themselves. Instead, they tend to be opinion leaders' friends and neighbors. Consumers trust positive word-of-mouth reviews from friends, family, and peers.[27] In fact, 50 percent of purchase decisions are influenced by word-of-mouth, and 92 percent of consumers trust recommendations from friends and family more than any other form of advertising.[28] Product discussions often drive Millennial conversations, so word-of-mouth marketing is particularly powerful among this demographic. According to Jeff Fromm, president of marketing consultancy firm FutureCast, Millennials are much more likely than other groups to discuss decisions with other people. Millennials' desire for social connection leads them to talk about their experiences in person, as well as on social media sites like YouTube and Instagram.[29]

While word-of-mouth marketing is important to Millennials, actually getting them to discuss products concretely can be difficult. According to Eric Pakurar, executive director and head of strategy at G2 USA, "They kind of ping-pong back and forth. They do a little research, then talk to their friends, and then do a little more research and check back with their friends and family."[30]

All word of mouth is not positive. Four out of five U.S. consumers report telling people around them about negative customer service experiences. Forty-two percent of consumers share customer service experiences on social media, roughly half of which is negative.[31] The early majority is an important link in the process of diffusing new ideas because they are positioned between earlier and later adopters. A dominant characteristic of the early majority is deliberateness.

LATE MAJORITY The late majority is the next 34 percent to adopt. The late majority adopts a new product because most of their friends have already adopted it. Because they also rely on group norms, their adoption stems from pressure to conform. This group tends to be older and below average in income and education. They depend mainly on word-of-mouth communication rather than on the mass media. The dominant characteristic of the late majority is skepticism.

LAGGARDS The final 16 percent to adopt are called laggards. Like innovators, laggards do not rely on group norms. Their independence is rooted in their ties to tradition. Thus, the past heavily influences their decisions. By the time laggards adopt an innovation, it has probably been outmoded and replaced by something else. For example, they may have bought their first color television set after flat screen televisions were already widely diffused. Laggards have the longest adoption time and the lowest socioeconomic status. They tend to be suspicious of new

products and alienated from a rapidly advancing society. The dominant value of laggards is tradition. Marketers typically ignore laggards, who do not seem to be motivated by advertising or personal selling and are virtually impossible to reach online.

Note that some product categories may never be adopted by 100 percent of the population. The adopter categories refer to all of those who will eventually adopt a product, not the entire population.

11-5b Product Characteristics and the Rate of Adoption

Five product characteristics can be used to predict and explain the rate of acceptance and diffusion of a new product:

- **Complexity:** the degree of difficulty involved in understanding and using a new product. The more complex the product, the slower is its diffusion.

- **Compatibility:** the degree to which the new product is consistent with existing values and product knowledge, past experiences, and current needs. Incompatible products diffuse more slowly than compatible products.

- **Relative advantage:** the degree to which a product is perceived as superior to existing substitutes. Because it can store and play back thousands of songs, the iPod and its many variants have a clear relative advantage over the portable CD player.

- **Observability:** the degree to which the benefits or other results of using the product can be observed by others and communicated to target customers. For instance, fashion items and automobiles are highly visible and more observable than personal-care items.

- **"Trialability":** the degree to which a product can be tried on a limited basis. It is much easier to try a new toothpaste or breakfast cereal, for example, than a new personal computer.

11-5c Marketing Implications of the Adoption Process

Two types of communication aid the diffusion process: *word-of-mouth communication* among consumers and communication from marketers to consumers. Word-of-mouth communication within and across groups, including social media and viral communication, speeds diffusion. Opinion leaders discuss new products with their followers and with other opinion leaders. Marketers must therefore ensure that opinion leaders have the types of information desired in the media that they use. Suppliers of some products, such as professional and health care services, rely almost solely on word-of-mouth communication for new business.

Many large-scale companies like Procter & Gamble, Cisco Systems, and Salesforce.com seek out opinion leaders among their employees. Some companies conduct surveys to identify opinion leaders while others use technology to map connections between individuals and postings. Once identified, these influential employees are provided with specially tailored communication training and are invited to attend senior management briefings. The hope is that these opinion leaders will field coworkers' questions and build positive buzz. Influencers are frequently rewarded for their skills with promotions and other forms of recognition.[32]

The second type of communication aiding the diffusion process is *communication directly from the marketer to potential adopters*. Messages directed toward early adopters should normally use different appeals than messages directed toward the early majority, the late majority, or the laggards. Early adopters are more important than innovators because they make up a larger group, are more socially active, and are usually opinion leaders.

As the focus of a promotional campaign shifts from early adopters to the early majority and the late majority, marketers should study the dominant characteristics, buying behavior, and media characteristics of these target markets. Then they should revise messages and media strategy to fit. The diffusion model helps guide marketers in developing and implementing promotion strategy.

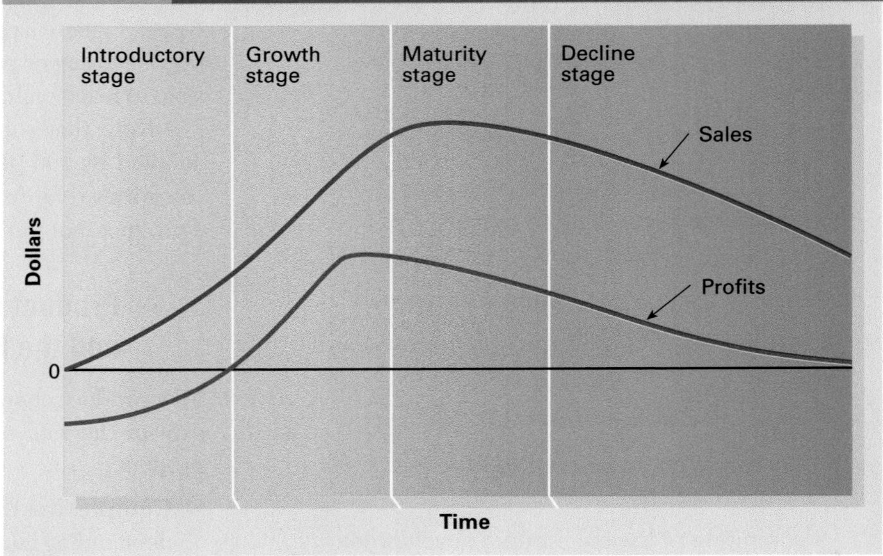

11-6 PRODUCT LIFE CYCLES

The product life cycle (PLC) is one of the most familiar concepts in marketing. Few other general concepts have been so widely discussed. Although some researchers and consultants have challenged the theoretical basis and managerial value of the PLC, many believe it is a useful marketing management

product life cycle (PLC) a concept that provides a way to trace the stages of a product's acceptance, from its introduction (birth) to its decline (death)

product category all brands that satisfy a particular type of need

diagnostic tool and a general guide for marketing planning in various life cycle stages.

The PLC is a biological metaphor that traces the stages of a product's acceptance, from its introduction (birth) to its decline (death). As Exhibit 11.2 shows, a product progresses through four major stages: introduction, growth, maturity, and decline.

The PLC concept can be used to analyze a brand, a product form, or a product category. The PLC for a product form is usually longer than the PLC for any one brand. The exception would be a brand that was the first and last competitor in a product form market. In that situation, the brand and product form life cycles would be equal in length. Product categories have the longest life cycles. A **product category** includes all brands that satisfy a particular type of need, such as shaving products, passenger automobiles, or soft drinks.

The time a product spends in any one stage of the life cycle may vary dramatically. Some products, such as fad items, move through the entire cycle in weeks. Fads are typically characterized by a sudden and unpredictable spike in sales followed by a rather abrupt decline. Examples of fad items are Silly Bandz, Beanie Babies, and Crocs. Other products, such as electric clothes washers and dryers, stay in the maturity stage for decades. Exhibit 11.2 illustrates the typical life cycle for a consumer durable good, such as a washer or dryer. In contrast, Exhibit 11.3 illustrates typical life cycles for styles (such as formal, business, or casual clothing), fashions (such as miniskirts or baggy jeans), and fads (such as leopard-print clothing). Changes in a product, its uses, its image, or its positioning can extend that product's life cycle.

EXHIBIT 11.2 FOUR STAGES OF THE PRODUCT LIFE CYCLE

EXHIBIT 11.3 PRODUCT LIFE CYCLES FOR STYLES, FASHIONS, AND FADS

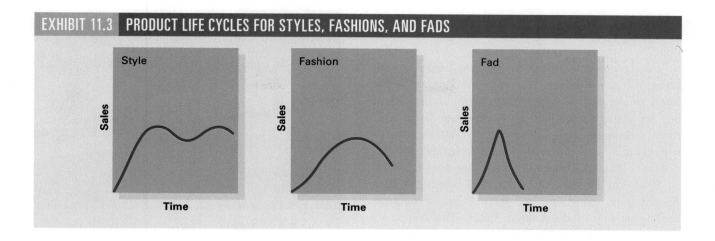

The PLC concept does not tell managers the length of a product's life cycle or its duration in any stage. It does not dictate marketing strategy. It is simply a tool to help marketers forecast future events and suggest appropriate strategies.

11-6a Introductory Stage

The **introductory stage** of the PLC represents the full-scale launch of a new product into the marketplace. Computer databases for personal use, room-deodorizing air-conditioning filters, and wind-powered home electric generators are all product categories that have recently entered the PLC. A high failure rate, little competition, frequent product modification, and limited distribution typify the introductory stage of the PLC.

Marketing costs in the introductory stage are normally high for several reasons. High dealer margins are often needed to obtain adequate distribution, and incentives are needed to get consumers to try the new product. Advertising expenses are high because of the need to educate consumers about the new product's benefits. Production costs are also often high in this stage, as product and manufacturing flaws are identified and corrected and efforts are undertaken to develop mass production economies.

Sales normally increase slowly during the introductory stage. Moreover, profits are usually negative because of R&D costs, factory tooling, and high introduction costs. The length of the introductory phase is largely determined by product characteristics, such as the product's advantages over substitute products, the educational effort required to make the product known, and management's commitment of resources to the new item. A short introductory period is usually preferred to help reduce the impact of negative earnings and cash flows. As soon as the product gets off the ground, the financial burden should begin to diminish. Also, a short introduction helps dispel some of the uncertainty as to whether the new product will be successful.

Promotion strategy in the introductory stage focuses on developing product awareness and informing consumers about the product category's potential benefits. At this stage, the communication challenge is to stimulate primary demand—demand for the product in general rather than for a specific brand. Intensive personal selling is often required to gain acceptance for the product among wholesalers and retailers. Promotion of convenience products often requires heavy consumer sampling and couponing. Shopping and specialty products demand educational advertising and personal selling to the final consumer.

11-6b Growth Stage

If a product category survives the introductory stage, it then advances to the **growth stage** of the life cycle. In this stage, sales typically grow at an increasing rate, many competitors enter the market, and large companies may start to acquire small pioneering firms. Profits rise rapidly in the growth stage, reach their peak, and begin declining as competition intensifies. Emphasis switches from primary demand promotion (e.g., promoting e-readers) to aggressive brand advertising and communication of the differences between brands (e.g., promoting Kindle versus Nook).

Distribution becomes a major key to success during the growth stage, as well as in later stages. Manufacturers scramble to sign up dealers and distributors and to build long-term

introductory stage the full-scale launch of a new product into the marketplace

growth stage the second stage of the product life cycle when sales typically grow at an increasing rate, many competitors enter the market, large companies may start to acquire small pioneering firms, and profits are healthy

relationships. Others are able to market direct to consumers using electronic media. Without adequate distribution, it is impossible to establish a strong market position.

As the economy recovers, more companies are entering the growth stage, and more workers are being hired. Because of this employment boom, staffing agencies are seeing a huge increase in revenues. On Assignment, a company that places temporary and permanent workers in several different industries, ranked third on *Fortune's* list of the fastest growing companies for 2014. In 2012, On Assignment acquired IT staffing agency ApexSystems, becoming the second largest infotech staffing agency in the United States. The company's stock rose 26.6 percent the day after the acquisition.[33]

11-6c Maturity Stage

A period during which sales increase at a decreasing rate signals the beginning of the maturity stage of the life cycle. New users cannot be added indefinitely, and sooner or later the market approaches saturation. Normally, this is the longest stage of the PLC. Many major household appliances are in the maturity stage of their life cycles.

For shopping products such as durable goods and electronics, and many specialty products, annual models begin to appear during the maturity stage. Product lines are lengthened to appeal to additional market segments. Service and repair assume more important roles as manufacturers strive to distinguish their products from others. Product design changes tend to become stylistic (How can the product be made different?) rather than functional (How can the product be made better?).

As prices and profits continue to fall, marginal competitors start dropping out of the market. Dealer margins also shrink, resulting in less shelf space for mature items, lower dealer inventories, and a general reluctance to promote the product. Thus, promotion to dealers often intensifies during this stage in order to retain loyalty.

Heavy consumer promotion by the manufacturer is also required to maintain market share. Cutthroat competition during this stage can lead to price wars. Another characteristic of the maturity stage is the emergence of "niche marketers" that target narrow, well-defined, underserved segments of a market. Starbucks Coffee targets its gourmet line at new, young, affluent coffee drinkers, the only segment of the coffee market that is growing.

maturity stage a period during which sales increase at a decreasing rate

decline stage a long-run drop in sales

Startbucks targets its gourmet line at new, young drinkers;—the only segment that is growing.

11-6d Decline Stage

A long-run drop in sales signals the beginning of the decline stage. The rate of decline is governed by how rapidly consumer tastes change or substitute products are adopted. Many convenience products and fad items lose their market overnight, leaving large inventories of unsold items, such as designer jeans. Others die more slowly. Landline telephone service is an example of a product in the decline stage of the product life cycle. Nearly 40 percent of American homes do not have a landline, which represents a continued steady increase since 2010—and a steady drop in the use of landlines.[34] People abandoning landlines to go wireless and households replacing landlines with Internet phones have both contributed to this long-term decline.

Some firms have developed successful strategies for marketing products in the decline stage of the PLC. They eliminate all nonessential marketing expenses and let sales decline as more and more customers discontinue purchasing the products. Eventually, the product is withdrawn from the market.

11-6e Implications for Marketing Management

The new-product development process, the diffusion process, and the PLC concept all have implications for marketing managers. The funnel shape of Exhibit 11.1 indicates that many new product ideas are necessary to produce one successful new product. The new-product development process is sometimes illustrated as a decay curve with roughly half of the ideas approved at one stage rejected at the next stage. While the actual numbers vary widely among firms and industries, the relationship between the stages can be generalized. This reinforces the notion that an organized effort to generate many ideas from various sources is important for any firm that wishes to produce a continuing flow of new products.

The major implication of the diffusion process to marketing managers is that the message may need to change over time. The targeted adopter and media may need to shift based on how various categories of adopters gather product information. A message developed for and targeted toward early adopters will not be perceived similarly by late majority adopters.

Exhibit 11.4 shows the relationship between the adopter categories and stages of the PLC. Note that the various categories of adopters buy products in different stages of the life cycle. Almost all sales in the maturity and decline stages represent repeat purchases.

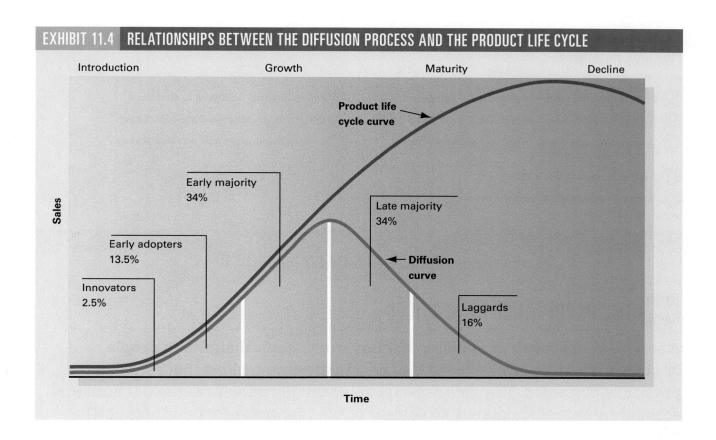

EXHIBIT 11.4 RELATIONSHIPS BETWEEN THE DIFFUSION PROCESS AND THE PRODUCT LIFE CYCLE

Introduction   Growth   Maturity   Decline

Product life cycle curve

Early majority 34%

Late majority 34%

Early adopters 13.5%

Diffusion curve

Innovators 2.5%

Laggards 16%

Sales

Time

STUDY TOOLS 11

LOCATED AT BACK OF THE TEXTBOOK
☐ Rip out Chapter Review Card

LOCATED AT WWW.CENGAGEBRAIN.COM
☐ Review Key Terms Flashcards and create your own
☐ Track your knowledge and understanding of key concepts in marketing
☐ Complete practice and graded quizzes to prepare for tests
☐ Complete interactive content within the MKTG Online experience
☐ View the chapter highlight boxes within the MKTG Online experience

12 | Services and Nonprofit Organization Marketing

LEARNING OUTCOMES

After studying this chapter, you will be able to...

12-1 Discuss the importance of services to the economy

12-2 Discuss the differences between services and goods

12-3 Describe the components of service quality and the gap model of service quality

12-4 Develop marketing mixes for services

12-5 Discuss relationship marketing in services

12-6 Explain internal marketing in services

12-7 Describe nonprofit organization marketing

12-8 Discuss global issues in services marketing

After you finish this chapter go to **PAGE 218** for **STUDY TOOLS**

12-1 THE IMPORTANCE OF SERVICES

A service is the result of applying human or mechanical efforts to people or objects. Services involve a deed, a performance, or an effort that cannot be physically possessed. The service sector substantially influences the U.S. economy, accounting for approximately 80 percent of the country's economic output. The service-oriented industries contributing to much of this output include technology, financial services, health care, and retail.[1]

The marketing process described in Chapter 1 is the same for all types of products, whether they are goods or services. In addition, although a comparison of goods and services marketing can be beneficial, in reality it is hard to distinguish clearly between manufacturing and service firms. Indeed, many manufacturing firms can point to service as a major factor in their success. For example, maintenance and repair services offered by the manufacturer are important to buyers of copy machines. Nevertheless, services have some unique characteristics that distinguish them from goods, and marketing strategies need to be adjusted for these characteristics.

12-2 HOW SERVICES DIFFER FROM GOODS

Services have four unique characteristics that distinguish them from goods. Services are intangible, inseparable, heterogeneous, and perishable.

service the result of applying human or mechanical efforts to people or objects

12-2a Intangibility

The basic difference between services and goods is that services are intangible performances. Because of their **intangibility**, they cannot be touched, seen, tasted, heard, or felt in the same manner that goods can be sensed.

Evaluating the quality of services before or even after making a purchase is harder than evaluating the quality of goods because, compared to goods, services tend to exhibit fewer search qualities. A **search quality** is a characteristic that can be easily assessed before purchase—for instance, the color of an appliance or automobile. At the same time, services tend to exhibit more experience and credence qualities. An **experience quality** is a characteristic that can be assessed only after use, such as the quality of a meal in a restaurant. A **credence quality** is a characteristic that consumers may have difficulty assessing even after purchase because they do not have the necessary knowledge or experience. Medical and consulting services are examples of services that exhibit credence qualities.

These characteristics also make it harder for marketers to communicate the benefits of an intangible service than to communicate the benefits of tangible goods. Thus, marketers often rely on tangible cues to communicate a service's nature and quality. For example, Travelers Insurance Company uses an umbrella symbol as a tangible reminder of the protection that insurance provides.

The facilities that customers visit, or from which services are delivered, are a critical tangible part of the total service offering. Messages about the organization are communicated to customers through such elements as the décor, the clutter or neatness of service areas, and the staff's manners and dress. Hotels know that guests form opinions quickly and are more willing than ever before to tweet them within the first fifteen minutes of their stay. Some hotels go to great lengths to make their guests feel at home.

intangibility the inability of services to be touched, seen, tasted, heard, or felt in the same manner that goods can be sensed

search quality a characteristic that can be easily assessed before purchase

experience quality a characteristic that can be assessed only after use

credence quality a characteristic that consumers may have difficulty assessing even after purchase because they do not have the necessary knowledge or experience

For example, Four Seasons makes sure that no plumbing is touching concrete at its hotels to create the quietest possible rooms. The company also gives all of its employees—from parking attendants to managers—the authority to act instantly when a guest makes a request. This allows Four Seasons to offer excellent personalized service from check-in to check-out.[2]

12-2b Inseparability

Goods are produced, sold, and then consumed. In contrast, services are often sold, produced, and consumed at the same time. In other words, their production and consumption are inseparable activities. This inseparability means that, because consumers must be present during the production of services like haircuts or surgery, they are actually involved in the production of the services they buy. That type of consumer involvement is rare in goods manufacturing.

Simultaneous production and consumption also means that services normally cannot be produced in a centralized location and consumed in decentralized locations, as goods typically are. Services are also inseparable from the perspective of the service provider. Thus, the quality of service that firms are able to deliver depends on the quality of their employees.

12-2c Heterogeneity

One great strength of McDonald's is consistency. Whether customers order a Big Mac in Chicago or Seattle, they know exactly what they are going to get. This is not the case with many service providers. Because services have greater heterogeneity, or variability of inputs and outputs, they tend to be less standardized and uniform than goods. For example, physicians in a group practice or barbers in a barbershop differ within each group in their technical and interpersonal skills. Because services tend to be labor intensive and production and consumption are inseparable, consistency and quality control can be hard to achieve.

Standardization and training help increase consistency and reliability. In the information technology sector, a number of certification programs are available to ensure that technicians are capable of working on (and within) complex enterprise software systems. Certifications such as the Cisco Certified Network Associate, CompTIA Security+, and Microsoft Certified Professional ensure a consistency of knowledge and ability among those who can pass these programs' rigorous exams.[3]

12-2d Perishability

Perishability is the fourth characteristic of services. Perishability refers to the inability of services to be stored, warehoused, or inventoried. An empty hotel room or airplane seat produces no revenue that day. The revenue is lost. Yet service organizations are often forced to turn away full-price customers during peak periods.

One of the most important challenges in many service industries is finding ways to synchronize supply and demand. The philosophy that some revenue is better than none has prompted many hotels to offer deep discounts on weekends and during the off-season.

12-3 SERVICE QUALITY

Because of the four unique characteristics of services, service quality is more difficult to define and measure than is the quality of tangible goods. Business executives rank the improvement of service quality as one of the most critical challenges facing them today.

12-3a Evaluating Service Quality

Research has shown that customers evaluate service quality by the following five components:

- **Reliability:** the ability to perform the service dependably, accurately, and consistently. Reliability is performing the service right the first time.

Quality service is a must if a company wants to keep the customers coming back.

Nejron Photo/Shutterstock.com

inseparability the inability of the production and consumption of a service to be separated; consumers must be present during the production

heterogeneity the variability of the inputs and outputs of services, which causes services to tend to be less standardized and uniform than goods

perishability the inability of services to be stored, warehoused, or inventoried

reliability the ability to perform a service dependably, accurately, and consistently

Has Discover Bank fallen into gap 4?

In 2015, Discover Bank was ordered to pay $16 million to student loan borrowers after overestimating minimum payment information and withholding important instructions on how to sign up for federal income tax benefits. These borrowers paid interest on loans that should have been deferred, and some even became delinquent on their accounts because they could not afford the payments. The bank fell into gap 4 in that it failed to properly communicate with its student customers.[4]

Alexey Rotanov/Shutterstock.com

This component has been found to be the one most important to consumers.

- **Responsiveness:** the ability to provide prompt service. Examples of responsiveness include calling the customer back quickly, serving lunch fast to someone who is in a hurry, or mailing a transaction slip immediately. The ultimate in responsiveness is offering service twenty-four hours a day, seven days a week. Priceline Group's global business, which operates in more than 220 countries and territories, shows responsiveness to its customers by hiring people who can answer calls in dozens of languages.[5]

- **Assurance:** the knowledge and courtesy of employees and their ability to convey trust. Skilled employees, who treat customers with respect and make customers feel that they can trust the firm, exemplify assurance.

- **Empathy:** caring, individualized attention to customers. Firms whose employees recognize customers and learn their specific requirements are providing empathy. LUX Resorts, a hospitality company based in Mauritius, recently initiated a company-wide plan to offer creative personalized service. Understanding that highly-scripted employees are often less able to empathize with customer needs, LUX's CEO started an educational program focused on getting employees to anticipate and understand guests' priorities. Knowing more about customers' wants and needs maximized employees' opportunities for providing great service, and two years after the program began, half of TripAdvisor's Top 10 list for Mauritius was filled with LUX properties.[6]

- **Tangibles:** the physical evidence of the service. The tangible parts of a service include the physical facilities, tools, and equipment used to provide the service, as well as the appearance of personnel.[7]

Overall service quality is measured by combining customers' evaluations for all five components.

12-3b The Gap Model of Service Quality

A model of service quality called the **gap model** identifies five gaps that can cause problems in service delivery and influence customer evaluations of service quality.[8] These gaps are illustrated in Exhibit 12.1.

- **Gap 1:** the gap between what customers want and what management thinks customers want. This gap results from a lack of understanding or a misinterpretation of the customers' needs, wants, or desires. A firm that does little or no customer satisfaction research is likely to experience this gap. To close gap 1, firms must stay attuned to customer wishes by researching customer needs and satisfaction.

- **Gap 2:** the gap between what management thinks customers want and the quality specifications that management develops to provide the service. Essentially, this gap is the result of management's inability to translate customers' needs into delivery systems within the firm. For example, KFC used to rate its

responsiveness the ability to provide prompt service

assurance the knowledge and courtesy of employees and their ability to convey trust

empathy caring, individualized attention to customers

tangibles the physical evidence of a service, including the physical facilities, tools, and equipment used to provide the service

gap model a model identifying five gaps that can cause problems in service delivery and influence customer evaluations of service quality

EXHIBIT 12.1 GAP MODEL OF SERVICE QUALITY

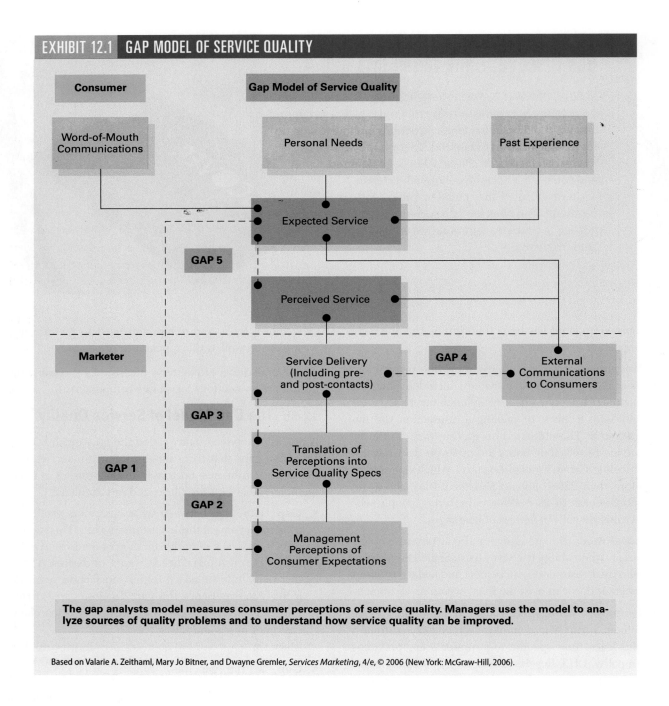

Gap Model of Service Quality

Consumer

Word-of-Mouth Communications

Personal Needs

Past Experience

Expected Service

GAP 5

Perceived Service

Marketer

Service Delivery (Including pre- and post-contacts)

GAP 4

External Communications to Consumers

GAP 3

Translation of Perceptions into Service Quality Specs

GAP 1

GAP 2

Management Perceptions of Consumer Expectations

The gap analysts model measures consumer perceptions of service quality. Managers use the model to analyze sources of quality problems and to understand how service quality can be improved.

Based on Valarie A. Zeithaml, Mary Jo Bitner, and Dwayne Gremler, *Services Marketing*, 4/e, © 2006 (New York: McGraw-Hill, 2006).

managers according to "chicken efficiency," or how much chicken they threw away at closing; customers who came in late would either have to wait for chicken to be cooked or settle for chicken several hours old.

- **Gap 3:** the gap between the service quality specifications and the service that is actually provided. If both gaps 1 and 2 have been closed, then gap 3 is due to the inability of management and employees to do what should be done. Management needs to ensure that employees have the skills and the proper tools to perform their jobs. Other techniques that help to close

gap 3 are training employees so they know what management expects and encouraging teamwork.

- **Gap 4:** the gap between what the company provides and what the customer is told it provides. This is clearly a communication gap. It may include misleading or deceptive advertising campaigns promising more than the firm can deliver or doing "whatever it takes" to get the business. To close this gap, companies need to create realistic customer expectations through honest, accurate communication about what the firms can provide.

- **Gap 5:** the gap between the service that customers receive and the service they want. This gap can be positive or negative. For example, if a patient expects to wait twenty minutes in the physician's office before seeing the physician but actually waits only ten minutes, the patient's evaluation of service quality will be high. However, a 40-minute wait would result in a lower evaluation. Nordstrom, a company whose service quality is legendary, consistently performs at a level above and beyond what customers expect, resulting in few to no signs of gap 5.[9]

When one or more of these gaps is large, service quality is perceived as low. As the gaps shrink, service quality perception improves. Chase Bank has joined a growing number of financial institutions working to close a persistent and wide gap 1—customers' desire for full-featured mobile banking. To meet the needs of highly mobile, technologically tuned-in customers, Chase has invested heavily in its banking app. Among other things, the app allows users to send money to friends, send wire transfers internationally, see statements, and log in using Touch ID on iPhones. It also has fun design features. For example, if someone uses the app in New York, he or she will see images of New York City.[10]

Several other companies consistently get their service quality right. According to a survey done by 24/7 Wall St. in collaboration with research survey group Zogby Analytics, the top five companies offering exceptional customer service in 2015 were

1. Amazon
2. Chick-fil-A
3. Apple
4. Marriott
5. Kroger[11]

These companies have three core beliefs in common: good service starts at the top, service is seen as a continual challenge, and companies work best when people want to work for them.

12-4 MARKETING MIXES FOR SERVICES

Services' unique characteristics—intangibility, inseparability of production and consumption, heterogeneity, and perishability—make marketing more challenging. Elements of the marketing mix (product, place, promotion, and pricing) need to be adjusted to meet the special needs created by these characteristics.

12-4a Product (Service) Strategy

A product, as defined in Chapter 10, is everything a person receives in an exchange. In the case of a service organization, the product offering is intangible and consists in large part of a process or a series of processes. Product strategies for service offerings include decisions on the type of process involved, core and supplementary services, standardization or customization of the service product, and the service mix.

SERVICE AS A PROCESS Two broad categories of things get processed in service organizations: people and objects. In some cases, the process is physical, or tangible, while in others the process is intangible. Based on these characteristics, service processes can be placed into one of four categories:

- *People processing* takes place when the service is directed at a customer. Examples are transportation services and health care.
- *Possession processing* occurs when the service is directed at customers' physical possessions. Examples are lawn care, dry cleaning, and veterinary services.
- *Mental stimulus processing* refers to services directed at people's minds. Examples are theater performances and education.
- *Information processing* describes services that use technology or brainpower directed at a customer's assets. Examples are insurance and consulting.[12]

Because customers' experiences and involvement differ for each of these types of services, marketing strategies may also differ. For example, people-processing services require customers to enter the *service factory*, which is a physical location, such as an aircraft, a physician's office, or a hair salon. In contrast, possession-processing services typically do not require the presence of the customer in the service factory. Marketing strategies for the former would therefore focus more on an attractive, comfortable physical environment and employee training on employee–customer interaction issues than would strategies for the latter.

CORE AND SUPPLEMENTARY SERVICE PRODUCTS The service offering can be viewed as a bundle of activities that includes the **core service**, which is the most basic benefit the customer is buying, and a group of **supplementary services** that support or enhance the core service. Exhibit 12.2 illustrates these concepts

core service the most basic benefit the consumer is buying

supplementary services a group of services that support or enhance the core service

EXHIBIT 12.2   CORE AND SUPPLEMENTARY SERVICES FOR A LUXURY HOTEL

Reservation

Room Phone

Parking

Core Delivery Process

Overnight rental of a bedroom

Room Service

Check-in/ Check-out

Pay TV

Supplementary Services

Porter

Meal

Delivery Processes for Supplementary Services

Source: Lovelock, Christopher H.; Wirtz, Jochen, *Services Marketing*, 7th, (c)2011. Electronically reproduced by permission of Pearson Education, Inc., Upper Saddle River, New Jersey.

for a luxury hotel. The core service is providing bedrooms for rent, which involves people processing. The supplementary services, some of which involve information processing, include food services, reservations, parking, phone, and television services.

In many service industries, the core service becomes a commodity as competition increases. Thus, firms usually emphasize supplementary services to create a competitive advantage. On the other hand, some firms are positioning themselves in the marketplace by greatly reducing supplementary services.

CUSTOMIZATION/STANDARDIZATION An important issue in developing the service offering is whether to customize or standardize it. Customized services are more flexible and respond to individual customers' needs. They also usually command a higher price. Standardized services are more efficient and cost less.

Instead of choosing to either standardize or customize a service, a firm may incorporate elements of both by adopting an emerging strategy called **mass customization**. Mass customization uses technology to deliver customized services on a mass basis, which results in giving each customer whatever she or he asks

mass customization a strategy that uses technology to deliver customized services on a mass basis

for. Application Programming Interface (API) banking represents a new way to think about banking services and how to deliver these services to different customer groups. For example, API banking could allow a bank to offer Millennials a mobile banking app with tools to pay down student debt while offering Baby Boomers a similar app but with special services focused on retirement planning.[13]

THE SERVICE MIX Most service organizations market more than one service. For example, TruGreen offers lawn care, shrub care, carpet cleaning, and industrial lawn services. Each organization's service mix represents a set of opportunities, risks, and challenges. Each part of the service mix should make a different contribution to achieving the firm's goals. To succeed, each service may also need a different level of financial support. Designing a service strategy, therefore, means deciding what new services to introduce to which target market, what existing services to maintain, and what services to eliminate.

12-4b Place (Distribution) Strategy

Distribution strategies for service organizations must focus on such issues as convenience, number of outlets, direct versus indirect distribution, location, and scheduling. A key factor influencing the selection of a service provider is *convenience*. An interesting example of this is Mac & Mia, a premium trunk club for children's clothing. This service targets parents of small children who have little or no time to shop. After a parent completes a style profile for his or her child at Mac & Mia's website, a company representative fills a box with a selection of hand-picked clothing and accessories and ships it out. Parents keep what they want and return what they don't within five days using an included prepaid envelope. The company provides busy parents an easy, fun, and convenient way to buy needed items for their kids.[14]

An important distribution objective for many service firms is the number of outlets to use or the number of outlets to open during a certain time. Generally, the intensity of distribution should meet, but not exceed, the target market's needs and preferences. Having too few outlets may inconvenience customers; having too many outlets may boost costs unnecessarily. Intensity of distribution may also depend on the image desired. Having only a few outlets may make the service seem more exclusive or selective.

The next service distribution decision is whether to distribute services to end-users *directly* or *indirectly* through other firms. Because of the intangible nature of services, many service firms have to use direct distribution or franchising. Examples include legal, medical, accounting, and personal-care services. The most-used form of direct distribution is the Internet. Most major airlines are now using online services to sell tickets directly to consumers, resulting in lower distribution costs for the airlines. Other firms with standardized service packages have developed indirect channels using independent intermediaries. For example, Banfield Pet Hospital formed a strategic partnership with PetSmart to offer veterinary services at PetSmart locations.

The *location* of a service most clearly reveals the relationship between its target market strategy and distribution strategy. For time-dependent service providers such as airlines, physicians, and dentists, *scheduling* is often a more important factor.

12-4c Promotion Strategy

Consumers and business users have more trouble evaluating services than goods because services are less tangible. In turn, marketers have more trouble promoting intangible services than tangible goods. Here are four promotion strategies they can try:

- **Stressing tangible cues:** A tangible cue is a concrete symbol of the service offering. To make their intangible services more tangible, hotels turn down the bedcovers and put mints on the pillows.

- **Using personal information sources:** A personal information source is someone consumers are familiar with (such as a celebrity) or someone they admire or can relate to personally. Service firms may seek to simulate positive word-of-mouth communication among present and prospective customers by using real customers in their ads.

- **Creating a strong organizational image:** One way to create an image is to manage the evidence, including the physical environment of the service facility, the appearance of the service employees, and the tangible items associated with a service (such as stationery, bills, and business cards). For example, McDonald's golden arches are instantly recognizable. Another way to create an image is through branding.

- **Engaging in postpurchase communication:** Postpurchase communication refers to the follow-up activities that a service firm might engage in after a customer transaction. Postcard surveys, telephone calls, and other types of follow-up show customers that their feedback matters.

AP Images/Susan Walsh

Celebrity is a powerful promotional tool for services and nonprofits alike. Here, actor and Eastern Congo Initiative founder Ben Affleck testifies before a Senate Foreign Relations Committee hearing on the Congo.

12-4d Price Strategy

Considerations in pricing a service are similar to the pricing considerations to be discussed in Chapter 19. However, the unique characteristics of services present two special pricing challenges.

First, in order to price a service, it is important to define the unit of service consumption. For example, should pricing be based on completing a specific service task (cutting a customer's hair), or should it be time based (how long it takes to cut a customer's hair)? Some services include the consumption of goods, such as food and beverages. Restaurants charge customers for food and drink rather than the use of a table and chairs.

Second, for services that are composed of multiple elements, the issue is whether pricing should be based on a "bundle" of elements or whether each element should be priced separately. A bundled price may be preferable when consumers dislike having to pay "extra" for every part of the service (e.g., paying extra for baggage or food on an airplane), and it is simpler for the firm to administer. Alternatively, customers may not want to pay for service elements they do not use. Many furniture stores now have "unbundled" delivery charges from the price of the furniture. Customers who wish to can pick up the furniture at the store, saving on the delivery fee.

Marketers should set performance objectives when pricing each service. Three categories of pricing objectives have been suggested:

- Revenue-oriented pricing focuses on maximizing the surplus of income over costs. This is the same approach that many manufacturing companies use. A limitation of this approach is that determining costs can be difficult for many services.

- Operations-oriented pricing seeks to match supply and demand by varying prices. For example, matching hotel demand to the number of available rooms can be achieved by raising prices at peak times and decreasing them during slow times.

- Patronage-oriented pricing tries to maximize the number of customers using the service. Thus, prices vary with different market segments' ability to pay, and methods of payment (such as credit) are offered that increase the likelihood of a purchase. Senior citizen and student discounts at movie theaters and restaurants are examples of patronage-oriented pricing.[15]

A firm may need to use more than one type of pricing objective. In fact, all three objectives probably need to be included to some degree in a pricing strategy, although the importance of each type may vary depending on the type of service provided, the prices that competitors are charging, the differing ability of various customer segments to pay, or the opportunity to negotiate price. For customized services (such as construction services), customers may also have the ability to negotiate a price.

12-5 RELATIONSHIP MARKETING IN SERVICES

Many services involve ongoing interaction between the service organization and the customer. Thus, they can benefit from relationship marketing, the strategy described in Chapter 1, as a means of attracting, developing, and retaining customer relationships. The idea is to develop strong loyalty by creating satisfied customers who will buy additional services from the firm and are unlikely to switch to a competitor. Satisfied customers are also likely to engage in positive word-of-mouth communication, thereby helping to bring in new customers.

Many businesses have found that it is more cost-effective to hang on to the customers they have than to focus only on attracting new ones. It has been estimated that companies spend seven dollars to market to an existing customer, but thirty-four dollars to market to a new one.[16]

Services that purchasers receive on a continuing basis (e.g., cable television, banking, insurance) can be considered membership services. This type of service naturally lends itself to relationship marketing. When services involve discrete transactions (e.g., in a movie theater, at a restaurant, or on public transportation), it may be more difficult to build membership-type relationships with customers. Nevertheless, services involving discrete transactions may be transformed into membership relationships using marketing tools. For example, the service could be sold in bulk (e.g., a theater series subscription or a commuter pass on public transportation). Or a service firm could offer special benefits to customers who choose to register with the firm (e.g., loyalty programs for hotels and airlines). The service firm that has a more formalized relationship with its customers has an advantage because it knows who its customers are and how and when they use the services offered.[17]

Relationship marketing can be practiced at four levels:

- **Level 1: Financial.** The firm uses pricing incentives to encourage customers to continue doing business with it. Frequent-flyer programs are an example of level 1 relationship marketing. This level of relationship marketing is the least effective in the long term because its price-based advantage is easily imitated by other firms.

- **Level 2: Social.** This level of relationship marketing also uses pricing incentives but seeks to build social bonds with customers. The firm stays in touch with customers, learns about their needs, and designs services to meet those needs. One example of this is when a company sends its customers birthday cards. Level 2 relationship marketing is often more effective than level 1 relationship marketing.

- **Level 3: Customization.** A customization approach encourages customer loyalty through intimate knowledge of individual customers (often referred to as *customer intimacy*) and the development of one-to-one solutions to fit customers' needs.

- **Level 4: Structural.** At this level, the firm again uses financial and social bonds but adds structural bonds to the formula. Structural bonds are developed by offering value-added services that are not readily available from other firms.[18] The MGM Grand hotel in Las Vegas offers an entire floor of Stay Well suites that feature air purification systems to reduce allergens and toxins in the air; healthy energizing lighting developed to reduce jet lag and regulate circadian rhythms; and vitamin C-infused water in showers to neutralize chlorine and soften skin and hair.[19]

12-6 INTERNAL MARKETING IN SERVICE FIRMS

Services are performances, so the quality of a firm's employees is an important part of building long-term relationships with customers. Employees who like their jobs and are satisfied with the firm they work for are more likely to deliver superior service to customers. In other words, a firm that makes its employees happy has a better chance of retaining customers. Thus, it is critical that service firms practice **internal marketing**, which means treating employees as customers and developing systems and benefits that satisfy their needs. While this strategy may also apply to goods manufacturers, it is even more critical in service firms. This is because in service industries, employees deliver the brand promise—their performance as a brand representative—directly to customers. To satisfy employees, companies have designed and instituted a wide variety of programs such as flextime, on-site day care, and concierge services. Google, the number-one ranked "Best Company to Work For" by *Fortune Magazine* seven years in a row, offers its employees benefits such as free chef-prepared organic foods, free health and dental insurance, subsidized massages, nap pods, and on-site phycians.[20]

Companies like Google have designed and instituted a wide variety of programs such as flextime, on-site daycare, and concierge service for their employees.

12-7 NONPROFIT ORGANIZATION MARKETING

A nonprofit organization is an organization that exists to achieve some goal other than the usual business goals of profit, market share, or return on investment. Both nonprofit organizations and private-sector service firms market intangible products, and both often require the customer to be present during the production process. Both for-profit and nonprofit services vary greatly from producer to producer and from day to day, even from the same producer.

Few people realize that nonprofit organizations account for more than twenty percent of the economic activity in the United States. The cost of government (i.e., taxes), the predominant form of nonprofit organization, has become the biggest single item in the American family budget—more than housing, food, or health care. Together, federal, state, and local governments collect tax revenues that amount to more than one-third of the U.S. gross domestic product (GDP). In addition to government entities, nonprofit organizations include hundreds of thousands of private museums, theaters, schools, and churches.

12-7a What Is Nonprofit Organization Marketing?

Nonprofit organization marketing is the effort by nonprofit organizations to bring about mutually satisfying exchanges with target markets. Although these organizations vary substantially in size and purpose and operate in different environments, most perform the following marketing activities:

- Identify the customers they wish to serve or attract (although they usually use other terms, such as clients, patients, members, or sponsors)

- Explicitly or implicitly specify objectives

- Develop, manage, and eliminate programs and services

- Decide on prices to charge (although they use other terms, such as fees, donations, tuition, fares, fines, or rates)

- Schedule events or programs, and determine where they will be held or where services will be offered

internal marketing treating employees as customers and developing systems and benefits that satisfy their needs

nonprofit organization an organization that exists to achieve some goal other than the usual business goals of profit, market share, or return on investment

nonprofit organization marketing the effort by nonprofit organizations to bring about mutually satisfying exchanges with target markets

- Communicate their availability through brochures, signs, public service announcements, or advertisements

Often, the nonprofit organizations that carry out these functions do not realize they are engaged in marketing.

12-7b Unique Aspects of Nonprofit Organization Marketing Strategies

Like their counterparts in business organizations, nonprofit managers develop marketing strategies to bring about mutually satisfying exchanges with target markets. However, marketing in nonprofit organizations is unique in many ways—including the setting of marketing objectives, the selection of target markets, and the development of appropriate marketing mixes.

OBJECTIVES In the private sector, profit motives are both objectives for guiding decisions and criteria for evaluating results. Nonprofit organizations do not seek to make a profit for redistribution to owners or shareholders. Rather, their focus is often on generating enough funds to cover expenses.

Most nonprofit organizations are expected to provide equitable, effective, and efficient services that respond to the wants and preferences of multiple constituencies. These include users, payers, donors, politicians, appointed officials, the media, and the general public. Nonprofit organizations cannot measure their success or failure in strictly financial terms.

The lack of a financial "bottom line" and the existence of multiple, diverse, intangible, and sometimes vague or conflicting objectives make prioritizing objectives, making decisions, and evaluating performance hard for nonprofit managers. They must often use approaches different from the ones commonly used in the private sector.

TARGET MARKETS Three issues relating to target markets are unique to nonprofit organizations:

- **Apathetic or strongly opposed targets:** Private-sector organizations usually give priority to developing those market segments that are most likely to respond to particular offerings. In contrast, nonprofit organizations must often target those who are apathetic about or strongly opposed to receiving their services, such as vaccinations and psychological counseling.

- **Pressure to adopt undifferentiated segmentation strategies:** Nonprofit organizations often adopt undifferentiated strategies (see Chapter 8) by default. Sometimes they fail to recognize the advantages of targeting, or an undifferentiated approach may appear to offer economies of scale and low per-capita costs. In other

Publicly funded nonprofit media companies like National Public Radio (NPR) and the Public Broadcasting Service (PBS) often hold fund drives to secure donations from patrons who appreciate their programming.

Gil C/Shutterstock.com

instances, nonprofit organizations are pressured or required to serve the maximum number of people by targeting the average user.

- **Complementary positioning:** The main role of many nonprofit organizations is to provide services, with available resources, to those who are not adequately served by private-sector organizations. As a result, the nonprofit organization must often complement, rather than compete with, the efforts of others. The positioning task is to identify underserved market segments and to develop marketing programs that match their needs rather than target the niches that may be most profitable. For example, a university library may see itself as complementing the services of the public library rather than as competing with it.

PRODUCT DECISIONS There are three product-related distinctions between business and nonprofit organizations:

- **Benefit complexity:** Nonprofit organizations often market complex behaviors or ideas. Examples include the need to exercise or eat right and the need to quit smoking. The benefits that a person receives are complex, long term, and intangible, and therefore are more difficult to communicate to consumers.

- **Benefit strength:** The benefit strength of many nonprofit offerings is quite weak or indirect. What are the direct, personal benefits to you of driving 55 miles per hour or donating blood? In contrast, most private-sector service organizations can offer customers direct, personal benefits in an exchange relationship.

- **Involvement:** Many nonprofit organizations market products that elicit very low involvement ("Prevent forest fires") or very high involvement ("Stop smoking"). The typical range for private-sector goods is much narrower. Traditional promotional tools may be inadequate to motivate adoption of either low- or high-involvement products.

PLACE (DISTRIBUTION) DECISIONS A nonprofit organization's capacity for distributing its service offerings to potential customer groups when and where they want them is typically a key variable in determining the success of those service offerings. For example, many large universities have one or more satellite campus locations to provide easier access for students in other areas. Some educational institutions also offer classes to students at off-campus locations through the use of interactive video technology or at home via the Internet.

The extent to which a service depends on fixed facilities has important implications for distribution decisions. Services like rail transit and lake fishing can be delivered only at specific points. Many nonprofit services, however, do not depend on special facilities.

PROMOTION DECISIONS Many nonprofit organizations are explicitly or implicitly prohibited from advertising, thus limiting their promotion options. Most federal agencies fall into this category. Other nonprofit organizations simply do not have the resources to retain advertising agencies, promotion consultants, or marketing staff. Nonprofit organizations have a few special promotion resources to call on, however:

- **Professional volunteers:** Nonprofit organizations often seek out marketing, sales, and advertising professionals to help them develop and implement promotion strategies. In some instances, an advertising agency donates its services in exchange for potential long-term benefits. Donated services create goodwill; personal contacts; and general awareness of the donor's organization, reputation, and competency.

- **Sales promotion activities:** Sales promotion activities that use existing services or other resources are increasingly being used to draw attention to the offerings of nonprofit organizations. Sometimes nonprofit charities even team up with other companies for promotional activities. For example, Columbia Sportswear, REI, Subaru, Aramark, and Southwest Airlines recently partnered with the U.S. National Park Foundation to create the "Find Your Park" campaign (http://findyourpark.com/share). This collaborative effort was launched to promote a 2016 Centennial Project contest showcasing 100 Find Your Park stories written by park visitors. The contest features prizes including annual national park passes, camping gear, adventure kits, and a fully guided weekend getaway for two.[21]

- **Public service advertising:** A **public service advertisement (PSA)** is an announcement that promotes a program of a federal, state, or local government or of a nonprofit organization. Unlike a commercial advertiser, the sponsor of the PSA does not pay for the time or space. Instead, it is donated by the medium. PSAs are used, for example, to help educate students about the dangers of misusing and abusing prescription drugs, as well as where to seek treatment for substance abuse problems. Lamar Advertising Company, one of the largest outdoor advertising firms in North America, donates millions of dollars' worth of advertising space each year to help law enforcement and nonprofit organizations communicate important information to the public.[22]

PRICING DECISIONS Five key characteristics distinguish the pricing decisions of nonprofit organizations from those of the profit sector:

- **Pricing objectives:** The main pricing objective in the profit sector is revenue or, more specifically, profit maximization, sales maximization, or target return on sales or investment. Many nonprofit organizations must also be concerned about revenue. Often, however, nonprofit organizations seek to either partially or fully defray costs rather

More than 200 Lamar billboards went up in Los Angeles to help identify two male assailants who severely beat a San Francisco Giants fan after a game.

Gina Ferazzi/Getty Images

public service advertisement (PSA) an announcement that promotes a program of a federal, state, or local government or of a nonprofit organization

First Lady Chirlane McCray announces a $78 million budget proposed by her husband, Mayor Bill de Blasio, for mental health services at a press conference at the Empire State Building.

than to achieve a profit for distribution to stockholders. Nonprofit organizations also seek to redistribute income—for instance, through taxation and sliding-scale fees. Moreover, they strive to allocate resources fairly among individuals or households or across geographic or political boundaries.

- **Nonfinancial prices:** In many nonprofit situations, consumers are not charged a monetary price but instead must absorb nonmonetary costs. The importance of those costs is illustrated by the large number of eligible citizens who do not take advantage of so-called "free" services for the poor. In many public assistance programs, about half the people who are eligible do not participate. Nonmonetary costs include time, embarrassment, and effort.

- **Indirect payment:** Indirect payment through taxes is common to marketers of "free" services, such as libraries, fire protection, and police protection. Indirect payment is not a common practice in the profit sector.

- **Separation between payers and users:** By design, the services of many charitable organizations are provided for those who are relatively poor and are largely paid for by those who are better off financially. Although examples of separation between payers and users can be found in the profit sector (such as insurance claims), the practice is much less prevalent.

- **Below-cost pricing:** An example of below-cost pricing is university tuition. Virtually all private and public colleges and universities price their services below full cost.

12-8 GLOBAL ISSUES IN SERVICES MARKETING

The international marketing of services is a major part of global business, and the United States has become the world's largest exporter of services. Competition in international services is increasing rapidly, but many U.S. service industries have been able to enter the global marketplace because of their competitive advantages. U.S. banks, for example, have advantages in customer service and collections management.

For both for-profit and nonprofit service firms, the first step toward success in the global marketplace is determining the nature of the company's core products. Then, the marketing mix elements (additional services, place, promotion, pricing, and distribution) should be designed to take into account each country's cultural, technological, and political environment. Pizza Hut creates pizza flavors that reflect its varying global locations. For example, customers can get Prawn Pizza in Australia, Cheesy Poutine (beef gravy, French fries, and cheese curds) Pizza in Canada, and Tuna Sweet Corn Melt Pizza in the United Kingdom.[23]

MKTG
ONLINE

REVIEW FLASHCARDS
ANYTIME, ANYWHERE!

**Create Flashcards
from Your StudyBits**

**Review Key Term
Flashcards Already
Loaded on the
StudyBoard**

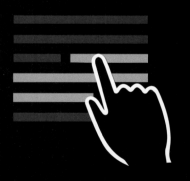

Access MKTG ONLINE at www.cengagebrain.com

13 | Supply Chain Management and Marketing Channels

LEARNING OUTCOMES

After studying this chapter, you will be able to…

13-1 Define the terms *supply chain* and *supply chain management* and discuss the benefits of supply chain management

13-2 Discuss the concepts of internal and external supply chain integration and explain why each of these types of integration is important

13-3 Identify the eight key processes of excellent supply chain management and discuss how each of these processes affects the end customer

13-4 Understand the importance of sustainable supply chain management to modern business operations

13-5 Discuss how new technology and emerging trends are impacting the practice of supply chain management

13-6 Explain what marketing channels and channel intermediaries are and describe their functions and activities

13-7 Describe common channel structures and strategies and the factors that influence their choice

13-8 Discuss omnichannel and multichannel marketing in both B-to-B and B-to-C structures and explain why these concepts are important

Alexander Kirch/Shutterstock.com

After you finish this chapter go to **PAGE 243** for **STUDY TOOLS**

13-1 SUPPLY CHAINS AND SUPPLY CHAIN MANAGEMENT

Many modern companies are turning to supply chain management for competitive advantage. A company's **supply chain** includes all of the companies involved in the upstream and downstream flow of products, services, finances, and information, extending from initial suppliers (the point of origin) to the ultimate customer (the point of consumption). The goal of **supply chain management** is to coordinate and integrate all of the activities performed by supply chain members into a seamless process, from the source to the point of consumption, ultimately giving supply chain managers "total visibility and control" of the materials, processes, money, and finished products both inside and outside the company they work for. The philosophy behind supply chain management is that by visualizing and exerting control over the entire supply chain, supply chain managers can balance supply and demand needs, maximize strengths, and increase efficiencies at each level of the chain.

supply chain the connected chain of all of the business entities, both internal and external to the company, that perform or support the logistics function

supply chain management a management system that coordinates and integrates all of the activities performed by supply chain members into a seamless process, from the source to the point of consumption, resulting in enhanced customer and economic value

Understanding and integrating supply and demand-related information at every level enables supply chain managers to optimize their decisions, reduce waste, and respond quickly to sudden changes in supply or demand.

Supply chain management, when performed well, reflects a completely customer-driven management philosophy. In the mass production era, manufacturers produced standardized products that were "pushed" down through marketing channels to consumers, who were convinced by salespeople to buy whatever was produced. In today's marketplace, however, customers who expect to receive product configurations and services matched to their unique needs are driving demand. The focus of businesses has shifted to determining how products and services are being "pulled" into the marketplace by customers, and on partnering with members of the supply chain to enhance customer

In today's marketplace, products are being driven by customer demand, and businesses' need to balance demand with supply in order to ensure economic profits.

value. For example, when Rolls-Royce launched its Ad Personam customer value program, the company used a build-to-order system that allowed every customer to design his or her car with more than a million combinations of leather, fabric, wood, and paint.[1] This differed from the mass-manufacturing approach companies used historically, whereby a company's focus on efficiency determined a far narrower range of cars and custom options.

This reversal of the flow of demand from "push" to "pull" has resulted in a radical reformulation of traditional marketing, production, and distribution functions toward a philosophy of supply chain agility. Agile companies synchronize their activities through the sharing of supply and demand market information, spend more time than their competitors focusing on activities that create direct customer benefits, partner closely with suppliers and service providers to reduce customer wait times for products, and constantly seek to reduce supply chain complexity through the evaluation and reduction (or elimination) of stock-keeping units (SKUs) that customers aren't buying, among other strategies. For example, Butterball has begun shipping cases of turkey meat to a central distribution center in advance of customer demand. The company uses advanced bar coding technology and customer analytics to route fresher shipments to grocery stores, optimizing its product replenishment.[2] By managing the product pipeline in this way, companies are able to reduce supply chain costs while at the same time offering better service levels, and in doing so, deliver more desirable products at better prices to customers.

13-1a Benefits of Effective Supply Chain Management

Supply chain management is a key means of differentiation for a firm, and therefore represents a critical component in marketing and corporate strategy. Companies that focus on supply chain management commonly report lower inventory, transportation, warehousing, and packaging costs; greater logistical flexibility; improved customer service; and higher revenues. Research has shown a clear relationship between supply chain performance and both profitability and company value. Additionally, because well-managed supply chains are able to provide better value to customers with only marginal incremental expenditure on company assets, best-in-class supply chain companies such as air conditioner manufacturer Lennox International are becoming significantly more valuable investments for investors. For many years, Lennox served its local and international customers alike from two distribution centers in Iowa. This centralized system resulted in long wait times and many unhappy customers. By moving to a more decentralized model with

19 locations around the world, Lennox reduced its average customer wait time to less than two days. The company's market share increased by more than 25 percent, leading to a much higher company value and increased customer satisfaction.[3]

Redesigning a supply chain can do more than just improve the bottom line. The Campbell Soup Company estimates that if it moved 10 percent of its truck-transported inventory to rail, it could both create more than $1 billion in savings and significantly reduce its overall carbon emissions.[4]

13-2 SUPPLY CHAIN INTEGRATION

A key principle of supply chain management is that multiple entities (firms and/or their functional areas) should work together to perform tasks as a single, unified system, rather than as multiple individual units acting in isolation. Companies in a world-class supply chain combine their resources, capabilities, and innovations across multiple business boundaries so they are used for the best interest of the entire supply chain as a whole. The goal is that the overall performance of the supply chain will be greater than the sum of its parts.

As companies become increasingly focused on supply chain management, they come to possess a supply chain orientation. This means that they develop management practices that are consistent with a "systems thinking" approach. Leading supply chain–oriented firms like Amazon, McDonald's, and Unilever possess five characteristics that, in combination, set them apart from their partners: [5]

1. *They are credible.* They have the capability to deliver on the promises they make.

2. *They are benevolent.* They are willing to accept short-term risks on behalf of others; are committed to others, and invest in others' success.

3. *They are cooperative.* They work with rather than against their partners when seeking to achieve goals.

4. *They have the support of top managers.* These managers possess the vision required to do things that benefit the entire supply chain in the short run so that they can enjoy greater company successes in the long run.

5. *They are effective at conducting and directing supply chain activity.* Thereby, they are better off in the long run financially than those who are not.

Management practices that reflect a highly coordinated effort between supply chain firms or across

supply chain agility an operational strategy focused on creating inventory velocity and operational flexibility simultaneously in the supply chain

supply chain orientation a system of management practices that are consistent with a "systems thinking" approach

business functions within the same or different firms are "integrated." In other words, **supply chain integration** occurs when multiple firms or their functional areas in a supply chain coordinate business processes so they are seamlessly linked to one another. In a world-class supply chain, the customer may not know where the business activities of one company or business unit end and where those of another begin—each actor keeps their own interests in mind, but all appear to be reading from the same script, and from time to time, each makes sacrifices that benefit the performance of the system as a whole.

In the modern supply chain, integration can be either internal or external to a specific company or, ideally, both. From an internal perspective, the very best companies develop a managerial orientation toward **demand-supply integration (DSI).** Under the DSI philosophy, those functional areas in a company charged with creating customer demand (such as marketing, sales, or research/development) communicate frequently and are synchronized with the parts of the business charged with fulfilling the created demand (purchasing, manufacturing, and logistics). Some companies, like Airbus, are beginning to co-locate their engineering, logistics, and procurement divisions in order to build synergies between them.[6] This type of alignment enhances customer satisfaction by ensuring that, for example, salespeople make promises to customers that can actually be delivered on by the company's logistics arm, or that raw materials being purchased actually meet customer specifications before they are placed into production. Simultaneously, the company gains efficiencies from ordering and using only those materials that lead directly to sales. In short, companies operating under a DSI philosophy are better at their business because all of the different divisions within the company "play from the same sheet of music."[7]

Additionally, the practice of world-class supply chain management requires that different companies act as if a single mission and leadership connect them. To accomplish this task across companies that have different ownership and interests, five types of external integration are sought by firms interested in providing top-level service to customers:[8]

- *Relationship integration* is the ability of two or more companies to develop social connections that serve to guide their interactions when working together. More specifically, relationship integration is the capability to develop and maintain a shared mental framework across companies that describes how they will depend on one another when working together. This includes the ways in which they will collaborate on activities or projects so that the customer gains the maximum amount of total value possible from the supply chain.

- *Measurement integration* reflects the idea that performance assessments should be transparent and measurable across the borders of different firms, and should also assess the performance of the supply chain as a whole while holding each individual firm or business unit accountable for meeting its own goals.

- *Technology and planning integration* refers to the creation and maintenance of information technology systems that connect managers across the firms in the supply chain. It requires information hardware and software systems that can exchange information when needed between customers, suppliers, and internal operational areas of each of the supply chain partners.

- *Material and service supplier integration* requires firms to link seamlessly to those outsiders that provide goods and services to them so that they can streamline work processes and thereby provide smooth, high-quality customer experiences. Both sides need to have a common vision of the total value creation process and be willing to share the responsibility for satisfying customer requirements to make supplier integration successful.

Airbus has co-located its engineering, logistics, and procurement divisions in order to build synergies between them. Here, an Airbus A350-900 makes its way to the Singapore Airshow.

Jordan Tan/Shutterstock.com

supply chain integration when multiple firms or business functions in a supply chain coordinate their activities and processes so that they are seamlessly linked to one another in an effort to satisfy the customer

demand-supply integration (DSI) a supply chain operational philosophy focused on integrating the supply-management and demand-generating functions of an organization

Max blain/Shutterstock.com

Relationally integrated supply chains have sets of rules, policies, and/or procedures that dictate how firms will work together and specify how conflicts among supply chain partners will be resolved.

- *Customer integration* is a competency that enables firms to offer long-lasting, distinctive, value-added offerings to those customers who represent the greatest value to the firm or supply chain. Highly customer-integrated firms assess their own capabilities and then match them to customers whose desires they can meet and who offer large enough sales potential for the linkage to be profitable over the long term.

Success in achieving both the internal and external types of integration is very important. Highly integrated supply chains (those that are successful in achieving many or all of these types of integration) have been shown to be better at satisfying customers, managing costs, delivering high-quality products, enhancing productivity, and utilizing company or business unit assets, all of which translate into greater profitability for the firms and their partners working together in the supply chain.

Integration involves a balance between barriers and enablers. Companies that work closely with their suppliers encounter problems such as corporate culture, information hoarding, and trust issues. For example, Häagen-Dazs and General Mills share information with their vanilla suppliers to increase yields and improve sustainability practices, but at the same time,

business processes bundles of interconnected activities that stretch across firms in the supply chain

customer relationship management (CRM) process allows companies to prioritize their marketing focus on different customer groups according to each group's long-term value to the company or supply chain

there is a danger. Giving supply chain partners this information enables those partners to share it with competitors. On the other hand, integration can be improved through long-term agreements, cross-organizational integrated product teams, and improved communication between partners. These factors all aid in integrating supply chain operations.[9]

13-3 THE KEY PROCESSES OF SUPPLY CHAIN MANAGEMENT

When firms practice good supply chain management, their functional departments or areas, such as marketing, research and development, and/or production, are integrated both within and across the linked firms. Integration, then, is "how" excellent supply chain management works. The business processes on which the linked firms work together represent the "what" of supply chain management—they are the objects of focus on which firms, departments, areas, and people work together when seeking to reduce supply chain costs or to generate additional revenues. **Business processes** are composed of bundles of interconnected activities that stretch across firms in the supply chain; they represent key areas that some or all of the involved firms are constantly working on to reduce costs and/or generate revenues for everyone throughout supply chain management. There are eight critical business processes on which supply chain managers must focus:

1. Customer relationship management
2. Customer service management
3. Demand management
4. Order fulfillment
5. Manufacturing flow management
6. Supplier relationship management
7. Product development and commercialization
8. Returns management[10]

13-3a Customer Relationship Management

The **customer relationship management (CRM) process** enables companies to prioritize their marketing focus on different customer groups according to each group's long-term value to the company or supply chain. Once higher-value customers are identified, firms should focus more on providing customized products and better service to this group than to others. The CRM process includes customer segmentation by value and subsequent generation of customer loyalty for the most attractive segments. This process provides a set of comprehensive principles for the initiation and maintenance of customer relationships and is often carried out with the assistance of specialized CRM computer software. For example, Boise Office Solutions recently spent more than $25 million on a CRM application to segment and better understand its 2.2 million customers. The initiative enabled the company to stratify its service levels based on customer needs, optimize its efforts, and, ultimately, positively impact the bottom line.[11]

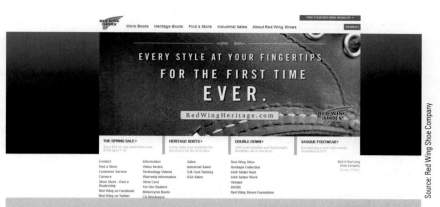

Source: Red Wing Shoe Company

Sales and Operations Planning quickly became a valuable asset to shoemaker Red Wing Shoes—known for their rugged work boots.

13-3b Customer Service Management

Whereas the CRM process is designed to identify and build relationships with good customers, the customer service management process is designed to ensure that those customer relationships remain strong. The **customer service management process** presents a multi-company, unified response system to the customer whenever complaints, concerns, questions, or comments are voiced. When the process is well executed, it can have a strong positive impact on revenues, often as a result of quick positive response to negative customer feedback, and sometimes even in the form of additional sales gained through the additional customer contact. Customers expect service from the moment a product is purchased until it is disposed of, and the customer service management process allows for touch points between the buyer and seller throughout this life cycle. The use of customer care software enables companies to enhance their customer service management process. Dell's customer support software, Clear View, enables staff members at the tech company's customer service command centers to view information from Dell's internal systems (as well as that of its partners) in real-time. This information is combined with a geographical system that allows Dell to match each customer's complaint with the proper service dispatch center, making its response both rapid and effective.[12]

13-3c Demand Management

The **demand management process** seeks to align supply and demand throughout the supply chain by anticipating customer requirements at each level and creating customer-focused plans of action prior to actual purchases being made. At the same time, demand management seeks to minimize the costs of serving multiple types of customers who have variable wants and needs. In other words, the demand management process allows companies in the supply chain to satisfy customers in the most efficient and effective ways possible. Activities such as collecting customer data, forecasting future demand, and developing activities that smooth out demand help bring available inventory into alignment with customer desires.

Though it is very difficult to predict exactly what items and quantities customers will buy prior to purchase, demand management can ease pressure on the production process and allow companies to satisfy most of their customers through greater flexibility in manufacturing, marketing, and sales programs. One key way this occurs is through the sharing of customer demand forecasts and data during **sales and operations planning (S&OP)** meetings. During these meetings, the

customer service management process presents a multi-company, unified response system to the customer whenever complaints, concerns, questions, or comments are voiced

demand management process seeks to align supply and demand throughout the supply chain by anticipating customer requirements at each level and creating demand-related plans of action prior to actual customer purchasing behavior

sales and operations planning (S&OP) a method companies use to align production with demand by merging tactical and strategic planning methods across functional areas of the business

demand-generating functions of the business (marketing and sales) work together with the production side of the business (procurement, production, and logistics) in a collaborative arrangement designed to both satisfy customers and minimize waste. When work boot manufacturer Red Wing Shoes implemented S&OP in 2013, it was able to reduce inventory by 27 percent while simultaneously increasing customer service rates by 8 to 10 percent, leading to significant costs savings that were passed along to customers.[13]

13-3d Order Fulfillment

One of the most fundamental processes in supply chain management is the order fulfillment process, which involves generating, filling, delivering, and providing on-the-spot service for customer orders. The order fulfillment process is a highly integrated process, often requiring persons from multiple companies and multiple functions to come together and coordinate to create customer satisfaction at a given place and time. The best order fulfillment processes reduce order cycle time—the time between order and customer receipt—as much as possible, while ensuring that the customer receives exactly what he or she wants. The shorter lead times are beneficial in that they allow firms to carry reduced inventory levels and free up cash that can be used on other projects. Overall, the order fulfillment process involves understanding and integrating the company's internal capabilities with customer needs, and matching these together so that the supply chain maximizes profits while minimizing costs and waste. Amazon now uses Kiva robots to help workers pack three to four times more orders per hour than before. These robots bring shelves of products to the human packers based on what is in each customer's order. The packers then pick out the correct items, pack them, and send the complete box off to another robot to be shipped. This process has greatly decreased Amazon's order cycle time recent research found that the work robots do at Amazon shaves more than an hour off the time needed to pick and pack the average order.[14]

13-3e Manufacturing Flow Management

The manufacturing flow management process is concerned with ensuring that firms in the supply chain have the needed resources to manufacture with flexibility and to move products through a multi-stage production process. Firms with flexible manufacturing have the ability to create a wide variety of goods and/or services with minimized costs associated with changing production techniques. The manufacturing flow process includes much more than simple production of goods and services—it means creating flexible agreements with suppliers and shippers so that unexpected demand bursts can be accommodated, without disruptions to customer service or satisfaction.

The goals of the manufacturing flow management process are centered on leveraging the capabilities held by multiple members of the supply chain to improve overall manufacturing output in terms of quality, delivery speed, and flexibility, all of which tie directly to profitability. Depending on the product, supply chain managers may choose between a lean or agile supply chain strategy. In a lean supply chain, products are built before demand occurs, but managers attempt to reduce as much waste as possible. Lean supply chains first appeared within the Toyota Production System (TPS) as early as the 1950s. Agile strategies lie on the other end of the continuum—they prioritize customer responsiveness more so than waste reduction. Instead of trying to forecast demand and reduce waste, agile supply chains wait for demand to occur and use communication and flexibility to fill that demand quickly.[15] In the United Kingdom, Tesco Grocery stores have become so agile that they plan afternoon shipments from distribution centers to stores only after reading morning sales data. This way, they can replenish inventory sold only hours before.[16]

13-3f Supplier Relationship Management

The supplier relationship management process is closely related to the manufacturing flow management process and contains several characteristics that parallel the customer relationship management process. The manufacturing flow management process is highly dependent on supplier relationships for flexibility. Furthermore, in a way similar to that found in the customer relationship management process, supplier relationship management provides structural support for developing and maintaining relationships with suppliers. Thus, by integrating these

order fulfillment process a highly integrated process, often requiring persons from multiple companies and multiple functions to come together and coordinate to create customer satisfaction at a given place and time

order cycle time the time delay between the placement of a customer's order and the customer's receipt of that order

manufacturing flow management process concerned with ensuring that firms in the supply chain have the needed resources to manufacture with flexibility and to move products through a multi-stage production process

supplier relationship management process supports manufacturing flow by identifying and maintaining relationships with highly valued suppliers

two ideas, supplier relationship management supports manufacturing flow by identifying and maintaining relationships with highly valued suppliers.

Just as firms benefit from developing close-knit, integrated relationships with customers, close-knit, integrated relationships with suppliers provide a means through which performance advantages can be gained. For example, careful management of supplier relationships is a key step toward ensuring that firms' manufacturing resources are utilized to their maximum potential. It is clear, then, that the supplier relationship management process has a direct impact on each supply chain member's bottom-line financial performance. In certain instances, it can be advantageous for the supply chain to integrate via a formal merger. American pharmaceutical company Bayer HealthCare recently purchased German-based Steigerwald Arzneimittelwerk, a pharmacy supplier that specializes in herbal medicines. Acquiring the supplier gave Bayer HealthCare access to new medications. At the same time, purchasing a supplier based in Germany gave Bayer HealthCare enhanced access to European markets. Managing supplier relationships not only gave Bayer HealthCare better access to supplies, it also offered a chance to broaden its customer base. The acquisition simply sealed the deal by making the partnership permanent.[17]

Titus Green assembles a recycled iPhone at a Green Citizen recycling facility in Burlingame, California. Green Citizen collects and disposes old electronics in the San Francisco Bay area, tracking each device to ensure that it is recycled back into raw material or refurbished and resold.

13-3g Product Development and Commercialization

The **product development and commercialization process** (discussed in detail in Chapter 11) includes the group of activities that facilitate the joint development and marketing of new offerings among a group of supply chain partner firms. In many cases, more than one supply chain entity is responsible for ensuring new product success. Commonly, a multi-company collaboration is used to execute new-product development, testing, and launch, among other activities. The capability for developing and introducing new offerings quickly is key for competitive success versus rival firms, so it is often advantageous to involve many supply chain partners in the effort. The process requires the close cooperation of suppliers and customers, who provide input throughout the process and serve as advisers and co-producers for the new offering(s).

Designing a new product with the help of suppliers and customers can enable a company to introduce features and cost-cutting measures into final products. Customers provide information about what they want from the product, while suppliers can help design for quality and manufacturability. Research has shown that when each supply chain partner shares responsibility for the design and manufacture of a new product, more obstacles can be identified early and opportunities for cost reduction are made possible. For example, Boeing involved a team of suppliers early in the development phase of its 787 Dreamliner aircraft, leading to a shift to a lighter composite material for the fuselage's outer shell. The lighter material is expected to make the aircraft substantially cheaper to operate on long haul flights.[18]

13-3h Returns Management

The final supply chain management process deals with situations in which customers choose to return a product to the retailer or supplier, thereby creating a reversed flow of goods within the supply chain. The **returns management process**

product development and commercialization process includes the group of activities that facilitates the joint development and marketing of new offerings among a group of supply chain partner firms

returns management process enables firms to manage volumes of returned product efficiently while minimizing returns-related costs and maximizing the value of the returned assets to the firms in the supply chain enables firms to manage volumes of returned product efficiently while minimizing returns-related costs and maximizing the value of the returned assets to the firms in the supply chain. Returns have the potential to affect a firm's financial position in a major and negative way if mishandled. In certain industries, such as apparel e-retailing, returns can amount to as much as 40 percent of sales volume.

In addition to the value of managing returns from a pure asset-recovery perspective, many firms are discovering that returns management also creates additional marketing and customer service touch points that can be leveraged for added customer value above and beyond normal sales and promotion-driven encounters. Handling returns quickly creates a positive image, and gives the company an additional opportunity to please the customer, and customers who have positive experiences with the returns management process can become very confident buyers who are willing to reorder, since they know any problems they encounter with purchases will be quickly and fairly rectified. In addition, the returns management process allows the firm to recognize weaknesses in product design and/or areas for potential improvement through the direct customer feedback that initiates the process.

Many major e-retailers, such as Zappos, have implemented extremely liberal return policies in order to reduce customers' sense of risk when making online purchases. Research shows that the ability to try products without being charged for returning them actually leads to greater revenues for companies. However, since returns generate more than $100 billion in supply chain costs every year, companies must carefully calculate whether the additional sales are truly worth it.[19]

Zappos' extremely liberal return policy reduces customers' sense of risk when making purchases.

goodluz/Shutterstock.com

13-4 SUSTAINABLE SUPPLY CHAIN MANAGEMENT

In response to the need for firms to both reduce costs and act as leaders in protecting the natural environment, many are adopting sustainable supply chain management principles as a key part of their supply chain strategy. **Sustainable supply chain management** involves the integration and balancing of environmental, social, and economic thinking into all phases of the supply chain management process. In doing so, the organization both better addresses current business needs and develops long-term initiatives that allow it to mitigate risks and avail itself of future opportunities in ways that preserve resources for future generations and ensure long-term viability. Such activities include environmentally friendly materials sourcing; the design of products with consideration given to their social and environmental impact; and end-of-life product management that includes easy recycling and/or clean disposal. By enacting sustainable supply chain management principles, companies can simultaneously generate cost savings, protect the Earth's natural resources, and ensure that socially responsible business practices are enacted. Recent research demonstrates a strong business case for supporting many sustainability initiatives. For example, the recycling of used pallets is both an environmentally sustainable practice and cheaper than purchasing new ones.[20]

UPS works continuously to develop a more sustainable supply chain. By integrating new transportation technology into its fulfillment networks, UPS mechanics and employees are able to facilitate package delivery in ways that are more fuel- and emissions-efficient—the proof lies in the more than 3 percent reduction in fuel use per package per year. UPS has logged more than 200 million miles on alternative fuel vehicles and offers carbon-neutral delivery in 36 countries.[21]

In addition to environmental sustainability, modern businesses are also balancing economic success with social sustainability practices like human rights, labor rights, employee diversity initiatives, and quality of life concerns. The benefits of social sustainability efforts have been demonstrated by retailers such as Lowe's Home Improvement and Walgreen Stores, where the hiring and training of disabled workers has increased

sustainable supply chain management a supply chain management philosophy that embraces the need for optimizing social and environmental costs in addition to financial costs

productivity in the host facilities by up to 20 percent. These companies have found that disabled workers are far less likely to miss work and are often as effective at performing job tasks as their abled counterparts—while frequently exceeding them in terms of process execution and safety standards.[22]

A common misconception surrounding both environmental and social sustainability is that their practice increases supply chain costs disproportionately, and therefore should be enacted only when business leaders are willing to act altruistically or for the purposes of good public relations.

13-5 TRENDS IN SUPPLY CHAIN MANAGEMENT

Several technological advances and business trends are affecting the job of the supply chain manager today. Some of the business trends that are affecting supply chain management include outsourcing logistics, maintaining a secure supply chain and minimizing supply chain risk, and maintaining a sustainable supply chain. While these trends exert pressure on managers to change the way their supply chains function, electronic distribution is being used and changed frequently to help make supply chain management more integrated and easier to track.

13-5a Outsourcing Logistics Functions

Partnering organizations are becoming increasingly efficient at dividing responsibility for supply chain management. Outsourcing, or contract logistics, is a rapidly growing initiative in which a manufacturer or supplier turns over an entire logistical function (often buying and managing transportation, warehousing, and/ or light postponed manufacturing) to an independent third-party logistics company (3PL). These service providers sell logistics solutions instead of physical products. Common 3PL products and services include managed warehouse space, transportation solutions, information sharing, manufacturing postponement, and enhanced technological innovations. When a firm's order fulfillment process is managed diligently, the amount of time between order placement and receipt of the customer's payment following order shipment (the *order-to-cash cycle*) is minimized as much as possible. Since many firms do not view order fulfillment as a core competency (versus, for example, product development or marketing), they often outsource this function to a 3PL that specializes in the order fulfillment process. The 3PL becomes a

semi-permanent part of the firm's supply chain and is assigned to manage one or more specialized functions.[23] For example, when Walmart outsourced portions of its transportation to 3PL company C.H. Robinson, it was able to focus on merchandising rather than shipping. This led to better in-stock levels, and accordingly, better sales.[24]

Other, more comprehensive partners, often known as fourth-party logistics companies (4PLs) or logistics integrators, create and manage entire solutions for getting products where they need to be, when they need to be there. Many times 3PLs and 4PLs provide a firm's only interaction with the customer, so they need to represent the needs and interests of the entire firm and supply chain. Developing and training these firms' employees to be empowered and to respond to the customer's needs in the best interest of the supply chain is becoming increasingly important.

Outsourcing enables companies to cut inventories, locate stock at fewer plants and distribution centers, and still provide the same level of service or even better. The companies then can refocus investment on their core business. In the hospitality industry, Avendra negotiates with suppliers to obtain virtually everything a hotel might need, from food and beverages to golf course maintenance. For example, by relying on Avendra to manage many aspects of the supply chain, companies like Fairmont Hotels & Resorts and Inter-Continental Hotels Group can concentrate on their core function—providing hospitality. The most progressive companies are engaging in vested outsourcing relationships, whereby both parties collaborate deeply to find mutually beneficial arrangements that allow both parties to "win" by reducing overall costs while achieving better performance.[25]

Because a logistics service provider is focused on logistical functions only, clients receive better service in a timely, efficient manner, thereby increasing their customers' satisfaction and boosting the perception of added value to a company's offerings. In many recent instances, North American companies have been offshoring, or outsourcing logistics to service providers located

outsourcing (contract logistics) a manufacturer's or supplier's use of an independent third party to manage an entire function of the logistics system, such as transportation, warehousing, or order processing

third-party logistics company (3PL) a firm that provides functional logistics services to others

fourth-party logistics company (4PL or logistics integrator) a consulting-based organization that assesses another's entire logistical service needs and provides integrated solutions, often drawing on multiple 3PLs for actual service

offshoring the outsourcing of a business process from one country to another for the purpose of gaining economic advantage in countries with lower labor costs, such as Vietnam and Bangladesh. However, as fuel costs have risen and security issues become more prominent, many companies have begun to relocate outsourced operations closer to home. **Nearshoring** to locations such as Mexico or the Caribbean nations ensures low costs while reducing supply chain risk. For example, General Motors recently built a plant in Toluca, Mexico, leading to a 40 percent savings on production costs when transportation and labor costs were considered together.[26] Nearshoring not only allows a company to manufacture its products more closely to major demand centers, it also gives the supplier a chance to make its presence known at a local level. Mexican-based IT firm Rural Sourcing Inc. has long worked with customers in Mexico, but an influx of American partners has led the company to grow an average of 150 percent annually over the last four years.[27]

13-5b Public-Private Partnerships

Sometimes, the magnitude of a supply chain dilemma is too great for a company and its suppliers or outsourcing partners to handle alone. Increasingly, this is leading firms to work together with government agencies in the form of **public-private partnerships (PPPs)**. PPPs are critical to the satisfaction of both company and societal interests and provide a mechanism by which very-large scale problems or opportunities can be addressed.

Though it is often assumed that industries and governments work poorly together (or in fact work against one another) when problems common to both emerge, a number of successful PPPs have formed over the past decade to diminish the negative impacts of potentially hazardous supply chain situations. For example, immediately following the September 11, 2001, terror attacks on the United States, representatives from both industry and government collaborated to develop the Customs-Trade Partnership Against Terrorism (C-TPAT) in an effort to protect U.S.-based supply chains from terrorist disruption. The program currently has more than 10,000 company participants and has, in general terms, been successful at protecting cargo inbound for the United States while only minimally impacting the performance of its members' supply chains. Similarly, governmental agencies like the Federal Emergency Management Agency (FEMA) and non-government organizations like the Red Cross have benefitted from the inclusion of commercial logistics expertise in their disaster response systems.[28] Efforts involving.

PPPs will likely factor into the solution of future national and global supply chain problems as well. For example, the dangerous combination of population growth and overuse of aging infrastructure has led to a situation whereby congestion and deterioration of roads imperils the timely shipment of goods. In response, a PPP negotiated between federal, state, and private stakeholders led to the construction of a 14.5-mile rail line connecting Bellevue, Washington and Seattle, Washington as well as eight miles of high-occupancy highway lanes across a floating bridge. The project cost more than $4 billion, shared between taxpayers and businesses in the two cities.[29] These sorts of

nearshoring the transfer of an offshored activity from a distant to a nearby country

public-private partnerships (PPPs) Critical to the satisfaction of both company and societal interests and provide a mechanism by which very large-scale problems or opportunities can be addressed

Efforts involving PPPs, like the Red Cross, will likely factor into the solution of future national and global supply chain.

PPP-led advancements will play a critical role in the price of retail goods in upcoming years due to the costs associated with product movement.[30]

13-5c Electronic Distribution

Electronic distribution is the most recent development in the logistics arena. Broadly defined, **electronic distribution** includes any kind of product or service that can be distributed electronically, whether over traditional forms such as fiber-optic cable or through satellite transmission of electronic signals. Companies like E*TRADE, Apple (iTunes), and Movies .com have built their business models around electronic distribution.

In the near future, however, electronic distribution will not be limited only to products and services that are mostly composed of information that can therefore be easily digitized. Experiments with **three-dimensional printing (3DP)** have been successful in industries such as auto parts, biomedical, and even fast food. Using 3DP technology, objects are built to precise specifications using raw materials at or near the location where they will be consumed. Charge Bikes prints customized titanium bicycle parts based on customer specifications, thus reducing the need to transport complete frames around the world before they can be assembled and sold.[31] Shipping raw materials such as powdered titanium is cheaper than shipping finished bicycles because it can be packaged in a perfectly cubic container, making transportation much more efficient and cost effective. Powdered titanium is used only when it is needed, so virtually no waste is produced during printing. Websites like 3DLT.com offer consumers templates for toys, dishes, and furniture that can be printed using the 3DP technology that is becoming increasingly available.[32]

Many industry experts project that 3DP (also referred to as *additive manufacturing*) will radically transform the ways global supply chains work by changing the basic platforms of business. With 3DP, smaller, localized supply chains will become the norm and small manufacturers will produce many more custom products than ever before over very short lead times. And because such platforms will remove much of the need for transportation of finished goods to distribution centers and retailers, 3DP is expected

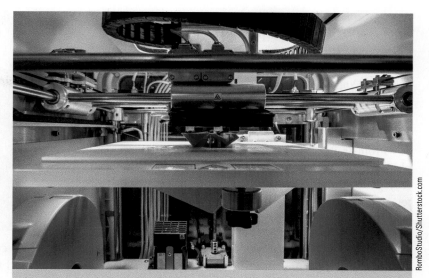

Using 3DP technology, objects are built to precise specifications using raw materials at or near the location where they will be consumed.

RomboStudio/Shutterstock.com

to have a very positive impact on businesses' carbon footprints and the environment at large. At the same time, these platforms should make it possible to deliver unique goods more quickly, creating perceptions of better service.[33]

13-5d Global Supply Chain Management

Global markets present their own sets of challenges for supply chain managers. Strategically, there are many reasons why a company might wish to globalize its supply chain. The allure of foreign markets is strong, due to increasing demand for imported products worldwide. Cheap labor advantages and trade barriers/tariffs have encouraged firms to expand their global manufacturing operations. At the same time, globalization has brought about great uncertainty for modern companies, and specifically, their supply chains. Moving operations offshore exposes companies to risks associated with geopolitical conflict, foreign nationalization of assets and knowledge diffusion, and highly variable quality standards. Foreign suppliers are often less reliable, and

electronic distribution
a distribution technique that includes any kind of product or service that can be distributed electronically, whether over traditional forms such as fiber-optic cable or through satellite transmission of electronic signals

three-dimensional printing (3DP) the creation of three-dimensional objects via an additive manufacturing (printing) technology that layers raw material into desired shapes

due to the lengthening of the supply chain, variability in transportation service can lead to service failures. It is important to consider how sourcing and logistics will be impacted by supply chain globalization.

From a supply management standpoint, it often makes sense to procure goods and services from offshore suppliers. From an economic perspective, lower labor rates, government subsidies, and low materials costs are attractive, but are sometimes outweighed by the costs of quality variation and loss of intellectual property. Still, moving offshore also exposes the company to new technologies, introduces competition to domestic suppliers who have become lackadaisical, and build brand equity. Companies moving offshore must carefully consider the pros and cons, and build supply management systems that can manage very diverse tasks. Logistically, it is critical for importers of all sizes to understand and cope with the legalities of trade in other countries. Shippers and distributors must be aware of the permits, licenses, and registrations they may need to acquire, and depending on the types of product they are importing, the tariffs, quotas, and other regulations that apply in each country. Sometimes, the complexities of handling overseas logistics are too great to overcome. As companies lengthen their global supply chains in search of cost advantages, other less obvious risks emanating from outside the immediate supply chain are also starting to come into play. Longer shipping lanes can expose shipments to natural disasters and extreme weather; political instability and trade restrictions can abruptly halt or slow shipments; fluctuations in currency values and border delays can diminish the value of products while they are on the path to the customer; and theft and piracy can present a greater threat due to increased time of exposure. For these reasons, many companies are

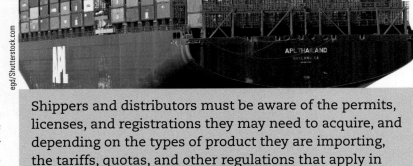

egd/Shutterstock.com

Shippers and distributors must be aware of the permits, licenses, and registrations they may need to acquire, and depending on the types of product they are importing, the tariffs, quotas, and other regulations that apply in each country.

now creating contingency plans so they can react quickly when something goes wrong.[34]

Indeed, as the world continues to globalize, supply chain management will undoubtedly continue to take on a globalized flavor. Worldwide, the resources needed to manufacture and sell increasingly demanded goods are becoming scarcer, and market boundaries are melting together. Free trade is expanding, and consumers in nations where demand has been traditionally low are viewing goods and placing orders via the Internet. Efforts to achieve world-class global supply chain management mean that the balancing of supply and demand—and the satisfaction of more and more customers worldwide—are becoming a reality for many companies.

13-5e Supply Chain Analytics and Technology

In addition to outsourcing, globalization, PPPs, and 3D printing, other advancements in data and technology are beginning to exert an impact on the effectiveness and efficiency of the supply chain. First, a rapidly increasing prevalence of powerful computers and methods for capturing customer, supplier, and company information over the past two decades has resulted in the appearance of **big data**, a colloquial term for the explosive availability of data that has traditionally been hard to capture, store, manage, and analyze. The emergence of big data has presented both great opportunities and significant problems for supply chain managers. There is indeed more information available about supply chain operations than ever before, but the challenge of extracting usable date from this information is also very great. In order to harvest more useful information, many companies are using **cloud computing** to collaborate on big data projects and analyze findings in a quick and cost-effective manner.

big data the rapidly collected and difficult-to-process large-scale datasets that have recently emerged, and which push the limits of current analytical capability

cloud computing the practice of using remote network servers to store, manage, and process data

As a result, many organizations are seeking to develop capabilities for **supply chain analytics**. Supply chain analytics programs that can interpret big data have great potential for improving supply chain operations. For example, the use of bigger and better data should allow supply chain forecasting to become more accurate; shipments to be rerouted in the event of traffic or bad weather; and warehouses to be stocked with exactly the products customers want (and none they don't want). Each of these ambitions, if realized, would offer lower prices for customers and lead to greater customer satisfaction.

Advanced technology enabled by big data is also improving supply chain operations. Fundamentally, the acquisition and analysis of big data allows a company to replace human reasoning with faster and more efficient decision making that is based on information rather than intuition. As a result, and combined with supply chain analytics, a company can automate many of its supply chain processes rather than using human labor. Many tasks that are done repetitively and require significant precision can be accomplished more cheaply and accurately by robots. For example, scientists at the University of California have developed robots—powered by cloud-based data about surgical patients—that are capable of performing basic hip and knee replacement surgery.[35] Cloud-based robots are already being used for large-scale production tasks like automobile and airplane manufacturing.

A final consideration related to technological advancement: sensory equipment that connects physical objects to decision-making analytics via the Internet is beginning to emerge. Recall the Internet of Things (IoT), which allows physical objects to relay specific information over the Internet without overt human interaction. The potential impact of the Internet of Things is tantalizing, but the technology is currently in its infant stage. Connections between cargo vessels or trucks and transportation networks may eventually lead to the development of smart transportation modes that re-route in real time based on local traffic

CLOUD COMPUTING

Makeitdouble/Shutterstock.com

patterns, weather events, and accidents. Alternatively, the traffic grid could react to a need for emergency supplies by enabling a sequence of green stoplights along a critical emergency route. The possibilities are essentially endless for the IoT to positively impact the supply chain. Many companies have already launched projects related to the development of IoT-enabled supply chain management strategies.

13-6 MARKETING CHANNELS AND CHANNEL INTERMEDIARIES

A marketing channel can be viewed as a canal or pipeline through which products, their ownership, communication, financing and payment, and accompanying risk flow to the consumer. A **marketing channel** (also called a **channel of distribution**) is a business structure of interdependent organizations that reaches from the point of production to the consumer and facilitates the downstream physical movement of goods through the supply chain. Channels represent the "place" or "distribution" element of the marketing mix (product, price, promotion, and place), in that they provide a route for company products and services to flow to the customer. In essence, the marketing channel is the "downstream" portion of the supply chain that connects a producer with the customer. Whereas "upstream" supply chain members are charged with moving component parts or raw materials to the producer, members of the marketing channel propel finished goods toward the customer, and/or provide services that facilitate additional customer value.

Many different types of organizations participate

> **supply chain analytics** data analyses that support the improved design and management of the supply chain
>
> **marketing channel (channel of distribution)** a set of interdependent organizations that eases the transfer of ownership as products move from producer to business user or consumer

Igor Strukov/Shutterstock.com

Sheila Fitzgerald/Shutterstock.com

MNStudio/Shutterstock.com

in marketing channels. **Channel members** (also called *intermediaries*, *resellers*, and *middlemen*) negotiate with one another, buy and sell products, and facilitate the change of ownership between buyer and seller in the course of moving finished goods from the manufacturer into the hands of the final consumer. As products move toward the final consumer, channel members facilitate the distribution process by providing specialization and division of labor, overcoming discrepancies, and providing contact efficiency.

13-6a How Marketing Channels Work

According to the concepts of *specialization and division of labor,* breaking down a complex task into smaller, simpler ones and assigning these to specialists creates greater efficiency and lower average production costs via economies of scale. Marketing channels attain economies of scale through specialization and division of labor by aiding upstream producers (who often lack the motivation, financing, or expertise) in marketing to end users or consumers. In most cases, such as for consumer goods like soft drinks, the cost of marketing directly to millions of consumers—taking and shipping individual orders—is prohibitive. For this reason, producers engage other channel members such as wholesalers and retailers to do what the producers

are not well suited to do. Some channel members can accomplish certain tasks more efficiently than others because they have built strategic relationships with key suppliers or customers or have unique capabilities. Their specialized expertise enhances the overall performance of the channel.

Because customers, like businesses, are specialized, they also rely on other entities for the fulfillment of most of their needs. Imagine what your life would be like if you had to grow your own food, make your own clothes, produce your own television shows, and assemble your own automobile! Luckily, members of marketing channels are available to undertake these tasks for us. However, not all goods and services produced by channel members exist in the form we'd most prefer, at least at first. Marketing channels are valuable because they aid producers in creating time, place, and exchange utility for customers, such that products become aligned with their needs. Producers, who sit at the top of the supply chain, provide **form utility** when they transform oats grown on a distant farm into the Cheerios that we like to eat for breakfast. **Time** and **place utility** are created by channel members, when, for example, a transport company hired by the producer physically moves boxes of cereal to a store near our homes in time for our next scheduled shopping trip. And the retailer, who is often the closest channel member to the customer, provides a desired product for some amount of money we are reasonably willing to give, creates **exchange utility** in doing so.

13-6b Functions and Activities of Channel Intermediaries

Intermediaries in a channel negotiate with one another, facilitate transfer of ownership for finished goods between buyers and sellers, and physically move products from the producer toward the final

channel members all parties in the marketing channel who negotiate with one another, buy and sell products, and facilitate the change of ownership between buyer and seller in the course of moving the product from the manufacturer into the hands of the final consumer

form utility the elements of the composition and appearance of a product that make it desirable

time utility the increase in customer satisfaction gained by making a good or service available at the appropriate time

place utility the usefulness of a good or service as a function of the location at which it is made available

exchange utility the increased value of a product that is created as its ownership is transferred

consumer. The most prominent difference separating intermediaries is whether they take title to the product. *Taking title* means they actually own the merchandise and control the terms of the sale—for example, price and delivery date. Retailers and merchant wholesalers are examples of intermediaries that take title to products in the marketing channel and resell them. **Merchant wholesalers** are organizations that facilitate the movement of products and services from the manufacturer to producers, resellers, governments, institutions, and retailers. All merchant wholesalers take title to the goods they sell, and most of them operate one or more warehouses where they receive finished goods, store them, and later reship them to retailers, manufacturers, and institutional clients. Since wholesalers do not dramatically alter the form of a good nor sell it directly to the consumer, their value hinges on their providing time and place utility and contact efficiency to retailers.

Other intermediaries do not take title to goods and services they market but do facilitate exchanges of ownership between sellers and buyers. **Agents and brokers** facilitate the sales of products downstream by representing the interests of retailers, wholesalers, and manufacturers to potential customers. Unlike merchant wholesalers, agents or brokers only facilitate sales and generally have little input into the terms of the sale. They do, however, get a fee or commission based on sales volume. For example, grocery chains often employ the services of food brokers, who provide expertise for a range of products within a category. The broker facilitates the sale of many different manufacturers' products to the grocery chain by marketing the producers' stocks, but the broker never actually takes ownership of any food products.

Many different variations in channel structures are possible, with choices made based in large part on the numbers and types of wholesaling intermediaries that are most desirable. Generally, product characteristics, buyer considerations, and market conditions determine the types and number of intermediaries the producer should use, as follows:

- Customized or highly complex products such as computers, specialty foods, or custom uniforms are usually sold through an agent or broker, who may represent one or multiple companies. In contrast, standardized product such as soda or toothpaste are often sold through a merchant wholesaler and retailer channel.

- Buyer considerations such as purchase frequency or customer wait time influence channel choice. When there is no time pressure, customers may save money on books by ordering online and taking direct distribution from a wholesaler. However, if a book is needed immediately, it will have to be purchased at retail—at the school bookstore—and will include a markup.

- Market characteristics such as how many buyers are in the market and whether they are concentrated in a general location also influence channel design. In a home sale, the buyer and seller are localized in one area, which facilitates the use of a simple agent/broker relationship, whereas mass-manufactured goods such as automobiles may require parts from all over the world and therefore many intermediaries.

Retailers are those firms in the channel that sell directly to consumers as their primary function. A critical role fulfilled by retailers within the marketing channel is that they provide contact efficiency for consumers. Suppose you had to buy your milk at a dairy, your meat at a stockyard, and so forth. You would spend a great deal of time, money, and energy just shopping for just a few groceries. Retailers simplify distribution by reducing the number of transactions required by consumers, and by making an assortment of goods available in one location. Consider the example illustrated in Exhibit 13.1. Four consumers each want to buy a tablet computer. Without a retail intermediary like Best Buy, tablet manufacturers Samsung, Asus, Microsoft, Apple, and Lenovo would each have to make four contacts to reach the four consumers who are in the target market, for a total of twenty transactions. But when Best Buy acts as an intermediary between the producer and consumers, each producer needs to make only one contact, reducing the number to nine transactions. This benefit to customers accrues whether the retailer operates in a physical store location or online format.

13-6c Channel Functions Performed by Intermediaries

Intermediaries in marketing channels perform three essential functions that enable goods to flow between producer and consumer. *Transactional* functions involve contacting and communicating with prospective buyers to make them aware of existing products and to explain their features, advantages, and benefits. Intermediaries in the channel also provide *logistical* functions. Logistical functions

merchant wholesaler an institution that buys goods from manufacturers and resells them to businesses, government agencies, and other wholesalers or retailers and that receives and takes title to goods, stores them in its own warehouses, and later ships them

agents and brokers wholesaling intermediaries who do not take title to a product but facilitate its sale from producer to end user by representing retailers, wholesalers, or manufacturers

retailer a channel intermediary that sells mainly to consumers

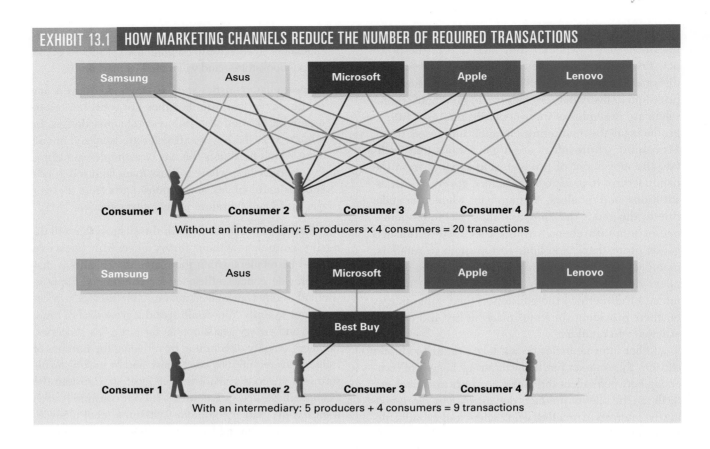

Without an intermediary: 5 producers x 4 consumers = 20 transactions

With an intermediary: 5 producers + 4 consumers = 9 transactions

typically include transportation and storage of assets, as well as their sorting, accumulation, consolidation, and/or allocation for the purpose of conforming to customer requirements. The third basic channel function, *facilitating*, includes research and financing. Research provides information about channel members and consumers by getting answers to key questions: Who are the buyers? Where are they located? Why do they buy? Financing ensures that channel members have the money to keep products moving through the channel to the ultimate consumer. Although individual members can be added to or deleted from a channel, someone in the channel must perform these essential functions. Producers, wholesalers, retailers, or consumers can perform them, and sometimes nonmember channel participants such as service providers elect to perform them for a fee.

13-7 CHANNEL STRUCTURES

A product can take any of several possible routes to reach the final consumer. Marketers and consumers each search for the most efficient channel from many available alternatives. Constructing

direct channel a distribution channel in which producers sell directly to consumers

channels for a consumer convenience good such as candy differs from doing the same for a specialty good like a Prada handbag. Exhibit 13.2 illustrates four ways manufacturers can route products to consumers. When possible, producers use a **direct channel** to sell directly to consumers in order to keep purchase prices low. Direct marketing activities—including telemarketing, mail order and catalog shopping, and forms of electronic retailing such as online shopping and shop-at-home television networks—are good examples of this type of channel structure. There are no intermediaries. Producer-owned stores and factory outlet stores—like Sherwin-Williams, Polo Ralph Lauren, Oneida, and WestPoint Home—are also examples of direct channels.

By contrast, when one or more channel members are small companies lacking in marketing power, an *agent/broker channel* may be the best solution. Agents or brokers bring manufacturers and wholesalers together for negotiations, but they do not take title to merchandise. Ownership passes directly from the producer to one or more wholesalers and/or retailers, who sell to the ultimate consumer.

Most consumer products are sold through distribution channels similar to the other two alternatives: the retailer channel and the wholesaler channel. A *retailer channel* is most common when the retailer is large and

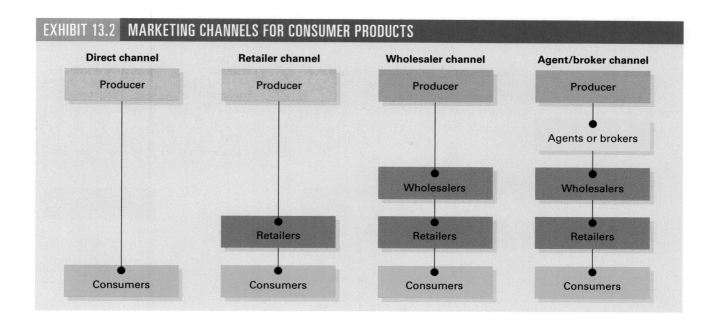

EXHIBIT 13.2 MARKETING CHANNELS FOR CONSUMER PRODUCTS

can buy in large quantities directly from the manufacturer. Walmart, Sears, and car dealers are examples of retailers that often bypass a wholesaler. A *wholesaler channel* is commonly used for low-cost items that are frequently purchased, such as candy, cigarettes, and magazines.

13-7a Channels for Business and Industrial Products

As Exhibit 13.3 illustrates, five channel structures are common in business and industrial markets. First, *direct channels* are typical in business and industrial markets. For example, manufacturers buy large quantities of raw materials, major equipment, processed materials, and supplies directly from other producers. Manufacturers that require suppliers to meet detailed technical specifications often prefer direct channels. For instance, Apple uses a direct channel to purchase high-resolution retina displays for its innovative iPad tablet line. To ensure sufficient supply for iPad manufacturing, Apple takes direct shipments of screens from Sharp, LG, and Samsung.[36]

Alternatively, companies selling standardized items of moderate or low value often rely on *industrial distributors*. In many ways, an industrial distributor is like a supermarket for organizations. Industrial distributors are wholesalers and channel members that buy and take title to products. Moreover, they usually keep inventories of their products and sell and service them. Often small manufacturers cannot afford to employ their own sales force. Instead, they rely on manufacturers' representatives or selling agents to sell to either

industrial distributors or users. Additionally, the Internet has enabled virtual distributors to emerge and has forced traditional industrial distributors to expand their business models. Many manufacturers and consumers are bypassing distributors and going direct, often via the Internet.

13-7b Alternative Channel Arrangements

Rarely does a producer use just one type of channel to move its product. It usually employs several different strategies, which include the use of multiple distribution, nontraditional channels, and strategic channel alliances. When a producer selects two or more channels to distribute the same product to target markets, this arrangement is called **dual or multiple distribution**. Dual or multiple distribution systems differ from single channel systems, and managers should recognize the differences. Multiple distribution channels must be organized and managed as a group, and managers must orchestrate their use in synchronization if whole system is to work well. As consumers increasingly embrace online shopping, more retailers are employing a multiple distribution strategy. This arrangement allows retailers to reach a wider customer base, but may also lead to competition between distribution channels through cannibalization (whereby one channel takes sales away from another). When multiple separate channels are used, they must all complement each other. Some customers use "showrooming" as a way

> **dual distribution (multiple distribution)** the use of two or more channels to distribute the same product to target markets

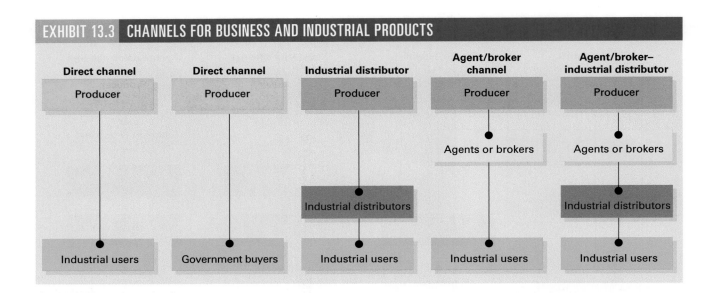

EXHIBIT 13.3 CHANNELS FOR BUSINESS AND INDUSTRIAL PRODUCTS

Direct channel	Direct channel	Industrial distributor	Agent/broker channel	Agent/broker–industrial distributor
Producer	Producer	Producer	Producer	Producer
			Agents or brokers	Agents or brokers
		Industrial distributors		Industrial distributors
Industrial users	Government buyers	Industrial users	Industrial users	Industrial users

of learning about products, but may then also shop as a way of making price comparisons. Regardless of which channel the customer chooses when making the final purchase, they should receive the same messages and "image" of the products.

The use of **nontraditional channels** may help differentiate a firm's product from the competition by providing additional information about products. Nontraditional channels include approaches such as mail-order television or video channels, or infomercials. Although nontraditional channels may limit a brand's coverage, they can give a producer serving a niche market a way to gain market access and customer attention without having to establish physical channel intermediaries and can also provide another sales avenue for larger firms.

Furthermore, companies often form **strategic channel alliances** that enable them to use another manufacturer's already-established channel. Alliances are used most often when the creation of marketing channel relationships may be too expensive and time consuming. For example, U.S.-based Vera Bradley, Inc. signed a deal with Mitsubishi Corporation and its partner Look, Inc. to distribute the former's handbags, luggage, and accessories in the Japanese department stores and boutiques in their respective networks. This alliance helps Vera Bradley reach new markets in foreign cities and diversifies its revenue base, while minimizing its risks of going abroad.[37]

In addition to using primary traditional and non-traditional channels to flow products toward customer markets, many businesses also employ secondary channels, using either an active or passive approach. For example, though most automobile manufacturers sell their finished products to end users through networks of owned or franchised dealers, they also sell cars to rental agencies such as Enterprise or Hertz, who then rent them to potential customers. Similarly, fashion apparel companies might distribute their premium products, such as silk ties or branded watches, through primary channels such as department stores or specialty stores, while using an off-brand or discount outlet for distribution of low-end products. In each case, the goal of the company is the same: to engage a segment of customers who might otherwise never experience the product by offering it at a more easily affordable price or under trial conditions.

Marketers must also be aware, however, that some unintended secondary channels also exist. In some countries, **gray marketing channels** may be used to sell stolen or counterfeited products, which could detract from the profitability of the primary and secondary channels controlled by the business. Counterfeit products such as North Face outerwear, Rolex watches, and Prada handbags can be very difficult to distinguish from the real thing, and their presence provides unintended competition for the producer when such products are distributed through unauthorized intermediaries.

nontraditional channels non-physical channels that facilitate the unique market access of products and services

strategic channel alliance a cooperative agreement between business firms to use the other's already established distribution channel

gray marketing channels secondary channels that are unintended to be used by the producer, and which often flow illegally obtained or counterfeit product toward customers

VERA BRADLEY

Vera Bradley signed a deal with Mitsubishi Corporation and its partner, Look, Inc., to distribute its handbags, luggage and accessories.

Along with marketing channels that move products downstream to end customers, retailers and manufacturers also manage channels that move products upstream, in the direction of the producer. These **reverse channels** enable consumers to return products to the retailer or manufacturer in the event of a product defect, or at the end of the product's useful life to the consumer. The retailers or manufacturers can then recycle the product and use components to manufacture new products, or refurbish and resell the same product in a secondary market. Several large companies, including Apple, Best Buy, and Walmart, offer opportunities to recycle items ranging from plastic bags and batteries to televisions and Christmas trees. Consumers and companies alike view reverse channels as not just a way to reduce the firm's environmental impact, but also as a means to gain some financial benefits as well.[38] For example, Apple will pay consumers for their old Apple products if they qualify for resale, or if their component parts are valuable for manufacturing new products.[39] **Drop and shop** programs use convenience to get consumers to recycle products, like batteries or cell phones, during a regular trip to the store.

13-7c Digital Channels

With technology changing rapidly, many companies are turning to digital channels to facilitate product distribution. **Digital channels** are pathways for moving product and information toward customers such that they can be sent and/or received with electronic devices, such as computers, smartphones, tablets, or video game consoles. Digital channels allow for either push- or pull-based information and product flows to occur, and sometimes simultaneously. For example, a downloaded video game or music file purchased by a customer can also include a digital ad for more games or a new music player.

In response to the growth of digital channels, customers are turning in droves to **M-commerce**, whereby a mobile device is used to assess, compare, and/or buy products. For example, suppose you need a ride from one point in Chicago to another. Instead of having to hail a cab or walk to the nearest elevated train station, you can use Uber's smartphone app to contact a local driver who will take you directly to your destination. A key advantage of Uber and similar apps is their frictionless payment interface. When you are done with your ride, you just get out of the car and walk away while the app charges your credit or debit card and pays the driver.[40] M-commerce is currently experiencing the largest growth in both retail and channel decision-making, in part because of its more than $20 billion annual revenue.

M-commerce also enables consumers using wireless mobile devices to connect to the Internet and shop. Essentially, M-commerce goes beyond text message advertisements to allow consumers to purchase goods and services using wireless mobile devices. M-commerce users adopt the new technology because it saves time and offers more convenience in a greater number of locations. The use of M-commerce has become increasingly important as users grow in both number and purchasing power. Consumers have become more reliant on digital technologies, as shown in the world's first fully digital generation, the Millennials, and firms that fail to react to this trend risk losing a rapidly growing group of M-commerce customers.[41]

Many major companies, ranging from Polo Ralph Lauren to Sears, already offer shopping on mobile phones, and the growth potential is huge. Along with smartphone use, consumers are

reverse channels channels that enable customers to return products or components for reuse or remanufacturing

drop and shop a system used by several retailers that allow customers to bring used products for return or donation at the entrance of the store

digital channels electronic pathways that allow products and related information to flow from producer to consumer

M-commerce the ability to conduct commerce using a mobile device for the purpose of buying or selling goods or services

Apps like Android Pay and Apple Pay allow users to pay for goods and services with their smartphones using near field communication (NFC) technology.

shopping with tablets just as much, if not more, than with company websites. One study even found that tablets accounted for twice as much in web-based sales as smartphone purchases.[42] M-commerce in the United States will exceed $41 billion by 2017 and sales made on mobile devices on a global scale will exceed $110 billion in the same time frame.[43] In the United States, 87 percent of adults own a cellphone, 45 percent own a smartphone, 31 percent own a tablet, and 26 percent own an e-reader.[44] Fifty-five percent of adults use the Internet on their mobile devices, and 31 percent report that they go online with their mobile device more than they do with a desktop or laptop computer.[45] The gap between the number of smartphones owned and smartphones used for purchases is closing rapidly. During the holiday season, about 30 percent of smartphone owners check prices using some kind of price comparison app or read reviews online while inside a store, and almost 50 percent use their smartphones to call a friend or family member for purchase advice.[46] Overall, more than two-thirds of Americans use their mobile devices to obtain shopping information.[47]

Along with smartphone technology, companies are starting to look into other digital channels with which to connect with their customers. Social shopping allows multiple retailers to sell products to customers through social media sites. Aaramshop brings hundreds of neighborhood grocery stores to customers through Facebook. Customers makes their purchases online and their specific neighborhood stores take care of delivering the items directly to customers' homes.[48] Home delivery extends beyond groceries in many heavily populated areas. In China and India, McDonald's has started delivering directly to its customers instead of making consumers come to them.

Firms are also using social media website as digital channels—even in some cases without offering a purchasing opportunity. Companies create profiles on websites like Pinterest or Facebook and use them not only to give customers information about their products, but also to collect customer information. According to one recent study, 38 percent of all online customers follow at least one retailer on a social networking site. Many customers use these website to find product information or get information on special deals, and those who follow a company's blog or profile on a social media site often end up clicking through to the firm's website.[49]

While some services group retailers together in order to bring products to customers, others allow consumers to combine and order larger amounts. Websites like Groupon and LivingSocial give customers the opportunity to fulfill their individual needs at group prices. Many of these sites are organized and managed by intermediaries between manufacturers and customers, but others may be customer initiated or even created by firms to better promote their own products and manage demand.[50]

13-7d Factors Affecting Channel Choice

Marketing managers must answer many questions before choosing a marketing channel. A book manufacturer must decide, for example, what roles physical and electronic distribution will play in the overall marketing strategy and how these two paths will fare against each other. In addition, managers must decide what level of distribution intensity is appropriate and must ensure that the channel strategy they choose is consistent with product, promotion, and pricing strategies. The choice of channels depends on a holistic analysis of market factors, product factors, and producer factors.

MARKET FACTORS Among the most important market factors affecting distribution channel choices are market considerations. Specifically, managers should

Levi Strauss launched Signature, a line of low cost jeans available exclusively at Walmart. According to the company, the Signature line offers superior fit, comfort, and style for less than $20.

answer the following questions: Who are the potential customers? What do they buy? Where do they buy? When do they buy? How do they buy? Additionally, the choice of channel depends on whether the producer is selling to consumers directly, or through other industrial buyers, due to differences in the buying routines of these groups. The geographic location and size of the market are also important factors guiding channel selection. As a rule, if the target market is concentrated in one or more specific areas, then direct selling through a sales force is appropriate, whereas intermediaries would be less expensive in broader markets.

PRODUCT FACTORS Complex, customized, and expensive products tend to benefit from shorter and more direct marketing channels. These types of products sell better through a direct sales force. Examples include pharmaceuticals, scientific instruments, airplanes, and mainframe computer systems. On the other hand, the more standardized a product is, the longer its distribution channel can be and the greater the number of intermediaries that can be involved without driving up costs. For example, with the exception of flavor and shape, the formula for chewing gum is fairly standard from producer to producer. As a result, the distribution channel for gum tends to involve many wholesalers and retailers.

The product stage in the life cycle is also an important factor in choosing a marketing channel. In fact, the choice of channel may change over the life of the

product. As products become more common and less intimidating to potential users, producers tend to look for alternative channels. Similarly, perishable products such as vegetables and milk have a relatively short life span, and fragile products like china and crystal require a minimum amount of handling. Therefore, both require fairly short marketing channels. Online retailers such as eBay facilitate the sale of unusual or difficult-to-find products that benefit from a direct channel.

PRODUCER FACTORS Several factors pertaining to the producer itself are important to the selection of a marketing channel. In general, producers with large financial, managerial, and marketing resources are better able to perform their own marketing, and thus will use more direct channels. These producers have the ability to hire and train their own sales forces, warehouse their own goods, and extend credit to their customers. Smaller or weaker firms, on the other hand, must rely on intermediaries to provide these services for them. Compared to producers with only one or two product lines, producers that sell several products in a related area are able to choose channels that are more direct. Sales expenses then can be spread over more products.

A producer's desire to control pricing, positioning, brand image, and customer support also tends to influence channel selection. For instance, firms that sell products with exclusive brand images, such as designer perfumes and clothing, usually avoid channels in which discount retailers are present. Manufacturers of upscale products, such as Gucci (handbags) and Godiva (chocolates), may sell their wares only in expensive stores in order to maintain an image of exclusivity. Many producers have opted to risk their image, however, and test sales in discount channels. For example, Levi Strauss expanded its distribution network to include JCPenney, Sears, and Walmart.

13-7e Levels of Distribution Intensity

Organizations have three options for intensity of distribution: intensive distribution, selective distribution, or exclusive distribution. **Intensive distribution** is a form of distribution aimed at maximum market coverage. Here, the manufacturer tries to have the product available in every outlet

intensive distribution a form of distribution aimed at having a product available in every outlet where target customers might want to buy it

Microsoft's Office 365 is a subscription service that gives users access to cloud storage and continuously-updated Office software for as low as $6.99 per month.

where potential customers might want to buy it. If buyers are unwilling to search for a product, it must be made very accessible to buyers. The next level of distribution, **selective distribution**, is achieved by screening dealers and retailers to eliminate all but a few in any single area. Because only a few are chosen, the consumer must seek out the product. For example, HBO selectively distributes its popular television shows through a series of its own subscription-based channels (HBO, HBO on Demand, and HBO Go for mobile devices) and sells subscriptions or single episodes through Apple, Amazon.com, and Sony's online stores but does not stream them through Netflix or Hulu Plus. The most restrictive form of market coverage is **exclusive distribution**, which entails only one or a few dealers within a given area. Because buyers may have to search or travel extensively to buy the product, exclusive distribution is usually confined to consumer specialty goods, a few shopping goods, and major industrial equipment. Products such as Rolls-Royce automobiles, Chris-Craft powerboats, and Pettibone tower cranes are distributed under exclusive arrangements.

EMERGING DISTRIBUTION STRUCTURES In recent years, rapid changes in technology and communication have led to the emergence of new, experimental distribution methods and channel structures.

For example, fashion flash sale sites like Gilt, JackThreads, and Ruelala have recently boomed in popularity. On these sites, new designer clothing items are made available every day—often at a discount from 15 to 80 percent, and always for an extremely limited time. The average fashion flash sale shopper is between 25 and 40 years of age and makes $100,000 a year—an ideal demographic for many marketers.

Another emerging channel structure involves renting items that are usually only sold to end consumers. For example, some websites allow customers to rent and return high fashion products (renttherunway.com and fashionrenting.com), handbags and accessories (lovemeandleaveme.com), and even furniture (fashionfurniture.com). Rental versus retail channels open up an entirely new customer base for certain products that were once reserved for a much smaller group.

For many years, subscription services such as book-of-the-month clubs have provided customers products periodically over time. More recently, subscription services have expanded far beyond books and magazines to include clothing (bombfell.com), shoes (shoedazzle.com), crafting kits (craftaholicsanonymous.net), and wine (www.clubw.com). Many websites require subscriptions to view premium content, and streaming media services like Spotify, Netflix, and OnLive offer a wholly new type of subscription service.

Digital marketplaces like Steam and the Google Play Store constitute another recent trend in marketing channels. Digital licensing adds an interesting facet to customer sales; instead of selling a tangible product, digital marketplaces sell the rights to songs, movies, and television shows through their websites and applications. Instead of leaving home to purchase a physical album, game, or movie, consumers can select specific media and download them directly to their computers or mobile devices.

13-8 OMNICHANNEL VERSUS MULTICHANNEL MARKETING

Marketing channels are valuable because they provide a route for products and services to reach the customer. Customers have different preferences, however, as to which channels to use when browsing, seeking information, comparing products to one another, and making a purchase. A single customer may use different channels

selective distribution a form of distribution achieved by screening dealers to eliminate all but a few in any single area

exclusive distribution a form of distribution that establishes one or a few dealers within a given area

for each of these activities, including both traditional and digital channels! For example, a customer might first learn about a new smartwatch when browsing a catalog, then conduct research about it on the company's website. She might later go to a physical retail location to try out the product, before finally purchasing the device using a mobile app. Because of these varying preferences through different stages of the shopping cycle, many companies have begun to employ a multichannel marketing strategy, whereby customers are offered information, goods, services, and/or support through one or more synchronized channels. Recent studies have demonstrated that customers who use multiple channels when shopping become more engaged during the purchase process, and tend to spend more than customers who shop one channel only. The exception is when customers are buying simple, utilitarian products that are well known and intended for frequent use. Since customers are already familiar with these product types, single-channel designs are just as effective.[51]

Because consumers use multiple channels during the shopping experience, it has become important for channel members to create a seamless shopping experience across all physical and digital channels. Facilitating such customer activities as checking a store's inventory online, purchasing an item through an app for in-store pickup, allowing online purchases to be returned in-store, and enabling mobile payment while shopping in-store are only a few strategies that producers and retailers are using to give customers the appearance that multiple channels are behaving as one.[52]

However, it is important to understand that the multichannel design does create redundancy and complexity in the firm's distribution system. Selling through multiple channels is typically accompanied by the construction of multiple, parallel supply chains, each with its own inventory, processes, and performance metrics.

Multichannel systems typically have meant that each channel would operate different transportation and distribution systems, hold and account for its own inventory, and otherwise act as independent sales and profit centers, with little knowledge of the operations of the other. This proved problematic for one retailer who was selling its products both in physical stores and on its website. The company had a distribution center in Kentucky for its Internet retailing business, and another near Chicago for its physical stores located there. When a customer in Chicago visited the local store looking for a certain product, the shelves were empty, and he was directed to order products from the company's website if he wanted one in time for the holidays. He did so, and the product was shipped to his home—at significant expense—from the Kentucky distribution center, while unused product sat only miles from his home in the Chicago distribution center, waiting to be stocked on local store shelves.

Because of situations like these, many companies are transitioning to an omnichannel distribution operation that supports their multichannel retail operations and unifies their retail interfaces so that all customers receive equal and efficient service. For example, retailers such as The Gap and Burberry allow customers to reserve items online for pickup in nearby stores, have employed a find-in-store feature on their websites that displays real-time stock information so customers can avoid unnecessary trips to the mall, and are beginning to provide in-store computer terminals or iPads for customers to search their websites for offerings the customer's local store may not carry. By making their inventory data available to customers in real-time, these retailers have effectively merged their multiple distribution channels in such a way that creates greater customer control over the shopping experience, leading to greater satisfaction and loyalty. We discuss further implications of this strategy in Chapter 15.

STUDY TOOLS 13

LOCATED AT BACK OF THE TEXTBOOK
☐ Rip out Chapter Review Card

LOCATED AT WWW.CENGAGEBRAIN.COM
☐ Review Key Terms Flashcards and create your own
☐ Track your knowledge and understanding of key concepts in marketing
☐ Complete practice and graded quizzes to prepare for tests
☐ Complete interactive content within the MKTG Online experience
☐ View the chapter highlight boxes within the MKTG Online experience

14 | Retailing

LEARNING OUTCOMES

After studying this chapter, you will be able to…

14-1 Explain the importance of the retailer within the channel and the U.S. economy

14-2 List and understand the different types of retailers

14-3 Explain why nonstore retailing is on the rise and list the advantages of its different forms

14-4 Discuss the different retail operations models and understand why they vary in strategy and format

14-5 Explain how retail marketing strategies are developed and executed

14-6 Discuss how services retailing differs from goods retailing

14-7 Understand how retailers address product/service failures and discuss the opportunities that service failures provide

14-8 Summarize current trends related to customer data, analytics, and technology

After you finish this chapter go to **PAGE 261** for **STUDY TOOLS**

gpointstudio/Shutterstock.com

14-1 THE IMPORTANCE OF RETAILING

Retailing represents all the activities directly related to the sale of goods and services to the ultimate consumer for personal, nonbusiness use. Retailing has enhanced the quality of our daily lives in countless ways. When we shop for groceries, hair care, clothes, books, or other products and services, we are doing business with **retailers**. The millions of goods and services provided by retailers mirror the diverse needs, wants, and trends of modern society. The U.S. economy depends heavily on the retail sector. Approximately two-thirds of the U.S. gross domestic product (GDP) comes from retail activity, and retail sales account for nearly 30 percent of all consumer spending.[1]

retailing all the activities directly related to the sale of goods and services to the ultimate consumer for personal, nonbusiness use

retailer a channel intermediary that sells mainly to consumers

Retailing affects everyone, both directly and indirectly. The retail industry consists of more than 3.7 million retail establishments and supports 42 million jobs, equal to about one in every four American jobs. A recent study suggests that 78 percent of current retail employees are satisfied with their jobs, and nearly 8 in 10 describe themselves as happy working in retail. According to the National Retail Federation, more than 98 percent of all retail businesses employ less than 50 people, indicating that small

businesses comprise most of the retailing industry. However, the industry is dominated by a small number of large companies. For example, if Walmart were a country, its sales would rank 28th in the world in GDP. That's right behind Norway, and ahead of Austria.[2] As the retail environment changes, so too do retailers. Trends and innovations relating to customer data, social media, and alternative forms of shopping are constantly developing, and retailers have no choice but to react. The *best* retailers actually lead the way by anticipating change and developing new and exciting ways to interact with customers. We discuss each of these issues and more in this chapter.

 TYPES OF RETAILERS AND RETAIL OPERATIONS

Retail establishments can be classified in several ways, such as type of ownership, level of service, product assortment, and price. These variables can be combined in several ways to create numerous unique retail operating models. Exhibit 14.1 depicts the major types of retailers and classifies them by their key differentiating characteristics.

14-2a Ownership Arrangement

Depending on its ownership arrangement, a retailer can gain advantages from having a broad brand identity, or from having the freedom to take risks and innovate. Retail ownership takes one of three forms—they can be independently owned, part of a chain, or a franchise outlet.

- An **independent retailer** is owned by a person or group and is not operated as part of a larger network. Around the world, most retailers are independent, with each owner operating a singular store within a local community.

- A **chain store** is a group of retailers (of one or more brand names) owned and operated by

independent retailer a retailer owned by a single person or partnership and not operated as part of a larger retail institution

chain store a store that is part of a group of the same stores owned and operated by a single organization

EXHIBIT 14.1 TYPES OF STORES AND THEIR CHARACTERISTICS

Type of Retailer	Level of Service	Product Assortment	Price	Gross Margin
Department store	Moderately high to high	Broad	Moderate to high	Moderately high
Specialty store	High	Narrow	Moderate to high	High
Supermarket	Low	Broad	Moderate	Low
Drugstore	Low to moderate	Medium	Moderate	Low
Convenience store	Low	Medium to narrow	Moderately high	Moderately high
Full-line discount store	Moderate to low	Medium to broad	Moderately low	Moderately low
Specialty discount store	Moderate to low	Medium to broad	Moderately low to low	Moderately low
Warehouse club	Low	Broad	Low to very low	Low
Off-price retailer	Low	Medium to narrow	Low	Low
Restaurant	Low to high	Narrow	Low to high	Low to high

a single organization. Under this form of ownership, a home office for the entire chain handles retail buying; creates unified operating, marketing, and other administrative policies; and works to ensure consistency across different locations. The Gap and Starbucks are retail chains.

- A **franchise** is a retail business where the operator is granted a license to operate and sell a product under the brand name of a larger supporting organizational structure, such as Subway or Supercuts. Under this arrangement, a **franchisor** originates the trade name, product, methods of operation, and so on. A **franchisee**, in return, pays the franchisor for the right to use its name, product, and business methods, and takes advantage of the franchisor's brand equity and operational expertise. The most successful franchises are increasingly services retailers. Three of the top five franchises recognized by Entrepreneur Magazine are primarily service rather than goods providers.[3]

14-2b Level of Service

The service levels that retailers provide range from full-service to self-service. Some retailers, such as exclusive clothing stores, offer very high or even customized service levels. They provide alterations,

credit, delivery, consulting, liberal return policies, layaway, gift-wrapping, and personal shopping. By contrast, retailers such as factory outlets and warehouse clubs offer virtually no service. After stock is set out for sale, the customer is responsible for any information gathering, acquisition, handling, use, and product assembly. At the extreme low end of the service continuum, a retailer may take the form of a product kiosk or vending machine.

14-2c Product Assortment

Retailers can also be categorized by the *width* and depth of their product lines. Width refers to the assortment of products offered; *depth* refers to the number of different brands offered within each assortment. Specialty stores such as Best Buy, Staples, and GameStop have the thinnest product assortments, usually carrying single or narrow product lines that are considerably deep. For example, a specialty pet store like PetSmart is limited to pet-related products, but may carry as many as twenty brands of dog food in a large variety of flavors, shapes, and sizes. On the other end of the spectrum, full-line discounters typically carry very wide assortments of merchandise that are fairly shallow.

Stores often modify their product assortments in order to accommodate factors in the external environment. For example, a recent shift in customer preference toward healthier food options—combined with support from regulatory bodies such as the Partnership for a Healthier America—has led many gas stations to

franchise a relationship in which the business rights to operate and sell a product are granted by the franchisor to the franchisee

franchisor the originator of a trade name, product, methods of operation, and the like that grants operating rights to another party to sell its product

franchisee an individual or business that is granted the right to sell another party's product

offer healthier food products such as fresh vegetables and whole grain cereals.[4] Similarly, food products ranging from milk to vitamins to dog treats have been excluded from retail product lines in order to better ensure customer safety. However, the type of product can influence customers' expectations about product assortments. Researchers recently found that customers expect less variety among items that are of higher quality.[5]

14-2d Price

Price is the fourth way to position retail stores. Traditional department stores and specialty stores typically charge the full "suggested retail price." In contrast, discounters, factory outlets, and off-price retailers use low prices and discounts to lure shoppers. The last column in Exhibit 14.1 shows the typical **gross margin**—how much the retailer makes as a percentage of sales after the cost of the goods sold is subtracted. (Margins will be covered in more detail in Chapter 19.) Today, prices in any store format might vary not just from day to day, but from minute to minute! Online retailers and traditional brick-and-mortar stores that have invested in electronic tagging systems are increasingly adopting dynamic pricing strategies that allow them to adjust to an item's surging popularity or slow movement in real time[6] The rise of smartphones and other mobile devices has added a new layer of complexity to pricing decisions. Customers have more information than ever before and can compare prices from dozens of retailers at once. Consequently, many are not willing to pay full price anymore. Recognizing this trend, some retailers have begun using pricing techniques to make customers believe that they are getting a bargain—even if they aren't. One well-known e-tailer was found liable for using misleading list prices to exaggerate customer savings. In other words, product list prices have become nothing more than a suggestion to deal-savvy consumers.[7]

14-2e Types of In-Store Retailers

Traditionally, retailers fall into one of several distinct types of retail stores, each of which features a product assortment, types of services, and price levels that

A recent shift in customer preference toward healthier food options has led many gas stations to offer healthier food products such as fresh vegetables and whole grain cereals.

align with the intended customers' shopping preferences. Recently, however, retailers began experimenting with alternative formats that blend the features and benefits of the traditional types. For instance, supermarkets are expanding their nonfood items and services, discounters are adding groceries, drugstores are becoming more like convenience stores, and department stores are experimenting with smaller stores. Nevertheless, many stores still fall into the traditional archetypes:

- **Department stores** such as JCPenney and Macy's carry a wide range of products and specialty goods, including apparel, cosmetics, housewares, electronics, and sometimes furniture. Each department acts as a separate profit center, but central management sets policies about pricing and the types of merchandise carried.

- **Specialty stores** typically carry a deeper but narrower assortment of merchandise within a single category of interest. The specialized knowledge of their salesclerks allows for more attentive customer service. The Children's Place, Williams-Sonoma, and Foot Locker are well-known specialty retailers.

gross margin the amount of money the retailer makes as a percentage of sales after the cost of goods sold is subtracted

department store a store housing several departments under one roof

specialty store a retail store specializing in a given type of merchandise

- **Supermarkets** are large, departmentalized, self-service retailers that specialize in food and some nonfood items. Some conventional supermarkets are being replaced by much larger *superstores*. Superstores offer one-stop shopping for food and nonfood needs, as well as services such as pharmacists, florists, salad bars, photo processing kiosks, and banking centers.

- **Drugstores** primarily provide pharmacy-related products and services, but many also carry an extensive selection of cosmetics, health and beauty aids, seasonal merchandise, greeting cards, toys, and some non-refrigerated convenience foods. As other retailer types have begun to add pharmacies and direct mail prescription services have become more popular, drugstores have competed by adding more services such as 24-hour drive-through windows and low-cost health clinics staffed by nurse practitioners.

- A **convenience store** resembles a miniature supermarket but carries a much more limited line of high-turnover convenience goods. These self-service stores are typically located near residential areas and offer exactly what their name implies: convenient locations, long hours, and fast service in exchange for premium prices. In exchange for higher prices, however, customers are beginning to demand more from convenience store management, such as higher quality food and lower prices on staple items such as gasoline and milk.

- **Discount stores** compete on the basis of low prices, high turnover, and high volume. Discounters can be classified into several major categories:

  - **Full-line discount stores** such as Walmart offer consumers very limited service and carry a vast assortment of well-known, nationally branded goods such as housewares, toys, automotive parts, hardware, sporting goods, garden items, and clothing.

  - **Supercenters** extend the full-line concept to include groceries and a variety of services, such as pharmacies, dry cleaning, portrait studios, photo finishing, hair salons, optical shops, and restaurants. For supercenter operators such as Target, customers are drawn in by food but end up purchasing other items from the full-line discount stock.

  - Single-line **specialty discount stores** such as Foot Locker offer a nearly complete selection of merchandise within a single category and use self-service, discount prices, high volume, and high turnover to their advantage. A **category killer** such as Best Buy is a specialty discount store that heavily dominates its narrow merchandise segment.

  - A **warehouse club** sells a limited selection of brand name appliances, household items, and groceries. These are sold in bulk from warehouse outlets on a cash-and-carry basis to members only. Currently, the leading stores in this category are Sam's Club, Costco, and BJ's Wholesale Club.

  - **Off-price retailers** such as TJ Maxx, Ross, and Marshall's sell at prices 25 percent or more below traditional department store prices because they buy inventory with cash and they don't require return privileges. These stores often sell manufacturers' overruns, irregular merchandise, and/or overstocks that they purchase at or below cost. A **factory outlet** is an off-price retailer that is owned and operated by a single manufacturer and carries one line of merchandise—its own. Manufacturers can realize higher profit margins using factory outlets than they would by disposing of the goods through independent wholesalers and retailers. **Used goods retailers** turn customers into suppliers: pre-owned items bought back from customers are resold to different customers. Used goods retailers can be either brick-and-mortar locations (such as Goodwill stores) or electronic marketplaces (such as eBay).

supermarket a large, departmentalized, self-service retailer that specializes in food and some nonfood items

drugstore a retail store that stocks pharmacy-related products and services as its main draw

convenience store a miniature supermarket, carrying only a limited line of high-turnover convenience goods

discount store a retailer that competes on the basis of low prices, high turnover, and high volume

full-line discount store a discount store that carries a vast depth and breadth of product within a single product category

supercenter a large retailer that stocks and sells a wide variety of merchandise including groceries, clothing, household goods, and other general merchandise

specialty discount store a retail store that offers a nearly complete selection of single-line merchandise and uses self-service, discount prices, high volume, and high turnover

category killer a large discount store that specializes in a single line of merchandise and becomes the dominant retailer in its category

warehouse club a large, no-frills retailer that sells bulk quantities of merchandise to customers at volume discount prices in exchange for a periodic membership fee

off-price retailer a retailer that sells at prices 25 percent or more below traditional department store prices because it pays cash for its stock and usually doesn't ask for return privileges

factory outlet an off-price retailer that is owned and operated by a manufacturer

used goods retailer a retailer whereby items purchased from one of the other types of retailers are resold to different customers

- **Restaurants** provide both tangible products—food and drink—and valuable services—food preparation and presentation. Most restaurants are also specialty retailers in that they concentrate their menu offerings on a distinctive type of cuisine—for example, Olive Garden Italian restaurants and Starbucks coffeehouses.

14-3 THE RISE OF NONSTORE RETAILING

The retailing formats discussed so far entail physical stores where merchandise is displayed and to which customers must travel in order to shop. In contrast, **nonstore retailing** enables customers to shop without visiting a physical store location. Nonstore retailing adds a level of convenience for customers who wish to shop from their current locations. Due to broader changes in culture and society, nonstore retailing is currently growing faster than in-store retailing. The major forms of nonstore retailing are automatic vending, direct retailing, direct marketing, and Internet retailing (or *e-tailing*). In response to the recent successes seen by nonstore retailers, traditional brick-and-mortar retailers have begun seeking a presence in limited nonstore formats. For example, Target has begun to heighten its Internet presence by offering movies via streaming video. The new Target Ticket platform allows customers to purchase movies and popular television shows cheaply and without subscription fees, which allows Target to compete with services such as Apple's iTunes and Netflix.[8] Target is also trying to compete with dominant e-tailers like Amazon by offering price matching, decreased shipping rates, and a mobile-friendly experience.[9]

- **Automatic vending** entails the use of machines to offer goods for sale—for example, the soft drink, candy, or snack vending machines commonly found in public places and office buildings. Retailers are continually seeking new opportunities to sell via vending. As a result, vending machines today sell merchandise such as DVDs, digital cameras, perfumes, and even ice cream. A key aspect of their continuing success is the proliferation of cashless payment systems in response to consumers' diminishing preference for carrying cash. Automatic vending has allowed marketers to tap into a new, unlikely audience: customers seeking luxury items on the

A pet owner stops by the world's first dog treat machine to buy a quick snack for her canine companion.

Vincent Boon/Getty Images

go. Vending machines in France are now being used to dispense high quality meat, while vending machines in other countries are being used to sell gold bars, champagne, and even luxury cars.[10]

- **Self-service technologies (SST)** comprise a form of automatic vending where services are the primary focus. Automatic teller

restaurant a retailer that provides both tangible products—food and drink—and valuable services—food preparation and presentation

nonstore retailing shopping without visiting a store

automatic vending the use of machines to offer goods for sale

self-service technologies (SST) technological interfaces that allow customers to provide themselves with products and/or services without the intervention of a service employee

machines, pay-at-the-pump gas stations, and movie ticket kiosks allow customers to make purchases that once required assistance from a company employee. However, as with any sort of self-service technology, automatic vending comes with failure risks due to human or technological error. Unless customers expect that they can easily recover from such errors, they may end up shopping elsewhere.

Naturally, some customers are frustrated with the growing trend toward self-service technology. Many can recall an incident of a self-service technology failure that left them begging to speak to a live human being. Some banks are attempting to avoid service failures at ATMs by re-introducing live interactions between customers and service employees. In the most advanced systems, ATM customers can video chat with a live teller at any hour, allowing for customized service based on customer preferences.[11]

- **Direct retailing** representatives sell products door-to-door, in offices, or at in-home sales parties. Companies like Avon, Mary Kay, and The Pampered Chef have used this approach for years. Social media selling has flourished among direct sellers seeking to increase the number of products and services sold. Many direct sellers now host digital parties on social media, where people can shop from the comfort of their own homes for items ranging from "do it yourself" manicures to weight loss body wraps. Man Cave, a new home sales party developed for men, has been described as "like Mary Kay on steroids." Man Cave representatives invite male friends and family over for testosterone-fueled parties at which Man Cave products are used and Man Cave foods are eaten. Affiliates earn commissions for the sale of beer mugs, grilling tools, frozen steaks, and other Man Cave products.[12]

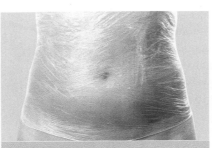

Weight loss body wraps are among the most popular products sold through Facebook and other social media today.

staras/Shutterstock.com

- **Direct marketing (DM)** includes techniques used to elicit purchases from consumers' homes, offices, and other convenient locations. Common DM techniques include telemarketing, direct mail, and mail-order catalogs. Shoppers using these methods are less bound by traditional shopping situations. Time-strapped consumers and those who live in rural or suburban areas are most likely to be DM shoppers because they value the convenience and flexibility it provides. DM occurs in several forms:

- **Telemarketing** is a form of DM that employs outbound and inbound telephone contacts to sell directly to consumers. Telemarketing is a highly effective marketing technique; recent estimates indicate that 5,000 U.S. companies will spend over $15 billion on inbound and outbound calls by 2015.[13]

- Alternatively, **direct mail** can be a highly efficient or highly inefficient retailing method, depending on the quality of the mailing list and the effectiveness of the mailing piece. With direct mail, marketers can precisely target their customers according to demographic, geographic, and/or psychographic characteristics. Direct mailers are becoming more sophisticated in targeting the right customers. **Microtargeting** based on data analytics of census data, lifestyle patterns, financial information, and past purchase and credit history allows direct mailers to pick out those most likely to buy their products.[14] U.S. companies spend more than $45 billion annually on direct marketing—a larger share of advertising expenditures than any other media except television. More than $11.5 billion of that is spent on data and software solutions intended to heighten customer responsiveness.[15] Microtargeting is also an effective tool for online retailing. Many companies have purchased access to online search engine data, making it easier than ever to pinpoint customer preferences. A customer's online search history enables retailers to match his or her specific customer wants through targeted digital advertisements.

direct retailing the selling of products by representatives who work door-to-door, office-to-office, or at home sales parties

direct marketing (DM) techniques used to get consumers to make a purchase from their home, office, or other nonretail setting

telemarketing the use of the telephone to sell directly to consumers

direct mail the delivery of advertising or marketing material to recipients of postal or electronic mail

microtargeting the use of direct marketing techniques that employ highly detailed data analytics in order to isolate potential customers with great precision

Back Stock	Floor Stock

Bugpha/iStock/Thinkstock; Thilak Piyadigama/iStock/Thinkstock

- **Shop-at-home television networks** such as HSN and QVC produce television shows that display merchandise to home viewers. Viewers can phone in their orders directly on toll-free lines and shop with their credit cards. The shop-at-home industry has quickly grown into a multibillion-dollar business with a loyal customer following and high customer penetration.

- **Online retailing**, or **e-tailing**, enables a customer to shop over the Internet and have items delivered directly to her door. Global online shopping accounts for more than $1.3 trillion in sales today and is expected to reach $2.5 trillion by 2018.[16] Online retailer Amazon sells more than 200 million products in the United States, including more than 5 million items in the clothing department and more than 20 million in the sports and outdoors department. Online, interactive shopping tools and live chats substitute for the in-store interactions with salespeople and product trials that customers traditionally use to make purchase decisions. Shoppers can look at a much wider variety of products online because physical space restrictions do not exist. While shopping, customers can take their time deciding what to buy.

In addition to retailer websites, consumers are increasingly using social media applications as shopping platforms. Social networking sites such as Facebook, Instagram, and Twitter enable users to immediately purchase items recommended by their social connections, a phenomenon known as *social shopping*. Companies are eager to establish direct linkages between social networking platforms and their own websites due to the belief that a product or service recommended by a friend will receive higher consideration from the potential customer.

 14-4 RETAIL OPERATIONS MODELS

The retail formats covered so far are co-aligned with unique operating models that guide the decisions made by their managers. Each operating model can be summarized as a set of guiding principles. For example, off-price retailers de-emphasize customer service and product selection in favor of lower prices, which are achieved through a greater focus on lean inventory management.

Alternatively, specialty shops generally adopt a high-service approach that is supported by an agile approach to inventory. By keeping a greater amount of **floor stock** (inventory displayed for sale to customers) and **back stock** (inventory held in reserve for potential future sale in a retailer's storeroom or stockroom) on hand, a broader range of customer demands can be accommodated. This operating model also implies higher prices for customers, however, so retail managers must make sure that they deliver on the promises their firms make to customers in order to secure their loyalty. At the same time, these retail managers must control demand via promotions and other sales events in order to sell off slow moving and perishable items, thereby making more room for items that are more popular.

Regardless of the type of stocking strategy a retailer chooses, there is always a chance that a wanted

shop-at-home television network a specialized form of direct response marketing whereby television shows display merchandise, with the retail price, to home viewers

online retailing (e-tailing) a type of shopping available to consumers with personal computers and access to the Internet

floor stock inventory displayed for sale to customers

back stock inventory held in reserve for potential future sale in a retailer's storeroom or stockroom

item will be out of stock. This is obviously bad for the retailer, but research suggests that there may be a bright side to stockouts. One recent study found that customers may view stockouts as an indication of how desirable a product is, and in turn, will buy an item that is similar to the out-of-stock item, regardless of whether they even wanted the original item.[17]

These sorts of tradeoffs have been partially responsible for the recent emergence of hybrid retail operating models. As an example of a hybrid strategy, the Spanish women's fashion retailer Zara employs a specialty retail format with a twist: It uses a mass merchandising inventory strategy. Zara offers high quality products and excellent customer service to draw customers into its stores but never replenishes specific inventory items that are sold. Rather, its designers and buyers are continually introducing new products in small or medium quantities. Once a product sells out, a new one replaces it, allowing for a very lean operation. This strategy not only lowers inventory costs (and thereby increases profitability) but also creates an aura of exclusivity around each piece that the retailer sells: Each skirt, blouse, and accessory is effectively a limited edition item. This strategy also has the ancillary benefit of driving customers back to the store in order to see what new products have arrived, and thus has the potential to increase repurchases.[18]

The tradeoffs inherent to retail operating models have both spurred the recent success of online-only retailers and led to a surge in online storefront development among retailers who have traditionally operated in physical formats only. A key advantage of online retail is that no physical retail store space is needed for displaying and selling merchandise. Lower cost remote distribution centers can be used since all of the showcasing occurs on the company's website. By moving online, a specialty store can gain the operational benefits of a mass merchandiser. It can showcase exclusive or trendy items in an almost-free space to potential customers located around the world, and can then fulfill demand from one of several localized distribution centers in a very short time. Fulfillment times are specified by the customer (according to their willingness to pay for greater shipping and delivery speed), and even this tradeoff is becoming less of a sticking point every year. Amazon's Prime subscription program, for example, includes free two-day shipping. The company has even introduced its own fleet of airplanes to decrease shipping times and minimize reliance on other shippers. Considering that there are about 60 million Prime members worldwide, shipping time is at the heart of what the Amazon customer values. Amazon has also opened a network of parcel lockers that allow customers to pick up their own orders, further decreasing delivery time and cost.[19] Startup company Deliv positioned itself as a cutting-edge crowdsourced courier service. Deliv provides its more than 250 national and regional U.S. retail partners (such as Macy's and Footlocker) a means of competing with Amazon by offering same-day home delivery.[20] It will be exciting to see how these advances continue to change retail strategies and operations in the years to come.

Today, most retail stores remain operationally and tactically similar to those that have been in business for hundreds of years; with one or more physical locations that the customer must visit in order to purchase a stocked product, and with strategies in place to attract customers to visit. The sorts of differences we have described among retail operating models imply that managing one type of store instead of another can involve very different experiences. But most of the decisions that retail managers make can be distilled down to six categories of activity, referred to as the retailing mix. These categories, described in the next section, are relatively universal to all forms of retailing, but are applied in different ways based on the retail format.

EXECUTING A RETAIL MARKETING STRATEGY

Retail managers develop marketing strategies based on the goals established by stakeholders and the overall strategic plans developed by company leadership. Strategic retailing goals typically focus on increasing total sales, reducing costs of goods sold, and improving financial ratios such as return on assets or equity. At the store level, more tactical retailing goals include increased store traffic, higher sales of a specific item, developing a more upscale image, and creating heightened public awareness of the retail operation and its products or services. The tactical strategies that retailers use to obtain their goals include having a sale, updating décor, and launching a new advertising campaign. The key strategic tasks that precede these tactical decisions are defining and selecting a target market and developing the retailing mix to successfully meet the needs of the chosen target market.

14-5a Defining a Target Market

The first and foremost task in developing a retail strategy is to define the target market. This process begins with market segmentation, the topic of Chapter 8. Successful retailing has always been based on knowing the customer. Sometimes retailing chains flounder when management loses sight of the customers the stores should be serving. Customers' desires and preferences change over their personal and professional lifespans, and it is important for retailers to be sensitive to these changes by migrating them to new and different products as their buying patterns evolve.

Target markets in retailing are often defined by demographics, geographic boundaries, and psychographics. For example, supermarket chain Publix recently introduced an app that makes shopping easier and more convenient for its customers. App users can even have groceries delivered directly to their homes to reduce shopping time. This app is targeted squarely at Millennials, who often have busy schedules and are technology savvy. Whole Foods, on the other hand, is opening smaller, more convenient, and more cost-effective store formats targeted at Millennials.[21] Determining a target market is a prerequisite to creating the retailing mix. For example, Target's merchandising approach for sporting goods is to match its product assortment to the demographics of the local store and region.

14-5b Choosing the Retailing Mix

As previously noted, defining a retail operation entails combining the elements of the retailing mix to come up with a single retailing method to attract the target market. The **retailing mix** consists of six Ps: the four Ps of the marketing mix (*product, promotion, place,* and *price*) plus *presentation* and *personnel* (see Exhibit 14.2). The combination of the six Ps projects a store's (or website's) image and influences customers' perceptions. Using these impressions, shoppers position one store or website against another. Managers must make sure that the positioning is aligned with target customers' expectations.

PRODUCT The first element in the retailing mix is the product offering, also called the product assortment or merchandise mix. Developing a product offering is essentially a question of the width and depth of the product assortment. Price, store/website design, displays, and service are important to customers in determining where to shop, but the most critical factor is merchandise selection. This reasoning also holds true for online retailers.

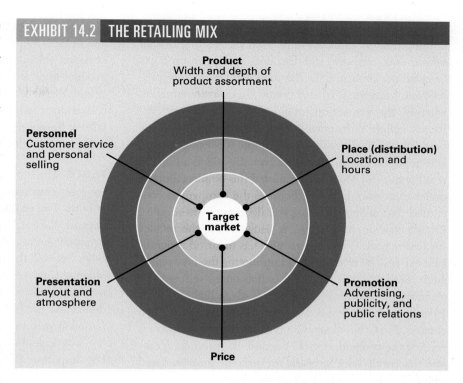

EXHIBIT 14.2 THE RETAILING MIX

Product
Width and depth of product assortment

Personnel
Customer service and personal selling

Place (distribution)
Location and hours

Target market

Presentation
Layout and atmosphere

Promotion
Advertising, publicity, and public relations

Price

Amazon.com, for instance, offers enormous width in its product assortment with millions of different items, including books, music, toys, videos, tools and hardware, health and beauty aids, electronics, and software. Conversely, online specialty retailers such as Lemon and Mint and Bridge 55 focus on a single category of merchandise, hoping to attract loyal customers with a larger depth of products at lower prices and excellent customer service. Many online retailers purposely focus on single product line niches that could never attract enough foot traffic to support a traditional brick-and-mortar store. For instance, websites such as bugbitingplants.com and petflytrap.com sell and ship live carnivorous plants in the United States. After determining what products will satisfy target customers' desires, retailers must find sources of supply and evaluate the products. When the right products are found, the retail buyer negotiates a purchase contract.

PROMOTION Retail promotion strategy includes advertising, public relations and publicity, and sales promotion. The goal is to help position the store or website in customers' minds. Retailers design intriguing ads, stage special events, and develop promotions aimed at their target markets. Today's grand-openings are a carefully orchestrated blend of advertising, merchandising, goodwill, and glitter. All the elements of an opening—press coverage, special events, media

retailing mix a combination of the six Ps—product, promotion, place, price, presentation, and personnel—to sell goods and services to the ultimate consumer

advertising, and store displays—are carefully planned. Other promotions that are often used successfully include sales events, coupons, and discounts for certain products or customer groups. One risk associated with store promotions, however, is **brand cannibalization**: a situation whereby the promotion intended to draw in new customers simply shifts current customers from buying one brand to another brand. For example, discount apparel and home decor store TJ Maxx recently added an online retail option. TJ Maxx has promoted this online shopping outlet cautiously, however, because the company is concerned that online shopping will decrease in-store sales. Cannibalization, in this case, is dangerous to the retailer for two reasons. First, the retailer has incurred a significant expense by setting up and promoting the new online store. Second, promoting the online outlet reduces the accuracy of sales forecasts, which leads to higher costs.[22] Brand cannibalization is dangerous to the retailer for two reasons. First, the retailer incurs significant expense in executing the promotion itself. Second, the promotion creates inaccurate sales forecasts for both the promoted and cannibalized products, leading to stockouts of the promoted brand and financial losses from discounting surplus inventory of the cannibalized brand. The latter types of losses can sometimes be significantly greater than the cost of the promotion itself. Therefore, retail managers should design their promotional activities carefully, with gaining new customers being the primary objective.

Much retail advertising is focused on the local level. Local advertising by retailers usually provides specific information about their stores, such as location, merchandise, hours, prices, and special sales. In contrast, national retail advertising generally focuses on image. For example, Target uses advertisements similar to designer fashion advertisements to depict high-quality goods. Paired with the ubiquitous red target and tag line "Expect more. Pay less," Target is demonstrating that it sells products that consumers normally aspire to own at prices they can afford.

Target's advertising campaigns also take advantage of cooperative advertising, another popular retail advertising practice. Traditionally, marketers would pay retailers to feature their products in store mailers, or a marketer would develop a television campaign for the product and simply tack on several retailers' names at the end. But Target's advertising uses a more collaborative trend by integrating products such as Tide laundry detergent or Coca-Cola into the actual campaign. Another common form of cooperative advertising involves promotion of exclusive products. For example, Target hires famous trendy designers for temporary partnerships, during which they develop reasonably priced product lines available exclusively at Target stores. Recently, Target teamed up with Neiman Marcus to offer a collection of holiday luxury items. These items were sold both at Target and Neiman Marcus stores, as well as on both stores' outlet web stores.

PLACE The retailing axiom "location, location, location" has long emphasized the importance of place to the retail mix. The physical *location* decision is important first because the retailer is making a large, semi-permanent commitment of resources that can reduce its future flexibility. Second, the physical location will almost inevitably affect the store's future growth and profitability. Many retailers work with consultants and/or city planners to determine the best sites for current sales as well as potential growth in the future.

Physical site location begins by choosing a community. Important factors to consider are the area's economic growth potential, the amount of competition, and geography. For instance, retailers like TJ Maxx and Walmart often build stores in new communities that are still under development. Fast-food restaurants tend to place a priority on locations with other fast-food restaurants because being located in clusters helps to draw customers for each restaurant. Even after careful research, however, the perfect location can be elusive in the face of changing markets. Mobile food trucks circumvent this problem by being able to relocate at will. By moving from spot to spot over the course of a day and parking outside events and heavily trafficked areas, mobile food trucks can maximize their exposure and adapt to changing markets.

After identifying a geographic region or community, retailers must choose a specific site. In addition to growth potential, the important factors to consider are neighborhood socioeconomic characteristics, traffic flows, land costs, zoning regulations, and public transportation. A particular site's visibility, parking, entrance and exit locations, accessibility, and safety and security issues are also important considerations.

A retailer should consider how its store fits into the surrounding environment. Retail decision makers probably would not locate a Dollar General store next door to a Neiman Marcus department store. Furthermore, brick-and-mortar retailers have to decide whether to have a freestanding unit or to become a tenant in a shopping center or mall. Large retailers like Target and sellers of shopping goods like furniture and cars often use an isolated, freestanding location. A freestanding store location may have the advantages of low site cost or rent and no

brand cannibalization the reduction of sales for one brand as the result of the introduction of a new product or promotion of a current product by another brand

The Victoria's Secret Fashion Show is a major part of the company's marketing strategy. Their "Angels" serve as key members of the company's marketing team.

nearby competitors. On the other hand, it may be hard to attract customers to a freestanding location, and no other retailers are around to share costs. To be successful, stores in isolated locations must become "destination stores." A **destination store** is a store consumers seek out and purposely plan to visit. Websites can also be destinations for shoppers. Amazon is a destination website for a wide variety of products, and Google is a destination website for search information.

Freestanding units are increasing in popularity as brick-and-mortar retailers strive to make their stores more convenient to access, more enticing to shop, and more profitable. Freestanding sites now account for more than half of all retail store construction starts in the United States as more and more retailers are deciding not to locate in pedestrian malls. Perhaps the greatest reason for developing a freestanding site is greater visibility. Retailers often feel they get lost in huge shopping centers and malls, but freestanding units can help stores develop an identity with shoppers. Also, an aggressive expansion plan may not allow time to wait for shopping centers to be built. Drugstore chains like Walgreens have been purposefully relocating their existing shopping center stores to freestanding sites, especially street corner sites for drive-through accessibility.

Shopping centers first appeared in the 1950s when the U.S. population started migrating to the suburbs. The first shopping centers were *strip centers*, typically located along busy streets. They usually included a supermarket, a variety store, and perhaps a few specialty stores. Then *community shopping centers* emerged, with one or two small department stores, more specialty stores, a couple of restaurants, and several apparel stores. These community shopping centers provided off-street parking and a broader variety of merchandise. *Regional malls* offering a much wider variety of merchandise started appearing in the mid-1970s. Regional malls are either entirely enclosed or roofed to allow shopping in any weather. Most are landscaped with trees, fountains, sculptures, and the like to enhance the shopping environment. They have acres of free parking. The *anchor stores* or *generator stores* (often major department stores) are usually located at opposite ends of the mall to create heavy foot traffic.

According to shopping center developers, *lifestyle centers* are emerging as the newest generation of shopping centers. Lifestyle centers typically combine outdoor shopping areas composed of upscale retailers and restaurants, with plazas, fountains, and pedestrian streets. They appeal to retail developers looking for an alternative to the traditional shopping mall, a concept rapidly losing favor among shoppers. Though shopping malls bring multiple retail locations together, location is often not the most important motivator for a customer to choose a specific store. Instead, most shoppers look for stores that guarantee product availability, more service employees, and time saving opportunities.

Many smaller specialty lines are opening shops inside larger stores to expand their retail opportunities without risking investment in a separate store. Toys"R"Us worked with Macy's to open stores-within-a-store at numerous Macy's locations. The 1,500-square-foot toy sections offered dolls, puzzles, and other potential stocking stuffers.[23] The Toys"R"Us modules reflect a popular trend of pop-up shops—tiny, temporary stores that stay in one location for only a few months. Pop-up shops help retailers reach a wide market while avoiding high rent at retail locations. They have become the marketing tool du jour for large companies.

PRICE Another important element in the retailing mix is price. Retailing's ultimate goal is to sell products to consumers, and the right price is critical to ensure sales. Because retail prices are usually based on the cost

destination store a store that consumers purposely plan to visit prior to shopping

of the merchandise, an essential part of pricing is efficient and timely buying. Another pricing strategy is "value-based pricing," which focuses on the value of the product to the customer more than the cost of the product to the supplier. Price is also a key element in a retail store's positioning strategy. Higher prices often indicate a level of quality and help reinforce the prestigious image of retailers, as they do for Lord & Taylor and Neiman Marcus. On the other hand, discounters and off-price retailers, such as Target and TJ Maxx, offer a good value for the money.

PRESENTATION The presentation of a retail store helps determine the store's image and positions the retail store in consumers' minds. For instance, a retailer that wants to position itself as an upscale store would use a lavish or sophisticated presentation. The main element of a store's presentation is its **atmosphere**, the overall impression conveyed by a store's physical layout, décor, and surroundings. The atmosphere might create a relaxed or busy feeling, a sense of luxury or efficiency, a friendly or cold attitude, a sense of organization or clutter, or a fun or serious mood. Urban Outfitters stores, targeted to Generation Y consumers, use raw concrete, original brick, rusted steel, and unfinished wood to convey an urban feel. These are the most influential factors in creating a store's atmosphere:

- *Employee type and density:* Employee type refers to an employee's general characteristics—for instance, neat, friendly, knowledgeable, or service oriented. Density is the number of employees per thousand square feet of selling space. Whereas low employee density creates a do-it-yourself, casual atmosphere, high employee density denotes readiness to serve the customer's every whim.

- *Merchandise type and density:* A prestigious retailer like Nordstrom or Neiman Marcus carries the best brand names and displays them in a neat, uncluttered arrangement. Discounters and off-price retailers often carry seconds or out-of-season goods crowded into small spaces and hung on long racks by category—tops, pants, skirts, and so on—creating the impression

Recent studies show that the type of music played can influence a customer's choice of product. What type of music do you think they play in the Disney Store? How do you think this affects customers' choices?

Alina Zamogilnykh/Shutterstock.com

that "We've got so much stuff, we're practically giving it away."

- *Fixture type and density:* Fixtures can be elegant (rich woods) or trendy (chrome and smoked glass); they can even consist of old, beat-up tables, as in an antiques store. The fixtures should be consistent with the general atmosphere the store is trying to create.

- *Sound:* Sound can be pleasant or unpleasant for a customer. Music can entice some customers to stay in the store longer and buy more or to eat quickly and leave a table for others. It can also control the pace of the store traffic, create an image, and attract or direct the shopper's attention. Recent studies show that the type of music played can even influence a customer's choice of product. Ethnic music increases the likelihood of a customer choosing a menu item from the same country, and country-western music increases customers' willingness to pay for functional, everyday products.[24]

- *Odors:* Smell can either stimulate or detract from sales. Research suggests that people evaluate merchandise more positively, spend more time shopping, and are generally in a better mood when an agreeable odor is present. Retailers use fragrances as an extension of their retail strategy.

- *Visual factors:* Colors can create a mood or focus attention and therefore are an important factor in atmosphere. Red, yellow, and orange are considered warm colors and are used when a feeling of warmth and closeness is desired. Cool colors like blue, green, and violet are used to open up closed-in places and create an air of elegance and cleanliness. Many retailers have found that natural lighting, either from windows or skylights, can lead to increased sales. Outdoor lighting can also affect a customer's choice of retailer.

The **layout** of retail stores is also a key factor in their success. The goal is to use all of the store's space effectively, including aisles, fixtures, merchandise displays, and non-selling areas. In addition to making shopping easy and convenient for the customer, an effective layout has a powerful influence on traffic patterns and purchasing behavior. Layout also includes where products are placed in the store. Many technologically advanced retailers are using a technique called *market-basket analysis* to sift through the

atmosphere the overall impression conveyed by a store's physical layout, décor, and surroundings

layout the internal design and configuration of a store's fixtures and products

data collected by their point-of-purchase scanning equipment. The analysis looks for products that are commonly purchased together to help retailers find ideal locations for each product. Walmart uses market-basket analysis to determine where in the store to stock products for customer convenience. Kleenex tissues, for example, are in the paper-goods aisle and also beside the cold medicines.

Retailers can better acquire and use assets when they customize store layouts and merchandise mixes to the tastes of local consumer bases. For example, O'Reilly Auto Parts designs each of its retail outlets with the wants and needs of local auto drivers in mind, creating a neighborhood-specific strategy for each location. By customizing layout and product mix to the vehicles owned and operated in a particular area, the company can simultaneously provide greater levels of availability and reduce inventory, creating savings that the company passes along to customers.[25]

PERSONNEL People are a unique aspect of retailing. Most retail sales involve a customer–salesperson relationship, if only briefly. Sales personnel provide their customers with the amount of service prescribed by the retail strategy of the store.

Retail salespeople serve another important selling function: They persuade shoppers to buy. They must therefore be able to persuade customers that what they are selling is what the customer needs. Salespeople are trained in two common selling techniques: trading up and suggestion selling. *Trading* up means persuading customers to buy a higher-priced item than they originally intended to purchase. To avoid selling customers something they do not need or want, however, salespeople should take care when practicing trading-up techniques. *Suggestion selling*, a common practice among most retailers, seeks to broaden customers' original purchases with related items. For example, if you buy a new printer at Office Depot, the sales representative will ask if you would like to purchase paper, a USB cable, and/or extra ink cartridges. Suggestion selling by sales or service associates should always help shoppers recognize true needs rather than sell them unwanted merchandise.

Providing great customer service is one of the most challenging elements in the retail mix because customer expectations for service vary greatly. What customers expect in a department store is very different from what they expect in a discount store. Customer expectations also change. Ten years ago, shoppers wanted personal, one-on-one attention. Today, many customers are happy to help themselves as long as they can easily find what they need.

 ## 14-6 RETAILING DECISIONS FOR SERVICES

The fastest-growing part of our economy is the service sector. Although distribution in the service sector is difficult to visualize, the same skills, techniques, and strategies used to manage inventory can also be used to manage service inventory, such as hospital beds, bank accounts, or airline seats. The quality of the planning and execution of distribution can have a major impact on costs and customer satisfaction.

Because service industries are so customer oriented, service quality is a priority. To manage customer relationships, many service providers, such as insurance carriers, physicians, hair salons, and financial services, use technology to schedule appointments, manage accounts, and disburse information. Service distribution focuses on four main areas:

- *Minimizing wait times:* Minimizing the amount of time customers wait in line is a key factor in maintaining the quality of service.

- *Managing service capacity:* If service firms don't have the capacity to meet demand, they must either turn down some prospective customers, let service levels slip, or expand capacity.

- *Improving service delivery:* Service firms are now experimenting with different distribution channels for their services. Choosing the right distribution channel can increase the times that services are available or add to customer convenience.

- *Establishing channel-wide network coherence:* Because services are to some degree intangible, service firms also find it necessary to standardize their service quality across different geographic regions to maintain their brand image.

14-7 ADDRESSING RETAIL PRODUCT/ SERVICE FAILURES

In spite of retailers' best intentions and efforts to satisfy each and every customer, all retailers inevitably disappoint a subset of their customers. In some cases, customer disappointment occurs by design. No retailer can be everything to every customer, and by making strategic decisions related to targeting, segmentation, and the retailing mix, retailers implicitly decide which customers will be delighted and which will probably leave the store unsatisfied. In other cases, service failures are unintentional. A product may be located where customers cannot easily find it (or it may remain in the stockroom, entirely out of customer view), or an employee may provide mistaken information about a product's features or benefits. Customers are generally indifferent to the reasons for retailer errors, and their reactions to mistakes such as product stockouts and unexpectedly poor quality products can range widely. Some may simply leave the store, while others will respond with anger or even revenge behaviors intended to prevent other customers from visiting the store.[26]

The best retailers have plans in place not only to recover from inevitable lapses in service but perhaps even to benefit from them. For these top-performing stores, service recovery is handled proactively as part of an overarching plan to maximize the customer experience. Actions that might be taken include:

- Notifying customers in advance of stockouts and explaining the reasons why certain products are not available

- Implementing liberal return policies designed to ensure that the customer can bring back any item for any reason (if the product fails to work as planned, or even if the customer simply doesn't like it)

- Issuing product recalls in conjunction with promotional offers that provide future incentives to repurchase

In short, the best retailers treat customer disappointments as opportunities to interact with and improve relations with their customers. Evidence indicates that successful handling of such failures can sometimes yield even higher levels of customer loyalty than if the failure had never occurred at all.

14-8 RETAILER AND RETAIL CUSTOMER TRENDS AND ADVANCEMENTS

Though retailing has been around for thousands of years, it continues to change every day. Retailers are constantly innovating. They are always looking for new products and services (or ways to offer them) that will attract new customers or inspire current ones to buy in greater quantities or more frequently. Many of the most interesting and effective retail innovations that have recently taken hold are related to the use of purchase and shopping

data to better understand customer wants and needs. Finding new and better ways to entice customers into a store—and then to spend more money once there—is another hotbed of innovation. This chapter concludes with an examination into emerging trends and recent advancements in retailing.

It is important to recognize that, fundamentally, retailers decide what to sell on the basis of what their target market wants to buy. They base these decisions on market research, past sales, fashion trends, customer requests, and other sources. Recently, the need for more and better information has led many retailers to use **big data analytics**, a process whereby retailers use complex mathematical models to make better product mix decisions. Dillard's, Target, and Walmart use big data analytics to determine which products to stock and at what prices, how to manage markdowns, and how to advertise to draw target customers. The data these and other companies collect at the point of sale and throughout their stores enable retailers and suppliers alike to gain better customer insights. For example, instead of simply unloading products into the distribution channel and leaving marketing, sales and relationship building to local dealers, auto manufacturers use websites to keep in touch with customers and prospects. They inquire about lifestyles, hobbies, and vehicle needs in an effort to develop long-lasting relationships in the hopes that these consumers will reward them with brand loyalty in the future.

Retailers are increasingly using **beacons**—devices that send out connecting signals to customers' smartphones and tablets. These devices recognize when a customer is in or near the store and indicate to an automated

big data analytics the process of discovering patterns in large data sets for the purposes of extracting knowledge and understanding human behavior

beacon a device that sends out connecting signals to customers' smartphones and tablets in order to bring them into a retail store or improve their shopping experience

system that the customer is ripe to receive a marketing message via e-mail or text. Beacons can also notify sales associates to offer (or not offer) a coupon at the point of sale. Some retailers are using an app called Swarm to map customer foot traffic data, which they use to make better decisions about product placement within the floor grid. Carefully designed beacons can even have an aesthetic appeal. At some retailers, cameras and beacons are built into mannequins located inside the store and in window displays. These beacons not only act as data collection devices, but also as primary displays for the clothing and jewelry that appeal to customers' eyes.[27]

RFID (Radio Frequency Identification) is not a new technology, but its use has increased greatly over the last few years. Traditionally used for inventory management purposes prior to items reaching the sales floor, retailers have begun using RFID to track items that customers pick up while shopping. This enables a retailer to instantly create a promotion for the specific item in a customer's hand. For example, if a customer picks up a set of sheets, the retailer can use RFID and digital advertising to suggest related items, such as pillowcases, blankets, and even paint colors that match the sheets. The advertisement can provide guidance as to where to find the promoted items in the store.

Retailers have recently begun using another emerging technology: facial recognition. Suppose a retailer scans a customer to determine the customer's gender and age group. The retailer can then cross-reference this data with the customer's location in the store, providing

Big retailers like Target use big data analytics to determine which products to stock and at what price.

Sergey Yechikov/Shutterstock.com

promotions and information with pinpoint accuracy. Facial recognition even allows retailers to identify customers, call them by their names, and target them with advertising as they walk through the retail space. Similarly, biometric sensors can be used to measure how long a customer views an ad or product in the store. This data can be used as a measure of interest and/or ad effectiveness.[28]

14-8a Shopper Marketing and Analytics

Shopper marketing is an emerging retailing trend that employs market data to best serve customers as they prepare to make a purchase. Shopper marketing focuses first on understanding how a brand's target consumers behave as shoppers in different channels and formats, and then using this information in business-based strategies and initiatives that are carefully designed to deliver balanced benefits to all stakeholders—brands, channel members, and customers. It may sound simple, but it is anything but. Whereas brand manufacturers used to advertise widely and tried to ensure that their products were available wherever consumers shopped, now they are placing far more emphasis on partnering with specific retailers or websites. Brand manufacturers work with retailers on everything from in-store initiatives to customized retailer-specific

Andrey_Popov/Shutterstock.com

> **shopper marketing** understanding how one's target consumers behave as shoppers, in different channels and formats, and leveraging this intelligence to generate sales or other positive outcomes

National toy store chain Toys'R'Us offers a click-and-collect service whereby customers can make purchases online and then pick their items up in-store.

the implications of this new method of customer research. One implication is the strategic alignment of customer segments. Brands' core target consumers are compared to retailers' most loyal shoppers in an effort to find intersecting areas where brands and retailers can pool their resources. The ideal outcome is a more focused marketing effort and a three-way win for brands, channel members, *and* customers.

Shopper marketing also has significant implications for retailers' supply chains. As in-store initiatives become more unique and short-term and products become more customized, supply chains must react more quickly to customer demand changes. Thus, shopper marketing has increased the need for sophisticated analytics and metrics. As with many modern business efforts, shopper marketing forces managers to coordinate better, measure more, think more creatively, and move faster.

products. Shopper marketing brings brand managers and account managers together to connect with consumers along the entire path-to-purchase, whether it be at home, on the go via mobile marketing, or in the store. Both manufacturers and retailers now think about consumers specifically while they are in shopping mode. They use **shopper analytics** to dig deeply into customers' shopping attitudes, perceptions, emotions, and behaviors—and are thereby able to learn how the shopping experience shapes these differences. More and more companies are conducting or participating in large-scale data analytics projects to better understand how shoppers think when they shop at a store or on a website and what factors influence their thought processes.

Shopper marketing is becoming increasingly popular as businesses see

shopper analytics searching for and discovering meaningful patterns in shopper data for the purpose of fine-tuning, developing, or changing market offerings

14-8b Future Developments in Retail Management

A retailing trend with great growth potential is the leveraging of technology to increase touchpoints with customers and thereby generate greater profitability. The use of mobile devices and social media while browsing, comparison shopping, and actually making a purchase is becoming extremely pervasive, leading retailers to rethink how they should appeal to shoppers in the decision-making mode. Recall that customers who "showroom" visit a physical retail store to examine product features or quality firsthand, but then eventually make the purchase online. This practice has motivated a showrooming response from retailers themselves, who reduce the amount of stock kept on hand, rent or lease smaller spaces, and ramp up their fulfillment capabilities at distribution centers. Showrooming and data analytics have even led to the development of virtual reality apps that enable customers to see themselves wearing articles of desired clothing without physically putting them on! These approaches have led some retailers to pursue a strategy of **retail channel omnification** (recall Chapter 13's discussion of omnichannel distribution operations). Retailers like Nordstrom used to treat their physical stores as entirely different businesses from their online stores, with each channel having a unique distribution system and a dedicated inventory. Now, retailers are combining these ventures into a single system that is responsible for delivering on customer demand regardless of whether it originated in a physical store or in cyberspace.[29] This single system avoids redundancies in inventory and transportation, saving costs and enabling retailers to offer competitive prices across their various outlets. Customers of Nordstrom, Nordstrom Rack, Nordstrom.com, hautelook.com, and nordstromrack.com can seamlessly transition between each of these channels when shopping, returning purchased goods or scheduling services such as alterations.

However, not all retailers are embracing omnification as the way of the future. The alternative strategy, **click-and-collect**, also enables customers to make their purchases online. Rather than waiting for orders to arrive at their homes, customers drive to physical stores to pick their orders up.[30] When retailers use this strategy, customers benefit from greater speed of delivery (in fact, they become the delivery vehicle), while retailers themselves benefit from the fact that customers must enter their stores in order to claim their purchases. Once inside, customers can be marketed to, increasing the likelihood that they will purchase add-on items or otherwise engage in impulse buying. It remains to be seen whether one or both of these strategies will stand the test of time, but it is certain that retailers are preparing for the inevitability of the Internet as an important shopping and purchasing medium for the foreseeable future.

Another fascinating trend is the use of artificial intelligence as a touch point for customers. Robots are replacing or augmenting retail employees at restaurants, supermarkets, and airports across the globe. As technology progresses, customers will begin to see virtual reality used in many retail contexts. Virtual reality enables customers to try items before they buy—even if those items don't actually exist yet. Currently, customers shopping online can use virtual dressing rooms to see how outfits might look on their own bodies. Imagine if customers could do the same for furniture or kitchen appliances! The integration of these new technologies will bring customers a shopping experience like they have never had before—both highly interactive and customized.[31]

> **retail channel omnification** the reduction of multiple retail channel systems into a single, unified system for the purpose of creating efficiencies or saving costs
>
> **click-and-collect** the practice of buying something online and then traveling to a physical store location to take delivery of the merchandise

STUDY TOOLS 14

LOCATED AT BACK OF THE TEXTBOOK
☐ Rip out Chapter Review Card

LOCATED AT WWW.CENGAGEBRAIN.COM
☐ Review Key Terms Flashcards and create your own
☐ Track your knowledge and understanding of key concepts in marketing
☐ Complete practice and graded quizzes to prepare for tests
☐ Complete interactive content within the MKTG Online experience
☐ View the chapter highlight boxes within the MKTG Online experience

15 | Marketing Communications

After you finish this chapter go to **PAGE 279** for **STUDY TOOLS**

15-1 THE ROLE OF PROMOTION IN THE MARKETING MIX

Few goods or services, no matter how well developed, priced, or distributed, can survive in the marketplace without effective promotion—communication by marketers that informs, persuades, and reminds potential buyers of a product in order to influence an opinion or elicit a response.

promotion communication by marketers that informs, persuades, and reminds potential buyers of a product in order to influence an opinion or elicit a response

promotional strategy a plan for the optimal use of the elements of promotion: advertising, public relations, personal selling, sales promotion, and social media

competitive advantage one or more unique aspects of an organization that cause target consumers to patronize that firm rather than competitors

Promotional strategy is a plan for the optimal use of the elements of promotion: advertising, public relations, personal selling, sales promotion, and social media. Promotion is a vital part of the marketing mix, informing consumers of a product's benefits and thereby positioning the product in the marketplace. As Exhibit 15.1 shows, the marketing manager determines the goals of the company's promotional strategy in light of the firm's overall goals for the marketing mix—product, place (distribution), promotion, and price. Using these overall goals, marketers combine the elements of the promotional strategy (the promotional mix) into a coordinated plan. The promotion plan then becomes an integral part of the marketing strategy for reaching the target market.

The main function of a marketer's promotional strategy is to convince target customers that the goods and services offered provide a competitive advantage over the competition. A **competitive advantage** is the set of unique features of a company and its products that are perceived by the target market as significant

Rawpixel.com/Shutterstock.com

and superior to those of the competition. Such features can include high product quality, rapid delivery, low prices, excellent service, or a feature not offered by the competition. Promotional strategies have changed a great deal over the years as many targeted customer segments have become more difficult to reach. Informative television advertisements are no longer enough, forcing marketers to think more creatively. Most modern campaigns utilize a variety of newer tactics—such as digital paid media, social media, and influencer marketing—in addition to more traditional media like television and print. Take, for instance, Dove's Real Strength Highlight Reel campaign for its Men+Care line of skin care products. This campaign was inspired by research showing that 86 percent of men feel the idea of masculinity has changed since their fathers' generation. Featuring Mike Greenberg from sports talk show Mike & Mike as the voiceover actor and NFL players Carson Palmer and Jordy Nelson as the primary spokespersons, Real Strength Highlight Reel celebrated athletes as strong people—not just strong players. In one ad, Palmer is shown styling his daughter's hair, while Nelson is shown teaching third grade.

Each video, posted on YouTube, garnered more than 2 million views within two months and reinforced the #RealStrength hashtag for Dove. The campaign then

EXHIBIT 15.1   **ROLE OF PROMOTION IN THE MARKETING MIX**

extended the conversation by encouraging men to post their own stories on Facebook, Twitter, and Instagram.[1]

15-2 MARKETING COMMUNICATION

Promotional strategy is closely related to the process of communication. As humans, we assign meaning to feelings, ideas, facts, attitudes, and emotions. Communication is the process by which meanings are exchanged or shared through a common set of symbols. When a company develops a new product, changes an old one, or simply tries to increase sales of an existing good or service, it must communicate its selling message to potential customers. Marketers communicate information about the firm and its products to the target market and various publics through their promotional programs.

In order to improve face-to-face communication between customers and store employees, Apple recently redesigned its Genius Bar customer service desk, rebranding it as the Genius Grove. Here, Genius Grove employees converse with customers during the grand opening of the company's new flagship store in San Francisco on May 21, 2016.

15-2a Interpersonal Communication

Communication can be divided into two major categories: interpersonal communication and mass communication. Interpersonal communication is direct, face-to-face communication between two or more people. When communicating face-to-face, people see the other person's reaction and can respond almost immediately. Apple salespeople are trained not only on Apple's products, but also on proper etiquette for interacting with customers. For example, salespeople must ask customers before touching their iPhones, thus highlighting the role of empathy in sales training. A salesperson speaking directly with a customer is an example of an interpersonal marketing communication.

15-2b Mass Communication

communication the process by which we exchange or share meaning through a common set of symbols

interpersonal communication direct, face-to-face communication between two or more people

mass communication the communication of a concept or message to large audiences

Mass communication involves communicating a concept or message to large audiences. A great number of marketing communications are directed to consumers as a whole, usually through a mass medium such as television or newspapers. When a company advertises, it generally does not personally know the people with whom it is trying to communicate. Furthermore, the company often cannot respond immediately to consumers' reactions to its messages (unless they are using social media or other Internet-based marketing tools). Any clutter from competitors' messages or other distractions in the environment can reduce the effectiveness of the mass-communication effort. Continuing the previous example, Apple uses many different mass media vehicles (including magazines and digital media) to reach its target audience.

15-2c The Communication Process

Marketers are both senders and receivers of messages. As *senders*, marketers attempt to inform, persuade, and remind the target market to take actions compatible with the need to promote the purchase of goods and services. As *receivers*, marketers listen to the target market in order to develop the appropriate messages, adapt existing messages, and spot new communication opportunities. In this way, most marketing communication is a two-way, rather than one-way, process. The two-way nature of the communication process is shown in Exhibit 15.2.

EXHIBIT 15.2 COMMUNICATION PROCESS

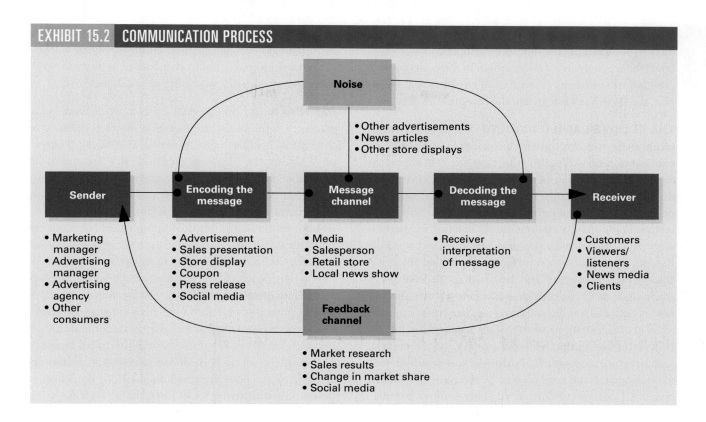

THE SENDER AND ENCODING The **sender** is the originator of the message in the communication process. In an interpersonal conversation, the sender may be a parent, a friend, or a salesperson. For an advertisement, press release, or social media campaign, the sender is the company or organization itself. It can sometimes be difficult to tell who the sender of a promotional message is, especially in the case of bold, avant-garde advertisements. For example, when Garnier wanted to drive awareness for its Fructis hair product line, it targeted digitally savvy women to create momentum around a new conversation. Garnier found that more than seven million women posted and tweeted every day using the hashtag #girlproblems. The number one complaint accompanying the hashtag was hair issues. Leveraging this trend, Garnier created the #girlproblems campaign, whereby the company produced humorous videos of men reading real #girlproblems posts as well as other humorous content featuring influential bloggers and comediennes. In this case, the sender was the Fructis brand, but the brand employed other senders like bloggers and spokespeople as well.[2]

Encoding is the conversion of the sender's ideas and thoughts into a message, usually in the form of words or signs. A basic principle of encoding is that what the source says is not what matters, but what the receiver hears. In the case of "Elevator Murder Experiment," the video encoded sentiments such as "you won't know what to expect" and "difficult ethical choices will need to be made"—provocative selling points for a gruesome action thriller.[2] One way of conveying a message the receiver will hear properly is to use concrete words and pictures.

MESSAGE TRANSMISSION Transmission of a message requires a **channel**—a voice, radio, newspaper, computer, smartphone, or other communication medium. A facial expression or gesture can also serve as a channel. For Garnier, the primary channel was video, which was then seeded on YouTube and Instagram. Garnier also posted owned content on BuzzFeed and the website www.onelessgirlproblem.com.[3] The response to these viral activities clearly created a lot of free publicity.

Reception occurs when the message is detected by the receiver and enters his or her frame of reference. In a two-way conversation such as a sales pitch given by a sales representative to a potential client, reception is normally high. Similarly, when the message is a recommendation from a friend, the reception is high as well. By contrast, the desired receivers may or may not detect the message when it

sender the originator of the message in the communication process

encoding the conversion of a sender's ideas and thoughts into a message, usually in the form of words or signs

channel a medium of communication—such as a voice, radio, or newspaper—for transmitting a message

is mass communicated because most media are cluttered by **noise**—anything that interferes with, distorts, or slows down the transmission of information. In some media overcrowded with advertisers, such as newspapers and television, the noise level is high and the reception level is low.

THE RECEIVER AND DECODING Marketers communicate their message through a channel to customers, or **receivers**, who will decode the message. It is important to note that there can be multiple receivers as consumers share their experiences and their recommendations online through social networks and other types of social media. Online conversations are becoming an increasingly influential way to promote products and services. Indeed, this new empowerment of the receiver has transformed marketing and advertising. Receivers can easily share new information with their friends and followers on social media, and those new receivers can then share that information as well. This leads to a more diverse interrelationship between senders and receivers of social media messages. **Decoding** is the interpretation of the language and symbols sent by the source through a channel. Common understanding between two communicators, or a common frame of reference, is required for effective communication. Therefore, marketing managers must ensure a proper match between the message to be conveyed and the target market's attitudes and ideas.

Even though a message has been received, it may not necessarily be properly decoded because of selective exposure, distortion, and retention. When people receive a message, they tend to manipulate it to reflect their own biases, needs, experiences, and knowledge. Therefore, differences in age, social class, education, culture, and ethnicity can lead to miscommunication. Further, because people do not always listen or read carefully, they can easily misinterpret what is said or written. In fact, researchers have found that consumers misunderstand a large proportion of both printed and televised communications. Bright colors and bold graphics have been shown to increase consumers' comprehension of marketing communication.

Even these techniques are not foolproof, however. The Garnier campaign was easily decoded and resonated with the target audience based on the BuzzFeed articles' trending status and the number of YouTube comments.[4]

Marketers targeting consumers in foreign countries must also worry about the translation and possible miscommunication of their promotional messages by other cultures. Global marketers must decide whether to standardize or customize the message for each global market in which they sell.

FEEDBACK In interpersonal communication, the receiver's response to a message is direct **feedback** to the source. Feedback may be verbal, as in saying "I agree" or "I do not like this new product." But it can also be nonverbal, as in nodding, smiling, frowning, or gesturing. Feedback can also occur digitally, as in a Facebook like, a comment on a blog post, or a message sent through a website contact form. Mass communicators are often cut off from direct feedback, so they must rely on market research, social media, or analysis of viewer responses for indirect feedback. They might use such measurements as the percentage of television viewers who recognized, recalled, or stated that they were exposed to the company's messages. Indirect feedback enables mass communicators to decide whether to continue, modify, or drop a message.

With the increase in online advertising, marketers are able to get more feedback than before the Internet became such a driving social force. Using web analytics, marketers can see how long customers stay on a website and which pages they view. Moreover, social media enable companies such as JetBlue Airways, Nike, American Airlines, and Comcast to provide instant feedback by responding to consumers' posts on Facebook and to complaints posted on Twitter.

The Internet and social media have had an impact on the communication model in two major ways. First, consumers are now able to become senders (as opposed to only brands being senders). A professional blogger who recommends a product, and thus influences a consumer's decision to buy it, is a sender. Everyday consumers who make casual recommendations on Facebook and Yelp are essentially senders as well. Clearly, the communication model is much more complicated today than it was just a few years ago. Second, the communication model shows the feedback channel as primarily impersonal and numbers driven. In the traditional communication process, marketers can see the results of customer behavior (for example, a drop or rise in sales) but are able to explain those changes only by using their judgment. Today, customers use social media platforms like Facebook, Twitter, and Instagram to comment publically on marketing efforts. These platforms enable marketers to personalize the feedback channel by opening the door for direct conversations with customers. However, because social media conversations occur in real time and are public, any negative posts or complaints are highly visible. Thus, many companies have crisis communication

noise anything that interferes with, distorts, or slows down the transmission of information

receiver the person who decodes a message

decoding interpretation of the language and symbols sent by the source through a channel

feedback the receiver's response to a message

ORDER YOUR COOLEST NOW!

Coolest Cooler

~~USD $499.99~~ USD $399.99

Includes one Coolest cooler, one battery pack and one removable Bluetooth speaker. Additional battery and speaker available for purchase.

Color   Classic Coolest

Clear selection

THE COOLEST "LOVE IT OR LEAVE IT" GUARANTEE

We guarantee that you will love the Coolest. If you don't, we will refund your money.

Try your Coolest for 30 days. If you're not happy, simply return the Coolest within 30 days of delivery. We'll refund you the purchase price, no questions asked (less any S&H).

30-DAY MONEY-BACK GUARANTEE

ORDER NOW AND GET FREE SHIPPING

Lock your order in now and we'll have your Coolest en route within 24 hours. Take advantage of this limited offer on FREE SHIPPING within the continental USA.

Source: Coolest Cooler

When COOLEST launched its innovative cooler, it used informative promotion to distinguish itself from seasoned competitors.

strategies to deal with negative information and promote good brand reputations.

15-3 THE GOALS OF PROMOTION

People communicate with one another for many reasons. They seek amusement, ask for help, give assistance or instructions, provide information, and express ideas and thoughts. Promotion, on the other hand, seeks to modify behavior and thoughts in some way. For example, promoters may try to persuade consumers to eat at Burger King rather than at McDonald's. Promotion also strives to reinforce existing behavior—for instance, getting consumers to continue dining at Burger King once they have switched. The source (the seller) hopes to project a favorable image or to motivate purchase of the company's goods and services.

Promotion can perform one or more of four tasks: *inform* the target audience, *persuade* the target audience, *remind* the target audience, or *connect* with the audience. The ability to *connect* to consumers is one task that can be facilitated through social media. Often a marketer will try to accomplish two or more of these tasks at the same time.

15-3a Informing

Informative promotion seeks to convert an existing need into a want or to stimulate interest in a new product. It

is generally more prevalent during the early stages of the product life cycle. People typically will not buy a product or service or support a nonprofit organization until they know its purpose and its benefits to them. Informative messages are important for promoting complex and technical products such as automobiles, computers, and investment services. For example, shortly after Google unveiled the Google Glass wearable computer and display, it released a series of commercials showing various practical uses for the device. A commercial titled "How It Feels" demonstrated point-of-view video and photo capture, messaging, video chatting, search, weather, mapping, and more. Even though it did not overtly explain the device's functions, the ad informed viewers how the device could record once-in-a-lifetime moments and provide the perfect solutions for life's little problems.[5] Informative promotion is also important for a "new" brand being introduced into an "old" product class. When modern-day cooler manufacturer COOLEST began its Kickstarter campaign, it used video to inform backers about its product's benefits. Unlike a traditional cooler, the COOLEST cooler features a rechargeable blender, a portable speaker, storage for plates and cutlery, and a USB outlet.[6] When the product launched, COOLEST again used informative promotion to distinguish itself from seasoned competitors. New products cannot establish themselves against more mature products unless potential buyers are aware of them, value their benefits, and understand their positioning in the marketplace.

15-3b Persuading

Persuasive promotion is designed to stimulate a purchase or an action. Persuasion typically becomes the main promotion goal when the product enters the growth stage of its life cycle. By this time, the target market should have general product awareness and some knowledge of how the product can fulfill its wants. Therefore, the promotional task switches from informing consumers about the product category to persuading them to buy the company's brand rather than that of the competitor. At this time, the promotional message emphasizes the product's real and perceived competitive advantages, often appealing to emotional needs such as love, belonging, self-esteem, and ego satisfaction. For example, advertisers of Android-based smartphones try to persuade users to purchase their companies' devices

The ALS Association received a boost to awareness thanks to pro golfer Chris Kennedy kicking off the campaign.

#ALSICEBUCKETCHALLENGE

Crystal Eye Studio/Shutterstock.com

instead of an iPhone (or even instead of another brand of Android phone). Advertising messages, therefore, highlight the unique technological benefits of Android phones such as a faster processors and larger screens.

Persuasion is important when the goal is to inspire direct action. The ALS Association experienced a huge increase in donations through the Ice Bucket Challenge. Pro Golfer Chris Kennedy kicked the vital hit off on his social network by pouring ice water over his head and then challenging others to do the same. The campaign spread all over Facebook and Twitter, was reported on cable television news shows, and eventually became part of popular culture. The effort raised $115 million, more than 20 times the usual donations received for that period of time. The "Ice Bucket Challenge" currently ranks as the largest social media fundraiser ever.[7] Persuasion can also be an important goal for very competitive mature product categories such as household items and soft drinks. In a marketplace characterized by many competitors, the promotional message often encourages brand switching and aims to convert some buyers into loyal users. Critics believe that some promotional messages and techniques can be too persuasive, causing consumers to buy products and services they don't really need.

15-3c Reminding

Reminder promotion is used to keep the product and brand name in the public's mind. This type of promotion prevails during the maturity stage of the life cycle. It assumes that the target market has already been persuaded of the merits of the good or service. Its purpose is simply to trigger a memory. Colgate toothpaste and other consumer products often use reminder promotion. Companies that produce products like automobiles and appliances advertise throughout the year in order to remind people about the brands when they are looking to purchase.

15-3d Connecting

The idea behind social media is to form relationships with customers and potential customers through technological ties such as Facebook, Twitter, YouTube, or other social media platforms. Indeed, some companies, such as Starbucks, have their own social networks that allow customers to share ideas, information, and feedback. By facilitating this exchange of information through a transparent process, brands are increasingly connecting with their customers in hopes they become brand advocates that promote the brand through their own social networks. Tools for connection include social networks, social games, social publishing tools, as well as social commerce. The ALS Association's "Ice Bucket Challenge" can also be considered an example of connecting since many people used videos posted to Facebook and Twitter to issue their challenges.

 THE PROMOTIONAL MIX

Most promotional strategies use several ingredients—which may include advertising, public relations, sales promotion, personal selling, and social media—to reach a target market. That combination is called the **promotional mix**. The proper promotional mix is the one that management believes will meet the needs of the target market and fulfill the organization's overall goals. Data plays a very important role in how marketers distribute funding among their promotional mix tactics. The more funds allocated to each promotional ingredient and the more managerial emphasis placed on each technique, the more important that element is thought to be in the overall mix.

promotional mix the combination of promotional tools—including advertising, public relations, personal selling, sales promotion, and social media—used to reach the target market and fulfill the organization's overall goals

15-4a Advertising

Almost all companies selling a good or a service use advertising, whether in the form of a multi-million-dollar campaign or a simple classified ad in a newspaper. **Advertising** is any form of impersonal paid communication in which the sponsor or company is identified. Traditional media—such as television, radio, newspapers, magazines, pay-per-click online advertising, display advertising, direct mail, billboards, and transit advertising (such as on buses and taxis and at bus stops)—are most commonly used to transmit advertisements to consumers. Other options include websites, e-mail, blogs, videos, and interactive games. Marketers' budgets are shifting more and more toward these digital options (including social media). However, as the Internet becomes a more vital component of many companies' promotion and marketing mixes, consumers and lawmakers are increasingly concerned about possible violations of consumers' privacy. Social networking sites like Facebook

Steve Granitz/Getty Images

Advertising can show up in any way, shape, or form. Here, actors Portia de Rossi (left) and Ellen DeGeneres arrive at the June 8, 2016 premiere of *Finding Dory* in front of a backdrop advertising Juicy Juice, Coppertone, and Kraft Macaroni & Cheese.

and Google+ are having to re-examine their privacy policies.

One of the primary benefits of advertising is its ability to communicate to a large number of people at one time. Cost per contact, therefore, is typically very low. Advertising has the advantage of being able to reach the masses (for example, through national television networks), but it can also be microtargeted to small groups of potential customers, such as television ads on a targeted cable network. Although the *cost per contact* in advertising is very low, the *total cost* to advertise is typically very high. This hurdle tends to restrict advertising on a national basis. Chapter 16 examines advertising in greater detail.

15-4b Public Relations

Concerned about how they are perceived by their target markets, organizations often spend large sums to build a positive public image. **Public relations** is the marketing function that evaluates public attitudes, identifies areas within the organization the public may be interested in, and executes a program of action to earn public understanding and acceptance. Public relations helps an organization communicate with its customers, suppliers, stockholders, government officials, employees, and the community in which it operates. Marketers use public relations not only to maintain a positive image but also to educate the public about the company's goals and objectives, introduce new products, and help support the sales effort.

A public relations program can generate favorable **publicity**—public information about a company, product, service, or issue appearing in the mass media as a news item. Social media sites like Twitter can provide large amounts of publicity quickly. Organizations generally do not pay for the publicity and are not identified as the source of the information, but they can benefit tremendously from it. However, although organizations do not directly pay for publicity, it should not be viewed as free. Preparing news releases, staging special events, and persuading media personnel to broadcast or print publicity messages costs money. Public relations and publicity are examined further in Chapter 16.

advertising impersonal, one-way mass communication about a product or organization that is paid for by a marketer

public relations the marketing function that evaluates public attitudes, identifies areas within the organization the public may be interested in, and executes a program of action to earn public understanding and acceptance

publicity public information about a company, product, service, or issue appearing in the mass media as a news item

15-4c Sales Promotion

Sales promotion consists of all marketing activities—other than personal selling, advertising, and public relations—that stimulate consumer purchasing and dealer effectiveness. Sales promotion is generally a short-run tool used to stimulate immediate increases in demand. Sales promotion can be aimed at end consumers, trade customers, or a company's employees. Sales promotions include free samples, contests, premiums, trade shows, vacation giveaways, and coupons. It also includes experiential marketing whereby marketers create events that enable customers to connect with brands. Forward-thinking companies like Groupon have combined social networks and sales promotions, and social media behemoths like Facebook are expanding their promotion platforms through built-in contest and sweepstakes tools. For example, Insurance company Esurance ran a television spot just before the 2015 Super Bowl instructing viewers to tweet the brand's hashtag for a chance to win $1 million. Twitter brand mentions spiked at 6:35 pm the night of the game, generating more than 9,000 Tweets per minute and trending nationally for 15 minutes. Esurance was the most mentioned brand of the game, ranking number one for first quarter Twitter data with 375,000 tweets. This approach was especially effective because Esurance's ad ran before the game, when ad prices were much less than the $5 million they cost to run during the game.[8]

Marketers often use sales promotion to improve the effectiveness of other ingredients in the promotional mix, especially advertising and personal selling. Research shows that sales promotion complements advertising by yielding faster sales responses. In many instances, more marketing money is spent on sales promotion than on advertising.

Many companies use social media to run contests and promote their products and services. Insurance company Esurance, for instance, ran a television spot just before the 2015 Super Bowl instructing viewers to retweet the brand's hashtag for a chance to win $1 million.

Source: Twitter

sales promotion marketing activities—other than personal selling, advertising, and public relations—that stimulate consumer buying and dealer effectiveness

personal selling a purchase situation involving a personal, paid-for communication between two people in an attempt to influence each other

15-4d Personal Selling

Personal selling is a purchase situation involving a personal, paid-for communication between two people in an attempt to influence each other. In this dyad, both the buyer and the seller have specific objectives they wish to accomplish. The buyer may need to minimize cost or assure a quality product, for instance, while the salesperson may need to maximize revenue and profits.

Traditional methods of personal selling include a planned presentation to one or more prospective buyers for the purpose of making a sale. Whether it takes place face-to-face or over the phone, personal selling attempts to persuade the buyer to accept a point of view. For example, a car salesperson may try to persuade a car buyer that a particular model is superior to a competing model in certain features, such as gas mileage. Once the buyer is somewhat convinced, the salesperson may attempt to elicit some action from the buyer, such as a test drive or a purchase. Frequently, in this traditional view of personal selling, the objectives of the salesperson are at the expense of the buyer, creating a win-lose outcome.

More current notions on personal selling emphasize the relationship that develops between a salesperson and a buyer. Initially, this concept was more typical in business-to-business selling situations, involving the sale of products like heavy machinery or computer systems. More recently, both business-to-business and business-to-consumer selling focus on building long-term relationships rather than on making a one-time sale.

Relationship selling emphasizes a win-win outcome and the accomplishment of mutual objectives that benefit both buyer and salesperson in the long term. Rather than focusing on a quick sale, relationship selling attempts to create a long-term, committed relationship based on trust, increased customer loyalty, and a continuation of the relationship between the salesperson and the customer. Personal selling, like other promotional mix elements, is increasingly dependent on the Internet. Most companies use their websites to attract potential buyers seeking information on products and services and to drive customers to their physical locations where personal selling can close the sale. Personal selling is discussed further in Chapter 17.

15-4e Content Marketing and Social Media

As promotional strategies change, and given brands' newfound ability to become publishers, content marketing has become a crucial part of promotion. Recall from Chapter 7 that content marketing entails developing valuable content for interested audience members and then using e-mail marketing, search engine optimization, paid search, and display advertising to pull customers to the company's website or social media channel so that they can learn about the brand or to make a purchase. Content created by brands is typically distributed through social media.

Recall that social media are promotion tools used to facilitate conversations and other interactions among people online. When used by marketers, these tools facilitate consumer empowerment. For the first time, consumers are able to speak directly to other consumers, the company, and web communities. Social media include blogs, microblogs (such as Twitter), video platforms (such as You Tube, Twitch, Periscope, and Vine), podcasting (online audio and video broadcasts), and social networks (such as Tumblr, Pinterest, Instagram, and Snapchat).

Initially, individuals used social media tools primarily for self-expression. For example, a lawyer might develop a blog to talk about politics because that is her hobby. Or a college freshman might develop a profile on Facebook to stay in touch with his high school friends. But soon, businesses saw that these tools could be used to engage with consumers as well. Indeed, social media have become a "layer" in promotional strategy. Social media are ubiquitous—it just depends on how deep that layer goes for each brand. The rise of streaming video, for example, has created a completely new way for marketers to manage their image, connect with consumers, and generate interest in and

desire for their companies' products. Blogging has also led to a new type of influencer marketing, whereby social media celebrities (including bloggers, tweeters, and other people with large social media audiences) promote brands and products. Now marketers are using social media as integral aspects of their campaigns and as a way to extend the benefits of their traditional media. Social media are discussed in more detail in Chapter 18.

15-4f The Communication Process and the Promotional Mix

The Internet has changed how businesses promote their brands. Traditionally, marketing managers have been in charge of defining the essence of the brand. This included complete brand control and mostly one-way communication between the brand and customers. All of the content and messages were focused on defining and communicating the brand value. The focus for many campaigns was pure entertainment, and the brand created all of the content for campaigns—from the website to television spots to print ads.

That approach has now changed. The consumer has much more control (which makes some brands quite nervous!). The communication space is increasingly controlled by the consumer, as is the brand message. Perception is reality as consumers have more control to adapt the brand message to fit their ideas. Instead of repetition, social media rely on the idea of customization and adaption of the message. Information is positioned as more valuable as opposed to being strictly entertaining. Probably the most important aspect is the idea of consumer-generated content, whereby consumers are able to both take existing content and modify it or to create completely new content for a brand. For example, Doritos has the "Crash the Super Bowl" promotion, where ordinary people are invited to create television commercials for Doritos that are then uploaded to www.crashthesuperbowl.com and voted on by millions of Doritos fans. The winning spots then run during the Super Bowl.

As a result of the impact of social media as well as the proliferation of new platforms, tools, and ideas, promotional tactics can also be categorized according to media type—paid, earned, or owned, as shown in Exhibit 15.3. **Paid media** is based on the traditional advertising model, whereby a brand pays for media space. Traditionally, paid media has included television,

paid media a category of promotional tactic based on the traditional advertising model, whereby a brand pays for media space

magazine, outdoor, radio, or newspaper advertising. Paid media also includes display advertising on website, pay-per-click advertising on search engines, and even promoted tweets on Twitter. Paid media is quite important, especially as it migrates to the Web. Paid media is used with other media types to develop an integrated message strategy. **Earned media** is based on a public relations or publicity model. The idea is to get people talking about the brand—whether through media coverage (as in traditional public relations) or through word of mouth (WOM). Word of mouth traditionally occurs face-to-face. Electronic word of mouth (EWOM), for example, sharing a movie review on a social media site, is growing rapidly. Earned media is often created when people talk and share content on social media. Additionally, search engine optimization (SEO), whereby companies embed key words into content to increase their positioning on search engine results pages (SERPs), can also be considered earned media. **Owned media** is a new form of promotional tactic where brands are becoming publishers of their own content in order to maximize the brand's value to customers as well as increase their search rank in Google. Owned media includes the company's websites as well as its official presence on Facebook, Twitter, YouTube channels, blogs, and other platforms. This media is controlled by the brand but continuously keeps the customer and his or her needs in mind as it creates videos, blog posts, contests, photos, and other pieces of content. Owned media, also called content marketing, is important for both B-to-B and B-to-C companies. The most effective campaigns typically employ all three types of media: owned media is created to increase WOM and earned media, and paid media is used to get the message out to target audiences.

The elements of the promotional mix differ in their ability to affect the target audience. For instance, promotional mix elements may communicate with the consumer directly or indirectly. The message may flow one way or two ways. Feedback may be fast or slow, a little or a lot. Likewise, the communicator may have varying degrees of control over message delivery, content, and flexibility. Exhibit 15.4 outlines characteristics among the promotional mix elements with respect

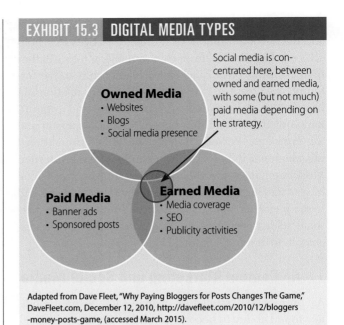

EXHIBIT 15.3 DIGITAL MEDIA TYPES

Owned Media
• Websites
• Blogs
• Social media presence

Social media is concentrated here, between owned and earned media, with some (but not much) paid media depending on the strategy.

Paid Media
• Banner ads
• Sponsored posts

Earned Media
• Media coverage
• SEO
• Publicity activities

Adapted from Dave Fleet, "Why Paying Bloggers for Posts Changes The Game," DaveFleet.com, December 12, 2010, http://davefleet.com/2010/12/bloggers-money-posts-game, (accessed March 2015).

to mode of communication, marketer's control over the communication process, amount and speed of feedback, direction of message flow, marketer's control over the message, identification of the sender, speed in reaching large audiences, and message flexibility.

From Exhibit 15.4, you can see that most elements of the promotional mix are indirect and impersonal when used to communicate with a target market, providing only one direction of message flow. For example, advertising, public relations, and sales promotion are generally impersonal, one-way means of mass communication. Because they provide no opportunity for direct feedback, it is more difficult to adapt these promotional elements to changing consumer preferences, individual differences, and personal goals.

Personal selling, on the other hand, entails direct two-way communication. The salesperson receives immediate feedback from the consumer and can adjust the message in response. Unlike other promotional tools, personal selling is very slow in dispersing the marketer's message to large audiences. Because a salesperson can communicate to only one person or a small group of persons at one time, it is a poor choice if the marketer wants to send a message to many potential buyers. Social media are also considered two-way communication, though not quite as immediate as personal selling. Social media can disperse messages to a wide audience and allow for engagement and feedback from customers through Twitter, Facebook, and blog posts.

earned media a category of promotional tactic based on a public relations or publicity model that gets customers talking about products or services

owned media a new category of promotional tactic based on brands becoming publishers of their own content in order to maximize the brands' value to customers

EXHIBIT 15.4 — CHARACTERISTICS OF THE ELEMENTS IN THE PROMOTIONAL MIX

	Advertising	Public Relations	Sales Promotion	Personal Selling	Social Media
Mode of Communication	Indirect and impersonal	Usually indirect and impersonal	Usually indirect and impersonal	Direct and face-to-face	Indirect but instant
Communicator Control over Situation	Low	Moderate to low	Moderate to low	High	Moderate
Amount of Feedback	Little	Little	Little to moderate	Much	Much
Speed of Feedback	Delayed	Delayed	Varies	Immediate	Intermediate
Direction of Message	One-way	One-way	Mostly one-way	Two-way	Two-way, multiple ways
Control over Message Content	Yes	No	Yes	Yes	Varies, generally no
Identification of Sponsor	Yes	No	Yes	Yes	Yes
Speed in Reaching Large Audience	Fast	Usually fast	Fast	Slow	Fast
Message Flexibility	Same message to all audiences	Usually no direct control over message audiences	Same message to varied targets	Tailored to prospective buyer	Some of the most targeted opportunities

15-5 PROMOTIONAL GOALS AND THE AIDA CONCEPT

The ultimate goal of any promotion is to get someone to buy a good or service or, in the case of nonprofit organizations, to take some action (for example, donate to a cause organization like Susan G. Komen). A classic model for reaching promotional goals is called the **AIDA concept**.[9] The acronym AIDA stands for *attention, interest, desire,* and *action*—the stages of consumer involvement with a promotional message. It mimics many "funnel-like" models that require audiences to move through a set of steps or stages.

15-5a The AIDA Model

This model proposes that consumers respond to marketing messages in a cognitive (thinking), affective (feeling), and conative (doing) sequence. First, a promotion manager may focus on attracting a consumer's *attention* by training a salesperson to use a friendly greeting and approach or by using loud volume, bold headlines, movement, bright colors, and the like in an advertisement. Next, a good sales presentation, demonstration, or advertisement creates *interest* in the product and then, by illustrating how the product's features will satisfy the consumer's needs, arouses *desire*. Finally, a special offer

or a strong closing sales pitch may be used to obtain purchase *action*.

The AIDA concept assumes that promotion propels consumers along the following four steps in the purchase-decision process:

1. **Attention:** The advertiser must first gain the attention of the target market. A firm cannot sell something if the market does not know that the good or service exists. When Apple introduced the iPad, it quickly became one of the largest electronics product launches in history. To create awareness and gain attention for its revolutionary tablet computer, Apple not only used traditional media advertising but also contacted influential bloggers and journalists so that they would write about the product in blogs, newspapers, and magazines. Because the iPad was a brand extension of the Apple computer, it required less effort than an entirely new brand would have. At the same time, because the iPad was an innovative new product line, the promotion had to get customers' attention and create awareness of a new idea from an established company.

2. **Interest:** Simple awareness of a brand seldom leads to a sale. The next step is to create interest in the product. A print ad cannot tell potential

> **AIDA concept** a model that outlines the process for achieving promotional goals in terms of stages of consumer involvement with the message; the acronym stands for attention, interest, desire, and action

customers all the features of the iPad. Therefore, Apple had to arrange iPad demonstrations and target messages to innovators and early adopters to create interest in the new tablet computer. To do this, Apple used both online videos on YouTube and personal demonstrations in Apple Stores. The iPad also received extensive media coverage from both online and traditional media outlets.

3. **Desire:** Potential customers for the Apple iPad may like the concept of a portable tablet computer, but they may not necessarily think that it is better than a laptop or smartphone. Therefore, Apple had to create brand preference with the iTunes Music Store, specialty apps, multiple functionality, and features such as better power management and a lighter weight unit. Specifically, Apple had to convince potential customers that the iPad was the best solution to their desire for a combination tablet computer and smartphone.

4. **Action:** Some potential target market customers may have been persuaded to buy an iPad but had yet to make the actual purchase. To motivate them to take action, Apple continued advertising to communicate the features and benefits more effectively. And the strategy worked—more than 250 million people own an iPad.[10]

Most buyers involved in high-involvement purchase situations pass through the four stages of the AIDA model on the way to making a purchase. The promoter's task is to determine where on the purchase ladder most of the target consumers are located and design a promotion plan to meet their needs. For example, if Apple learned from its market research that many

EXHIBIT 15.5 THE PROMOTIONAL MIX AND AIDA

	Attention	Interest	Desire	Action
Advertising	●	●	○	●
Public Relations	●	●	○	●
Sales Promotion	○	○	●	●
Personal Selling	○	●	●	●
Social Media	●	●	○	○

● Very effective   ○ Somewhat effective   ● Not effective

potential customers were in the desire stage but had not yet bought an iPad for some reason, it could place advertising on Facebook and Google, and perhaps in video games, to target younger individuals and professionals with messages motivating them to buy an iPad.

The AIDA concept does not explain how all promotions influence purchase decisions. The model suggests that promotional effectiveness can be measured in terms of consumers progressing from one stage to the next. However, the order of stages in the model, as well as whether consumers go through all steps, has been much debated. A purchase can occur without interest or desire, perhaps when a low-involvement product is bought on impulse. Regardless of the order of the stages or consumers' progression through these stages, the AIDA concept helps marketers by suggesting which promotional strategy will be most effective.[11]

15-5b AIDA and the Promotional Mix

Exhibit 15.5 depicts the relationship between the promotional mix and the AIDA model. It shows that although advertising does have an impact in the later stages, it is most useful in gaining attention for goods or services. By contrast, personal selling reaches fewer people at first. Salespeople are more effective at creating customer interest for merchandise or a service and at creating desire. For example, advertising may help a potential computer purchaser gain knowledge about competing brands, but the salesperson may be the one who actually encourages the buyer to decide a particular brand is the best choice. The salesperson also has the advantage of having the computer physically there to demonstrate its capabilities to the buyer.

Public relations' greatest impact is as a method of gaining attention for a company, good, or service. Many companies can attract attention and build goodwill by sponsoring community events that benefit worthy causes such as an anti-bullying campaign or a global poverty program. Such sponsorships project a positive

The four steps of the AIDA process describe how consumers make purchases. These steps are:

1. **ATTENTION:** First, Apple uses a number of media outlets to gain the attention of the target market.

2. **INTEREST:** Next, it arranges iPad demonstrations and develops target messages to create interest among innovators and early adopters.

3. **DESIRE:** Then, Apple creates brand preference and convinces potential customers that they want the new iPad.

4. **ACTION:** Finally, having been attracted to the new iPad and convinced that they need it, customers purchase the iPad.

iStockphotos.com/Hocus-focus

image of the firm and its products into the minds of consumers and potential consumers. Book publishers push to get their titles on the best-seller lists of major publications, such as *Publishers Weekly* or the *New York Times*. Book authors make appearances on talk shows and at bookstores to personally sign books and speak to fans. They also frequently engage with fans on social media like Facebook and Twitter.

Sales promotion's greatest strength is in creating strong desire and purchase intent. Coupons and other price-off promotions are techniques used to persuade customers to buy new products. Frequent-buyer sales promotion programs, popular among retailers, allow consumers to accumulate points or dollars that can be redeemed for goods. Frequent buyer programs tend to increase purchase intent and loyalty and encourage repeat purchases.

Social media are a strong way to gain attention and interest in a brand, particularly if content goes viral. It can then reach a massive audience. Social media are also effective at engaging with customers and enabling companies to maintain interest in the brand if properly managed.

15-6 INTEGRATED MARKETING COMMUNICATIONS

Ideally, marketing communications from each promotional mix element (personal selling, advertising, sales promotion, social media, and public relations) should be integrated. That is, the message reaching the consumer should be the same regardless of whether it is from an advertisement, a salesperson in the field, a magazine article, a Facebook fan page, or a coupon in a newspaper insert.

From the consumer's standpoint, a company's communications are already integrated. Consumers do not think in terms of the five elements of promotion: personal selling, advertising, sales promotion, public relations, and social media. Instead, everything is an "ad." The only people who recognize the distinctions among these communications elements are the marketers themselves.

Unfortunately, many marketers neglect this fact when planning promotional messages and fail to integrate their communication efforts from one element to the next. The most common rift typically occurs between personal selling and the other elements of the promotional mix.

This unintegrated, disjointed approach to promotion has propelled many companies to adopt the concept of **integrated marketing communications (IMC)**. IMC is the careful coordination of all promotional messages—traditional advertising, direct marketing, social media, interactive, public relations, sales promotion, personal selling, event marketing, and other communications—for a product or service to assure the consistency of messages at every contact point where a company meets the consumer. Following the concept of IMC, marketing managers carefully work out the roles that various promotional elements will play in the marketing mix. Timing of promotional activities is coordinated, and the results of each campaign are carefully monitored to improve future use of the promotional mix tools. Typically, a marketing communications director is appointed who has overall responsibility for integrating the company's marketing communications.

The IMC concept has been growing in popularity for several reasons. First, the proliferation of thousands of media choices beyond traditional television has made promotion a more complicated task. Instead of promoting a product just through mass-media options, like television and magazines, promotional messages today can appear in many varied sources.

Further, the mass market has also fragmented—more selectively segmented markets and an increase in niche marketing have replaced the traditional broad market groups that marketers promoted to in years past. Finally, marketers have slashed their advertising spending in favor of promotional techniques that generate immediate sales responses and those that are more easily measured, such as direct marketing. Online advertising has earned a bigger share of the budget as well due to its measurability. Thus, the interest in IMC is largely a reaction to the scrutiny that marketing communications has come under and, particularly, to suggestions that uncoordinated promotional activity leads to a strategy that is wasteful and inefficient.

integrated marketing communications (IMC) the careful coordination of all promotional messages for a product or a service to ensure the consistency of messages at every contact point at which a company meets the consumer

Hilch/Shutterstock.com

15-7 FACTORS AFFECTING THE PROMOTIONAL MIX

Promotional mixes vary a great deal from one product and one industry to the next. Normally, advertising and personal selling are used to promote goods and services. These primary tools are often supported and supplemented by sales promotion. Public relations help develop a positive image for the organization and the product line. Social media have been used more for consumer goods, but business-to-business marketers are increasingly using these media. A firm may choose not to use all five promotional elements in its promotional mix, or it may choose to use them in varying degrees. The particular promotional mix chosen by a firm for a product or service depends on several factors: the nature of the product, the stage in the product life cycle, target market characteristics, the type of buying decision, funds available for promotion, and whether a push or a pull strategy will be used.

15-7a Nature of the Product

Characteristics of the product itself can influence the promotional mix. For instance, a product can be classified as either a business product or a consumer product. (Refer to Chapters 7 and 10.) As business products are often custom-tailored to the buyer's exact specifications, they are often not well suited to mass promotion. Therefore, producers of most business goods rely more heavily on personal selling than on advertising, but advertising still serves a purpose in the promotional mix. Advertising

Print media advertising often includes coupons soliciting the potential customer.

in trade media can also help locate potential customers for the sales force. For example, print media advertising often includes coupons soliciting the potential customer to "fill this out for more detailed information."

By contrast, because consumer products generally are not custom-made, they do not require the selling efforts of a company representative who can tailor them to the user's needs. Thus, consumer goods are promoted mainly through advertising or social media to create brand familiarity. Television and radio advertising, consumer-oriented magazines, and increasingly the Internet and other highly targeted media are used to promote consumer goods, especially nondurables. Sales promotion, the brand name, and the product's packaging are about twice as important for consumer goods as for business products. Persuasive personal selling is important at the retail level for goods such as automobiles and appliances.

The costs and risks associated with a product also influence the promotional mix. As a general rule, when the costs or risks of buying and using a product or service increase, personal selling becomes more important. Inexpensive items cannot support the cost of a salesperson's time and effort unless the potential volume is high. On the other hand, expensive and complex machinery, cars, and new homes represent a considerable investment. A salesperson must assure buyers that they are spending their money wisely and not taking an undue financial risk.

Social risk is an issue as well. Many consumer goods are not products of great social importance because they do not reflect social position. People do not experience much social risk in buying a loaf of bread. However, buying many specialty products such as jewelry and clothing involves a social risk. Many consumers depend on sales personnel for guidance in making the "proper" choice.

15-7b Stages in the Product Life Cycle

The product's stage in its life cycle is a big factor in designing a promotional mix (see Exhibit 15.6). During the *introduction stage*, the basic goal of promotion is to inform the target audience that the product is available. Initially, the emphasis is on the general product class—for example, smartphones. This emphasis gradually changes to gaining attention for a particular brand, such as Apple, Samsung, Google Nexus, Sony, LG, or Motorola. Typically, both extensive advertising and public relations inform the target audience of the product class or brand and heighten awareness levels.

EXHIBIT 15.6 PRODUCT LIFE CYCLE AND THE PROMOTIONAL MIX

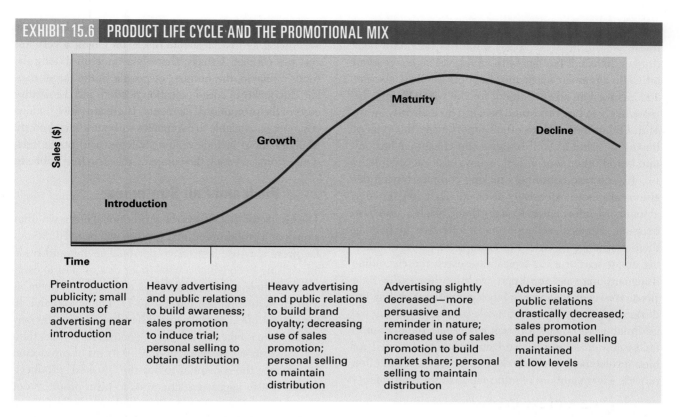

Preintroduction publicity; small amounts of advertising near introduction	Heavy advertising and public relations to build awareness; sales promotion to induce trial; personal selling to obtain distribution	Heavy advertising and public relations to build brand loyalty; decreasing use of sales promotion; personal selling to maintain distribution	Advertising slightly decreased—more persuasive and reminder in nature; increased use of sales promotion to build market share; personal selling to maintain distribution	Advertising and public relations drastically decreased; sales promotion and personal selling maintained at low levels

Sales promotion encourages early trial of the product, and personal selling gets retailers to carry the product.

When the product reaches the *growth stage* of the life cycle, the promotion blend may shift. Often a change is necessary because different types of potential buyers are targeted. Although advertising and public relations continue to be major elements of the promotional mix, sales promotion can be reduced because consumers need fewer incentives to purchase. The promotional strategy is to emphasize the product's differential advantage over the competition. Persuasive promotion is used to build and maintain brand loyalty during the growth stage. By this stage, personal selling has usually succeeded in getting adequate distribution for the product.

As the product reaches the *maturity stage* of its life cycle, competition becomes fiercer, and thus persuasive and reminder advertising are emphasized more strongly. Sales promotion comes back into focus as product sellers try to increase their market share.

All promotion, especially advertising, is reduced as the product enters the *decline stage*. Nevertheless, personal selling and sales promotion efforts may be maintained, particularly at the retail level.

15-7c Target Market Characteristics

A target market characterized by widely scattered potential customers, highly informed buyers, and brand loyal repeat purchasers generally requires a promotional mix with more advertising and sales promotion and less personal selling. Sometimes, however, personal selling is required even when buyers are well informed and geographically dispersed. Although industrial installations may be sold to well-educated people with extensive work experience, salespeople must be present to explain the product and work out the details of the purchase agreement.

Often firms sell goods and services in markets where potential customers are hard to locate. Print advertising can be used to find them. The reader is invited to go online, call, or mail in a reply card for more information. As the online queries, calls, or cards are received, salespeople are sent to visit the potential customers.

15-7d Type of Buying Decision

The promotional mix also depends on the type of buying decision—for example, a routine decision or a complex decision. For routine consumer decisions like buying toothpaste, the most effective promotion calls attention to the brand or reminds the consumer about the brand. Advertising, and especially sales promotion, are the most productive promotion tools to use for routine decisions.

If the decision is neither routine nor complex, advertising and public relations help establish awareness for the good or service. Suppose a man is looking for a bottle of wine to serve to his dinner guests. As a beer drinker, he is not familiar with wines, yet he has read an article in a popular magazine about Silver Oak Cabernet and has seen an advertisement for the wine. He may be more likely to buy this brand because he is already aware of it. Online reviews are often important in this type of buying decision as well because the consumer has any number of other consumers' reviews easily accessible.

By contrast, consumers making complex buying decisions are more extensively involved. They rely on large amounts of information to help them reach a purchase decision. Personal selling is most effective in helping these consumers decide. For example, consumers thinking about buying a car typically research the car online using corporate and third-party websites like Kelley Blue Book. However, few people buy a car without visiting the dealership. They depend on a salesperson to provide the information they need to reach a decision. In addition to online resources, print advertising may also be used for high-involvement purchase decisions because it can often provide a large amount of information to the consumer.

15-7e Available Funds

Money, or the lack of it, may easily be the most important factor in determining the promotional mix. A small, undercapitalized manufacturer may rely heavily on free publicity if its product is unique. If the situation warrants a sales force, a financially strained firm may turn to manufacturers' agents, who work on a commission basis with no advances or expense accounts. Even well capitalized organizations may not be able to afford the advertising rates of publications like *Time, Sports Illustrated*, and the *Wall Street Journal*, or the cost of running television commercials during *Modern Family, The Voice*, or the Super Bowl. The price of a high-profile advertisement in these media could support several salespeople for an entire year.

When funds are available to permit a mix of promotional elements, a firm will generally try to optimize its return on promotion dollars while minimizing the *cost per contact*, or the cost of reaching one member of the target market. In general, the cost per contact is very high for personal selling, public relations, and sales promotions like sampling and demonstrations.

push strategy a marketing strategy that uses aggressive personal selling and trade advertising to convince a wholesaler or a retailer to carry and sell particular merchandise

On the other hand, given the number of people national advertising and social media reach, they have a very low cost per contact. Usually, there is a trade-off among the funds available, the number of people in the target market, the quality of communication needed, and the relative costs of the promotional elements. There are plenty of low-cost options available to companies without a huge budget. Many of these include online strategies and public relations efforts, in which the company relies on free publicity.

15-7f Push and Pull Strategies

The last factor that affects the promotional mix is whether a push or a pull promotional strategy will be used. Manufacturers may use aggressive personal selling and trade advertising to convince a wholesaler or a retailer to carry and sell their merchandise. This approach is known as a **push strategy** (see Exhibit 15.7). The wholesaler, in turn, must often push the merchandise forward by persuading the retailer to handle the goods. The retailer then uses advertising, displays, and other forms of promotion to convince the consumer to buy the "pushed" products. Walmart uses aggressive discounts to push products out of its stores. For example, First Lady Michelle Obama praised the retailer for using drastically reduced prices to push fresh meat, produce, and other healthy options to consumers in low-income areas. The move proved to be a win-win strategy. Fresh foods generated 70 percent of Walmart's sales growth in recent years, and customers have saved more than $2.3 billion on fresh fruits and vegetables by shopping at Walmart.[12] This concept also applies to services.

Lay's calls attention to its commitment to natural ingredients as a distinguishing attribute in order to help customers make a routine buying decision— purchasing Lay's snack food.

EXHIBIT 15.7 PUSH STRATEGY VERSUS PULL STRATEGY

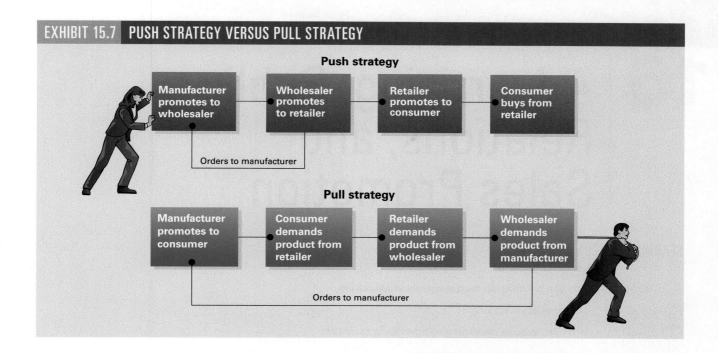

Push strategy

Manufacturer promotes to wholesaler → Wholesaler promotes to retailer → Retailer promotes to consumer → Consumer buys from retailer

Orders to manufacturer

Pull strategy

Manufacturer promotes to consumer → Consumer demands product from retailer → Retailer demands product from wholesaler → Wholesaler demands product from manufacturer

Orders to manufacturer

At the other extreme is a **pull strategy**, which stimulates consumer demand to obtain product distribution. Rather than trying to sell to the wholesaler, the manufacturer using a pull strategy focuses its promotional efforts on end consumers or opinion leaders. Social media and content marketing are the most recent (and best) example of pull strategy. The idea is that social media content does not interrupt a consumer's experience with media (like a commercial interrupts your favorite television program). Instead, the content invites customers to experience it on social media or a website. Consumer demand pulls the product through the channel of distribution (see Exhibit 15.7). Heavy sampling, introductory consumer advertising, cents-off campaigns, and couponing are part of a pull strategy.

Rarely does a company use a pull or a push strategy exclusively. Instead, the mix will emphasize one of these strategies. For example, pharmaceutical companies generally use a push strategy (personal selling and trade advertising) to promote their drugs and therapies to physicians. Sales presentations and advertisements in medical journals give physicians the detailed information they need to prescribe medication to their patients. Most pharmaceutical companies supplement this push promotional strategy with a pull strategy targeted directly to potential patients through advertisements in consumer magazines and on television.

pull strategy a marketing strategy that stimulates consumer demand to obtain product distribution

STUDY TOOLS 15

LOCATED AT BACK OF THE TEXTBOOK

☐ Rip out Chapter Review Card

LOCATED AT WWW.CENGAGEBRAIN.COM

☐ Review Key Terms Flashcards and create your own

☐ Track your knowledge and understanding of key concepts in marketing

☐ Complete practice and graded quizzes to prepare for tests

☐ Complete interactive content within the MKTG Online experience

☐ View the chapter highlight boxes within the MKTG Online experience

Advertising, Public Relations, and Sales Promotion

LEARNING OUTCOMES

After studying this chapter, you will be able to...

16-1 Discuss the effects of advertising on market share and consumers

16-2 Identify the major types of advertising

16-3 Discuss the creative decisions in developing an advertising campaign

16-4 Describe media evaluation and selection techniques

16-5 Discuss the role of public relations in the promotional mix

16-6 Define and state the objectives of sales promotion and the tools used to achieve them

After you finish this chapter go to PAGE 301 for STUDY TOOLS

16-1 THE EFFECTS OF ADVERTISING

Advertising was defined in Chapter 15 as impersonal, one-way mass communication about a product or organization that is paid for by a marketer.
It is a popular form of promotion, especially for consumer packaged goods and services. Increasingly, as more and more marketers consolidate their operations, advertising is seen as an international endeavor. Promotion makes up a large part of most brands' budgets. Typically, promotional spending is divided into *measured* and *unmeasured media*. Measured media ad spending includes network and cable TV, newspapers, magazines, radio, outdoor, and Internet (though paid search and social media are not included).

Unmeasured media spending includes direct marketing, promotions, co-op, coupons, catalogs, product placement, and event marketing. Every year, total media spending increases approximately 4 percent in the United States and 4.6 percent worldwide. The United States is, by far, the largest spender ($178 billion). China, Japan, the United Kingdom, and Brazil round out the top five countries in terms of advertising spending. The Asia-Pacific region is the fastest-growing market, recently increasing by more than 7 percent annually.[1] The top 25 largest U.S. advertisers spend more than $53 billion each year. Procter & Gamble (P&G) is by far the largest advertiser, spending almost $4.7 billion annually on its host of brands. Telecommunications companies like AT&T ($3.3 billion total spend)

Savvapanf Photo/Shutterstock.com

and automotive companies like General Motors ($3.1 billion total spend) are also top spenders.[2]

Advertising and marketing services, agencies, and other firms that provide marketing and communications services employ millions of people across America. Just as the producers of goods and services need marketers to build awareness of their products, media outlets such as magazines and websites need marketing teams to coordinate with producers and transmit those messages to customers. The longer one thinks about the business of marketing, the more unique positions within the industry become apparent. One particular area that has continued to see rapid growth is the data side of marketing. Companies are collecting huge amounts of information and need skilled, creative, web-savvy people to interpret the data coming in from web, mobile, and other digital ad campaigns. One Microsoft study estimates that 90 percent of enterprise companies have a dedicated budget for addressing data analytics. Forty-nine percent of the demand for data analytics is driven by sales and marketing departments. According to IDC program vice president Dan Vesset, "A lot of the ultimate potential is in the ability to discover potential connections, and to predict potential outcomes in a way that wasn't really possible before. Before, you only looked at these things in hindsight."[3]

16-1a Advertising and Market Share

The five most valuable U.S. brands are Apple ($170 billion —up 43 percent from the previous year), Google ($120 billion—up 12 percent), Coca-Cola ($78 billion), Microsoft ($67 billion), and IBM ($65 billion). These were all top brands the year before, but some shifted in rank. Most of these brands were built over many years by heavy advertising and marketing investments long ago. Google is the only exception—its brand value was built using digital platforms.[4] Today's advertising dollars for successful consumer brands are spent on maintaining brand awareness and market share.

New brands with a small market share tend to spend proportionately more for advertising and sales promotion than those with a large market share, typically for two reasons. First, beyond a certain level of spending for advertising and sales promotion, diminishing returns set in. That is, sales and market share improvements slow down and eventually decrease no matter how much is spent on advertising and sales promotion. This phenomenon is called the **advertising response function**. Understanding the advertising response function helps marketers use budgets wisely. A market leader like Johnson & Johnson's Neutrogena typically spends proportionately less on advertising than a newer line such as Unilever's Vaseline Spray & Go brand. Neutrogena has already captured the attention of the majority of its target market. It only needs to remind customers of its product.

The second reason new brands tend to require higher spending for advertising and sales promotion is that a certain minimum level of exposure is needed to measurably affect purchase habits. If Vaseline advertised its Spray & Go moisturizers in only one or two publications and bought only one or two television spots, it would not achieve the exposure needed to penetrate consumers' perceptual defenses and affect purchase intentions.

16-1b The Effects of Advertising on Consumers

Advertising affects peoples' daily lives, informing them about products and services and influencing their attitudes, beliefs, and ultimately, their purchases. Advertising affects the television programs people watch, the content of the newspapers they read, the politicians they elect, the medicines they take, and the toys their children play with. Consequently, the influence of advertising on the U.S. socioeconomic system has been the subject of extensive debate in nearly all corners of society.

Interestingly, despite a proliferation of new technology options, consumers still spend a lot of time consuming traditional media (where much of advertising exists). The average person, for example, spends more than 250 minutes a day watching television and 329 minutes a day using

Most Valuable U.S. Brands:

- Apple ($170 billion)
- Google ($120 billion)
- Coca-Cola ($78 billion)
- Microsoft ($67 billion)
- IBM ($65 billion)

Eric Milos/Shutterstock.com

digital media devices like desktops, laptops, and tablets.[5] Americans report an average of 5.3 leisure hours a day, and most of it is spent watching TV. As a result, American consumers are exposed to thousands of advertising messages each year.[6]

Though advertising cannot change consumers' deeply rooted values and attitudes, advertising may succeed in transforming a person's negative attitude toward a product into a positive one. For instance, serious or dramatic advertisements are more effective at changing consumers' negative attitudes. Humorous ads, on the other hand, have been shown to be more effective at shaping attitudes when consumers already have a positive image of an advertised brand.

Advertising also reinforces positive attitudes toward brands. A brand with a distinct personality is more likely to have a larger base of loyal customers and market share. The more consistent a brand's personality, the more likely a customer will build a relationship with that brand over his or her lifetime. Consider Apple, for example. Sixty percent of iPhone users report they would switch to Apple's latest iPhone without considering any other options, admitting to "blind loyalty."[7] This is why market leaders spend billions of dollars annually to reinforce and remind their loyal customers about the benefits of their products.

Advertising can also affect the way consumers rank a brand's attributes. In years past, car ads emphasized such brand attributes as roominess, speed, and low maintenance. Today, however, car marketers have added technology, safety, versatility, customization, and fuel efficiency to the list.

16-2 MAJOR TYPES OF ADVERTISING

A firm's promotional objectives determine the type of advertising it uses. If the goal of the promotion plan is to improve the image of the company or the industry, **institutional advertising** may be used. In contrast, if the advertiser wants to enhance the sales of a specific good or service, **product advertising** should be used.

advertising response function a phenomenon in which spending for advertising and sales promotion increases sales or market share up to a certain level but then produces diminishing returns

institutional advertising a form of advertising designed to enhance a company's image rather than promote a particular product

product advertising a form of advertising that touts the benefits of a specific good or service

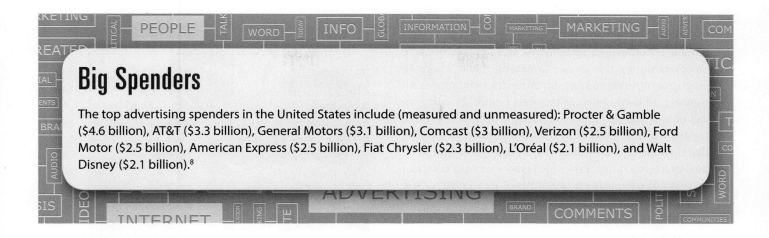

16-2a Institutional Advertising

Historically, advertising in the United States has been product and service oriented. Today, however, companies market multiple products and need a different type of advertising. Institutional advertising, or corporate advertising, is designed to establish, change, or promote the corporation's identity as a whole. It usually does not ask the audience to do anything but maintain a favorable attitude toward the advertiser and its goods or services. A beer company running a series of television spots advocating designated driving is an example of institutional advertising.

A form of institutional advertising called **advocacy advertising** is typically used to safeguard against negative consumer attitudes and to enhance the company's credibility among consumers who already favor its position. Corporations often use advocacy advertising to express their views on controversial issues. For example, in celebration of the one-year anniversary of New York's Marriage Equality Act, Nabisco's Oreo posted a gay pride-themed image (an Oreo cookie with six rainbow-colored layers of cream filling) on its Facebook page. Accompanying the image were the phrases "Pride" and "Proudly support love!" Responses to the images were mixed: "I'm never eating Oreos again. This is just disgusting," wrote one commenter, while another replied, "I didn't think it was possible for me to love Oreo's more than I already did!!" Though controversial, the post drew a considerable amount of support from fans, generating approximately 15,000 shares and 87,000 "likes."[9] Similarly, breakfast cereal Cheerios drew both praise and criticism for a commercial depicting a biracial family. Alternatively, an advocacy campaign might refute criticism or blame, or ward off increases in regulation, damaging legislation, or the unfavorable outcome of a lawsuit.

16-2b Product Advertising

Unlike institutional advertising, product advertising promotes the benefits of a specific good or service. The product's stage in its life cycle often determines which type of product advertising is used: pioneering advertising, competitive advertising, or comparative advertising.

PIONEERING ADVERTISING Pioneering advertising is intended to stimulate primary demand for a new product or product category. Heavily used during the introductory stage of the product life cycle, pioneering advertising offers consumers in-depth information about the benefits of the product class. Pioneering advertising also seeks to create interest and, as such, can be quite innovative in its own right. For example, Motorola placed an ad for its new flagship smartphone, the Moto X, in *Wired*. The Moto X is highly customizable, featuring more than twenty different back plate and accent colors. Built in Austin, Texas, the Moto X is the first smartphone of its kind to be so customizable. Using an embedded LED array, microchip, and battery, the print ad allows the reader to push eleven different colored buttons, changing the color of the Moto X Smartphone pictured in the ad. A demonstration of the ad can be seen at www.youtube.com/watch?v=iMrZmSPpIRw.[10]

COMPETITIVE ADVERTISING Firms use competitive or brand advertising when a product enters the growth phase of the product life cycle and other companies begin to enter the marketplace. Instead of building demand for the

advocacy advertising a form of advertising in which an organization expresses its views on controversial issues or responds to media attacks

pioneering advertising a form of advertising designed to stimulate primary demand for a new product or product category

product category, the goal of **competitive advertising** is to influence demand for a specific brand. Often, promotion becomes less informative and appeals more to emotions during this phase. Generally, this is where an emphasis on branding begins. Advertisements focus on showing subtle differences between brands, building recall of a brand name, and creating a favorable attitude toward the brand. GEICO uses competitive advertising that discusses the attributes of the brand, how little time it takes to get a quote, how much customers can save, and the ease of submitting a claim. All of its campaigns use humor to promote the brand above others in the industry but without actively comparing GEICO with other insurance companies.

COMPARATIVE ADVERTISING Comparative advertising directly or indirectly compares two or more competing brands on one or more specific attributes. Some advertisers even use comparative advertising against their own brands. Products experiencing slow growth or those entering the marketplace against strong competitors are more likely to employ comparative claims in their advertising. In contrast to GEICO's "Fifteen minutes can save you 15 percent or more on car insurance" tagline that does not explicitly mention any other insurance company, 21st Century Insurance takes on its major competitors directly in its "Shopping Carts" television ad campaign. The ad features two cars, one labeled GEICO, the other 21st Century. As shopping carts pour down on the cars like rain, a voiceover explains that since both cars are covered, both get the same repairs.[11] Then the commercial goes on to explain that 21st Century Insurance customers who switch from GEICO save an average of $508 a year.[12] 21st Century is explicitly comparing its insurance rates with those of its main competitors and capitalizing on customers' desire for great coverage at the lowest prices.

Before the 1970s, comparative advertising was allowed only if the competing brand was veiled and unidentified. In 1971, however, the Federal Trade Commission (FTC) fostered the growth of comparative advertising by saying that the advertising provided information to the customer and that advertisers were more skillful than the government in communicating

GEICO uses competitive advertising that discusses attributes of the brand.

this information. Federal rulings prohibit advertisers from falsely describing competitors' products and allow competitors to sue if ads show their products or mention their brand names in an incorrect or false manner. FTC rules also apply to advertisers making false claims about their own products.

 16-3

CREATIVE DECISIONS IN ADVERTISING

Advertising strategies are typically organized around an advertising campaign. An **advertising campaign** is a series of related advertisements focusing on a common theme, slogan, and set of advertising appeals. It is a specific advertising effort for a particular product that extends for a defined period of time.

Before any creative work can begin on an advertising campaign, it is important to determine what goals or objectives the advertising should achieve. An **advertising objective** identifies the specific communication task that a campaign should accomplish for a specified target audience during a specified period. The objectives of a specific advertising campaign often depend on the overall corporate objectives and the product being advertised.

---

competitive advertising
a form of advertising designed to influence demand for a specific brand

comparative advertising
a form of advertising that compares two or more specifically named or shown competing brands on one or more specific attributes

advertising campaign a series of related advertisements focusing on a common theme, slogan, and set of advertising appeals

advertising objective a specific communication task that a campaign should accomplish for a specified target audience during a specified period

What form of advertising is the Kellogg Company using in this Pop-Tarts advertisement? What does that say about the Pop-Tarts brand?

The DAGMAR approach (Defining Advertising Goals for Measured Advertising Results) is one method of setting objectives. According to this method, all advertising objectives should precisely define the target audience, the desired percentage change in some specified measure of effectiveness, and the time frame in which that change is to occur.

Once objectives are defined, creative work can begin on the advertising campaign. Advertising campaigns often follow the AIDA model, which was discussed in Chapter 15. Depending on where consumers are in the AIDA process, the creative development of an advertising campaign might focus on creating attention, arousing interest, stimulating desire, or ultimately leading to the action of buying the product. Specifically, creative decisions include identifying product benefits, developing and evaluating advertising appeals, executing the message, and evaluating the effectiveness of the campaign.

16-3a Identifying Product Benefits

A well-known rule of thumb in the advertising industry is "Sell the sizzle, not the steak"—that is, in advertising, the goal is to sell the benefits of the product, not its attributes. Customers buy benefits, not attributes. An attribute is simply a feature of the product such as its easy-open package, special formulation, or new lower price. A benefit is what consumers will receive or achieve by using the product, such as convenience or ease of use. A benefit should answer the consumer's question "What's in it for me?" Benefits might be such things as pleasure, improved health, savings, or relief. A quick test to determine whether you are offering attributes or benefits in your advertising is to ask "So?" Consider this example:

- **Attribute:** "DogsBestFriend is an all-natural skin care lotion for dogs that combines traditional medicines and Nigella sativa seed oils with the newest extraction technology." "So . . . ?"

- **Benefit:** "So . . . DogsBestFriend acts as a natural replacement for hydrocortisone, antihistamines, and topical antibiotics that is powerful enough to combat inflammation, itching, and pain, yet safe enough to use on dogs of all ages."[13]

16-3b Developing and Evaluating Advertising Appeals

An **advertising appeal** identifies a reason for a person to buy a product. Developing advertising appeals, a challenging task, is typically the responsibility of the creative team (e.g., art directors and copywriters) in the advertising agency. Advertising appeals typically play off consumers' emotions or address some need or want consumers have.

Advertising campaigns can focus on one or more advertising appeals. Often the appeals are quite general, thus allowing the firm to develop a number of subthemes or mini campaigns using both advertising and sales promotion. Several possible advertising appeals are listed in Exhibit 16.1.

Choosing the best appeal from those developed usually requires market research. Criteria for evaluation include desirability, exclusiveness, and believability. The appeal first must make a positive impression on and be desirable to the target market. It must also be exclusive or unique. Consumers must be able to distinguish the advertiser's message from competitors' messages. Most importantly, the appeal should be believable. An appeal that makes extravagant claims not only wastes promotional dollars but also creates ill will for the advertiser.

The advertising appeal selected for the campaign becomes what advertisers call its **unique selling proposition**. The unique selling proposition often becomes all or part of the campaign's slogan. The

advertising appeal a reason for a person to buy a product

unique selling proposition a desirable, exclusive, and believable advertising appeal selected as the theme for a campaign

EXHIBIT 16.1 COMMON ADVERTISING APPEALS

Appeal	Goal
Profit	Lets consumers know whether the product will save them money, make them money, or keep them from losing money.
Health	Appeals to those who are body conscious or who want to be healthy; love or romance is used often in selling cosmetics and perfumes.
Fear	Can center around social embarrassment, growing old, or losing one's health; because of its power, requires advertiser to exercise care in execution.
Admiration	Frequently highlights celebrity spokespeople.
Convenience	Is often used for fast-food restaurants and microwave foods.
Fun and Pleasure	Are the keys to advertising vacations, beer, amusement parks, and more.
Vanity and Egotism	Are used most often for expensive or conspicuous items such as cars and clothing.
Environmental Consciousness	Centers around protecting the environment and being considerate of others in the community.

Snickers candy bar is known for its ability to stop hunger. In order to emphasize this attribute, the company recently changed the logo on its packaging to words associated with hunger, such as "snippy" and "grouchy." This move helped the brand stand out in a crowded snack market.[14]

16-3c Executing the Message

Message execution is the way an advertisement port-rays its information. In general, the AIDA plan (see Chapter 15) is a good blueprint for executing an advertising message. Any ad should immediately draw the reader's, viewer's, or listener's attention. The advertiser must then use the message to hold interest, create desire for the good or service, and ultimately motivate a purchase.

The style in which the message is executed is one of the most creative elements of an advertisement. Exhibit 16.2 lists some examples of executional styles used by advertisers. Executional styles often dictate what type of media is to be employed to convey the message. For example, scientific executional styles lend themselves well to print advertising, where more information can be conveyed. Testimonials by athletes are one of the more popular executional styles.

Injecting humor into an advertisement is a popular and effective executional style. Humorous executional styles are more often used in radio and television advertising than in print or magazine advertising, where humor is less easily communicated. Recall that humorous ads are typically used for lower-risk, low-involvement, routine purchases such as candy, cigarettes, and casual jeans than for higher-risk purchases or for products that are expensive, durable, or flamboyant.[15]

Sometimes an executional style must be modified to make a marketing campaign more effective. Nowhere is this more evident than in the political realm, where advertisements for issues and candidates must account for ever-changing poll numbers and public sentiments. In Barack Obama's second presidential election, campaign advertisements taking aim at the president shifted in tone from sharply combative and accusatory to concerned—even mournful—about the state of the economy. According to Republican pollster Frank Luntz, focus group research revealed that ads that attacked Obama too personally turned people off in ways that kept them turned off. The Republican campaign shifted its executional style, opting for advertisements that appealed to citizens' worries and frustrations. In one ad, a forlorn-looking woman declares, "I supported President Obama because he spoke so beautifully. But since then, things have gone from bad to much worse." The 2016 presidential election brought a whole new style of appeal as the campaigns of Democrat Bernie Sanders and Republican Donald Trump targeted disenfranchised and angry voters.[16]

16-3d Post-Campaign Evaluation

Evaluating an advertising campaign can be the most demanding task facing advertisers. How can an advertiser assess if the campaign led to an increase in sales or market share or elevated awareness of the product? Many advertising campaigns aim to create an image for the good or service instead of asking for action, so their real effect is unknown. So many variables shape the effectiveness of an

Snickers recently changed the logo on its packaging to words associated with hunger, such as "snippy" and "grouchy." This move helped the brand stand out in a crowded snack market.

EXHIBIT 16.2 ELEVEN COMMON EXECUTIONAL STYLES FOR ADVERTISING

Executional Style	Description
Slice-of-Life	Depicts people in normal settings, such as at the dinner table or in their car. McDonald's often uses slice-of-life styles showing youngsters munching on french fries from Happy Meals on family outings.
Lifestyle	Shows how well the product will fit in with the consumer's lifestyle. As his Volkswagen Jetta moves through the streets of the French Quarter, a Gen X driver inserts a techno music CD and marvels at how the rhythms of the world mimic the ambient vibe inside his vehicle.
Spokesperson/Testimonial	Can feature a celebrity, company official, or typical consumer making a testimonial or endorsing a product. Sheryl Crow represented Revlon's Colorist hair coloring, while Beyoncé Knowles was named the new face of American Express. Dell Inc. founder Michael Dell touts his vision of the customer experience via Dell in television ads.
Fantasy	Creates a fantasy for the viewer built around use of the product. Carmakers often use this style to let viewers fantasize about how they would feel speeding around tight corners or down long country roads in their cars.
Humorous	Advertisers often use humor in their ads, such as Snickers' "Not Going Anywhere for a While" campaign featuring hundreds of souls waiting, sometimes impatiently, to get into heaven.
Real/Animated Product Symbols	Creates a character that represents the product in advertisements, such as the Energizer Bunny or Starkist's Charlie the Tuna. GEICO's suave gecko and disgruntled cavemen became cult classics for the insurance company.
Mood or Image	Builds a mood or image around the product, such as peace, love, or beauty. De Beers ads depicting shadowy silhouettes wearing diamond engagement rings and diamond necklaces portrayed passion and intimacy while extolling that "a diamond is forever."
Demonstration	Shows consumers the expected benefit. Many consumer products use this technique. Laundry detergent spots are famous for demonstrating how their product will clean clothes whiter and brighter. Fort James Corporation demonstrated in television commercials how its Dixie Rinse & ReUse disposable stoneware product line can stand up to the heat of a blowtorch and survive a cycle in a clothes washer.
Musical	Conveys the message of the advertisement through song. For example, Nike's ads depicted a marathoner's tortured feet and a surfer's thigh scarred by a shark attack while strains of Joe Cocker's "You Are So Beautiful" could be heard in the background.
Scientific	Uses research or scientific evidence to give a brand superiority over competitors. Pain relievers like Advil, Bayer, and Excedrin use scientific evidence in their ads.

ad that advertisers often must guess whether their money has been well spent. Nonetheless, marketers spend considerable time studying advertising effectiveness and its probable impact on sales, market share, or awareness.

Testing ad effectiveness can be done before and/or after the campaign. Before a campaign is released, marketing managers use pretests to determine the best advertising appeal, layout, and media vehicle. After advertisers implement a campaign, they use several monitoring techniques to determine whether the campaign has met its original goals. Even if a campaign has been highly successful, advertisers still typically do a post-campaign analysis to identify how the campaign might have been more efficient and what factors contributed to its success.

16-4 MEDIA DECISIONS IN ADVERTISING

A major decision for advertisers is the choice of medium—the channel used to convey a message to a target market. Media planning, therefore, is the series of decisions advertisers make regarding the selection and use of media, enabling the marketer to optimally and cost-effectively communicate the message to the target audience. Specifically, advertisers must determine which types of media will best communicate the benefits of their product or service to the target audience and when and for how long the advertisement will run.

Promotional objectives and the appeal and executional style of the advertising strongly affect the selection of media. Both creative and media decisions are made at the same time: creative work cannot be completed without knowing which medium will be used to convey the message to the target market. In many cases, the advertising objectives dictate the medium and the creative approach to be used. For example, if the objective is to demonstrate how fast a product operates, a television commercial that shows this action may be the best choice.

In 2015, U.S. advertisers spent about $180 billion

medium the channel used to convey a message to a target market

media planning the series of decisions advertisers make regarding the selection and use of media, allowing the marketer to optimally and cost-effectively communicate the message to the target audience

Best of the Best

According to *Advertising Age*, the best advertising campaigns of the 21st century are

1. Dove's "Real Beauty"
2. Nike's "Nike+"
3. BMW's "BMW Films"
4. Old Spice's "The Man Your Man Could Smell Like"
5. Red Bull's "Stratos"[17]

on paid media monitored by national reporting services—newspapers, magazines, radio, television, the Internet, and outdoor/cinema. This number is forecasted to be close to $190 billion for 2016.[18] The remainder was spent on unmonitored media such as direct mail, trade exhibits, cooperative advertising, brochures, coupons, catalogs, and special events. More than 36 percent of every media dollar goes toward television ads (cable, syndicated, spot, and network); almost 28 percent toward Internet ads; 11 percent toward newspaper ads; 9.6 percent toward magazine ads; 9.5 percent toward radio ads; and 5 percent toward outdoor/cinema ads.[19] But these traditional mass-market media are declining in usage as more targeted media are emerging. Future growth lies primarily in the digital realm, both in paid media (display ads, video ads, and search ads) and earned media (social media).

16-4a Media Types

Advertising media are channels that advertisers use in mass communication. The six major advertising media are newspapers, magazines, radio, television, the Internet, and outdoor media. Exhibit 16.3 summarizes the advantages and disadvantages of some of these major channels. In recent years, however, alternative media channels have emerged that give advertisers innovative ways to reach their target audience and avoid advertising clutter.

NEWSPAPERS Newspapers are one of the oldest forms of media. The advantages of newspaper advertising include geographic flexibility and timeliness. Although there has been a decline in circulation as well as in the number of newspapers, nationally, there are still several major newspapers including the *Wall Street Journal*, *USA Today*, the *New York Times*, the *Los Angeles Times*, and the *Washington Post*. But most newspapers are local. Because newspapers are generally a mass-market medium, however, they may not be the best vehicle for marketers trying to reach a very narrow market. Newspaper advertising also encounters

EXHIBIT 16.3	ADVANTAGES AND DISADVANTAGES OF MAJOR ADVERTISING MEDIA	
Medium	**Advantages**	**Disadvantages**
Newspapers	Geographic selectivity and flexibility; short-term advertiser commitments; news value and immediacy; year-round readership; high individual market coverage; co-op and local tie-in availability; short lead time	Little demographic selectivity; limited color capabilities; low pass-along rate; may be expensive
Magazines	Good reproduction, especially for color; demographic selectivity; regional selectivity; local market selectivity; relatively long advertising life; high pass-along rate	Long-term advertiser commitments; slow audience buildup; limited demonstration capabilities; lack of urgency; long lead time
Radio	Low cost; immediacy of message; can be scheduled on short notice; relatively no seasonal change in audience; highly portable; short-term advertiser commitments; entertainment carryover	No visual treatment; short advertising life of message; high frequency required to generate comprehension and retention; distractions from background sound; commercial clutter
Television	Ability to reach a wide, diverse audience; low cost per thousand; creative opportunities for demonstration; immediacy of messages; entertainment carryover; demographic selectivity with cable stations	Short life of message; some consumer skepticism about claims; high campaign cost; little demographic selectivity with network stations; long-term advertiser commitments; long lead times required for production; commercial clutter
Internet	Fastest-growing medium; ability to reach a narrow target audience; relatively short lead time required for creating web-based advertising; moderate cost; ability to measure ad effectiveness; ability to engage consumers through search engine marketing, social media, display advertising, and mobile marketing	Most ad exposure relies on "click-through" from display ads; measurement for social media needs much improvement; not all consumers have access to the Internet, and many consumers are not using social media
Outdoor Media	Repetition; moderate cost; flexibility; geographic selectivity	Short message; lack of demographic selectivity; high "noise" level distracting audience

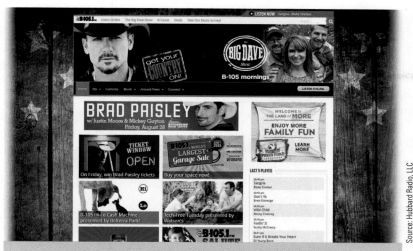

Future growth in advertising lies in the digital realm; this includes display ads, video ads, search ads and banner ads.

Source: Hubbard Radio, LLC

distractions from competing ads and news stories. Therefore, one company's ad may not be particularly visible.

The main sources of newspaper ad revenue are local retailers, classified ads, and cooperative advertising. In **cooperative advertising**, the manufacturer and the retailer split the costs of advertising the manufacturer's brand. For example, Estée Lauder may split the cost of an advertisement with Macy's department store provided that the ad focuses on Estée Lauder's products. One reason manufacturers use cooperative advertising is the impracticality of listing all their dealers in national advertising. Also, cooperative advertising encourages retailers to devote more effort to the manufacturer's lines.

MAGAZINES Magazines are another traditional medium that has been successful. Some of the top magazines according to circulation include *AARP*, *Better Homes and Gardens*, *Reader's Digest*, *National Geographic*, and *Good Housekeeping*. However, compared to the cost of other media, the cost per contact in magazine advertising is usually high. The cost per potential customer may be much lower, however, because magazines are often targeted to specialized audiences and thus reach more potential customers.

RADIO Radio has several strengths as an advertising medium: selectivity and audience segmentation, a large out-of-home audience, low unit and production costs, timeliness, and geographic flexibility. Local advertisers are the most frequent users of radio advertising, contributing over 75 percent of all radio ad revenue. Like newspapers, radio also lends itself well to cooperative advertising.

TELEVISION Television broadcasters include network television, independent stations, cable television, and direct broadcast satellite television. Network television reaches a wide and diverse market, and cable television and direct broadcast satellite systems, such as DIRECTV and DISH Network, broadcast a multitude of channels devoted to highly segmented markets. Because of its targeted channels, cable television is often characterized as "narrowcasting" by media buyers. DIRECTV is testing the ability to serve ads based on household data (as opposed to demographic and geographic data). To stay relevant amidst new technologies, DIRECTV and other television-focused companies are beginning to recognize the need for better audience targeting.

Advertising time on television can be very expensive, especially for network and popular cable channels. Special events and first-run prime-time shows for top-ranked television programs command the highest rates for a typical commercial. For example, running a thirty-second spot during the sitcom *How to Get Away with Murder* on *ABC* costs $252,934, while running one during NFL Sunday Football costs $603,000. Cable programs like ESPN's *Monday Night Football* command similarly hefty price tags.[20] A thirty-second spot during the Super Bowl costs approximately $5 million.[21] Despite its high cost, many brands feel that a Super Bowl ad is a good investment given the earned media leading up to the game, during the game, and after the game.[22] An alternative to a commercial spot is the **infomercial**, a 30-minute or longer advertisement, which is relatively inexpensive to produce and air. Advertisers say the infomercial is an ideal way to present complicated information to potential customers, which other advertising vehicles typically do not allow time to do. Beachbody's P90X and Insanity exercise DVDs are advertised through infomercials.

One of the most significant trends of concern to television advertising is the rise in popularity of digital video recorders (DVRs) and on-demand viewing. For every hour of television programming, an average of 20 minutes is dedicated to nonprogram material (ads, public service announcements, and network promotions), so the popularity of DVRs among ad-weary viewers is hardly surprising. Like marketers and advertisers, networks are also highly concerned about ad skipping. If consumers are not watching advertisements, then marketers will spend

cooperative advertising an arrangement in which the manufacturer and the retailer split the costs of advertising the manufacturer's brand

infomercial a 30-minute or longer advertisement that looks more like a television talk show than a sales pitch

a greater proportion of their advertising budgets on alternative media, and a critical revenue stream for networks will disappear.

THE INTERNET Online advertising has become a versatile medium to target specific groups. U.S. digital ad revenues exceed $50 billion annually and are expected to increase to $82 billion annually by 2018. This figure is projected to grow to more than $163 billion by 2016, at which point it will represent 26 percent of all advertising expenditures.[23] Online advertising includes search engine marketing (e.g., pay-per-click ads like Google AdWords), display advertising (e.g., banner ads, video ads), social media advertising (e.g., Facebook ads), e-mail marketing, and mobile marketing (including mobile advertising and SMS). Some online channels like Google offer the ability to *audience buy* (whereby advertisers can purchase ad space targeted to a highly specific group), but others, such as Turner Digital's FunnyOrDie.com, believe the complex cookie-based strategy poses too many risks.[24]

Popular Internet sites and search engines generally sell advertising space to marketers to promote their goods and services. Internet surfers click on these ads to be linked to more information about the advertised product or service. Both leading advertisers and companies whose ad budgets are not as large have become big Internet advertisers. Because of the relative low cost and high targetability, search engines generate nearly half of all Internet ad revenue. The fastest-growing platform for Internet advertising is the mobile space.[25]

Another popular Internet advertising format is **advergaming**, whereby companies put ad messages in web-based, mobile, console, or handheld video games to advertise or promote a product, service, organization, or issue. *Gamification*, the process of using game mechanics and a gaming mindset to engage an audience, is increasingly important for marketers to know about and utilize. Challenges, rewards, incentives, and competition are all important aspects in social media games like *Candy Crush Saga and Clash of Clans*.[26] Some games amount to virtual commercials; others encourage players to buy in-game items and power-ups to advance; and still others allow advertisers to sponsor games or buy ad space for product placements. Many of these are social games, played on Facebook or mobile networks, where players can interact with one another. Social gaming has

advergaming placing advertising messages in web-based, mobile, console, or handheld video games to advertise or promote a product, service, organization, or issue

Realistic sports games like EA's FIFA 16 feature advertisements on uniforms, stadium walls, and even replay segments to simulate advertisement-heavy television broadcasts.

a huge audience—according to Facebook CEO Mark Zuckerberg, 235 million people play social games on Facebook every month. The Facebook gaming market is projected to more than double in the next three years, attracting 554 million people and generating $5.6 billion.[27]

More than three-fourths of Americans have mobile phones, and over one-third of those are smartphones. Fifty-five percent of mobile phone owners access the Web on their phones, making mobile websites and apps more important.[28] Mobile advertising has substantial upside potential given that there are more than six billion cell phone users in the world, and an increasing number of those users have smartphones or tablets with Internet access. U.S. mobile advertising is finally reaching its tipping point, earning almost $40 billion annually. This accounts for nearly all growth in digital advertising. The primary reason is that people are spending more of their time (19.4 percent) on mobile devices rather than on desktops and laptops.[29] As devices such as the iPad continue to grow in popularity, mobile advertising spending will continue to grow worldwide.

OUTDOOR MEDIA Outdoor or out-of-home advertising is a flexible, low-cost medium that may take a variety of forms. Examples include billboards, skywriting, giant inflatables, mini billboards in malls and on bus stop shelters, signs in sports arenas, and lighted moving signs in bus terminals and airports, as well as ads painted on cars, trucks, buses, water towers, manhole covers, drinking glass coasters, and even people, called "living advertising." The plywood scaffolding surrounding downtown construction sites often holds ads, which in places like Manhattan's Times Square, can reach over a million viewers a day.

Outdoor advertising reaches a broad and diverse market and is therefore ideal for promoting convenience products and services as well as directing consumers to local businesses. One of outdoor advertising's main advantages over other media is that its exposure frequency is very high, yet the amount of clutter from competing ads is very low. Outdoor advertising also can be customized to local marketing needs, which is why local businesses are the leading outdoor advertisers in any given region.

ALTERNATIVE MEDIA To cut through the clutter of traditional advertising media, advertisers are developing new media vehicles, like shopping carts in grocery stores, computer screen savers, interactive kiosks in department stores, advertisements run before movies at the cinema, posters on bathroom stalls, and *advertainments*—mini movies that promote a product and are shown online.

Marketers are looking for more innovative ways to reach captive and often bored commuters. For instance, subway systems are now showing ads via lighted boxes installed along tunnel walls. Other advertisers seek consumers at home. Some marketers have begun replacing hold music on customer service lines with advertisements and movie trailers. This strategy generates revenue for the company being called and catches undistracted consumers for advertisers. The trick is to amuse and interest this captive audience without annoying them during their ten- to fifteen-minute wait. After Yahoo! CEO Marissa Mayer called her company's on-hold message "garbage," audio production startup Jingle Punks hired Canadian rapper Snow (known for his 1992 hit song "Informer") to write a humorous on-hold jingle for Yahoo! (you can hear the jingle at www.youtube.com/watch?v=vRmVDADlnOU). Yahoo! has yet to implement the jingle, however.[30]

16-4b Media Selection Considerations

An important element in any advertising campaign is the **media mix**, the combination of media to be used. Media mix decisions are typically based on several factors: cost per contact, cost per click, reach, frequency, target audience considerations, flexibility of the medium, noise level, and the life span of the medium.

There are a number of factors to consider before committing to any sort of advertising medium; this includes flexibility of the medium, noise level, and the life span of the medium.

Cost per contact, also referred to as **cost per thousand (CPM)**, is the cost of reaching one member of the target market. Naturally, as the size of the audience increases, so does the total cost. Cost per contact enables an advertiser to compare the relative costs of specific media vehicles (such as television versus radio or magazine versus newspaper), or more specifically, within a media category (such as *People* versus *US Weekly*). Thus, an advertiser debating whether to spend local advertising dollars for television spots or radio spots could consider the cost per contact of each. Alternatively, if the question is which magazine to advertise in, she might choose the one with the greater reach. In either case, the advertiser can pick the vehicle with the lowest cost per contact to maximize advertising punch for the money spent. **Cost per click** is the cost associated with a consumer clicking on a display

media mix the combination of media to be used for a promotional campaign

cost per contact (cost per thousand or CPM) the cost of reaching one member of the target market

cost per click the cost associated with a consumer clicking on a display or banner ad

or banner ad. Although there are several variations, this option enables the marketer to pay only for "engaged" consumers—those who opted to click on an ad.

Reach is the number of target customers who are exposed to a commercial at least once during a specific period, usually four weeks. Media plans for product introductions and attempts at increasing brand awareness usually emphasize reach. For example, an advertiser might try to reach seventy percent of the target audience during the first three months of the campaign. Reach is related to a medium's ratings, generally referred to in the industry as *gross ratings points*, or *GRP*. A television program with a higher GRP means that more people are tuning in to the show and the reach is higher. Accordingly, as GRP increases for a particular medium, so does cost per contact.

Because the typical ad is short-lived, and often only a small portion of an ad may be perceived at one time, advertisers repeat their ads so that potential customers will remember the message. **Frequency** is the number of times an individual is exposed to a given message during a specific period. Advertisers use average frequency to measure the intensity of a specific medium's coverage. For example, Coca-Cola might want an average exposure frequency of five for its Powerade television ads. That means that each of the television viewers who saw the ad saw it an average of five times.

Media selection is also a matter of matching the advertising medium with the product's target market. If marketers are trying to reach teenage females, they might select *Teen Vogue* magazine. A medium's ability to reach a precisely defined market is its **audience selectivity**. Some media vehicles, like general newspapers and network television, appeal to a wide cross section of the population. Others—such as *Brides*, *Popular Mechanics*, *Architectural Digest*, *Lucky*, MTV, ESPN, and Christian radio stations— appeal to very specific groups.

The *flexibility* of a medium can be extremely important to an advertiser. For example, because of layouts and design, the lead time for magazine advertising is considerably longer than for other media types and so is less flexible. By contrast, radio and Internet advertising provide maximum flexibility. If necessary, an advertiser can change a radio ad on the day it is aired.

Noise level is the level of distraction experienced by the target audience in a medium. Noise can be created by competing ads, as when a street is lined with billboards or when a television program is cluttered with competing ads. Whereas newspapers and magazines have a high noise level, direct mail is a private medium with a low noise level. Typically, no other advertising media or news stories compete for direct mail readers' attention.

Media have either a short or a long *life span*, which means that messages can either quickly fade or persist as tangible copy to be carefully studied. A radio commercial may last less than a minute, but advertisers can overcome this short life span by repeating radio ads often. In contrast, a magazine has a relatively long life span, which is further increased by a high pass-along rate.

Media planners have traditionally relied on the above factors in selecting an effective media mix, with reach, frequency, and cost often the overriding criteria. Well-established brands with familiar messages, however, probably need fewer exposures to be effective, while newer or unfamiliar brands likely need more exposures to become familiar. In addition, today's media planners have more media options than ever before. (Today, there are over 1,600 television networks across the country, whereas forty years ago there were only three.)

The proliferation of media channels is causing *media fragmentation* and forcing media planners to pay as much attention to where they place their advertising as to how often the advertisement is repeated. That is, marketers should evaluate reach *and* frequency in

reach the number of target consumers exposed to a commercial at least once during a specific period, usually four weeks

frequency the number of times an individual is exposed to a given message during a specific period

audience selectivity the ability of an advertising medium to reach a precisely defined market

There are many ways for viewers to avoid watching commercials, such as using a DVR.

Zealot/Shutterstock.com

New media like virtual reality, holographic displays, and augmented reality mobile games will give marketers all-new ways to advertise.

assessing the effectiveness of advertising. In certain situations, it may be important to reach potential consumers through as many media vehicles as possible. When this approach is considered, however, the budget must be large enough to achieve sufficient levels of frequency to have an impact. In evaluating reach versus frequency, therefore, the media planner ultimately must select an approach that is most likely to result in the ad being understood and remembered when a purchase decision is being made.

Advertisers also evaluate the qualitative factors involved in media selection. These include such things as attention to the commercial and the program, involvement, program liking, lack of distractions, and other audience behaviors that affect the likelihood that a commercial message is being seen and, hopefully, absorbed. While advertisers can advertise their product in as many media as possible and repeat the ad as many times as they like, the ad still may not be effective if the audience is not paying attention. Additional research highlights the benefits of cross-media advertising campaigns.[31]

16-4c Media Scheduling

After choosing the media for the advertising campaign, advertisers must schedule the ads. A **media schedule** designates the medium or media to be used (such as magazines, television, or radio), the specific vehicles (such as *People* magazine, the show *Scandal* on television, or Rush Limbaugh's national radio program), and the insertion dates of the advertising.

There are four basic types of media schedules:

- A **continuous media schedule** allows the advertising to run steadily throughout the advertising period. Examples include Ivory soap and Charmin toilet tissue, which may have an ad in the newspaper every Sunday and a television commercial on NBC every Wednesday at 7:30 p.m. over a three-month time period. Products in the later stages of the product life cycle, which are advertised on a reminder basis, often use a continuous media schedule.

- With a **flighted media schedule**, the advertiser may schedule the ads heavily every other month or every two weeks to achieve a greater impact with an increased frequency and reach at those times. Movie studios might schedule television advertising on Wednesday and Thursday nights, when moviegoers are deciding which films to see that weekend.

- A **pulsing media schedule** combines continuous scheduling with flighted scheduling. It is continuous advertising that is simply heavier during the best sale periods. A retail department store may advertise on a year-round basis but place more advertising during certain sale periods such as Thanksgiving, Christmas, and back-to-school. Or beer may be advertised more heavily during the summer months and football season given the higher consumption levels at those times.

- Certain times of the year call for a **seasonal media schedule**. Products like Sudafed

media schedule designation of the media, the specific publications or programs, and the insertion dates of advertising

continuous media schedule a media scheduling strategy in which advertising is run steadily throughout the advertising period; used for products in the later stages of the product life cycle

flighted media schedule a media scheduling strategy in which ads are run heavily every other month or every two weeks to achieve a greater impact with an increased frequency and reach at those times

pulsing media schedule a media scheduling strategy that uses continuous scheduling throughout the year coupled with a flighted schedule during the best sales periods

seasonal media schedule a media scheduling strategy that runs advertising only during times of the year when the product is most likely to be used

cold tablets and Coppertone sunscreen, which are used more during certain times of the year, tend to follow a seasonal strategy.

Research comparing continuous media schedules and flighted ones suggests that continuous schedules are more effective than are flighted ones at driving sales through television advertisements. This research suggests that it may be important to reach a potential customer as close as possible to the time at which he makes a purchase. Therefore, the advertiser should maintain a continuous schedule over as long a period of time as possible. Often called *recency planning*, this theory of scheduling is now commonly used for scheduling television advertising for frequently purchased products such as Coca-Cola and Tide detergent. Recency planning's main premise is that advertising works by influencing the brand choice of people who are ready to buy. Mobile advertising may be one of the most promising tactics for contacting consumers when they are thinking about a specific product. For example, a GPS-enabled mobile phone can get text messages for area restaurants around lunchtime to advertise specials to professionals working in a big city.

 ## 16-5 PUBLIC RELATIONS

Public relations is the element in the promotional mix that evaluates public attitudes, identifies issues that may elicit public concern, and executes programs to gain public understanding and acceptance. Public relations is a vital link in a forward-thinking company's marketing communication mix. Marketing managers plan solid public relations campaigns that fit into overall marketing plans and focus on targeted audiences. These campaigns strive to maintain a positive image of the corporation in the eyes of the public. As such, they should capitalize on the factors that enhance the firm's image and minimize the factors that could generate a negative image. The concept of earned media is based on public relations and publicity.

Publicity is the effort to capture media attention—for example, through articles or editorials in publications or through

human-interest stories on radio or television programs. Corporations usually initiate publicity through press releases that further their public relations plans. A company about to introduce a new product or open a new store may send press releases to the media in the hope that the story will be published or broadcast. Savvy publicity can often create overnight sensations or build up a reserve of goodwill with consumers. Corporate donations and sponsorships can also create favorable publicity.

16-5a Major Public Relations Tools

Public relations professionals commonly use several tools, many of which require an active role on the part of the public relations professional, such as writing press releases

public relations the element in the promotional mix that evaluates public attitudes, identifies issues that may elicit public concern, and executes programs to gain public understanding and acceptance

publicity an effort to capture media attention, often initiated through press releases that further a corporation's public relations plans

Remigio Pereira faced a publicity nightmare after changing the lyrics of the Canadian national anthem to "all lives matter" during the 2016 MLB All-Star Game. Pereira, who also held up an "All Lives Matter" sign during the performance, met widespread public outrage and was promptly let go from The Tenors singing group after the incident.

AP Images/Gregory Bull

The Many Duties of Public Relations Departments

Public relations departments may perform any or all of the following functions:

- **Press relations:** Placing positive, newsworthy information in the news media or in the hands of influential bloggers to attract attention to a product, a service, or a person associated with the firm or institution

- **Product publicity:** Publicizing specific products or services through a variety of traditional and online channels

- **Corporate communication:** Creating internal and external messages to promote a positive image of the firm or institution

- **Public affairs:** Building and maintaining local, national, or global community relations

- **Lobbying:** Influencing legislators and government officials to promote or defeat legislation and regulation

- **Employee and investor relations:** Maintaining positive relationships with employees, shareholders, and others in the financial community

- **Crisis management:** Responding to unfavorable publicity or a negative event placement, often at a much lower cost than in mass media like television ads

and engaging in proactive media relations. Sometimes, however, these techniques create their own publicity.

NEW-PRODUCT PUBLICITY Publicity is instrumental in introducing new products and services. Publicity can help advertisers explain what's different about their new product by prompting free news stories or positive word of mouth about it. During the introductory period, an especially innovative new product often needs more exposure than conventional, paid advertising affords. Public relations professionals write press releases or develop videos in an effort to generate news about their new product. They also jockey for exposure of their product or service at major events, on popular television and news shows, or in the hands of influential people. Consider the publicity Apple generated for the release of the iPad Air, which included press coverage in traditional media as well as online blogs and forums. That was a small part of the entire marketing campaign.

PRODUCT PLACEMENT Marketers are increasingly using product placement to reinforce brand awareness and create favorable attitudes. **Product placement** is a strategy that involves getting one's product, service, or name to appear in a movie, television show, radio program, magazine, newspaper, video game, video or audio clip, book, or commercial for another product; on the Internet; or at special events. Including an actual product, such as a can of Pepsi, adds a sense of realism to a movie, television show,

video game, book, or similar vehicle that cannot be created by a can simply marked "soda." Product placements are arranged through barter (trade of product for placement), through paid placements, or at no charge when the product is viewed as enhancing the vehicle it is placed in.

Global product placement expenditures total about $8 billion annually ($4.3 billion in the United States alone).[32] More than two-thirds of product placements are in movies and television shows, but placements in other alternative media are growing, particularly on the Internet and in video games. Digital technology now enables companies to "virtually" place their products in any audio or video production. Virtual placement not only reduces the cost of product placement for new productions but also enables companies to place their products in previously produced programs, such as reruns of television shows. Overall, companies obtain valuable product exposure, brand reinforcement, and increased sales through product placement.

CONSUMER EDUCATION Some major firms believe that educated consumers are more loyal customers. Financial planning firms often sponsor free educational seminars on money management, retirement

> **product placement** a public relations strategy that involves getting a product, service, or company name to appear in a movie, television show, radio program, magazine, newspaper, video game, video or audio clip, book, or commercial for another product; on the Internet; or at special events

planning, and investing in the hope that the seminar participants will choose the sponsoring organization for their future financial needs.

SPONSORSHIP Sponsorships are increasing both in number and as a proportion of companies' marketing budgets. Currently sitting at about $32 billion annually, U.S. sponsorship spending is likewise increasing.[33] Probably the biggest reason for the increasing use of sponsorships is the difficulty of reaching audiences and differentiating a product from competing brands through the mass media.

With **sponsorship**, a company spends money to support an issue, cause, or event that is consistent with corporate objectives, such as improving brand awareness or enhancing corporate image. The biggest category of sponsorships is sports, which accounts for almost 70 percent of spending in sponsorships and has seen steady growth in recent years.[34] Nonsports categories include entertainment tours and attractions, causes, arts, festivals, fairs and annual events, and association and membership organizations.

Although the most popular sponsorship events are still those involving sports, music, or the arts, companies have recently been turning to more specialized events such as tie-ins with schools, charities, and other community service organizations. Marketers sometimes even create their own events tied around their products. For example, energy drink manufacturer Red Bull hosted Stratos, a multimillion-dollar event where Austrian Felix Baumgartner skydived from the edge of space—nearly twenty-four miles above Earth's surface. Baumgartner became the first human to break the sound barrier in free fall, reaching 834 miles per hour before touching down safely in New Mexico. A major marketing victory for Red Bull, Stratos set its own record as the most-watched YouTube live stream of all time—more than eight million viewers tuned in to the event.[35]

Corporations sponsor issues as well as events. Sponsorship issues are quite diverse, but the three most popular are education, health care, and social programs. Firms often donate a percentage of sales or profits to a worthy cause favored by their target market.

Corporations sponsor events in an attempt to market their product. The yearly Rose Bowl game has been sponsored by companies like Citi and Northwestern Mutual.

sponsorship a public relations strategy in which a company spends money to support an issue, cause, or event that is consistent with corporate objectives, such as improving brand awareness or enhancing corporate image

EXPERIENTIAL MARKETING While the Internet enables consumers to connect with their favorite brands in a virtual environment, there is often nothing like experiencing the real thing live and in person. Experiential marketing involves engaging with consumers in a way that enables them to feel the brand—not just read about it. Experiential and event marketing have increased in recent years, with most of the growth coming from the world's largest brands. Examples of experiential marketing include American Express's Small Business Saturday, which promotes shopping at local businesses, and Clear Channel's effort to run a carnival-style dunk tank in New York City's Times Square.[36]

COMPANY WEBSITES Companies are increasingly using the Internet in their public relations strategies. Company websites are used to introduce new products; provide information to the media, including social media news releases; promote existing products; obtain consumer feedback; communicate legislative and regulatory information; showcase upcoming events; provide links to related sites (including corporate and non-corporate blogs, Facebook, Twitter, and Instagram); release financial information; interact with customers and potential customers; and perform many more marketing activities. In addition, social media are playing a larger role in how companies interact with customers online, particularly through sites like Facebook, Yelp, or Twitter. Indeed, online reviews (good and bad) from opinion leaders and other consumers help marketers sway purchasing decisions in their favor.

16-5b Managing Unfavorable Publicity

Although marketers try to avoid unpleasant situations, crises do happen. In our free-press environment, publicity is not easily controlled, especially in a crisis. Crisis management is the coordinated effort to handle the effects of unfavorable publicity, ensuring fast and accurate communication in times of emergency.

When the Villa Fresh Italian Kitchen ran "Dub the Dew," an online contest to name a green apple–flavored variety of Mountain Dew exclusive to the restaurant, it was not long before Internet trolls descended. These digital pranksters submitted absurd and offensive names (such as "diabeetus," "gushing granny," and "Hitler did nothing wrong"), and then voted their submissions to the top of the contest leaderboard en masse. The contest's website was quickly taken offline, and Mountain Dew tweeted that the contest "lost to the internet." In an attempt to manage the crisis, the Villa Fresh Italian Kitchen issued an apologetic statement: "'Dub the Dew,' a local market promotional campaign that was created by one of our customers—not Mountain Dew—was compromised. We are working diligently with our customer's team to remove all offensive content that was posted and putting measures in place to ensure this doesn't happen again."[37]

 ## 16-6 SALES PROMOTION

In addition to using advertising and public relations, marketing managers can use sales promotion to increase the effectiveness of their promotional efforts. Sales promotion consists of marketing communication activities other than advertising, personal selling, and public relations, in which a short-term incentive motivates consumers or members of the distribution channel to purchase a good or service immediately, either by lowering the price or by adding value.

Sales promotion is usually cheaper than advertising and easier to measure. A major national television advertising campaign often costs $10 million or more to create, produce, and place. In contrast, promotional campaigns using the Internet or direct marketing methods can cost less than half that amount. It is also very difficult to determine how many people buy a product or service as a result of radio or television ads. With sales promotion, marketers know the precise number of coupons redeemed or the number of contest entries received.

Sales promotion usually has more effect on behavior than on attitudes. Giving the consumer an incentive to make an immediate purchase is the goal of sales promotion, regardless of the form it takes. Sales promotion is usually targeted toward either of two distinctly different markets. **Trade sales promotion** is directed to members of the marketing channel, such as wholesalers and retailers. **Consumer sales promotion** is targeted to the ultimate consumer market. The objectives of a promotion depend on the general behavior of targeted customers Exhibit 16.4. For example, marketers who are targeting loyal users of their product need to reinforce existing behavior or increase product usage. An effective tool for strengthening brand loyalty is the *frequent buyer program*, which rewards consumers for repeat purchases. Other types of promotions are more effective with customers who are prone to brand switching or with those who are loyal to a competitor's product. A cents-off coupon, free sample, or eye-catching display in a store will often entice shoppers to try a different brand.

Once marketers understand the dynamics occurring within their product category and determine the particular customers and behaviors they want to influence, they can then go about selecting promotional tools to achieve these goals.

16-6a Tools for Trade Sales Promotion

As we'll discuss in section 16-6b, consumer promotions pull a product through the channel by creating demand. However, trade promotions *push* a product through the distribution channel (see Chapter 13). When selling to members of the distribution channel, manufacturers use many of the same sales promotion tools used in consumer promotions, such as sales contests premiums and point-of-purchase displays. Several tools, however, are unique to manufacturers and intermediaries:

- **Trade allowances:** A **trade allowance** is a price reduction offered by manufacturers to intermediaries such as wholesalers and retailers. The price reduction or rebate is given in exchange for doing something specific, such as allocating space for a new product or buying

crisis management a coordinated effort to handle all the effects of unfavorable publicity or another unexpected unfavorable event

sales promotion marketing communication activities other than advertising, personal selling, and public relations, in which a short-term incentive motivates consumers or members of the distribution channel to purchase a good or service immediately, either by lowering the price or by adding value

trade sales promotion promotion activities directed to members of the marketing channel, such as wholesalers and retailers

consumer sales promotion promotion activities targeted to the ultimate consumer market

trade allowance a price reduction offered by manufacturers to intermediaries such as wholesalers and retailers

EXHIBIT 16.4 TYPES OF CONSUMERS AND SALES PROMOTION GOALS

Type of Buyer	Desired Results	Sales Promotion Examples
Loyal customers People who buy your product most or all of the time	Reinforce behavior, increase consumption, change purchase timing	• Loyalty marketing programs, such as frequent buyer cards or frequent shopper clubs • Bonus packs that give loyal consumers an incentive to stock up or premiums offered in return for proofs of purchase
Competitor's customers People who buy a competitor's product most or all of the time	Break loyalty, persuade to switch to your brand	• Sampling to introduce your product's superior qualities compared to their brand • Sweepstakes, contests, or premiums that create interest in the product
Brand switchers People who buy a variety of products in the category	Persuade to buy your brand more often	• Any promotion that lowers the price of the product, such as coupons, price-off packages, and bonus packs • Trade deals that help make the product more readily available than competing products
Price buyers People who consistently buy the least expensive brand	Appeal with low prices or supply added value that makes price less important	• Coupons, price-off packages, refunds, or trade deals that reduce the price of the brand to match that of the brand that would have been purchased

From *Sales Promotion Essentials*, 2nd ed., by Don E. Schultz, William A. Robinson, and Lisa A. Petrison, published by McGraw-Hill Education.

something during special periods. For example, a local Best Buy outlet could receive a special discount for running its own promotion on Sony surround sound systems.

- **Push money:** Intermediaries receive **push money** as a bonus for pushing the manufacturer's brand through the distribution channel. Often the push money is directed toward a retailer's salespeople. LinoColor, the leading high-end scanner company, produces a Picture Perfect Rewards catalog filled with merchandise retailers can purchase with points accrued for every LinoColor scanner they sell.

- **Training:** Sometimes a manufacturer will train an intermediary's personnel if the product is rather complex—as frequently occurs in the computer and telecommunications industries. For example, representatives of major pharmaceutical companies receive extensive training because they need to provide accurate information to doctors and nurses.

- **Free merchandise:** Often a manufacturer offers retailers free merchandise in lieu of quantity discounts. Occasionally, free merchandise is used as payment for trade allowances normally provided through other sales promotions. Instead of giving a retailer a price reduction for buying a certain quantity of merchandise, the manufacturer may throw in extra merchandise "free" (i.e., at a cost that would equal the price reduction).

- **Store demonstrations:** Manufacturers can also arrange with retailers to perform an in-store demonstration. Food manufacturers often send representatives to grocery stores and supermarkets to let customers sample a product while shopping.

- **Business meetings, conventions, and trade shows:** Trade association meetings, conferences, and conventions are an important aspect of sales promotion and a growing, multi-billion-dollar market. At these shows, manufacturers, distributors, and other vendors have the chance to display their goods or describe their services to potential customers. Companies participate in trade shows to attract and identify new prospects, serve current customers, introduce new products, enhance corporate image, test the market response to new products, enhance corporate morale, and gather competitive product information.

Trade promotions are popular among manufacturers for many reasons. Trade sales promotion tools help manufacturers gain new distributors for their products, obtain wholesaler and retailer support for consumer sales promotions, build or reduce dealer inventories, and improve trade relations. Car manufacturers annually sponsor dozens of auto shows for consumers. The shows attract millions of consumers, providing dealers with increased store traffic as well as good leads.

push money money offered to channel intermediaries to encourage them to "push" products—that is, to encourage other members of the channel to sell the products

16-6b Tools for Consumer Sales Promotion

Marketing managers must decide which consumer sales promotion devices to use in a specific campaign. The methods chosen must suit the objectives to ensure success of the overall promotion plan. The popular tools for consumer sales promotion, discussed in the following pages, have also been easily transferred to online versions to entice Internet users to visit sites, purchase products, or use services on the Web.

iStockphoto.com/Magnez2

American Express is experimenting with Twitter to offer cardholders great deals at participating businesses.

COUPONS AND REBATES A **coupon** is a certificate that entitles consumers to an immediate price reduction when the product is purchased. Coupons are a particularly good way to encourage product trial and repurchase. They are also likely to increase the amount of a product bought. Coupons can be distributed in stores as instant coupons on packaging, on shelf displays with pull-off coupon dispensers, and at cash registers, printed based on what the customer purchased; through freestanding inserts (FSIs); and through various Internet daily deal sites.

FSIs, the promotional coupons inserts found in newspapers, are the traditional way of circulating printed coupons. FSIs are used to distribute approximately 80 percent of coupons. Such traditional types of coupon distribution, which also include direct mail and magazines, have been declining for several years, as consumers use fewer coupons. About 3 billion coupons are redeemed annually. Mobile coupons have a much higher redemption rate than paper coupons.[38]

The Internet is changing the face of coupons. In addition to Internet coupon sites such as Valpak.com and Coolsavings.com, and social coupon sites such as Groupon and LivingSocial, there are also deal sites like DealSurf.com that aggregate offers from different sites for convenience. While daily deal sites have been quite popular with consumers, sites like Groupon and Living-Social are coming under some fire as many small businesses claim they lose money or drown under the flood of coupon redemptions. American Express is using Twitter to drive card use. After syncing their credit cards to their Twitter accounts, American Express customers can send tweets using an approved hashtag (or "cashtag") to pay for items purchased through third-party retailers.

Cardholders can also receive automatic discounts from partner businesses on Twitter when they make purchases with their American Express cards.[39]

A **rebate** is similar to a coupon in that a rebate offers the purchaser a price reduction; however, because the purchaser must mail in a rebate form and usually some proof of purchase, the reward is not as immediate. Manufacturers prefer rebates for several reasons. Rebates allow manufacturers to offer price cuts to consumers directly. Manufacturers have more control over rebate promotions because they can be rolled out and shut off quickly. Further, because buyers must fill out forms with their names, addresses, and other data, manufacturers use rebate programs to build customer databases. Perhaps the best reason of all to offer rebates is that although rebates are particularly good at enticing purchase, most consumers never bother to redeem them—only about 40 percent of consumers eligible for rebates collect them.[40]

PREMIUMS A **premium** is an extra item offered to the consumer, usually in exchange for some proof that the promoted product has been purchased. Premiums reinforce the consumer's purchase decision, increase consumption, and persuade nonusers to switch brands. A longstanding example of the use of premiums is the McDonald's Happy Meal, which rewards children with a small toy. Premiums can also include more product for the regular price, such as two-for-the-price-of-one bonus packs or packages that include more of the product. Some companies attach a premium to the product's package, such as a small sample of a complementary hair product attached to a shampoo bottle.

LOYALTY MARKETING PROGRAMS A **loyalty marketing program** builds long-term, mutually

coupon a certificate that entitles consumers to an immediate price reduction when the product is purchased.

rebate a cash refund given for the purchase of a product during a specific period

premium an extra item offered to the consumer, usually in exchange for some proof of purchase of the promoted product

loyalty marketing program a promotional program designed to build long-term, mutually beneficial relationships between a company and its key customers

beneficial relationships between a company and its key customers. One of the most popular types of loyalty programs, the **frequent buyer program**, rewards loyal consumers for making multiple purchases. The objective of loyalty marketing programs is to build long-term, mutually beneficial relationships between a company and its key customers.

There are almost three billion loyalty program memberships in the United States; the average household has signed up for 18 programs.[41] Popularized by the airline industry through frequent-flyer programs, loyalty marketing enables companies to strategically invest sales promotion dollars in activities designed to capture greater profits from customers already loyal to the product or company. Co-branded credit cards are an increasingly popular loyalty marketing tool. Most department stores only offer loyalty programs if a customer opens their branded credit card. However, high-end chain Bloomingdales recently changed its rewards program to include anyone who will sign up. Members of the new Loyalist program receive one point for each dollar they spend and receive a $25 gift card after earning 5,000 points. While Bloomingdale's credit card holders receive more points per dollar spent, the company is hoping to monitor a greater number of its shoppers' spending habits by enabling non-cardholders to join Loyalist.[42]

Through loyalty programs, shoppers receive discounts, alerts on new products, and other types of enticing offers. In exchange, retailers are able to build customer databases that help them better understand customer preferences.

CONTESTS AND SWEEPSTAKES Contests and sweepstakes are generally designed to create interest in a good or service, often to encourage brand switching. *Contests* are promotions in which participants use some skill or ability to compete for prizes. A consumer contest usually requires entrants to answer questions, complete sentences, or write a paragraph about the product and submit proof of purchase. Winning a *sweepstakes*, on the other hand, depends on chance, and participation is free. Sweepstakes usually draw about ten times more entries than contests do.

While contests and sweepstakes may draw considerable interest and publicity, generally they are not effective tools for generating long-term sales. To increase their effectiveness, sales promotion managers must make certain the award will appeal to the target market. Offering several smaller prizes to many winners instead of one huge prize to just one person often will increase the effectiveness of the promotion, but there is no denying the attractiveness of a jackpot-type prize.

SAMPLING Sampling allows the customer to try a product risk-free. In a recent study, in-store sampling proved to be the most successful promotional tactic when researchers introduced a new dairy product to grocery stores. In-store sampling events increased sales 116 percent, outperforming aisle displays (70 percent), ad circulars (63 percent), and temporary price reductions (48 percent).[43]

Samples can be directly mailed to the customer, delivered door-to-door, packaged with another product, or

Baby formula companies like Enfamil, will send samples to expectant mothers or homes where baby's were recently born.

frequent buyer program a loyalty program in which loyal consumers are rewarded for making multiple purchases of a particular good or service

sampling a promotional program that allows the consumer the opportunity to try a product or service for free

demonstrated or distributed at a retail store or service outlet. Sampling at special events is a popular, effective, and high profile distribution method that permits marketers to piggyback onto fun-based consumer activities—including sporting events, college fests, fairs and festivals, beach events, and chili cook-offs. Distributing samples to specific location types, such as health clubs, churches, or doctors' offices, is also one of the most efficient methods of sampling. Online sampling is catching up in popularity, however, with the growth of social media. Branded products not only run contests through Facebook, but also connect with fans, show commercials, and offer samples of new products in exchange for "liking" the brand.

POINT-OF-PURCHASE PROMOTION A **point-of-purchase (P-O-P) display** includes any promotional display set up at the retailer's location to build traffic, advertise the product, or induce impulse buying. P-O-P displays include shelf "talkers" (signs attached to store shelves), shelf extenders (attachments that extend shelves so products stand out), ads on grocery carts and bags, end-aisle and floor-stand displays, television monitors at supermarket checkout counters, in-store audio messages, and audiovisual displays. One big advantage of the P-O-P display is that it offers manufacturers a captive audience in retail stores. According to POPAI's Shopper Engagement Study, approximately 76 percent of all retail purchase decisions are made in-store. Fifty-seven percent of shoppers buy more than they anticipated once in the store, so P-O-P displays can be very effective.[44] Other strategies to increase sales include adding cards to the tops of displays, changing messages on signs on the sides or bottoms of displays, adding inflatable or mobile displays, and using signs that advertise the brand's sports, movie, or charity tie-in.

16-6c Trends in Sales Promotion

The biggest trend in sales promotion on both the trade and consumer side has been the increased use of the Internet. Social media-, e-mail-, and website-based promotions have expanded dramatically in recent years. Marketers are now spending billions of dollars annually on such promotions. Sales promotions online have proved both effective and cost-efficient—generating response rates three to five times higher than off-line promotions. The most effective types of online sales promotions are free merchandise, sweepstakes, free shipping with purchases, and coupons. One major goal of retailers is to add potential customers to their databases and expand marketing touch points.

Marketers have discovered that online coupon distribution provides another vehicle for promoting their products. The redemption rate of online coupons has been growing substantially while total coupon redemption has remained steady.[45] Online coupons can help marketers lure new customers, and with the speed of online feedback, marketers can track the success of a coupon in real time and adjust it based on changing market conditions.[46]

Online versions of loyalty programs are also popping up, and although many types of companies have these programs, the most successful are those run by hotel and airline companies. A final major trend in sales promotion is the utilization of sales promotions on social media and at the point of purchase. Google's Zero Moment of Truth (ZMOT) insights illustrate how important consumer feedback is to consumer purchases, highlighting the importance of behavioral data when serving up a targeted sales promotion.[47]

> **point of purchase (P-O-P) display** a promotional display set up at the retailer's location to build traffic, advertise the product, or induce impulse buying

17 | Personal Selling and Sales Management

LEARNING OUTCOMES

After studying this chapter, you will be able to...

17-1 Understand the sales environment

17-2 Describe personal selling

17-3 Discuss the key differences between relationship selling and traditional selling

17-4 List and explain the steps in the selling process

17-5 Understand the functions of sales management

17-6 Describe the use of customer relationship management in the selling process

After you finish this chapter go to **PAGE 319** for **STUDY TOOLS**

Yuganov Konstantin/Shutterstock.com

17-1 THE SALES ENVIRONMENT

Many people around the world work in some form of selling. Traditionally, salespeople engage in direct face-to-face contact with customers. This can take place either at the salesperson's place of business or at a secondary location (such as when a salesperson travels door-to-door or meets a customer at her office or home). Salespeople can be consumer-focused (as in the case of retail) or business-focused.

In many cases, consumer-focused salespeople require customers to come directly to a retail store, shortening the sales process time. Even though many retailers use multiple customer relationship management processes (including information kiosks, websites, and self-checkouts), one-to-one interactions are often key to retail success. Most major retailers use trained salespeople—not just order takers—to enhance the customer experience. Nordstrom's, for example, offers a retail management internship that provides both hands-on selling experience and classroom learning for students looking for careers in retail management and sales.[1] By having knowledgeable salespeople, retailers can help their customers select the products or services that are best for them.

As previously discussed, some consumer-focused salespeople travel to their customers' locations. For example, many home improvement and maintenance salespeople meet potential customers at their homes. Certain cosmetics, small appliances, and magazine subscriptions are sold directly to customers at their homes. These salespeople are considered direct salespeople. Companies such as CUTCO Cutlery, AVON, and Mary Kay Cosmetics have been very successful in direct selling.

Business-focused salespeople call on other companies to sell their products. These business-to-business

salespeople often spend a good deal of time traveling to customer locations to make sales calls, and the sales process generally takes a longer period of time. Often, business-to-business salespeople have more extensive sales training, are required to travel more, and receive a higher level of compensation.

The sales environment changes constantly as new competitors enter the market and old competitors leave. The ways that customers interact with salespeople and learn about products and suppliers are changing due to the rapid increase in new sales technologies. In order for companies to successfully sell products or services using a sales force, they must be very effective at personal selling, sales management, customer relationship management, and technology—all of which play critical roles in building strong long-term relationships with customers.

17-2 PERSONAL SELLING

As mentioned in Chapter 15, *personal selling* is a purchase situation involving a personal, paid-for communication between two people in an attempt to influence each other. In a sense, all businesspeople are salespeople. An individual may become a plant manager, a chemist, an engineer, or a member of any profession and yet still have to sell. During a job search, applicants must "sell" themselves to prospective employers in an interview. Personal selling offers several advantages over other forms of promotion:

- Personal selling provides a detailed explanation or demonstration of the product. This capability is especially needed for complex or new goods and services.

- The sales message can be varied according to the motivations and interests of each prospective customer. Moreover, when the prospect has questions or raises objections, the salesperson is there to provide explanations and guidance. By contrast, advertising and sales promotion can respond only to the questions and objections that the copywriter *thinks* are important to customers.

- Personal selling should only be directed toward qualified prospects. Other forms of promotion include some unavoidable waste because many people in the audience are not prospective customers.

- Costs can be controlled by adjusting the size of the sales force (and resulting expenses) in one-person increments. On the other hand, advertising and sales promotion must often be purchased in fairly large amounts.

- Perhaps the most important advantage is that personal selling is considerably more effective than other forms of promotion in obtaining a sale and gaining a satisfied customer.
- Personal selling also has several limitations compared to other forms of promotion:
  - Cost per contact is much greater than for mass forms of communication, leading companies to be highly selective about where and when they use salespeople.
  - If the sales force is not properly trained, the message provided can be inconsistent and inaccurate. Continual sales force management and training are necessary.
  - Salespeople can convince customers to buy unneeded products or services. This can lead to increased levels of cognitive dissonance among buyers if a salesperson is being pushed to meet certain quotas.

Personal selling often works better than other forms of promotion given certain customer and product characteristics. Generally speaking, personal selling becomes more important as the number of potential customers decreases, as the complexity of the product increases, and as the value of the product grows (see Exhibit 17.1). For highly complex goods such as business jets and private communication systems, a salesperson is needed to determine the prospective customer's needs and wants, explain the product's benefits and advantages, and propose the exact features and accessories that will best meet the client's needs. Many upscale clothing retailers offer free personal shopping, whereby consultants select and suggest designer clothing they believe will fit the customer's style and specified need. Bloomingdales'

EXHIBIT 17.1	COMPARISON OF PERSONAL SELLING AND ADVERTISING/SALES PROMOTION

Personal selling is more important if . . .	Advertising and sales promotion are more important if . . .
The product has a high value.	The product has a low value.
It is a custom-made product.	It is a standardized product.
There are few customers.	There are many customers.
The product is technically complex.	The product is easy to understand.
Customers are concentrated.	Customers are geographically dispersed.
Examples: Insurance policies, custom windows, airplane engines	**Examples:** Soap, magazine subscriptions, cotton T-shirts

personal shoppers help customers select gifts for others, provide guidance tailored to the individual's personal tastes, coordinate gift wrapping and alterations, help navigate the entire store from clothing to home goods, and even schedule reminders for special occasions.[2]

Technology plays an increasingly important role in personal selling. Instead of being handed traditional sales pamphlets and brochures, consumers are now able to easily learn about products and services by searching the Internet before entering a store. Many consumers compare product features, prices, and quality online before even deciding which store to visit. Even after entering a store, consumers use their smartphones to browse competitors' websites while evaluating products. In addition to their own research, consumers are being bombarded with in-store messages, coupons, and sale information using beacon technology like Apple's iBeacon. Suffice to say, consumers are more educated about products and services today than they've ever been before.

This shift in technology has changed the dynamic of how information is obtained. If salespeople do not stay well informed about the products they're selling, consumers may enter the store knowing even more than they do. This reduces the ability of the salesperson to build trust and confidence.

Social media are increasingly being used to make sales. For social media to be successful in this capacity, however, customers and organizations alike must understand and be comfortable with the technology.[3] LinkedIn, Facebook, blogs, and Twitter are not only a place to make sales; they can also help establish a salesperson's expertise within a field. With more than 400 million members, LinkedIn positions itself as the world's largest professional network.[4] In addition to its networking function, LinkedIn offers sales solutions to help salespeople find prospects, qualify leads, and make product recommendations to decision makers.[5] LinkedIn also provides free advice on how to effectively sell using social media, including a six-step guide to aid salespeople in successful social selling.[6] LinkedIn also provides actionable social selling tips, making it a great resource for salespeople looking to harness the power of technology themselves.[7]

17-3 RELATIONSHIP SELLING

Historically, marketing theory and practice concerning personal selling have focused almost entirely on planned presentations to prospective customers for the sole purpose of making sales. Marketers were mostly concerned with making one-time sales and then moving on to the next prospect.

Traditional Personal Selling	Relationship or Consultative Selling
Sell products (goods and services)	Sell advice, assistance, and counsel
Focus on closing sales	Focus on improving the customer's bottom line
Limited sales planning	Consider sales planning as top priority
Spend most contact time telling customers about product	Spend most contact time attempting to build a problem-solving environment with the customer
Conduct "product-specific" needs assessment	Conduct discovery in the full scope of the customer's operations
"Lone wolf" approach to the account	Team approach to the account
Proposals and presentations based on pricing and product features	Proposals and presentations based on profit impact and strategic benefits to the customer
Sales follow-up is short term, focused on product delivery	Sales follow-up is long term, focused on long-term relationship enhancement

Source: Robert M. Peterson, Patrick, L. Schul, and George H. Lucas Jr., "Consultative Selling: Walking the Walk in the New Selling Environment, "*National Conference on Sales Management Proceedings*, March 1996; and Ari Walker, *7 Ways to Stop "Selling" and Start Building Relationships*, http://marketing.about.com/od/salestraining/a/stopselling .htm (accessed March 2015).

Jack Frog/Shutterstock.com

Technology is leading the way in selling in all forms of business.

Traditional personal selling methods attempted to persuade the buyer to accept a point of view or convince the buyer to take some action. Frequently, the objectives of the salesperson were at the expense of the buyer, creating a win–lose outcome. Although this type of sales approach has not disappeared entirely, it is being used less and less often by professional salespeople.

By contrast, modern views of personal selling emphasize the relationship that develops between a salesperson and a buyer. **Relationship selling**, or **consultative selling**, is a multistage process that emphasizes personalization, win–win outcomes, and empathy as key ingredients in identifying prospects and developing them as long-term, satisfied customers. The focus, therefore, is on building mutual trust between the buyer and seller through the delivery of long-term, value-added benefits that are anticipated by the buyer.

Relationship or consultative salespeople, therefore, become consultants, partners, and problem solvers for their customers. They strive to build long-term relationships with key accounts by developing trust over time. The emphasis shifts from a one-time sale to a long-term relationship in which the salesperson works with the customer to develop solutions for enhancing the customer's bottom line. The end result of relationship selling tends to be loyal customers who purchase from the company time after time, often with an increased share-of-purchase. A relationship selling strategy focused on retaining customers is often less expensive to a company than having to constantly prospect for and sell to new customers. Relationship selling provides many advantages over traditional selling in the consumer goods market. Still, relationship selling is more often used in selling situations for industrial-type goods, such as heavy machinery and computer systems, and services, such as airlines and insurance, than in selling situations for consumer goods. Exhibit 17.2 lists the key differences between traditional personal selling and relationship or consultative selling.

relationship selling (consultative selling) a sales practice that involves building, maintaining, and enhancing interactions with customers in order to develop long-term satisfaction through mutually beneficial partnerships

STEPS IN THE SELLING PROCESS

Completing a sale requires multiple steps. The **sales process**, or **sales cycle**, is simply the set of steps a salesperson goes through to sell a particular product or service. The sales process can be unique for each product or service offered. The actual sales process depends on the features of the product or service, characteristics of customer segments, and internal processes in place within the firm (such as how leads are gathered).

Some sales take only a few minutes to complete, but others may take much longer. Sales of technical products (like a Boeing or Airbus airplane) and customized goods and services typically take many months, perhaps even years, to complete. On the other end of the spectrum, sales of less technical products (like stationery) are generally more routine and often take less than a day to complete. Whether a salesperson spends a few minutes or a few years on a sale, there are seven basic steps in the personal selling process:

1. Generating leads
2. Qualifying leads
3. Approaching the customer and probing needs
4. Developing and proposing solutions
5. Handling objections
6. Closing the sale
7. Following up

Like other forms of promotion, the steps of selling follow the AIDA concept discussed in Chapter 16. Once a salesperson has located and qualified a prospect with the authority to buy, he or she tries to get the prospect's attention. A thorough needs assessment turned into an effective sales proposal and presentation should generate interest. After developing the customer's initial desire (preferably during the presentation of the sales proposal), the salesperson seeks action in the close by trying to get an agreement to buy. Follow-up after the sale, the final step in the selling process, not only lowers cognitive dissonance (refer to Chapter 6) but also may open up opportunities for repeat business, cross-sales of related products and services, and new customer referrals.

Traditional selling and relationship selling follow the same basic steps. They differ in the relative importance placed on key steps in the process. Traditional selling efforts are transaction oriented, focusing on generating as many leads as possible, making as many presentations as possible, and closing as many sales as possible. Minimal effort is placed on asking questions to identify customer needs and wants or matching these needs and wants to the benefits of the product or service. Often, traditional selling efforts allow little time for following up and ensuring that customers are satisfied with the products or services they received. Again, these types of sales generally generate lower levels of customer satisfaction and can result in more win-lose transactions for salespeople.

By contrast, salespeople practicing relationship selling emphasize a long-term investment in the time and effort needed to uncover each customer's specific needs and wants and meet them with the product or service offering. By doing their homework up front, salespeople often create the conditions necessary for a relatively straightforward close. In general, customers are more satisfied, engage in more repeat business, and provide higher shares-of-purchase over longer periods of time with relationship salespeople. In the following sections, we will examine each step of the personal selling process.

17-4a Step 1: Generating Leads

Initial groundwork must precede communication between the potential buyer and the salesperson. **Lead generation**, or **prospecting**, is the identification of those firms and people most likely to buy the seller's offerings. These firms or people become "sales leads" or "prospects."

Sales leads can be obtained in many different ways, most notably through advertising, trade shows and conventions, social media, webinars, or direct mail and telemarketing programs. Favorable publicity also helps to create leads. Company records of past client purchases

sales process (sales cycle) the set of steps a salesperson goes through in a particular organization to sell a particular product or service

lead generation (prospecting) identification of those firms and people most likely to buy the seller's offerings

urbanbuzz/Shutterstock.com

are another excellent source of leads. Many sales professionals are also securing valuable leads from their firm's website.

A basic unsophisticated method of lead generation is done through **cold calling**—a form of lead generation in which the salesperson approaches potential buyers without any prior knowledge of the prospects' needs or financial status. Although cold calling is still used in generating leads, many sales managers have realized the inefficiencies of having their top salespeople use their valuable selling time searching for the proverbial "needle in a haystack." Passing the job of cold calling to a lower-cost employee, typically an internal sales support person, allows salespeople to spend more time and use their relationship-building skills on prospects who have already been identified.

Another way to gather a lead is through a **referral**—a recommendation from a customer or business associate. The advantages of referrals over other forms of prospecting are highly qualified leads, higher closing rates, larger initial transactions, and shorter sales cycles. Referrals are often as much as ten times more productive in generating sales than are cold calls. Unfortunately, although many clients are willing to give referrals, most salespeople do not ask for them. Effective sales training can help to overcome this reluctance to ask for referrals. To increase the number of referrals, some companies even pay or send small gifts to customers or suppliers that provide referrals. Generating referrals is one area that social media and technology can usually make much more efficient.

Salespeople should build strong networks to help generate leads. **Networking** is using friends, business contacts, coworkers, acquaintances, and fellow members in professional and civic organizations to identify potential clients. Indeed, a number of national networking clubs have been started for the sole purpose of generating leads and providing valuable business advice. Increasingly, sales professionals are also using online networking sites like LinkedIn to connect with targeted leads and clients around the world, 24 hours a day.

17-4b Step 2: Qualifying Leads

When a prospect shows interest in learning more about a product, the salesperson has the opportunity to follow up, or qualify, the lead. Typically, unqualified prospects give vague or incomplete answers to a salesperson's specific questions, try to evade questions on budgets, and request changes in standard procedures like prices and terms of sale. In contrast, qualified leads are real prospects who answer questions, value the salesperson's time, and are realistic about money and when they are prepared to buy.

Lead qualification involves determining whether the prospect has three things:

1. **A recognized need:** The most basic criterion for determining whether someone is a prospect for a product is a need that is not being satisfied. The salesperson should first consider prospects who are aware of a need but should not disregard prospects who have not yet recognized that they have one. With a little more information about the product, they may decide they do have a need for it. Preliminary questioning can often provide the salesperson with enough information to determine whether there is a need.

2. **Buying power:** Buying power involves both authority to make the purchase decision and access to funds to pay for it. To avoid wasting time and money, the salesperson needs to identify the purchasing authority and his or her ability to pay before making a presentation. Organizational charts and information about a firm's credit standing can provide valuable clues.

3. **Receptivity and accessibility:** The prospect must be willing to see the salesperson and be accessible to the salesperson. Some prospects simply refuse to see salespeople. Others, because of their stature in their organization, will see only a salesperson or sales manager with similar stature.

Often the task of lead qualification is handled by a telemarketing group or a sales support person who prequalifies the lead for the salesperson. Prequalification systems free sales representatives from the time-consuming task of following up on leads to determine need, buying power and receptiveness. Prequalification systems may even set up initial appointments with the prospect for the salesperson. The result is more time for the sales force to spend in front of interested customers.

Companies are increasingly using their websites and other software to qualify leads. When qualifying leads online,

cold calling a form of lead generation in which the salesperson approaches potential buyers without any prior knowledge of the prospects' needs or financial status

referral a recommendation to a salesperson from a customer or business associate

networking a process of finding out about potential clients from friends, business contacts, coworkers, acquaintances, and fellow members in professional and civic organizations

lead qualification determination of a sales prospect's (1) recognized need, (2) buying power, and (3) receptivity and accessibility

companies want visitors to register, indicate the products and services they are interested in, and provide information on their time frames and resources. Leads from the Internet can then be prioritized (those indicating short time frames, for instance, are given a higher priority) and then transferred to salespeople. Enticing visitors to register also enables companies to customize future electronic interactions.

Personally visiting unqualified prospects wastes valuable salesperson time and company resources. Many leads often go unanswered because salespeople are given no indication as to how qualified the leads are in terms of interest and ability to purchase. Inside salespeople and sales support staff assess leads to maximize successful meetings, while CRM systems provide resources to increase lead follow-up rates. Still, salespeople only follow up on 10 to 15 percent of leads.

17-4c Step 3: Approaching the Customer and Probing Needs

Before approaching customers, the salesperson should learn as much as possible about the prospect's organization and its buyers. This process, called the **preapproach**, describes the "homework" that must be done by the salesperson before contacting the prospect. This may include visiting company website, consulting standard reference sources such as Moody's, Standard & Poor's, or Dun & Bradstreet, or contacting acquaintances or others who may have information about the prospect. Reading the prospect's social media sites (following the company's Twitter feed and reading its Facebook page, for example) is a great way to get to know the company culture, become acquainted with customer needs, and learn more about daily activities.[8] Another preapproach task is to determine whether the actual approach should be a personal visit, a phone call, a letter, or some other form of communication. Note that the preapproach applies to most business-to-business sales and outside consumer sales, but it is usually not possible when consumers approach salespeople in the retail store environment.

During the sales approach, the salesperson either talks to the prospect or secures an appointment to probe the prospect further about his or her needs. Experts on relationship selling suggest that salespeople should begin developing mutual trust with their prospect during the approach. Salespeople must sell themselves before they can sell the product. Small talk that projects sincerity and some suggestion of friendship is encouraged to build rapport with the prospect, but remarks that could be construed as insincere should be avoided.

The salesperson's ultimate goal during the approach is to conduct a **needs assessment** to find out as much as possible about the prospect's situation. The salesperson should be determining how to maximize the fit between what he or she can offer and what the prospective customer wants. As part of the needs assessment, the consultative salesperson must know everything there is to know about the following:

- **The product or service:** Product knowledge is the cornerstone for conducting a successful needs analysis. The consultative salesperson must be an expert on his or her product or service, including technical specifications, features and benefits, pricing and billing procedures, warranty and service support, performance comparisons with the competition, other customers' experiences with the product, and current advertising and promotional campaign messages. For example, a salesperson who is attempting to sell a Canon copier to a doctor's office should be very knowledgeable about Canon's selection of copiers, their attributes, capabilities, technological specifications, and postpurchase servicing.

- **Customers and their needs:** The salesperson should know more about customers than he knows about himself. That's the secret to relationship and consultative selling, where the salesperson acts not only as a supplier of products and services but also as a trusted consultant and adviser. The professional salesperson brings each client business-building ideas and solutions to problems. For example, if the Canon salesperson is asking the "right" questions, then he or she should be able to identify copy-related areas where the doctor's office is losing or wasting money. Rather than just selling a copier, the Canon salesperson can act as a consultant on how the doctor's office can save money and time.

- **The competition:** The salesperson must know as much about the competitor's company and products as he or she knows about his or her own company. Competitive intelligence includes many factors: who the competitors are and what is known about them, how their products and services compare, advantages and disadvantages, and strengths and weaknesses. For example, if the competitor's Xerox copy machine is less expensive than the Canon copier, the doctor's

preapproach a process that describes the "homework" that must be done by a salesperson before he or she contacts a prospect

needs assessment a determination of the customer's specific needs and wants and the range of options the customer has for satisfying them

office may be leaning toward purchasing the Xerox. But if the Canon salesperson can point out that the cost of long-term maintenance and toner cartridges is lower for the Canon copier, offsetting its higher initial cost, the salesperson may be able to persuade the doctor's office to purchase the Canon copier.

- **The industry:** Knowing the industry requires active research by the salesperson. This means attending industry and trade association meetings, reading articles published in industry and trade journals, keeping track of legislation and regulation that affect the industry, being aware of product alternatives and innovations from domestic and foreign competition, and having a feel for economic and financial conditions that may affect the industry. It is also important to be aware of economic downturns, as businesses may be looking for less expensive financing options.

Creating a *customer profile* during the approach helps salespeople optimize their time and resources. This profile is then used to help develop an intelligent analysis of the prospect's needs in preparation for the next step, developing and proposing solutions. Customer profile information is typically stored and manipulated using sales force automation software packages designed for use on laptop computers, smartphones, or tablets. Sales force automation software provides sales reps with a computerized and efficient method of collecting customer information for use during the entire

The Real Deal

Firms that sell complex products generally offer the most extensive training programs. Once applicants are hired at General Electric (GE), they enter one of the many "rotational" training programs depending on their interest and major. For example, the Sales and Marketing Commercial Leadership Program (CLP) is geared toward developing skills needed for a successful career at GE. The program ranges from one to two years, depending on which GE business area the employee selects, and includes several rotations between business headquarters and the field. On completing the program, the new employees are better prepared to sell GE products because of their high level of product knowledge and on-the-job experience interacting with customers.[9]

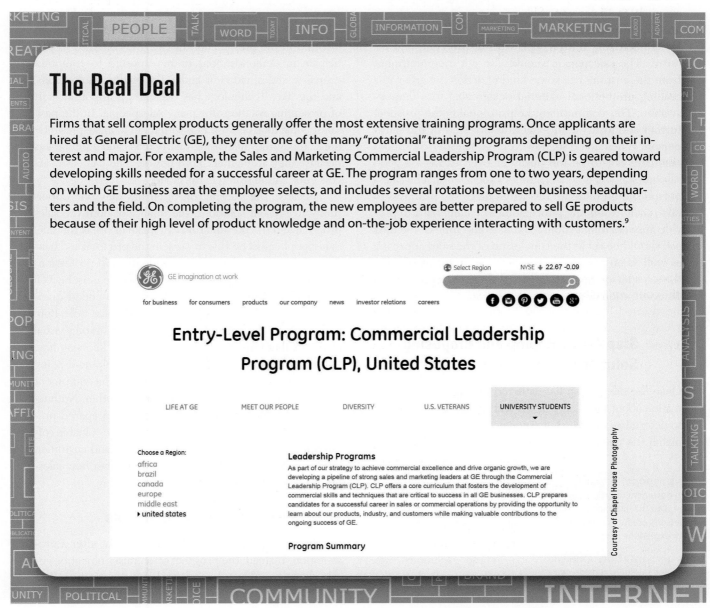

Courtesy of Chapel House Photography

sales process. Further, customer and sales data stored in a computer database can be easily shared among sales team members. The information can also be appended with industry statistics, sales or meeting notes, billing data, and other information that may be pertinent to the prospect or the prospect's company. The more salespeople know about their prospects, the better they can meet their needs.

A salesperson should wrap up the sales approach and need-probing mission by summarizing the prospect's need, problem, and interest. The salesperson should also get a commitment from the customer to some kind of action, whether it is reading promotional material or agreeing to a demonstration. This commitment helps to qualify the prospect further and justify additional time invested by the salesperson. When doing so, however, the salesperson should take care not to be too pushy or overbearing—a good salesperson will read a customer's social cues. The salesperson should reiterate the action he or she promises to take, such as sending information or calling back to provide answers to questions. The date and time of the next call should be set at the conclusion of the sales approach as well as an agenda for the next call in terms of what the salesperson hopes to accomplish, such as providing a demonstration or presenting a solution.

A sales presentation is a formal meeting in which a salesperson has an opportunity to present a sales proposal.

antoniodiaz/Shutterstock.com

17-4d Step 4: Developing and Proposing Solutions

Once the salesperson has gathered the appropriate information about the client's needs and wants, the next step is to determine whether her company's products or services match the needs of the prospective customer. The salesperson then develops a solution, or possibly several solutions, in which the salesperson's product or service solves the client's problems or meets a specific need.

These solutions are typically presented to the client in the form of a sales

sales proposal a formal written document or professional presentation that outlines how the salesperson's product or service will meet or exceed the prospect's needs

sales presentation a meeting in which the salesperson presents a sales proposal to a prospective buyer

proposal presented at a sales presentation. A **sales proposal** is a written document or professional presentation that outlines how the company's product or service will meet or exceed the client's needs. The **sales presentation** is the formal meeting in which the salesperson has the opportunity to present the sales proposal. The presentation should be explicitly tied to the prospect's expressed needs. Further, the prospect should be involved in the presentation by being encouraged to participate in demonstrations or by exposure to computer exercises, slides, video or audio, flip charts, photographs, and the like. Technology has become an important part of presenting solutions for many salespeople. In the past, salespeople took desktop PCs with them to make presentations. Today, they increasingly carry iPads and other tablets because they are lighter, more flexible, and can easily access information stored in the cloud.

Because the salesperson often has only one opportunity to present solutions, the quality of both the sales proposal and the presentation can make or break the sale. Salespeople must be able to present the proposal and handle any customer objections confidently and professionally. For a powerful presentation, salespeople must be well prepared, use direct eye contact, ask open-ended questions, be poised, use hand gestures and voice inflection, and focus on the customer's needs. Incorporating visual elements that impart valuable information, knowing how to operate the audio/visual or computer equipment being used for the presentation, and making sure the equipment works will make the presentation flow smoother. Nothing loses customers faster than a boring or ill-prepared presenter, and equipment mishaps can consume valuable (often limited) time for both the salesperson and customer. Often, customers are more likely to remember how salespeople present themselves than what they say.

17-4e Step 5: Handling Objections

Rarely does a prospect say "I'll buy it" right after a presentation. Instead, the prospect often raises objections or asks questions about the proposal and the product. The potential buyer may insist that the price is too high or that the good or service will not satisfy the present need.

One of the first lessons every salesperson learns is that objections to the product should not be taken personally as confrontations or insults. A good salesperson considers objections a legitimate part of the purchase decision. To handle objections effectively, the salesperson should anticipate specific objections (such as concerns about price), fully investigate the objection with the customer, be aware of what the competition is offering, and, above all, stay calm.

Often salespeople can use objections to close the sale. The customer may try to pit suppliers against each other to drive down the price, so the salesperson should be prepared to point out weaknesses in the competitor's offer and stand by the quality and value of his or her own proposal.

Closing and negotiating require courage and skill. It is often a team effort when companies complete business deals.

17-4f Step 6: Closing the Sale

At the end of the presentation, the salesperson should ask the customer how he or she would like to proceed. If the customer exhibits signs that he or she is ready to purchase, all questions have been answered, and objections have been met, then the salesperson can try to close the sale. Customers often give signals during or after the presentation that they are ready to buy or are not interested. Examples include changes in facial expressions, gestures, and questions asked. The salesperson should look for these signals and respond appropriately.

Closing requires courage and skill. A salesperson should keep an open mind when asking for the sale and be prepared for both a positive and a negative outcome.[10] Often, a salesperson will be told "no" flat out. In such a case, the salesperson must be resilient and must be able to handle this type of rejection gracefully and effectively. The typical salesperson makes hundreds—potentially even thousands—of sales calls every year. Many of these are repeat calls to the same group of clients in an attempt to make a single sale. Building and developing a good relationship with the customer is very important. Often, if the salesperson has developed a strong relationship with the customer, only minimal efforts are needed to close a sale (increasing the salesperson's closure rate).

Negotiation often plays a key role in the closing of the sale. **Negotiation** is the process during which both the salesperson and the prospect offer special concessions in an attempt to arrive at a sales agreement. For example, the salesperson may offer a price cut, free installation, or a trial order. Effective negotiators, however, avoid using price as a negotiation tool and are able to show increased value in their products or services. Because companies spend millions on advertising and product development to create value, when salespeople give in to price negotiations too quickly, it decreases the value of the product. Salespeople should also be prepared to ask for trade-offs and try to avoid giving unilateral concessions. Moreover, if the customer asks for a 5 percent discount, the salesperson should ask for something in return, such as higher volume or more flexibility in delivery schedules.

More and more U.S. companies are expanding their marketing and selling efforts into global markets. Salespeople selling in foreign markets should tailor their presentations and closing styles to each market. Different personalities and skills will be successful in some countries and absolute failures in others. For instance, if a salesperson is an excellent closer and always focuses on the next sale, doing business in Latin America might be difficult because customers there prefer to take a long time building a personal relationship with their suppliers. Similarly, personal space and physical contact are treated differently in different cultures. In many European and South American cultures, it is customary to kiss a business associate on both cheeks instead of shaking hands.[11]

17-4g Step 7: Following Up

A salesperson's responsibilities do not end with making the sale and placing the order. One of the most important aspects of the job is

negotiation the process during which both the salesperson and the prospect offer special concessions in an attempt to arrive at a sales agreement

follow-up—the final step in the selling process, in which the salesperson must ensure delivery schedules are met, goods or services perform as promised, and buyers' employees are properly trained to use the products.

In the traditional sales approach, follow-up with the customer is generally limited to successful product delivery and performance. A basic goal of relationship selling is to motivate customers to come back again and again by developing and nurturing long-term relationships. Exhibit 17.3 depicts the time involved in the sales process and how those elements relate to the traditional and relationship selling approaches.

Most businesses depend on repeat sales, and repeat sales depend on thorough and continued follow-up by the salesperson. When customers feel abandoned, cognitive dissonance arises and repeat sales decline. Today, this issue is more pertinent than ever because customers are far less loyal to brands and vendors. Buyers are more inclined to look for the best deal, especially when they experience poor postsale follow-up. Automated e-mail follow-up marketing—a combination of sales automation and Internet technology—is one tool that some marketers are using in an effort to enhance customer satisfaction and bring in more business. After the initial contact with a prospect, a software program automatically sends a series of personalized e-mail messages over a period of time. Another approach is to use contact software like GoToMeeting, which facilitates live face-to-face exchanges via video conferencing and direct access to cloud-based datacenters.

17-4h The Impact of Technology on Personal Selling

Will the increasingly sophisticated technology now available at marketers' fingertips eliminate the need for salespeople? Experts agree that a relationship between the salesperson and customer will always be necessary. Technology, however, can certainly help to improve that relationship. Cell phones, laptops, text messaging,

follow-up the final step of the selling process, in which the salesperson ensures delivery schedules are met, goods or services perform as promised, and the buyers' employees are properly trained to use the products

EXHIBIT 17.3 RELATIVE AMOUNT OF TIME SPENT IN THE KEY STEPS OF THE SELLING PROCESS

Source: Data from Robert M. Peterson, Patrick L. Schul, and George H. Lucas Jr., "Consultative Selling: Walking the Walk in the New Selling Environment," *National Conference on Sales Management Proceedings*, March 1996; and Mark Ellwood, *How Sales Reps Spend Their Time*, http://paceproductivity.com/files/How_Sales_Reps_Spend_Their_Time.pdf (accessed March 2015).

e-mail, and electronic organizers allow salespeople to be more accessible to both clients and the company. Moreover, the Internet provides salespeople with vast resources of information on clients, competitors, and the industry. This is not always advantageous, however, as some buyers now expect salespeople to be reachable 24 hours a day, seven days a week.

E-business—buying, selling, marketing, collaborating with partners, and servicing customers electronically using the Internet—has had a significant impact on personal selling. Virtually all large companies and most medium and small companies are involved in e-commerce and consider it to be necessary to compete in today's marketplace. For customers, the Web has become a powerful tool, providing accurate and up-to-date information on products, pricing, and order status. The Internet also facilitates cost-effective processing of orders and service requests. Although on the surface the Internet might appear to be a threat to the job security of salespeople, the Web is actually freeing sales reps from tedious administrative tasks like shipping catalogs, placing routine orders, or tracking orders. This leaves them more time to focus on the needs of their clients.

17-5 SALES MANAGEMENT

There is an old adage in business that nothing happens until a sale is made. Without sales, there is no need for accountants, production workers, or even a company president. Sales provide the fuel that keeps the corporate engines humming. Companies such as Cisco Systems, International Paper, Johnson Controls, and thousands of other manufacturers would cease to exist without successful salespeople. Even companies such as Procter & Gamble (P&G) and Kraft Foods, which mainly sell consumer goods and use extensive advertising campaigns, still rely on salespeople to move products through the channel of distribution. Thus, sales management must be one of every firm's most critical specialties. Effective sales management stems from a success-oriented sales force that accomplishes its mission economically and efficiently. Poor sales management can lead to unmet sales and profit objectives or even to the downfall of the corporation.

Just as selling is a personal relationship, so is sales management. Although the sales manager's basic job is to maximize sales at a reasonable cost while also maximizing profits, he or she also has many other important responsibilities and decisions:

1. Defining sales goals and the sales process
2. Determining the sales force structure
3. Recruiting and training the sales force
4. Compensating and motivating the sales force
5. Evaluating the sales force

Part of sales management is defining sales goals for the sales force.

iStockphoto.com/Hocus-focus

17-5a Defining Sales Goals and the Sales Process

Effective sales management begins with a determination of sales goals. Without goals to achieve, salesperson performance would be mediocre at best, and the company would likely fail. Like any marketing objective, sales goals should be stated in clear, precise, and measurable terms and should always specify a time frame for their completion. Overall sales force goals are usually stated in terms of desired dollar sales volume, market share, and/or profit level. For example, a life insurance company may have a goal to sell $50 million in life insurance policies annually, to attain a 12 percent market share, and/or to achieve $4 million in profits. Individual salespeople are also assigned goals in the form of quotas. A **quota** is a statement of the salesperson's sales goals, usually based on sales volume alone, but sometimes including other focuses such as key accounts (those with greatest potential), new account generation, volume of repeat sales, profit margin, and specific product mixes sold.

17-5b Determining the Sales Force Structure

Because personal selling is so costly, no sales department can afford to be disorganized. Proper design helps the sales manager organize and delegate sales duties and provide direction for salespeople. Sales departments are most often organized by geographic regions, product lines, marketing functions performed (such as account development or account maintenance), markets, industries, individual clients, or accounts. For example, the sales force for Hewlett-Packard (HP) could be organized into sales territories covering New England, the Midwest, the South, and the West Coast or into distinct groups selling different product lines. HP salespeople might also be assigned to specific industries or markets (such as the telecommunications industry), or to key clients (such as AT&T, Virgin Mobile, and Verizon).

Market or industry-based structures and key account structures are gaining popularity in today's competitive selling environment, especially with the emphasis on relationship selling. Being familiar with one industry or market allows sales reps to become experts in their fields and thereby offer better solutions and service. Further, by organizing the sales force around specific customers, many companies hope to improve customer service, encourage collaboration with other arms of the company, and unite salespeople in customer-focused sales teams.

> **quota** a statement of the salesperson's sales goals, usually based on sales volume

17-5c Recruiting and Training the Sales Force

Sales force recruitment should be based on an accurate, detailed description of the sales task as defined by the sales manager. For example, GE uses its website to provide prospective salespeople with explanations of different career entry paths and video accounts of what it is like to have a career at GE. Aside from the usual characteristics such as level of experience or education, what traits should sales managers look for in applicants?

- **Ego strength:** Great salespeople should have a strong, healthy self-esteem and the ability to bounce back from rejection.

- **Sense of urgency and competitiveness:** These traits push their sales to completion, as well as help them persuade people.

- **Assertiveness:** Effective salespeople have the ability to be firm in one-to-one negotiations, to lead the sales process, and to get their point across confidently without being overbearing or aggressive.

- **Sociable:** Wanting to interact with others is a necessary trait for great salespeople.

- **Risk takers:** Great salespeople are willing to put themselves in less-than-assured situations, and in doing so, often are able to close unlikely sales.

- **Capable of understanding complex concepts and ideas:** Quick thinking and comprehension allow salespeople to quickly grasp and sell new products or enter new sales areas.

- **Creativity:** Great salespeople develop client solutions in creative ways.

- **Empathetic:** Empathy—the ability to place oneself in someone else's shoes—enables salespeople to understand the client.

In addition to these traits, almost all successful salespeople say their sales style is relationship oriented rather than transaction oriented.[12]

After the sales recruit has been hired and given a brief orientation, initial training begins. A new salesperson generally receives instruction in company policies and practices, selling techniques, product knowledge, industry and customer characteristics, and nonselling duties such as filling out sales and market information reports and using a sales automation computer program. Many companies provide new salespeople with sales coaches, who provide individualized one-on-one feedback in an experiential-based learning environment. This way, the new hire can acquire additional and more nuanced skills for long-term success.[13] Continuous training then keeps salespeople up-to-date on changes in products and services, technology, the competitive landscape, and sales techniques, among other issues. Continuous training can occur during sales meetings, annual meetings, or during the course of everyday business.

Training can take place in a classroom environment, in the field, or using online modules. When conducting job training in the field via a live sales call, the trainer should be a more experienced salesperson or sales manager. This type of training provides real world experience for the trainee, but may reduce the effectiveness of the call because it often entails a reduced selling time. Another form of training involves the trainee working in inside sales, primarily phone-based sales, for an extended period of time before being given an outside territory to cover. This enables the trainee to develop selling skills with less-important and/or less-established accounts before facing the challenges of outside sales.

17-5d Compensating and Motivating the Sales Force

Compensation planning is one of the sales manager's toughest jobs. Only good planning will ensure that compensation attracts, motivates, and retains good salespeople. Generally, companies and industries with lower levels of compensation suffer higher turnover rates. This increases costs (including training and recruiting costs), decreases sales effectiveness, and harms relationship management. Therefore, compensation needs to be competitive enough to attract and motivate the best salespeople. Firms sometimes take profit into account when developing their compensation plans. Instead of paying salespeople on overall volume, they pay according to the profitability achieved from selling each product.

Still other companies tie a part of the salesperson's total compensation to customer satisfaction. As the emphasis on relationship selling increases, many sales managers believe that a portion of a salesperson's compensation should be tied to a client's satisfaction. To determine this, sales managers can survey clients on a salesperson's ability to create realistic expectations and his or her responsiveness to customer needs. At PeopleSoft, a division of Oracle, structure, culture, and strategies are all built around customer satisfaction. Sales force compensation is tied to both sales quotas and a satisfaction metric that enables clients to voice their opinions on the services provided.

Although a compensation-based plan motivates a salesperson to sell, sometimes it is not enough to produce the volume of sales or the profit margin required by sales management. Sales managers therefore often offer rewards or incentives, such as recognition at ceremonies, plaques, and/or monetary-based rewards such as vacations, merchandise, pay raises, and cash bonuses. Cash awards are the most popular sales incentive and are used by virtually all companies. Mary Kay Cosmetics offers a unique type of incentive whereby salespeople can earn the use of different types of vehicles—from a lowly Ford Fiesta all the way up to the coveted pink Mary Kay Cadillac. To qualify for these vehicles, salespeople must reach certain sales quotas.[14]

Recognition and rewards may help increase overall sales volume, add new accounts, improve morale and goodwill, move slow items, and bolster slow sales. They can also be used to achieve short- and long-term objectives such as reducing overstocked inventory and meeting a monthly or quarterly sales goal. In motivating their sales force, however, sales managers must be careful not to encourage unethical behavior.

17-5e Evaluating the Sales Force

The final task of sales managers is evaluating the effectiveness and performance of the sales force. To evaluate the sales force, the sales manager needs feedback—that is, regular information from salespeople. Typical performance measures include sales volume, contribution-to-profit, calls per order, sales or profits per call, or percentage of calls achieving specific goals such as sales of products that the firm is heavily promoting.

Performance information helps the sales manager monitor a salesperson's progress through the sales cycle and pinpoint where breakdowns might be occurring. For example, by learning the number of prospects an individual salesperson has in each step of the sales cycle process and determining where prospects are falling out of the sales cycle, a manager can determine how effective a salesperson might be at lead generation, needs assessment, proposal generation, presenting, closing, and follow-up stages. This information can then tell a manager which sales skills might need to be reassessed or retrained. For example, if a sales manager notices that a sales rep seems to be letting too many prospects slip away after presenting proposals, it might mean he or she needs help with developing proposals, handling objections, or closing sales.

17-6 CUSTOMER RELATIONSHIP MANAGEMENT AND THE SALES PROCESS

As we have discussed throughout the text, customer relationship management (CRM) is the ultimate goal of a new trend in marketing that focuses on understanding customers as individuals instead of as part of a group. To do so, marketers are making their communications more customer specific using the CRM cycle, covered in Chapter 8, and by developing relationships with their customers through touch points and data mining. CRM was initially popularized as one-to-one marketing. But CRM is a much broader approach to understanding and serving customer needs than is one-to-one marketing.

Throughout the text, our discussion of a CRM system has assumed two key points. First, customers take center stage in any organization. Second, the business must manage the customer relationship across all points of customer contact throughout the entire organization. By identifying customer relationships, understanding the customer base, and capturing customer data, marketers and salespeople can leverage the information not only to develop deeper relationships but also to close more sales with loyal customers in a more efficient manner.

17-6a Identify Customer Relationships

Companies that have CRM systems follow a customer-centric focus or model. **Customer-centric** is an internal management philosophy similar to the marketing concept discussed in Chapter 1. Under this philosophy, the company customizes its product and service offering based on data generated through interactions between the customer and the company. This philosophy transcends all functional areas of the business, producing an internal system where all of the company's decisions and actions are a direct result of customer information.

Each unit of a business typically has its own way of recording what it learns, and perhaps even has its own customer information system. The departments' different interests make it difficult to pull all of the customer information together in one place using a common format. To

> **customer-centric** a philosophy under which the company customizes its product and service offerings based on data generated through interactions between the customer and the company

overcome this problem, companies using CRM rely on knowledge management. **Knowledge management** is a process by which customer information is centralized and shared in order to enhance the relationship between customers and the organization. Information collected includes experiential observations, comments, customer actions, and qualitative facts about the customer.

As Chapter 1 explained, *empowerment* involves delegating authority to solve customers' problems. Usually, organizational representatives, salespeople for example, are able to make changes during interactions with customers through phone, fax, e-mail, social media, or face-to-face.

An **interaction** occurs when a customer and a company representative exchange information and develop learning relationships. With CRM, the customer—not the organization—defines the terms of the interaction, often by stating his or her preferences. The organization responds by designing products and services around customers' desired experiences. Social media have created numerous new ways for companies to interact with customers—see Chapter 18 for more on this topic.

The success of CRM—building lasting and profitable relationships—can be directly measured by the effectiveness of the interaction between the customer and the organization. In fact, what further differentiates CRM from other strategic initiatives is the organization's ability to establish and manage interactions with its current customer base. The more latitude (empowerment) a company gives its representatives, the more likely the interaction will conclude in a way that satisfies the customer.

| EXHIBIT 17.4 | CUSTOMER-CENTRIC APPROACH FOR MANAGING CUSTOMER INTERACTIONS |

customers, generate and manage knowledge about them, negotiate mutually satisfying commitments, and build long-term relationships.

Exhibit 17.4 illustrates the customer-centric approach for managing customer interactions. Following a customer-centric approach, an interaction can occur through different communication channels, such as a phone, the Internet, or a salesperson. Any activity or touch point a customer has with an organization, either directly or indirectly, constitutes an interaction.

Companies that effectively manage customer interactions recognize that data provided by customers affect a wide variety of **touch points**. In a CRM system, touch points are all areas of a business where customers have contact with the company and data might be gathered. Touch points might include: a customer registering for a particular service; a customer communicating with customer service for product information; a customer completing and returning the warranty information card for a product; or a customer talking with salespeople, delivery personnel, and product installers. Data gathered at these touch points, once interpreted, provide information that affects touch points inside the company. Interpreted information may be redirected to marketing research to develop profiles of extended warranty purchasers, to production to analyze recurring problems and repair components, to accounting to establish cost-control models for repair service calls, and to sales for better customer profiling and segmentation.

knowledge management the process by which customer information is centralized and shared in order to enhance the relationship between customers and the organization

interaction the point at which a customer and a company representative exchange information and develop learning relationships

touch points areas of a business where customers have contact with the company and data might be gathered

17-6b Understand Interactions of the Current Customer Base

The interaction between the customer and the organization is the foundation on which a CRM system is built. Only through effective interactions can organizations learn about the expectations of their

WEB-BASED INTERACTIONS Web-based interactions are an increasingly popular touch point for customers to communicate with companies on their own terms. Web users can evaluate and purchase products, make reservations, input preferential data, and provide customer feedback on services and products. Data from these web-based interactions are then captured, compiled, and used to segment customers, refine marketing efforts, develop new products, and deliver a degree of individual customization to improve customer relationships.

SOCIAL CRM As social media have become more popular, many companies have begun to use these media for "social CRM." ZDNet journalist Paul Greenberg recently named Lithium, Microsoft, Salesforce. com, Blackbaud, and SAP as companies to watch in the field of social CRM.[15] Essentially, social CRM takes the most successful aspects of traditional CRM, such as behavioral targeting, and expands them to include ways to engage customers through social media. This new

GET UNDER THE SKIN OF YOUR MAN.
TAKE OUR VALENTINE QUIZ.

MR. ACTION   MR. SENSITIVE

MR. SMOOTH   MR. EXTREME

FIND HIS PERFECT VALENTINE GIFT
Take our quiz to find the perfect products for your man
and for your chance to WIN A ROMANTIC BREAK!

Go to
facebook.com/LorealParisUK

L'ORÉAL
MEN EXPERT

EXPERT AT BEING A MAN

L'Oreal Paris/Advertising Archive

This advertisement for L'Oréal directs a highly segmented group of customers to its Facebook page, where the company will continue to engage them through social CRM.

paradigm includes a new customer recommendation value called the *net promoter score*. The net promoter score measures how much a customer influences the behavior of other customers through recommendations on social media. Its ultimate purpose is to gather all consumer interactions into a single database so that they can be analyzed and used to improve communication. Social CRM also enables marketers to focus more on the relationship aspect of CRM. For example, REI empowers customers to "carve your own adventure" through its YouTube channel. JetBlue uses Facebook and Twitter to provide advice and updates to travelers. To use social CRM effectively, companies must understand which sites customers use, whether they post opinions, and who the major influencers in the category are. They can then marry this information with behavioral data like purchases and purchase frequency.

POINT-OF-SALE INTERACTIONS Another touch point is through **point-of-sale interactions** in stores or at information kiosks. Many point-of-sale software programs enable customers to easily provide information about themselves without feeling violated. The information is then used for marketing and merchandising activities and to accurately identify the store's best customers and the types of products they buy. Data collected at point-of-sale interactions are also used to increase customer satisfaction through the development of in-store services and customer recognition promotions.

17-6c Capture Customer Data

Vast amounts of data can be obtained from the interactions between an organization and its customers. Therefore, in a CRM system, the issue is not how much data can be obtained, but rather what types of data should be acquired and how the data can effectively be used for relationship enhancement.

The traditional approach for acquiring data from customers is through channel interactions. Channel interactions include store visits, conversations with salespeople, interactions via the Web, traditional phone conversations, and wireless communications. In a CRM system, channel interactions are viewed as prime information sources based on the channel selected to initiate the interaction rather than on the data acquired. In some cases, companies use online chat to answer questions customers have about products they are looking for. For example, 24 Hour Fitness has an online chat window that opens when a potential customer begins

point-of-sale interactions
a touch point in stores or information kiosks that uses software to enable customers to easily provide information about themselves without feeling violated

to review the website. If the visitor remains on the site, the online chat window asks if he or she needs help finding something specific.

Interactions between the company and the customer facilitate the collection of large amounts of data. Companies can obtain not only simple contact information (name, address, phone number) but also data pertaining to the customer's current relationship with the organization—past purchase history, quantity and frequency of purchases, average amount spent on purchases, sensitivity to promotional activities, and so forth.

In this manner, a large amount of information can be captured from one individual customer across several touch points. Multiply this by the thousands of customers across all of the touch points within an organization, and the volume of data can rapidly become unmanageable for company personnel. The large volume of data resulting from a CRM initiative can be managed effectively only through technology. Once customer data are collected, the question of who owns those data becomes extremely salient. In its privacy statement, Toysmart.com declared that it would never sell information registered at its website—including children's names and birth dates—to a third party. When the company filed for bankruptcy protection, it said that the information it collected constituted a company asset that needed to be sold off to pay creditors. Despite the outrage at this announcement, many dot-coms closing their doors found they had little in the way of assets and followed Toysmart's lead.

17-6d **Leverage Customer Information**

Data mining can be used to identify the most profitable customers and prospects. Managers can then design tailored marketing strategies to best appeal to the identified segments. In CRM, this is commonly referred to as leveraging customer information to facilitate enhanced relationships with customers. Exhibit 17.5 shows some common CRM marketing database applications.

CAMPAIGN MANAGEMENT Through campaign management, all areas of the company participate in the development of programs targeted to customers. Campaign management involves monitoring and leveraging customer interactions to sell a company's products and to increase customer service. Campaigns are based directly

campaign management
developing product or service offerings customized for the appropriate customer segment and then pricing and communicating these offerings for the purpose of enhancing customer relationships

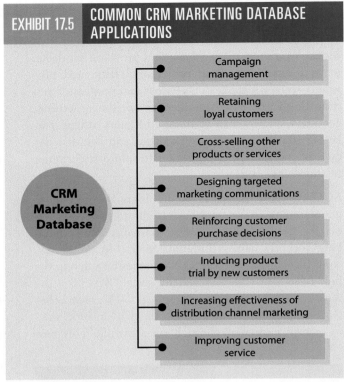

EXHIBIT 17.5 COMMON CRM MARKETING DATABASE APPLICATIONS

CRM Marketing Database
- Campaign management
- Retaining loyal customers
- Cross-selling other products or services
- Designing targeted marketing communications
- Reinforcing customer purchase decisions
- Inducing product trial by new customers
- Increasing effectiveness of distribution channel marketing
- Improving customer service

on data obtained from customers through various interactions. Campaign management includes monitoring the success of the communications based on customer reactions through sales, orders, callbacks to the company, and so on. If a campaign appears unsuccessful, it is evaluated and changed to better achieve the company's desired objective.

Campaign management involves developing customized product and service offerings for the appropriate customer segment, pricing these offerings attractively, and communicating these offers in a manner that enhances customer relationships. Customizing product and service offerings requires managing multiple interactions with customers, as well as giving priority to those products and services that are viewed as most desirable for a specifically designated customer. Even within a highly defined market segment, individual customer differences will emerge. Therefore, interactions among customers must focus on individual experiences, expectations, and desires.

RETAINING LOYAL CUSTOMERS If a company has identified its best customers, then it should make every effort to maintain and increase their loyalty. When a company retains an additional 5 percent of its customers each year, profits will increase by as much as 125 percent. What's more, improving customer retention by a mere 2 percent can decrease costs by as much as 10 percent.

Loyalty programs reward loyal customers for making multiple purchases. The objective is to build long-term, mutually beneficial relationships between a company and its key customers. More than 4,000 small- and medium-sized businesses across thirty-five states have teamed up with reward management firm Belly to develop unique rewards programs, such as getting to throw eggs at a food truck after a specified number of purchases or having the owner of your favorite bagel store sing to you after buying 100 bagels. The individualized rewards reflect each business's personality and (ideally) those of its customers, making the rewards programs highly motivating.[16] In addition to rewarding good customers, loyalty programs provide businesses with a wealth of information about their customers and shopping trends, which can be used to make future business decisions.

The process by which customers enroll in loyalty programs is easier than ever before. Key Ring, for example, enables users to enroll in numerous rewards programs without filling out hundreds of forms or carrying a wallet full of plastic reward cards. More than a mobile wallet for loyalty cards, Key Ring provides a total shopping solution, including access to exclusive deals from a number of retailers and brands.[17]

CROSS-SELLING OTHER PRODUCTS AND SERVICES

CRM provides many opportunities to cross-sell related products. Marketers can use the database to match product profiles and consumer profiles so that they can cross-sell customers products that match their demographic, lifestyle, or behavioral characteristics. The financial services industry uses cross-selling better than most other industries do. Cross-selling is a key part of Wells Fargo's strategy, for example, and is a large contributor to the company's success in the industry. After engaging with customers to determine their financial needs and aspirations, Wells Fargo reps work to determine how the company's wide range of products can synergize to meet or exceed those financial goals.[18]

Internet companies use product and customer profiling to reveal cross-selling opportunities while customers surf their sites. Past purchases, tracking programs, and the site a surfer is referred from give online marketers clues about the surfer's interests and what items to cross-sell. Amazon, for example, has used profiling to better meet customer needs for years. The company systematically compares individuals' shopping habits and online activities to other Amazon customers to make better tailored recommendations. Customers are also able to proactively rate products, review products, add products to wishlists, recommend products, and save products for a later purchase—all of which make for a more customized customer experience.[19]

DESIGNING TARGETED MARKETING COMMUNICATIONS Using transaction and purchase data, a database allows marketers to track customers' relationships to the company's products and services and modify the marketing message accordingly.

Customers can also be segmented into infrequent users, moderate users, and heavy users. A segmented communications strategy can then be developed based on which group the customer falls into. Communications to infrequent users might encourage repeat purchases through a direct incentive such as a limited-time price discount for ordering again. Online marketers for retailers like GNC and Newegg send out periodic e-mails with discounts to customers who made previous purchases. Communications to moderate users may use fewer incentives and more reinforcement of past purchase decisions. Communications to heavy users would be designed around loyalty and reinforcement of the purchase rather than around price promotions.

STUDY TOOLS 17

LOCATED AT BACK OF THE TEXTBOOK
☐ Rip Out Chapter Review Card

LOCATED AT WWW.CENGAGEBRAIN.COM
☐ Review Key Terms Flashcards and create your own
☐ Track your knowledge and understanding of key concepts in marketing
☐ Complete practice and graded quizzes to prepare for tests
☐ Complete interactive content within the MKTG Online experience
☐ View the chapter highlight boxes within the MKTG Online experience

18 | Social Media and Marketing

LEARNING OUTCOMES

After studying this chapter, you will be able to...

18-1 Describe social media, how they are used, and their relations to integrated marketing communications

18-2 Explain how to create a social media campaign

18-3 Evaluate the various methods of measurement for social media

18-4 Explain consumer behavior on social media

18-5 Describe the social media tools in a marketer's toolbox and how they are useful

18-6 Describe the impact of mobile technology on social media

18-7 Understand the aspects of developing a social media plan

After finishing this chapter go to **PAGE 337** for **STUDY TOOLS**

18-1 WHAT ARE SOCIAL MEDIA?

The most exciting thing to happen to marketing and promotion in recent years is the increasing use of online technology to promote brands, particularly using social media. Social media have changed the way that marketers can communicate with their brands—from mass messages to intimate conversations. As marketing moves into social media, marketers must remember that for most people, social media are meant to be a social experience, not a marketing experience. In fact, the term *social media* means different things to different people, though most people think it refers to digital technology. The American Bar Association uses a definition developed by social media expert Brian Solis. According to Solis, **social media** is "any tool or service that uses the Internet to facilitate conversations."[1] However, social media can also be defined relative to traditional advertising like television and magazines: whereas traditional marketing media offer a mass media method of interacting with consumers, social media offer more one-to-one ways to meet consumers.

social media any tool or service that uses the Internet to facilitate conversations

Social media have several implications for marketers and the ways that they interact with their customers. First, marketers must realize that they often do not control the content on social media sites. Consumers are sharing their thoughts, wishes, and experiences about brands with the world through social media. Because of this level of visibility and discussion, marketers must realize that having a great ad campaign is not enough—the product or service must be great, too.

Second, the ability to share experiences quickly and with such large numbers of people amplifies the impact of word of mouth in ways that can affect a company's bottom line. Singer Katy Perry has more than 85 million Twitter followers, and as such, has a very large reach.[2] YouTube is the company with the largest Twitter presence (more than 61 million followers), and Coca-Cola is the most liked brand on Facebook with more than 97 million fans.[3] The total reach of these brands is difficult to quantify, but it is unquestionably massive. Many companies use mascots to drive their marketing messages on social media. For example, Progressive auto insurance's perky saleswoman Flo has almost 5.5 million Facebook fans that read her posts about Progressive products. According to the company,

> "Interaction and engagement [on social media] is something that you don't necessarily see in traditional media. That's why we [at Ford] continue to accelerate our digital advertising investment to more than 25% of our media dollars."[4]
>
> —JIM FARLEY, FORD GLOBAL SALES AND MARKETING VICE PRESIDENT

since Flo began appearing in ads, the company has seen yearly gains in the number of policies taken out.[5]

Third, social media allow marketers to listen. Domino's Pizza listened to what was being posted about

Due to her more than 85 million Twitter followers, singer Katy Perry has a very large reach on social media.

conversations. Social media are designed for people to socialize with each other. They have changed how and where conversations take place, even globalizing human interaction through rapidly evolving technology. Google+ Hangouts, a popular facet of the fledgling Google+ social network, allows individuals around the world to video chat in real time. Competing with products such as Apple's FaceTime and Microsoft's Skype, Hangouts offers unique innovations such as live streaming and recording. Various companies have used Hangouts to conduct team meetings and webinars, offer consulting services, and host live press conferences. Bakespace.com has successfully utilized Hangouts as a potent marketing platform. The company interacts with customers, shares recipes, and hosts chats with celebrity chefs using Hangouts. And as a chef might say, the proof is in the pudding—Bakespace.com has more than 450,000 people in its Hangouts circle, compared to just 14,000 fans on Facebook.[7] Clearly, conversations are happening online; it is up to the marketer to decide if engaging in those conversations will be profitable and to find the most effective method of entering the conversation.

Companies are beginning to understand the implications of their employees' activities on social media. In fact, there have been several examples of employees getting fired for airing their personal feelings on social media platforms. To combat this, many companies have begun developing social media policies as to what can be posted and what is inappropriate. Some companies have rules concerning corporate blogs, Facebook, Twitter, LinkedIn, comments, and even passwords. Adidas has adopted an "encouraging but strict" approach whereby employees may state their affiliation with Adidas but must also state that any personal views are just that—personal. Obviously, employees are still prohibited from sharing sensitive information. Similarly, Best Buy has a clear set of social media guidelines stating that any negative posts regarding religion, race, or ethnicity will not be tolerated.[8] Having a social media policy can certainly help mitigate risk, but it is not a guarantee that employees won't occasionally slip up.

Marketers are interested in online communication because it is wildly popular: brands, companies, individuals, and celebrities all promote their messages online. In fact, some social media are becoming so important that celebrities, sports stars, and even hotels

its products (much of which was not nice) and decided to use that information to change its product. Social media, along with traditional marketing research, allowed Domino's to gain the insight needed to completely reinvent its pizza. Dell and Gatorade have taken social media monitoring to a whole new level as they literally put social media at the center of their marketing efforts. Premium sportswear company Lululemon was forced to acknowledge manufacturing problems after comments critical of the company's product quality were posted across its social media sites.[6]

Fourth, social media provide more sophisticated methods of measuring how marketers meet and interact with consumers than traditional advertising does. Currently, social media include tools and platforms like social networks, blogs, microblogs, and media sharing sites, which can be accessed through a growing number of devices including smartphones, e-readers, televisions, tablets, video game consoles, and netbooks. This technology changes daily, offering consumers new ways to experience social media platforms. As such, social media must constantly innovate to keep up with consumer demands.

Finally, social media allow marketers to have much more direct and meaningful conversations with customers. Social media offer a form of relationship building that will ultimately bring the customer and brand closer. Indeed, the culture of *participation* that social media foster may well prove to be a fifth "P" for marketing.

At the basic level, consumers of social media want to exchange information, collaborate with others, and have

are hiring coaches to help them strike the correct tone. Britney Spears, Carly Rae Jepsen, and Will.I.Am all have coaches that help them navigate the perilous landscape of Twitter. Coaches instruct clients on best practices and advise them how to leverage their personal brands in online spaces. They also monitor clients' Twitter feeds in real time, acting as editor, security guard, and advisor all at once. Some celebrities have social media advisors accompany them to galas and award shows, but coaches are often underutilized by the entertainment elite. As one celebrity coach noted, "It can get really busy if you're doing interviews on the red carpet, and it's just nice to have someone with you who can say, 'Hey, you should take a picture with your other-famous-person friend right now. Here you go, now you should tweet it.'"[9]

Some companies go so far as to require Facebook and Twitter training for high-profile employees. Approximately 30 percent of Adobe's employees have gone through some form of social media training. According to Cory Edwards, head of Adobe's Social Business Center of Excellence, Adobe's social media training "helps employees understand key principles such as disclosure and who to contact with questions. Guided by a set of core Adobe principles, the program aims to build employee social media fluency through awareness, empowerment, and excellence."[10]

18-1a How Consumers Use Social Media

Before beginning to understand how to leverage social media for brand building, it is important to understand which social media consumers are using and how they are using them. It is safe to assume that many of your customers are active on Facebook. Targeting can be accomplished by using less ubiquitous platforms. Tencent QQ, Qzone, and Sina Weibo are the largest social media platforms in China, for example. Match.com, OkCupid, and Tinder are great platforms to reach young adult singles. Y8 and Big Fish Games offer a wide variety of social games. Teens tend to use platforms like Snapchat, Instagram, Twitch, Yik Yak, and Tumblr. While Facebook is used widely by older teens and adults, its popularity among younger consumers is decreasing.[11]

Videos are another of the most popular tools by which marketers reach consumers, and YouTube is by far the largest online video repository—it has more content than any major television network. Twitter's Vine, which limits videos to six seconds in length, is also widely popular. Flickr, Twitter, Periscope, and blogs—all of which will be discussed in more detail later on—are some of the other most popular social media destinations among consumers. A few key usage numbers:

- There are 3.4 billion Internet users around the world; 2.3 billion are active social media users.

- There are 3.8 billion unique mobile users around the world; 1.96 billion are mobile social media users.

- 10 years ago, 7 percent of the U.S. population used one or more social networking sites. Today, 65 percent of the population uses social networking sites. Of those with access to the Internet, a massive majority of 76 percent use social media.

- Usage has started to plateau; most of the current growth is occurring among those age 65 and older.[12]

- The most popular platforms overall are Facebook, YouTube, Twitter, Google+, Instagram, and LinkedIn. But this varies dramatically by age group—the most popular platforms among 16- to 24-year-olds include Snapchat, Kik, and Instagram.[13]

The bottom line, according to Universal McCann's Comparative Study on Social Media Trends, is that "if you are online, you are using social media."[14]

Increased usage of alternative platforms like smartphones and tablet computers has further contributed to the proliferation of social media usage. In the United States, 90 percent of American adults own a cell phone, while 66 percent own a smartphone. These numbers jump to 98 percent and 85 percent for adults age eighteen to twenty-nine. Among all adults, 55 percent access the Internet on a mobile phone, and 40 percent have accessed a social media website.[15] Tablet usage has hit critical mass among mobile surfers—one in four smartphone users owns a tablet as well. According to Mark Donovan, senior vice president of mobile at ComScore, "Tablets are one of the most rapidly adopted consumer technologies in history and are poised to fundamentally disrupt the way people engage with the digital world both on-the-go and perhaps most notably, in the home."[16] The overall impact of tablet computing on social media (and thus the discipline of marketing) is yet to be seen, but given the incredible impact that the smartphone has had in its short life span, tablets could indeed prove to be game changing.

SOCIAL COMMERCE A new area of growth in social media is **social commerce**, which combines social media with the basics of e-commerce. Social commerce is a subset of

social commerce a subset of e-commerce that involves the interaction and user contribution aspects of social online media to assist online buying and selling of products and services

e-commerce that involves the interaction and user contribution aspects of social online media to assist online buying and selling of products and services.[17] Basically, social commerce relies on user-generated content on website to assist consumers with purchases. Pinterest lets users collect ideas and products from all over the Web and "pin" favorite items to individually curated pinboards. Other users browse boards by theme, keyword, or product; click on what they like; and either visit the originating sites or re-pin the items on their own pinboards. Social commerce sites often include ratings and recommendations (as Amazon.com does) and social shopping tools (as Groupon does). In general, social commerce sites are designed to help consumers make more informed decisions on purchases and services.

Social commerce generated almost $24 billion in sales in 2014, with nearly half of all online sales coming through social media sites.[18] There are seven types of social commerce:

- Peer-to-peer sales platforms (like eBay and Etsy)
- Social networking websites driven by sales (like Pinterest and Twitter)
- Group buying platforms (like Groupon and Social Living)
- Peer recommendation sites (like Yelp and JustBoughtIt)
- User-curated shopping sites (like The Fancy and Lyst)
- Participatory commerce platforms (like Kickstarter and Threadless)
- Social shopping sites (like Motilo and GoTryItOn).[19]

As companies migrate to social commerce sites such as Pinterest, consumer interactions across the sites may change. One way that companies are leveraging Pinterest's user base is by running promotions. For example, Favorite Family Recipes offered two iPads as prizes for users who followed and pinned the logos of thirteen associated Pinterest boards. This type of promotion can undermine the authenticity that many consumers rely on when using social commerce sites. However, some companies hope to cultivate authentic relationships by staying away from promotions. Whole Foods pins items that relate to the company's values but are not promotional or linked back to the Whole Foods site. Customers have built a relationship with Whole Foods based on upcycled products and recipes, rather than free products.[20]

18-1b Social Media and Integrated Marketing Communications

While marketers typically employ a social media strategy alongside traditional channels like print and broadcast, many budget pendulums are swinging toward social media. Forrester Research predicts that mobile marketing, social media, e-mail marketing, display advertising, and search marketing will grow to more than 35 percent of spending in the next few years, equaling spending on television today. The bulk of this budget will still go to search marketing and display advertising, but substantial investments will also be made in mobile marketing and social media.[21]

A unique consequence of social media is the widespread shift from one-to-many communication to many-to-many communication. Instead of simply putting a brand advertisement on television with no means for feedback, marketers

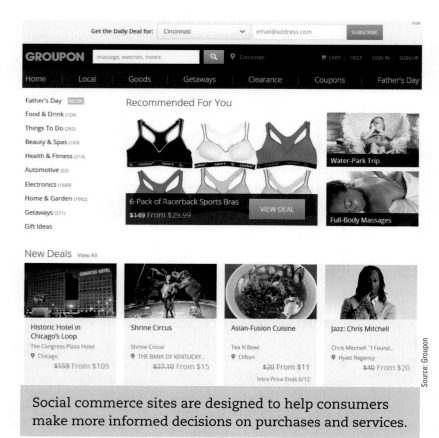

Source: Groupon

Social commerce sites are designed to help consumers make more informed decisions on purchases and services.

can use social media to have conversations with consumers, forge deeper relationships, and build brand loyalty. Social media also allow consumers to connect with each other, share opinions, and collaborate on new ideas according to their interests.

With social media, the audience is often in control of the message, the medium, the response, or all three. This distribution of control is often difficult for companies to adjust to, but the focus of social marketing is unavoidably on the audience, and the brand must adapt to succeed. The interaction between producer and consumer becomes less about entertaining and more about listening, influencing, and engaging.

Using consumers to develop and market products is called **crowdsourcing**. Crowdsourcing describes how the input of many people can be leveraged to make decisions that used to be based on the input of only a few people.[22] Companies get feedback on marketing campaigns, new product ideas, and other marketing decisions by asking customers to weigh in. One company called Talenthouse is offering up the crowd to help musicians fulfill all sorts of needs—for example, someone to design album art or sew a dress for a lead singer. Talenthouse has users submit work to be voted on by Facebook and Twitter peers. The winner gets the job (though the musician has the final say in who wins). Some musicians see Talenthouse as a way to gain publicity or to help aspiring artists. English singer-songwriter Ellie Goulding set up a contest for Talenthouse competitors to submit a photograph that showed people connecting with music at a concert or festival. The winner received £1,000 (about $1,500), a new laptop, special promotion, and a job as the official photographer for an Ellie Goulding concert.[23] Crowdsourcing offers a way for companies to engage heavy users of a brand and receive input, which in turn increases those users' brand

advocacy and lessens the likelihood that a change will be disliked enough to drive away loyal customers.

18-2 CREATING AND LEVERAGING A SOCIAL MEDIA CAMPAIGN

Social media is an exciting new field, and its potential for expanding a brand's impact is enormous. Because the costs are often minimal and the learning curve is relatively low, some organizations are tempted to dive headfirst into social media. As with any marketing campaign, however, it is always important to start with a strategy. For most organizations, this means starting with a marketing or communications plan. Important evaluative areas such as situation analysis, objectives, and evaluation are still essential. It is important to link communication objectives (for example, improving customer service) to the most effective social media tools (for example, Twitter) and to be able to measure the results to determine if the objectives were met. It is also important to understand the various types of media involved.

The new communication paradigm created by a shift to social media marketing raises questions about categorization. In light of the convergence of traditional and digital media, researchers have explored different ways that interactive marketers can categorize media types, namely owned, earned, and paid media (recall these concepts from Chapter 15). The purpose of owned media is to develop deeper relationships with customers. A brand's Facebook presence, YouTube channel, Twitter presence, Pinterest presence, and presence on other social platforms constitute owned media. Additional content such as videos, webinars, recommendations, ratings, and blog posts are also considered owned media since they are sharable on social media platforms. In an interactive space, media are *earned* through word of mouth or online buzz about something the brand is doing. Earned media include viral videos, retweets, comments on blogs, and other forms of customer feedback resulting from a social media presence. When consumers pass along brand information in the form of retweets, blog comments, or ratings and recommendations, this is an example of earned media. In other words, the word of mouth is spread online rather than face-to-face. Paid media are similar to marketing efforts that utilize traditional media, like newspaper,

Rawpixel.com/Shutterstock.com

crowdsourcing using consumers to develop and market products

magazine, and television advertisements. In an interactive space, paid media include display advertising, paid search words, and other types of direct online advertising.[24] Ads purchased on Facebook, for example, are considered paid media since the brand is paying for the text-based or visual ad that shows up on the right-hand side of Facebook profiles.

As a result, social media can really be thought of as an additional "layer" that many brands decide to develop. Some layers are quite deep—Doritos, Old Spice, and Nike can be said to have deeper layers of social media since these are brands that people talk about. Other brands, for example, many B-to-B brands, may have a more shallow social media layer and provide access on only one or two social media platforms. At the end of the day, it really depends on the type of product being sold and the customer's propensity to participate in social media.

To leverage all three types of media, marketers must follow a few key guidelines. First, they must maximize owned media by reaching out beyond their existing websites to create portfolios of digital touch points. This is especially true for brands with tight budgets, as the organization may not be able to afford much paid media. Second, marketers must recognize that public and media relations no longer translates into earned media. Instead, marketers must learn how to listen and respond to stakeholders. This will stimulate word of mouth. Finally, marketers must understand that paid media must serve as a catalyst to drive customer engagement and expand into emerging channels.[25] If balanced correctly, all three types of media can be powerful tools for interactive marketers.

18-2a The Listening System

The first action a marketing team should take when initiating a social media campaign is simple—it should just listen. Customers are on social media and assume that the brand is there as well. They expect a new level of engagement with brands. Developing an effective listening system is necessary to both understanding and engaging an online audience. Marketers must not only hear what is being said about the brand, the industry, the competition, and the customer, but they must also pay attention to who is saying what and act upon that information. The specific ways that customers and noncustomers rate, rank, critique, praise, deride, recommend, snub, and generally discuss brands are all important.

social media monitoring the process of identifying and assessing what is being said about a company, individual, product, or brand

Thus, social media have created a new method of market research: customers telling marketers what they want and need (and do not want and do not need).

Once a company has started listening, it typically wants to develop a more formalized approach. **Social media monitoring** is the process of identifying and assessing what is being said about a company, individual, product, or brand. It can involve sentiment analysis and *text mining* specific key words on social networking website, blogs, discussion forums, and other social media. Negative comments and complaints are of particular importance, both because they can illuminate unknown brand flaws and because they are the comments that tend to go viral. Listening is important because consumers believe that if negative comments about a brand go unanswered, that brand is insincere, and consumers will take their business elsewhere. Failure to respond to criticism typically leads to a larger crisis. Online tools such as Google Alerts, Social Mention, HootSuite, TweetReach, and Klout are extremely helpful in monitoring social media. Larger companies typically use an enterprise system such as Salesforce.com's Radian6 CRM software to monitor social media.

18-2b Social Media Objectives

After establishing a listening platform, the organization should develop a list of objectives for its social media team to accomplish. These objectives must be developed with a clear understanding of how social media change the communication dynamic with and for customers. Remember, attempting to reach a mass audience with a static message will never be as successful as influencing people through conversation. Marketing managers must set objectives that reflect this reality. Here are some practical ideas that marketing managers should consider when setting social media objectives:

- **Listen and learn:** Monitor what is being said about the brand and competitors, and glean insights about audiences. Use online tools and do research to implement the best social media practices. If you have established a listening strategy, this objective should already be accomplished.

- **Build relationships and awareness:** Open dialogues with stakeholders by giving them compelling content across a variety of media. Engage in conversations, and answer customers' questions candidly. This will both increase web traffic and boost your search engine ranking. This is where crowdsourcing can be useful for product development and communication campaign feedback.

Social media monitoring has become so important that several tech companies have begun offering it as a standalone service. Some of the leaders in the field include Sysomos, Oracle, Salesforce, and Lithium.

- **Promote products and services:** The clearest path to increasing the bottom line using social media is to get customers talking about products and services, which ultimately translates into sales.

- **Manage your reputation:** Develop and improve the brand's reputation by responding to comments and criticism that appear on blogs and forums. Additionally, organizations can position themselves as helpful and benevolent by participating in other forums and discussions. Social media make it much easier to establish and communicate expertise.

- **Improve customer service:** Customer comments about products and services will not always be positive. Use social media to search out displeased customers and engage them directly in order to solve their service issues.

18-3 EVALUATION AND MEASUREMENT OF SOCIAL MEDIA

Social media have the potential to revolutionize the way organizations communicate with stakeholders. Given the relative ease and efficiency with which organizations can use social media, a positive return on investment (ROI) is likely for many—if not most—organizations. A Forrester Research report found that 95 percent of marketers planned to increase or maintain their investments in social media. However, though they understand that it is a worthwhile investment, most marketers have not been able to figure out how to measure the benefits of social media.

As with traditional advertising, marketers lack hard evidence as to the relative effectiveness of these tools. Some marketers accept this unknown variable and focus on the fact that social media are less about ROI than about deepening relationships with customers; others work tirelessly to better understand the measurement of social media's effectiveness. A recent Ragan/NASDAQ OMX Corporate Solutions survey found that 40 percent of marketers are unsure of what evaluative tools to use, and about 70 percent are only "somewhat satisfied" or "not satisfied at all" with how their companies measure social media. "I'm not sure what to measure or how," said one survey participant. "I know it's important, but I can't show my boss how many retweets a post received and expect him to care."[26]

While literally hundreds of metrics have been developed to measure social media's value, these metrics are meaningless unless they are tied to key performance indicators.[27] For example, a local coffee shop manager may measure the success of her social media presence by the raw number of friends on Facebook and followers on Twitter she has accumulated. But these numbers depend entirely on context. The rate of accumulation, investment per fan and follower, and comparison to similarly sized coffee shops are all important metrics to consider. Without context, measurements are meaningless. This is a hot topic, and several marketing blogs cover the areas of social media measurement.

18-4 SOCIAL BEHAVIOR OF CONSUMERS

Social media have changed the way that people interact in their everyday lives. Some say that social media have made people smarter by giving people (especially children) access to so much information and interactivity. Social media allow people to stay in touch in ways never before experienced. Social media have also reinvented civic engagement (recall that the ALS Association's "Ice Bucket Challenge" grew worldwide through social media like Facebook and Twitter). Social media have drastically changed the advertising business from an industry based on mass-media models (for example, television) to an industry based on relationships and conversations. This all has implications for how consumers use social media and the purposes for which they use those media.[28]

Social media has reinvented civic engagement—see the ALS Ice Bucket Challenge as a prime example.

Marcos Mesa Sam Wordley/Shutterstock.com

Many social media marketers will simply need to start with good measurable objectives, determine what needs to be measured, and figure it out. Still, some social media metrics to consider include

- **Buzz:** volume of consumer-created buzz for a brand based on posts and impressions, by social channel, by stage in the purchase channel, by season, and by time of day.

- **Interest:** number of "likes," fans, followers, and friends; growth rates; rate of virality or pass along; and change in pass along over time.

- **Participation and Engagement:** number of comments, ratings, social bookmarks, subscriptions, page views, uploads, downloads, embeds, retweets, Facebook posts, pins, and time spent with social media platform.

- **Search engine ranks and results:** increases and decreases on searches and changes in key words.

- **Influence:** media mentions, influences of bloggers reached, influences of customers reached, and second-degree reach based on social graphs.

- **Sentiment analysis:** positive, neutral, and negative sentiment; trends of sentiment; and volume of sentiment.

- **Website metrics:** clicks, click-through rates, and percentage of traffic.

Once objectives have been determined and measurement tools have been implemented, it is important to identify the consumer the marketer is trying to reach. Who is using social media? What types of social media do they use? How do they use social media? Are they just reading content, or do they actually create it? Does Facebook attract younger users? Do Twitter users retweet viral videos? These types of questions must be considered because they determine not only which tools will be most effective but also, more importantly, whether launching a social media campaign even makes sense for a particular organization.

Understanding an audience necessitates understanding how that audience uses social media. In *Groundswell*, Charlene Li and Josh Bernoff of Forrester Research identify six categories of social media users:

1. **Creators:** Those who produce and share online content like blogs, websites, articles, and videos

2. **Critics:** Those who post comments, ratings, and reviews of products and services on blogs and forums

3. **Collectors:** Those who use RSS feeds to collect information and vote for websites online

4. **Joiners:** Those who maintain a social networking profile and visit other sites

5. **Spectators:** Those who read blogs, listen to podcasts, watch videos, and generally consume media

6. **Inactives:** Those who do none of these things[29]

A Forrester Research study determined that 24 percent of social media users function as creators, 36 percent function as critics, 23 percent function as collectors, 68 percent function as joiners, 73 percent function as spectators, and 14 percent function—or rather, do not function—as inactives.[30] Participation in most categories has slowed slightly, prompting analysts to recommend that marketers re-examine how they are engaging with their customers online.

Despite the apparent slowdown, research also shows that more social networking "rookies" are classified as joiners. Another bright spot is a new category, "conversationalists," or people who post status updates on social networking sites and microblogging services such as Twitter. Conversationalists represent 36 percent of users.[31] This type of classification gives marketers a general idea of who is using social media and how to engage them. It is similar to any type of market segmentation—especially the 80/20 rule. Those who are creating content and active on social media could be those consumers most likely to actively engage with a brand as well as actively post negative comments on social media. The critics and collectors make up most of this group. However, it is important not to miss the joiners and spectators, because they are eager to follow and act on the comments of their fellow customers.

18-5 SOCIAL MEDIA TOOLS: CONSUMER- AND CORPORATE-GENERATED CONTENT

Given that it is important for marketers to engage with customers on social media for the reasons mentioned earlier, there are a number of tools and platforms that can be employed as part of an organization's social media strategy. Blogs, microblogs, social networks, media creation and sharing sites, social news sites, location-based social networking sites, review sites, and virtual worlds and online gaming all have their place in a company's social marketing plan. These are all tools in a marketing manager's toolbox, available when applicable to the marketing plan but not necessarily to be used all at once. Because of the breakneck pace at which technology changes, this list of resources will surely look markedly different five years from now. More tools emerge every day, and branding strategies must keep up with the ever-changing world of technology. For now, the resources highlighted in this section remain a marketer's strongest set of platforms for conversing and strengthening relationships with customers.

18-5a Blogs

Blogs have become staples in many social media strategies and are often a brand's social media centerpiece. A blog is a publicly accessible web page that functions as an interactive journal, whereby readers can post comments on the author's entries. Some experts believe that every company should have a blog that speaks to current and potential customers, not as consumers, but as people.[32] Blogs allow marketers to create content in the form of posts, which ideally build trust and a sense of authenticity in customers. Once posts are made, audience members can provide feedback through comments. Because it opens a dialogue and gives customers a voice, the comments section of a blog post is one of the most important avenues of conversation between brands and consumers.

Blogs can be divided into two broad categories: corporate and professional blogs, and noncorporate blogs such as personal blogs. **Corporate blogs** are sponsored by a company or one of its brands and are maintained by one or more of the company's employees. They disseminate marketing-controlled information and are effective platforms for developing thought leadership, fostering better relationships with stakeholders, maximizing search engine optimization, attracting new customers, endearing the organization with anecdotes and stories about brands, and providing an active forum for testing new ideas. Many companies, however, have moved away from corporate blogs, replacing the in-depth writing and comment monitoring that come with blog maintenance with the quick, easy, and more social Facebook, Twitter, or Tumblr. Coca Cola, Walmart, and AllState operate some of the best big company corporate blogs. All are known for their creative and engaging content and the authenticity of their tone.[33]

On the other hand, **noncorporate blogs** are independent and not associated with the marketing efforts of any particular company or brand. Because these blogs contain information not controlled by marketers, they are perceived to be more authentic than corporate blogs. Mommy bloggers, women who review children's products and discuss family-related topics on their personal blogs, use noncorporate blogs. The goal of mommy blogs is to share parenting tips and experiences and become part of a community. Food blogs are especially popular, particularly those posting restaurant reviews, diet and exercise tips, and recipes.

blog a publicly accessible web page that functions as an interactive journal, whereby readers can post comments on the author's entries

corporate blogs blogs that are sponsored by a company or one of its brands and maintained by one or more of the company's employees

noncorporate blogs independent blogs that are not associated with the marketing efforts of any particular company or brand

Because of the popularity of these and other types of blogs, many bloggers receive products and/or money from companies in exchange for a review. Many bloggers disclose where they received the product or if they were paid, but an affiliation is not always clear. Because of this, bloggers must disclose any financial relationship with a company per Federal Trade Commission rules. Marketing managers need to understand the rules behind offering complimentary products to bloggers before using them as a way to capitalize on the high potential for social buzz; four out of five noncorporate bloggers post brand or product reviews. Even if a company does not have a formal social media strategy, chances are the brand is still out in the blogosphere, whether or not a marketing manager approached a blogger.

18-5b Microblogs

Microblogs are blogs that entail shorter posts than traditional blogs. Twitter, the most popular microblogging platform, requires that posts be no more than 140 characters in length. However, there are several other platforms, including Tumblr, Plurk, and, of course, Facebook's status updates. Unlike Twitter, these platforms allow users to post longer pieces of text, videos, images, and links. While some microblogs (such as Tumblr) do not have text length limits, their multimedia-based cultures discourage traditional blog-length text posts. The content posted on microblogs ranges from five-paragraph news stories to photos of sandwiches with the ingredients as captions (scanwiches.com). While Tumblr is growing rapidly, Twitter, originally designed as a short messaging system used for internal communication, is wildly popular and is used as a communication and research tool by individuals and brands around the world. Twitter is effective for disseminating breaking news, promoting longer blog posts and campaigns, sharing links, announcing events, and promoting sales. By following, retweeting, responding to potential customers' tweets, and tweeting content that inspires customers to engage the brand, corporate Twitter users can lay a foundation for meaningful two-way conversation quickly and effectively. Celebrities also flock to Twitter to interact with fans, discuss tour dates, and efficiently promote themselves directly to fans. Research has found that when operated correctly, corporate Twitter accounts are well respected and well received. Twitter can be used to build communities, aid in customer service, gain prospects, increase awareness, and, in the case of nonprofits, raise funds.

The ways a business can use microblogs to successfully engage with customers are almost limitless. A wide variety of companies find Tumblr's easy and customizable format a great way to promote an individual brand. Mashable uses its Tumblr to give a glimpse inside the offices and share the company's sense of humor. Ace Hotel, located in New York, Portland, Seattle, and Palm Springs, shows off its properties and local art exhibits on a spare, gallery-like Tumblr. Lure Fishbar shows off its delectable food on its Tumblr.[34]

18-5c Social Networks

Social networking sites allow individuals to connect—or network—with friends, peers, and business associates. Connections may be made around shared interests, shared environments, or personal relationships. Depending on the site, connected individuals may be able to send each other messages, track each other's activity, see each other's personal information, share multimedia, comment on each other's blog and microblog posts—or do all of these things. Depending on a marketing team's goals, several social networks might be engaged as part of a social media strategy: Facebook is the largest social network; Instagram and Snapchat are popular among younger audiences; LinkedIn is geared toward professionals and businesses who use it to recruit employees; and niche networks like Twitch, SoundCloud, Grindr, BlackPlanet, and ChristianMingle.com cater to specialized markets. There is a niche social network for just about every demographic and interest. Beyond those already established, an organization may decide to develop a brand-specific social network or community. Although each social networking site is different, some marketing goals can be accomplished on any such site. Given the right strategy, increasing awareness, targeting audiences, promoting products, forging relationships, highlighting expertise and leadership, attracting event participants, performing research, and generating new business are attainable marketing goals on any social network.

microblogs blogs with strict post length limits

social networking sites websites that allow individuals to connect—or network—with friends, peers, and business associates

Chonlachai/Shutterstock.com

FACEBOOK Facebook originated as a community for college students that opened to the general public as its popularity grew. It now has almost 1.5 billion monthly active users, making it the largest social networking site by far. Growth in new profiles is highest among baby boomers using Facebook as a way to connect with old friends and keep up with family. Facebook is popular not only with individuals, but also with groups and companies. How an individual uses Facebook differs from the way a group or company uses Facebook, as you can see in Exhibit 18.1. Individual Facebook users create profiles, while brands, organizations, and nonprofit causes operate as pages. As opposed to individual profiles, all pages are public and are thus subject to search engine indexing.

By maintaining a popular Facebook page, a brand not only increases its social media presence, it also helps to optimize search engine results. Pages often include photo and video albums, brand information, and links to external sites. One of the most useful page features is the Timeline. The Timeline allows a brand to communicate directly with fans via status updates, which enables marketers to build databases of interested stakeholders. When an individual becomes a fan of your organization or posts on your Timeline, that information is shared with the individual's friends, creating a mini viral marketing campaign. Other Facebook marketing tools include groups, applications, and ads. Facebook is an extremely important platform for social marketers.

Facebook has proved to be fertile ground for new marketing ideas and campaigns. Many companies use Facebook as a way to share photos of the business they are doing, whether that is images of the plant where the product is made or finished construction on a new project. Offering guides relevant to a company's product

Source: Spark Networks, Inc.

There is a niche social network for just about every demographic and interest.

or service as a way to educate interested customers has worked well for Kitchen Cabinet Kings, which found that educated customers make more purchases. Threadless' Voting Hub Facebook page allows fans to share, promote, and vote on new T-shirt designs.[35]

LINKEDIN LinkedIn is used primarily by professionals who wish to build their personal brands online and businesses that are recruiting employees and freelancers. LinkedIn features many of the same services as Facebook (profiles, status updates, private messages, company pages, and groups) but is oriented around business and professional connections—it is designed to be information-rich rather than multimedia-rich. LinkedIn serves as a virtual rolodex, providing recruiters and job seekers alike a network to connect and conduct business. LinkedIn's question-and-answer forum, endorsement system, job classifieds platform, and acquisition of presentation-hosting website SlideShare set it apart from Facebook as a truly business-oriented space.[36] LinkedIn is the most effective social media platform for B-to-B marketing, as many use it for lead generation. Some companies use LinkedIn for recruiting, and others use it for thought leadership. Indeed, company pages on LinkedIn can serve as an effective hub for products and services, promotional videos, and company news.

18-5d Media Sharing Sites

Media sharing sites allow users to upload and distribute multimedia content like videos and photos. YouTube, Flickr, Pinterest, Instagram, Vine, and Snapchat are particularly useful to brands' social marketing strategies because they add

media sharing sites websites that allow users to upload and distribute multimedia content like videos and photos

---

EXHIBIT 18.1	FACEBOOK LINGO

Non-Individual (Usually Corporate)	Individual
Page	Profile
Fan of a page, tells fan's friends that the user is a fan, creates mini viral campaign	Friend a person, send private messages, write on the wall, see friend-only content
Public, searchable	Privacy options, not searchable unless user enabled

Ask Me Anything

Politicians, celebrities, and business leaders from all walks of life have used Reddit's Ask Me Anything (AMA) series to promote their issues, projects, and products. After an AMA is posted, Reddit users ask questions—sometimes complex or controversial questions—and the poster answers them as he or she chooses. Some of the site's most popular AMAs have included Bill Gates, Molly Ringwald, Snoop Lion, Neil deGrasse Tyson, Louis C.K., and President Barack Obama.[38]

a vibrant interactive channel on which to disseminate content. Suffice to say, the distribution of user-generated content has changed markedly over the past few years. Today, organizations can tell compelling brand stories through videos, photos, and audio.

Photo sharing sites allow users to archive and share photos. Flickr, Picasa, Twitpic, Photobucket, Facebook, and Imgur all offer free photo hosting services that can be utilized by individuals and businesses alike. Instagram is often used by brands to engage younger audience members. Snapchat is also useful, but since photos and videos are only visible for a few seconds, complex marketing messages cannot easily be conveyed.

Video creation and distribution have also gained popularity among marketers because of video's rich ability to tell stories. YouTube, the highest-trafficked video-based website and the third-highest-trafficked site overall, allows users to upload and stream their videos to an enthusiastic and active community.[37] YouTube is not only large (in terms of visitors), but it also attracts a diverse base of users: age and gender demographics are remarkably balanced.

Many entertainment companies and movie marketers have used YouTube as a showcase for new products, specials, and movie trailers. User-generated content can also be a powerful tool for brands that can use it effectively. While YouTube is still the champ, Vine is quickly becoming another popular platform for corporate promotion.

A podcast, another type of user-generated media, is a digital audio or video file that is distributed serially for other people to listen to

or watch. Podcasts can be streamed online, played on a computer, uploaded to a portable media player, or downloaded onto a smartphone. Podcasts are like radio shows that are distributed through various means and not linked to a scheduled time slot. While they have not experienced the exponential growth rates of other digital platforms, podcasts have amassed a steadily growing number of loyal devotees. For example, Etsy, an online marketplace for handmade and vintage wares, offers a podcast series introducing favorite craftspeople to the world—driving business for those individuals.

18-5e Social News Sites

Social news sites allow users to decide which content is promoted on a given website by voting that content up or down. Users post news stories and multimedia on crowdsourced sites such as Reddit for the community to vote on. The more interest from readers, the higher the story or video is ranked. Marketers have found that these sites are useful for promoting campaigns, creating conversations around related issues, and building website traffic.

If marketing content posted to a crowdsourced site is voted up, discussed, and shared enough to be listed among the most popular topics of the day, it can go viral across other sites, and eventually, the entire web. Social bookmarking sites such as Delicious and StumbleUpon are similar to social news sites but the objective of their users is to collect, save, and share interesting and valuable links. On these sites, users categorize links with short, descriptive tags. Users can search the site's database of links by specific tags or can add their own tags to others' links. In this way, tags serve as the foundation for

social news sites websites that allow users to decide which content is promoted on a given website by voting that content up or down

Rvlsoft/Shutterstock.com

Live video streaming apps like Facebook Live and Periscope are changing the way we share and consume media. Comedians like Kevin Hart (pictured), Chris Hardwick, Annie Lederman, and Jim Gaffigan have embraced Periscope as a way to connect with fans and increase awareness.

information gathering and sharing on social bookmarking sites.[39]

18-5f Location-Based Social Networking Sites

Considered by many to be the next big thing in social marketing, location sites like Foursquare and Loopt should be on every marketer's radar. Essentially, **location-based social networking sites** combine the fun of social networking with the utility of location-based Global Positioning System (GPS) technology. Foursquare, one of the most popular location sites, treats location-based micronetworking as a game: Users earn badges and special statuses based on their number of visits to particular locations. Users can write and read short reviews and tips about businesses, organize meet-ups, and see which Foursquare-using friends are nearby. Foursquare updates can also be posted to linked Twitter and Facebook accounts for followers and friends

to see. Location sites such as Foursquare are particularly useful social marketing tools for local businesses, especially when combined with sales promotions like coupons, special offers, contests, and events. Location sites can be harnessed to forge lasting relationships with and deeply ingrained loyalty from customers.[40] For example, a local restaurant can allow consumers to check in on Foursquare using their smartphones and receive coupons for that day's purchases. Since the location site technology is relatively new, many brands are still figuring out how best to utilize Foursquare. Facebook added Places to capitalize on this location-based technology, which allows people to "check in" and share their location with their online friends. It will be interesting to see how use of this technology grows over time.

18-5g Review Sites

Individuals tend to trust other people's opinions when it comes to purchasing. According to Nielsen Media Research, more than 70 percent of consumers said that they trusted online consumer opinions. This percentage is much higher than that of consumers who trust traditional advertising. Based on the early work of Amazon .com and eBay to integrate user opinions into product and seller pages, countless website allowing users to voice their opinions have sprung up across every segment of the Internet market. **Review sites** allow consumers to post, read, rate, and comment on opinions regarding all kinds of products and services. For example, Yelp, the most active local review directory on the Web, combines customer critiques of local businesses with business information and elements of social networking to create an engaging, informative experience. On Yelp, users scrutinize local restaurants, fitness centers, tattoo parlors, and other businesses, each of which has a detailed profile page. Business owners and representatives can edit their organizations' pages and respond to Yelp reviews both privately and publicly. Yelp even rewards its most popular (and prolific) reviewers with Elite status. Businesses like Worthington, Ohio's Pies & Pints will throw Elite-only parties to allow these esteemed Yelpers to try out their restaurant, hoping to receive a favorable review. A Tiki Beach Party for Yelp Elites at Montreal, Canada's Le Lab garnered thirteen reviews averaging five stars out of five.[41] By giving marketers the opportunity to respond to their customers directly

location-based social networking sites website that combine the fun of social networking with the utility of location-based GPS technology

review sites websites that allow consumers to post, read, rate, and comment on opinions regarding all kinds of products and services

and put their businesses in a positive light, review sites certainly serve as useful tools for local and national businesses.

18-5h Virtual Worlds and Online Gaming

Online gaming presents additional opportunities for marketers to engage with consumers. These include massive multiplayer online (MMO) games such as *World of Warcraft, Destiny,* and *EVE Online*; competitive online games such as *League of Legends, Overwatch,* and *Street Fighter V*; and online communities (or virtual worlds) such as *Sec-*

In many sports games, such as EA's UFC 2, in-game advertisements increase the authenticity of the experience.

ond Life, Poptropica, and *Habbo Hotel*. Although these virtual worlds are unfamiliar to and even intimidating for many traditional marketers, the field is becoming an important, viable, and growing consideration. More than 155 million Americans play video games, and approximately 42 percent play regularly (at least three hours per week). Research firm Newzoo estimates that the global market for games will reach $103 billion in 2017, representing an almost 70 percent increase over 2016.[42]

One particular area of growth is social gaming. The number of people playing games on Facebook like *Words with Friends, FarmVille,* and *Trivia Crack* grew to 550 million in 2016—an increase of almost 50 percent over the previous year.[43] Much of these games' revenue comes from in-game advertising, as virtual world environments are often fertile grounds for branded content. Organizations such as IBM and the American Cancer Society have developed profitable trade presences in *Second Life*, but others have abandoned the persistent online community as its user base has declined—the average number of users logged into *Second Life* has dropped almost 25 percent in the last four years.[44]

The average player of social games is a 35-year-old male (users who play on mobile devices tend to be younger), but women make up nearly 48 percent of social gamers. Facebook is by far the largest social network for gaming, though up-and-comer hi5 is hoping to win over more users with its large variety of games. The top five games on Facebook are Candy Crush Saga, Clash of

Clans, Candy Crush Soda Saga, Farm Heroes Saga, and 8 Ball Pool, which together entice more than 50 million users every day.[45] These games are attractive because they can be played in just five minutes.

Many mobile games use advertising to generate revenue for the game developers and publishers. As long as the ads are not overly intrusive, most users opt to play free versions of games with ads over paid versions that do not have ads. Another popular strategy is to give an ad-free game away for free and then charge small sums of money for in-game items and power-ups. These microtransactions account for 79 percent of app revenue in the United States and 94 percent of app revenue in China and Japan. Microtransactions have become a popular source of revenue in non-mobile games as well. In 2016, *League of Legends*, the most popular eSports game in the world, generated more than $1.3 billion from in-game microtransactions alone.[46]

MMOs tend to draw a different group of consumers—18- to 34-year-old males. In MMO environments, thousands of people play simultaneously. Regardless of the type of experience, brands must be creative in how they integrate ads into games. Social and realistic titles are the most appropriate for marketing and advertising (as opposed to fantasy games). Promotions typically include special events, competitions, and sweepstakes, and for some games, having ads actually increases the authenticity. For example, Nike offers shoes in life simulator *The Sims Online* that allow players to run faster, while replays in football franchise *Madden* are sponsored by real-life companies.

18-6 SOCIAL MEDIA AND MOBILE TECHNOLOGY

While much of the excitement in social media has been based on website and new technology uses, much of the growth lies in new platforms. These platforms include the multitude of smartphones as well as iPads and other tablets. The major implication of this development is that consumers now can access popular website like Facebook, Mashable, Twitter, and Foursquare from all their various platforms.

18-6a Mobile and Smartphone Technology

Worldwide, there are more than six billion mobile phones in use, 17 percent of which are smartphones.[47] It is no surprise, then, that the mobile platform is such an effective marketing tool—especially when targeting a younger audience. Smartphones up the ante by allowing individuals to do nearly everything they can do with a computer—from anywhere. With a smartphone in hand, reading a blog, writing an e-mail, scheduling a meeting, posting to Facebook, playing a multiplayer game, watching a video, taking a picture, using GPS, and surfing the Internet might all occur during one ten-minute bus ride. Smartphone technology, often considered the crowning achievement in digital convergence and social media integration, has opened the door to modern mobile advertising as a viable marketing strategy.

The global mobile advertising market hit two significant milestones in 2016: it surpassed $100 billion in annual spending, and it accounted for more than 50 percent of all digital ad expenditures for the first time. The $102 billion spent globally on ads served to mobile phones and tablets worldwide represents a nearly 430 percent increase over the last three years.[48] There are several reasons for the recent popularity of mobile marketing. First, an effort to standardize mobile platforms has resulted in a low barrier to entry. Second, especially given mobile marketing's younger audiences, there are more consumers than ever acclimating to once-worrisome privacy and pricing policies. Third, because most people carry their smartphones with them at all times, mobile marketing is uniquely effective at garnering customer attention in real time. Fourth, mobile marketing is measurable: metrics and usage statistics make it an effective tool for gaining insight into consumer behavior. Fifth, in-store notification technology such as Apple's iBeacon can send promotional messages based on real-time interactions with customers. Finally, mobile marketing's response rate is higher than that of traditional media types like print and broadcast advertisement. Some common mobile marketing tools include

- **SMS (short message service):** 160-character text messages sent to and from cell phones. SMS is typically integrated with other tools.
- **MMS (multimedia messaging service):** Similar to SMS but allows the attachment of images, videos, ringtones, and other multimedia to text messages.
- **Mobile website (MOBI and WAP website):** website designed specifically for viewing and navigation on mobile devices.
- **Mobile ads:** Visual advertisements integrated into text messages, applications, and mobile website. Mobile ads are often sold on a cost-per-click basis.
- **Bluetooth marketing:** A signal is sent to Bluetooth-enabled devices, allowing marketers to send targeted messages to users based on their geographic locations.
- **Smartphone applications (apps):** Software designed specifically for mobile and tablet devices.

A popular use for barcode scanning apps is the reading and processing of Quick Response (QR) codes. When scanned by a smartphone's QR reader app, a QR code takes the user to a specific site with content about or a discount for products or services. Uses range from donating to a charity by scanning the code to simply checking out the company's website for more information. For example, Modify Watches offers a watch face with no hands. Instead it has a QR code that, when scanned, shows the correct time.[49]

Another smartphone trend is called "near field communication" (NFC), which uses small chips hidden in or behind products that, when touched by compatible devices, will transfer the information on the chip to the device. Barnes & Noble is hoping to work with publishers to ship hardcover books containing NFC chips to Barnes & Noble stores. The chips will be embedded with editorial reviews about that book from Barnes & Noble's website. When a NOOK user touches the hardcover with her NOOK, the book reviews will display on her tablet, helping her make a purchase decision.[50] The Samsung Galaxy S6 smartphone can track users' eye movements and shift screen content depending on where they are looking. While a relatively new technology, eye tracking has interesting implications for mobile marketing in the near future.[51]

Finally, mobile marketing is particularly powerful when combined with geo-location platforms such as Foursquare, whereby people can "check in" to places and receive benefits and special offers. These platforms allow retailers and other businesses to incentivize multiple visits, visits at certain times of the day, and positive customer reviews.

18-6b Apps and Widgets

Given the widespread adoption of Apple's iPhone, Android-based phones, and other smartphones, it is no surprise that millions of apps have been developed for the mobile market. Dozens of new and unique apps that harness mobile technology are added to mobile marketplaces every day. While many apps perform platform-specific tasks, others convert existing content into a mobile-ready format. Whether offering new or existing content, when an app is well branded and integrated into a company's overall marketing strategy, it can create buzz and generate customer engagement.

Web widgets, also known as gadgets and badges, are software applications that run entirely within existing online platforms. Essentially, a web widget allows a developer to embed a simple application such as a weather forecast, horoscope, or stock market ticker into a website, even if the developer did not write (or does not understand) the application's source code. From a marketing perspective, widgets allow customers to display company information (such as current promotions, coupons, or news) on their own websites or smartphone home screens. Widgets are often cheaper than apps to develop, can extend an organization's reach beyond existing platforms, will broaden the listening system, and can make an organization easier to find.[52]

18-7 THE SOCIAL MEDIA PLAN

To effectively use the tools in the social media toolbox, it is important to have a clearly outlined social media plan. The social media plan is linked to larger plans such as a promotional plan or marketing plan and should fit appropriately into the objectives and steps in those plans (for more

Twin Design/Shutterstock.com

information, review Chapters 2 and 16). It is important to research throughout the development of the social media plan to keep abreast of the rapidly changing social media world. There are six stages involved in creating an effective social media plan:

1. **Listen to customers:** This is covered in more detail in section 18-2a.

2. **Set social media objectives:** Set objectives that can be specifically accomplished through social media, with special attention to how to measure the results. Numerous metrics are available, some of which are mentioned throughout the chapter.

3. **Define strategies:** This includes examining trends and best practices in the industry.

4. **Identify the target audience:** This should line up with the target market defined in the marketing plan, but in the social media plan, pay special attention to how that audience participates and behaves online.

5. **Select the tools and platforms:** Based on the result of Step 4, choose the social media tools and platforms that will be most relevant. These choices are based on the knowledge of where the target audience participates on social media.

6. **Implement and monitor the strategy:** Social media campaigns can be fluid, so it is important to keep a close eye on what is successful and what is not. Then, based on the observations, make changes as needed. It also becomes important, therefore, to go back to the listening stage to interpret how consumers are perceiving the social media campaign.

Listening to customers and industry trends, as well as continually revising the social media plan to meet the needs of the changing social media market, are keys to successful social media marketing. There are numerous industry leaders sharing some of their best practices, and sources such as *Fast Company* and the *Wall Street Journal* report regularly on how large and small companies are successfully using social media to gain market share and sales. A good example of using social media strategies is HubSpot, a company that practices what it preaches. HubSpot advocates the benefits of building valuable content online and then using social media

EXHIBIT 18.2   SOCIAL MEDIA TRENDS

Trend	Change	Where Is It Now?
Yik Yak	Anonymous geolocated messaging	
Microsoft Office 365, Google Drive	Integration with file hosting	
Ello	Challengers to Facebook's dominance	
Facebook buying Oculus	Integration into virtual reality	
The Internet of Things	Integration into wearables, appliances, apparel, and more	
Apple Pay, Google Wallet, Bitcoin, and NFC- enabled payment options	Replace credit cards with various forms of digital payment	
Loot Crate, Trunk Club, and NatureBox	Online and subscription-based personal shopping	
Twitch, Meerkat, and Periscope	Live video streaming for everybody	
Tinder and Grindr	The mainstreaming of geolocated dating apps	

to pull customers to its website. Social engine profiles have increased HubSpot's website traffic, which has made its lead generation program much more effective.

18-7a The Changing World of Social Media

As you read through the chapter, some of the trends that are noted may already seem ancient to you. The rate of change in social media is astounding—usage statistics change daily for sites like Facebook and Twitter. Some things that are in the rumor mill as we write this may have exploded in popularity; others may have fizzled out without even appearing on your radar. In Exhibit 18.2, we have listed some of the items that seem to be on the brink of exploding on to the social media scene. Take a moment to fill in the current state of each in the third column. Have you heard of it? Has it come and gone? Maybe it is still rumored, or maybe it has petered out. This exercise highlights not only the speed with which social media change but also the importance of keeping tabs on rumors. Doing so may give you a competitive advantage by being able to understand and invest in the next big social media site.

STUDY TOOLS 18

LOCATED AT BACK OF THE TEXTBOOK

☐ Rip out Chapter Review Card

LOCATED AT WWW.CENGAGEBRAIN.COM

☐ Review Key Terms Flashcards and create your own

☐ Track your knowledge and understanding of key concepts in marketing

☐ Complete practice and graded quizzes to prepare for tests

☐ Complete interactive content within the MKTG Online experience

☐ View the chapter highlight boxes within the MKTG Online experience

19 | Pricing Concepts

After finishing this chapter go to **PAGE 359** for **STUDY TOOLS**

LEARNING OUTCOMES

After studying this chapter, you will be able to…

19-1 Discuss the importance of pricing decisions to the economy and to the individual firm

19-2 List and explain a variety of pricing objectives

19-3 Explain the role of demand in price determination

19-4 Understand the concepts of dynamic pricing and yield management systems

19-5 Describe cost-oriented pricing strategies

19-6 Demonstrate how the product life cycle, competition, distribution and promotion strategies, customer demands, the Internet and extranets, and perceptions of quality can affect price

19-7 Describe the procedure for setting the right price

19-8 Identify the legal constraints on pricing decisions

19-9 Explain how discounts, geographic pricing, and other pricing tactics can be used to fine-tune a base price

JaysonPhotography/Shutterstock.com

19-1 THE IMPORTANCE OF PRICE

Price means one thing to the consumer and something else to the seller. To the consumer, it is the cost of something. To the seller, price is revenue—the primary source of profits. In the broadest sense, price allocates resources in a free-market economy. Marketing managers are frequently challenged by the task of price setting, but they know that meeting the challenge of setting the right price can have a significant impact on the firm's bottom line. Organizations that successfully manage prices do so by creating a pricing infrastructure within the company. This means defining pricing goals, searching for ways to create greater customer value, assigning authority and responsibility for pricing decisions, and creating tools and systems to continually improve pricing decisions. The importance of creating the right pricing strategy cannot be overstated.

19-1a What Is Price?

Price is that which is given up in an exchange to acquire a good or service. Price also plays two roles in the evaluation of product alternatives: as a measure of sacrifice and as an information cue. To some degree, these are two opposing effects.

THE SACRIFICE EFFECT OF PRICE Price is, again, "that which is given up," which means what is sacrificed to get a good or service. In the United States, the sacrifice is usually money, but it can be other things as well. It may also be time lost while waiting to acquire the good or service. Price might also include lost dignity for individuals who lose their jobs and must rely on charity. For a college student, paying tuition might mean skipping a vacation, buying a less luxurious car, or waiting longer to buy a first house.

THE INFORMATION EFFECT OF PRICE Consumers do not always choose the lowest-priced product in a category, such as shoes, cars, or wine, even when the products are otherwise similar. One explanation of this behavior, based upon research, is that we infer quality information from price. That is, higher quality equals higher price. The information effect of price may also extend to favorable price perceptions by others because higher prices can convey the

> **"Trying to set the right price is one of the most stressful and pressure-filled tasks of the marketing manager."**

prominence and status of the purchaser to other people. Thus, both a Swatch and a Rolex can tell time accurately, but they convey different meanings. The price–quality relationship will be discussed later in the chapter.

VALUE IS BASED UPON PERCEIVED SATISFACTION
Consumers are interested in obtaining a "reasonable price." "Reasonable price" really means "perceived reasonable value" at the time of the transaction. One of your authors purchased a new juice machine for around $60 so he could quickly prepare fresh-squeezed orange juice in the morning. The machine worked just fine for about a year and a half, but one morning, it made a strange noise and that was the last of the fresh orange juice. The warranty was only good for a year, so the author

> **price** that which is given up in an exchange to acquire a good or service

had to buy a new machine. He did not receive the expected perceived reasonable value from the original juice machine.

19-1b The Importance of Price to Marketing Managers

As noted in the chapter introduction, prices are the key to revenues, which in turn are the key to profits for an organization. **Revenue** is the price charged to customers multiplied by the number of units sold. Revenue is what pays for every activity of the company: production, finance, sales, distribution, and so on. What is left over (if anything) is **profit**. Managers usually strive to charge a price that will earn a fair profit.

$$\textbf{Price} \times \textbf{Units} = \textbf{Revenue}$$

To earn a profit, managers must choose a price that is not too high or too low—a price that equals the perceived value to target consumers. If, in consumers' minds, a price is set too high, the perceived value will be less than the cost, and sale opportunities will be lost.

19-2 PRICING OBJECTIVES

To survive in today's highly competitive marketplace, companies need pricing objectives that are specific, attainable, and measurable. Realistic pricing goals then require continual monitoring to determine the effectiveness of the company's strategy. For convenience, pricing objectives can be divided into three categories: profit oriented, sales oriented, and status quo.

19-2a Profit-Oriented Pricing Objectives

Profit-oriented pricing objectives include profit maximization, satisfactory profits, and target return on investment.

PROFIT MAXIMIZATION *Profit maximization* means setting prices so that total revenue is as large as possible relative to total costs. Profit maximization does not always signify unreasonably high prices, however. Both price and profits depend on the type of competitive environment a firm faces, such as whether it is in a monopoly position (being the only seller) or in a much more competitive situation. Also, remember that a firm cannot charge a price higher than the product's perceived value. Sometimes managers say that their company is trying to maximize profits—in other words, trying to make as much money as possible. Although this goal may sound impressive to stockholders, it is not good enough for planning.

In attempting to maximize profits, managers can try to expand revenue by increasing customer satisfaction, or they can attempt to reduce costs by operating more efficiently. A third possibility is to attempt to do both. Some companies may focus too much on cost reduction at the expense of the customer. Lowe's lost market share when it cut costs by reducing the number of associates on the floor. Customer service declined—and so did revenue. When firms rely too heavily on customer service, however, costs tend to rise to unacceptable levels. United States' airlines used to serve full meals on two-hour flights and offered pillows and blankets to tired customers. This proved to be unsustainable. A company can maintain or slightly cut costs while increasing customer loyalty through customer service initiatives, loyalty programs, customer relationship management programs, and allocating resources to programs that are designed to improve efficiency and reduce costs.

SATISFACTORY PROFITS Satisfactory profits are a reasonable level of profits. Rather than maximizing profits, many organizations strive for profits that are satisfactory to the stockholders and management—in other words, a level of profits consistent with the level of risk an organization faces. In a risky industry, a satisfactory profit may be thirty-five percent. In a low-risk industry, it might be seven percent.

TARGET RETURN ON INVESTMENT The most common profit objective is a target **return on investment (ROI)**, sometimes called the firm's return on total assets. ROI measures management's overall effectiveness in generating profits with the available assets. The higher the firm's ROI, the better off the firm is. Many companies use a target ROI as their main pricing goal. In summary, ROI is a percentage that puts a firm's profits into perspective by showing profits relative to investment.

Return on investment is calculated as follows:

$$\text{Return on investment} = \frac{\textbf{Net profits after taxes}}{\textbf{Total assets}}$$

revenue the price charged to customers multiplied by the number of units sold

profit revenue minus expenses

return on investment (ROI) net profit after taxes divided by total assets

Assume that in 2017 Rimer Systems had assets of $4.5 million, net profits of $550,000, and a target ROI of ten percent. This was the actual ROI:

$$\text{ROI} = \frac{\$550,000}{\$4,500,000} = 12.2 \text{ percent}$$

As you can see, the ROI for Rimer Systems exceeded its target, which indicates that the company prospered in 2017.

Comparing the 12.2 percent ROI with the industry average provides a more meaningful picture, however. Any ROI needs to be evaluated in terms of the competitive environment, risks in the industry, and economic conditions. Generally speaking, firms seek ROIs in the ten to thirty percent range. In some industries, such as the grocery industry, however, a return of under five percent is common and acceptable.

A company with a target ROI can predetermine its desired level of profitability. The marketing manager can use the standard, such as ten percent ROI, to determine whether a particular price and marketing mix are feasible.

In addition, however, the manager must weigh the risk of a given strategy even if the return is in the acceptable range.

19-2b Sales-Oriented Pricing Objectives

Sales-oriented pricing objectives are based on market share as reported in dollar or unit sales. Firms strive for either market share or to maximize sales.

MARKET SHARE Market share is a company's product sales as a percentage of total sales for that industry. Sales can be reported in dollars or in units of product. It is very important to know whether market share is expressed in revenue or units because the results may be different. Consider four companies competing in an industry with 2,000 total unit sales and total industry revenue of $4,000 (see Exhibit 19.1). Company A has the largest unit market share at 50 percent, but it has only 25 percent of the revenue market share. In contrast, Company D has only a 15 percent unit share but the largest revenue share: 30 percent. Usually, market share is expressed in terms of revenue and not units.

Many companies believe that maintaining or increasing market share is an indicator of the effectiveness of their marketing mix. Larger market shares have indeed often meant higher profits, thanks to greater economies of scale, market power, and ability to compensate top-quality management. Conventional wisdom also says that market share and ROI are strongly related. For the most part they are; however, many companies with low market share survive and even prosper. To succeed with a low market share, companies often need to compete in industries with slow growth and few product changes—for instance, industrial supplies. Otherwise, they must vie in an industry that makes frequently bought items, such as consumer convenience goods.

The conventional wisdom about market share and profitability is not always reliable, however. Because of extreme competition in some industries, many market share leaders either do not reach their target ROI or actually lose money. Procter & Gamble switched from market share to ROI objectives after realizing that profits do not automatically follow from a large market share.

SALES MAXIMIZATION Rather than strive for market share, sometimes companies try to maximize sales. A firm with the objective of maximizing sales ignores profits, competition, and the marketing environment as long as sales are rising.

If a company is strapped for funds or faces an uncertain future, it may try to generate a maximum amount of cash in the short run. Management's task when using this objective is to calculate which price–quantity relationship generates the greatest cash revenue. Sales maximization can also be effectively used on a temporary basis to sell off excess inventory. It is not uncommon to find Christmas cards, ornaments, and other seasonal items discounted at 50 to 70 percent off retail prices after the holiday season has ended.

Maximization of cash should never be a long-run

market share a company's product sales as a percentage of total sales for that industry

EXHIBIT 19.1	TWO WAYS TO MEASURE MARKET SHARE (UNITS AND REVENUE)				
Company	Units Sold	Unit Price	Total Revenue	Unit Market Share	Revenue Market Share
A	1,000	$1.00	$1,000	50	25
B	200	4.00	800	10	20
C	500	2.00	1,000	25	25
D	300	4.00	1,200	15	30
Total	2,000		$4,000		

It is not uncommon to find Christmas cards, ornaments, and other seasonal items discounted at 50 to 70 percent off retail prices after the holiday season has ended.

objective because cash maximization may mean little or no profitability.

19-2c Status Quo Pricing Objectives

Status quo pricing seeks to maintain existing prices or to meet the competition's prices. This third category of pricing objectives has the major advantage of requiring little planning. It is essentially a passive policy.

Often, firms competing in an industry with an established price leader simply meet the competition's prices. These industries typically have fewer price wars than those with direct price competition. In other cases, managers regularly shop competitors' stores to ensure that their prices are comparable.

Status quo pricing often leads to suboptimal pricing. This occurs because the strategy ignores customers' perceived value of both the firm's goods or services and those offered by its competitors. Status quo pricing also ignores demand and costs. Although the policy is simple to implement, it can lead to a pricing disaster.

> **status quo pricing** a pricing objective that maintains existing prices or meets the competition's prices
>
> **demand** the quantity of a product that will be sold in the market at various prices for a specified period
>
> **supply** the quantity of a product that will be offered to the market by a supplier at various prices for a specified period
>
> **elasticity of demand** consumers' responsiveness or sensitivity to changes in price
>
> **elastic demand** a situation in which consumer demand is sensitive to changes in price
>
> **inelastic demand** a situation in which an increase or a decrease in price will not significantly affect demand for the product

19-3 THE DEMAND DETERMINANT OF PRICE

After marketing managers establish pricing goals, they must set specific prices to reach those goals. The price they set for each product depends mostly on two factors: the demand for the good or service and the cost to the seller for that good or service. When pricing goals are mainly sales oriented, demand considerations usually dominate. Other factors, such as distribution and promotion strategies, perceived quality, needs of large customers, the Internet, and the stage of the product life cycle, can also influence price.

19-3a The Nature of Demand

Demand is the quantity of a product that will be sold in the market at various prices for a specified period. The quantity of a product that people will buy depends on its price. The higher the price, the fewer goods or services consumers will demand. Conversely, the lower the price, the more goods or services they will demand.

Supply is the quantity of a product that will be offered to the market by a supplier or suppliers at various prices for a specified period. At higher prices, manufacturers earn more capital and can produce more products.

19-3b Elasticity of Demand

To appreciate the concept of demand , you should understand elasticity. **Elasticity of demand** refers to consumers' responsiveness or sensitivity to changes in price. **Elastic demand** is a situation in which consumer demand is sensitive to price changes. Conversely, **inelastic demand** means that an increase or a decrease in price will not significantly affect demand for the product.

FACTORS THAT AFFECT ELASTICITY Several factors affect elasticity of demand, including the following:

- **Availability of substitutes:** When many substitute products are available, the consumer can easily switch from one product to another, making demand more elastic. The same is true in reverse: A person with complete renal failure will pay whatever is charged for a kidney transplant because there is no substitute.

- **Price relative to purchasing power:** If a price is so low that it is an inconsequential part of an individual's budget, demand will be inelastic. If the price of pepper doubles, for example, people won't stop putting pepper on their eggs or buying more when they run out.

- **Product durability:** Consumers often have the option of repairing durable products (like cars and washing machines) rather than replacing them, thus prolonging their useful life. In other words, people are sensitive to the price increase, and demand is more elastic.

- **A product's other uses:** The greater the number of different uses for a product, the more elastic demand tends to be. If a product has only one use, as may be true of a new medicine, the quantity purchased probably will not vary as price varies. A person will consume only the prescribed quantity, regardless of price. On the other hand, a product like steel has many possible applications. As its price falls, steel becomes more economically feasible in a wider variety of applications, thereby making demand relatively elastic.

Examples of both elastic and inelastic demand abound in everyday life. A 50 percent-plus drop in oil prices recently created some short-run elasticity in demand, but perhaps not as much as one might think. Most people will not rush out and buy a gigantic gas-guzzling SUV just because gasoline prices fall. They may, however, take a longer vacation than originally planned. Most people's driving habits do not change that much during waves of lower gas prices. Instead, they either save the extra money or spend it on other things. On the other hand, demand for tickets to certain sporting and concert events is highly inelastic. The Rolling Stones are still selling out concerts with tickets priced at up to $400. For years, luxury goods companies like LVMH (known for brands like Louis Vuitton, Givenchy, Dom Perignon, Christian Dior, and Bvlgari) regularly priced items 25 to 40 percent higher in Hong Kong and China than in Europe.[1] As the euro began to fall in value against the Chinese yuan, that gap increased to more than 60 percent. Sales began to fall among LVMH and other luxury goods manufacturers in China, indicating that demand for luxury goods was elastic in the Chinese market. However, it turned out that Chinese consumers were still buying luxury goods—they were just buying them outside of China. In 2015, overseas purchases of luxury goods by

The Rolling Stones are still selling out concerts with tickets priced at up to $400.

Chinese customers increased about as much as they fell in Hong Kong and mainland China.

19-4 THE POWER OF DYNAMIC PRICING AND YIELD MANAGEMENT SYSTEMS

When competitive pressures are high, a company must know when it should raise or lower prices to maximize its revenues. More and more companies are turning to **dynamic pricing** to help adjust prices. Dynamic pricing is the ability to adjust prices very quickly, often in real time. This technology has come to the aid of brick-and-mortar retailers, enabling them to compete more effectively with online alternatives. In order to make sure they're getting the best prices, many consumers keep Amazon and other e-commerce sites open on their smartphones while shopping in-store. Rather than sticking with the set prices that give them the profit margins they want, physical retailers increasingly have to tweak their pricing in real time to match—or at least approach—those of their online rivals.

Nebraska Furniture Mart used to have a team of employees at each of its four locations update printed price labels by hand—a time-consuming effort to

dynamic pricing the ability to change prices very quickly, often in real time

Dynamic Pricing to the Extreme

Pioneered by Amazon but adopted by countless on-line retailers, database- and cookie-based dynamic pricing uses a customer's purchase history, location, Internet history, and usage statistics to arrive at a final sale price. For example, Home Depot displays products to mobile device users that are often $100 more expensive than those displayed to desktop computer users.

Hotel-booking websites Cheaptickets and Orbitz charge users an average $12 more per night if they aren't logged in; Travelocity charges users $15 less per night if they access the site from an Apple mobile device; and Expedia and Hotels.com steer users at random to pricier products.[2]

Safeway's "Just for U" app uses dynamic pricing to create exclusive personalized offers for users. At checkout, users scan a club card to redeem their unique discounts.[3]

The city of San Francisco recently installed sensors in 18,250 parking spots. The city uses traffic data to adjust meter and garage parking prices to match demand. While parking rates were previously static no matter how many spots were available, they now range from 25 cents to $6.00 an hour depending on demand. San Francisco also provides real-time parking availability maps via the SFpark app. The city estimates that the sensors and app have reduced the total distance driven looking for parking spots by 30 percent.[4]

Freshplum's machine learning algorithm can predict which customers will leave a website with-out buying anything with 99 percent-plus accuracy. When integrated into an e-commerce platform, the program can offer this group of customers a steeper discount than normal to entice them to purchase before leaving. Visitors to sites with active Freshplum promotions are 36 percent more likely to buy.[5]

maintain the company's pledge to offer the lowest prices on televisions, dishwashers, sofas, and flooring. But now, using long-range wireless transmitters connected to digital price displays, a single worker can update the entire chain's prices quickly and remotely. Besides enabling Nebraska Furniture Mart to quickly change its prices, digital display systems can integrate with smartphone apps and GPS to lead customers directly to items. They can even trigger a shelf price display to flash as the customer approaches.

While digital pricing has better equipped brick-and-mortar stores to compete with online alternatives, it can't totally bring them up to the same level. With some exceptions, Nebraska Furniture Mart limits pricing changes to one per day, before the stores open, so a customer doesn't take an item off the shelf only to find that its price has gone up when he or she gets to the cash register. Chief Information Officer David Bash says, "I know Amazon makes price changes all day long, but that would drive our customers nuts. At 10 a.m., when the store opens, we are the lowest price in our categories. At 10:05 we can't guarantee that."[6]

Developed in the airline industry, **yield management systems (YMS)** use complex mathematical software to profitably fill unused capacity. The

yield management systems (YMS) a technique for adjusting prices that uses complex mathematical software to profitably fill unused capacity by discounting early purchases, limiting early sales at these discounted prices, and overbooking capacity

software employs techniques such as discounting early purchases, limiting early sales at these discounted prices, and overbooking capacity. One of the key inputs in airlines' yield management systems is what has been the historical pattern of demand for a specific flight.

Now dynamic pricing and YMS are spreading beyond service industries as their popularity increases. The lessons of airlines and hotels are not entirely applicable to other industries, however, because plane seats and hotel beds are perishable—if they go empty, the revenue opportunity is lost forever. So it makes sense to slash prices to move toward capacity if it's possible to do so without reducing the prices that other customers pay. Cars and steel are not so perishable, but the capacity to make them is. An underused factory is a lost revenue opportunity. So it makes sense to cut prices to use up capacity if it is possible to do so while getting other customers to pay full price.

19-5 THE COST DETERMINANT OF PRICE

Sometimes companies minimize or ignore the importance of demand and decide to price their products largely or solely on the basis of costs. Prices determined strictly on the basis of costs may be too high for the target market, thereby reducing or eliminating sales. On the other hand, cost-based prices may be too low, causing the firm to earn a lower return than it should. Nevertheless, costs should generally be part of any price determination, if only as a floor below which a good or service must not be priced in the long run.

The idea of cost may seem simple, but it is actually a multifaceted concept, especially for producers of goods and services. A **variable cost** is a cost that varies with changes in the level of output; an example of a variable cost is the cost of materials. In contrast, a **fixed cost** does not change as output is increased or decreased. Examples include rent and executives' salaries. Costs can be used to set prices in a variety of ways. While markup pricing is relatively simple, break-even pricing uses more complicated concepts of cost.

19-5a Markup Pricing

Markup pricing, the most popular method used by wholesalers and retailers to establish a selling price, does not directly analyze the costs of production. Instead, **markup pricing** uses the cost of buying the product

from the producer, plus amounts for profit and for expenses not otherwise accounted for. The total determines the selling price.

A retailer, for example, adds a certain percentage to the cost of the merchandise received to arrive at the retail price. An item that costs the retailer $1.80 and is sold for $2.20 carries a markup of forty cents, which is a markup of 22 percent of the cost ($0.40 ÷ $1.80). Retailers tend to discuss markup in terms of its percentage of the retail price—in this example, 18 percent ($0.40 ÷ $2.20). The difference between the retailer's cost and the selling price (40 cents) is the gross margin.

The formula for calculating the retail price given a certain desired markup is as follows:

$$\text{Retail price} = \frac{\text{Cost}}{1 - \text{Desired return on Sales}}$$

$$= \frac{\$1.80}{1.00 - 0.18}$$

$$= \$2.20$$

If the retailer wants a 30 percent return, then:

$$\text{Retail price} = \frac{\$1.80}{1.00 - 0.30}$$

$$= \$2.57$$

The reason that retailers and others speak of markups on selling price is that many important figures in financial reports, such as gross sales and revenues, are sales figures, not cost figures.

To use markup based on cost or selling price effectively, the marketing manager must calculate an adequate gross margin—the amount added to cost to determine price. The margin must ultimately provide adequate funds to cover selling expenses and profit. Once an appropriate margin has been determined, the markup technique has the major advantage of being easy to employ.

Markups are often based on experience. For example, many small retailers markup merchandise 100 percent over cost. (In other words, they double the cost.) This tactic is called **keystoning**. Some other factors that influence markups are the merchandise's appeal to customers, past response to the markup (an implicit

variable cost a cost that varies with changes in the level of output

fixed cost a cost that does not change as output is increased or decreased

markup pricing the cost of buying the product from the producer, plus amounts for profit and for expenses not otherwise accounted for

keystoning the practice of marking up prices by 100 percent, or doubling the cost

EXHIBIT 19.2   COSTS, REVENUES, AND BREAK-EVEN POINT FOR AMY'S CANDLES

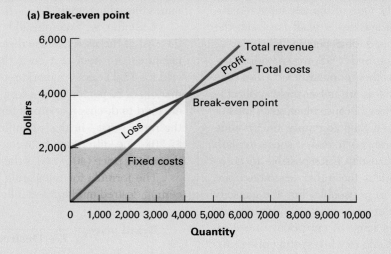

(a) Break-even point

(b) Costs and revenues

Output	Total fixed costs	Average variable costs	Total variable costs	Average total costs	Average revenue (price)	Total revenue	Total costs	Profit or loss
500	$2,000	$0.50	$ 250	$4.50	$1.00	$ 500	$2,250	($1,750)
1,000	2,000	0.50	500	2.50	1.00	1,000	2,500	(1,500)
1,500	2,000	0.50	750	1.83	1.00	1,500	2,750	(1,250)
2,000	2,000	0.50	1,000	1.50	1.00	2,000	3,000	(1,000)
2,500	2,000	0.50	1,250	1.30	1.00	2,500	3,250	(750)
3,000	2,000	0.50	1,500	1.17	1.00	3,000	3,500	(500)
3,500	2,000	0.50	1,750	1.07	1.00	3,500	3,750	(250)
*4,000	2,000	0.50	2,000	1.00	1.00	4,000	4,000	0
4,500	2,000	0.50	2,250	0.94	1.00	4,500	4,250	250
5,000	2,000	0.50	2,500	0.90	1.00	5,000	4,500	500
5,500	2,000	0.50	2,750	0.86	1.00	5,500	4,750	750
6,000	2,000	0.50	3,000	0.83	1.00	6,000	5,000	1,000

*Break-even point

demand consideration), the item's promotional value, the seasonality of the good, its fashion appeal, the product's traditional selling price, and competition. Most retailers avoid any set markup because of such considerations as promotional value and seasonality.

19-5b Break-Even Pricing

break-even analysis a method of determining what sales volume must be reached before total revenue equals total costs

Now, let's take a closer look at the relationship between sales and cost. **Break-even analysis** determines what sales volume must be reached before the company breaks even (its total costs equal total revenue) and no profits are earned.

The typical break-even model assumes a given fixed cost and a constant average variable cost (total cost divided by quantity of output). Suppose that Amy's Candles, a hypothetical firm, has fixed costs of $2,000 and that the cost of labor and materials for each unit produced is fifty cents. Assume that it can sell up to 6,000 units of its product at $1 without having to lower its price.

Exhibit 19-2a illustrates Amy's Candles' break-even point. As Exhibit 19.2b indicates, Amy's Candles' total variable costs increase by fifty cents every time a new unit is produced, and total fixed costs remain constant at

$2,000 regardless of the level of output. Therefore, for 4,000 units of output, Amy's Candles has $2,000 in fixed costs and $2,000 in total variable costs (4,000 units × $0.50), or $4,000 in total costs.

The advantage of break-even analysis is that it provides a quick estimate of how much the firm must sell to break even and how much profit can be earned if a higher sales volume is obtained. If a firm is operating close to the break-even point, it may want to see what can be done to reduce costs or increase sales.

Break-even analysis is not without several important limitations. Sometimes it is hard to know whether a cost is fixed or variable. If labor wins a tough guaranteed-employment contract, are the resulting expenses a fixed cost? More important than cost determination is the fact that simple break-even analysis ignores demand. How does Amy's Candles know it can sell 4,000 units at $1? Could it sell the same 4,000 units at $2 or even $5?

19-6 OTHER DETERMINANTS OF PRICE

Other factors besides demand and costs can influence price. For example, the stages in the product life cycle, the competition, the product distribution strategy, The Internet and extranets, the promotion strategy, customer loyalty, demands of large customers, and the perceived quality can all affect pricing.

19-6a Stages in the Product Life Cycle

As a product moves through its life cycle (see Chapter 11), the demand for the product and the competitive conditions tend to change:

- **Introductory stage:** Management usually sets prices high during the introductory stage. One reason is that it hopes to recover its development costs quickly. In addition, demand originates in the core of the market (the customers whose needs ideally match the product's attributes) and thus is relatively inelastic. On the other hand, if the target market is highly price sensitive, management often finds it better to price the product at the market level or lower. When companies introduce highly innovative products such as consumer electronics, medical devices, and pharmaceuticals, they must properly estimate the elasticity or demand for those products. This is particularly true today, when some life cycles are measured in months, not years.

- **Growth stage:** As the product enters the growth stage, prices generally begin to stabilize for several reasons. First, competitors have entered the market, increasing the available supply. Second, the product has begun to appeal to a broader market. Finally, economies of scale are lowering costs, and the savings can be passed on to the consumer in the form of lower prices.

- **Maturity stage:** Maturity usually brings further price decreases as competition increases and inefficient, high-cost firms are eliminated. Distribution channels become a significant cost factor, however, because of the need to offer wide product lines for highly segmented markets, extensive service requirements, and the sheer number of dealers necessary to absorb high-volume production. The manufacturers that remain in the market toward the end of the maturity stage typically offer similar prices. At this stage, price increases are usually cost initiated, not demand initiated. Nor do price reductions in the late phase of maturity stimulate much demand. Because demand is limited and producers have similar cost structures, the remaining competitors will probably match price reductions.

- **Decline stage:** The final stage of the life cycle may see further price decreases as the few remaining competitors try to salvage the last vestiges of demand. When only one firm is left in the market, prices begin to stabilize. In fact, prices may eventually rise dramatically if the product survives and moves into the specialty goods category, as horse-drawn carriages and vinyl records have.

19-6b Competition, Price Matching, and Customer Loyalty

Competition varies during the product life cycle, of course, and so at times it may strongly affect pricing decisions. Although a firm may not have any competition at first, the high prices it charges may eventually induce another firm to enter the market.

Fast food giants McDonald's, Burger King, and Wendy's have been going head-to-head for years in their efforts to attract cost-conscious customers. A recent McDonald's promotion, McPick2, offered two items for two dollars. One way to counter a competitor's prices is price matching. The four biggest British supermarket chains all offer price matching guarantees, ensuring that customers cannot save money by shopping elsewhere. When a shopper pays more for an item than it would cost at another store, he or she receives a voucher saying, "Your shopping would have been cheaper elsewhere, so here is a voucher for the difference."[7]

In 2015, Target announced that it would price match online retailers Amazon and Walmart.com.

On the face of it, it seems that fierce competition is driving down prices. And this is often the case. However, economists warn that price matching may actually result in higher prices. A car dealership worried about losing clients to a lower-priced rival may offer a price matching guarantee. The hope is that the guarantee will persuade customers not to shop around; they will always pay the lowest price available by sticking with the usually higher-priced dealership. As a result, cutting prices no longer wins the competitor new business. Instead, it means lower profits on existing sales. Thus, the competitor will likely conclude that prices and profit margins are better left high.

Recall the British supermarket chains that give vouchers as a way to meet their price-matching guarantees. In order for a voucher to have value, the customer must return to the same supermarket chain. In this way, price matching can be a tool for building customer loyalty. And the more return customers the store gains over time, the greater the sales volume. Companies attempt to build customer loyalty in many ways. One approach is to offer discounts to regular patrons. This can lead to a loyalty-discount cycle, whereby loyal customers receive deeper discounts that in turn further increase their customer loyalty—resulting in downward pressure on the issuing firm's long-term pricing strategy.[8] Discounts can be an excellent tool to build customer loyalty, but care must be taken not to compromise profit goals. There are many other creative and industry-specific ways

extranet a private electronic network that links a company with its suppliers and customers

to reward loyalty. For example, airlines use unfilled seats to award free travel and upgrades to loyal customers. Some companies give branded gifts to drive customer loyalty. Hotel chains build databases on their most loyal customers so they can automatically serve the room and amenity preferences of frequent customers.

19-6c Distribution Strategy

An effective distribution network can sometimes overcome other minor flaws in the marketing mix. For example, although consumers may perceive a price as being slightly higher than normal, they may buy the product anyway if it is being sold at a convenient retail outlet.

Adequate distribution for a new product can often be attained by offering a larger-than-usual profit margin to distributors. A variation on this strategy is to give dealers a large trade allowance to help offset the costs of promotion and further stimulate demand at the retail level.

19-6d The Impact of the Internet and Extranets

The Internet, **extranets** (private electronic networks), and wireless setups are linking people, machines, and companies around the globe—and connecting sellers and buyers as never before. These links are enabling buyers to quickly and easily compare products and prices, putting them in a better bargaining position. At the same time, the technology allows sellers to collect detailed data about customers' buying habits, preferences, and even spending limits so that sellers can tailor their products and prices.

USING SHOPPING BOTS A shopping bot is a program that searches the Web for the best price for a particular item that you wish to purchase. Bot is short for robot. Shopping bots theoretically give pricing power to the consumer. The more information that the shopper has, the more efficient his or her purchase decision will be.

There are two general types of shopping bots. The first is the broad-based type that searches (trawls) a wide range of product categories such as Google Shopping, Nextag, and PriceGrabber. These sites operate using a Yellow Pages type of model in that they list every retailer they can find. The second is the niche-oriented type that searches for prices for only one type of product such as consumer electronics (CNET), event tickets (SeatGeek), or travel-related services (Kayak).

Shopping bots have been around for quite some time, and security protocols have been developed by some Internet retailers to limit bot trawls. Still, shopping bots remain a powerful and impactful marketing tool to this day.

INTERNET AUCTIONS The Internet auction business is huge. Among the most popular consumer auction sites are:

- **www.onlineauction.com:** Charges a small monthly fee rather than listing and final value fees
- **www.ebay.com:** The most popular auction site, with more than 100 million buyers and sellers.
- **www.ebid.com:** The second largest Internet auction site; fees are less than eBay's.

Even though consumers are spending billions on Internet auctions, business-to-business auctions are likely to be the dominant form in the future. In a reverse auction, the buyer, rather than the seller, specifies the item or service that he or she is looking for. Sellers then compete to offer the lowest price to win the bid. A private company called FedBid has used reverse auctions to position itself between the federal government and private businesses. FedBid uses reverse auctions to put lucrative government contracts up for bid. In theory, since the lowest bid wins, the process can save taxpayers money by encouraging businesses to offer the best possible prices. Critics suggest that awarding government contracts based solely on price means that the government risks ending up with inferior products and services. For example, should the federal government award the next contract for a Navy aircraft carrier solely on the basis of price? Supporters contend that many items that the government purchases (such as automobiles, tools, painting services, and groundskeeping services) are entirely suitable for a reverse auction.

19-6e Promotion Strategy

Price is often used as a promotional tool to increase consumer interest. In many cases, consumer perceptions of a store's prices are more impactful than the actual prices themselves. For example, Whole Foods is perceived as significantly more expensive than other grocery stores despite having prices that are largely in line with competitors. Whole Foods has made a concerted effort to change its pricing image by promoting lower prices and adding new lower-priced options. Similarly, Nordstrom is perceived as a pricier alternative to Macy's even though it has similar prices in many categories and lower prices in other categories. Clearly, price promotion alone does not always create a low price image. Upscale ambiance, expensive specialty offerings, premier locations, a high level of service, and a lack of price matching contribute to a high price image as well.[9]

Often, the amount saved is the most important information when promoting a discount. For example, starting with a retail price of $80, a 40 percent discount creates a savings of $32 for a net sale price of $58. Of these four numbers—80, 40, 32, and 58—the most effective one to promote is the absolute savings of $32.[10]

19-6f Demands of Large Customers

Manufacturers find that their large customers such as department stores often make specific pricing demands that the suppliers must agree to. Department stores are making greater-than-ever demands on their suppliers to cover the heavy discounts and markdowns on their own selling floors. They want suppliers to guarantee their stores' profit margins, and they insist on cash rebates if the guarantee is not met. They are also exacting fines for violations of ticketing, packing, and shipping rules. Cumulatively, the demands are nearly wiping

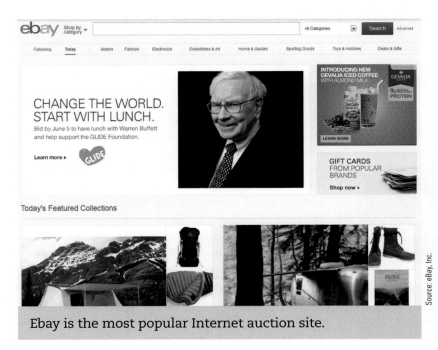

Ebay is the most popular Internet auction site.

Source: eBay, Inc.

out profits for all but the very biggest suppliers, according to fashion designers and garment makers.

Walmart is the largest retailer in the world, and the company uses that size to encourage companies to meet its needs. When Walmart decided that its grocery department needed to have everyday low prices instead of periodic rollbacks, it talked to its major suppliers, such as ConAgra, Quaker Oats, and McCormick & Co., to discuss the possibility of offering a consistently lower price to drive business. Some companies, like ConAgra, are struggling to lower costs while grain and other ingredients are steadily increasing in price. Other companies, like Kraft, have been steadily lowering costs and are having an easier time meeting Walmart's demands. Walmart's demands are not all about keeping prices low, however. The company recently instituted a policy requiring suppliers to evaluate and disclose the full environmental costs of their products. The risk of not working with Walmart? Either your product is important enough to drive traffic that Walmart keeps the item, or you lose the world's biggest sales outlet.

19-6g The Relationship of Price to Quality

As mentioned at the beginning of the chapter, when a purchase decision involves uncertainty, consumers tend to rely on a high price as a predictor of good quality. Reliance on price as an indicator of quality seems to occur for all products, but it reveals itself more strongly for some items than for others. Among the products that benefit from this phenomenon are coffee, aspirin, shampoo, clothing, furniture, whiskey, education, and many services. In the absence of other information, people typically assume that prices are higher because the products contain better materials, because they are made more

Quaker Oats and several other companies have felt the pinch of Walmart's strict pricing demands.

carefully, or, in the case of professional services, because the provider has more expertise.

Researchers have found that price promotions of higher priced, higher quality brands tend to attract more business than do similar promotions of lower priced and lower quality brands. Higher prices increase expectation and set a reference point against which people can evaluate their consumption experiences. Passengers on expensive full-service airlines like Delta, United, and American complain about service failures much more often than do customers of low-cost airlines like Spirit, Southwest, and Easy Jet. A bad experience with a higher priced product or service tends to increase the level of disappointment. Finally, products that generate strong emotions, such as perfumes and fine watches, tend to get more "bang for the buck" in price promotions.[11]

 ### HOW TO SET A PRICE ON A PRODUCT

Setting the right price on a product is a four-step process, as illustrated in Exhibit 19.3 and discussed throughout this chapter:

1. Establish pricing goals.
2. Estimate demand, costs, and profits.
3. Choose a price strategy to help determine a base price.
4. Fine-tune the base price with pricing tactics.

19-7a Establish Pricing Goals

The first step in setting the right price is to establish pricing goals. Recall that pricing objectives fall into three categories: profit oriented, sales oriented, and status quo. These goals are derived from the firm's overall objectives. A good understanding of the marketplace and of the consumer can sometimes tell a manager very quickly whether a goal is realistic.

All pricing objectives have trade-offs that managers must weigh. A profit maximization objective may require a bigger initial investment than the firm can commit to or wants to commit to. Reaching the desired market share often means sacrificing short-term profit because without careful management, long-term profit goals may not be met. Meeting the competition is the easiest pricing goal to implement. But can managers really afford to ignore demand and costs, the life cycle stage, and other considerations? When creating pricing objectives, managers must consider these trade-offs in light of the target

Bloomberg/Getty Images

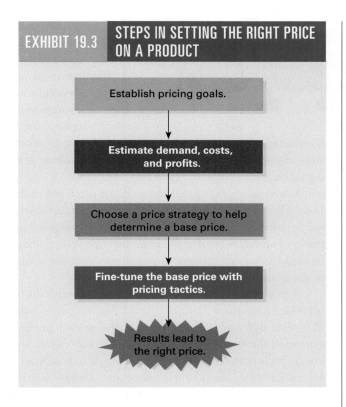

EXHIBIT 19.3 — STEPS IN SETTING THE RIGHT PRICE ON A PRODUCT

Establish pricing goals.

↓

Estimate demand, costs, and profits.

↓

Choose a price strategy to help determine a base price.

↓

Fine-tune the base price with pricing tactics.

↓

Results lead to the right price.

customer, the environment, and the company's overall objectives.

19-7b Estimate Demand, Costs, and Profits

Recall that total revenue is a function of price and quantity demanded and that quantity demanded depends on elasticity. Elasticity is a function of the perceived value to the buyer relative to the price. The types of questions managers consider when conducting marketing research on demand and elasticity are key. Some questions for market research on demand and elasticity are:

• What price is so low that consumers would question the product's quality?

• What is the highest price at which the product would still be perceived as a bargain?

• What is the price at which the product is starting to be perceived as expensive?

• What is the price at which the product becomes too expensive for the target market?

After establishing pricing goals, managers should estimate total revenue

at a variety of prices. This usually requires marketing research. Next, they should determine corresponding costs for each price. They are then ready to estimate how much profit, if any, and how much market share can be earned at each possible price. Managers can study the options in light of revenues, costs, and profits. In turn, this information can help determine which price can best meet the firm's pricing goals.

19-7c Choose a Price Strategy

The basic, long-term pricing framework for a good or service should be a logical extension of the pricing objectives. The marketing manager's chosen **price strategy** defines the initial price and gives direction for price movements over the product life cycle.

The price strategy sets a competitive price in a specific market segment based on a well-defined positioning strategy. Changing a price level from premium to super premium may require a change in the product itself, the target customers served, the promotional strategy, or the distribution channels.

A company's freedom in pricing a new product and devising a price strategy depends on the market conditions and the other elements of the marketing mix. If a firm launches a new item resembling several others already on the market, its pricing freedom will be restricted. To succeed, the company will probably have to charge a price close to the average market price. In contrast, a firm that introduces a totally new product with no close substitutes will have considerable pricing freedom.

The conventional wisdom is that store brands such as Target's Archer Farms and Kroger's Simple Truth should be priced lower than manufacturer's national brands. In fact, private label products are priced an average of 29 percent less than their national brand counterparts.[12] However, savvy retailers doing pricing strategy research have found that store brands do not necessarily have to be cheap. When store brands are positioned as gourmet or specialty items, consumers will even pay more for them than for gourmet national brands.

Companies that do serious planning when creating a price strategy usually select from three basic approaches: price

Sheila Fitzgerald/Shutterstock.com

> **price strategy** a basic, long-term pricing framework that establishes the initial price for a product and the intended direction for price movements over the product life cycle

skimming, penetration pricing, and status quo pricing.

PRICE SKIMMING

Price skimming is sometimes called a "market-plus" approach to pricing because it denotes a high price relative to the prices of competing products. The term *price skimming* is derived from the phrase "skimming the cream off the top." Companies often use this strategy for new products when the product is perceived by the target market as having unique advantages. Often companies will use skimming and then lower prices over time. This is called "sliding down the demand curve." Manufacturers sometimes maintain skimming prices throughout a product's life cycle. A manager of the factory that produces Chanel purses (retailing for over $2,000 each) told one of your authors that it takes back unsold inventory and destroys it rather than selling it at a discount.

Price skimming works best when there is strong demand for a good or service. Apple, for example, uses skimming when it brings out a new iPhone or Watch. As new models are unveiled, prices on older versions are normally lowered. Firms can also effectively use price skimming when a product is well protected legally, when it represents a technological breakthrough, or when it has in some other way blocked the entry of competitors. Managers may follow a skimming strategy when production cannot be expanded rapidly because of technological difficulties, shortages, or constraints imposed by the skill and time required to produce a product (such as fine china, for example).

A successful skimming strategy enables management to recover its product development costs quickly. Even if the market perceives an introductory price as too high, managers can lower the price. Firms often believe it is better to test the market at a high price and then lower the price if sales are too slow. Successful skimming strategies are not limited to products. Well-known athletes, lawyers, and celebrity hairstylists are experts at price skimming. Naturally, a skimming strategy will encourage competitors to enter the market.

PENETRATION PRICING

Penetration pricing is at the opposite end of the spectrum from skimming. Penetration pricing means charging a relatively low price for a product when it is first rolled out as a way to reach the mass market. The low price is designed to capture a large share of a substantial market, resulting in lower production costs. If a marketing manager has made obtaining a large market share the firm's pricing objective, penetration pricing is a logical choice.

Penetration pricing does mean lower profit per unit, however. Therefore, to reach the break-even point, it requires a higher volume of sales than would a skimming policy. The recovery of product development costs may be slow. As you might expect, penetration pricing tends to discourage competition.

A penetration strategy tends to be effective in a price-sensitive market. Price should decline more rapidly when demand is elastic because the market can be expanded through a lower price. The ultra-low-cost airline Spirit is now among the most profitable U.S. airlines. Its cut-rate fares include little more than a seat—nearly everything else is sold à la carte. The only complimentary item in the cabin is ice. If you want water with your ice, it costs $3.00. Yet this airline maintains the highest load numbers in the industry and it continues its rapid growth. Clearly, price matters.[13]

If a firm has a low fixed cost structure and each sale provides a large contribution to those fixed costs, penetration pricing can boost sales and provide large increases in profits—but only if the market size grows or if competitors choose not to respond. Low prices can attract additional buyers to the market. The increased sales can justify production expansion or the adoption of new technologies, both of which can reduce costs. And, if firms have excess capacity, even low-priced business can provide incremental dollars toward fixed costs.

Penetration pricing can also be effective if an experience curve will cause costs per unit to drop significantly. The experience curve proposes that per-unit costs will go down as a firm's production experience increases. Manufacturers that fail to take advantage of these effects will find themselves at a competitive cost disadvantage relative to others that are further along the curve.

The big advantage of penetration pricing is that it typically discourages or blocks competition from entering a market. The disadvantage is that penetration means gearing up for mass production to sell a large volume at a low price. If the volume fails to materialize, the company will face huge losses from building or converting a factory to produce the failed product.

Carlos Yudica/Shutterstock.com

price skimming a pricing policy whereby a firm charges a high introductory price, often coupled with heavy promotion

penetration pricing a pricing policy whereby a firm charges a relatively low price for a product when it is first rolled out as a way to reach the mass market

STATUS QUO PRICING The third basic price strategy a firm may choose is status quo pricing. Recall that this pricing strategy means charging a price identical to or very close to the competition's price. Although status quo pricing has the advantage of simplicity, its disadvantage is that the strategy may ignore demand or cost or both. If the firm is comparatively small, however, meeting the competition may be the safest route to long-term survival.

19-8 THE LEGALITY OF PRICE STRATEGY

As mentioned in Chapter 4, some pricing decisions are subject to government regulation. Among the issues that fall into this category are unfair trade practices, price fixing, price discrimination, and predatory pricing.

19-8a Unfair Trade Practices

In more than half of the United States, **unfair trade practice acts** put a floor under wholesale and retail prices. Selling below cost in these states is illegal. Wholesalers and retailers must usually take a certain minimum percentage markup on their combined merchandise cost and transportation cost. The most common markup figures are 6 percent at the retail level and 2 percent at the wholesale level. If a specific wholesaler or retailer can provide conclusive proof that operating costs are lower than the minimum required figure, lower prices may be allowed.

The intent of unfair trade practice acts is to protect small local firms from giants like Walmart, which operates very efficiently on razor-thin profit margins. State enforcement of unfair trade practice laws has generally been lax, however, partly because low prices benefit local consumers.

19-8b Price Fixing

Price fixing is an agreement between two or more firms on the price they will charge for a product. Suppose two or more executives from competing firms meet to decide how much to charge for a product or to decide which of them will submit the lowest bid on a certain contract. Such practices are illegal under the Sherman Act and the Federal Trade Commission Act. Offenders have received fines and sometimes prison terms. Price fixing is one area where the law is quite clear, and the U.S. Justice Department's enforcement is vigorous.

19-8c Price Discrimination

The Robinson-Patman Act of 1936 prohibits any firm from selling to two or more different buyers, within a reasonably short time, commodities (not services) of like grade and quality at different prices where the result would be to substantially lessen competition. The act also makes it illegal for a seller to offer two buyers different supplementary services and for buyers to use their purchasing power to force sellers into granting discriminatory prices or services.

The Robinson-Patman Act provides three defenses for a seller charged with price discrimination (in each case the burden is on the seller to prove the defense):

- **Cost:** A firm can charge different prices to different customers if the prices represent manufacturing or quantity discount savings.

- **Market conditions:** Price variations are justified if designed to meet fluid product or market conditions. Examples include the deterioration of perishable goods, the obsolescence of seasonal products, a distress sale under court order, and a legitimate going-out-of-business sale.

- **Competition:** A reduction in price may be necessary to stay even with the competition. Specifically, if a competitor undercuts the price quoted by a seller to a buyer, the law authorizes the seller to lower the price charged to the buyer for the product in question.

19-8d Predatory Pricing

Predatory pricing is the practice of charging a very low price for a product with the intent of driving competitors out of business or out of a market. Once competitors have been driven out, the firm raises its prices. This practice is illegal under the Sherman Act and the Federal Trade Commission Act. To prove predatory pricing, the Justice Department must show that the predator—the destructive company—explicitly tried to ruin a competitor and that the predatory price was below the predator's average variable cost.

Prosecutions for predatory pricing suffered a major setback when a federal judge threw out a predatory pricing suit filed by the Department of Justice against American

unfair trade practice acts laws that prohibit wholesalers and retailers from selling below cost

price fixing an agreement between two or more firms on the price they will charge for a product

predatory pricing the practice of charging a very low price for a product with the intent of driving competitors out of business or out of a market

Sixty independent pet supply retailers met in March 2016 to discuss rampant predatory pricing among their online competitors. These online-only storefronts, which frequently sell products at or below wholesale prices, recently began targeting customers of brick-and-mortar retailers with aggressive print and digital ad campaigns.

Airlines. The Department of Justice argued that the definition should be updated and that the test should be whether there was any business justification, other than driving away competitors, for American's aggressive pricing. Under that definition, the Department of Justice attorneys thought they had a great case. Whenever a fledgling airline tried to get a toehold in the Dallas market, American would meet its fares and add flights. As soon as the rival retreated, American would jack its fares back up.

Under the average variable cost definition, however, the case would have been almost impossible to win. The reason is that, like a high-tech industry, the airline industry has high fixed costs and low marginal costs. Once a flight is scheduled, the marginal cost of providing a seat for an additional passenger is almost zero. Thus, it is very difficult to prove that an airline is pricing below its average variable cost. The judge was not impressed by the Department of Justice's argument, however, and kept the average variable cost definition of predatory pricing.

19-9 TACTICS FOR FINE-TUNING THE BASE PRICE

After managers understand both the legal and the marketing consequences of price strategies, they should set a base price—the general price level at which the company expects to sell the good or service. The general price level is correlated with the pricing policy: above the market (price skimming), at the market (status quo pricing), or below the market (penetration pricing). The final step, then, is to fine-tune the base price.

Fine-tuning techniques are approaches that do not change the general price level. They do, however, result in changes within a general price level. These pricing tactics allow the firm to adjust for competition in certain markets, meet ever-changing government regulations, take advantage of unique demand situations, and meet promotional and positioning goals. Fine-tuning pricing tactics include various sorts of discounts, geographic pricing, and other pricing strategies.

19-9a Discounts, Allowances, Rebates, and Value-Based Pricing

A base price can be lowered through the use of discounts and the related tactics of allowances, rebates, low or zero percent financing, and value-based pricing. Managers use the various forms of discounts to encourage customers to do what they would not ordinarily do, such as paying cash rather than using credit, taking delivery out of season, or performing certain functions within a distribution channel. The following are the most common tactics:

- **Quantity discounts:** When buyers get a lower price for buying in multiple units or above a specified dollar amount, they are receiving a quantity discount. A cumulative quantity discount is a deduction from list price that applies to the buyer's total purchases made during a specific period; it is intended to encourage customer loyalty. In contrast, a noncumulative quantity discount is a deduction from list price that applies to a single order rather than to the total volume of orders placed during a certain period. It is intended to encourage orders in large quantities.

- **Cash discounts:** A cash discount is a price reduction offered to a consumer, an industrial user, or a

---

base price the general price level at which the company expects to sell the good or service

quantity discount a price reduction offered to buyers buying in multiple units or above a specified dollar amount

cumulative quantity discount a deduction from list price that applies to the buyer's total purchases made during a specific period

noncumulative quantity discount a deduction from list price that applies to a single order rather than to the total volume of orders placed during a certain period

cash discount a price reduction offered to a consumer, an industrial user, or a marketing intermediary in return for prompt payment of a bill

marketing intermediary in return for prompt payment of a bill. Prompt payment saves the seller carrying charges and billing expenses and allows the seller to avoid bad debt.

Coprid/Shutterstock.com

- **Functional discounts:**
When distribution channel intermediaries, such as wholesalers or retailers, perform a service or function for the manufacturer, they must be compensated. This compensation, typically a percentage discount from the base price, is called a **functional discount** (or **trade discount**). Functional discounts vary greatly from channel to channel, depending on the tasks performed by the intermediary.

- **Seasonal discounts:** A **seasonal discount** is a price reduction for buying merchandise out of season. It shifts the storage function to the purchaser. Seasonal discounts also enable manufacturers to maintain a steady production schedule year-round.

- **Gambled price discounts:** The customer receives a discount based upon the outcome of a probabilistic gamble (and which is therefore uncertain). Discounts involving uncertainty have been growing in popularity recently. Sears' Super Scratch event involved customers receiving a scratch-and-save card that granted savings up to $500. After paying, the cashier scratched the card to reveal the discount. This is similar to a *roll-the-dice discount*, which involves paying for the item and then rolling dice to determine the discount. Several apparel chains (such as Jack Jones and Mustang Jeans) and restaurants (such as Hooters) have conducted roll-the-dice campaigns. Research shows that regular price discounts can create expectations of lower prices. This can have a negative impact on profitability. Gambled price discounts, however, tend not to create long-run expectations of lower prices.[14]

- **Promotional allowances:** A **promotional allowance** (also known as a **trade allowance**) is a payment to a dealer for promoting the manufacturer's products. It is both a pricing tool and a promotional device. As a pricing tool, a promotional allowance is like a functional discount. If, for example, a retailer runs an ad for a manufacturer's product, the manufacturer may pay half the cost.

- **Rebates:** A **rebate** is a cash refund given for the purchase of a product during a specific period. The advantage of a rebate over a simple price reduction for stimulating demand is that a rebate is a temporary inducement that can be taken away without altering the basic price structure. A manufacturer that uses a simple price reduction for a short time may meet resistance when trying to restore the price to its original, higher level.

- **Coupons:** A coupon is a discount offered via paper, a card, a printable web page, or an electronic code. U.S. marketers issue more than 310 billion coupons each year, 2.75 billion of which are redeemed. This redemption rate of less than 1 percent has held steady for many years.[15] Insurance companies often raise copays on expensive drugs to get consumers to switch to low-cost alternatives. However, drug manufacturers have begun advertising "no copay" coupons for certain high-price drugs, leaving the insurance companies to pay the balance. The pharmaceutical industry now spends about $7 billion a year on copay coupons and discount cards.[16] When patients have a copay of $50, they are four times less likely to fill a prescription.[17] Drug companies say that they are just making their drugs more affordable for consumers, but are not offering similar discounts to insurance providers. Some pharmacy benefit managers, such as Express Scripts and CUS Health, have begun banning drugs from their programs because of high costs and coupon copays. United Health Group, the nation's largest health insurer, now bans 35 specialty drugs including growth hormones and medicines for pulmonary hypertension and infertility.[18]

- **Zero percent financing:** To get consumers into automobile showrooms, manufacturers sometimes offer zero percent financing, which enable purchasers to borrow money to pay for new cars with no interest charge. This tactic creates a huge increase in sales, but is not without its costs. A five-year interest-free car loan

functional discount (trade discount) a discount to wholesalers and retailers for performing channel functions

seasonal discount a price reduction for buying merchandise out of season

promotional allowance (trade allowance) a payment to a dealer for promoting the manufacturer's products

rebate a cash refund given for the purchase of a product during a specific period

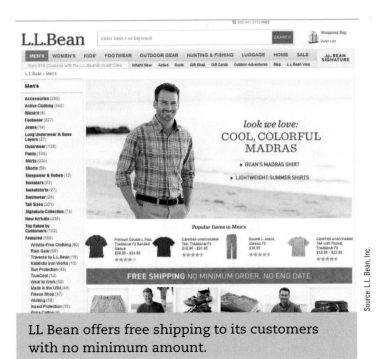

LL Bean offers free shipping to its customers with no minimum amount.

Source: L.L. Bean, Inc.

and associated costs, and then determines the appropriate price. The basic assumption is that the firm is customer driven, seeking to understand the attributes customers want in the goods and services they buy and the value of that bundle of attributes to customers. Because very few firms operate in a pure monopoly, however, a marketer using value-based pricing must also determine the value of competitive offerings to customers. Customers determine the value of a product (not just its price) relative to the value of alternatives. In value-based pricing, therefore, the price of the product is set at a level that seems to the customer to be a good price compared with the prices of other options.

Research has found that loyal customers become even more loyal when they receive discounts. Also, customers who are loyal because of superior service and quality are less likely to bargain over price.[21]

19-9b Geographic Pricing

Because many sellers ship their wares to a nationwide or even a worldwide market, the cost of freight can greatly affect the total cost of a product. Sellers may use several different geographic pricing tactics to moderate the impact of freight costs on distant customers. The following methods of geographic pricing are the most common:

- **FOB origin pricing:** FOB origin pricing, also called FOB factory or FOB shipping point, is a price tactic that requires the buyer to absorb the freight costs from the shipping point ("free on board"). The farther buyers are from sellers, the more they pay, because transportation costs generally increase with the distance merchandise is shipped.

- **Uniform delivered pricing:** If the marketing manager wants total costs, including freight, to be equal for all purchasers of identical products, the firm will adopt uniform delivered pricing, or "postage stamp" pricing. With **uniform delivered pricing**, the seller pays the actual freight charges and bills every purchaser an identical, flat freight charge. This is sometimes called *postage stamp pricing* because a person can send a letter across the street or across the country for the same price.

- **Zone pricing:** A marketing manager who wants to equalize total costs among buyers within large geographic areas—but not necessarily all of the seller's market area—may modify the base price with a zone-pricing tactic. **Zone pricing** is a modification of

typically represents a loss of more than $3,000 for the car's manufacturer.

- **Free shipping:** Free shipping is another method of lowering the price for purchasers. Zappos, Nordstrom, and L.L. Bean offer free shipping with no minimum order amount. However, since shipping is an expense to the seller, it must be built into the cost of the product. Amazon spends about $6.6 billion on shipping but brings in only about $3.1 billion in payments for shipping.[19] Amazon, Best Buy, and Gap recently raised their minimum order requirements to receive free shipping. Based on a study of 113 major retailers, a customer must spend an average of $82 on merchandise to qualify for free shipping.[20]

VALUE-BASED PRICING Value-based pricing, also called *value pricing*, is a pricing strategy that has grown out of the quality movement. Value-based pricing starts with the customer, considers the competition

value-based pricing setting the price at a level that seems to the customer to be a good price compared to the prices of other options

FOB origin pricing a price tactic that requires the buyer to absorb the freight costs from the shipping point ("free on board")

uniform delivered pricing a price tactic in which the seller pays the actual freight charges and bills every purchaser an identical, flat freight charge

zone pricing a modification of uniform delivered pricing that divides the United States (or the total market) into segments or zones and charges a flat freight rate to all customers in a given zone

uniform delivered pricing. Rather than using a uniform freight rate for the entire United States (or its total market), the firm divides it into segments or zones and charges a flat freight rate to all customers in a given zone.

- **Freight absorption pricing:** In freight absorption pricing, the seller pays all or part of the actual freight charges and does not pass them on to the buyer. The manager may use this tactic in intensely competitive areas or as a way to break into new market areas.

- **Basing-point pricing:** With basing-point pricing, the seller designates a location as a basing point and charges all buyers the freight cost from that point, regardless of the city from which the goods are shipped. Thanks to several adverse court rulings, basing-point pricing has waned in popularity. Freight fees charged when none were actually incurred, called *phantom freight*, have been declared illegal.

19-9c Other Pricing Tactics

Unlike geographic pricing, other pricing tactics are unique and defy neat categorization. Managers use these tactics for various reasons—for example, to stimulate demand for specific products, to increase store patronage, and to offer a wider variety of merchandise at a specific price point. Such pricing tactics include a single-price tactic, flexible pricing, professional services pricing, price lining, leader pricing, bait pricing, odd–even pricing, price bundling, and two-part pricing.

SINGLE-PRICE TACTIC A merchant using a single-price tactic offers all goods and services at the same price (or perhaps two or three prices). Dollar Tree and Dollar Bill chains sell everything for $1 or less. Such a strategy can be quite successful. The 280-store chain 99 Cents Only sold for $1.6 billion.[22]

FLEXIBLE PRICING Flexible pricing (or variable pricing) means that different customers pay different prices for essentially the same merchandise bought in equal quantities. This tactic is often found in the sale of shopping goods, specialty merchandise, and most industrial goods except supply items. Car dealers and many appliance retailers commonly follow the practice. It allows the seller to adjust for competition by meeting another seller's price. Thus, a marketing manager with a status quo pricing objective might readily adopt the tactic. Flexible pricing also enables the seller to close a sale with price-conscious consumers.

The obvious disadvantages of flexible pricing are the lack of consistent profit margins, the potential ill will of

Flexible pricing allows a seller to close a sale with price-conscious consumers.

high-paying purchasers, the tendency for salespeople to automatically lower the price to make a sale, and the possibility of a price war among sellers.

PROFESSIONAL SERVICES PRICING Professional services pricing is used by people with lengthy experience, training, and often certification by a licensing board—for example, lawyers, physicians, and family counselors. Professionals sometimes charge customers at an hourly rate, but sometimes fees are based on the solution of a problem or performance of an act (such as an eye examination) rather than on the actual time involved.

Those who use professional pricing have an ethical responsibility not to overcharge a customer. Because demand is sometimes highly inelastic, such as when a person requires heart surgery to survive, there may be a temptation to charge "all the traffic will bear."

PRICE LINING When a seller establishes a series of prices for a type of merchandise, it creates a price line. Price lining is the practice of offering a product line with several items at specific price points. Wireless providers use price lining for cell phones that are purchased with a two-year contract. The top

---

freight absorption pricing a price tactic in which the seller pays all or part of the actual freight charges and does not pass them on to the buyer

basing-point pricing a price tactic that charges freight from a given (basing) point, regardless of the city from which the goods are shipped

single-price tactic a price tactic that offers all goods and services at the same price (or perhaps two or three prices)

flexible pricing (variable pricing) a price tactic in which different customers pay different prices for essentially the same merchandise bought in equal quantities

price lining the practice of offering a product line with several items at specific price points

tier is usually priced at $299 (the highest the market will pay), and subsequent tiers are $249, $199, $149, $99, and $49.

Price lining reduces confusion for both the salesperson and the consumer. The buyer may be offered a wider variety of merchandise at each established price. Price lines may also enable a seller to reach several market segments. For buyers, the question of price may be quite simple: all they have to do is find a suitable product at the predetermined price. Moreover, price lining is a valuable tactic for the marketing manager, because the firm may be able to carry a smaller total inventory than it could without price lines. The results may include fewer markdowns, simplified purchasing, and lower inventory carrying charges.

Price lines also present drawbacks, especially if costs are continually rising. Sellers can offset rising costs in three ways. First, they can begin stocking lower-quality merchandise at each price point. Second, sellers can change the prices, although frequent price line changes confuse buyers. Third, sellers can accept lower profit margins and hold quality and prices constant. This third alternative has short-run benefits, but its long-run handicaps may drive sellers out of business.

LEADER PRICING Leader pricing (or **loss-leader pricing**) is an attempt by the marketing manager to attract customers by selling a product near or even below cost in the hope that shoppers will buy other items once they are in the store. This type of pricing appears weekly in the newspaper advertising of supermarkets. Leader pricing is normally used on well-known items that consumers can easily recognize as bargains.

Leader pricing is not limited to products. Health clubs offer a one-month free trial as a loss leader.

BAIT PRICING In contrast to leader pricing, which is a genuine attempt to give the consumer a reduced price, bait pricing is deceptive. **Bait pricing** tries to get consumers into a store through false or misleading price advertising and then uses high-pressure selling to persuade them to buy more expensive merchandise. You may have seen this ad or a similar one:

> REPOSSESSED . . . Singer slant-needle sewing machine . . . take over 8 payments of $5.10 per month . . . ABC Sewing Center.

This is bait. When a customer goes in to see the machine, a salesperson says that it has just been sold or else shows the prospective buyer a piece of junk. Then the salesperson says, "But I've got a really good deal on this fine new model." This is the switch that may cause a susceptible consumer to walk out with a $400 machine. The Federal Trade Commission considers bait pricing a deceptive act and has banned its use in interstate commerce. Most states also ban bait pricing, but sometimes enforcement is lax.

ODD-EVEN PRICING Odd–even pricing (or **psychological pricing**) means pricing at odd-numbered prices to connote a bargain and pricing at even-numbered prices to imply quality. For years, many retailers have priced their products in odd numbers—for example, $99.95—to make consumers feel they are paying a lower price for the product. Even-numbered pricing is often used for "prestige" items, such as a fine perfume at $100 a bottle or a good watch at $1,000. The demand curve for such items would also be sawtoothed, except that the outside edges would represent even-numbered prices and, therefore, elastic demand.

PRICE BUNDLING Price bundling is marketing two or more products in a single package for a special price. For example, Microsoft offers "suites" of software that bundle spreadsheets, word processing, graphics, e-mail, Internet access, and groupware for networks of microcomputers. Price bundling can stimulate demand for the bundled items if the target market perceives the price as a good value.

Services like hotels and airlines sell a perishable commodity (hotel rooms and airline seats) with relatively fixed costs. Bundling can be an important income stream for these businesses because the variable costs tend to be low—for instance, the cost of cleaning a hotel room. To account for this variability, hotels sometimes charge a resort fee that covers things like use of the gym, pool, and Wi-Fi.

Bundling is also widely used in the telecommunications industry. Companies offer local service, long distance, DSL Internet service, wireless, and even cable television in various bundled configurations. Telecom companies use bundling as a way to protect their market share and fight off competition by locking customers into a group of services. For consumers, comparison shopping may be difficult since they may not be able to determine how much they are really paying for each component of the bundle.

You inevitably encounter bundling when you go to a fast food restaurant. McDonald's Happy Meals and Value

leader pricing (loss-leader pricing) a price tactic in which a product is sold near or even below cost in the hope that shoppers will buy other items once they are in the store

bait pricing a price tactic that tries to get consumers into a store through false or misleading price advertising and then uses high-pressure selling to persuade consumers to buy more expensive merchandise

odd-even pricing (psychological pricing) a price tactic that uses odd-numbered prices to connote bargains and even-numbered prices to imply quality

price bundling marketing two or more products in a single package for a special price

Meals are bundles, and customers can trade up these bundles by super sizing them. Super sizing provides a greater value to the customer and creates more profits for the fast food chain.

TWO-PART PRICING **Two-part pricing** means establishing two separate charges to consume a single good or service. Consumers sometimes prefer two-part pricing because they are uncertain about the number and the types of activities they might use at places like an amusement park. Also, the people who use a service most often pay a higher total price. Two-part pricing can increase a seller's revenue by attracting consumers who would not pay a high fee even for unlimited use. For example, a health club might be able to sell only 100 memberships at $700 annually with unlimited use of facilities, for a total revenue of $70,000. However, it could sell 900 memberships at $200 with a guarantee of using the racquetball courts ten times a month. Every use over ten would require the member to pay a $5 fee. Thus, membership revenue would provide a base of $180,000, with some additional usage fees throughout the year.

PAY WHAT YOU WANT To many people, paying what you want or what you think something is worth is a very risky tactic. Obviously, it would not work for expensive durables like automobiles. Imagine someone paying $1 for a new BMW! Yet this model has worked in varying degrees in digital media marketplaces, restaurants, and other service businesses. One of your authors has patronized a restaurant close to campus that asks diners to pay what they think their meals are worth. After several years, the restaurant is still in business. The owner says

HamsterMan/Shutterstock.com

that the average lunch donation is around $8 for lunch. Social pressures can come into play in a "pay what you want" environment because an individual does not want to appear poor or cheap to his or her peers.

PACKAGE CONTENT REDUCTION Manufacturers can keep the price and package size the same while reducing the amount of content, thereby increasing the price per ounce or pound.[23]

19-9d Consumer Penalties

More and more businesses are adopting **consumer penalties**—extra fees paid by consumers for violating the terms of a purchase agreement. Airlines often charge a fee for changing a return date on a ticket. Businesses impose consumer penalties for two reasons: they will allegedly (1) suffer an irrevocable revenue loss and/or (2) incur significant additional transaction costs should customers be unable or unwilling to complete their purchase obligations. For the company, these customer payments are part of doing business in a highly competitive marketplace. With profit margins in many companies increasingly coming under pressure, organizations are looking to stem losses resulting from customers not meeting their obligations. Some medical professionals charge a penalty fee if you don't show up for an appointment. However, the perceived unfairness of a penalty may affect some consumers' willingness to patronize a business in the future.

two-part pricing a price tactic that charges two separate amounts to consume a single good or service

consumer penalty an extra fee paid by the consumer for violating the terms of the purchase agreement

---

STUDY TOOLS 19

LOCATED AT BACK OF THE TEXTBOOK
☐ Rip out Chapter Review Card

LOCATED AT WWW.CENGAGEBRAIN.COM
☐ Review Key Terms Flashcards and create your own

☐ Track your knowledge and understanding of key concepts in marketing

☐ Complete practice and graded quizzes to prepare for tests

☐ Complete interactive content within the MKTG Online experience

☐ View the chapter highlight boxes within the MKTG Online experience

ENDNOTES

1

1. "Definition of Marketing," *American Marketing Association*, www.marketingpower.com/AboutAMA/Pages/DefinitionofMarketing.aspx (accessed February 16, 2016).

2. Lydia Dishman, "Secrets of America's Happiest Companies," *Fast Company*, January 10, 2013, www.fastcompany.com/3004595/secrets-americas-happiest-companies (accessed February 17, 2016).

3. "100 Best Companies to Work For 2016: Google (Alphabet)," *Fortune*, http://fortune.com/best-companies/google-alphabet-1/ (accessed March 28, 2016).

4. Philip Kotler and Kevin Lane Keller, *A Framework for Marketing Management*, 6th ed. (Upper Saddle River, NJ: Prentice Hall, 2016),

5. Josh Lowensohn, "Apple's Thunderbolt Cable Gets a Price Drop, Shorter Version," *CNET*, January 9, 2013, http://news.CNET.com/8301-13579_3-57563157-37/apples-thunderbolt-cable-gets-a-price-drop-shorter-version (accessed February 18, 2016).

6. Mark J. Miller, "Kellogg's is Open for Breakfast – and Your Opinion on Its Brands," *Brand Channel*, January 20, 2015, www.brandchannel.com/home/post/2015/01/20/150120-Kellogg-Open-for-Breakfast (accessed February 20, 2016).

7. Jeff Youngs, "2015 U.S. Customer Service Index (CSI) Study," *J.D. Power and Associates*, http://jdpower.com/cars/articles/jd-power-studies/2015-us-customer-service-index-study-results (accessed February 18, 2016)

8. Ian Paul, "RIM at CES: 5 Things to Know about BlackBerry 10," *PC World*, January 10, 2013, www.pcworld.com/article/2024740/rim-at-ces-5-things-to-know-about-blackberry-10.html (accessed February 18, 2016).

9. "Consumers are Willing to Put Their Money Where Their Heart Is When It Comes to Goods and Services From Companies Committed to Social Responsibility," *Nielsen*, June 17, 2014, www.nielsen.com/us/en/press-room/2014/global-consumers-are-willing-to-put-their-money-where-their-heart-is.html (accessed February 18, 2016).

10. Marc Gunther, "Unilever's CEO has a green thumb," *Fortune*, June 10, 2013, 125–130, http://connection.ebscohost.com/c/articles/89584471/unilevers-ceo-has-green-thumb (accessed February 18, 2016).

11. A.G. Laffey and Ron Charon, cited in George S. Day and Christine Moorman, *Strategy from the Outside In: Profiting from Customer Value*, (New York City, NY: McGraw-Hill, 2010), 235.

12. George Day and Christine Moorman, *Strategy From the Outside In*, New York, McGraw-Hill, 2010.

13. "The Customer Is Not an Interruption in Our Work; He Is the Purpose of It," *Quote Investigator*, August 2, 2012, http://quoteinvestigator.com/2012/08/02/gandhi-customer (accessed February 18, 2016).

14. George Day and Christine Moorman, *Strategy From the Outside In*, New York, McGraw-Hill, 2010.

15. *Ibid*.

16. "Using Advertising to Engage the Price-Sensitive Consumer," *Dunnhumby*, http://info.dunnhumby.com/pricesensitivity2013 (accessed February 18, 2016).

17. Rob Brunner, "America Shacks Up," *FastCompany*, July/August 2015, 77–95.

18. Michael B. Sauder, Sam Stebbins and Thomas C. Frolich, "Customer Service Hall of Shame," *Yahoo*, July 27, 2015, http://finance.yahoo.com/news/customer-hall-shame-151103637.html (accessed February 18, 2016).

19. "Coastal.com Receives STELLAService Elite Seal for Outstanding Customer Service," *Fort Mill Times*, January 2, 2013, www.businesswire.com/news/home/20130102005748/en/Coastal.com-Receives-STELLAService-Elite-Seal-Outstanding-Customer (accessed February 19, 2016).

20. Rosa Say, "The Six Basic Needs of Customers," *Lifehack*, April 27, 2013, www.lifehack.org/articles/work/the-six-basic-needs-of-customers.html (accessed February 19, 2016).

21. Humayun Khan, "How Nordstrom Made Its Brand Synonymous with Customer Service," *Shopify*, October 2, 2014, https://www.shopify.com/blog/15517012-how-nordstrom-made-its-brand-synonymous-with-customer-service-and-how-you-can-too (accessed February 19, 2016).

22. Harley Manning, "How The 'Most Improved' Companies Raised Their Customer Experience Game Last Year," *Harley Manning's Blog*, April 25, 2011, http://blogs.forrester.com/harley_manning/11-04-25-how_the_most_improved_companies_raised_their_customer_experience_game_last_year (accessed February 21, 2016).

23. Jason Fried, "Marketing Without Marketing," *INC.*, December 2013/January 2014, 116.

24. Michael B. Sauder, Sam Stebbins and Thomas C. Frolich, "Customer Service Hall of Shame."

25. David Kirkaday, "12 Service Values Ritz Carlton Uses (And You Can Too)," www.davidkirkaldy.com/12-service-values-ritz-carlton-uses-and-you-can-too/ (accessed February 21, 2016).

26. Ian Percy, "Is Your Mission Statement Strange?" *RetailWire*, July 7, 2015, www.retailwire.com/discussion/18390/is-your-mission-statement-strange (accessed February 21, 2016).

27. Shalini Ramachandran and Jeffrey A. Trachtenberg, "End of Era for Britannica," *The Wall Street Journal*, March 14, 2013, http://online.wsj.com/news/articles/SB10001424052702304450004577280143864147250 (accessed February 21, 2016).

28. "Canne 2013: Yaris – It's a Car Case Study," Publicis Groupe, http://publicisgroupe.com/#/en/videos/info/id/20114 (accessed February 21, 2016).

29. Peter Dahlstrom and David Edelman, "The Coming Era of 'On-Demand' Marketing," *McKinsey*, April 2013, www.mckinsey.com/insights/marketing_sales/the_coming_era_of_on-demand_marketing (accessed February 21, 2016).

30. U.S. Census Bureau, "U.S. & World Population Clocks," February 21, 2016, www.census.gov/main/www/popclock.html.

31. Nina Golgowski, "Average American Consumes One Ton of Food a Year While Equating a Gallon of Soda a Week," *Daily Mail*, January 1, 2012, www.dailymail.co.uk/news/article-2080940/Average-American-consumes-ton-food-year-equating-gallon-soda-week.html (accessed February 21, 2016).

2

1. Dale Buss, "McDonald's Trims Menu, Expands Customization to Turn Around Brand," *Brand Channel*, December 11, 2014, www.brandchannel.com/home/post/2014/12/11/141211-McDonalds-DIY-Burgers.aspx?utm_campaign=141211-McDonalds-DIY-Burgers&utm_source=newsletter&utm_medium=email (accessed February 22, 2016)

2. Tom Ryan, "Walmart Shutters Express," *RetailWire*, January 18, 2016, http://retailwire.com/discussion/18789/walmart-shutters-express (accessed March 28, 2016).

3. Dale Buss, "Starbucks Goes Back to the Bean in 'Big Bet' on Upscale Coffee Lovers," *Brand Channel*, December 5, 2014, www.brandchannel.com/home/post/141205-Starbucks-Roastery.aspx (accessed February 22, 2016).

4. Dan Caplinger, "Why Amazon.com, Zynga, and Deckers Outdoor Soared Today," *The Motley Fool*, October 25, 2013, www.fool.com/investing/general/2013/10/25/why-amazoncom-zynga-and-deckers-outdoor-soared-tod.aspx (accessed February 22, 2016).

5. John Kell, "McDonald's Promotions, New Menu Items Fail to Jolt U.S. Sales," *Fortune*, July 23, 2015, http://fortune.com/2015/07/23/mcdonalds-sales-breakfast-menu (accessed February 22,, 2016).

6. Dale Buss, "Abbott Labs Expands Into Healthy Snacks with 'Decadent' Curate Bars," *Brand Channel*, February 10, 2016, http://brandchannel.com/2016/02/10/abbott-labs-curate-bars-021016/ (accessed March 28, 2016).

7. Liz Hull, "New Harley is Roaring After Women: Firm Launches Two Bikes Designed for Ladies," *Daily Mail*, July 8, 2014, http://dailymail.co.uk/news/article-2652350/Now-Harley-roaring-women-Firm-launches-two-bikes-designed-ladies.html (accessed February 22, 2016).

8. "GoPro Hero 3 HD Camera Picked as Top Device in 2013 according to iTrustNews," *PRWeb*, January 5, 2013, www.prweb.com/releases/prwebgopro-hero-3/gopro-hero-hd/prweb10293699.htmp (accessed February 22, 2016).

9. Douglas Imaralu, "Can Africa Save Blackberry?" *Ventures*, May 30, 2014, www.ventures-africa.com/2014/05/can-africa-save-blackberry/ (accessed February 22, 2016).

10. "Church's Chicken Purple Pepper Sauce Back by Popular Demand and Brand New Honey Buffalo BBQ Sauce to Complement Church's Fan Favorite Chicken Strips," *Restaurant News Release*, January 13, 2014, www.restaurantnewsrelease.com/churchs-chicken-purple-pepper-sauce-back-by-popular-demand-and-brand-new-honey-buffalo-bbq-sauce-to-complement-churchs-fan-favorite-tender-strips/8534625/ (accessed February 22, 2016).

11. Peter Burrows and Jim Aley, "Why the iPad's Success May Spell the End of the Computer Industry as We Know It," *Bloomberg Businessweek*, March 26–April 1, 2012, 4–5. http://magsreview .com/bloomberg-businessweek/bloomberg -businessweek-march-26-2012/3264-nice-try.html (accessed February 22, 2016).

12. Dave Walker, "'Under the Gunn,' Starring 'Project Runway's' Tim Gunn, Debuts on Lifetime," *NOLA*, January 16, 2014, www.nola.com/tv/index .ssf/2014/01/under_the_gunn_starring_projec.html (accessed February 22, 2016).

13. Matthew Stern, "Starbucks Dumps Tea Bar Concept, Keeps Tea," *RetailWire*, January 27, 2016, http:// retailwire.com/discussion/18809/starbucks -dumps-tea-bar-concept-keeps-tea (accessed March 28, 2016).

14. Matthew Garrahan, "Dr Dre Beats New Paths in Music," *Financial Times*, January 11, 2013, www .ft.com/intl/cms/s/2/70a003d4-5bd7-11e2-bf31 -00144feab49a.html (accessed February 15, 2015); Todd Martens, "Beats Aligns with TopSpin, Picks Daisy Subscription Service Chief," January 10, 2013, www.latimes.com/entertainment/envelope /cotown/la-et-ct-beats-partners-with-topspin-daisy -subscription-service-20130110,0,305852.story (accessed February 22, 2016).

15. "Ben & Jerry's Ice Cream - Ben & Jerry's Mission Statement," Ben & Jerry's, www.benjerry .com/activism/mission-statement (accessed February 22, 2016).

16. Damon Poeter, "Report: Dell 'In Talks' to Go Private," *PC Magazine*, January 14, 2013, www .pcmag.com/article2/0,2817,2414282,00.asp (accessed February 11, 2015); Donna Guglielmo, "Dell Officially Goes Private: Inside the Nastiest Tech Buyout Ever," *Forbes.com*, October 30, 2013, www.forbes.com/sites/connieguglielmo/2013/10/30 /you-wont-have-michael-dell-to-kick-around -anymore/ (accessed February 22, 2016).

17. Sheila Shayon, "Kodak Emerges from Bank-ruptcy with Focus on Digital Imaging, Commercial Printing," *Brand Channel*, April 9, 2013, www .brandchannel.com/home/post/2013/09/04/Kodak -Emerges-From-Bankruptcy (accessed February 22, 2016).

18. Teresa Cedarholm, "Overview: Southwest Airlines," Market Realist, July 21, 2014, http:// marketrealist.com/2014/07/overview-southwest -airlines/ (accessed February 22, 2016).

19. David Aaker, "Why Uniqlo is Winning," *Marketing News*, January 2015, p. 24.

20. "Blue Bell History," www.bluebell.com/the _little_creamery/our_history.html (accessed February 22, 2016).

21. "Our Story," *The Chef's Garden*, www.chefs -garden.com/our-story (accessed February 22, 2016); "Research and Development," *The Chef's Garden*, www.chefs-garden.com/research-and -development (accessed February 22, 2016).

22. Daniel B. Kline, "Amazon's Sustainable Competitive Advantage," *The Motley Fool*, May 18, 2015, http:// fool.com/investing/general/2015/05/18 /amazons-sustainable-competitive-advantage.aspx, (accessed February 22, 2016).

23. "How to Play the Email Game," *The Email Game*, http://emailgame.baydin.com/index.html (accessed February 22, 2016).

24. "Talent Management Framework: Human Resources, Role and Strategies at Google," *Russia Robinson*, June 23, 2014,. https://russiarobinson .wordpress.com/2014/06/23/talent-management -framework-human-resources-role-and-strategies -at-google-inc/ (accessed February 24, 2016).

3

1. "Social Control: From Hunter Gatherer Bands to the United Nations." *Anthropology Now*, April 17, 2014, http://anthropologynow.wordpress.com /tag/social-control (accessed January 16, 2015).

2. "Slapping a 'Natural' Label on Everything," *Bloomberg Businessweek*, November 5, 2015, 62.

3. Kimberlee Morrison, "Yelp Pays $450,000 FTC fine for COPPA Violation," *Social Times*, September 22, 2014, www.adweek.com/socialtimes /yelp-pays-450000-ftc-fine-coppa-violation/204977 (accessed January, 14, 2015).

4. "Compliance," *Google*, https://support.google .com/work/answer/6056694?hl=en (accessed March 14, 2016).

5. "Consumers Seek a Dialogue Rather Than a Monologue," *Quirk's Marketing Research Review*, December, 2015, 12.

6. "Hoaxwagen," *Fortune*, March 15, 2016, 99–115.

7. Catherine Rainbow, "Descriptions of Ethical Theories and Principles," *Davidson College*, www .bio.davidson.edu/people/kabernd/indep/carainbow /Theories.htm (accessed January 10, 2015). Reprinted with permission.

8. "VW Scandal Threatens to Upend CEP," *Wall Street Journal*, September 23, 2015, A1, A2.

9. Clifford Atiyeh, "Everything You Need to Know About the VW Diesel Emissions Scandal," *Car and Driver*, April 5, 2016, http://blog.caranddriver.com /everything-you-need-to-know-about-the-vw-diesel -emissions-scandal/ (accessed April 14, 2016).

10. Ibid.

11. "Moral Development: Lawrence Kohlberg and Carol Gilligan," *Academia.edu*, www.academia .edu/7829090/Moral_Development_Lawrence _Kohlberg_and_Carol_Gilligan (accessed January 11, 2015).

12. Anusorn Singhapakdi, Scott Vitell, and Kenneth Kraft, "Moral Intensity and Ethical Decision Making of Marketing Professionals," *Journal of Business Research*, 36, no. 3, (1996): 245–255; Ishmael Akaah and Edward Riordan, "Judgments of Marketing Profes-sionals about Ethical Issues in Marketing Research: A Replication and Extension," *Journal of Marketing Research*, 26, no. 1, (1989): 112–120; see also Shelby Hunt, Lawrence Chonko, and James Wilcox, "Ethi-cal Problems of Marketing Researchers," *Journal of Marketing Research*, 21, no. 3, (1984): 309–324; Kenneth Andrews, "Ethics in Practice," *Harvard Business Review*, September 1989, 99–104; Thomas Dunfee, Craig Smith, and William T. Ross, Jr., "Social Contracts and Marketing Ethics," *Journal of Marketing*, 63, no. 3, (1999): 14–32; Jay Handelman and Stephen Arnold, "The Role of Marketing Actions with a Social Dimension: Appeals to the Institutional Environment," *Journal of Marketing*, 63, no. 3 (1999): 33–48; David Turnipseed, "Are Good Soldiers Good? Exploring the Link between Organizational Citizenship Behavior and Personal Ethics," *Journal of Business Research*, 55, no. 1, (2002): 1–15; and O.C. Ferrell, John Fraedrich, and Linda Ferrell, *Business Ethics: Ethical Decision Making and Cases*. 10th ed. (Stamford, CT: Cengage Learning) 2015, 128–137.

13. "A Strong Ethical Culture Is Key to Cutting Misconduct on the Job," *Ethics Resource Center*, June 23, 2010, http://ethics.org/news/strong-ethical -culture-key-cutting-misconduct-job (accessed January 12, 2015); "Workplace Ethics in Transition," *Ethics.org*, www.ethics.org/resource/webcasts (accessed January 12, 2015).

14. Ibid.

15. "Message from Larry Merlo, President and CEO," *CVS Health*, February 5, 2014, http:// cvshealth.com/newsroom/message-larry-merlo (accessed April 15, 2016).

16. Author's estimate.

17. "State of Ethics in Large Companies," *Ethics and Compliance Initiative*, https://ethics.org/eci /research/eci-research/nbes/nbes-reports/large -companies (accessed April 15, 2016).

18. Susan Jakes, "Interactive: Visualizing China's Massive Corruption Crackdown," *Foreign Policy*, January 21, 2016, http://foreignpolicy.com/2016 /01/21/interactive-visualizing-chinas-massive -corruption-crackdown/ (accessed April 15, 2016).

19. "Burger King Drops Supplier Linked to Horsemeat," *Times Union*, www.timesunion.com /news/ (accessed January 19, 2015).

20. "Apple IPO Makes Instant Millionaires," EDN, December 12, 2014, www.edn.com/electronics -blogs/edn-moments/44032761/ (accessed January 16, 2015).

21. "Here's What You Don't Know About Microsoft, Today's Best Dow Stock," *The Motley Fool*, March 18, 2014, www.fool.com /investing/general/2014/03/18 (accessed January 16, 2015).

22. "The Benefits and Costs of Socially Responsible Investing," *Morningstar*, January 7, 2015, http:// news.morningstar.com/articlenet/article .aspx?id=679225 (accessed April 15, 2016); Saurabh Mishra and Sachin B. Modi, "Corporate Social Responsibility and Shareholder Wealth: The Role of Marketing Capability," *Journal of Marketing*, January 2016, 26–46.

23. Christian Homburg, Marcel Stierl, and Torsten Bornemann, "Corporate Social Responsibility in Business-to-Business Markets: How Organizational Customers Account for Supplier Corporate Social Responsibility Engagement," *Journal of Marketing*, November 2013, 53–72; Daniel Korschun, C.B. Bhattacharya, and Scott Swain, "Corporate Social Responsibility, Customer Orientation, and the Job Performance of Frontline Employees," *Journal of Marketing*, May 2014, 20–37; Farnoosh Khodakarami, J. Andrew Petersen, and Rajkumar Venkatesan, "Developing Donor Relationships: The Role of the Breadth of Giving." *Journal of Marketing*, July 2015, 77–93; Charles Kang, Frank Germann, and Rajdeep Grewal, "Washing Away Your Sins? Corporate Re-sponsibility, Corporate Social Irresponsibility, and Firm Performance," *Journal of Marketing*, March 2016, 59–79.

24. "The ROI of Morality," *Marketing News*, February 2015.

25. "The Halo Effect," *The Economist*, June 27, 2015, 56.

26. "Made Greener Coffee Refill Tumbler, 16 fl. oz." *Starbucks*, http://store.starbucks.com /made-greener-coffee-refill-tumbler/011039302, default,pd.html (accessed January 18, 2015).

27. "It Pays to be Green: Corporate Social Respon-sibility Meets the Bottom Line," *Nielsen*, June 17, 2014, www.nielsen.com/us/en/insights/news/2014 (accessed January 19, 2015).

28. Ibid.

29. "UN Global Compact Participants," *United Nations*, www.unglobalcompact.org /ParticipantsandStakeholders/index.html (accessed March 17, 2016).

30. "Certified B Corporations," *B Corporation*, www.bcorporation.net (accessed March 15, 2016).

31. "2015 Year in Review," *B Corporation*, January 5, 2016, https://bcorporation.net/blog/2015-year-in -review (accessed April 15, 2016).

32. "Marketing to the Green Consumer," *Mintel*, www.mintel.com/marketing-to-the-green-consumers-us-March-2014 (accessed January 18, 2015). To better understand the notion of "greenness" see: Andrew Gershoff and Judy Frels, "What Makes It Green? The Role of Centrality of Green Attributes in Evaluations of the Greenness of Products," *Journal of Marketing*, January 2015, 97–110.

33. Serena Ng, "Laundry Detergent from Jessica Alba's Honest Company Contains Ingredient It Pledged to Avoid," *Wall Street Journal*, March 10, 2016, www.wsj.com/articles/laundry-detergent-from-jessica-albas-honest-co-contains-ingredient-it-pledged-to-avoid-1457647350 (accessed April 15, 2016).

34. Jefferson Graham, "Jessica Alba's Honest Co. Accused of Not Using Green Ingredients," *USA TODAY*, March 11, 2016, www.usatoday.com/story/tech/2016/03/10/jessica-albas-honest-co-accused-not-using-green-ingredients/81619486 (accessed April 15, 2016).

35. "Poop → Water; Dow Chemical Is Turning Sewage Into a Refreshing Drink," *Bloomberg Businessweek*, December 7, 2015, 78–82.

36. "Clean Bill of Health," *Marketing News*, August 2015. 28–29.

37. "Profiting From Poor Africans," *Bloomberg Businessweek*, December 7, 2015. 72–77.

38. "The Tao of Rose," *Fortune*, September 15, 2015, 155–161.

39. *Ibid*.

40. "Great Strides," *Fast Company*, February 2016, 44–46.

41. Ibid.

42. Author's estimate.

43. Michelle Andrews, Xueming Luo, Zheng Fang, and Jaakko Aspara, "Cause Marketing Effectiveness and the Moderating Role of Price Discounts," *Journal of Marketing*, November 2014, 120–142.

44. "The Right to R&R", *Marketing News*, November 2014, 12–14.

45. "2015 Halo Award: Best Message Focused Campaign," *Cause Marketing* Forum, www.causemarketingforum.com/site/c.bkLUKcOTLkK4E/b.6381409/apps/s/content.asp?ct=14695337 (accessed March 19, 2016).

46. "2015 Halo Award: Best Social Service Campaign," *Cause Marketing Forum*, www.causemarketingforum.com/site/c.bkLUKcOTLkK4E/b.6381409/apps/s/content.asp?ct=14695413 (accessed March 17, 2016)

4

1. "Asian-American Shoppers Make Health a Priority," *Quirk's Marketing Research Review*, August 2015, 16–17.

2. Haresh Kumar, "Mobile Commerce Trends to Buy Into," *Marketing Insights*, Spring 2016, 20–21.

3. "A New Way to Shop," *Curbside*, www.shopcurbside.com (accessed March 23, 2016).

4. Kumar, "Mobile Commerce…," 21.

5. "Yellow Cab Taxi Company Goes Bankrupt Due to Competition," *Tech Monkey*, January 9, 2016, http://techmymoney.com/2016/01/09/san-francico-taxi-company-goes-bankrupt-due-to-competition (accessed March 22, 2016).

6. "Bankruptcy Filing: Competition Killed the Room Store," Furniture Today, www.furnituretoday.com/article/526958-bankruptcy-filing-competition-killed-room-store (accessed March 22, 2016).

7. "Why Sport Authority's Bankruptcy May be a Good Thing," *Fortune*, http://fortune. com.2016/03/02/bankruptcy-sports-authority (accessed March 22, 2016).

8. "Internet of Things (IoT)," *Cisco*, www.cisco.com/web/solutions/trends/iot/overview.html (accessed March 22, 2016).

9. "Social Networking Fact Sheet," *Pew*, www.pewinternet.org/fact-sheets/ (accessed January 21, 2015).

10. "Digital Social & Mobile Worldwide in 2015."

11. "Social Media Update 2014," *Pew*, January 9, 2015, www.pewinternet.org/2015/01/09/social-media-update-2014/ (accessed January 21, 2015).

12. "Social Networks Are Driving Car Sales," *Quirk's Marketing Research Review*, June 2015. 8.

13. Ryan Holmes, "5 Trends That Will Change How Companies Use Social Media in 2016," *Fast Company*, www.fastcompany.com/3054347/the-future-of-work/5-trends-that-will-change-how-companies-use-social-media-in-2016 (accessed March 23, 2016).

14. Ibid.

15. "Wendy's Pretzel Bacon Cheeseburger Love Songs," *CIO*, www.cio.com/article/2369784/social-media/155992-14-Must-See-Social-Media-Marketing-success-stories.html (accessed January 21, 2015).

16. "#AdidasNeo: Involve Your Brand Ambassadors," *Talkwalker*, http://blog.talkwalker.com/en/5-social-media-campaigns-inspiration-2016-strategy-social-media-analytics/ (accessed March 23, 2016).

17. "eBags:#Travel Tip Tuesdays," *Salesforce*, www.salesforce.com/blog/2015/12/2015-most-brilliant-social-media-campaigns.html (accessed March 21, 2016).

18. Current World Population," *Worldometers*, www.worldometers.info/world-population/ (accessed May 13, 2016).

19. J. Walker Smith, "Togetherness, Not Singleness," *Marketing News*, December 2015, 16–17.

20. Ibid.

21. Ibid; "The Global Flight from the Family," *Wall Street Journal*, February 21–22, 2015, A11.

22. "Tweens by the Numbers: A Rundown of Recent Stats," *Chicago Now*, February 20, 2014, www.chicagonow.com/tween-us/2014/12 (accessed March 24, 2016).

23. Ibid.

24. "Report on Media Use by Tweens and Teens," *CHC Online*, December 7, 2015, www.chconline.org/media-use-by-tweens-and-teens/ (accessed March 25, 2016).

25. "What Do Tweens Want?" *School Library Journal*, October 8, 2015, www.slj.com/2015/10/programs/what-do-tweens-want/# (accessed March 25, 2016).

26. "The Digital World of Teens," *Pinterest*, www.pinterest.com/pin/16466354861535005 (accessed January 22, 2015).

27. "Teens Spend a Mind-Boggling 9 Hours a Day Using Media, Report Says," *CNN*, November 3, 2015, www.cnn.com/2015/11/03/health/teens-tweens-media-screen-use-report/ (accessed March 24, 2016).

28. Ibid.

29. Ibid.

30. "Why Teens Are the Most Elusive and Valuable Customers in Tech," Inc., www.inc.com/issie-lapowsky/inside-massive-tech-land-grab-teenabers.html (accessed January 22, 2015).

31. Author's estimate.

32. "Teenage Consumer Spending Statistics," *Statistics Brain*, www.statisticsbrain.com/teenage-consumer-spending-statistics/ (accessed March 19, 2016).

33. Lindsay Woolman, "Teen Consumer Spending Habits," *Lovetoknow*, http://teens.lovetoknow.com/Teen_Consumer_Spending_Habits (accessed May 13, 2016).

34. "Myths About Millennials," *The Economist*, August 1, 2015, 60.

35. "How Aging Millennials Will Affect Technology Consumption," *Wall Street Journal*, May 18, 2015, B6.

36. "10 New Findings About the Millennial Consumer," *Forbes*, January 20, 2015, www.forbes.com/sites/danschawbel/2015/01/20/10-new-findings-about-the-millennial-consumer/2/ (accessed March 24, 2016).

37. "Generations Are More Than Labels," *Marketing News*, November 2015, 28–29.

38. "Study Examines How to Keep Millennial Workers Happy," *Quirk's Marketing Research Review*, August 2015, 18–19.

39. "A Millennial's Field Guide to Mastering Your Career," *Fortune*, January 1, 2016, 83–88.

40. "Millennials: Love Them or Let Them Go," *Wall Street Journal*, May 6, 2015, B1, B7.

41. "A 'Kids Table' for Young Office Workers," *Wall Street Journal*, May 6, 2015, B7.

42. "10 New Findings…"; Millennial's Attention Divided Across Devices More Than Other Age Groups, Study Finds," *Marketing News*, April 2015, 5.

43. "Get to Know Gen X: The Small But Mighty Generation," *Centro*, September 17, 2015. www.centro.net/blog/get-to-know-gen-x-the-small-but-mighty-generation (accessed March 25, 2016).

44. Rieva Lesonsky, "Gen X: How to Market to the Forgotten Generation," *American Express*, September 15, 2014, www.AmericanExpress.com/us/small-business/openforum/articles/gen-x-how-to-market-to-the-forgotten-generation (accessed January 22, 2015).

45. "This is Why Gen X Will Never Be Able to Retire," Time, July 9, 2015, www.time.com/3935428/this-is-why-gen-x-will-never-be-able-to-retire (accessed March 27, 2015).

46. "Reality Still Bites for Gen-X—and Our Independent Streak Is Making Things Worse," *Salon*, June 11, 2015, www.salon.com/2015.com/2015/06/11/reality-still-bites-for-gen-x-and-our-independent-steak-is-making-it-worse (accessed March 24, 2015).

47. "Gen X Is 50; Are We Going to Call Them Boomers Now?" *Media Post*, February 9, 2015, www.mediapost.com/publications/article/243372/gen-x-is-50-are-we-going-to-call-them-boomers-now.html (accessed March 21, 2015).

48. "Get to Know…"

49. Ibid.

50. "The Baby Boom Cohort in the United States: 2012 to 2060," *United States Census Bureau*, May 2014, www.census.gov/prod/2014pubs/p25-1141.pdf (accessed January 22, 2015).

51. "Generations Are More Than Labels," Marketing News, November 2015, 28–29.

52. "Are You Ready for the 'Majority-Minority Demographic'?" Media Post, April 10, 2014, www.mediapost.com/publications/article/223044/are-you-ready-for-the-majority-minority-demographis.html (accessed March 23, 2016).

53. "From Minor to Major," *The Economist,* March 14, 2015, 3–16.

54. Ibid.

55. "Five Insights for Researching Hispanic Consumers in 2016," *Media Post,* December 8, 2015, www.mediapost.com/puclications/article/264267 /five-insights-for-reaching-hispanic-consumers -in-2016 (accessed March 26, 2016).

56. Ibid.

57. "Hispanic Millennials Require New Marketing Strategies," *Hispanic Marketing,* March 3, 2016, http://hispanic-marketing.com/hispanic-millennials -require-new-marketing-strategies/ (accessed March 28, 2016).

58. Ibid.

59. "Hispanic Media: Fact Sheet," Journalism.org, April 29, 2015, www.journalism.org/2015/04/29 /hispanic-media-fact-sheet/ (accessed March 28, 2016).

60. "Hispanic Media Spending Down 6.6% in 2015, Up 7.99% in 2016." *Hispanic Ad,* March 23, 2016, www.hispanicad.com/agency/marketing/hispanic -media-spending-down-66-2015-79-2016-report (accessed March 28, 2016).

61. "Five Insights For Reaching Hispanic…"

62. "2000 National Population Projections," *United States Census Bureau,* www.census.gov/population /projections/data/national/natsum.html (accessed March 29, 2016); "Connecting Through Culture: African Americans Favor Diverse Advertising," *Nielsen,* October 20, 2014, www.nielsen.com/us /en/insights/news/2014/connecting-through-culture -african-americans-favor-diverse-advertising.html (accessed March 29, 2016).

63. "African-American Consumers: The Untold Story," Nielsen, www.sites/nielsen.com /africanamericans/ (accessed March 29, 2016)

64. Ibid.

65. Ibid.

66. "How Fox's Marketing Fanned the Flames of Empire, One of the Biggest New Shows in Years – The Strategy Behind a Breakout Hit," *Adweek,* January 29, 2015, www.adweek.com/news /television/how-foxs-marketing-fanned-flames -empire-one-biggest-new-shows-years-162612 (accessed March 29, 2016).

67. "How Blacks Are Influencing Media, Marketing and Advertising," *BET,* www.bet.com/news/national /photos/Nielsen-company/ (accessed January 23, 2015).

68. "Usher's Honey Nut Commercial Knows Its Audience," *Businessweek,* August 21, 2014, www .businessweek.com/articles/2014-08-21/ushers -honey-nut-cheerios-commercial-knows-its-audience (accessed January 23, 2015).

69. "Asian Immigrants in the United States Today," *American* Progress, May 21, 2015, www .americanprogress.org/issues/immigration /news/2015/05/21/13690/asian-immigrants-in-the -united-states-today/ (accessed March 28, 2016).

70. "The Rise of Asian Americans," *Pew,* www .pewsocialtrends.org/asianamericans-graphics / (accessed March 28, 2016).

71. "The Minority Model Is Losing Patience," *The Economist,* October 3, 2015, 23–25.

72. "Asian-American Shoppers…"

73. "The Rise of Asian…"

74. "The Rise of Asian…"

75. "Asian-American Shoppers…"

76. "January Real Median Household Income at Another Post-Recession High," *Advisor Perspectives,* March 15, 2016, www.advisorperspectives.com /dshort/updates/Median-household-income-update (accessed March 28, 2016).

77. "Weekly Commentary March 24, 2016," *Exencial,* www.exencialwealth.com/newsletters -and-commentaries/ (accessed March 29, 2016).

78. "The Employment Situation," *Bureau of Labor Statistics,* March 4, 2016, www.bls.gov/news.release /pdf/empsit.pdf (accessed March 29, 2016).

79. "Fast Facts: Income of Young Adults," *Institute of Education Sciences,* http://nces .ed.gov/fastfacts/display.asp?id=77 (accessed January 23, 2015).

80. "What Is the Current Inflation Rate," *Inflation Data,* March 16, 2016, www.inflationdata.com /inflation/inflation_rate/Currentinflation.asp (accessed March 29, 2016).

81. "The 20 Countries With the Highest Inflation Rate in 2015," *Statista,* www.statista .com/statistics/268225/countries-with-the-highest -inflation-rate/ (accessed March 27, 2016).

82. "Innovation: A Look Inside the Idea Factory," *Wired,* www.wired.co.uk/promotions/shell-lets-go /innovation/the-idea-factory (accessed January 24, 2015).

83. "Innovation is the Buzzword Du Jour," *Marketing News,* March 2015, 42–50.

84. "The Death of American Research and Development," *Fortune,* January 1, 2016, 9–10.

85. "Look Who's Driving R&D Now," Bloomberg Businessweek, June 8, 2015, 18–20.

86. "Innovation-Smart Table," *Bloomberg Businessweek,* November 30, 2015, 39.

87. "20 Tips on Google's 20 Percent Time in Your Classroom," *Learning Personalized,* www .learningpersonalized.com/2015/01/06/20-tips -on-googles-20-percent-time-in-your-classroom / (accessed January 24, 2015).

88. "Zara Builds Its Business Around RFID," *Wall Street Journal,* September 19, 2014, B1-B2.

89. Ibid.

90. "The Disruption Factor," Fortune, December 15, 2015, S1-S5.

91. Ibid.

92. "2015 Annual Report," United States Securities and Exchange Commission, February 11, 2016, www.sec.gov/Archives /edgar/data/37996/000003799616000092 /f1231201510-k.htm (accessed May 13, 2016).

93. Jobs and the Clever Robot," *Wall Street Journal,* February 25, 2015, A1, A10.

94. "Benefits of ObamaCare: Advantage of ObamaCare," *Obamacare Facts,* http://obamacarefacts .com/benefitsofobamacare/ (accessed January 24, 2015.

95. Maryann Tobin, "How Consumer Protection Laws Affect Advertising," LeadsCon, www .leadscon.com/how-consumer-protection-laws -affect-advertising/ (accessed March 30, 2016).

96. "Bureau of Consumer Protection," *Federal Trade Commission,* www.ftc.gov/about-ftc/bureaus -offices/bureau-consumer-protection (accessed January 24, 2015).

97. "Total Media Ad Spending Growth Slows Worldwide," *eMarketer,* September 15, 2015, www .emarketer.com/Article/total-media-ad-spending -growth-slows-worldwide/1012981 (accessed March 30, 2016).

98. "Acxiom InfoBase Consumer List Mailing List," *NextMark,* http://Lists.nextmark.com /market?page=order/online/datacard&id=131838 (accessed January 24, 2015).

99. "Personic X Lifestage Analysis," *Lab 3 Marketing,* http://Lab3marketing.com/direct-marketing /data-analytics/personicX-lifestage-analysis (accessed January 24, 2015).

100. "Americans' Attitudes About Privacy, Security and Surveillance," Pew, May 20, 2015, www .pewinternet.org/2015/05/20/americans-attitudes -about-privacy-security-and-surveillance/ (accessed March 29, 2016).

101. "Internet Provides Face Privacy Fight", *Wall Street Journal,* March 20, 2016, B4.

102. "FBI Says It Cracked Terrorists' iPhone," *Wall Street Journal,* March 29, 2016, A1, A5.

103. "By the Numbers: 110+ Amazing Amazon Statistics," *Expanded* Ramblings, January 28, 2016, www.expandedramblings.com/index.php/Amazon -statistics/ (accessed March 30, 2016).

104. "Mobile Shoppers Looking for Products Start at Amazon," *Media Post,* August 7, 2015, www .mediapost.com/publications/article/255689/mobile -shoppers-looking-for-products-start-at-amazon .html (accessed March 30, 2016).

5

1. "World Trade Records Biggest Reversal Since Crises," *Financial Times,* February 26, 2016, www.ft.com/cms/s/2/9e2533d6-dbd8-11e4-9ba -3abc1e7247e4.html#axzz44yOEeYT7 (accessed April 1, 2016).

2. "Top 20 Facts About Manufacturing," *National Association of Manufacturers,* www.nam.org /Newsroom/top-20-facts-about-manufacturing/ (accessed April 1, 2016).

3. "The Engine That Pulled Us Out of Recession," *Wall Street Journal,* March 19, 2015, A13.

4. Ibid.

5. "U.S. Exports 1950–2015," *Trading Economics,* www.tradingeconomics.com/united-states/exports (accessed January 25, 2015).

6. "The Economic Benefits of U.S. Trade," Executive Office of the President of the United States, May 2015, 3–4.

7. Ibid.

8. "EXIM Bank Releases Its FY2015 Annual Report," *EXIM Bank,* January 14, 2016, www.exim .gov/news/exim-bank-releases-its-fy-2015-annual -report (accessed April 2, 2016).

9. "State Trade Expansion Program/– Fact Sheet-2016-01," *U.S. Small Business Administration,* www.sba.gov/managing-business/exporting /step (accessed April 2, 2016).

10. "Five Myths about Imports," *Wall Street Journal,* May 20, 2014, A11.

11. Ibid.

12. "The Economic Benefits…"

13. "Companies Jump on IT Insourcing Bandwagon," *Laser Fiche,* November 2, 2015, www .laserfiche.com/simplicity/companies-jump-on-it -insourcing-bandwagon/ (accessed April 4, 2016).

14. "An Inconvenient Trust About Free Trade," *Bloomberg Businessweek,* April 4, 2016, 608.

15. Ibid.

16. "Why Trade Critics Are Getting Traction," *Wall Street Journal,* March 30, 2016, A11.

17. Author's estimates; "The 2015 Global Innovation 1000: Innovations New World Order," October 17, 2015, www.strategyand.pwc.com/reports/2015 -global-innovation-1000-media-report (accessed April 5, 2016).

18. Theodore Levitt, "The Globalization of Markets," *Harvard Business Review,* May 1983, 92–100.

19. "GNI Per Capita Ranking," *World Bank,* February 17, 2016, www.data.worldbank.org

/data-catalog/GNI-per-capita-Atlas-and-PPP-table (accessed April 6, 2016).

20. Ibid.

21. Nick Timiraos, "The Most Expensive Cities in the World to Live," *Wall Street Journal*, March 10, 2016, http://blogs.wsj.com/economics/2016/03/10/the-most-expensive-cities-in-the-world-to-live/ (accessed April 8, 2016).

22. "United States Balance Of Trade 1950–2016," *Trading Economics*, www.tradingeconomics.com/united-states-balance-of-trade (accessed April 8, 2016).

23. "Trade Seen Weighing on Growth," *Wall Street Journal*, April 6, 2016, A2.

24. "World GDP Ranking 2015," *Knoema*, http://knoema.com/nwnfkne/world-gdp-ranking-2015-data-and-charts (accessed April 9, 2016).

25. "Asia Rich Outnumber North America," *Wall Street Journal*, September 16, 2015, C3.

26. "The Last BRIC Standing," *Fortune*, January 2, 2016, 72–73.

27. *Doing Business 2016*, 13th ed., World Bank Group, Washington, D.C. 2–4.

28. Ibid.

29. "Wal-Mart Fights Back in China," *Wall Street Journal*, April 14, 2014, A1–A14.

30. "McDonald's Will Open Over 60 Restaurants in Russia in 2016," *Business Insider*, January 25, 2016, http://businessinsider.com/r-mcdonalds-to-open-more-than-60-restaurants-in-russia-in-2016-2016-1 (accessed May 23, 2016).

31. "Renault Tries to Fix Russian Misadventure," *Wall Street Journal*, April 22, 2016, A1, A10.

32. "Forces That Opened Borders Show Signs of Sputtering," *Wall Street Journal*, April 4, 2016, A2.

33. Ibid.

34. "Understanding the WTO," *World Trade Organization*, www.wto.org.english/thewtoe/tife/org6_e.htm (accessed April 13, 2016).

35. "China Defends Trade Policies After U.S. Files Case at W.T.O.," *New York Times*, February 13, 2015, www.nytimes/com/2015/02/13/business/international/China-defends-trade-policies-after-us-files-case-at-wto.html (accessed April 12, 2016).

36. "Global Trade After the Failure of the Doha Round," *New York Times*, January 2, 2016, www.nytimes/com/2016/01/01/opinion/global-trade-after-the-failure-of-the-doha-round.htm (accessed April 12, 2016).

37. "The Asian Way Out of a European Impasse," *Businessweek*, November 13, 2015, 14.

38. "Free Exchange," *The Economist*, November 14, 2015, 76.

39. "The Pacific Alliance is a Great Brand in Search of a Shared Product," *The Economist*, March 14, 2015, 39.

40. Ibid.

41. Ibid.

42. "Advantages of NAFTA," *About.com*, March 23, 2016, http://useconomy.about.com/od/tradepolicy/p/NAFTA_Advantage.htm (accessed April 15, 2016).

43. Ibid.

44. "A Tale of Two NAFTA Towns," *Bloomberg Businessweek*, April 11, 2016, 12–13.

45. "Photo of the Month: March 2016," *Heron*, http://heron.org/engage/pulse/photo-month-nafta-jobs-and-campaign-rhetoric (accessed April 15, 2016).

46. "NAFTA May Have Saved Many Autoworkers' Jobs," *New York Times*, March 29, 2016, www.nytimes/com/2016/03/30/business/economy/nafta0may-have-saved-many-autoworkers-jobs.html?_r=o. (accessed April 15, 2016).

47. "Dominican Republic-Central America-United States Free Trade Agreement (CAFTA-DR)," *Export.gov*, http://export.gov/FTA/cafta-dr/index.asp (accessed March 19, 2015).

48. "GDP Data for All Countries," *Economy Watch*, April 15, 2016, www.economywatch.com/economic-indicators/GDP_Current_Prices_US_Dollars/ (accessed April 15, 2016).

49. "America and the European Union Have Reached a Deal on Data Protection," *The Economist*, February 6, 2016, 50.

50. "France Orders Facebook to Fix Privacy Issues," *Wall Street Journal*, February 9, 2016, B4.

51. "Microsoft Nods to EU's Data-Protection Fears," *Wall Street Journal*, November 12, 2015, B1, B4.

52. "IMF Halts Mozambique Lending," *Wall Street Journal*, April 16–17, 2016, B2.

53. "G-20 Puts Tax Havens on Notice," *Wall Street Journal*, April 16–17, 2016, A12.

54. "The Four Global Forces Breaking All the Trends," *McKinsey & Company*, April 2016, www.mckinsey.com/business-functions/strategy-and-corporate-finance/our-insights/the-four-global-forces-breaking-all-the-trends (accessed April 18, 2016).

55. "Slow Growth Clouds Fight Against Poverty," *Wall Street Journal*, January 20, 2016, R7.

56. "Urban World: The Global Consumers to Watch," *McKinsey & Company*, March 2016, http://mckinsey.com/global-themes/urbanization/urban-world-the-global-consumers-to-watch/ (accessed April 19, 2016).

57. Ibid.

58. Ibid.

59. Ibid.

60. "The Four Global Forces…"

61. "The Four Global Forces…"

62. "U.S. and World Population Clock," U.S. Census Bureau, April 19, 2016, www.census.gov/popclock/ (accessed April 19, 2016); "Freshwater Crises," *National Geographic*, http://environment.nationalgeographic.com/environment/freshwater/freshwater-crises/ (accessed April 19, 2016).

63. Ibid.

64. "Exporting is Good for Your Bottom Line," *International Trade Administration*, www.trade.gov/cs/factsheet.asp (accessed April 22, 2016).

65. "Event Information By Type For Trade Mission," *Export.gov*, http://export.gov/eac/show_short_trade_events.asp (accessed April 23, 2016).

66. "Fast-Food Franchises Get Creative When They Go Abroad," *Wall Street Journal*, May 26, 2015, www.wsj.com/articles/fast-food-franchises-get-creative-when-they-go-abroad-1432318075 (accessed April 24, 2016).

67. "Exhibit A in GE's Case for Alston Deal," *New York Times*, May 23, 2014, www.nytimes.com/2014/05/26/business/international/generalelectric_joint_venture_in_France.html (accessed April 23, 2016).

68. "Qualcomm Forms Joint Venture In China To Take On Intel," *Fortune*, http://fortune.com/2016/01/17/qualcomm-server-china/ (accessed April 24, 2016).

69. "Bureau of Economic Analysis Releases Two New Data Sets to Deepen Understanding of U.S. Economy," *U.S. Bureau of Economic Analysis*, December 3, 2015, https://blog.bea.gov/.category/direct-investment (accessed April 24, 2016).

70. Foreign Direct Investment in the United States – 2016 Report: (Washington: Organization for International Investment: 2016) 1–12.

71. "2015 Select USA Investment Summit is Now Open for Business," *United States Department of Commerce*, January 8, 2015, www.commerce.gov/blog/category/138 (accessed April 24, 2016).

72. "How Procter & Gamble is Conquering Emerging Markets," *The Motley Fool*, www.fool.com/investing/general/2013/10/27/how-procter-gamble-is-conquering-emerging-markets.aspx (accessed April 30, 2016).

73. "What is Selling Where? Pringles Chips," *Wall Street Journal*, April 24, 2013, D3.

74. "How Domino's Won India," *Fast Company*, February 2015, 54.

75. "Cereal Makers Tweak Recipes for Emerging Markets," *Wall Street Journal*, September 28, 2015, B6.

76. David Aaker, "Lessons from Lifebuoy," *Marketing News*, January 2016, 16–17.

77. "McDonald's to Expand Reach in China," *Wall Street Journal*, April 2, 2016, B6.

78. Ibid.

79. "Thomson Reuters World-Check," *Thomson Reuters*, https://risk.thomsonreuters.com/products/world-check (accessed April 29, 2016).

80. "The Big Mac Index: After the Dips," *The Economist*, January 9, 2016, 60.

81. "Understanding Antidumping and Countervailing Duty Investigations," *U.S. International Trade Commission*, https://www.usitc.gov/press_room/usad.htm (accessed May 1, 2016).

82. Ibid.

83. "Suggested Reading about Countertrade," *Exporter-Sources.com*, http://exporters-sources.com/suggested-reading-about-countertrade (accessed January 30, 2015).

84. "Countertrade," *All About Countertrade*, http://allaboutcountertrade.blogspot.com (accessed May 1, 2016).

85. "13 Businesses with Brilliant Global Marketing Strategies," *HubSpot*, July 29, 2015, http://blog.hubspot.com/blog/tabid/6307/bid/33857/10-Businesses-We-Admire-for-Brilliant-Global-Marketing.aspx (accessed May 3, 2016).

86. Ibid.

87. "Red Bull Ad Sparks Social Media Outburst From Kenyans," *Jambonewspot*, January 15, 2015, www.jambonewspot.com/video-redbull-ad-sparks-social-media-outburst-kenyans/ (accessed January 31, 2015).

88. Ibid.

89. Ibid.

1. The material on hedonic and utilitarian value was partially adapted from Barry Babin and Eric Harris, *CB* 6th ed., Cengage Learning, 2015, 28–29.

2. Tonya Williams Bradford, "Beyond Fungible: Transforming Money into Moral and Social Resources," *Journal of Marketing*, March 2015, 79–97; "Budget Allocation Signals Consumers' Need States, Research Finds" *Marketing News*, April 2015, 7.

3. "By the Numbers: 100 Amazing Google Statistics and Facts," *DMR*, February 25, 2016, www.expandedramblings.com/index.php/by-the-numbers-a-gigantic-list-of-google-stats-and-facts/ (accessed January 20, 2016).

4. Eric Anderson and Duncan Simester, "Reviews Without a Purchase: Low Ratings, Loyal Customers,

and Deception," *Journal of Marketing Research,* June 2014, 249–269.

5. Masroor Ahmed, "Is Social Media the Biggest Influencer of Buying Decisions?" *Social Media Today,* May 31, 2015, www.socialmediatoday.com/marketing/masroor/2015-05-28/social-media-biggest-influencer-buying-decisions (accessed April 15, 2016).

6. "Good Tidings for Retail," *Marketing News,* December 2014, 14.

7. Edwin von Bommel, David Edelman, and Kelly Ungerman, "Digitizing the Consumer Decision Journey," *McKinsey,* June 2014, www.mckinsey.com/insights/marketing_sales/digitizing_the_consumer_decision_journey/ (accessed February 17, 2015).

8. Ashish Kumar, Ram Bezawada, Rishika Rishika, Ramkumar Janakiraman, and P.K. Kannan, "From Social to Sale: The Effects of Firm-Generated Content in Social Media on Customer Behavior," *Journal of Marketing,* January 2016, 7–25.

9. Uma Karmarkar, Baba Shiv, and Brian Kuntson, "Cost Conscious? The Neural and Behavioral Impact of Price Primacy on Decision Making," *Journal of Marketing Research,* August 2015, 467–481.

10. "Survey: 3 in 4 Americans Make Impulse Purchases," *CreditCards.com,* November 23, 2014, www.creditcards.com/credit-card-news/impulse-purchase-survey.php (accessed February 17, 2015).

11. Don Schultz, "The Path Not Taken," *Marketing Insights,* September/October 2015, 12–13.

12. Sam Hui, Yanliu Huang, Jacob Suher, and Jeff Inman, "Deconstructing the First Moment of Truth: Understanding Unplanned Consideration and Purchase Conversion Using In-Store Video Tracking," *Journal of Marketing Research,* August 2013, 445–462.

13. Iiro Jussila, Anssi Tarkiainen, Marko Sarstedt, and Joe Hair, "Individual Psychological Ownership: Concepts, Evidence and Implications for Research in Marketing," *Journal of Marketing Theory and Practice,* March 2015, 121–139; Bernadette Kamleitner and Silva Feuchtl, "As If It Were Mine": Imaginary Works by Inducing Psychological Ownership," *Journal of Marketing Theory and Practice,* March 2015, 208–223.

14. Suzanne Shu and Joann Peck, "Psychological Ownership and Affective Reaction: Emotional Attachment Process Variables and the Endowment Effect," *Journal of Consumer Psychology,* March 2011, 439–452; Colleen Patricia Kirk, Bernard McSherry and Scott Swain, "Investing the Self: The Effect of Nonconscious Goals on Investor Psychological Ownership and Word-of-Mouth Intentions," *Journal of Behavioral and Experimental Economics,* January 2015, 186–194.

15. Colleen Patricia Kirk, Scott Swain, and James Gaskin, "I'm Proud of It: Consumer Technology Appropriation and Psychological Ownership," *Journal of Marketing Theory and Practice,* February 2015, 166–184.

16. Crystal Collier and Gavin Sinter, "Meet Them Where They Want to Be," *Quirk's Marketing Research Review,* October 2014, 58–62.

17. Julio Sevilla and Joseph Redden, "Limited Availability Reduces the Rate of Satiation," *Journal of Marketing Research,* April 2014, 205–217.

18. David Edelman, "Branding in the Digital Age: You're Spending Your Money in All the Wrong Places," *Harvard Business Review,* December 2010, https://hbr.org/2010/12/branding-in-the-digital-age-youre-spending-your-money-in-all-the-wrong-places (accessed April 15, 2016).

19. David Edelman and Marc Singer, "The New Consumer Decision Journey," *McKinsey & Company,* October 2015, www.mckinsey.com/insights/marketing_sales/the_new_consumer_decision_journey (accessed April 15, 2016).

20. David Edelman and Marc Singer, "Competing on Customer Journeys," *Harvard Business Review,* November 2015, https://hbr.org/2015/11/competing-on-customer-journeys (accessed January 12, 2016).

21. Samantha Cross and Mary Gilly, "Cultural Competence and Cultural Compensatory Mechanisms in Binational Households," *Journal of Marketing,* May 2014, 121–139.

22. "Most Expensive Cars in the World: Top 10 List 2014–2015," *The Supercars,* www.thesupercars.org/top-cars/most-expensive-cars-in-the-world-top-10-list/ (accessed February 18, 2015).

23. "2015 Poverty Guidelines," January 22, 2015, *United States Department of Health and Human Services,* http://aspe.hhs.gov/poverty/15poverty.cfm (accessed February 18, 2015).

24. Hans Risselada, Peter Verdoef, and Tammo Bijmolt, "Dynamic Effects of Social Influence and Direct Marketing on the Adoption of High-Technology Products," *Journal of Marketing,* March 2014, 52–68.

25. This section was partially adapted from Babin and Harris, 156–157.

26. "Is Women's Empowerment Marketing the New 'Pink It and Shrink It'?" *Entrepreneur,* February 9, 2015, www.entrepreneur.com/article/242677 (accessed February 20, 2015).

27. "Industry Statistics Shows Growth in Men Engaging in Online Shopping," *Mobile Commerce Insider,* June 18, 2013, www.mobilecommerceinsider.com/topics/mobilecommerceinsider/articles/342484-industry-statistics-show-growth-men-engaging-online-shopping.html (accessed January 29, 2014).

28. "Reach Over 45 Million American Families," *eTarget Media,* www.etargetmedia.com/family-lists.html (accessed February 20, 2015).

29. "Messes and Wrong Guesses," *The Wall Street Journal,* February 15–16, 2014, C4.

7

1. Michael D. Hutt and Thomas W. Speh, *Business Marketing Management,* 12th ed. (Boston: Cengage, 2017).

2. Jeffrey Cohen "20 Most Important Stats from the 2015 B2B Content Marketing Report," *Social Media B2B,* October 6, 2014, www.socialmediab2b.com/2014/10/b2b-content-marketing-report-statistics-2015.com (accessed March 22, 2016).

3. Autumn Truong, "5 B2B Social Media Lessons Cisco Learned in 2014," *Social Media B2B,* January 20, 2015 www.socialmediab2b.com (accessed March 22, 2016).

4. "Online Measurement," *Nielsen,* www.nielsen.com/us/en/nielsen-solutions/nielsen-measurement/nielsen-online-measurement.html (accessed March 22, 2016).

5. "2014 Social Media Benchmarking Report," *B2B Marketing Magazine,* www.b2bmarketing.net/magazine (accessed March 22, 2016).

6. Meghan Keaney Anderson, "10 Exceptional B2B Content Marketing Examples," *Hubspot,* June 9, 2015, http://blog.hubspot.com/blog/tabid/6307/bid/33505/10-B2B-Companies-That-Create-Exceptional-Content.aspx (accessed March 18, 2016).

7. "3 Ways B2B Companies Must Market Themselves in 2016," *Forbes,* January 5, 2016, http://forbes.com/sites/ajagrawal/2016/01/05/3-ways-b2b-companies-must-market-themselves-in-2016/#7e8c732a7557 (accessed March 17, 2016).

8. Brian Stelter, "ABC and Yahoo Expand Partnership," *CNN Money,* March 12, 2015, http://money.cnn.com/2015/03/12/media/yahoo-abc-partnership-expansion/ (accessed March 18, 2016).

9. Eric Griffin, "12 Amazon Fire TV Tips for Streaming Fans," *PC Mag,* February 19, 2015, www.pcmag.com/slideshow/story/332129/12-amazon-fire-tv-tips-for-streaming-fans (accessed March 22, 2016).

10. Sheila Shayon, "Sustainable Alliances: 5 Questions with Caterpillar Sr. Tech Pro Mark Kelly," *Brandchannel,* March 16, 2016, http://brandchannel.com/2016/03/16/5-questions-caterpillar-031616/ (accessed March 22, 2016).

11. Robert M. Morgan and Shelby D. Hunt, "The Commitment-Trust Theory of Relationship Marketing," *Journal of Marketing,* 58, no. 3, 1994, 23.

12. Ibid.

13. Nils Pratley, "Phones 4U Has Only Itself to Blame," *The Guardian,* September 15, 2014, www.theguardian.com/business/nils-pratley-on-finance/2014/sep/15/phones-4u-administrators (accessed March 22, 2016).

14. "Microsoft Signs Agreements with Leading Companies and Government Institutions in China," *Microsoft,* September 23, 2015, https://blogs.microsoft.com/firehose/2015/09/23/microsoft-signs-agreements-with-leading-companies-and-government-institutions-in-china/ (accessed March 18, 2016).

15. Stephen Dinan, "Fed Spending Soars in 2015; Taxes Spike," *Washington Times,* October 15, 2015, http://washingtontimes.com/news/2015/oct/15/fed-spending-soars-2015-taxes-rise-faster/ (accessed March 18, 2016).

16. Ibid.

17. Ibid.

18. Ibid.

19. Alan Levin and Susanna Ray, "Boeing 878 Dreamlines Is Grounded Worldwide by Regulators," *Bloomberg,* January 17, 2013, www.bloomberg.com/news/2013-01-16/boeing-787-dreamliner-fleet-grounded-by-u-s-after-emergency.html (accessed March 22, 2016).

20. Jim Melvin, "S.C. Forestry Industry Has Plenty of Room for Growth," *The Times and Democrat,* February 21, 2016, http://thetandd.com/business/agriculture/s-c-forestry-industry-has-plenty-of-room-for-growth/article_e7659d8d-6adf-5024-abee-3300df0a2220.html (accessed March 22, 2016).

21. Jon Hilkevitch, "CTA Seeks More Bids for New Rail Cars," *Chicago Tribune,* October 16, 2014, http://chicagotribune.com/news/local/breaking/ct-cta-rail-cars-met-1016-20141016-story.html (accessed March 22, 2016).

22. Hutt and Speh.

23. Paul Demery, "Alibaba.com Looks for Growth Among U.S. Suppliers," *Internet Retailer,* February 4, 2015, www.internetretailer.com/2015/02/04/alibabacom-looks-growth-among-us-suppliers (accessed March 22, 2016).

24. Daisuke Wakabayashi and Lorraine Luk, "Apple Watch: Faulty Taptic Engine Slows Rollout," *Wall Street Journal,* April 29, 2015, http://wsj.com/articles/apple-watch-faulty-taptic-engine-slows-roll-out-1430339460?mod=LS1 (accessed March 22, 2016).

25. Wayne Faulkner, "International Paper to Invest Millions in Riegelwood Mill, but Cut Jobs," *Star News Online*, March 31, 2015, http://starnewsonline.com/article/20150331/articles/150339957 (accessed March 21, 2016).

26. Hutt and Speh.

27. Ibid.

28. Stuart Leung, "Selling to Executives: Bringing Your Sales "A" Game to the C-Level," *SalesForce Blog*, February 24, 2014, http://blogs.salesforce.com/company/2014/02/selling-to-c-level-executives.html (accessed March 22, 2016).

29. Ibid.

30. Hutt and Speh.

31. Ibid.

8

1. "Biting Off the High End of the Market," *Inc.*, February 2015, 25 (accessed March 19, 2016).

2. "Target Announces Store Growth Plans for 2015," https://corporate.target.com/press/releases/2015/02/target-announces-store-growth-plans-for-2015 (accessed March 19, 2016).

3. Rebecca Spera, "CrossFit for Kids Focuses on Fun," *ABC*, January 21, 2015, http://abc13.com/health/crossfit-for-kids-focuses-on-fun/482997/ (accessed March 19, 2016).

4. Sheila Shayton, "Never Mind Millennials—Gen Z May be the Hardest Marketing Nut to Crack," *Brand Channel*, August 20, 2014, www.brandchannel.com/home/post/2014/08/20/140820-Gen-Z-Marketing (accessed March 19, 2016).

5. Katy Steinmetz, "Move Over Millennials," *Time*, December 28, 2015–January 4, 2016, 134.

6. Sheila Shayton, "Never Mind Millennials—Gen Z May be the Hardest Marketing Nut to Crack."

7. Jennifer Chan, "Aéropostale Debuts Pretty Little Liars Clothing Line—See the Pics!" http://www.eonline.com/news/497450/aeropostale-debuts-pretty-little-liars-clothing-line-see-the-pics, January 9, 2014 (accessed March 19, 2016).

8. "Who are Millennials?" *Millennial Marketing*, http://www.millennialmarketing.com/who-are-millennials/ (accessed February 23, 2015).

9. Joanna Franchini, "3 Ways to Tap into What Really Matters to Millennials, and All People," November 3, 2015, http://www.adweek.com/news/advertising-branding/why-blindly-chasing-after-millennials-short-sighted-strategy-167914 (accessed March 19, 2016).

10. Ryan Rudominer, "Corporate Social Responsibility Matters: Ignore Millennials at Your Peril," http://www.huffingtonpost.com/ryan-rudominer/corporate-social-responsi_9_b_9155670 (accessed February 2, 2016).

11. Mindy Weinstein, "A Trillion-Dollar Demographic: 10 Brands That Got Millennial Marketing Right," July 23, 2015, https://www.searchenginejournal.com/trillion-dollar-demographic-10-brands-got-millennial-marketing-right/135969/ (accessed March 19, 2016).

12. William F. Schroer, "Generations X, Y, Z and the Others," *The Social Librarian*, www.socialmarketing.org/newsletter/features/generation3.htm (accessed March 20, 2016).

13. "Dine Out Vancouver," *Tourism Vancouver*, 2 http://www.tourismvancouver.com/events/festivals-and-events/dine-out-vancouver (accessed March 20, 2016).

14. David Wright, "50+ Facts and Fiction: Size, Wealth and Spending of 50+ Consumers," March 9, 2015, https://www.immersionactive.com/resources/size-wealth-spending-50-consumers/ (accessed March 21, 2016).

15. Christine Birkner, "Senior Moment," *Marketing News*, September 2014, 12–13.

16. Neil Howe, "The Silent Generation, The Lucky Few," *Forbes*, August 13, 2014, http://forbes.com/sites/neilhowe/2014/08/13/the-silent-generation-the-lucky-few-part-3-of-7/#22a92a161e54 (accessed March 21, 2016).

17. Stephen M. Golant, "Aging in the American Suburbs: A Changing Population," *Aging Well*, www.agingwellmag.com/news/ex_06309_01.shtml (accessed March 21, 2016).

18. Bridget Brennan, "Top 10 Things Everyone Should Know about Women Consumers," *Forbes*, January 21, 2015, http:// forbes.com/sites/bridgetbrennan/2015/01/21/top-10-things-everyone-should-know-about-women-consumers/#906c88d2897d (accessed March 21, 2016).

19. "Men, Women and Money: How We View Finances Differently," *TransAmerica*, www.transamerica.com/yourlife/retirement/education/men-women-money-how-we-view-finances-differently (accessed March 21, 2016).

20. Dana Hull, "Tesla Asked Women What They Wanted and Came Up with Model X SUV," *Bloomberg*, September 17, 2015, http:// bloomberg.com/news/articles/2015-09-18/tesla-asked-women-what-they-wanted-and-came-up-with-model-x-suv (accessed March 21, 2016).

21. Nolan Shea, "What Guys Like: Men Grow Comfortable with Grooming Routines," *Brand Channel*, December 17, 2015, http://brandchannel.com/2015/12/17/mens-grooming-routines-121715/ (accessed March 21, 2016).

22. Ana Swanson, "What Super Bowl Manvertising Says About Men's New Role in America," *The Washington Post*, February 2, 2015, www.washingtonpost.com/blogs/wonkblog/wp/2015/02/02/what-super-bowl-manvertising-says-about-mens-new-role-in-america (accessed March 21, 2016).

23 Judy Bankman, "Junk Food Marketing Makes Big Moves in Developing Countries," *Civil Eats*, October 2, 2013, http://civileats.com/2013/10/02/junk-food-marketing-makes-big-moves-in-developing-countries/ (accessed March 22, 2016).

24. Jilian Mincer and Lisa Baertlein, "Dollar Stores in Fight to Double Down on Low-Income Shoppers," Daily Finance, August 25, 2014, http://dailyfinance.com/2014/08/25/dollar-stores-battle-low-income-shoppers/ (accessed March 21, 2016).

25. Vincent Bastien, "Marketing to a High-End Consumer, Using the Luxury Strategy," *Entrepreneur*, September 20, 2015, http:// entrepreneur.com/article/250745 (accessed March 22, 2016).

26. Monica Watrous, "Reaching the Hispanic Consumer," *Food Business News*, December 5, 2014, http:// foodbusinessnews.net/articles/news_home/Consumer_Trends/2014/12/Reaching_the_Hispanic_consumer.aspx?ID=%7B692B9084-6CE2-4D60-8E51-2CA0BFF974F1%7D&cck=1 (accessed March 22, 2016).

27. "About Us," *Fashion Fair*, http:// fashionfair.com/aboutus.php (accessed March 22, 2016)

28. Paul Bedard, "Census: Marriage Rate at 93-year Low, Even Including Same-Sex Couples," *Washington Examiner*, September 18, 2014, http:// washingtonexaminer.com/census-marriage-rate-at-93-year-low-even-including-same-sex-couples/article/2553600 (accessed March 22, 2016).

29. "Why You Need a Brand Ambassador Program (and 4 Companies that Are Doing It Right)," April 3, 2014, http://thenextweb.com/entrepreneur/2014/04/03/need-brand-ambassador-program-4-companies-right (accessed March 22, 2016).

30. Laurie Sullivan, "Nielsen Taps eXelate's Data Pipeline," *MediaPost*, August 27, 2013, www.mediapost.com/publications/article/207917/nielsen-taps-exelates-data-pipeline.html (accessed March 22, 2016); "The Start-Up Hunter," *Nielsen*, June 27, 2013, www.nielseninnovate.com/start-hunter (accessed March 22, 2016).

31. Will Greenwald, "Sling TV," *PC Magazine*, February 17, 2015, www.pcmag.com/article2/0,2817,2475619,00.asp (accessed March 22, 2016).

32. Joseph F. Kovar, "Actfio Looks to Simplify Storage Product Line, Channel Program," *CRN*, February 1, 2013, www.crn.com/news/storage/240147697/actifio-looks-to-simplify-storage-product-line-channel-program.htm (accessed March 22, 2016).

33. "Amazon Webstore," *Amazon*, http://webstore.amazon.com/ (accessed March 22, 2016).

34. Sarah Nassuer, "If Your Fridge Could Talk…" *Wall Street Journal*, December 17, 2014, D1, D2 (accessed March 22, 2016).

35. Noelle Buhidar, "Calling All Bargain Hunters," *RetailMeNot*, May 29, 2015, http:// retailmenot.com/blog/flash-sale-sites.html (accessed March 22, 2016).

36. "Campus Solutions," Zipcar, http:// zipcar.com/universities/solutions (accessed March 22, 2016).

37. Kurt Marko, "Apple's Product Cannibalization Means Cook Might Eat His Own Words," *Forbes*, April 30, 2015, http://forbes.com/sites/kurtmarko/2015/04/30/time-for-apple-hybrid/#7838c9c829b0 (accessed March 24, 2016).

38. Laura Fagan, "How Birchbox Used CR to Successfully Scale Their Business," April 1, 2014, http://blogs.salesforce.com/company/2014/04/birchbox.html (accessed March 24, 2016).

39. "All Brands," *Coca-Cola*, www.thecoca-colacompany.com/brands/brandlist.html (accessed February 24, 2015).

40. Dale Buss, "A Return to Salad Days? 5 Questions with Ruby Tuesday CMO Dave Skena," *Brand Channel*, March 9, 2016, www.brandchannel.com/2016/03/09/5-questions-ruby-tuesday (accessed April 19, 2016).

41. "Nutrition Guide," *Kentucky Fried Chicken*, www.kfc.com/nutrition/pdf/kfc_nutrition.pdf (accessed March 24, 2016).

42. "Our Brands," *Gap Inc.*, www.gapinc.com/content/gapinc/html/aboutus/ourbrands.html (accessed March 24, 2016).

43. Graham Robertson, "How to Find Your Brand's E-M-O-T-I-O-N-A-L Brand Positioning," *Beloved Brands*, November 3, 2014, http://beloved-brands.com/2014/11/03/emotional-brand-positioning/ (accessed March 24, 2016).

44. Susan Gunelius, "Kia Rolls Out Brand Repositioning Ad Campaign," *Corporate Eye*, January 9, 2015, www.corporate-eye.com/main/kia-rolls-out-brand-repositioning-ad-campaign (accessed March 24, 2016).

9

1. "The Mechanics of Modern-Day Brand Affinity," *Marketing News*, March 2015, 32–39.

2. "Center-Stores Doing Just Fine, Thank You," *Quirk's Marketing Research Review*, January 2016, 14–16.

3. Ibid.

4. "Connected Devices Gaining in Popularity," *Quirk's Marketing Research Review*, March 2015, 16–17.

5. "This Just In: We Pamper Our Pets," *Quirk's Marketing Research Review*, October 2015, 18.

6. "The Top 20 Valuable Facebook Statistics – Updated July 2016," *Zephoria*, July 2016, https://zephoria.com/top-15-valuable-facebook-statistics/ (accessed July 18, 2016).

7. "Buy Signal: Facebook Widens Data Targeting," *Wall Street Journal*, April 10, 2013, B4.

8. "Zuckerberg's New Tools," *Marketing Insights*, Spring 2013, 5.

9. "Block This," *Business Week*, October 5, 2015, 37–38.

10. Ibid.

11. Parmy Olson, "We Know Everything," *Forbes*, November 18, 2013, 68–70.

12. Ibid.

13. "8 Ways Big Data Will Transform Marketing in 2015," *Marketing News*, February 2015, 6–7.

14. "What is Apache Hadoop?" *Apache*, www.hadoop.apache.org/#What+Is+Apache+Hadoop%3F (accessed February 23, 2015).

15. "Ten Big Data Case Studies in a Nutshell," *SearchCIO*, http://searchcio.techtarget.com/opinion/Ten-big-data-case-studies-in-a-nutshell (accessed February 23, 2015).

16. "6 Big Data Examples from Big Global Brands," *Teradata*, http://blogs.teradata.com/data-points/big-data-examples-from-global-brands/ (accessed January 29, 2016).

17. "What is Watson Analytics," *Marketing News*, February 2016, 30–15; "Google Analytics in 2016," *Marketing News*, February 2016, 8–9.

18. "Travelers Cite Least-Favorite Airplane Passenger Types," *Quirk's Marketing Research Review*, January 2016, 8–9.

19. Carl McDaniel and Roger Gates, *Marketing Research*, 10th ed. John Wiley & Sons, 2015, 171.

20. "The Science of Shopping," *Indiana University*, http://Kelley.iu.edu/Marketing/Research/Labs/shopability1.htmp (accessed February 24, 2015).

21. "Viva Vantage Named 2015 Product of the Year," *PR Newswire*, www.prnewswire.com/news-releases/viva-vantage-named-2015-product-of-the-year-30032887/html (accessed February 25, 2015).

22. "Methodological Analysis from the Pew Research Center," *Google*, www.google.com/insights/consumersurveys/news (accessed February 4, 2016).

23. "Election Reopens Debate Over Online Polling," *National Journal*, www.nationaljournal.com/politics/election-reopens-debate-over-online-polling-10121130 (accessed February 24, 2015).

24. "Character Counts, Characters Count," *Quirk's Marketing Research Review*, July 2013, 48–51.

25. "Brand + TV + iPad: The New Research Triangle," *Quirk's Marketing Research Review*, March 2014, 36–41.

26. "Screen Size Correlates with Completion Rates," *Quirk's Marketing Research Review*, April 2014, 8.

27. "Easy Answers," *Quirk's Marketing Research Review*, February 2015, 32–36.

28. "Instant Insight," *Marketing News*, February 2013, 46–49.

29. "That's the Spot" *Quirk's Marketing Research Review*, July 2014, 38–45.

30. Ibid.

31. "Behavior Scan CPG TV Ad Testing," *IRI Worldwide*, www.iriworldwide.com/Product Solutions/AllProductsDetail/productID/29.aspx (accessed February 25, 2015).

10

1. Marl J. Miller, "CES 2016: Under Armour Goes All In on Fitness Tech with Healthbox," *Brandchannel*, January 5, 2016, www.brandchannel.com/2016/01/05/under-armour-healthbox-010516/ (accessed July 18, 2016).

2. "Cat's Pride Introduces New Fresh & Light Ultimate Care," *Cat's Pride*, March 7, 2016, http://catspride.com/cat-matters/in-the-news/ (accessed July 18, 2016).

3. Dale Buss, "SeaWorld CEO Joel Manby Details Rebrand to Orca Conservation," *Brandchannel*, March 24, 2016, http://brandchannel.com/2016/03/24/seaworld-joel-manby-032416/ (accessed July 18, 2016).

4. Sarah Halzach, "Target's New Strategy: We Need More Than Just Minivan Moms," *Washington Post*, March 4, 2015, www.washingtonpost.com/news/business/wp/2015/03/04/targets-new-strategy-we-need-more-than-just-minivan-moms (accessed April 6, 2016).

5. "Three New Krispy Kreme Ready-to-Drink Iced Coffee Flavors Now Available in Grocery Stores Nationwide," *Krispy Kreme*, July 21, 2015, http://investor.krispykreme.com/press-releases/press-release-details/2015/Three-New-Krispy-Kreme-Ready-to-Drink-Iced-Coffee-Flavors-Now-Available-in-Grocery-Stores-Nationwide/default.aspx (accessed April 6, 2016).

6. Gregg Keizer, "Apple Recovers Top 'Brand Value' Spot from Google with $247B Assessment," *Computer World*, May 27, 2015, www.computerworld.com/article/2927453/it-industry/apple-recovers-top-brand-value-spot-from-google-with-247b-assessment.html (accessed April 6, 2016).

7. Dale Buss, "Toyota Axes Scion Brand, Rolls Models into Toyota Lineup," *Brandchannel*, February 4, 2016, http://brandchannel.com/2016/02/04/toyota-axes-scion-020416/ (accessed July 18, 2016).

8. Ron Margulis, "Will Store Brands Outcompete National Rivals in Fresh Categories?" *RetailWire*, November 19, 2015, www.retailwire.com/discussion/18679/will-store-brands-outcompete-national-rivals-in-fresh-categories (accessed April 6, 2016).

9. Eugene Kim, "Amazon Quietly Launched 7 Fashion Brands while Ramping Up Hiring for its Own Clothing Line," *Business Insider*, February 22, 2016, www.businessinsider.com/amazon-owns-7-private-label-fashion-brands-2016-2 (accessed July 18, 2016).

10. Monica Watrous, "Why Millennials Love Store Brands," *Food Business News*, April 10, 2015, www.foodbusinessnews.net/articles/news_home/Consumer_Trends/2015/04/Why_millennials_love_store_bra.aspx?ID=%7B44ECC337-75C5-4647-A302-BBA7B1248ED3%7D (accessed April 6, 2016).

11. Keith Nunes, "Kroger Succeeding with Simple Truth," *Meat+Poultry*, March 9, 2015, www.meatpoultry.com/articles/news_home/Trends/2015/03/Kroger_succeeding_with_Simple.aspx?ID=%7B45586455-1818-4988-A981-FEA683EF49DA%7D&cck=1 (accessed April 6, 2016).

12. "Brands & Products: Brand Browser," *Church & Dwight*, www.churchdwight.com/brands-and-products/brand-browser.aspx (accessed April 6, 2016).

13. "Bruegger's Bagels and Jamba Juice Launch Co-Branded Concept," *Bruegger's*, February 25, 2016, https://www.brueggers.com/news/brueggers-jamba-juice-cobranded-concept-melrose/ (accessed July 18, 2016).

14. "Doc Popcorn, Dippin' Dots to Debut First Co-Brand Store," *Business Wire*, February 10, 2015, www.businesswire.com/news/home/20150210005273/en/Doc-Popcorn-Dippin'-Dots-Debut-Co-Brand-Store (accessed April 6, 2016).

15. "Copyright vs. Trademark vs. Patent," *Law Mart*, www.lawmart.com/forms/difference.htm (accessed April 6, 2016).

16. Maira Sutton, "Copyright Law as a Tool for State Censorship of the Internet," *Electronic Frontier Foundation*, December 3, 2014, https://www.eff.org/deeplinks/2014/12/copyright-law-tool-state-internet-censorship (accessed April 6, 2016).

17. Dominic Patten, "'Empire' & Fox Win Trademark Suit in Time for Season 2 Spring Return," *Deadline*, February 3, 2016, http://deadline.com/2016/02/empire-fox-trademark-infringement-lawsuit-order-lee-daniels-1201695714 (accessed July 18, 2016).

18. Chantal Fernandez, "Gucci Loses Trademark Infringement Case Against Guess in France," *Fashionista*, February 2, 2015, http://fashionista.com/2015/02/french-court-rejects-gucci-trademark-claims-against-guess-paris-france (accessed April 12, 2016); "Counterfeit Combat," *Inc.*, March 2015, 68–69.

19. "11 Ridiculous Fast Food Chain Ripoffs in China," *Elite Readers*, November 25, 2015, www.elitereaders.com/ridiculous-fast-food-chain-ripoffs-in-china/2/ (accessed April 12, 2016).

20. Molly Soat, "Misunderstood Measures," *Marketing News*, January 2015, 18–19.

21. "Diet Coke Unveils New Packaging Design," *Beverage Industry*, January 28, 2016, www.bevindustry.com/articles/89056-diet-coke-unveils-new-packaging-design (accessed July 18, 2016).

22. Nathan Rao, "'Wrap Rage' Soars Over Packaging We Can't Open," *Express*, January 28, 2014, www.express.co.uk/news/uk/456493/Wrap-Rage-soars-over-packaging-we-can-t-open (accessed April 12, 2016).

23. Anne Marie Mohan, "Six Packaging Trends for 2016," *Pack World*, February 15, 2016, www.packworld.com/trends-and-issues/global/six-packaging-trends-2016 (accessed July 18, 2016).

24. Kristin Hohenadel, "One Designer's Lonely Crusade to Make Packing Disappear," *Slate*, April 2, 2014, www.slate.com/blogs/the_eye/2014/04/02/how_to_eliminate_packaging_waste_the_disappearing_package_by_aaron_mickelson.html (accessed April 12, 2016).

25. "Food Safety Innovation: Smart Packaging," *Mobile Future*, October 7, 2015, http://mobilefuture.org/food-safety-innovation-smart-packaging (accessed April 12, 2016).

26. "About Green Seal," April 12, 2016, *Green Seal*, www.greenseal.org/AboutGreenSeal.aspx (accessed July 18, 2016).

11

1. "The Most Innovative Companies of 2016," *Fast Company*, www.fastcompany.com/most-innovative-companies (accessed April 11, 2016).

2. "Phases of Development," *Pfizer*, www.pfizer.com/research/clinical_trials/phases_of_development (accessed April 11, 2016).

3. Barry Jaruzelski, Kevin Schwartz, and Volker Staack, "The 2015 Global Innovation 1000: Innovation's New World Order (study report)," *strategy&*, October 27, 2015, www.strategyand.pwc.com/reports/2015-global-innovation-1000-media-report (accessed April 11, 2016).

4. Dieter Bohn, "Hands-on with the new 12-inch MacBook with Retina Display," *The Verge*, March 9,

2015, www.theverge.com/2015/3/9/8173685/macbook-retina-display-usb-type-c-hands-on-video (accessed April 11, 2016).

5. Mike Esterl, "Gatorade Sets Its Sights on Digital Fitness," *The Wall Street Journal*, March 10, 2016, www.wsj.com/articles/gatorade-sets-its-sights-on-digital-fitness-1457640150 (accessed April 11, 2016).

6. "Moleskine World," *Moleskine*, www.moleskine.com/moleskine_world (accessed April 11, 2016).

7. Jeanine Poggi, "Inside Taco Bell's Not-So-Secret Super Bowl Product Launch," *Ad Age*, February 7, 2016, http://adage.com/article/special-report-super-bowl/inside-taco-bell-s-secret-super-bowl-product-launch/302553/ (accessed April 11, 2016).

8. Carly Page, "iPhone 6 Release Date, Price and Specs," *The Inquirer*, February 3, 2015, www.theinquirer.net/inquirer/news/2323136/iphone-6-rumours-price-features-and-release-date (accessed April 11, 2016).

9. Steven J. Erwing, "Mercedes Renames Utility Vehicles, Repositions Maybach as Sub-brand," *Autoblog*, November 11, 2014, www.autoblog.com/2014/11/11/mercedes-name-changes-gl-maybach/ (accessed April 11, 2016).

10. Jacob Morgan, "Five Uncommon Internal Innovation Examples," *Forbes*, April 8, 2015, www.forbes.com/sites/jacobmorgan/2015/04/08/five-uncommon-internal-innovation-examples/ (accessed April 11, 2016).

11. Bill George, "The World's Most Innovative Company," *Huffington Post*, October 10, 2015, www.huffingtonpost.com/bill-george/the-worlds-most-innovativ_b_8406556.html (accessed April 11, 2016).

12. Michelle Greenwald, "NikeID, Coca-Cola Freestyle and Other Brands Mastering Infinite Customization," *Forbes*, October 8, 2014, www.forbes.com/sites/michellegreenwald/2014/10/08/infinite-customization-12-category-examples-6-key-questions-to-ask/ (accessed April 11, 2016).

13. Tyler Falk, "How Google's Secretive Lab Innovates: Rewarding Failure," *ZDNet*, January 27, 2014, www.zdnet.com/article/how-googles-secretive-lab-innovates-reward-failure/ (accessed April 11, 2016).

14. "Fuld & Company Is the World's Preeminent Research and Consulting Firm in the Field of Competitive Intelligence," *Fuld & Company*, www.fuld.com/company (accessed April 11, 2016).

15. Liz Welch, "Success, One Board at a Time," *Inc.*, March 2014, 24–25.

16. David Kramer, "US Seeing Its Lead in R&D Slipping Against Other Nations," *Physicstoday*, February 2014, http://scitation.aip.org/content/aip/magazine/physicstoday/news/10.1063/PT.5.1010 (accessed April 11, 2016).

17. "Company Profile," *Continuum*, http://continuuminnovation.com/about/company-profile (accessed April 11, 2016).

18. Jen Hansegard, "Lego's Plan to Find the Next Big Hit: Crowdsource It," *Wall Street Journal*, February 25, 2015, http://blogs.wsj.com/digits/2015/02/25/legos-plan-to-find-the-next-big-hit-crowdsource-it/ (accessed April 11, 2016).

19. Eddie Makuch, "Ubisoft's Open-world Racer The Crew Has Been in Development for Six Years," *Gamespot*, May 15, 2014, www.gamespot.com/articles/ubisoft-s-open-world-racer-the-crew-has-been-in-development-for-six-years/1100-6419658/ (accessed April 11, 2016); Eddie Makuch, "Watch Dogs Sells 4 Million Copies in First Week, Needs 2 Million More to Match Assassin's Creed Lifetime Tally," *Gamespot*, June 3, 2014, www.gamespot.com/articles/watch-dogs-sells-4-million-copies-in-first-week-needs-2-million-more-to-match-assassin

/Survey-Reveals-U.S.-Consumers-Feel-Businesses-Lead (accessed April 11, 2016).

20. Michael D. Hutt and Thomas W. Speh, *Business Marketing Management*, 12th ed. (Cincinnati: Cengage Learning, 2015).

21. "Wheaties™ Fans Select Anthony Pettis as America's NEXT Bow Champion," *PR Newswire*, September 3, 2014, www.prnewswire.com/news-releases/wheaties-fans-select-anthony-pettis-as-americas-next-box-champion-273732841.html (accessed April 11, 2016).

22. Mary Vanac, "Meet Wendy's Ciabatta Bacon Cheeseburger," *Columbus Dispatch*, January 27, 2014, www.dispatch.com/content/blogs/the-bottom-line/2014/01/wendys-bringing-bacon-cheeseburger-back-with-ciabatta-bun.html (accessed April 11, 2016).

23. John Dodge, "Dark Barrel Latte: Starbucks Has No Immediate Plan To Serve Beer-Flavored Drink In Chicago," *CBS Chicago*, September 24, 2014, http://chicago.cbslocal.com/2014/09/24/dark-barrel-latte-starbucks-has-no-immediate-plan-to-serve-beer-flavored-drink-in-chicago/ (accessed April 11, 2016).

24. "P&G Everyday," *Procter & Gamble*, www.pgeveryday.com/pgeds/index.jsp (accessed April 11, 2016).

25. Copernicus Marketing Consulting and Research, "Top 10 Reasons for New Product Failure," *GreenBook*, www.greenbook.org/marketing-research.cfm/top-10-reasons-for-new-product-failure (accessed April 11, 2016).

26. Sage McHugh, "8 Biggest Product Fails of 2014," *Alternet*, December 5, 2014 www.alternet.org/economy/8-biggest-product-fails-2014 (accessed April 11, 2016).

27. Susan Gunelius, "Data Proves Word-of-Mouth Marketing Works—Infographic," *Newstex*, February 12, 2014, http://newstex.com/2014/02/12/data-proves-word-of-mouth-marketing-works-infographic/ (accessed April 11, 2016).

28. Ibid.

29. Micah Solomon, "2015 Is The Year of the Millennial Customer: 5 Key Traits These 80 Million Consumers Share," *Forbes*, December 29, 2014, www.forbes.com/sites/micahsolomon/2014/12/29/5-traits-that-define-the-the-80-million-millennial-customers-coming-your-way/#5173e08f2a81 (accessed April 11, 2016).

30. Ibid.

31. "Survey Reveals U.S. Consumers Feel Businesses Lead in Recognizing the Value of Listening to Feedback," *BusinessWire*, January 28, 2014, www.businesswire.com/news/home/20140128005598/en.

32. Rachael Feintzeig, "Boss's Next Demand: Make Lots of Friends," *Wall Street Journal*, February 12, 2014, B1.

33. Vivian Giang, "100 Fastest-Growing Companies," *Fortune*, http://fortune.com/100-fastest-growing-companies/on-assignment-3/ (accessed April 11, 2016).

34. Robert Channick, "40% of Homes Now Without a Landline," *Chicago Tribune*, July 8, 2014, www.chicagotribune.com/business/breaking/chi-landlines-survey-20140708-story.html (accessed April 11, 2016).

12

1. "U. S. Economic Outlook," *Focus Economics*, April 5, 2016, www.focus-economics.com/countries/united-states (accessed July 18, 2016).

2. Dinah Eng, "Building Great Service at the Four Seasons," *Fortune*, April 1, 2016, pp. 31–32.

3. Ed Jones, "Top 10 IT Certifications to Target in 2015," *Cloud Computing Intelligence*, January 5, 2015, www.cloudcomputingintelligence.com/item/1733-the-top-it-certifications-to-target-in-2015 (accessed April 16, 2016).

4. Clark Howard, "Companies that Stink: 2015's Customer Service Hall of Shame," *Clark Howard*, January 4, 2016, www.clarkhoward.com/companies-that-failed-their-customers-in-2015 (accessed July 18, 2016).

5. Darren Hudson, "How I Did It…Priceline's CEO on Creating an In-House Multilingual Customer Service Operation," April 2016, *Harvard Business Review*, pp. 37–40.

6. "Revolutionizing Customer Service," April 2016, *Harvard Business Review*, pp. 26–27.

7. Dwayne Gremler, Mary Jo Bitner, and Valarie Zeithaml, *Services Marketing* (New York: McGraw-Hill, 2012).

8. Ibid.

9. Pam Goodfellow, "L.L. Bean, Amazon and Nordstrom are Customer Service Champions, According to Customers," *Forbes*, March 29, 2016, www.forbes.com/sites/forbesinsights/2016/03/29/l-l-bean-amazon-and-nordstrom-are-customer-service-champions-according-to-consumers/#4170693d7bc2 (accessed July 18, 2016).

10. Nick Clement, "The Best Mobile Banking Apps," *Forbes*, December 22, 2015, www.forbes.com/sites/nickclements/2015/12/22/the-best-mobile-banking-apps/#77bc8cf97902 (accessed April 16, 2016).

11. Michael B.Sauter, Thomas C. Frohlich and Sam Stebbins, *USA Today*, "2015's Customer Service Hall of Fame," August 2, 2015, www.usatoday.com/story/money/business/2015/07/24/24-7-wall-st-customer-service-hall-fame/30599943 (accessed April 17, 2016).

12. Much of the material in this section is based on Christopher H. Lovelock and Jochen Wirtz, *Services Marketing*, 7th ed. (Upper Saddle River, NJ: Prentice Hall, 2011).

13. Zac Townsend, "Era of Mass Customization in Banking," *Bank Innovation*, April 17, 2014, http://bankinnovation.net/2014/04/era-of-mass-customization-in-banking (accessed April 19, 2016).

14. Wendy Donahue, "Mac & Mia Trunk Club for Kids Makes Shopping Easy for Busy Moms," *The Charlotte Observer*, February 11, 2015, www.charlotteobserver.com/incoming/article10430567.html (accessed April 19, 2016).

15. Lovelock and Wirtz, *Services Marketing*.

16. Iris Kuo, "How to Keep Them Coming Back," April 2016, *Inc.*, pp. 80–81.

17. Ibid.

18. Much of the material in this section is based on Dwayne Gremler, Mary Jo Bitner, and Valarie Zeithaml, *Services Marketing*, (New York: McGraw-Hill), 2012.

19. Mia Taylor, "5 Hotels Opening in 2015 that Embody Latest Travel Trends," *MainStreet*, December 24, 2014, www.mainstreet.com/article/5-hotels-opening-in-2015-that-embody-latest-travel-trends (accessed April 19, 2016).

20. "100 Best Companies to Work For 2016," *Fortune*, March 15, 2016, pp. 143–165.

21. Joe Waters, "10 Best Cause Marketing Campaigns of 2015," *Selfish Giving*, January 5, 2016, www.selfishgiving.com/blog/ten-best-cause-marketing-promotions-2015 (accessed April 19, 2016); Katie Jackson, "Why You Should Care About the 'Find Your Park' Campaign," *Outside*, April 30, 2015, www.outsideonline.com/1969631/why-you-should-care-about-find-your-park-campaign (accessed April 19, 2016).

22. "Our Company," *Lamar*, www.lamar.com/About (accessed April 19, 2016).

23. "Pizza Hut International," *Pizza Hut*, https://order.pizzahut.com/international (accessed April 19, 2016).

13

1. Hannah Elliott, "Rolls Royce's Bespoke Program Puts Virtually No Limits on Customization," *Pittsburgh Post-Gazette*, February 20, 2015.

2. Elliot Maras, "How Agile Are Today's Foodservice Supply Chains?" *Food Logistics*, October 16, 2015, www.foodlogistics.com/article/12117374 /how-agile-are-todays-foodservice-supply-chains (accessed April 21, 2016).

3. "Predicting the Unpredictable: Lennox Takes a New Approach to Demand Modeling," *SupplyChainBrain*, December 18, 2015, www.supplychainbrain.com/content/index. php?id=5032&cHash=081010&tx_ttnews [tt_news]=35798 (accessed April 21, 2016).

4. "Campbell Soup Company 2013 Performance Update of the corporate Social Responsibility Report," *Campbell Soup Company*, www .campbellcsr.com/Download/_pdf/Campbells _2013Update_CSR_Report.pdf (accessed April 21, 2016).

5. "Gartner Announces Rankings of Its 2015 Supply Chain Top 25," *Gartner*, May 14, 2015, www .gartner.com/newsroom/id/3053118 (accessed April 21, 2016).

6. "Production," *Airbus*, www.airbus.com/company /aircraft-manufacture/how-is-an-aircraft-built /production/ (accessed April 21, 2016).

7. Mark A. Moon, *Demand and Supply Integration: The Key to World-Class Demand Forecasting*. New York: Financial Times Press, 2013.

8. Much of this section is based on material adapted from Donald J. Bowersox, David J. Closs, and Theodore P. Stank, *21st Century Logistics: Making Supply Chain Integration a Reality*, Oak Brook, IL: Council of Logistics Management, 1999; Barbara Flynn, Michiya Morita, and Jose Machuca, *Managing Global Supply Chain Relationships: Operations, Strategies and Practices*, Business Science, Hershey, New York, 2010; and David Sims, "Integrated Supply Chains Maximize Efficiencies and Savings," *ThomasNet*, July 23, 2013, http:// news.thomasnet.com/imt/2013/07/23/integrated -supply-chains-maximize-efficiencies-and-savings (accessed March 2015).

9. "Häagen-Dazs and General Mills to Help Smallholder Vanilla Farmers Increase Yields and Improve Sustainability Practices in Madagascar," *CSRwire*, February 20, 2013, www.csrwire.com /press_releases/35228-H-agen-Dazs-and-General -Mills-to-Help-Smallholder-Vanilla-Farmers -Increase-Yields-and-Improve-Sustainability -Practices-in-Madagascar (accessed January 2015).

10. Much of this and the following sections are based on material adapted from the edited volume Douglas M. Lambert, ed., *Supply Chain Management: Processes, Partnerships and Performance*, Sarasota, FL: Supply Chain Management Institute, 2004; and "The Supply Chain Management Processes," *Supply Chain Management Institute*, www.ijlm.org/Our-Relationship-Based-Business -Model.htm (accessed March 2015).

11. Christopher Milliken, "A CRM Success Story," *Computer World*, November 7, 2002, www.computerworld.com/article/2578532/crm/a -crm-success-story.html (accessed April 21, 2016).

12. James A. Cooke, "Inside Dell's Global Command Centers," *DC Velocity*, September 24, 2012, www.dcvelocity.com/articles/20120924-inside-dells -global-command-centers (accessed January 2015).

13. Stephanie Grothe, "How They Did It: Red Wing Shoes' Journey to S&OP," *Supply Chain Management Review*, May/June 2014.

14. John Letzing, "Amazon Adds That Robotic Touch," *Wall Street Journal*, March 20, 2012, http://online.wsj.com/article/SB10001424052702304 7244045772919032447962 14.htm (accessed March 2015); Donna Tam, "Meet Amazon's Busiest Employee—The Kiva Robot," *CNET*, November 20, 2014, www.cnet.com/news/meet-amazons -busiest-employee-the-kiva-robot/ (accessed March 2015).

15. Tony Hines, *Supply Chain Strategies: Demand Driven and Customer Focused*, 2nd ed., New York: Routledge, 2013.

16. Robert J. Bowman, "In Modern Retail Replenishment, Once a Day Isn't Enough," *SupplyChainBrain*, April 15, 2013, www.supplychainbrain.com/content /index.php?id=5032&cHash=081010&tx_ttnews [tt_news]=21625 (accessed April 21, 2016).

17. "Bayer HealthCare to Purchase Pharmacy Supplier Steigerwald Arzneimittelwerk," *Zenopa*, May 17, 2013, www.zenopa.com/news/801587313 /bayer-healthcare-to-purchase-pharmacy-supplier -steigerwald-arzneimittelwerk (accessed March 3, 2015).

18. Kenneth J. Petersen, Robert Handfield, and Gary Ragatz, "Supplier Integration into New Product Development: Coordinating Product, Process, and Supply Chain Design," *Journal of Operations Management*, 23, no. 3-4, (2005): 371–388; and Stephen Trimble, "Analysis: US South Rises on Airbus, Boeing Expansion," *Flight Global*, www.flightglobal .com (accessed February 2015).

19. J. Andrew Petersen and V. Kumar, "Can Product Returns Make You Money?" *MIT Sloan Management Review*, April 1, 2010, http://sloanreview.mit .edu/article/can-product-returns-make-you-money/ (accessed April 21, 2016).

20. Lauren Levy, "Sustainable Pallets, Packages & More," *Food Logistics*, May 17, 2013, www .foodlogistics.com/article/10944473/sustainable -pallets-packages-more (accessed April 21, 2016).

21. UPS, "Logistics of Sustainability," *Compass*, Spring 2012, 10.

22. Steve Szilagyi, keynote address, *Warehousing Education and Research Council* Annual Conference, Atlanta, GA, May 2012; and Judy Owen, "Lowe's Ramps Up Disability Inclusion," *Forbes*, April 2013.

23. Martin Christopher, *Logistics and Supply Chain Management*, 4th ed. (New York: Prentice Hall/Financial Times, 2010).

24. "Walmart Honors C.H. Robinson with First Ever 3PL Award," *C.H. Robinson*, March 26, 2015, www.chrobinson.com/en/us/Newsroom/Press -Releases/2015/03-26-2015_Walmart-Honors -CH-Robinson-with-First-Ever-3PL-Award/ (accessed April 21, 2016).

25. Kate Vitasek and Karl Manrodt, *Vested: How P&G, McDonalds, and Microsoft are Redefining Winning in Business Relationships* (New York: Palgrave MacMillan, 2012).

26. Shelly K. Schwartz, "What's the Next Global Manufacturing Superpower?" *CNBC*, September 18, 2012, www.cnbc.com/id/49007307 (accessed April 21, 2016).

27. Dinah Wisenberg Brin, "Need Technology Experts? Try Rural America," *CNBC*, February 20, 2013, www.cnbc.com/id/100470457 (accessed March 2015).

28. Wesley S. Randall, "Public-Private Partnerships in Supply Chain Management," *Journal of Business Logistics*, December 2013.

29. "Project Delivery," *Federal Highway Administration*, www.fhwa.dot.gov/ipd/project_delivery/ (accessed April 21, 2016).

30. "Federal Highway Administration," *U.S. Department of Transportation*, www.fhwa.dot.gov/ (accessed March 3, 2015).31. "Printing Titanium Bicycle Parts. A Charge Bikes Collaboration with EADS," *Vimeo*, August 14, 2012, http://vimeo .com/47522348 (accessed January 2015).

32. "Home," *3DLT*, www.3dlt.com (accessed March 2015).

33. Hans-Georg Kaltenbrunner, "How 3D Printing is Set to Shake Up Manufacturing Supply Chains," *The Guardian*, November 25, 2014.

34. J. Paul Dittmann, *Managing Risk in the Global Supply Chain*, Global Supply Chain Institute: Knoxville, TN, 2014.

35. John Markoff, "New Research Center Aims to Develop Second Generation of Surgical Robots," *The New York Times*, October 23, 2014.

36. Eric Savitz, "Apple Screens for iPad3 in Short Supply," *Forbes*, March 1, 2012, 9.

37. "Vera Bradley Strikes International Agreement," *Inside Indiana Business*, June 4, 2014, www .insideindianabusiness.com/newsitem.asp?id=65477 (accessed March 3, 2015).

38. "Takeback Programs," *South Carolina Department of Health and Environmental Control*, www.scdhec.gov/environment/lwm/recycle/e-cycle /takeback_programs.htm(accessed February 2015).

39. "Frequently Asked Questions About the Apple Recycling Program," *Apple*, www.apple .com/recycling/includes/recycling-faq.html (accessed January 2015).

40. Aaron Strout, "Frictionless Mobile Commerce: 5 Examples of Companies that are Leading," *Marketing Land*, www.marketingland.com (accessed January 2015).

41. Alex Hamilton, "M-Commerce Causing Sales Figures to Explode," *TechRadar*, www.techradar .com (accessed February 2015).

42. "Retailers Leveraging Tablets to Elevate Brand, Boost Sales," *Retailing Insight*, http://retailinginsight. com/industrynews8.html (accessed January 2015).

43. "What Is the Size of the M-Commerce Market in the US?" *Quora*, www.quora.com/Mobile -Commerce-1/What-is-the-size-of-the-m-commerce -market-in-the-US (accessed January 2015).

44. Joanna Brenner, "Pew Internet: Mobile," *Pew Mobile*, September 13, 2013, http:// pewinternet.org/Commentary/2012/February/Pew -Internet-Mobile.aspx (accessed January 2015).

45. Ibid.

46. Aaron Smith, "In-store Mobile Commerce During the 2012 Holiday Shopping Season," *Pew Internet*, January 31, 2013, http://pewinternet.org /Reports/2013/in-store-mobile-commerce.aspx (accessed January 2015).

47. Ibid.

48. Jack Uldrich, "The Future of Retail Isn't So Foreign," *Jump the Curve*, January 30, 2013, http://jumpthecurve.net/retail-marketing /the-future-of-retail-isnt-so-foreign/ (accessed January 2015).

49. "Survey Finds Consumers Using Pinterest to Engage With Retailers More Than Facebook, Twitter," *Retailing Insight*, http://retailinginsight .com/industrynews9.html (accessed January 2015).

50. Wang, J. J., Zhao, X., and Li, J. J. (2013). "Group Buying: A Strategic Form of Consumer

Collective," *Journal of Retailing* 89(3), 338–351.

51. Taurn Kushwaha and Venkatesh Shankar, "Are multichannel customers really more valuable? The moderating role of product category characteristics," *Journal of Marketing*, 77, no. 4, 67–85.

52. Jennifer Lonoff Schiff, "Eight Ways to Create a Successful Multichannel Customer Experience," *CIO Magazine*, February 23, 2015.

14

1. "Monthly & Annual Retail Trade," *United States Census Bureau*, March 12, 2015, www.census.gov/retail (accessed February 2015).

2. "Home," *National Retail Federation*, www.nrf.com (accessed April 21, 2016); Benjamin Snyder, "9 Facts about Walmart that Will Surprise You," *Fortune*, June 6, 2015, http://fortune.com/2015/06/06/walmart-facts/ (accessed April 21, 2016).

3. Jason Daley, "The 2015 Franchise 500," *Entrepreneur*, December 16, 2014.

4. "Kwik Trip Recognized for Providing Healthier Options," *NACS*, February 22, 2016, www.nacsonline.com/Media/Daily/Pages/ND0222161.aspx#.VuMQu5MrLX4 (accessed April 21, 2016).

5. K. Kwak, S. D. Duvvuri, and G. J. Russell, "An Analysis of Assortment Choice in Grocery Retailing," *Journal of Retailing* 91, no. 1, (2015): 19–33.

6. Susan Johnston, "Beware These Online Retail Pricing Strategies," *US News and World Report*, June 24, 2013.

7. David Streitfeld, "It's Discontinued, but Is It a Deal? How List Prices Lost Their Meaning," *New York Times*, March 6, 2016, www.nytimes.com/2016/03/06/technology/its-discounted-but-is-it-a-deal-how-list-prices-lost-their-meaning.html?_r=0 (accessed April 21, 2016).

8. Alaric Dearment, "Target Tackles Movie Streaming," *Retailing Today*, September 25, 2013, http://retailingtoday.com/article/target-tackles-movie-streaming (accessed February 2015).

9. Phil Wahba, "How Do Target and Walmart Stack Up in the E-commerce Wars?" *Fortune*, March 11, 2015, http://fortune.com/2015/03/11/target-walmart/ (accessed April 21, 2016).

10. Leslie Wu, "Rise of the Machines: What Meat Vending Machines Mean for French Dining Habits," *Forbes*, February 29, 2016, www.forbes.com/sites/lesliewu/2016/02/29/rise-of-the-machines-what-meat-vending-machines-mean-for-french-dining-habits/#46340ef71c37 (accessed April 21, 2016); Moe Thet War, "10 Weird Things You Can Buy from Vending Machines," *Gadgette*, December 24, 2015, www.gadgette.com/2015/12/24/10-weird-things-you-can-buy-from-vending-machines/ (accessed April 21, 2016).

11. "Bank of America Adds Human Touch to New ATMs," *Bank of America*, April 4, 2013, http://newsroom.bankofamerica.com/press-release/consumer-banking/bank-america-adds-human-touch-new-atms (accessed April 21, 2016).

12. "Man Cave—Home Parties for Men," *Man Cave*, www.mancaveworldwide.com (accessed March 2015).

13. "Telemarketing in the 21st Century," *BusinessTM*, http://businesstm.com/home-based/telemarketing-in-the-21st-century.html (accessed January 2015).

14. Tianyi Jiang and Alexander Tuzhilin, "Dynamic Microtargeting: Fitness-based Approach to Predicting Individual Preferences," *Knowledge and Information Systems* 19, no. 3, (2009): 337–60.

15. Al Urbanski, "Big Money for Big Data: Marketers will Spend $11.5B in 2015," *Direct Marketing News*, www.dmnews.com (accessed February 2015).

16. "Market Research on Digital Media, Internet Marketing," *eMarketer*, www.emarketer.com (accessed March 2015).

17. Y. Huang and Y. C. Zhang, "The Out-of-Stock (OOS) Effect on Choice Shares of Available Options," *Journal of Retailing* (2015).

18. Ashley Lutz, "Zara's Genius Business Model Could Destroy JCPenney and Sears," *Business Insider*, March 4, 2013, www.businessinsider.com/zaras-genius-business-model-2013-3 (accessed April 1, 2015).

19. Davey Alba, "Forget Drones: Amazon Is Going to Fly Its Own Planes," *Wired*, March 10, 2016, www.wired.com/2016/03/amazon-going-use-planes-move-merchandise/ (accessed April 21, 2016); Emma Thomasson and Nikola Rotscheroth, "Amazon to Open Parcel Locker Network across Europe," *The Globe and Mail*, February 19, 2016, www.theglobeandmail.com/report-on-business/international-business/european-business/amazon-to-open-parcel-locker-network-across-europe/article28810793/ (accessed April 21, 2016).

20. Lydia Dishman, "The Entrepreneur Who Is Beating Amazon at Same-day Delivery," *Fast Company*, www.fastcompany.com/3042207/strong-female-lead/the-entrepreneur-who-is-beating-amazon-at-same-day-delivery (accessed March 13, 2015).

21. Mallory Schlossberg and Ashley Lutz, "The Top 100 Brands for Millennials," *Business Insider*, November 14, 2015, www.businessinsider.com/top-100-millennial-brands-2015-5 (accessed April 21, 2016); Hadley Malcolm, "Whole Foods to Open Chain for Millennials," *USA TODAY*, May 7, 2015, www.usatoday.com/story/money/2015/05/07/whole-foods-cheaper-millennial-chain/70934302/ (accessed April 21, 2016).

22. Taryn Luna, "Retailer T.J. Maxx Quietly Relaunches Online Store," *Boston Globe*, September 18, 2013, www.bostonglobe.com/business/2013/09/17/without-advance-notice-maxx-launches-its-online-store/8HKY5v2OjjV9NK9ofO3DGN/story.html (accessed April 21, 2016).

23. Tiffany Hsu, "Toys R Us to Open Holiday Pop-up Shops in Macy's," *Los Angeles Times*, October 10, 2012, http://articles.latimes.com/2012/oct/10/business/la-fi-mo-toys-r-us-holiday-popup-macys-20121010 (accessed January 2015).

24. A. C. North, L. P. Sheridan, and C. S. Areni, "Music Congruity Effects on Product Memory, Perception, and Choice," *Journal of Retailing* (2015).

25. Adam Blair, "The Drive to Localize," *RIS News*, May 7, 2011, http://risnews.edgl.com/retail-news/The-Drive-to-Localize72436 (accessed March 2015).

26. Haithem Zourrig, Jean-Charles Chebat, and Roy Toffoli, "Consumer Revenge Behavior: A Cross-Cultural Perspective," *Journal of Business Research* 62, no. 10, (2009): 995–1001.

27. Christopher Ratcliff, "iBeacons: The Hunt for Stats," *Econsultancy.com*, August 26, 2014; Rachel Abrams, "Psst! It's Me, the Mannequin," *New York Times*, 2015, A8.

28. "Taking a Look at NRF16: Trends in Retail Industrial Technology," *Digital Signage Today*, February 18, 2016, www.digitalsignagetoday.com/articles/taking-a-look-at-nrf16-trends-in-retail-industry-technology/ (accessed April 21, 2016).

29. Ben Kersey, "Wal-Mart Tries a Blended Channel Approach to Survive in a Digital World," *The Verge*, November 23, 2012, www.theverge.com/2012/11/23/3681694/walmart-hybrid-model (accessed January 2015).

30. Stuart Miller, "Customers Have High Expectations for Click and Collect," *Real Business*, November 28, 2013, http://realbusiness.co.uk/article/24866-customers-have-high-expectations-for-click-and-collect (accessed March 2015).

31. "Taking a Look at NRF16: Trends in Retail Industrial Technology," *Digital Signage Today*; Matt Novak, "China Is Kicking America's Ass in the Robot Waiter Wars," *Gizmodo*, February 17, 2016, http://gizmodo.com/china-is-kicking-americas-ass-in-the-robot-waiter-wars-1759635384 (accessed April 21, 2016); Joe Bates, "Introducing NAO the Robot at Tokyo Haneda Airport," *Airport World*, February 15, 2016, www.airport-world.com/news/general-news/5448-introducing-nao-the-robot-at-tokyo-haneda-airport.html (accessed April 21, 2016).

15

1. "Dove Men+Care Launches 'Real Strength' Campaign on Sports' Biggest Stage to Celebrate the Caring Side of Modern Men" *PR Newswire*, January 20, 2015, http://prnewswire.com/news-releases/dove-mencare-launches-real-strength-campaign-on-sports-biggest-stage-to-celebrate-the-caring-side-of-modern-men-300022814.html (accessed April 7, 2016); Jeanine Poggie, "See Dove Men's Super Bowl Ad Celebrating Dads Unilever Brand Kicks Off 'Real Strength' Campaign," *Advertising Age*, January 20, 2015, http://adage.com/article/special-report-super-bowl/dove-men-care-super-bowl-ad-celebrating-dads/296665/ (accessed April 8, 2016).

2. "#OneLessGirlProblem," *Garnier*, www.onelessgirlproblem.com (accessed April 7, 2016); "Garnier Sleek and Shine," *BuzzFeed*, www.buzzfeed.com/garniersleekandshine (accessed April 7, 2016).

3. Ibid.

4. Ibid.

5. Steve Dent, "Google Glass' Now-like UI Finally Revealed, Just Accept and Say 'ok,'" *Engadget*, February 20, 2013, www.engadget.com/2013/02/20/google-glass-how-it-feels-video (accessed April 7, 2016).

6. "COOLEST COOLER," *Kickstarter*, https://kickstarter.com/projects/ryangrepper/coolest-cooler-21st-century-cooler-thats-actually?ref=most_funded (accessed April 8, 2016).

7. "Ice Bucket Challenge," *ALS Association*, http://alsa.org/fight-als/ice-bucket-challenge.html (accessed March 16, 2016).

8. Lauren Johnson, "Esurance's Super Bowl Pregame Ad Helped Generate 9,000 Tweets a Minute: Cash Giveaway Garnered Huge Twitter Chatter," *Advertising Age*; February 7, 2016, http://adweek.com/news/technology/esurances-1st-quarter-super-bowl-ad-helped-generate-9000-tweets-minute-169495 (accessed April 7, 2016).

9. The AIDA concept is based on the classic research of E. K. Strong Jr. as theorized in *The Psychology of Selling and Advertising* (New York: McGraw-Hill, 1925) and "Theories of Selling," *Journal of Applied Psychology*, 9, 1925, 75–86.

10. "How Many People in America Own an iPad?" *Answers*, http://wiki.answers.com/Q/How_many_people_in_America_own_an_iPad?#slide=2 (accessed April 8, 2016).

11. Thomas E. Barry and Daniel J. Howard, "A Review and Critique of the Hierarchy of Effects in Advertising," *International Journal of Advertising*, 9, 1990, 121–135.

12. Diana Reese, "Why Is Michelle Obama Praising Walmart in Springfield, Mo.?" *Washington Post*, March 1, 2013, www.washingtonpost.com/blogs/she -the-people/wp/2013/03/01/why-is-michelle-obama -praising-walmart-in-springfield-mo (accessed April 7, 2016).

16

1. "Marketers," *Advertising Age 2016 Edition Marketing Fact Pack*, 6.

2. Ibid.

3. Darryl K. Taft, "IBM's Not-so-secret Weapon: Big Data," *eWeek*, February 26, 2013, www.eweek.com/database/ibms-not-so-secret -weapon-big-data-marketing (accessed April 8, 2016).

4. "The World's Most Valuable Brands," *Forbes*, www.forbes.com/powerful-brands/ (accessed April 8, 2016).

5. "How Americans Use Leisure Time," *Advertising Age 2016 Edition Marketing Fact Pack*, 30.

6. "Time Spent Using Media," *Advertising Age 2016 Edition Marketing Fact Pack*, 21.

7. Matthew Sparkes, "iPhone Owners Admit Having 'Blind Loyalty' to Apple," *Telegraph*, February 12, 2014, www.telegraph.co.uk/technology/apple /10632787/iPhone-owners-admit-having-blind -loyalty-to-Apple.html (accessed April 7, 2016).

8. "25 Largest US Advertisers," *Advertising Age 2016 Edition Marketing Fact Pack*, 8.

9. David Griner, "Oreo Surprises 26 Million Facebook Fans with Gay Pride Post," *Adweek*, June 25, 2012, www.adweek.com/adfreak/oreo-surprises -26-million-facebook-fans-gay-pride-post-141440 (accessed April 7, 2016).

10. Oussama Jebali, "First Interactive Print Ad Featuring LED Light and Battery by Motorola," *Esprit Mobile*, January 21, 2014, http://espritmobile .com/first-interactive-print-ad-featuring-led-light -and-battery-by-motorola/ (accessed April 8, 2016).

11. "'Shopping Carts' Commercial—21st Century Auto Insurance: Same Great Coverage for Less," *YouTube*, February 22, 2012, www.youtube.com /watch?v=CDoAmgIfj_U (accessed April 8, 2016).

12. Ibid.

13. John Babish, "Ithaca, NY Company, Bionexus, Introduces First Natural Skin Care Lotion for Dogs Containing Standardized Nigella Sativa Extracts," *PRNewswire*, April 17, 2012, www.facebook.com /permalink.php?id=118344488181338&story _fbid=419853818042564 (accessed April 8, 2016).

14. Tim Nudd, "Snickers Swaps Out Its Brand Name for Hunger Symptoms on Painfully Honest Packaging So You Can Call Out Your Irritable Friends," *Advertising Age*, September 21, 2015, www.adweek.com/adfreak/snickers-swaps-out-its -brand-name-hunger-symptoms-painfully-honest -packaging-167061 (accessed April 8, 2016).

15. Lauren Cleave, "What Do We Really Think about Humour in Advertising?", http://adgrad .co.uk/?author=4 (accessed April 7, 2016).

16. Neil King Jr., "Anti-Obama Ads Take Elegiac Tone," *The Wall Street Journal*, May 4, 2012, http://online.wsj.com/article/SB10001424052702303 877604577383950339656854.html (accessed April 8, 2016).

17. "Media—Share of Ad Spending by Medium," *Advertising Age 2016 Edition Marketing Fact Pack*, 14.

18. Ibid.

19. "The Top 15 Campaigns of the 21st Century," *Advertising Age*, http://adage.com/lp/top15/#intro (accessed April 6, 2016).

20. Alex Kantrowitz, "$70 Billion TV Ad Market Easing into Digital Direction," *Advertising Age*, October 14, 2013, http://adage.com/article /media/70-billion-tv-ad-market-eases-digital -direction/244699/ (accessed April 8, 2016).

21. Jeanine Poggi, "TV Ad Prices: Football Is Still King," *Advertising Age*, October 20, 2013, http://adage.com/article/media/tv-ad-prices -football-king/244832/ (accessed April 7, 2016).

22. "Cost for a 30-Second Television Spot," *Advertising Age 2016 Edition Marketing Fact Pack*, 18–19.

23. "US Ad Spending Totals by Medium from Kantar Media," *Advertising Age 2016 Edition Marketing Fact Pack*, 14.

24. David Kaplan, "For Turner Digital, Audience Buying Risk Outweighs Reward," *AdExchanger*, October 9, 2012, www.adexchanger.com/online -advertising/for-turner-digital-audience-buying-risk -outweighs-reward (accessed April 8, 2016).

25. "IAB Internet Advertising Revenue Report: 2012 Full Year Results," *PricewaterhouseCoopers*, April 2013, www.iab.net/media/file/IAB_Internet _Advertising_Revenue_Report_FY_2012.pdf (accessed April 8, 2016); "Mobile Ad Spend to Top $100 Million Worldwide in 2016, 51% of Digital Marketing," *eMarketer*, April 2, 2015, www.emarketer.com/Article/Mobile-Ad-Spend -Top-100-Billion-Worldwide-2016-51-of-Digital -Market/1012299 (accessed April 7, 2016).

26. "Most Popular Facebook Games in February 2016"; *Statista*; www.statista.com/statistics/267003 /most-popular-social-games-on-facebook-based-on -daily-active-users/ (accessed May 2, 2016).

27. "Facebook vs. Non-Facebook Social Network Gaming Ecosystem and Market Analysis 2013– 2018," *MarketWatch*, February 4, 2014, www .marketwatch.com/story/facebook-vs-non-facebook -social-network-gaming-ecosystem-and-market -analysis-2013-2018-2014-02-04 (accessed April 8, 2016).

28. Joanna Brenner, "Pew Internet: Mobile," *Pew Research Center*, January 31, 2013, http://pewinternet .org/Commentary/2012/February/Pew-Internet -Mobile.aspx (accessed March 2015); "Mobile Ad Spend to Top $100 Million Worldwide in 2016, 51% of Digital Marketing," *eMarketer*, April 2, 2015; www.emarketer.com/Article/Mobile-Ad-Spend -Top-100-Billion-Worldwide-2016-51-of-Digital -Market/1012299 (accessed April 7, 2016).

29. Alex Kantrowitz, "Mobile Ad Revenue Explodes, Finally," *Advertising Age*, December 16, 2013, 6.

30. Owen Thomas, "New Marissa Mayer's Complaint about Yahoo's Hold Music Has Turned into a Music Video," *Business Insider*, February 4, 2013, www. businessinsider.com/yahoo-earnings-hold-music- video-snow-rapper-2013-2 (accessed April 8, 2016).

31. John Moulding, "ABC Proves the Value of the Unified TV/Digital Ad Buy," *Videonet*, October 23, 2013, www.v-net.tv/abc-proves-the-value-of-the -unified-tvdigital-ad-buy/(accessed April 8, 2016).

32. Kathy Crosett, "Online Product Placement to Increase," *Ad-ology*, January 10, 2013, www .marketingforecast.com/archives/22200 (accessed April 8, 2016).

33. "US Ad Spending Forecast from Zenith Opti-media," *Advertising Age 2016 Edition Marketing Fact Pack*, 14.

34. Ibid.

35. Jennifer Wang, "10 Marketing Masterworks," *Entrepreneur*, February 18, 2013, www.entrepreneur .com/article/225462 (accessed April 8, 2016).

36. Edmund Lawler, "The Rise of Experiential Marketing," *Advertising Age*, November 18, 2013, C1–C2.

37. Philip Caulfield, "Web Pranksters Hijack Restaurant's Mountain Dew Naming Contest," *New York Daily News*, August 15, 2012 www.nydailynews .com/news/national/web-pranksters-hijack-mountain -dew-online-crowdsourced-naming-effort-new-green -apple-flavored-soda-article-1.1136204 (accessed April 8, 2016).

38. "Inmar 2015 Coupon Trends—Year End 2015," *Inmar*, February, 2016,http://go.inmar.com/rs /inmar/images/Inmar_2015_Coupon_Trends_Report .pdf (accessed May 8, 2016).

39. Caitlin McGarry, "Pay by Hashtag: Twitter Wants to Get Inside Your Wallet," *TechHive*, January 24, 2014, www.techhive.com/article /2090822/pay-by-hashtag-twitter-wants-to-get -inside-your-wallet.html (accessed April 8, 2016); Andrew R. Johnson, "@AmericanExpress Tries #Deals via Twitter," *The Wall Street Journal*, March 7, 2012, www.wsj.com/articles/SB1000142405297 0204781804577267402969728444 (accessed April 8, 2016).

40. Donna L. Montaldo, "How to Avoid the Rebate Rip-off," *About.com*, http://couponing.about.com /od/bargainshoppingtips/a/hub_rebate.htm (accessed March 2015).

41. Martin Moylan, "Retailers' Loyalty Programs Popular with Consumers," *Minnesota Public Radio*, January 2, 2013, http://minnesota.publicradio.org /display/web/2013/01/02/business/retail-rewards -programs (accessed April 8, 2016).

42. Elizabeth Holmes, "At Bloomies, Loyalty for All," *The Wall Street Journal*, February 24, 2012, B5.

43. Kelly Short, "Study Shows In-store Sampling Events Outperform Other Top In-store Marketing Tactics," *Interactions*, February 28, 2013, www .interactionsmarketing.com/news/?p=352 (accessed April 8, 2016).

44. Jim Tierney, "Study Shows Most Customers Make Purchase Decisions In the Store," *Loyalty360*, November 11, 2013, http://loyalty360.org/resources /article/study-shows-most-customers-make-purchase -decisions-in-the-store (accessed April 8, 2016).

45. Don Davis, "Consumers Redeem 141% More Digital Coupons in 2013," *Internet Retailer*, January 16, 2014, www.internetretailer.com/2014/01/16 /consumers-redeem-141-more-digital-coupons -2013 (accessed April 8, 2016).

46. Rachel King, "Google Trying out Real-time, Targeted Digital Coupons with Zavers," *ZDNet*, January 11, 2013, www.zdnet.com/google-trying -out-real-time-targeted-digital-coupons-with -zavers-7000009722/ (accessed April 8, 2016).

47. "Zero Moment of Truth (ZMOT)," *Google*, www.thinkwithgoogle.com/collections/zero -moment-truth.html (accessed April 8, 2016).

17

1. "Nordstrom Careers," *Nordstrom*, http://about .nordstrom.com/careers/ (accessed March 18, 2016).

2. "Personal Shoppers," *Bloomingdales*, www1 .bloomingdales.com/about/shopping/personal.jsp (accessed March 18, 2016).

3. Rodrigo Guesalaga, "The Use of Social Media in Sales: Individual and Organizational Antecedents, and the Role of Customer Engagement in Social Media," *Industrial Marketing Management,* in press, (accessed March 18, 2016).

4. "What is LinkedIn?," *LinkedIn*, www.linkedin .com/static?key=what_is_linkedin&trk=hb_what (accessed March 18, 2016).

5. "Sales Navigator Product Datasheet," *LinkedIn*, https://business.linkedin.com/sales-solutions/site-forms/sales-navigator-datasheet (accessed March 18, 2016).

6. Alex Hisaka, "The 6-step Guide to Successful Social Selling on LinkedIn – Sales Solutions Blog," *LinkedIn*, January 22, 2015, http://sales.linkedin.com/blog/the-6-step-guide-to-successful-social-selling-on-linkedin/ (accessed March 18, 2016).

7. "Social Selling tips: 10 Actionable Sale Tips LinkedIn Sales Solutions," *Linkedin*, https://business.linkedin.com/sales-solutions/resources/social-selling/top-sales-tips (accessed March 18, 2016).

8. Kim Garst, "Find Prospects on Social Media and Turn Them into Customers," *Huffington Post*, February 18, 2014, www.huffingtonpost.com/kim-garst/find-prospects-on-social-_b_4785711.html (accessed March 18, 2016).

9. "Leadership Program," *General Electric*, www.ge.com/careers/students/clp/index.html (accessed March 18, 2016).

10. Jeff S. Johnson, Scott B. Friend, Brian N. Rutherford, and G. Alexander Hamwi (2015), "Absolute versus Relative Sales Failure," *Journal of Business Research,* 69, 596–603.

11. Linda Ray, "Examples of Cultural Differences in Business," *Demand Media*, http://smallbusiness.chron.com/examples-cultural-differences-business-21958.html (accessed March 18, 2016).

12. Weitz, Castleberry, and Tanner, *Selling*, 17–22.

13. Zahed Subhan, Roger Brooksbank, Scott Rader, Duncan Steel, and Kimberley Mackey (2014), "Running an Effective Induction Program for New Sales Recruits: Lessons from the Financial Services Industry," *Journal of Selling*, 14 (1), 20–32.

14. Peter Criscione, "Mary Kay's Top Salespeople are Pretty in Pink," *Brampton Guardian*, February 25, 2014, www.mississauga.com/news-story/4384280-mary-kay-s-top-salespeople-are-pretty-in (accessed March 18, 2016).

15. Paul Greenberg, "And the Winners of the 2016 CRM Watchlist are…," *ZDNet*, February 16, 2016, www.zdnet.com/article/and-the-winners-of-the-2016-crm-watchlist-are/ (accessed March 18, 2016).

16. Heather Clancy, "7 Apps to Take Your Customer Loyalty Program Mobile," *ZDNet*, January 27, 2014, www.zdnet.com/7-apps-to-take-your-customer-loyalty-program-mobile-7000025654/ (accessed March 18, 2016); Jessica Bruder, "A Customer Loyalty Program (From Some of the Folks Who Brought You Groupon)," *New York Times*, February 21, 2012, http://boss.blogs.nytimes.com/2012/02/21/a-customer-loyalty-program-from-some-of-the-folks-who-brought-you-groupon (accessed March 18, 2016).

17. "The Key Ring Story – From Scrappy Startup to Market Leader," *Key Ring*, www.keyringapp.com/about/story (accessed March 18, 2016).

18. Saul Perez, "Why Cross-Selling is Part of Wells Fargo's Strategy," *Market Realist*, October 10, 2014, http://finance.yahoo.com/news/why-cross-selling-part-wells-130018022.html;_ylt=aolevx (accessed March 18, 2016).

19. "About Recommendations," *Amazon,* www.amazon.com/gp/help/customer/display.html/ref=help_search_1-1?ie=UTF8&nodeId=16465251&qid=1426340118&sr=1-1 (accessed March 18, 2016).

18

1. "Social Media and the New Reality for Law Practice," *LegalWire*, February 24, 2013, www.legalwire.co.uk/?dt_portfolio=legal-profession-2-0-social-media-and-the-new-reality-for-law-firms (accessed May 2016).

2. Shanyndi Raice, Mike Ramsey, and Sam Schechner, "Facebook Gains Two Big Advertisers' Support," *The Wall Street Journal*, June 20, 2012, B6.

3. "Twitter: Most Followers," *FriendOrFollow*, http://friendorfollow.com/twitter/most-followers/ (accessed April 2016).

4. "Facebook Statistics—Brands," *Socialbakers*, www.socialbakers.com/statistics/facebook/pages/total/brands/ (accessed April 2016).

5. Ibid.

6. Lululemon Practiced Textbook Crisis PR During Yoga Pants Frenzy," *PR Daily*, www.prdaily.com/Main/Articles/Lululemon_practiced_textbook_crisis_PR_during_yoga_14137.aspx# (accessed May 2016).

7. David Moth, "Six Brands that Have Been Busy Experimenting with Google Hangouts," *Econsultancy*, http://econsultancy.com/us/blog/62774-six-brands-that-have-been-busy-experimenting-with-google-hangouts (accessed May 2016).

8. 5 Terrific Examples of Company Social Media Policies, *Hire Rabbit*, http://blog.hirerabbit.com/5-terrific-examples-of-company-social-media-policies/ (accessed May 2016).

9. Tessa Stuart, "Secrets of a Celebrity Twitter Coach," *BuzzFeed*, February 19, 2013, www.buzzfeed.com/tessastuart/secrets-of-a-celebrity-twitter-coach#.wiM2vVjgE (accessed April 2016).

10. Cory Edwards, "A Shift in Social Media Training for Employees," *Adobe*, December 17, 2013, http://blogs.adobe.com/digitalmarketing/social-media/a-social-shift-in-social-media-training-for-employees/ (accessed April 2016).

11. Parmy Olson, "Teenagers Say Goodbye to Facebook and Hello to Messenger Apps," *The Guardian*, November 9, 2013, www.theguardian.com/technology/2013/nov/10/teenagers-messenger-apps-facebook-exodus (accessed May 2016).

12. Dave Chaffey, "Global Social Media Research Summary 2016," *Smart Insights*, www.smartinsights.com/social-media-marketing/social-media-strategy/new-global-social-media-research-/ (accessed July 21, 2016).

13. Ibid.

14. "SBANC Newsletter—June 5th, 2012," *International Council for Small Business*, June 5, 2012, www.icsb.org/article.asp?messageID=983 (accessed April 2016).

15. Aaron Smith, "US Smart Phone Users 2015," *Pew Research Center*, April 1, 2015, http://pewinternet.org (accessed April 10, 2016).

16. Steven Musil, "U.S. Tablet Usage Hits 'Critical Mass' ComScore Reports," *CNet*, June 10, 2012, http://news.cnet.com/8301-13579_3-57450079-37/u.s-tablet-usage-hits-critical-mass-comscore-reports (accessed May 2016).

17. Sid Gandotra, "Why Social Commerce Matters," *Social Media Today*, November 6, 2012, http://socialmediatoday.com/sid-gandotra/974961/social-commerce-socialmedia-ecommerce (accessed May 2016).

18. Janessa Rivera, "Gartner Says CRM Will Be at the Heart of Digital Initiatives for Years to Come," *Gartner*, February 12, 2014, www.gartner.com/newsroom/id/2665215 (accessed April 2016).

19. Lauren Indvik, "The 7 Species of Social Commerce," *Mashable*, May 10, 2013, http://mashable.com/2013/05/10/social-commerce-definition/ (accessed July 21, 2016).

20. "Giveaway!!! Pin It to Win It! An iPad Mini for Two Lucky Winners!!!" *Favorite Family Recipes*, March 10, 2013, www.favfamilyrecipes.com/2013/03/giveaway-pin-it-to-win-it-an-ipad-mini-for-two-lucky-winners.html (accessed May 2016); Lauren Indvik, "How Brands Are Using Promotions to Market on Pinterest," *Mashable*, March 7, 2012, http://mashable.com/2012/03/07/pinterest-brand-marketing (accessed May 2016).

21. "Complimentary White Paper: Forrester's US Interactive Marketing Forecast through 2016," *Adobe Marketing Cloud*, http://success.adobe.com/en/na/programs/products/digitalmarketing/migration12/1208_21408_forrester_interactive_marketing_forecast.html (accessed May 2016).

22. Eric Mosley, "Crowdsource your Performance Reviews," *Harvard Business Review*, June 15, 2013, http://blogs.hbr.org/cs/2012/06/crowdsource_your_performance_r.html (accessed May 2016).

23. "Photograph for Ellie Goulding with HP Connected Music," *Talenthouse*, www.talenthouse.com/photograph-for-ellie-goulding-and-hp-connected-music#description (accessed May 2016).

24. "Paid Media Marketing," *Greenlight*, www.greenlightdigital.com/paid-media (accessed May 2016).

25. Ibid.

26. Russell Working, "Most Unhappy with Social Media Measurement, Survey Says," *Ragan Communications*, www.ragan.com/Main/Articles/Most_unhappy_with_social_media_measurement_survey_45919.aspx (accessed May 2016).

27. "Key Performance Indicators," *Intrafocus*, June 2013, www.google.com/url?sa=t&rct=j&q=&esrc=s&source=web&cd=1&ved=0CB4QFjAA&url=http%3A%2F%2Fwww.intrafocus.com%2Fwp-content%2Fuploads%2F2014%2F06%2FKey-Performance-Indicators.docx&ei=W1wEVaShMYiZNtrPgKAJ&usg=AFQjCNEBG-PWazcH1Hxz5LXOH2UewiQZ4w&bvm=bv.88198703,d.eXY (accessed April 2016).

28. Andy Williams, "How Social Media Has Changed the Way We Complain," *Koozai*, February 25, 2013, www.koozai.com/blog/branding/reputation-management/how-social-media-has-changed-the-way-we-complain (accessed May 2016); Bob Fine, "How Social Media Has Changed Politics: It's Not Just Tactics," *The Social Media Monthly*, January 18, 2013, http://thesocialmediamonthly.com/how-social-media-has-changed-politics-its-not-just-tactics (accessed May 2016); "How Social Media Has Changed the Way We Communicate," *Information Gateway*, January 24, 2013, www.informationgateway.org/social-media-changed-communicate (accessed May 2016).

29. Charlene Li and Josh Bernoff, *Groundswell: Winning in a World Transformed by Social Technologies*, revised ed. (Boston: Harvard Business Press, 2011).

30. Gina Sverdlov, "Global Social Technographics Update: US and EU Mature, Emerging Markets Show Lots of Activity," *Forrester*, January 4, 2012, http://blogs.forrester.com/gina_sverdlov/12-01-04-global_social_technographics_update_2011_us_and_eu_mature_emerging_markets_show_lots_of_activity (accessed April 2016); "What's the Social Technographics Profile of Your Customer?" *Forrester Empowered*, http://empowered.forrester.com/tool_consumer.html (accessed May 2016).

31. "Forrester: Social Media Use in US and EU Maturing, More Passive Than Emerging Markets," *Paige ONeill*, http://paigeoneill.com/2012/01/05/forrester-social-media-use-in-us-and-eu-maturing-more-passive-than-emerging-markets/ (accessed May 2016).

32. Shanna Mallon, "Should Every Company Have a Blog?" *The Media Revolution*, January 30, 2014,

www.blogworld.com/2014/01/30/should-every
-company-have-a-blog/ (accessed May 2016).

33. Schaefer, Mark (January 12, 2015) "The 10
Best Big Company Blogs in the Worlds," *Businesses
Grow,* www.businessesgrow.com/2015/01/12/best
-company-blogs/ (accessed May 2016).

34. Lauren Drell, "The Quick and Dirty Guide to
Tumblr for Small Business," *Mashable,*
February 18, 2012, http://mashable.
com/2012/02/18/tumblr-small-biz-guide (accessed
April 2016).

35. Chris Erasmus, "The Voting Hub Facebook
Page," *Threadless,* February 16, 2014,
www.threadless.com/forum/post/990069/the_voting
_hub_facebook_page/ (accessed May 2016).

36. Josh Bersin, "Facebook Vs. LinkedIn—What's
the Difference?" *Forbes,* May 21, 2012, www
.forbes.com/sites/joshbersin/2012/05/21/facebook
-vs-linkedin-whats-the-difference (accessed May
2016).

37. "Top Sites," *Alexa,* www.alexa.com/topsites (accessed May 2016).

38. Rob Walker, "How Reddit's Ask Me Anything
Became Part of the Mainstream Media Circuit,"
Yahoo, March 13, 2013, http://news.yahoo.com
/how-reddit-s-ask-me-anything-became-part-of
-the-mainstream-media-circuit--130755591.html
(accessed May 2016); "Top Scoring Links: IAmA,"
Reddit, www.reddit.com/r/IAmA/top/ (accessed
May 2016).

39. Tony Nguyen, "The Importance of Social Bookmarking and RSS in SEO," *Business Review
Center,* October 18, 2012, http://businessreview-
center.com/social-bookmarking-and
-rss (accessed May 2016).

40. Jordan Slabaugh, "4 Ways to Get Customers on
Your Side," *iMedia Connection,* January 29, 2014,
www.imediaconnection.com/content/35808.asp
(accessed May 2016).

41. "Yelp Elite Event: Tiki Beach Party at Le Lab"
Yelp, www.yelp.com/biz/yelp-elite-event-tiki-beach
-party-at-le-lab-montr%C3%A9al (accessed May
2016).

42. "Global Games Market Will Reach 102.9 Billion in 2017," *Newzoo,* May 14, 2015, https://new-
zoo.com/insights/articles/global-games-market
-will-reach-102-9-billion-2017-2/ (accessed April
2016).

43. Emanuel Maiberg, "Top 25 Facebook Games
of May 2013," *Inside Social Games,* May 1, 2013,
www.insidesocialgames.com/2013/05/01/the-top
-25-facebook-games-of-may-2013/ (accessed
March 2015).

44. "Second Life Grid Survey—Economic Metrics," *GridSurvey,* March 15, 2013, http://gridsur-
vey.com/economy.php (accessed May 2016); Matt
Weinberger, "This Company Was 13 Years Early
to Virtual Reality—and It's Getting Ready to Try
Again," *Business Insider,* March 29, 2015, www
.businessinsider.com/second-life-is-still-around
-and-getting-ready-to-conquer-virtual
-reality-2015-3 (accessed July 21, 2016); Charles
Poladian, "Facebook Paid $2.5 Billion to Game
Developers in 2015, but Don't Call It Farmville,"
IBTimes, March 29, 2016, www.ibtimes.com

/facebook-paid-25-billion-game-developers
-2015-dont-call-it-farmville-2336856 (accessed
April 2016).

45. "Most Popular Facebook Games as of
February 2016, Based on Number of Daily Active
Users (in Millions)," *Statista,* www.statista.com
/statistics/267003/most-popular-social-games-on
-facebook-based-on-daily-active-users/ (accessed
April 2016).

46. John Gaudiosi, "This Company Is Hosting the
First Ever eSports Event at Madison Square Garden," *Fortune,* June 9, 2015, http://fortune
.com/2015/06/09/riot-games-esports/ (accessed
April 2016).

47. "Global Mobile Statistics 2013 Part A: Mobile
Subscribers; Handset Market Share; Mobile Operators," *mobiThinking,* March 2013, http://mobithink-
ing.com/mobile-marketing-tools/latest
-mobile-stats/a (accessed May 2016).

48. Ingrid Lunden, "Digital Ads Will Be 22%
Of All U.S. Ad Spend In 2013, Mobile Ads 3.7%;
Total Global Ad Spend In 2013 $503B," *Tech-
Crunch,* September 1, 2013, http://techcrunch
.com/2013/09/30/digital-ads-will-be-22-of-all-u
-s-ad-spend-in-2013-mobile-ads-3-7-total-gobal
-ad-spend-in-2013-503b-says-zenithoptimedia/ (accessed May 2016).

49. "Modify QR Code Watch—Because Simply
Reading Time on Your Watch Is Soooo 2011,"
Modify Watches, February 23, 2012, www
.modifywatches.com/blog/qr-code-watch (accessed
May 2016).

50. JP Mangalindan, "Barnes & Noble CEO: NFC
Coming to the Nook," *CNN,* May 1, 2012, http://
tech.fortune.cnn.com/2012/05/01/nook (accessed
May 2016).

51. "The Next Big Thing is Almost Here—Samsung Galaxy S6," *T-Mobile,* https://explore
.t-mobile.com/samsung-galaxy-s6-and-s6
-edge?cmpid=ADV_PG_sTubibNN&002
=2200112&004=18774752225&005
=79090275441&006=70390625225&007
=Search&008=&025=c&026=&gclid=
CNzwgaW4rcQCFeJr7AodmDUAOg
(accessed May 2016).

52. Daniel Howley, "The Best iPhone Widgets
You're Not Using," *Yahoo,* January 24, 2015, https://
www.yahoo.com/tech/the-best-iphone-widgets
-youre-not-using-108954809304.html (accessed
May 2016).

19

1. "Luxury of Premium Pricing in China Is Looking
Unaffordable," *The Wall Street Journal,* June 13–14,
2015, B14.

2. "Can You Trust That Web Price?" *The Wall
Street Journal,* October 23, 2014, B1.

3. "Personalized Pricing," *Business Week,* January 2,
2014, 47–48; Koert van Ittersum, Brian Wansink,
Joost Pennings, and Daniel Sheehan, "Smart Shopping Carts: How Real Time Feedback Influences
Spending," *Journal of Marketing,* November 2013,
21–36.

4. "SFPark Called a Success, Will Expand
Throughout the City," June 21, 2014, *SFGate,*
www.sfgate.com/bayarea/article/SFpark-called
-a-success-willexpand-throughout-5568645.php
(accessed February 26, 2015).

5. "How Much Did You Pay for That Lipstick?"
Forbes, April 14, 2015, 46–49.

6. Spencer Soper, "Stores Try Fixed Prices That
Aren't So Fixed," *Businessweek,* July 27, 2015–August 2, 2015, 22–23.

7. "Guaranteed Profits," *The Economist,*
February 14, 2016, 68.

8. "The Effect of Customer Loyalty on Retail Pricing," *Marketing News,* January 2016, 3.

9. Ryan Hamilton and Alexander Chernev, "Low
Prices Are Just the Beginning: Price Image in Retail
Management," *Journal of Marketing,* November
2013, 1–20.

10. Keith Coulter and Anne Roggeveen, "Price
Number Relationships and Deal Processing Flu-
ency: The Effects of Approximation Sequence and
Number Multiples," *Journal of Marketing Research,*
February 2014, 69–82.

11. Aylin Aydini, Marco Bertini, and Anja Lam-
brecht, "Price Promotion for Emotional Impact,"
Journal of Marketing, July 2014, 80–96.

12. "Future of Private Labels Looks Bright,"
McLoone, January 31, 2014, www.mccloone
.com/blog/future-of-private-labels-looks-bright/
(accessed February 27, 2015).

13. "Spirit Airlines: The Power of a Clear Strategy,"
Strongbrands, February 2, 2015, http://timcalkins
.com/branding-insights/spirit-airlines-power-clear
-strategy/ (accessed February 28, 2015).

14. Sascha Alavi, Torsten Bornemann, and Jan Wi-
eseke, "Gambled Price Discounts: A Remedy to the
Negative Side Effects of Regular Price Discounts,"
Journal of Marketing, March 2015, 62–78.

15. "Annual Topline View CPE Coupon Facts,"
NCH Marketing, https://www2.nchmarketing
.com/ResourceCenter/assets/0/22/28/76/226/457
/4bfe051da14f4f8f9e8bc7e48d9e510a.pdf (accessed
January 26, 2016).

16. "That Drug Coupon Isn't Really Clipping
Costs," *Businessweek,* December 28, 2015, 21–22.

17. Ibid.

18. Ibid.

19. "Free Shipping Is Getting More Expensive,"
The Wall Street Journal, October 22, 2014, www.wsj
.com/articles/free-shipping-is-going-to-cost-you
-more-1414003507 (accessed February 28, 2015).

20. Ibid.

21. Jan Wieseke, Sascha Alavi, and Johannes Ha-
bel, "Willing to Pay More, Eager to Pay Less: The
Role of Consumer Loyalty in Price Negotiations,"
Journal of Marketing, November 2014, 17–37.

22. "The Psychology Behind the Sweet Spots of
Pricing," *Fast Company,* www.fastcompany
.com/1826172/psychology-behind-sweet-spots
-pricing (accessed February 28, 2015).

23. "Same Package, Same Price, Less Product,"
The Wall Street Journal, June 12, 2015, B1–B2.

INDEX

1-1 Define the term *marketing*. Marketing is the activity, set of institutions, and processes for creating, communicating, delivering, and exchanging offerings that have value for customers, clients, partners, and society at large. Marketing also requires all facets of a company to work together to pool ideas and resources. One major goal of marketing is to create an exchange. An exchange has five conditions, as listed below. Even if all five conditions are met, however, an exchange might not occur. People engage in marketing whether or not an exchange happens.

Five conditions of exchange

1. There must be at least two parties.
2. Each party has something that might be of value to the other party.
3. Each party is capable of communication and delivery.
4. Each party is free to accept or reject the exchange offer.
5. Each party believes it is appropriate or desirable to deal with the other party.

Google offers many amenities to its employees, part of the reason *Fortune* ranked it as the best company to work for from 2012 to 2016

Zuma Press, Inc./Alamy Stock Photo

marketing the activity, set of institutions, and processes for creating, communicating, delivering, and exchanging offerings that have value for customers, clients, partners, and society at large (p. 2)

exchange people giving up something in order to receive something else they would rather have (p. 3)

1-2 Describe four marketing management philosophies. The role of marketing and the character of marketing activities within an organization are strongly influenced by the organization's marketing philosophy and orientation. A production-oriented organization focuses on the internal capabilities of the firm rather than on the desires and needs of the marketplace. A sales orientation is based on the beliefs that people will buy more products and services if aggressive sales techniques are used and that high sales volumes produce high profits. A market-oriented organization focuses on satisfying customer wants and needs while meeting organizational objectives. A societal marketing orientation goes beyond a market orientation to include the preservation or enhancement of individuals' and society's long-term best interests.

production orientation a philosophy that focuses on the internal capabilities of the firm rather than on the desires and needs of the marketplace (p. 4)

sales orientation the belief that people will buy more goods and services if aggressive sales techniques are used and that high sales result in high profits (p. 4)

marketing concept the idea that the social and economic justification for an organization's existence is the satisfaction of customer wants and needs while meeting organizational objectives (p. 5)

market orientation a philosophy that assumes that a sale does not depend on an aggressive sales force but rather on a customer's decision to purchase a product;

it is synonymous with the marketing concept (p. 5)

societal marketing orientation the idea that an organization exists not only to satisfy customer wants and needs and to meet organizational objectives but also to preserve or enhance individuals' and society's long-term best interests (p. 6)

1-3 Discuss the differences between sales and market orientations. First, sales-oriented firms focus on their own needs; market-oriented firms focus on customers' needs and preferences. Second, sales-oriented companies consider themselves to be deliverers of goods and services, whereas market-oriented companies view themselves as satisfiers of customers. Third, sales-oriented firms direct their products to everyone; market-oriented firms aim at specific segments of the population. Fourth, sales-oriented organizations place a higher premium on making a sale, while market-oriented businesses seek a long-term relationship with the customer. Finally, sales-oriented businesses pursue maximum sales volume through intensive promotion, whereas market-oriented businesses pursue customer satisfaction through coordinated activities.

iStockphoto.com/2007 Getty Images/Justin Sullivan

In 2015, *Fast Company* named Starbucks' Howard Schultz as he top customer-focused CEO in the United States. Schultz has taken several steps to improve the customer experience at Starbucks, such as installing espresso machines with lower profiles so that baristas can look customers in the eyes while making drinks.

customer value the relationship between benefits and the sacrifice necessary to obtain those benefits (p. 7)

customer satisfaction customers' evaluation of a good or service in terms of whether it has met their needs and expectations (p. 7)

relationship marketing a strategy that focuses on keeping and improving relationships with current customers (p. 9)

empowerment delegation of authority to solve customers' problems quickly—usually by the first person the customer notifies regarding a problem (p. 10)

teamwork collaborative efforts of people to accomplish common objectives (p. 10)

customer relationship management (CRM) a company-wide business strategy designed to optimize profitability, revenue, and customer satisfaction by

focusing on highly defined and precise customer groups (p. 11)

on-demand marketing delivering relevant experiences, integrated across both physical and virtual environments, throughout the consumer's decision and buying process (p. 11)

1-4 **Describe several reasons for studying marketing.** First, marketing affects the allocation of goods and services that influence a nation's economy and standard of living. Second, an understanding of marketing is crucial to understanding most businesses. Third, career opportunities in marketing are diverse, profitable, and expected to increase significantly during the coming decade. Fourth, understanding marketing makes consumers more informed.

2-1 **Understand the importance of strategic planning.** Strategic planning is the basis for all marketing strategies and decisions. These decisions affect the allocation of resources and ultimately the financial success of the company.

strategic planning the managerial process of creating and maintaining a fit between the organization's objectives and resources and the evolving market opportunities (p. 14)

2-2 **Define strategic business units (SBUs).** An SBU should have these characteristics: a distinct mission and a specific target market, control over its resources, its own competitors, a single business, and plans independent from other SBUs in the organization. Each SBU has its own rate of return on investment, growth potential, and associated risks, and requires its own strategies and funding.

strategic business unit (SBU) a subgroup of a single business or collection of related businesses within the larger organization (p. 15)

2-3 **Identify strategic alternatives and know a basic outline for a marketing plan.** Ansoff's opportunity matrix presents four options to help management develop strategic alternatives: market penetration, market development, product development, and diversification. A marketing plan should define the business mission, perform a situation analysis, define objectives, delineate a target market, and establish components of the marketing mix.

market penetration a marketing strategy that tries to increase market share among existing customers (p. 16)

market development a marketing strategy that entails attracting new customers to existing products (p. 16)

product development a marketing strategy that entails the creation of new products for present markets (p. 16)

diversification a strategy of increasing sales by introducing new products into new markets (p. 17)

portfolio matrix a tool for allocating resources among products or strategic business units on the basis of relative market share and market growth rate (p. 17)

star in the portfolio matrix, a business unit that is a fast-growing market leader (p. 18)

cash cow in the portfolio matrix, a business unit that generates more cash than it needs to maintain its market share (p. 18)

problem child (question mark) in the portfolio matrix, a business unit that shows rapid growth but poor profit margins (p. 18)

dog in the portfolio matrix, a business unit that has low growth potential and a small market share (p. 18)

planning the process of anticipating future events and determining strategies to achieve organizational objectives in the future (p. 20)

marketing planning designing activities relating to marketing objectives and the changing marketing environment (p. 20)

marketing plan a written document that acts as a guidebook of marketing activities for the marketing manager (p. 20)

2-4 **Develop an appropriate business mission statement.** The firm's mission statement establishes boundaries for all subsequent decisions, objectives, and strategies. A mission statement should focus on the market(s) the organization is attempting to serve rather than on the good or service offered.

mission statement a statement of the firm's business based on a careful analysis of benefits sought by present and potential customers and an analysis of existing and anticipated environmental conditions (p. 21)

marketing myopia defining a business in terms of goods and services rather than in terms of the benefits customers seek (p. 21)

2-5 **Describe the components of a situation analysis.** In the situation (or SWOT) analysis, the firm should identify its internal strengths (S) and weaknesses (W) and also examine external opportunities (O) and threats (T). When examining external opportunities and threats, marketing managers must analyze aspects of the marketing environment in a process called environmental scanning.

SWOT analysis identifying internal strengths (S) and weaknesses (W) and also examining external opportunities (O) and threats (T) (p. 22)

environmental scanning collection and interpretation of information about forces, events, and relationships in the external environment that may affect the future of the organization or the implementation of the marketing plan (p. 22)

2-6 **Identify sources of competitive advantage.** There are three types of competitive advantage: cost, product/service differentiation, and niche. Sources of cost competitive advantage include experience curves, efficient labor, no-frills goods and services, government subsidies, product design, reengineering, production innovations, and new methods of service delivery. A product/service differentiation competitive advantage exists when a firm provides something unique that is valuable to buyers beyond just low price. Niche competitive advantages come from targeting unique segments with specific needs and wants.

competitive advantage a set of unique features of a company and its products that are perceived by the target market as significant and superior to those of the competition (p. 22)

cost competitive advantage being the low-cost competitor in an industry while maintaining satisfactory profit margins (p. 22)

experience curves curves that show costs declining at a predictable rate as experience with a product increases (p. 23)

product/service differentiation competitive advantage the provision of something that is unique and valuable to buyers beyond simply offering a lower price than that of the competition (p. 23)

niche competitive advantage the advantage achieved when a firm seeks to target and effectively serve a small segment of the market (p. 24)

sustainable competitive advantage an advantage that cannot be copied by the competition (p. 24)

2-7 **Explain the criteria for stating good marketing objectives.** Objectives should be realistic, measurable, time specific, and compared to a benchmark. They must also be consistent and indicate the priorities of the organization. Good marketing objectives communicate marketing management philosophies, provide management direction, motivate employees, force executives to think clearly, and form a basis for control.

marketing objective a statement of what is to be accomplished through marketing activities (p. 25)

2-8 **Discuss target market strategies.** Targeting markets begins with a market opportunity analysis (MOA), which describes and estimates the size and sales potential of market segments that are of interest to the firm. In addition, an assessment of key competitors in these market segments is performed. After the market segments are described, one or more may be targeted by the firm.

marketing strategy the activities of selecting and describing one or more target markets and developing and maintaining a marketing mix that will produce mutually satisfying exchanges with target markets (p. 25)

market opportunity analysis (MOA) the description and estimation of the size and sales potential of market segments that are of interest to the firm and the assessment of key competitors in these market segments (p. 26)

2-9 **Describe the elements of the marketing mix.** The marketing mix is a blend of product, place, promotion, and pricing strategies (the four Ps) designed to produce mutually satisfying exchanges with a target market. The starting point of the marketing mix is the product offering. Place (distribution) strategies are concerned with making products available when and where customers want them. Promotion includes advertising, public relations, sales promotion, and personal selling. Price is what a buyer must give up in order to obtain a product.

marketing mix (four Ps) a unique blend of product, place (distribution), promotion, and pricing strategies designed to produce mutually satisfying exchanges with a target market (p. 26)

2-10 **Explain why implementation, evaluation, and control of the marketing plan are necessary.** Before a marketing plan can work, it must be implemented—that is, people must perform the actions in the plan. The plan should also be evaluated to see if it has achieved its objectives. Poor implementation can be a major factor in a plan's failure, but working to gain acceptance can be accomplished with task forces. Once implemented, one major aspect of control is conducting and following through on a marketing audit.

implementation the process that turns a marketing plan into action assignments and ensures that these assignments are executed in a way that accomplishes the plan's objectives (p. 28)

evaluation gauging the extent to which the marketing objectives have been achieved during the specified time period (p. 28)

control provides the mechanisms for evaluating marketing results in light of the plan's objectives and for correcting actions that do not help the organization reach those objectives within budget guidelines (p. 28)

marketing audit a thorough, systematic, periodic evaluation of the objectives, strategies, structure, and performance of the marketing organization (p. 28)

2-11 **Identify several techniques that help make strategic planning effective.** First, management must realize that strategic planning is an ongoing process and not a once-a-year exercise. Second, good strategic planning involves a high level of creativity. The last requirement is top management's support and participation.

3-1 Explain the determinants of a civil society.

Societal order is created through the six modes of social control. Ethics are the moral principles or values that generally govern the conduct of an individual or a group. Laws come into being when ethical rules and guidelines are codified into law. Formal and informal groups have codes of conduct that prescribe acceptable and desired behaviors of their members. Self-regulation involves the voluntary acceptance of standards established by nongovernmental entities. The media play a key role in informing the public about the actions of individuals and organizations—both good and bad. An informed and engaged society can help mold individual and corporate behavior.

social control any means used to maintain behavioral norms and regulate conflict (p. 30)

behavioral norms standards of proper or acceptable behavior. Several modes of social control are important to marketing (p. 30)

ethics the moral principles or values that generally govern the conduct of an individual or a group (p. 30)

3-2 Explain the concept of ethical behavior.

Ethics are the standards of behavior by which conduct is judged. Standards that are legal may not always be ethical. An ethics violation offends a person's sense of justice or fairness. Ethics basically constitute the unwritten rules developed to guide interactions. Many ethical questions arise from balancing a business's need to produce profit for shareholders against its desire to operate honestly and with concern for environmental and social issues.

Several ethical theories apply to marketing. Deontological theory states that people should adhere to their obligations and duties when analyzing an ethical dilemma. Utilitarian ethical theory says that the choice that yields the greatest benefit to the most people is the choice that is ethically correct. The casuist ethical theory compares a current ethical dilemma with examples of similar ethical dilemmas and their outcomes. Moral relativists believe in time-and-place ethics, that is, ethical truths depend on the individuals and groups holding them. Virtue ethics suggests that individuals become able to solve ethical dilemmas when they develop and nurture a set of virtues.

deontological theory ethical theory that states that people should adhere to their obligations and duties when analyzing an ethical dilemma (p. 32)

utilitarian ethical theory ethical theory that is founded on the ability to predict the consequences of an action (p. 33)

casuist ethical theory ethical theory that compares a current ethical dilemma with examples of similar ethical dilemmas and their outcomes (p. 33)

moral relativism an ethical theory of time-and-place ethics; that is, the belief that ethical truths depend on the individuals and groups holding them (p. 33)

virtue a character trait valued as being good (p. 33)

3-3 Describe ethical behavior in business.

Business ethics may be viewed as a subset of the values of society as a whole, with a foundation based on the cultural values and norms that constitute a culture's morals. The ethical conduct of businesspeople is shaped by societal elements, including family, education, and religious institutions. Morals are the rules people develop as a result of cultural values and norms. As members of society, businesspeople are morally obligated to consider the ethical implications of their decisions. Ethical decision making can be grouped into three basic approaches. The first approach examines the consequences of decisions. The second approach relies on rules and laws to guide decision making. The third approach is based on a theory of moral development that places individuals or groups in one of three developmental stages: preconventional morality, conventional morality, or postconventional morality.

In addition to personal influences, there are many business influences on ethical decision making. Some of the most influential include the extent of ethical problems within the organization, top management's actions on ethics, potential magnitude of the consequences, social consensus, probability of a harmful outcome, length of time between the decision and the onset of consequences, and the number of people affected.

Many companies develop a code of ethics to help their employees make ethical decisions. A code of ethics can help employees identify acceptable business practices, be an effective internal control on behavior, help employees avoid confusion when determining whether decisions are ethical, and facilitate discussion about what is right and wrong.

Studies show that ethical beliefs vary little from country to country. However, there are enough cultural differences, such as the practice of bribery or gift giving, that laws such as the Foreign Corrupt Practices Act (FCPA) have been put in place to discourage and attempt to modify the current acceptance of such practices.

morals the rules people develop as a result of cultural values and norms (p. 34)

code of ethics a guideline to help marketing managers and other employees make better decisions (p. 36)

Foreign Corrupt Practices Act (FCPA) a law that prohibits U.S. corporations from making illegal payments to public officials of foreign governments to obtain business rights or to enhance

their business dealings in those countries (p. 36)

CHAPTER REVIEW

CHAPTER 3 LEARNING OUTCOMES / KEY TERMS

3-4 **Discuss corporate social responsibility.** Corporate social responsibility (CSR) is a business's concern for society's welfare. Responsibility in business refers to a firm's concern for the way its decisions affect society. Stakeholder theory says that social responsibility means paying attention to the interest of every affected stakeholder in every aspect of a firm's operation, including employees, management, customers, the local community, suppliers, and owners. According to the pyramid of corporate social responsibility, CSR has four components: economic, legal, ethical, and philanthropic. These are intertwined, yet the most fundamental is earning a profit. If a firm does not earn a profit, the other three responsibilities are moot.

corporate social responsibility (CSR) a business's concern for society's welfare (p. 38)

stakeholder theory ethical theory stating that social responsibility is paying attention to the interest of every affected stakeholder in every aspect of a firm's operation (p. 38)

pyramid of corporate social responsibility a model that suggests corporate social responsibility is composed of economic, legal, ethical, and philanthropic responsibilities and that a firm's economic performance supports the entire structure (p. 40)

3-5 **Describe the arguments for and against society responsibility.** Most businesspeople believe they should do more than pursue profits. Although a company must consider its economic needs first, it must also operate within the law, do what is ethical and fair, and be a good corporate citizen. Sustainability is the concept that socially responsible companies will outperform their peers by focusing on the world's social problems and viewing them as an opportunity to earn profits and help the world at the same time. Social responsibility is growing, but it can be costly and the benefits are not always immediate. In addition, some surveys report that consumer desire to purchase responsible products does not always translate to actually purchasing those products. One branch of social responsibility is green marketing, which aids the environment and often the bottom line of a business.

sustainability the idea that socially responsible companies will outperform their peers by focusing on the world's social problems and viewing them as opportunities to build profits and help the world at the same time (p. 42)

green marketing the development and marketing of products designed to minimize negative effects on the physical environment or to improve the environment (p. 43)

3-6 **Explain cause-related marketing.** Cause-related marketing is the cooperative effort between a for-profit firm and a nonprofit organization. It is different from philanthropy, which is a specific, tax-deductible donation. Cause-related marketing is very popular because it can enhance the reputation of the corporation and also make additional profit for the company. However, consumers sometimes come to believe that every company is tied to a cause, resulting in consumer cause fatigue.

EXHIBIT 3.3 **THE PYRAMID OF CORPORATE SOCIAL RESPONSIBILITY**

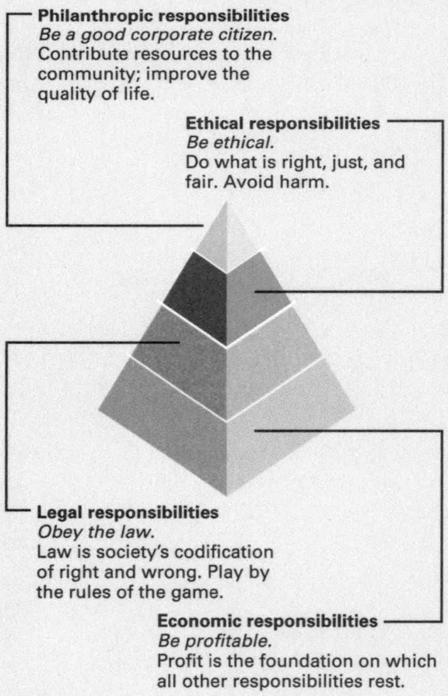

Philanthropic responsibilities
Be a good corporate citizen.
Contribute resources to the community; improve the quality of life.

Ethical responsibilities
Be ethical.
Do what is right, just, and fair. Avoid harm.

Legal responsibilities
Obey the law.
Law is society's codification of right and wrong. Play by the rules of the game.

Economic responsibilities
Be profitable.
Profit is the foundation on which all other responsibilities rest.

cause-related marketing the cooperative marketing efforts between a for-profit firm and a nonprofit organization (p. 45)

CHAPTER 4 LEARNING OUTCOMES / KEY TERMS

4-1 Discuss the external environment of marketing and explain how it affects a firm. The external marketing environment consists of social, demographic, economic, technological, political and legal, and competitive variables. Marketers generally cannot control the elements of the external environment. Instead, they must understand how the external environment is changing and the impact of that change on the target market. Then marketing managers can create a marketing mix to effectively meet the needs of target customers.

target market a group of people or organizations for which an organization designs, implements, and maintains a marketing mix intended to meet the need of that group, resulting in mutually satisfying exchanges (p. 48)

4-2 Describe the social factors that affect marketing. Within the external environment, social factors are perhaps the most difficult for marketers to anticipate. Several major social trends are currently shaping marketing strategies. First, people of all ages have a broader range of interests, defying traditional consumer profiles. Second, social media, web-based, and mobile technology change how people and marketers interact by allowing one-to-one, one-to-many, and many-to-many communications. Because Facebook is about human-to-human interaction, companies are turning to it and other forms of social media with ever-increasing speed.

component lifestyles the practice of choosing goods and services that meet one's diverse needs and interests rather than conforming to a single, traditional lifestyle (p. 51)

4-3 Explain the importance to marketing managers of current demographic trends. There are more than 7 billion people alive today. China has the largest population with 1.38 billion people; India is second with 1.32 billion. Census data puts the U.S. population at more than 318 million, with metropolitan areas growing and rural areas shrinking in population. Marketers are faced with increasingly experienced consumers among the younger generations such as tweens and teens. Because the population is also growing older, marketers are offering more products that appeal to middle-aged and older consumers.

demography the study of people's vital statistics, such as age, race and ethnicity, and location (p. 53)

Millennials people born between 1979 and 1994 (p. 54)

Generation X people born between 1965 and 1978 (p. 55)

baby boomers people born between 1946 and 1964 (p. 56)

4-4 Explain the importance to marketing managers of growing ethnic markets. The minority population today is about 118 million. By 2050, around one in three U.S. residents will be Hispanic. The United States will flip completely to a majority-minority makeup in 2041. Many companies are creating departments and product lines to target multicultural market segments effectively. Companies have quickly found that ethnic markets are not homogeneous.

4-5 Identify consumer and marketer reactions to the state of the economy. The annual median household income in the United States in 2016 was approximately $57,000, though the median household income varies widely from state to state. During a time of inflation, marketers generally attempt to maintain level pricing to avoid losing customer brand loyalty. During times of recession, many marketers maintain or reduce prices to counter the effects of decreased demand; they also concentrate on increasing production efficiency and improving customer service. The Great Recession was the largest economic downturn since the Great Depression. While the causes of recession are very complex, this one began with the collapse of inflated housing prices.

purchasing power a comparison of income versus the relative cost of a standard set of goods and services in different geographic areas (p. 59)

inflation a measure of the decrease in the value of money, expressed as the percentage reduction in value since the previous year (p. 60)

recession a period of economic activity characterized by negative growth, which reduces demand for goods and services (p. 60)

4-6 Identify the impact of technology on a firm. Technological success is based upon innovation, and innovation requires imagination and risk taking. Monitoring new technology and encouraging research and development (R&D) of new technology are essential to keeping up with competitors in today's marketing environment. Innovation through R&D needs to be stimulated by upper management and fostered in creative environments. Although developing new technology internally is a key to creating and maintaining a long-term competitive advantage, external technology is also important to managers.

basic research pure research that aims to confirm an existing theory or to learn more about a concept or phenomenon (p. 61)

applied research research that attempts to develop new or improved products (p. 61)

4-7 **Discuss the political and legal environment of marketing.** All marketing activities are subject to state and federal laws and the rulings of regulatory agencies. Marketers are responsible for remaining aware of and abiding by such regulations. Some key federal agencies that affect marketing are the Consumer Product Safety Commission, the Food and Drug Administration, and the Federal Trade Commission. Many laws, including privacy laws, have been passed to protect the consumer as well. In 2012, the FTC called for online data collectors to adopt better privacy policies and asked Congress to pass comprehensive privacy legislation. Despite federal efforts, online tracking has become widespread and pervasive.

Consumer Product Safety Commission (CPSC) a federal agency established to protect the health and safety of consumers in and around their homes (p. 65)

Food and Drug Administration (FDA) a federal agency charged with enforcing regulations against selling and distributing adulterated, misbranded, or hazardous food and drug products (p. 65)

Federal Trade Commission (FTC) a federal agency empowered to prevent persons or corporations from using unfair methods of competition in commerce (p. 65)

4-8 **Explain the basics of foreign and domestic competition.** The competitive environment encompasses the number of competitors a firm must face, the relative size of the competitors, and the degree of interdependence within the industry. Declining population growth, rising costs, and shortages of resources have heightened domestic competition.

EXHIBIT 4.2 **PRIMARY U.S. LAWS PROTECTING CONSUMERS**

Legislation	Impact on Marketing
Federal Food and Drug Act of 1906	Prohibits adulteration and misbranding of foods and drugs involved in interstate commerce; strengthened by the Food, Drug, and Cosmetic Act (1938) and the Kefauver-Harris Drug Amendment (1962).
Federal Hazardous Substances Act of 1960	Requires warning labels on hazardous household chemicals.
Kefauver-Harris Drug Amendment of 1962	Requires that manufacturers conduct tests to prove drug effectiveness and safety.
Consumer Credit Protection Act of 1968	Requires that lenders fully disclose true interest rates and all other charges to credit customers for loans and installment purchases.
Child Protection and Toy Safety Act of 1969	Prevents marketing of products so dangerous that adequate safety warnings cannot be given.
Public Health Smoking Act of 1970	Prohibits cigarette advertising on television and radio and revises the health hazard warning on cigarette packages.
Poison Prevention Labeling Act of 1970	Requires safety packaging for products that may be harmful to children.
National Environmental Policy Act of 1970	Established the Environmental Protection Agency to deal with various types of pollution and organizations that create pollution.
Public Health Cigarette Smoking Act of 1971	Prohibits tobacco advertising on radio and television.
Consumer Product Safety Act of 1972	Created the Consumer Product Safety Commission, which has authority to specify safety standards for most products.
Child Protection Act of 1990	Regulates the number of minutes of advertising on children's television.
Children's Online Privacy Protection Act of 1998	Empowers the FTC to set rules regarding how and when marketers must obtain parental permission before asking children marketing research questions.
Aviation Security Act of 2001	Requires airlines to take extra security measures to protect passengers, including the installation of stronger cockpit doors, improved baggage screening, and increased security training for airport personnel.
Homeland Security Act of 2002	Protects consumers against terrorist acts; created the Department of Homeland Security.
Do Not Call Law of 2003	Protects consumers against unwanted telemarketing calls.
CAN-SPAM Act of 2003	Protects consumers against unwanted e-mail, or spam.
Credit Card Act of 2009	Provides many credit card protections.
Restoring American Financial Stability Act of 2010	Created the Consumer Financial Protection Bureau to protect consumers against unfair, abusive, and deceptive financial practices.
Patient Protection and Affordable Care Act	Overhauled the U.S. health care system; mandated and subsidized health insurance for individuals.

CHAPTER 5 LEARNING OUTCOMES / KEY TERMS

5-1 Discuss the importance of global marketing.
Businesspeople who adopt a global vision are better able to identify global marketing opportunities, understand the nature of global networks, create effective global marketing strategies, and compete against foreign competition in domestic markets. Large corporations have traditionally been the major global competitors, but more and more small businesses are entering the global marketplace. Despite fears of job losses to other countries with cheaper labor, there are many benefits to globalization, including the reduction of poverty and increased standards of living.

global marketing marketing that targets markets throughout the world (p. 68)

global vision recognizing and reacting to international marketing opportunities, using effective global marketing strategies, and being aware of threats from foreign competitors in all markets (p. 68)

gross domestic product (GDP) the total market value of all final goods and services produced in a country for a given time period (p. 70)

outsourcing sending U.S. jobs abroad (p. 70)

inshoring returning production jobs to the United States (p. 71)

5-2 Discuss the impact of multinational firms on the world economy. Multinational corporations are international traders that regularly operate across national borders. Because of their vast size and financial, technological, and material resources, multinational corporations have great influence on the world economy. They have the ability to overcome trade problems, save on labor costs, and tap new technology. There are critics and supporters of multinational corporations, and the critics question the actual benefits of bringing capital-intensive technology to impoverished nations. Many countries block foreign investment in factories, land, and companies to protect their economies.

Some companies presume that markets throughout the world are more and more similar, so some global products can be standardized across global markets.

multinational corporation a company that is heavily engaged in international trade, beyond exporting and importing (p. 72)

capital intensive using more capital than labor in the production process (p. 73)

global marketing standardization production of uniform products that can be sold the same way all over the world (p. 73)

multidomestic strategy when multinational firms enable individual subsidiaries to compete independently in domestic markets (p. 74)

5-3 Describe the external environment facing global marketers. Global marketers face the same environmental factors as they do domestically: culture, economic and technological development, the global economy, political structure and actions, demography, and natural resources. Cultural considerations include societal values, attitudes and beliefs, language, and customary business practices. A country's economic and technological status depends on its stage of industrial development, which, in turn, affects average family incomes. A global marketer today must be fully aware of the intertwined nature of the global economy. The political structure is shaped by political ideology and such policies as tariffs, quotas, boycotts, exchange controls, trade agreements, and market groupings. Demographic variables include the size of a population and its age and geographic distribution. A shortage of natural resources also affects the external environment by dictating what is available and at what price.

EXHIBIT 5.1	MEMBERS OF THE G-20		
Argentina	European Union	Italy	South Africa
Australia	France	Japan	Republic of Korea
Brazil	Germany	Mexico	Turkey
Canada	India	Russia	United Kingdom
China	Indonesia	Saudi Arabia	United States

balance of trade the difference between the value of a country's exports and the value of its imports over a given period (p. 75)

balance of payments the difference between a country's total payments to other countries and its total receipts from other countries (p. 75)

Mercosur the largest Latin American trade agreement; includes Argentina, Bolivia, Brazil, Chile, Colombia, Ecuador, Paraguay, Peru, Uruguay, and Venezuela (p. 78)

Uruguay Round a trade agreement to dramatically lower trade barriers worldwide; created the World Trade Organization (p. 78)

World Trade Organization (WTO) a trade organization that replaced the old General Agreement on Tariffs and Trade (GATT) (p. 78)

General Agreement on Tariffs and Trade (GATT) a trade agreement that contained loopholes enabling countries to avoid trade-barrier reduction agreements (p. 78)

North American Free Trade Agreement (NAFTA) an agreement between Canada, the United States, and Mexico that created the world's then-largest free trade zone (p. 79)

Dominican Republic-Central America Free Trade Agreement (CAFTA-DR) a trade agreement instituted in 2005 that includes Costa Rica, the Dominican Republic, El Salvador, Guatemala, Honduras, Nicaragua, and the United States (p. 80)

European Union (EU) a free trade zone encompassing 28 European countries (p. 80)

World Bank an international bank that offers low-interest loans, advice, and information to developing nations (p. 81)

International Monetary Fund (IMF) an international organization that acts as a lender of last resort, providing loans to troubled nations, and also works to promote trade through financial cooperation (p. 81)

Group of Twenty (G-20) a forum for international economic development that promotes discussion between industrial and emerging-market countries on key issues related to global economic stability (p. 82)

5-4 **Identify the various ways of entering the global marketplace.** Firms use the following strategies to enter global markets, in descending order of risk and profit: direct investment, joint venture, contract manufacturing, licensing and franchising, and exporting.

EXHIBIT 5.2 **RISK LEVELS FOR FIVE METHODS OF ENTERING THE GLOBAL MARKETPLACE**

exporting selling domestically produced products to buyers in other countries (p. 84)

buyer for export an intermediary in the global market that assumes all ownership risks and sells globally for its own account (p. 84)

export broker an intermediary who plays the traditional broker's role by bringing buyer and seller together (p. 84)

export agent an intermediary who acts like a manufacturer's agent for the exporter; the export agent lives in the foreign market (p. 84)

licensing the legal process whereby a licensor allows another firm to use its manufacturing process, trademarks, patents, trade secrets, or other proprietary knowledge (p. 85)

contract manufacturing private label manufacturing by a foreign company (p. 85)

joint venture when a domestic firm buys part of a foreign company or joins with a foreign company to create a new entity (p. 85)

direct foreign investment active ownership of a foreign company or of overseas manufacturing or marketing facilities (p. 86)

5-5 **List the basic elements involved in developing a global marketing mix.** A firm's major consideration is how much it will adjust the four Ps—product, promotion, place (distribution), and price—within each country. One strategy is to use one product and one promotion message worldwide. A second strategy is to create new products for global markets. A third strategy is to keep the product basically the same but alter the promotional message. A fourth strategy is to slightly alter the product to meet local conditions.

exchange rate the price of one country's currency in terms of another country's currency (p. 88)

floating exchange rates a system in which prices of different currencies move up and down based on the demand for and the supply of each currency (p. 89)

dumping the sale of an exported product at a price lower than that charged for the same or a like product in the "home" market of the exporter (p. 89)

countertrade a form of trade in which all or part of the payment for goods or services is in the form of other goods or services (p. 90)

5-6 **Discover how the Internet is affecting global marketing.** Simply opening an e-commerce site can open the door for international sales. International carriers, such as UPS, can help solve logistics problems. Language translation software can help an e-commerce business become multilingual. Yet cultural differences and old-line rules, regulations, and taxes hinder rapid development of e-commerce in many countries. Not only do global marketers use social media for understanding consumers, but they also use social media to build their brands as they expand internationally.

6-1 **Explain why marketing managers should understand consumer behavior.** An understanding of consumer behavior reduces marketing managers' uncertainty when they are defining a target market and designing a marketing mix.

consumer behavior processes a consumer uses to make purchase decisions, as well as to use and dispose of purchased goods or services; also includes factors that influence purchase decisions and product use (p. 92)

value a personal assessment of the net worth one obtains from making a purchase, or the enduring belief that a specific mode of conduct is personally or socially preferable to another mode of conduct (p. 93)

perceived value the value a consumer *expects* to obtain from a purchase (p. 93)

utilitarian value a value derived from a product or service that helps the consumer solve problems and accomplish tasks (p. 93)

hedonic value a value that acts as an end in itself rather than as a means to an end (p. 94)

6-2 **Analyze the components of the consumer decision-making process.** The consumer decision-making process begins with need recognition, when stimuli trigger awareness of an unfulfilled want. If additional information is required to make a purchase decision, the consumer may engage in an internal or external information search. The consumer then evaluates the alternatives using the additional information and establishes purchase guidelines. Finally, a purchase decision is made.

consumer decision-making process a five-step process used by consumers when buying goods or services (p. 94)

need recognition result of an imbalance between actual and desired states (p. 94)

want recognition of an unfulfilled need and a product that will satisfy it (p. 94)

stimulus any unit of input affecting one or more of the five senses: sight, smell, taste, touch, hearing (p. 95)

internal information search the process of recalling past information stored in the memory (p. 95)

external information search the process of seeking information in the outside environment (p. 95)

nonmarketing-controlled information source a product information source that is not associated with advertising or promotion (p. 95)

marketing-controlled information source a product information source that originates with marketers promoting the product (p. 96)

evoked set (consideration set) a group of brands resulting from an information search from which a buyer can choose (p. 97)

6-3 **Explain the consumer's postpurchase evaluation process.** Consumer postpurchase evaluation is influenced by prepurchase expectations, the prepurchase information search, and the consumer's general level of self-confidence. When a purchase creates cognitive dissonance, consumers tend to react by seeking positive reinforcement for the purchase decision, avoiding negative information about the purchase decision, or revoking the purchase decision by returning the product.

cognitive dissonance inner tension that a consumer experiences after recognizing an inconsistency between behavior and values or opinions (p. 100)

6-4 **Identify the types of consumer buying decisions and discuss the significance of consumer involvement.** Consumer decision making falls into three broad categories: routine response behavior, limited decision making, and extensive decision making. High-involvement decisions usually include an extensive information search and a thorough evaluation of alternatives. By contrast, low-involvement decisions are characterized by brand loyalty and a lack of personal identification with the product.

involvement the amount of time and effort a buyer invests in the search, evaluation, and decision processes of consumer behavior (p. 100)

routine response behavior the type of decision making exhibited by consumers buying frequently purchased, low-cost goods and services; requires little search and decision time (p. 101)

limited decision making the type of decision making that requires a moderate amount of time for gathering information and deliberating about an unfamiliar brand in a familiar product category (p. 101)

extensive decision making the most complex type of consumer decision making, used when buying an unfamiliar, expensive product or an infrequently bought item; requires use of several criteria for evaluating options and much time for seeking information (p. 101)

showrooming the practice of examining merchandise in a physical retail location without purchasing it, and then shopping online for a better deal on the same item (p. 103)

6-5 **Describe how some marketers are reconceptualizing the consumer decision making process.** The balance of power has shifted largely from the marketer to the consumer. The consumer decision journey begins when a stimulus causes a consumer to research a number of products, continues through to purchase, and ends with a feedback loop of ratings, rankings, and referrals. In order to minimize the "consider and evaluate" phases of the consumer journey, a company must have four distinct but interconnected capabilities: automation, proactive personalization, contextual interaction, and journey innovation.

6-6 **Identify and understand the cultural factors that affect consumer buying decisions.** Cultural influences on consumer buying decisions include one's subcultures and social class, as well as the values, language, myths, customs, rituals, laws, and artifacts transmitted from one generation to the next.

culture the set of values, norms, attitudes, and other meaningful symbols that shape human behavior and the artifacts, or products, of that behavior as they are transmitted from one generation to the next (p. 106)

subculture a homogeneous group of people who share elements of the overall culture as well as unique elements of their own group (p. 107)

social class a group of people in a society who are considered nearly equal in status or community esteem, who regularly socialize among themselves both formally and informally, and who share behavioral norms (p. 108)

6-7 **Identify and understand the social factors that affect consumer buying decisions.** Consumers seek out others' opinions for guidance on products with image-related attributes or because attribute information is lacking. Consumers may use products to identify with a reference group or to follow an opinion leader. Family members also influence purchase decisions.

reference group all of the formal and informal groups in society that influence an individual's purchasing behavior (p. 110)

primary membership group a reference group with which people interact regularly in an informal, face-to-face manner, such as family, friends, and coworkers (p. 110)

secondary membership group a reference group with which people associate less consistently and more formally than a primary membership group, such as a club, professional group, or religious group (p. 110)

aspirational reference group a group that someone would like to join (p. 110)

norm a value or attitude deemed acceptable by a group (p. 110)

nonaspirational reference group a group with which an individual does not want to associate (p. 110)

opinion leader an individual who influences the opinions of others (p. 111)

socialization process how cultural values and norms are passed down to children (p. 112)

separated self-schema a perspective whereby a consumer sees himself or herself as distinct and separate from others (p. 113)

connected self-schema a perspective whereby a consumer sees himself or herself as an integral part of a group (p. 113)

6-8 **Identify and understand the individual factors that affect consumer buying decisions.** Men and women differ in their social and economic roles, and that affects consumer buying decisions. A consumer's age generally indicates what products he or she may be interested in purchasing. Marketers often define their target markets in terms of life cycle stage, following changes in consumers' attitudes and behavioral tendencies as they mature. Finally, certain products reflect consumers' personality, self-concept, and lifestyle.

personality a way of organizing and grouping the consistencies of an individual's reactions to situations (p. 115)

self-concept how consumers perceive themselves in terms of attitudes, perceptions, beliefs, and self-evaluations (p. 115)

ideal self-image the way an individual would like to be perceived (p. 115)

real self-image the way an individual actually perceives himself or herself (p. 115)

6-9 **Identify and understand the psychological factors that affect consumer buying decisions.** Perception allows consumers to recognize their consumption problems. Motivation is what drives consumers to take action to satisfy specific consumption needs. Almost all consumer behavior results from learning, which is the process that creates changes in behavior through experience.

perception the process by which people select, organize, and interpret stimuli into a meaningful and coherent picture (p. 115)

selective exposure a process whereby a consumer notices certain stimuli and ignores others (p. 116)

selective distortion a process whereby a consumer changes or distorts information that conflicts with his or her feelings or beliefs (p. 116)

selective retention a process whereby a consumer remembers only that information that supports his or her personal beliefs (p. 116)

motive a driving force that causes a person to take action to satisfy specific needs (p. 117)

Maslow's hierarchy of needs a method of classifying human needs and motivations into five categories in ascending order of importance: physiological, safety, social, esteem, and self-actualization (p. 117)

learning a process that creates changes in behavior, immediate or expected, through experience and practice (p. 118)

stimulus generalization a form of learning that occurs when one response is extended to a second stimulus similar to the first (p. 119)

stimulus discrimination a learned ability to differentiate among similar products (p. 119)

CHAPTER 7 LEARNING OUTCOMES / KEY TERMS

7-1 Describe business marketing. Business marketing provides goods and services that are bought for use in business rather than for personal consumption. Intended use, not physical characteristics, distinguishes a business product from a consumer product.

business marketing (industrial, business-to-business, B-to-B, or B2B marketing) the marketing of goods and services to individuals and organizations for purposes other than personal consumption (p. 120)

business product (industrial product) a product used to manufacture other goods or services, to facilitate an organization's operations, or to resell to other customers (p. 120)

consumer product a product bought to satisfy an individual's personal wants or needs (p. 120)

7-2 Describe trends in B-to-B Internet marketing. B-to-B companies use the Internet in three major ways. First, they use their websites to facilitate communication and orders. Second, they use digital marketing to increase brand awareness. Third, they use digital marketing—primarily in the form of content marketing—to position their businesses as thought leaders and therefore generate sales leads. Content marketing, a strategic marketing approach focused on creating and distributing valuable, relevant, and consistent content, has played an important role for B-to-B marketers. As they build reputations in their business areas, many B-to-B marketers use social media to share content, increase awareness, and build relationships and community. Some metrics that are particularly useful for increasing the success of a social media campaign are awareness, engagement, and conversion.

Content marketing a strategic marketing approach that focuses on creating and distributing content that is valuable, relevant and consistent. (p. 122)

7-3 Discuss the role of relationship marketing and strategic alliances in business marketing. Relationship marketing entails seeking and establishing long-term alliances or partnerships with customers. A strategic alliance is a cooperative agreement between business firms. Firms form alliances to leverage what they do well by partnering with others that have complementary skills. Although the concepts of relationship marketing and strategic alliances are relatively new to American marketers, these ideas have long been used by marketers in other cultures.

strategic alliance (strategic partnership) a cooperative agreement between business firms (p. 124)

relationship commitment a firm's belief that an ongoing relationship with another firm is so important that the relationship warrants maximum efforts at maintaining it indefinitely (p. 124)

trust the condition that exists when one party has confidence in an exchange partner's reliability and integrity (p. 124)

keiretsu a network of interlocking corporate affiliates (p. 125)

7-4 Identify the four major categories of business market customers. Producer markets consist of for-profit individuals and organizations that buy products to use in producing other products, as components of other products, or in facilitating business operations. Reseller markets consist of wholesalers and retailers that buy finished products to resell for profit. Government markets include federal, state, county, and city governments that buy goods and services to support their own operations and serve the needs of citizens. Institutional markets consist of very diverse nonbusiness institutions whose main goals do not include profit.

original equipment manufacturers (OEMs) individuals and organizations that buy business goods and incorporate them into the products they produce for eventual sale to other producers or to consumers (p. 125)

7-5 Explain the North American Industry Classification System. The North American Industry Classification System (NAICS) provides a way to identify, analyze, segment, and target business and government markets. Organizations can be identified and compared by a numeric code indicating business sector, subsector, industry group, industry, and industry subdivision. NAICS is a valuable tool for analyzing, segmenting, and targeting business markets.

EXHIBIT 7.1 HOW NAICS WORKS

The more digits in the NAICS code, the more homogeneous the groups at that level.

NAICS Level	NAICS Code	Description
Sector	51	Information
Subsector	513	Broadcasting and telecommunications
Industry group	5133	Telecommunications
Industry	51332	Wireless telecommunications carriers, except satellite
Industry subdivision	513321	Paging

© Cengage Learning

North American Industry Classification System (NAICS) a detailed numbering system developed by the United States, Canada, and Mexico to classify North American business establishments by their main production processes (p. 127)

7-6 **Explain the major differences between business and consumer markets.** In business markets, demand is derived, inelastic, joint, and fluctuating. Purchase volume is much larger than in consumer markets, customers are fewer and more geographically concentrated, and distribution channels are more direct. Buying is approached more formally using professional purchasing agents, more people are involved in the buying process, negotiation is more complex, and reciprocity and leasing are more common. And, finally, selling strategy in business markets normally focuses on personal contact rather than on advertising.

derived demand the demand for business products (p. 127)

joint demand the demand for two or more items used together in a final product (p. 128)

multiplier effect (accelerator principle) phenomenon in which a small increase or decrease in consumer demand can produce a much larger change in demand for the facilities and equipment needed to make the consumer product (p. 129)

business-to-business online exchange an electronic trading floor that provides companies with integrated links to their customers and suppliers (p. 129)

reciprocity a practice whereby business purchasers choose to buy from their own customers (p. 130)

7-7 **Describe the seven types of business goods and services.** Major equipment includes capital goods such as heavy machinery. Accessory equipment is typically less expensive and shorter lived than major equipment. Raw materials are extractive or agricultural products that have not been processed. Component parts are finished or near-finished items to be used as parts of other products. Processed materials are used to manufacture other products. Supplies are consumable and not used as part of a final product. Business services are intangible products that many companies use in their operations.

major equipment (installations) capital goods such as large or expensive machines, mainframe computers, blast furnaces, generators, airplanes, and buildings (p. 130)

accessory equipment goods, such as portable tools and office equipment, that are less expensive and shorter-lived than major equipment (p. 130)

raw materials unprocessed extractive or agricultural products, such as mineral ore, lumber, wheat, corn, fruits, vegetables, and fish (p. 130)

component parts either finished items ready for assembly or products that need very little processing before becoming part of some other product (p. 131)

processed materials products used directly in manufacturing other products (p. 131)

supplies consumable items that do not become part of the final product (p. 131)

business services expense items that do not become part of a final product (p. 132)

7-8 **Discuss the unique aspects of business buying behavior.** Business buying behavior is distinguished by five fundamental characteristics. First, buying is normally undertaken by a buying center consisting of many people who range widely in authority level. Second, business buyers typically evaluate alternative products and suppliers based on quality, service, and price—in that order. Third, business buying falls into three general categories: new buys, modified rebuys, and straight rebuys. Fourth, the ethics of business buyers and sellers are often scrutinized. Fifth, customer service before, during, and after the sale plays a big role in business purchase decisions.

EXHIBIT 7.2 **BUYING CENTER ROLES FOR COMPUTER PURCHASES**

Role	Illustration
Initiator	Division general manager proposes to replace company's computer network.
Influencers/evaluators	Corporate controller's office and vice president of information services have an important say in which system and vendor the company will deal with.
Gatekeepers	Corporate departments for purchasing and information services analyze company's needs and recommend likely matches with potential vendors.
Decider	Vice president of administration, with advice from others, selects vendor the company will deal with and system it will buy.
Purchaser	Purchasing agent negotiates terms of sale.
Users	All division employees use the computers.

buying center all those people in an organization who become involved in the purchase decision (p. 132)

new buy a situation requiring the purchase of a product for the first time (p. 134)

modified rebuy a situation in which the purchaser wants some change in the original good or service (p. 134)

straight rebuy a situation in which the purchaser reorders the same goods or services without looking for new information or investigating other suppliers (p. 134)

8-1 Describe the characteristics of markets and market segments. A market is composed of individuals or organizations with the ability and willingness to make purchases to fulfill their needs or wants. A market segment is a group of individuals or organizations with similar product needs as a result of one or more common characteristics.

market people or organizations with needs or wants and the ability and willingness to buy (p. 136)

market segment a subgroup of people or organizations sharing one or more characteristics that cause them to have similar product needs (p. 136)

market segmentation the process of dividing a market into meaningful, relatively similar, and identifiable segments or groups (p. 137)

8-2 Explain the importance of market segmentation. Before the 1960s, few businesses targeted specific market segments. Today, segmentation is a crucial marketing strategy for nearly all successful organizations. Market segmentation enables marketers to tailor marketing mixes to meet the needs of particular population segments. Segmentation helps marketers identify consumer needs and preferences, areas of declining demand, and new marketing opportunities.

8-3 Discuss the criteria for successful market segmentation. Successful market segmentation depends on four basic criteria: (1) a market segment must be substantial and have enough potential customers to be viable; (2) a market segment must be identifiable and measurable; (3) members of a market segment must be accessible to marketing efforts; and (4) a market segment must respond to particular marketing efforts in a way that distinguishes it from other segments.

8-4 Describe the bases commonly used to segment consumer markets. Five bases are commonly used for segmenting consumer markets. Geographic segmentation is based on region, size, density, and climate characteristics. Demographic segmentation is based on age, gender, income level, ethnicity, and family life cycle characteristics. Psychographic segmentation includes personality, motives, and lifestyle characteristics. Benefits sought is a type of segmentation that identifies customers according to the benefits they seek in a product. Finally, usage segmentation divides a market by the amount of product purchased or consumed.

segmentation bases (variables) characteristics of individuals, groups, or organizations (p. 138)

geographic segmentation segmenting markets by region of a country or the world, market size, market density, or climate (p. 138)

demographic segmentation segmenting markets by age, gender, income, ethnic background, and family life cycle (p. 139)

family life cycle (FLC) a series of stages determined by a combination of age, marital status, and the presence or absence of children (p. 141)

psychographic segmentation segmenting markets on the basis of personality, motives, lifestyles, and geodemographics (p. 143)

geodemographic segmentation segmenting potential customers into neighborhood lifestyle categories (p. 143)

benefit segmentation the process of grouping customers into market segments according to the benefits they seek from the product (p. 143)

usage-rate segmentation dividing a market by the amount of product bought or consumed (p. 144)

80/20 principle a principle holding that 20 percent of all customers generate 80 percent of the demand (p. 144)

8-5 Describe the bases for segmenting business markets. Business markets can be segmented on two general bases. First, businesses may segment markets based on company characteristics, such as customers' geographic location, type of company, company size, and product use. Second, companies may segment customers based on the buying processes those customers use.

satisficers business customers who place an order with the first familiar supplier to satisfy product and delivery requirements (p. 145)

optimizers business customers who consider numerous suppliers (both familiar and unfamiliar), solicit bids, and study all proposals carefully before selecting one (p. 145)

8-6 List the steps involved in segmenting markets. Six steps are involved when segmenting markets: (1) selecting a market or product category for study; (2) choosing a basis or bases for segmenting the market; (3) selecting segmentation descriptors; (4) profiling and evaluating segments; (5) selecting target markets; and (6) designing, implementing, and maintaining appropriate marketing mixes.

8-7 Discuss alternative strategies for selecting target markets. Marketers select target markets using three different strategies: undifferentiated targeting, concentrated targeting, and multisegment targeting. An undifferentiated targeting strategy assumes that all members of a market have similar needs that can be met with a single marketing mix. A concentrated targeting strategy focuses all marketing efforts on a single market segment. Multisegment targeting is a strategy that uses two or more marketing mixes to target two or more market segments.

target market a group of people or organizations for which an organization designs, implements, and maintains a marketing mix intended to meet the needs of that group, resulting in mutually satisfying exchanges (p. 146)

undifferentiated targeting strategy a marketing approach that views the market as one big market with no individual segments and thus uses a single marketing mix (p. 146)

concentrated targeting strategy a strategy used to select one segment of a market for targeting marketing efforts (p. 147)

niche one segment of a market (p. 147)

multisegment targeting strategy a strategy that chooses two or more well-defined market segments and develops a distinct marketing mix for each (p. 148)

cannibalization a situation that occurs when sales of a new product cut into sales of a firm's existing products (p. 148)

8-8 Explain how CRM can be used as a targeting tool. Companies that successfully implement CRM tend to customize the goods and services offered to their customers based on data generated through interactions between carefully defined groups of customers and the company. CRM relies on four things to be successful: personalization, time savings, loyalty, and technology. Although mass marketing will probably continue to be used, the advantages of CRM cannot be ignored.

8-9 Explain how and why firms implement positioning strategies and how product differentiation plays a role. Positioning is used to influence consumer perceptions of a particular brand, product line, or organization in relation to competitors. The term position refers to the place that the offering occupies in consumers' minds. To establish a unique position, many firms use product differentiation, emphasizing the real or perceived differences between competing offerings. Products may be differentiated on the basis of attribute, price and quality, use or application, product user, product class, competitor, or emotion. Some firms, instead of using product differentiation, position their products as being similar to competing products or brands. Sometimes products or companies are repositioned in order to sustain growth in slow markets or to correct positioning mistakes.

---

positioning developing a specific marketing mix to influence potential customers' overall perception of a brand, product line, or organization in general (p. 149)

position the place a product, brand, or group of products occupies in consumers' minds relative to competing offerings (p. 149)

product differentiation a positioning strategy that some firms use to distinguish their products from those of competitors (p. 150)

perceptual mapping a means of displaying or graphing, in two or more dimensions, the location of products, brands, or groups of products in customers' minds (p. 150)

repositioning changing consumers' perceptions of a brand in relation to competing brands (p. 151)

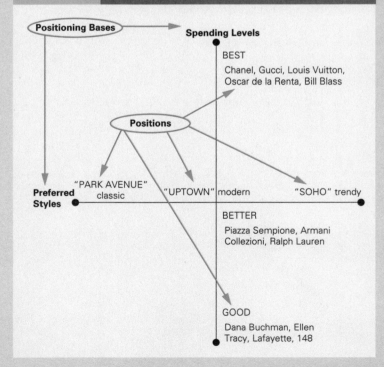

| EXHIBIT 8.3 | PERCEPTUAL MAP AND POSITIONING STRATEGY FOR SAKS DEPARTMENT STORES |

CHAPTER 9 LEARNING OUTCOMES / KEY TERMS

9-1 **Define marketing research and explain its importance to marketing decision making.** Marketing research is a process of collecting and analyzing data for the purpose of solving specific marketing problems. Practically speaking, marketers use marketing research to improve the decision-making process, trace problems, serve customers, gauge the value of goods and services, understand the marketplace, and measure customer service efforts.

marketing research the process of planning, collecting, and analyzing data relevant to a marketing decision (p. 152)

9-2 **Describe the steps involved in conducting a marketing research project.** The marketing research process involves several basic steps. First, the researcher and the decision maker must agree on a problem statement or set of research objectives. Social media and big data may be helpful in this pursuit. The researcher then creates an overall research design to specify how primary data will be gathered and analyzed. Before collecting data, the researcher decides whether the group to be interviewed will be a probability or nonprobability sample. Field service firms are often hired to carry out data collection. Once data have been collected, the researcher analyzes them using statistical analysis. The researcher then prepares and presents oral and written reports, with conclusions and recommendations, to management. As a final step, the researcher determines whether the recommendations were implemented and what could have been done to make the project more successful.

marketing research problem determining what information is needed and how that information can be obtained efficiently and effectively (p. 155)

marketing research objective the specific information needed to solve a marketing research problem; the objective should be to provide insightful decision-making information (p. 155)

management decision problem a broad-based problem that uses marketing research in order for managers to take proper actions (p. 155)

secondary data data previously collected for any purpose other than the one at hand (p. 155)

big data the exponential growth in the volume, variety, and velocity of information and the development of complex, new tools to analyze and create meaning from such data (p. 157)

research design specifies which research questions must be answered, how and when the data will be gathered, and how the data will be analyzed (p. 159)

primary data information that is collected for the first time; used for solving the particular problem under investigation (p. 159)

survey research the most popular technique for gathering primary data, in which a researcher interacts with people to obtain facts, opinions, and attitudes (p. 160)

mall intercept interview a survey research method that involves interviewing people in the common areas of shopping malls (p. 160)

computer-assisted personal interviewing an interviewing method in which the interviewer reads questions from a computer screen and enters the respondent's data directly into the computer (p. 161)

computer-assisted self-interviewing an interviewing method in which a mall interviewer intercepts and directs willing respondents to nearby computers where each respondent reads questions off a computer screen and directly keys his or her answers into the computer (p. 161)

central-location telephone (CLT) facility a specially designed phone room used to conduct telephone interviewing (p. 161)

executive interview a type of survey that usually involves interviewing business people at their offices concerning industrial products or services (p. 161)

focus group seven to ten people who participate in a group discussion led by a moderator (p. 162)

open-ended question an interview question that encourages an answer phrased in the respondent's own words (p. 162)

closed-ended question an interview question that asks the respondent to make a selection from a limited list of responses (p. 163)

scaled-response question a closed-ended question designed to measure the intensity of a respondent's answer (p. 163)

observation research a research method that relies on four types of observation: people watching people, people watching an activity, machines watching people, and machines watching an activity (p. 163)

mystery shoppers researchers posing as customers who gather observational data about a store (p. 163)

behavioral targeting (BT) a form of observation marketing research that combines a consumer's online activity with psychographic and demographic profiles compiled in databases (p. 164)

social media monitoring the use of automated tools to monitor online buzz, chatter, and conversations (p. 164)

ethnographic research the study of human behavior in its natural context; involves observation of behavior and physical setting (p. 164)

experiment a method of gathering primary data in which the researcher alters one or more variables while observing the effects of those alterations on another variable (p. 165)

sample a subset from a larger population (p. 165)

universe the population from which a sample will be drawn (p. 165)

probability sample a sample in which every element in the population has a known statistical likelihood of being selected (p. 166)

random sample a sample arranged in such a way that every element of the population has an equal chance of being selected as part of the sample (p. 166)

nonprobability sample any sample in which little or no attempt is made to get a representative cross section of the population (p. 166)

convenience sample a form of nonprobability sample using respondents who are convenient or readily accessible to the researcher—for example, employees, friends, or relatives (p. 166)

measurement error an error that occurs when there is a difference between the information desired by the researcher and the information provided by the measurement process (p. 166)

sampling error an error that occurs when a sample somehow does not represent the target population (p. 166)

frame error an error that occurs when a sample drawn from a population differs from the target population (p. 166)

random error an error that occurs when the selected sample is an imperfect representation of the overall population (p. 166)

field service firm a firm that specializes in interviewing respondents on a subcontracted basis (p. 167)

cross-tabulation a method of analyzing data that lets the analyst look at the responses to one question in relation to the responses to one or more other questions (p. 167)

9-3 **Discuss the profound impact of the Internet on marketing research.** The Internet has simplified the secondary data search process. Internet survey research is surging in popularity. Internet surveys can be created rapidly, are reported in real time, are relatively inexpensive, and are easily personalized.

Often, researchers use the Internet to contact respondents who are difficult to reach by other means. The Internet can also be used to conduct focus groups, to distribute research proposals and reports, and to facilitate collaboration between the client and the research supplier.

9-4 **Describe the growing importance of mobile research.** Mobile survey traffic now accounts for approximately 30 percent of interview responses. Mobile surveys are designed to fit into the brief cracks of time that open up when a person waits for a plane, is early for an appointment, commutes to work on a train, or stands in a line. Marketers strive to engage respondents in the moment

because mobile research provides immediate feedback when a consumer makes a decision to purchase, consumes a product, or experiences some form of promotion. Mobile research has also expanded into qualitative research. Using an app, respondents can participate in bulletin board and research community discussions.

9-5 **Discuss the growing importance of scanner-based research.** A scanner-based research system enables marketers to monitor a market panel's exposure and reaction to such variables as advertising, coupons, store displays, packaging, and price. By

analyzing these variables in relation to the panel's subsequent buying behavior, marketers gain useful insight into sales and marketing strategies.

scanner-based research a system for gathering information from a single group of respondents by continuously monitoring the advertising, promotion, and pricing they are exposed to and the things they buy (p. 172)

InfoScan a scanner-based sales-tracking service for the consumer packaged-goods industry (p. 172)

neuromarketing a field of marketing that studies the body's responses to marketing stimuli (p. 172)

9-6 **Explain when marketing research should be conducted.** Because acquiring marketing information can be time-consuming and costly, deciding to acquire additional decision-making information depends on managers' perceptions of its quality, price, and timing. Research, therefore, should

be undertaken only when the expected value of the information is greater than the cost of obtaining it. A customer relationship management system is integral to analyzing, transforming, and leveraging customer data.

9-7 **Explain the concept of competitive intelligence.** Intelligence is analyzed information, and it becomes decision-making intelligence when it has implications for the organization. By helping managers assess their competition and vendors,

competitive intelligence (CI) leads to fewer surprises. CI is part of a sound marketing strategy, helps companies respond to competitive threats, and helps reduce unnecessary costs.

competitive intelligence (CI) an intelligence system that helps managers assess their competition and vendors in order to become more efficient and effective competitors (p. 173)

10-1 | **Define the term *product*.** A product is anything, desired or not, that a person or organization receives in an exchange. The basic goal of purchasing decisions is to receive the tangible and intangible benefits associated with a product. Tangible aspects include packaging, style, color, size, and features. Intangible qualities include service, the retailer's image, the manufacturer's reputation, and the social status associated with a product. An organization's product offering is the crucial element in any marketing mix.

product everything, both favorable and unfavorable, that a person receives in an exchange (p. 174)

10-2 | **Classify consumer products.** Consumer products are classified into four categories: convenience products, shopping products, specialty products, and unsought products. Convenience products are relatively inexpensive and require limited shopping effort. Shopping products are of two types: homogeneous and heterogeneous. Because of the similarity of homogeneous products, they are differentiated mainly by price and features. In contrast, heterogeneous products appeal to consumers because of their distinct characteristics. Specialty products possess unique benefits that are highly desirable to certain customers. Finally, unsought products are either new products or products that require aggressive selling because they are generally avoided or overlooked by consumers.

convenience product a relatively inexpensive item that merits little shopping effort (p. 175)

shopping product a product that requires comparison shopping because it is usually more expensive than a convenience product and is found in fewer stores (p. 176)

specialty product a particular item for which consumers search extensively and are very reluctant to accept substitutes (p. 176)

unsought product a product unknown to the potential buyer or a known product that the buyer does not actively seek (p. 176)

10-3 | **Define the terms *product item*, *product line*, and *product mix*.** A product item is a specific version of a product that can be designated as a distinct offering among an organization's products. A product line is a group of closely related products offered by an organization. An organization's product mix includes all the products it sells. Product mix width refers to the number of product lines an organization offers. Product line depth is the number of product items in a product line. Firms modify existing products by changing their quality, functional characteristics, or style. Product line extension occurs when a firm adds new products to existing product lines.

EXHIBIT 10.1 | **CAMPBELL'S PRODUCT LINES AND PRODUCT MIX**

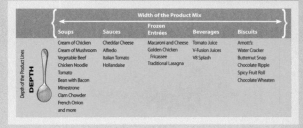

product item a specific version of a product that can be designated as a distinct offering among an organization's products (p. 176)

product line a group of closely related product items (p. 177)

product mix all products that an organization sells (p. 177)

product mix width the number of product lines an organization offers (p. 177)

product line depth the number of product items in a product line (p. 177)

product modification changing one or more of a product's characteristics (p. 178)

planned obsolescence the practice of modifying products so those that have already been sold become obsolete before they actually need replacement (p. 179)

product line extension adding additional products to an existing product line in order to compete more broadly in the industry (p. 179)

10-4 | **Describe marketing uses of branding.** A brand is a name, term, or symbol that identifies and differentiates a firm's products. Established brands encourage customer loyalty and help new products succeed. Branding strategies require decisions about individual, family, manufacturers', and private brands.

EXHIBIT 10.3 | **COMPARISON OF MANUFACTURER'S AND PRIVATE BRANDS FROM THE RESELLERS PERSPECTIVE**

Key Advantages of Carrying Manufacturers' Brands	Key Advantages of Carrying Private Brands
• Heavy advertising to the consumer by manufacturers such as Procter & Gamble helps develop strong consumer loyalties.	• A wholesaler or retailer can usually earn higher profits on its own brand. In addition, because the private brand is exclusive, there is less pressure to mark down the price to meet competition.
• Well-known manufacturers' brands, such as Kodak and Fisher-Price, can attract new customers and enhance the dealer's (wholesaler's or retailer's) prestige.	• A manufacturer can decide to drop a brand or a reseller at any time or even become a direct competitor to its dealers.
• Many manufacturers offer rapid delivery, enabling the dealer to carry less inventory.	• A private brand ties the customer to the wholesaler or retailer. A person who wants a DieHard battery must go to Sears.
• If a dealer happens to sell a manufacturer's brand of poor quality, the customer may simply switch brands and remain loyal to the dealer.	• Wholesalers and retailers have no control over the intensity of distribution of manufacturers' brands. Walmart store managers don't have to worry about competing with other sellers of Sam's American Choice products or Ol' Roy dog food. They know that these brands are sold only in Walmart and Sam's Club stores.

brand a name, term, symbol, design, or combination thereof that identifies a seller's products and differentiates them from competitors' products (p. 180)

brand name that part of a brand that can be spoken, including letters, words, and numbers (p. 180)

brand mark the elements of a brand that cannot be spoken (p. 180)

brand equity the value of a company or brand name (p. 180)

global brand a brand that obtains at least a one-third of its earnings from outside its home country, is recognizable outside its home base of customers, and has publicly available marketing and financial data (p. 180)

brand loyalty consistent preference for one brand over all others (p. 181)

manufacturer's brand the brand name of a manufacturer (p. 182)

private brand a brand name owned by a wholesaler or a retailer (p. 182)

captive brand a brand manufactured by a third party for an exclusive retailer, without evidence of that retailer's affiliation (p. 182)

individual branding using different brand names for different products (p. 182)

family branding marketing several different products under the same brand name (p. 183)

co-branding placing two or more brand names on a product or its package (p. 183)

trademark the exclusive right to use a brand or part of a brand (p. 183)

service mark a trademark for a service (p. 183)

generic product name identifies a product by class or type and cannot be trademarked (p. 184)

10-5 **Describe marketing uses of packaging and labeling.** Packaging has four functions: containing and protecting products; promoting products; facilitating product storage, use, and convenience; and facilitating recycling and reducing environmental damage As a tool for promotion, packaging identifies the brand and its features. It also serves the critical function of differentiating a product from competing products and linking it with related products from the same manufacturer. The label is an integral part of the package, with persuasive and informational functions. In essence, the package is the marketer's last chance to influence buyers before they make a purchase decision.

persuasive labeling a type of package labeling that focuses on a promotional theme or logo, and consumer information is secondary (p. 186)

informational labeling a type of package labeling designed to help consumers make proper product selections and lower their cognitive dissonance after the purchase (p. 186)

universal product codes (UPCs) a series of thick and thin vertical lines (bar codes) readable by computerized optical scanners that represent numbers used to track products (p. 187)

10-6 **Discuss global issues in branding and packaging.** In addition to brand piracy, international marketers must address a variety of concerns regarding branding and packaging, including choosing a brand name policy, translating labels and meeting host-country labeling requirements, making packages aesthetically compatible with host-country cultures, and offering the sizes of packages preferred in host countries.

Global Branding Considerations	Global Packaging Considerations
One name	Labeling
Modify or adapt one name	Aesthetics
Different names in different markets	Climate

10-7 **Describe how and why product warranties are important marketing tools.** Just as a package is designed to protect the product, a warranty protects the buyer and gives essential information about the product. A warranty confirms the quality or performance of a good or service. An express warranty is a written guarantee. Express warranties range from simple statements—such as "100 percent cotton" (a guarantee of quality) and "complete satisfaction guaranteed" (a statement of performance)—to extensive documents written in technical language. In contrast, an implied warranty is an unwritten guarantee that the good or service is fit for the purpose for which it was sold. All sales have an implied warranty under the Uniform Commercial Code.

Express warranty = written guarantee

Implied warranty = unwritten guarantee

warranty a confirmation of the quality or performance of a good or service (p. 188)

express warranty a written guarantee (p. 188)

implied warranty an unwritten guarantee that the good or service is fit for the purpose for which it was sold (p. 188)

11-1 Explain the importance of developing new products and describe the six categories of new products. New products are important to sustain growth and profits and to replace obsolete items. New products can be classified as new-to-the-world products (discontinuous innovations), new product lines, additions to existing product lines, improvements or revisions of existing products, repositioned products, or lower-priced products. To sustain or increase profits, a firm must innovate.

new product a product new to the world, the market, the producer, the seller, or some combination of these (p. 191)

11-2 Explain the steps in the new-product development process. First, a firm forms a new-product strategy by outlining the characteristics and roles of future products. Then new-product ideas are generated by customers, employees, distributors, competitors, vendors, and internal research and development personnel. Once a product idea has survived initial screening by an appointed screening group, it undergoes business analysis to determine its potential profitability. If a product concept seems viable, it progresses into the development phase, in which the technical and economic feasibility of the manufacturing process is evaluated. The development phase also includes laboratory and use testing of a product for performance and safety. Following initial testing and refinement, most products are introduced in a test market to evaluate consumer response and marketing strategies. Finally, test market successes are propelled into full commercialization. The commercialization process involves starting up production, building inventories, shipping to distributors, training a sales force, announcing the product to the trade, and advertising to consumers.

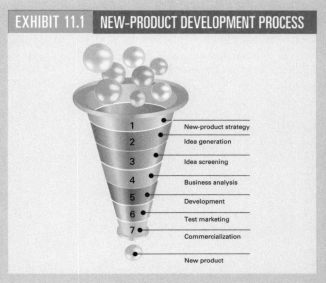

EXHIBIT 11.1   NEW-PRODUCT DEVELOPMENT PROCESS

1. New-product strategy
2. Idea generation
3. Idea screening
4. Business analysis
5. Development
6. Test marketing
7. Commercialization

New product

new-product strategy a plan that links the new-product development process with the objectives of the marketing department, the business unit, and the corporation (p. 192)

product development a marketing strategy that entails the creation of marketable new products; the process of converting applications for new technologies into marketable products (p. 194)

brainstorming the process of getting a group to think of unlimited ways to vary a product or solve a problem (p. 195)

screening the first filter in the product development process, which eliminates ideas that are inconsistent with the organization's new-product strategy or are obviously inappropriate for some other reason (p. 195)

concept test a test to evaluate a new-product idea, usually before any prototype has been created (p. 195)

business analysis the second stage of the screening process where preliminary figures for demand, cost, sales, and profitability are calculated (p. 195)

development the stage in the product development process in which a prototype is developed and a marketing strategy is outlined (p. 196)

simultaneous product development a team-oriented approach to new-product development (p. 197)

test marketing the limited introduction of a product and a marketing program to determine the reactions of potential customers in a market situation (p. 197)

simulated (laboratory) market testing the presentation of advertising and other promotional materials for several products, including a test product, to members of the product's target market (p. 198)

commercialization the decision to market a product (p. 198)

11-3 Understand why some products succeed and others fail. Despite the amount of time and money spent on developing and testing new products, a large proportion of new-product introductions fail. Products fail for a number of reasons. Failure can be a matter of degree—absolute failure occurs when a company cannot recoup its development, marketing, and production costs, while relative product failure occurs when the product returns a profit but fails to achieve sales, profit, or market share goals.

11-4 Discuss global issues in new-product development. A marketer with global vision seeks to develop products that can easily be adapted to suit local needs. The goal is not simply to develop a standard product that can be sold worldwide. Smart global marketers also look for good product ideas worldwide.

11-5 Explain the diffusion process through which new products are adopted. The diffusion process is the spread of a new product from its producer to ultimate adopters. Adopters in the diffusion process belong to five categories: innovators, early adopters, the early majority, the late majority, and laggards. Product characteristics that affect the rate of adoption include product complexity, compatibility with existing social values, relative advantage over existing substitutes, visibility, and "trialability." The diffusion process is facilitated by word-of-mouth communication and communication from marketers to consumers.

innovation a product perceived as new by a potential adopter (p. 200)

diffusion the process by which the adoption of an innovation spreads (p. 200)

11-6 **Explain the concept of product life cycles.** All brands and product categories undergo a life cycle with four stages: introduction, growth, maturity, and decline. The rate at which products move through these stages varies dramatically. Marketing managers use the product life cycle concept as an analytical tool to forecast a product's future and devise effective marketing strategies.

product life cycle (PLC) a concept that provides a way to trace the stages of a product's acceptance, from its introduction (birth) to its decline (death) (p. 202)

product category all brands that satisfy a particular type of need (p. 202)

introductory stage the full-scale launch of a new product into the marketplace (p. 203)

growth stage the second stage of the product life cycle when sales typically grow at an increasing rate, many competitors enter the market, large companies may start to acquire small pioneering firms, and profits are healthy (p. 203)

maturity stage a period during which sales increase at a decreasing rate (p. 204)

decline stage a long-run drop in sales (p. 204)

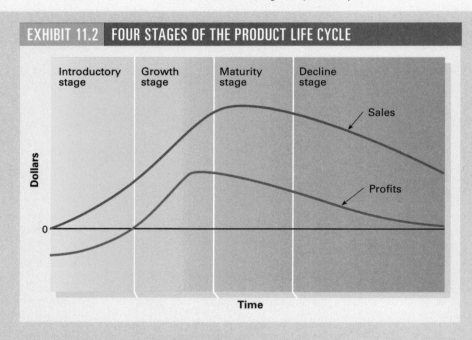

EXHIBIT 11.2 **FOUR STAGES OF THE PRODUCT LIFE CYCLE**

12-1 **Discuss the importance of services to the economy.** The service sector plays a crucial role in the U.S. economy. In 2016, service industries accounted for 80 percent of U.S. economic output. Services have unique characteristics that distinguish them from goods, and marketing strategies need to be adjusted for these characteristics.

service the result of applying human or mechanical efforts to people or objects (p. 206)

12-2 **Discuss the differences between services and goods.** Services are distinguished by four characteristics. Services are intangible performances in that they lack clearly identifiable physical characteristics, making it difficult for marketers to communicate their specific benefits to potential customers. The production and consumption of services occurs simultaneously. Services are heterogeneous because their quality depends on such elements as the service provider, individual consumer, location, and the like. Finally, services are perishable in the sense that they cannot be stored or saved. As a result, synchronizing supply with demand is particularly challenging in the service industry.

intangibility the inability of services to be touched, seen, tasted, heard, or felt in the same manner that goods can be sensed (p. 207)

search quality a characteristic that can be easily assessed before purchase (p. 207)

experience quality a characteristic that can be assessed only after use (p. 207)

credence quality a characteristic that consumers may have difficulty assessing even after purchase because they do not have the necessary knowledge or experience (p. 207)

inseparability the inability of the production and consumption of a service to be separated; consumers must be present during the production (p. 208)

heterogeneity the variability of the inputs and outputs of services, which causes services to tend to be less standardized and uniform than goods (p. 208)

perishability the inability of services to be stored, warehoused, or inventoried (p. 208)

12-3 **Describe the components of service quality and the gap model of service quality.** Service quality has five components: reliability (ability to perform the service dependably, accurately, and consistently), responsiveness (providing prompt service), assurance (knowledge and courtesy of employees and their ability to convey trust), empathy (caring, individualized attention), and tangibles (physical evidence of the service).

The gap model identifies five key discrepancies that can influence customer evaluations of service quality. When the gaps are large, service quality is low. As the gaps shrink, service quality improves. Gap 1 is found between customers' expectations and management's perceptions of those expectations. Gap 2 is found between management's perception of what the customer wants and specifications for service quality. Gap 3 is found between service quality specifications and delivery of the service. Gap 4 is found between service delivery and what the company promises to the customer through external communication. Gap 5 is found between customers' service expectations and their perceptions of service performance.

reliability the ability to perform a service dependably, accurately, and consistently (p. 208)

responsiveness the ability to provide prompt service (p. 209)

assurance the knowledge and courtesy of employees and their ability to convey trust (p. 209)

empathy caring, individualized attention to customers (p. 209)

tangibles the physical evidence of a service, including the physical facilities, tools, and equipment used to provide the service (p. 209)

gap model a model identifying five gaps that can cause problems in service delivery and influence customer evaluations of service quality (p. 209)

12-4 **Develop marketing mixes for services.** "Product" (service) strategy issues include what is being processed (people, possessions, mental stimulus, information), core and supplementary services, customization versus standardization, and the service mix. Distribution (place) decisions involve convenience, number of outlets, direct versus indirect distribution, and scheduling. Stressing tangible cues, using personal sources of information, creating strong organizational images, and engaging in postpurchase communication are effective promotion strategies. Pricing objectives for services can be revenue oriented, operations oriented, patronage oriented, or any combination of the three.

core service the most basic benefit the consumer is buying (p. 211)

supplementary services a group of services that support or enhance the core service (p. 211)

mass customization a strategy that uses technology to deliver customized services on a mass basis (p. 212)

12-5 **Discuss relationship marketing in services.** Relationship marketing in services involves attracting, developing, and retaining customer relationships. There are four levels of relationship marketing: level 1 focuses on pricing incentives; level 2 uses pricing incentives and social bonds with customers; level 3 focuses on customization; and level 4 uses pricing, social bonds, and structural bonds to build long-term relationships.

12-6 **Explain internal marketing in services.** Internal marketing means treating employees as customers and developing systems and benefits that satisfy their needs. Employees who like their jobs and are happy with the firm they work for are more likely to deliver good service.

internal marketing treating employees as customers and developing systems and benefits that satisfy their needs (p. 215)

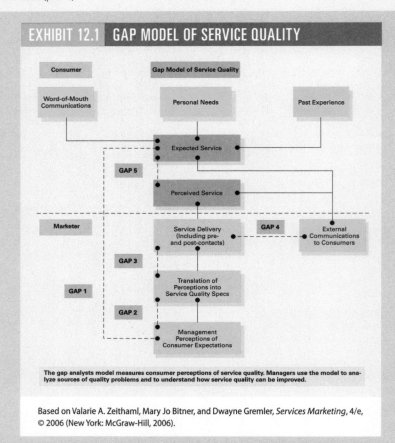

EXHIBIT 12.1   GAP MODEL OF SERVICE QUALITY

The gap analysts model measures consumer perceptions of service quality. Managers use the model to analyze sources of quality problems and to understand how service quality can be improved.

Based on Valarie A. Zeithaml, Mary Jo Bitner, and Dwayne Gremler, *Services Marketing*, 4/e, © 2006 (New York: McGraw-Hill, 2006).

12-7 **Describe nonprofit organization marketing.** Nonprofit organizations pursue goals other than profit, market share, and return on investment. Nonprofit organization marketing facilitates mutually satisfying exchanges between nonprofit organizations and their target markets. Several unique characteristics distinguish nonbusiness marketing strategy, including a concern with services and social behaviors rather than manufactured goods and profit; a difficult, undifferentiated, and in some ways marginal target market; a complex product that may have only indirect benefits and elicit very low involvement; distribution that may or may not require special facilities depending on the service provided; a relative lack of resources for promotion; and prices only indirectly related to the exchange between the producer and the consumer of services.

nonprofit organization an organization that exists to achieve some goal other than the usual business goals of profit, market share, or return on investment (p. 215)

nonprofit organization marketing the effort by nonprofit organizations to bring about mutually satisfying exchanges with target markets (p. 215)

public service advertisement (PSA) an announcement that promotes a program of a federal, state, or local government or of a nonprofit organization (p. 217)

12-8 **Discuss global issues in services marketing.** The United States has become the world's largest exporter of services. Although competition is keen, the United States has a competitive advantage because of its vast experience in many service industries. To be successful globally, service firms must adjust their marketing mix for the environment of each target country.

CHAPTER 13 LEARNING OUTCOMES / KEY TERMS   CHAPTER REVIEW

13-1 Define the terms *supply chain* and *supply chain management* and discuss the benefits of supply chain management. Management coordinates and integrates all of the activities performed by supply chain members into a seamless process from the source to the point of consumption. The benefits of supply chain management include reduced inventory, transportation, warehousing, and packaging costs; greater supply chain flexibility; improved customer service; and higher revenues.

supply chain the connected chain of all of the business entities, both internal and external to the company, that perform or support the logistics function (p. 220)

supply chain management a management system that coordinates and integrates all of the activities performed by supply chain members into a seamless process, from the source to the point of consumption, resulting in enhanced customer and economic value (p. 220)

supply chain agility an operational strategy focused on creating inventory velocity and operational flexibility simultaneously in the supply chain (p. 222)

13-2 Discuss the concepts of internal and external supply chain integration and explain why each of these types of integration is important. In the modern supply chain, integration can be either internal or external. Internally, the very best companies develop a managerial orientation toward demand-supply integration. Externally, five types of integration are sought by firms interested in providing top-level service to customers: relationship integration, measurement integration, technology and planning integration, material and service supplier integration, and customer integration.

supply chain orientation a system of management practices that are consistent with a "systems thinking" approach (p. 222)

supply chain integration when multiple firms or business functions in a supply chain coordinate their activities and processes so that they are seamlessly linked to one another in an effort to satisfy the customer (p. 223)

demand-supply integration (DSI) a supply chain operational philosophy focused on integrating the supply-management and demand-generating functions of an organization (p. 223)

13-3 Identify the eight key processes of excellent supply chain management and discuss how each of these processes affects the end customer. The key processes that leading supply chain companies focus on are (1) customer relationship management, (2) customer service management, (3) demand management, (4) order fulfillment, (5) manufacturing flow management, (6) supplier relationship management, (7) product development and commercialization, and (8) returns management.

business processes bundles of interconnected activities that stretch across firms in the supply chain (p. 224)

customer relationship management (CRM) process allows companies to prioritize their marketing focus on different customer groups according to each group's long-term value to the company or supply chain (p. 224)

customer service management process presents a multi-company, unified response system to the customer whenever complaints, concerns, questions, or comments are voiced (p. 225)

demand management process seeks to align supply and demand throughout the supply chain by anticipating customer requirements at each level and creating demand-related plans of action prior to actual customer purchasing behavior (p. 225)

sales and operations planning (S&OP) a method companies use to align production with demand by merging tactical and strategic planning methods across functional areas of the business (p. 225)

order fulfillment process a highly integrated process, often requiring persons from multiple companies and multiple functions to come together and coordinate to create customer satisfaction at a given place and time (p. 226)

order cycle time the time delay between the placement of a customer's order and the customer's receipt of that order (p. 226)

manufacturing flow management process concerned with ensuring that firms in the supply chain have the needed resources to manufacture with flexibility and to move products through a multi-stage production process (p. 226)

supplier relationship management process supports manufacturing flow by identifying and maintaining relationships with highly valued suppliers (p. 226)

product development and commercialization process includes the group of activities that facilitates the joint development and marketing of new offerings among a group of supply chain partner firms (p. 227)

returns management process enables firms to manage volumes of returned product efficiently while minimizing returns-related costs and maximizing the value of the returned assets to the firms in the supply chain (p. 227)

13-4 Understand the importance of sustainable supply chain management to modern business operations. Sustainable supply chain management involves the integration and balancing of environmental, social, and economic thinking into all phases of the supply chain management process.

sustainable supply chain management a supply chain management philosophy that embraces the need for optimizing social and environmental costs in addition to financial costs (p. 228)

13-5 Discuss how new technology and emerging trends are impacting the practice of supply chain management. Some of the business trends affecting supply chain management include outsourcing logistics, public-private partnerships, electronic distribution, maintaining a secure supply chain, and new analytics tools. While these changes exert pressure on managers to change the way their supply chains function, they also help make supply chain management more integrated and easier to track.

outsourcing (contract logistics) a manufacturer's or supplier's use of an independent third party to manage an entire function of the logistics system, such as transportation, warehousing, or order processing (p. 229)

third-party logistics company (3PL) a firm that provides functional logistics services to others (p. 229)

fourth-party logistics company (4PL or logistics integrator) a consulting-based organization that assesses another's entire logistical service needs and provides integrated solutions, often drawing on multiple 3PLs for actual service (p. 229)

offshoring the outsourcing of a business process from one country to another for the purpose of gaining economic advantage (p. 229)

nearshoring the transfer of an offshored activity from a distant to a nearby country (p. 230)

public-private partnerships (PPPs) Critical to the satisfaction of both company and societal interests and provide a mechanism by which very-large scale problems or opportunities can be addressed (p. 230)

electronic distribution a distribution technique that includes any kind of product or service that can be distributed electronically, whether over traditional forms such as fiber-optic cable or through satellite transmission of electronic signals (p. 231)

three-dimensional printing (3DP) the creation of three-dimensional objects via an additive manufacturing (printing) technology that layers raw material into desired shapes (p. 231)

big data the rapidly collected and difficult-to-process large-scale datasets that have recently emerged, and which push the limits of current analytical capability (p. 232)

cloud computing the practice of using remote network servers to store, manage, and process data (p. 232)

supply chain analytics data analyses that support the improved design and management of the supply chain (p. 233)

13-6 **Explain what marketing channels and channel intermediaries are and describe their functions and activities.** A marketing channel is a business structure of interdependent organizations that reach from the point of production to the consumer. Intermediaries negotiate with one another, buy and sell products, and facilitate the change of ownership between buyer and seller. Retailers are those firms in the channel that sell directly to consumers.

---

marketing channel (channel of distribution) a set of interdependent organizations that eases the transfer of ownership as products move from producer to business user or consumer (p. 233)

channel members all parties in the marketing channel who negotiate with one another, buy and sell products, and facilitate the change of ownership between buyer and seller in the course of moving the product from the manufacturer into the hands of the final consumer (p. 234)

form utility the elements of the composition and appearance of a product that make it desirable (p. 234)

time utility the increase in customer satisfaction gained by making a good or service available at the appropriate time (p. 234)

place utility the usefulness of a good or service as a function of the location at which it is made available (p. 234)

exchange utility the increased value of a product that is created as its ownership is transferred (p. 234)

merchant wholesaler an institution that buys goods from manufacturers and resells them to businesses, government agencies, and other wholesalers or retailers and that receives and takes title to goods, stores them in its own warehouses, and later ships them (p. 235)

agents and brokers wholesaling intermediaries who do not take title to a product but facilitate its sale from producer to end user by representing retailers, wholesalers, or manufacturers (p. 235)

retailer a channel intermediary that sells mainly to consumers (p. 235)

13-7 **Describe common channel structures and strategies and the factors that influence their choice.** When possible, producers use the direct channel to sell directly to consumers. When one or more channel members are small companies, an agent/broker channel may be the best solution. Most consumer products are sold through distribution channels similar to the retailer channel and the wholesaler channel. Dual distribution may be used to distribute the same product to target markets, and companies often form strategic channel alliances to use already-established channels. Managers must be sure that the channel strategy chosen is consistent with market factors, product factors, and producer factors.

---

direct channel a distribution channel in which producers sell directly to consumers (p. 236)

dual distribution (multiple distribution) the use of two or more channels to distribute the same product to target markets (p. 237)

nontraditional channels non-physical channels that facilitate the unique market access of products and services (p. 238)

strategic channel alliance a cooperative agreement between business firms to use the other's already established distribution channel (p. 238)

gray marketing channels secondary channels that are unintended to be used by the producer, and which often flow illegally obtained or counterfeit product toward customers (p. 238)

reverse channels channels that enable customers to return products or components for reuse or remanufacturing (p. 239)

drop and shop a system used by several retailers that allow customers to bring used products for return or donation at the entrance of the store (p. 239)

digital channels electronic pathways that allow products and related information to flow from producer to consumer (p. 239)

M-commerce the ability to conduct commerce using a mobile device for the purpose of buying or selling goods or services (p. 239)

intensive distribution a form of distribution aimed at having a product available in every outlet where target customers might want to buy it (p. 241)

selective distribution a form of distribution achieved by screening dealers to eliminate all but a few in any single area (p. 242)

exclusive distribution a form of distribution that establishes one or a few dealers within a given area (p. 242)

13-8 **Discuss multichannel and omnichannel marketing in both B-to-B and B-to-C structures and explain why these concepts are important.** In multichannel marketing strategies customers are offered information, goods, services, and/or support through one or more synchronized channels. While it can promote better consumer behavior, the multichannel design also creates redundancy and complexity in the firm's distribution system. Many companies are transitioning to omnichannel distribution operations that support their multichannel retail operations and unify their retail interfaces.

CHAPTER 14 LEARNING OUTCOMES / KEY TERMS

14-1 **Explain the importance of the retailer within the channel and the U.S. economy** Retailing represents all the activities directly related to the sale of goods and services to the ultimate consumer for personal, nonbusiness use, and has enhanced the quality of our daily lives. When we shop for groceries, hair styling, clothes, books, and many other products and services, we are doing business with retailers. Retailing affects all people directly or indirectly. Trends and innovations relating to customer data, social media, and alternative forms of shopping are constantly developing, and retailers have no choice but to react.

retailing all the activities directly related to the sale of goods and services to the ultimate consumer for personal, nonbusiness use (p. 244)

retailer a channel intermediary that sells mainly to consumers (p. 244)

14-2 **List and understand the different types of retailers** Retail establishments can be classified according to ownership, level of service, product assortment, and price. These variables can be combined in several ways to create various retail operating models. Retail ownership takes one of three forms: independent, part of a chain, or a franchise outlet. The service levels that retailers provide range from full-service to self-service. Retailers can also be categorized by the width and depth of their product lines. Price is the fourth way to position retail stores. Many stores fall into the basic types of retailers, but some companies have begun to experiment with alternative formats.

independent retailer a retailer owned by a single person or partnership and not operated as part of a larger retail institution (p. 245)

chain store a store that is part of a group of the same stores owned and operated by a single organization (p. 245)

franchise a relationship in which the business rights to operate and sell a product are granted by the franchisor to the franchisee (p. 246)

franchisor the originator of a trade name, product, methods of operation, and the like that grants operating rights to another party to sell its product (p. 246)

franchisee an individual or business that is granted the right to sell another party's product (p. 246)

gross margin the amount of money the retailer makes as a percentage of sales after the cost of goods sold is subtracted (p. 247)

department store a store housing several departments under one roof (p. 247)

specialty store a retail store specializing in a given type of merchandise (p. 247)

supermarket a large, departmentalized, self-service retailer that specializes in food and some nonfood items (p. 248)

drugstore a retail store that stocks pharmacy-related products and services as its main draw (p. 248)

convenience store a miniature supermarket, carrying only a limited line of high-turnover convenience goods (p. 248)

discount store a retailer that competes on the basis of low prices, high turnover, and high volume (p. 248)

full-line discount store a discount store that carries a vast depth and breadth of product within a single product category (p. 248)

supercenter a large retailer that stocks and sells a wide variety of merchandise including groceries, clothing, household goods, and other general merchandise (p. 248)

specialty discount store a retail store that offers a nearly complete selection of single-line merchandise and uses self-service, discount prices, high volume, and high turnover (p. 248)

category killer a large discount store that specializes in a single line of merchandise and becomes the dominant retailer in its category (p. 248)

warehouse club a large, no-frills retailer that sells bulk quantities of merchandise to customers at volume discount prices in exchange for a periodic membership fee (p. 248)

off-price retailer a retailer that sells at prices 25 percent or more below traditional department store prices because it pays cash for its stock and usually doesn't ask for return privileges (p. 248)

factory outlet an off-price retailer that is owned and operated by a manufacturer (p. 248)

used goods retailer a retailer whereby items purchased from one of the other types of retailers are resold to different customers (p. 248)

restaurant a retailer that provides both tangible products—food and drink—and valuable services—food preparation and presentation (p. 249)

14-3 **Explain why nonstore retailing is on the rise and list the advantages of its different forms** Nonstore retailing enables customers to shop without visiting a physical store location. It adds a level of convenience for customers who wish to shop from their current locations. Due to broader changes in culture and society, nonstore retailing is currently growing faster than in-store retailing. The major forms of nonstore retailing are automatic vending, direct retailing, direct marketing, and Internet retailing.

nonstore retailing shopping without visiting a store (p. 249)

automatic vending the use of machines to offer goods for sale (p. 249)

self-service technologies (SST) technological interfaces that allow customers to provide themselves with products and/or services without the intervention of a service employee (p. 249)

direct retailing the selling of products by representatives who work door-to-door, office-to-office, or at home sales parties (p. 250)

direct marketing (DM) techniques used to get consumers to make a purchase from their home, office, or other nonretail setting (p. 250)

telemarketing the use of the telephone to sell directly to consumers (p. 250)

direct mail the delivery of advertising or marketing material to recipients of postal or electronic mail (p. 250)

microtargeting the use of direct marketing techniques that employ highly detailed data analytics in order to isolate

potential customers with great precision (p. 250)

shop-at-home television network a specialized form of direct response marketing whereby television shows display

merchandise, with the retail price, to home viewers (p. 251)

online retailing (e-tailing) a type of shopping available to consumers with personal computers and access to the Internet (p. 251)

14-4 Discuss the different retail operations models and understand why they vary in strategy and format Retail formats are co-aligned with unique operating models that guide the decisions made by their managers. Each operating model can be summarized as a set of guiding principles. Today, most retail stores remain operationally and tactically similar to those that have been in business for hundreds of years; with one or more physical locations that the customer must visit in order to purchase a stocked product, and with strategies in place to attract customers to visit.

floor stock inventory displayed for sale to customers (p. 251)

back stock inventory held in reserve for potential future sale in a retailer's storeroom or stockroom (p. 251)

14-5 Explain how retail marketing strategies are developed and executed Retail managers develop marketing strategies based on the goals established by stakeholders and the overall strategic plans developed by company leadership. Strategic retailing goals typically focus on increasing total sales, reducing costs of goods sold, and improving financial ratios such as return on assets or equity. The first and foremost task in developing a retail strategy is to define the target market. Then comes combining the elements of the retailing mix to come up with a single retailing method to attract that target market.

retailing mix a combination of the six Ps—product, promotion, place, price, presentation, and personnel—to sell goods and services to the ultimate consumer (p. 253)

brand cannibalization the reduction of sales for one brand as the result of the

introduction of a new product or promotion of a current product by another brand (p. 254)

destination store a store that consumers purposely plan to visit prior to shopping (p. 255)

atmosphere the overall impression conveyed by a store's physical layout, décor, and surroundings (p. 256)

layout the internal design and configuration of a store's fixtures and products (p. 256)

14-6 Discuss how services retailing differs from goods retailing The fastest-growing part of our economy is the service sector. Although distribution in the service sector is difficult to visualize, the same skills, techniques, and strategies used to manage inventory can also be used to manage service inventory, such as hospital beds, bank accounts, or airline seats. Because service industries are so customer oriented, service quality is a priority.

14-7 Understand how retailers address product/service failures and discuss the opportunities that service failures provide No retailer can be everything to every customer, and by making strategic decisions related to targeting, segmentation, and the retailing mix, retailers implicitly decide which customers will be delighted and which will probably leave the store unsatisfied. The best retailers have plans in place not only to recover from inevitable lapses in service but also perhaps even to benefit from them.

14-8 Summarize current trends related to customer data, analytics, and technology Retailers are constantly innovating. They are always looking for new products and services (or ways to offer them) that will attract new customers or inspire current ones to buy in greater quantities or more frequently. Big data analytics, shopper marketing, mobile technology, and social media are at the front of this innovation. Some retailers have turned to channel omnification, while others have embraced click-and-collect.

big data analytics the process of discovering patterns in large data sets for the purposes of extracting knowledge and understanding human behavior (p. 258)

beacon a device that sends out connecting signals to customers' smartphones and tablets in order to bring them into a retail store or improve their shopping experience (p. 258)

shopper marketing understanding how one's target consumers behave as shoppers, in different channels and formats, and leveraging this intelligence to generate sales or other positive outcomes (p. 259)

shopper analytics searching for and discovering meaningful patterns in shopper data for the purpose of fine-tuning, developing, or changing market offerings (p. 260)

retail channel omnification the reduction of multiple retail channel systems into a single, unified system for the purpose of creating efficiencies or saving costs (p. 261)

click-and-collect the practice of buying something online and then traveling to a physical store location to take delivery of the merchandise (p. 261)

15-1 **Discuss the role of promotion in the marketing mix.** Promotional strategy is the plan for using the elements of promotion—advertising, public relations, sales promotion, personal selling, and social media—to meet the firm's overall objectives and marketing goals. Based on these objectives, the elements of the promotional strategy become a coordinated promotion plan. The promotion plan then becomes an integral part of the total marketing strategy for reaching the target market along with product, distribution, and price. Promotional strategies have changed a great deal over the years as many target customer segments have become harder and harder to reach.

promotion communication by marketers that informs, persuades, and reminds potential buyers of a product in order to influence an opinion or elicit a response (p. 262)

promotional strategy a plan for the optimal use of the elements of promotion: advertising, public relations, personal selling, sales promotion, and social media (p. 262)

competitive advantage one or more unique aspects of an organization that cause target consumers to patronize that firm rather than competitors (p. 262)

15-2 **Describe the communication process.** The communication process has several steps. When an individual or organization has a message it wishes to convey to a target audience, it encodes that message using language and symbols familiar to the intended receiver and sends the message through a channel of communication. Noise in the transmission channel distorts the source's intended message. Reception occurs if the message falls within the receiver's frame of reference. The receiver decodes the message and usually provides feedback to the source. Normally, feedback is direct for interpersonal communication and indirect for mass communication. The Internet and social media have had an impact on the communication model in two major ways: consumers are now able to become senders, and marketers can personalize the feedback channel by initiating direct conversations with customers.

communication the process by which we exchange or share meaning through a common set of symbols (p. 264)

interpersonal communication direct, face-to-face communication between two or more people (p. 264)

mass communication the communication of a concept or message to large audiences (p. 264)

sender the originator of the message in the communication process (p. 265)

encoding the conversion of a sender's ideas and thoughts into a message, usually in the form of words or signs (p. 265)

channel a medium of communication—such as a voice, radio, or newspaper—for transmitting a message (p. 265)

noise anything that interferes with, distorts, or slows down the transmission of information (p. 266)

receiver the person who decodes a message (p. 266)

decoding interpretation of the language and symbols sent by the source through a channel (p. 266)

feedback the receiver's response to a message (p. 266)

15-3 **Explain the goals and tasks of promotion.** The fundamental goals of promotion are to induce, modify, or reinforce behavior by informing, persuading, reminding, and connecting. Informative promotion explains a good's or service's purpose and benefits. Promotion that informs the consumer is typically used to increase demand for a general product category or to introduce a new good or service. Persuasive promotion is designed to stimulate a purchase or an action. Promotion that persuades the consumer to buy is essential during the growth stage of the product life cycle, when competition becomes fierce. Reminder promotion is used to keep the product and brand name in the public's mind. Promotions that remind are generally used during the maturity stage of the product life cycle. Connection promotion is designed to form relationships with customers and potential customers using social media. Connecting encourages customers to become brand advocates and share their experiences via social media.

15-4 **Discuss the elements of the promotional mix.** The elements of the promotional mix include advertising, public relations, sales promotion, personal selling, and social media. Advertising is a form of impersonal, one-way mass communication paid for by the source. Public relations is the function of promotion concerned with a firm's public image. Sales promotion is typically used to back up other components of the promotional mix by stimulating immediate demand. Personal selling typically involves direct communication, in person or by telephone; the seller tries to initiate a purchase by informing and persuading one or more potential buyers. Finally, social media are promotion tools used to facilitate conversations among people online.

promotional mix the combination of promotional tools—including advertising, public relations, personal selling, sales promotion, and social media—used to reach the target market and fulfill the organization's overall goals (p. 268)

advertising impersonal, one-way mass communication about a product or organization that is paid for by a marketer (p. 269)

public relations the marketing function that evaluates public attitudes, identifies areas within the organization the public may be interested in, and executes a program of action to earn public understanding and acceptance (p. 269)

publicity public information about a company, product, service, or issue appearing in the mass media as a news item (p. 269)

sales promotion marketing activities—other than personal selling, advertising, and public relations—that stimulate consumer buying and dealer effectiveness (p. 270)

personal selling a purchase situation involving a personal, paid-for communication between two people in an attempt to influence each other (p. 270)

paid media a category of promotional tactic based on the traditional advertising model, whereby a brand pays for media space (p. 271)

earned media a category of promotional tactic based on a public relations or publicity model that gets customers talking about products or services (p. 272)

owned media a new category of promotional tactic based on brands becoming publishers of their own content in order to maximize the brands' value to customers (p. 272)

15-5

Discuss the AIDA concept and its relationship to the promotional mix. The AIDA model outlines the four basic stages in the purchase decision-making process, which are initiated and propelled by promotional activities: (1) attention, (2) interest, (3) desire, and (4) action. The components of the promotional mix have varying levels of influence at each stage of the AIDA model. Advertising is a good tool for increasing awareness and knowledge of a good or service. Sales promotion is effective when consumers are at the purchase stage of the decision-making process. Personal selling is most effective in developing customer interest and desire.

AIDA concept a model that outlines the process for achieving promotional goals in terms of stages of consumer involvement with the message; the acronym stands for attention, interest, desire, and action (p. 273)

15-6

Discuss the concept of integrated marketing communications. Integrated marketing communications is the careful coordination of all promotional messages for a product or service to ensure the consistency of messages at every contact point where a company meets the consumer—advertising, sales promotion, personal selling, public relations, and social media, as well as direct marketing, packaging, and other forms of communication. Marketing managers carefully coordinate all promotional activities to ensure that consumers see and hear one message. Integrated marketing communications has received more attention in recent years due to the proliferation of media choices, the fragmentation of mass markets into more segmented niches, and the decrease in advertising spending in favor of promotional techniques that generate an immediate sales response.

integrated marketing communications (IMC) the careful coordination of all promotional messages for a product or a service to ensure the consistency of messages at every contact point at which a company meets the consumer (p. 275)

15-7

Describe the factors that affect the promotional mix. Promotion managers consider many factors when creating promotional mixes. These factors include the nature of the product, product life cycle stage, target market characteristics, the type of buying decision involved, availability of funds, and feasibility of push or pull strategies. As products move through different stages of the product life cycle, marketers will choose to use different promotional elements. Characteristics of the target market, such as geographic location of potential buyers and brand loyalty, influence the promotional mix, as does whether the buying decision is complex or routine. The amount of funds a firm has to allocate to promotion may also help determine the promotional mix. Last, if a firm uses a push strategy to promote the product or service, the marketing manager might choose to use aggressive advertising and personal selling to wholesalers and retailers. If a pull strategy is chosen, then the manager often relies on aggressive mass promotion, such as advertising and sales promotion, to stimulate consumer demand.

push strategy a marketing strategy that uses aggressive personal selling and trade advertising to convince a wholesaler or a retailer to carry and sell particular merchandise (p. 278)

pull strategy a marketing strategy that stimulates consumer demand to obtain product distribution (p. 279)

EXHIBIT 15.7 PUSH STRATEGY VERSUS PULL STRATEGY

CHAPTER 16 LEARNING OUTCOMES / KEY TERMS

16-1 **Discuss the effects of advertising on market share and consumers.** Advertising helps marketers increase or maintain brand awareness and, subsequently, market share. Typically, more is spent to advertise new brands with a small market share than to advertise older brands. Brands with a large market share use advertising mainly to maintain their share of the market.

Although advertising can seldom change strongly held consumer attitudes and values, it may transform a consumer's negative attitude toward a product into a positive one. By emphasizing different brand attributes, advertisers can change their appeal in response to consumers' changing needs or try to achieve an advantage over competing brands.

advertising response function a phenomenon in which spending for advertising and sales promotion increases sales or market share up to a certain level but then produces diminishing returns (p. 282)

16-2 **Identify the major types of advertising.** Advertising is any form of nonpersonal, paid communication in which the sponsor or company is identified. The two major types of advertising are institutional advertising and product advertising. Institutional advertising is not product oriented; rather, its purpose is to foster a positive company image among the general public, investment community, customers, and employees. Product advertising is designed mainly to promote goods and services, and it is classified into three main categories: pioneering, competitive, and comparative. A product's place in the product life cycle is a major determinant of the type of advertising used to promote it.

institutional advertising a form of advertising designed to enhance a company's image rather than promote a particular product (p. 282)

product advertising a form of advertising that touts the benefits of a specific good or service (p. 282)

advocacy advertising a form of advertising in which an organization expresses its views on controversial issues or responds to media attacks (p. 283)

pioneering advertising a form of advertising designed to stimulate primary demand for a new product or product category (p. 283)

competitive advertising a form of advertising designed to influence demand for a specific brand (p. 284)

comparative advertising a form of advertising that compares two or more specifically named or shown competing brands on one or more specific attributes (p. 284)

16-3 **Discuss the creative decisions in developing an advertising campaign.** Before any creative work can begin on an advertising campaign, it is important to determine what goals or objectives the advertising should achieve. The objectives of a specific advertising campaign often depend on the overall corporate objectives and the product being advertised and are often determined using the DAGMAR approach. Once objectives are defined, creative work can begin (e.g., identifying the product's benefits, developing possible advertising appeals, evaluating and selecting the advertising appeals, executing the advertising message, and evaluating the effectiveness of the campaign).

advertising campaign a series of related advertisements focusing on a common theme, slogan, and set of advertising appeals (p. 284)

advertising objective a specific communication task that a campaign should accomplish for a specified target audience during a specified period (p. 284)

advertising appeal a reason for a person to buy a product (p. 285)

unique selling proposition a desirable, exclusive, and believable advertising appeal selected as the theme for a campaign (p. 285)

16-4 **Describe media evaluation and selection techniques.** Media evaluation and selection make up a crucial step in the advertising campaign process. Major types of advertising media include newspapers, magazines, radio, television, the Internet, and outdoor media. Recent trends in advertising media include shopping carts, computer screen savers, interactive kiosks, advertisements run before movies, posters on bathroom stalls, and advertainments. Promotion managers choose the advertising campaign's media mix on the basis of the following variables: cost per contact, reach, frequency, characteristics of the target audience, flexibility of the medium, noise level, and the life span of the medium.

medium the channel used to convey a message to a target market (p. 287)

media planning the series of decisions advertisers make regarding the selection and use of media, allowing the marketer to optimally and cost-effectively communicate the message to the target audience (p. 287)

cooperative advertising an arrangement in which the manufacturer and the retailer split the costs of advertising the manufacturer's brand (p. 289)

infomercial a 30-minute or longer advertisement that looks more like a television talk show than a sales pitch (p. 289)

advergaming placing advertising messages in web-based, mobile, console, or handheld video games to advertise or promote a product, service, organization, or issue (p. 290)

media mix the combination of media to be used for a promotional campaign (p. 291)

cost per contact (cost per thousand or CPM) the cost of reaching one member of the target market (p. 291)

cost per click the cost associated with a consumer clicking on a display or banner ad (p. 291)

reach the number of target consumers exposed to a commercial at least once during a specific period, usually four weeks (p. 292)

frequency the number of times an individual is exposed to a given message during a specific period (p. 292)

audience selectivity the ability of an advertising medium to reach a precisely defined market (p. 292)

media schedule designation of the media, the specific publications or programs, and the insertion dates of advertising (p. 293)

continuous media schedule a media scheduling strategy in which advertising is run steadily throughout the advertising period; used for products in the later stages of the product life cycle (p. 293)

flighted media schedule a media scheduling strategy in which ads are run

heavily every other month or every two weeks to achieve a greater impact with an increased frequency and reach at those times (p. 293)

pulsing media schedule a media scheduling strategy that uses continuous scheduling throughout the year coupled with a flighted schedule during the best sales periods (p. 293)

seasonal media schedule a media scheduling strategy that runs advertising only during times of the year when the product is most likely to be used (p. 293)

16-5 **Discuss the role of public relations in the promotional mix.** Public relations is a vital part of a firm's promotional mix. A company fosters good publicity to enhance its image and promote its products. Popular public relations tools include new-product publicity, product placement, consumer education, sponsorship, and company websites. An equally important aspect of public relations is managing unfavorable publicity in a way that is least damaging to a firm's image.

public relations the element in the promotional mix that evaluates public attitudes, identifies issues that may elicit public concern, and executes programs to gain public understanding and acceptance (p. 294)

publicity an effort to capture media attention, often initiated through press releases that further a corporation's public relations plans (p. 294)

product placement a public relations strategy that involves getting a product, service, or company name to appear in a movie, television show, radio program, magazine, newspaper, video game, video or audio clip, book, or commercial for another product; on the Internet; or at special events (p. 295)

sponsorship a public relations strategy in which a company spends money to

support an issue, cause, or event that is consistent with corporate objectives, such as improving brand awareness or enhancing corporate image (p. 296)

crisis management a coordinated effort to handle all the effects of unfavorable publicity or another unexpected unfavorable event (p. 297)

16-6 **Define and state the objectives of sales promotion and the tools used to achieve them.** Marketing managers can use sales promotion to increase the effectiveness of their promotional efforts. Sales promotion can target either trade or consumer markets. Trade promotions may push a product through the distribution channel using sales contests, premiums, P-O-P displays, trade allowances, push money, training, free merchandise, store demonstrations, and business meetings. Consumer promotions may push a product through the distribution channel using coupons, rebates, premiums, loyalty marketing programs or frequent buyer programs, contests, sweepstakes, sampling, and P-O-P displays.

sales promotion marketing communication activities other than advertising, personal selling, and public relations, in which a short-term incentive motivates consumers or members of the distribution channel to purchase a good or service immediately, either by lowering the price or by adding value (p. 297)

trade sales promotion promotion activities directed to members of the marketing channel, such as wholesalers and retailers (p. 297)

consumer sales promotion promotion activities targeted to the ultimate consumer market (p. 297)

trade allowance a price reduction offered by manufacturers to intermediaries such as wholesalers and retailers (p. 297)

push money money offered to channel intermediaries to encourage them to "push" products—that is, to encourage other members of the channel to sell the products (p. 298)

coupon a certificate that entitles consumers to an immediate price reduction when the product is purchased. (p. 299)

rebate a cash refund given for the purchase of a product during a specific period (p. 299)

premium an extra item offered to the consumer, usually in exchange for some proof of purchase of the promoted product (p. 299)

loyalty marketing program a promotional program designed to build

long-term, mutually beneficial relationships between a company and its key customers (p. 299)

frequent buyer program a loyalty program in which loyal consumers are rewarded for making multiple purchases of a particular good or service (p. 300)

sampling a promotional program that allows the consumer the opportunity to try a product or service for free (p. 300)

point of purchase (P-O-P) display a promotional display set up at the retailer's location to build traffic, advertise the product, or induce impulse buying (p. 301)

17-1 Understand the sales environment. Salespeople can be consumer-focused (as in the case of retail) or business-focused. The sales environment changes constantly as new competitors enter the market and old competitors leave. The ways that customers interact with salespeople and learn about products and suppliers are changing due to the rapid increase in new sales technologies. In order for companies to successfully sell products or services using a sales force, they must be very effective at personal selling, sales management, customer relationship management, and technology—all of which play critical roles in building strong long-term relationships with customers.

17-2 Describe personal selling. Personal selling is direct communication between a sales representative and one or more prospective buyers in an attempt to influence each other in a purchase situation. Broadly speaking, all businesspeople use personal selling to promote themselves and their ideas. Personal selling offers several advantages over other forms of promotion. Generally speaking, personal selling becomes more important as the number of potential customers decreases, as the complexity of the product increases, and as the value of the product grows. Technology plays an increasingly important role in personal selling. If salespeople do not stay well informed about the products they're selling, consumers may enter the store knowing even more than they do.

17-3 Discuss the key differences between relationship selling and traditional selling. Relationship selling is the practice of building, maintaining, and enhancing interactions with customers to develop long-term satisfaction through mutually beneficial partnerships. Traditional selling, on the other hand, is transaction focused. That is, the salesperson is most concerned with making a one-time sale and moving on to the next prospect. Salespeople practicing relationship selling spend more time understanding a prospect's needs and developing solutions to meet those needs.

EXHIBIT 17.2   KEY DIFFERENCES BETWEEN TRADITIONAL SELLING AND RELATIONSHIP SELLING

Traditional Personal Selling	Relationship or Consultative Selling
Sell products (goods and services)	Sell advice, assistance, and counsel
Focus on closing sales	Focus on improving the customer's bottom line
Limited sales planning	Consider sales planning as top priority
Spend most contact time telling customers about product	Spend most contact time attempting to build a problem-solving environment with the customer
Conduct "product-specific" needs assessment	Conduct discovery in the full scope of the customer's operations
"Lone wolf" approach to the account	Team approach to the account
Proposals and presentations based on pricing and product features	Proposals and presentations based on profit impact and strategic benefits to the customer
Sales follow-up is short term, focused on product delivery	Sales follow-up is long term, focused on long-term relationship enhancement

Source: Robert M. Peterson, Patrick, L. Schul, and George H. Lucas Jr., "Consultative Selling: Walking the Walk in the New Selling Environment, "*National Conference on Sales Management Proceedings*, March 1996; and Ari Walker, *7 Ways to Stop "Selling" and Start Building Relationships*, http://marketing.about.com /od/salestraining/a/stopselling.htm (accessed March 2015).

relationship selling (consultative selling) a sales practice that involves building, maintaining, and enhancing interactions with customers in order to develop long-term satisfaction through mutually beneficial partnerships (p. 305)

17-4 List and explain the steps in the selling process. The selling process is composed of seven basic steps: (1) generating leads, (2) qualifying leads, (3) approaching the customer and probing needs, (4) developing and proposing solutions, (5) handling objections, (6) closing the sale, and (7) following up. The actual sales process depends on the features of the product or service, characteristics of customer segments, and internal processes in place within the firm (such as how leads are gathered). Some sales take only a few minutes to complete, but others may take much longer. Like other forms of promotion, the steps of selling follow the AIDA concept.

sales process (sales cycle) the set of steps a salesperson goes through in a particular organization to sell a particular product or service (p. 306)

lead generation (prospecting) identification of those firms and people most likely to buy the seller's offerings (p. 306)

cold calling a form of lead generation in which the salesperson approaches potential buyers without any prior knowledge of the prospects' needs or financial status (p. 307)

referral a recommendation to a salesperson from a customer or business associate (p. 307)

networking a process of finding out about potential clients from friends, business contacts, coworkers, acquaintances, and fellow members in professional and civic organizations (p. 307)

lead qualification determination of a sales prospect's (1) recognized need, (2) buying power, and (3) receptivity and accessibility (p. 307)

preapproach a process that describes the "homework" that must be done by a salesperson before he or she contacts a prospect (p. 308)

needs assessment a determination of the customer's specific needs and wants and the range of options the customer has for satisfying them (p. 308)

sales proposal a formal written document or professional presentation that outlines how the salesperson's product or

service will meet or exceed the prospect's needs (p. 310)

sales presentation a meeting in which the salesperson presents a sales proposal to a prospective buyer (p. 310)

negotiation the process during which both the salesperson and the prospect offer

special concessions in an attempt to arrive at a sales agreement (p. 311)

follow-up the final step of the selling process, in which the salesperson ensures delivery schedules are met, goods or services perform as promised, and the buyers' employees are properly trained to use the products (p. 312)

17-5 **Understand the functions of sales management.** The sales manager's basic job is to maximize sales at a reasonable cost while also maximizing profits. The sales manager's responsibilities include (1) defining sales goals and the sales process,

(2) determining the sales force structure, (3) recruiting and training the sales force, (4) compensating and motivating the sales force, and (5) evaluating the sales force.

quota a statement of the salesperson's sales goals, usually based on sales volume (p. 313)

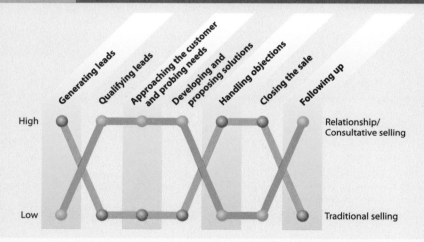

EXHIBIT 17.3 **RELATIVE AMOUNT OF TIME SPENT IN THE KEY STEPS OF THE SELLING PROCESS**

Source: Data from Robert M. Peterson, Patrick L. Schul, and George H. Lucas Jr., "Consultative Selling: Walking the Walk in the New Selling Environment, "*National Conference on Sales Management Proceedings*, March 1996; and Mark Ellwood, *How Sales Reps Spend Their Time*, http://paceproductivity.com/files/How_Sales_Reps_Spend_Their_Time.pdf (accessed March 2015).

17-6 **Describe the use of customer relationship management in the selling process.** Companies that have CRM systems follow a customer-centric focus or model. The interaction between the customer and the organization is the foundation on which a CRM system is built. Only through effective interactions

can organizations learn about the expectations of their customers, generate and manage knowledge about them, negotiate mutually satisfying commitments, and build long-term relationships. If a company has identified its best customers, then it should make every effort to maintain and increase their loyalty.

customer-centric a philosophy under which the company customizes its product and service offerings based on data generated through interactions between the customer and the company (p. 315)

knowledge management the process by which customer information is centralized and shared in order to enhance the relationship between customers and the organization (p. 316)

interaction the point at which a customer and a company representative exchange information and develop learning relationships (p. 316)

touch points areas of a business where customers have contact with the company and data might be gathered (p. 316)

point-of-sale interactions a touch point in stores or information kiosks that

uses software to enable customers to easily provide information about themselves without feeling violated (p. 317)

campaign management developing product or service offerings customized for the appropriate customer segment and then pricing and communicating these offerings for the purpose of enhancing customer relationships (p. 318)

CHAPTER 18 LEARNING OUTCOMES / KEY TERMS

18-1 **Describe social media, how they are used, and their relation to integrated marketing communications.** Social media, commonly thought of as digital technology, offer a way for marketers to communicate one-on-one with consumers and measure the effects of those interactions. Social media include social networks, microblogs, and media sharing sites, all of which are used by the majority of adults. Smartphones and tablet computers have given consumers greater freedom to access social media on the go, which is likely to increase usage of social media sites. Many advertising budgets are allotting more money to online marketing, including social media, mobile marketing, and search marketing.

social media any tool or service that uses the Internet to facilitate conversations (p. 320)

social commerce a subset of e-commerce that involves the interaction and user contribution aspects of social online media to assist online buying and selling of products and services (p. 323)

crowdsourcing using consumers to develop and market products (p. 325)

18-2 **Explain how to create a social media campaign.** A social media campaign should take advantage of owned media, earned media, and paid media. To use these types of media in a social media campaign, first implement an effective listening system. Marketers can interact with negative feedback, make changes, and effectively manage their online presence. Paying attention to the ways that competing brands attract and engage with their customers can be particularly enlightening for both small businesses and global brands. Second, develop a list of objectives that reflects how social media dynamically communicate with customers and build relationships.

social media monitoring the process of identifying and assessing what is being said about a company, individual, product, or brand (p. 326)

18-3 **Evaluate the various methods of measurement for social media.** Most marketers have not been able to figure out how to measure the benefits of social media. Hundreds of metrics have been developed to measure social media's value, but these metrics are meaningless unless they are tied to key performance indicators. Some social media metrics to consider include buzz, interest, participation, search engine rank and results, influence, sentiment analysis, and website metrics.

18-4 **Explain consumer behavior on social media.** To effectively leverage social media, marketers must understand who uses social media and how they use it. If a brand's target market does not use social media, a social media campaign might not be useful. There are six categories of social media users: creators, critics, collectors, joiners, spectators, and inactives. A new category is emerging called "conversationalists," who post status updates on social networking sites or microblogs.

18-5 **Describe the social media tools in a marketer's toolbox and how they are useful.** A marketer has many tools to implement a social media campaign. However, new tools emerge daily, so these resources will change rapidly. Some of the strongest social media platforms are blogs, microblogs, social networks, media creation and sharing sites, social news sites, location-based social networking sites, and virtual worlds and online gaming. Blogs allow marketers and consumers to create content in the form of posts, which ideally build trust and a sense of authenticity in customers. Microblogs allow brands to follow, repost, respond to potential customers, and post content that inspires customers to engage the brand, laying a foundation for meaningful two-way conversation. Social networks allow marketers to increase awareness, target audiences, promote products, forge relationships, attract event participants, perform research, and generate new business. Media sharing sites give brands an interactive channel to disseminate content. Social news sites are useful to marketers to promote campaigns, create conversations, and build website traffic. Location-based social networking sites can forge lasting relationships and loyalty in customers. Review sites allow marketers to respond to customer reviews and comments about their brand. Online and mobile gaming are fertile grounds for branded content and advertising.

blog a publicly accessible web page that functions as an interactive journal, whereby readers can post comments on the author's entries (p. 329)

corporate blogs blogs that are sponsored by a company or one of its brands and maintained by one or more of the company's employees (p. 329)

noncorporate blogs independent blogs that are not associated with the marketing efforts of any particular company or brand (p. 329)

microblogs blogs with strict post length limits (p. 330)

social networking sites websites that allow individuals to connect—or network—with friends, peers, and business associates (p. 330)

media sharing sites websites that allow users to upload and distribute multimedia content like videos and photos (p. 331)

social news sites websites that allow users to decide which content is promoted on a given website by voting that content up or down (p. 332)

location-based social networking sites websites that combine the fun of social networking with the utility of location-based GPS technology (p. 333)

review sites websites that allow consumers to post, read, rate, and comment on opinions regarding all kinds of products and services (p. 333)

18-6 **Describe the impact of mobile technology on social media.** The mobile platform is such an effective marketing tool—especially when targeting a younger audience. There are six reasons for the popularity of mobile marketing: (1) mobile platforms are standardized, (2) fewer consumers are concerned about privacy and pricing policies, (3) advertising can be done in real time, (4) mobile marketing is measurable, (5) in-store notification technology such as Apple's iBeacon can send promotional messages based on real-time interactions with customers, and (6) there is a higher response rate than with traditional advertising. Because of the rapid growth of smartphones, well-branded, integrated apps allow marketers to create buzz and generate customer engagement. Widgets allow customers to post a company's information to its site, are less expensive than apps, and broaden that company's exposure.

18-7 **Understand the aspects of developing a social media plan.** The social media plan should fit into the overall marketing plan and help marketers meet the organization's larger goals. There are six stages in creating an effective social media plan; (1) listening, (2) setting social media objectives, (3) defining strategies, (4) identifying the target audience, (5) selecting the appropriate tools and platforms, and (6) implementing and monitoring the strategy. Listening and revising the social media plan to accommodate changing market trends and needs is key to an effective social media plan.

EXHIBIT 18.2	SOCIAL MEDIA TRENDS	
Trend	**Change**	**Where Is It Now?**
Yik Yak	Anonymous geolocated messaging	
Microsoft Office 365, Google Drive	Integration with file hosting	
Ello	Challengers to Facebook's dominance	
Facebook buying Oculus	Integration into virtual reality	
The Internet of Things	Integration into wearables, appliances, apparel, and more	
Apple Pay, Google Wallet, Bitcoin, and NFC- enabled payment options	Replace credit cards with various forms of digital payment	
Loot Crate, Trunk Club, and NatureBox	Online and subscription-based personal shopping	
Twitch, Meerkat, and Periscope	Live video streaming for everybody	
Tinder and Grindr	The mainstreaming of geolocated dating apps	

19-1 **Discuss the importance of pricing decisions to the economy and to the individual firm.** Pricing plays an integral role in the U.S. economy by allocating goods and services among consumers, governments, and businesses. Pricing is essential in business because it creates revenue, which is the basis of all business activity.

price that which is given up in an exchange to acquire a good or service (p. 339)

revenue the price charged to customers multiplied by the number of units sold (p. 340)

profit revenue minus expenses (p. 340)

19-2 **List and explain a variety of pricing objectives.** Profit-oriented pricing is based on profit maximization, a satisfactory level of profit, or a target return on investment (ROI). Sales-oriented pricing focuses on either maintaining a percentage share of the market or maximizing dollar or unit sales. Status quo pricing aims to maintain the status quo by matching competitors' prices.

return on investment (ROI) net profit after taxes divided by total assets (p. 340)

market share a company's product sales as a percentage of total sales for that industry (p. 341)

status quo pricing a pricing objective that maintains existing prices or meets the competition's prices (p. 342)

19-3 **Explain the role of demand in price determination.** When establishing prices, a firm must first determine demand for its product. A typical demand schedule shows an inverse relationship between quantity demanded and price: when price is lowered, sales increase; when price is increased, the quantity demanded falls. Elasticity of demand is the degree to which the quantity demanded fluctuates with changes in price. If consumers are sensitive to changes in price, demand is elastic; if they are insensitive to price changes, demand is inelastic.

demand the quantity of a product that will be sold in the market at various prices for a specified period (p. 342)

supply the quantity of a product that will be offered to the market by a supplier

at various prices for a specified period (p. 342)

elasticity of demand consumers' responsiveness or sensitivity to changes in price (p. 342)

elastic demand a situation in which consumer demand is sensitive to changes in price (p. 342)

inelastic demand a situation in which an increase or a decrease in price will not significantly affect demand for the product (p. 342)

19-4 **Understand the concepts of dynamic pricing and yield management systems.** Dynamic pricing allows companies to adjust prices on the fly to meet demand. Yield management systems use complex mathematical software to fill unused capacity profitably. These systems are used in both service and retail businesses and are substantially raising revenues.

dynamic pricing the ability to change prices very quickly, often in real time (p. 343)

yield management systems (YMS) a technique for adjusting prices that uses complex mathematical software to profitably fill unused capacity by discounting early purchases, limiting early sales at these discounted prices, and overbooking capacity (p. 344)

19-5 **Describe cost-oriented pricing strategies.** Wholesalers and retailers commonly use markup pricing to cover expenses and turn a profit. With this strategy, they tack an extra amount on to the manufacturer's original price. With break-even pricing, a firm determines how much it must sell to break even; this amount in turn is used as a reference point for adjusting price.

variable cost a cost that varies with changes in the level of output (p. 345)

fixed cost a cost that does not change as output is increased or decreased (p. 345)

markup pricing the cost of buying the product from the producer, plus amounts

for profit and for expenses not otherwise accounted for (p. 345)

keystoning the practice of marking up prices by 100 percent, or doubling the cost (p. 345)

break-even analysis a method of determining what sales volume must be reached before total revenue equals total costs (p. 346)

19-6 **Demonstrate how the product life cycle, competition, distribution and promotion strategies, customer demands, the Internet and extranets, and perceptions of quality can affect price.** The price of a product normally changes as it moves through the life cycle and as demand for the product and competitive conditions change. Management often sets a high price at the introductory stage, and the high price tends to attract competition. The competition usually drives prices down because individual competitors lower prices to gain market share. Adequate distribution for a new product can sometimes be obtained by offering a larger-than-usual profit margin to wholesalers and retailers. The Internet enables consumers to compare products and prices quickly and efficiently. Perceptions of quality can also influence pricing strategies.

WWW.CENGAGEBRAIN.COM

extranet a private electronic network that links a company with its suppliers and customers (p. 348)

19-7 Describe the procedure for setting the right price.

The process of setting the right price on a product involves four major steps: (1) establishing pricing goals; (2) estimating demand, costs, and profits; (3) choosing a price policy to help determine a base price; and (4) fine-tuning the base price with pricing tactics. A price strategy establishes a long-term pricing framework for a good or service. The three main types of price policies are price skimming, penetration pricing, and status quo pricing.

price strategy a basic, long-term pricing framework that establishes the initial price for a product and the intended direction for price movements over the product life cycle (p. 351)

price skimming a pricing policy whereby a firm charges a high introductory price, often coupled with heavy promotion (p. 352)

penetration pricing a pricing policy whereby a firm charges a relatively low price for a product when it is first rolled out as a way to reach the mass market (p. 352)

19-8 Identify the legal constraints on pricing decisions.

Government regulation helps monitor four major areas of pricing: unfair trade practices, price fixing, price discrimination, and predatory pricing. Many states have enacted unfair trade practice acts that protect small businesses from large firms that operate on extremely thin profit margins. The Sherman Act and the Federal Trade Commission Act prohibit both price fixing and predatory pricing. The Robinson-Patman Act of 1936 makes it illegal for firms to discriminate between two or more buyers in terms of price. Predatory pricing is the practice of charging a very low price for a product with the intent of driving competitors out of business or out of a market.

unfair trade practice acts laws that prohibit wholesalers and retailers from selling below cost (p. 353)

price fixing an agreement between two or more firms on the price they will charge for a product (p. 353)

predatory pricing the practice of charging a very low price for a product with the intent of driving competitors out of business or out of a market (p. 353)

19-9 Explain how discounts, geographic pricing, and other pricing tactics can be used to fine-tune a base price.

Discounts, allowances, and rebates give lower prices to those who pay promptly, order a large quantity, or perform some function for the manufacturer. Geographic pricing tactics are used to moderate the impact of shipping costs on distant customers. A variety of other pricing tactics stimulate demand for certain products, increase store patronage, and offer more merchandise at specific prices.

base price the general price level at which the company expects to sell the good or service (p. 354)

quantity discount a price reduction offered to buyers buying in multiple units or above a specified dollar amount (p. 354)

cumulative quantity discount a deduction from list price that applies to the buyer's total purchases made during a specific period (p. 354)

noncumulative quantity discount a deduction from list price that applies to a single order rather than to the total volume of orders placed during a certain period (p. 354)

cash discount a price reduction offered to a consumer, an industrial user, or a marketing intermediary in return for prompt payment of a bill (p. 354)

functional discount (trade discount) a discount to wholesalers and retailers for performing channel functions (p. 355)

seasonal discount a price reduction for buying merchandise out of season (p. 355)

promotional allowance (trade allowance) a payment to a dealer for promoting the manufacturer's products (p. 355)

rebate a cash refund given for the purchase of a product during a specific period (p. 355)

value-based pricing setting the price at a level that seems to the customer to be a good price compared to the prices of other options (p. 356)

FOB origin pricing a price tactic that requires the buyer to absorb the freight costs from the shipping point ("free on board") (p. 356)

uniform delivered pricing a price tactic in which the seller pays the actual freight charges and bills every purchaser an identical, flat freight charge (p. 356)

zone pricing a modification of uniform delivered pricing that divides the United States (or the total market) into segments or zones and charges a flat freight rate to all customers in a given zone (p. 356)

freight absorption pricing a price tactic in which the seller pays all or part of the actual freight charges and does not pass them on to the buyer (p. 357)

basing-point pricing a price tactic that charges freight from a given (basing) point, regardless of the city from which the goods are shipped (p. 357)

single-price tactic a price tactic that offers all goods and services at the same price (or perhaps two or three prices) (p. 357)

flexible pricing (variable pricing) a price tactic in which different customers pay different prices for essentially the same merchandise bought in equal quantities (p. 357)

price lining the practice of offering a product line with several items at specific price points (p. 357)

leader pricing (loss-leader pricing) a price tactic in which a product is sold near or even below cost in the hope that shoppers will buy other items once they are in the store (p. 358)

bait pricing a price tactic that tries to get consumers into a store through false or misleading price advertising and then uses high-pressure selling to persuade consumers to buy more expensive merchandise (p. 358)

odd-even pricing (psychological pricing) a price tactic that uses odd-numbered prices to connote bargains and even-numbered prices to imply quality (p. 358)

price bundling marketing two or more products in a single package for a special price (p. 358)

two-part pricing a price tactic that charges two separate amounts to consume a single good or service (p. 359)

consumer penalty an extra fee paid by the consumer for violating the terms of the purchase agreement (p. 359)

MKTG
ONLINE

STUDY YOUR WAY
WITH STUDYBITS!

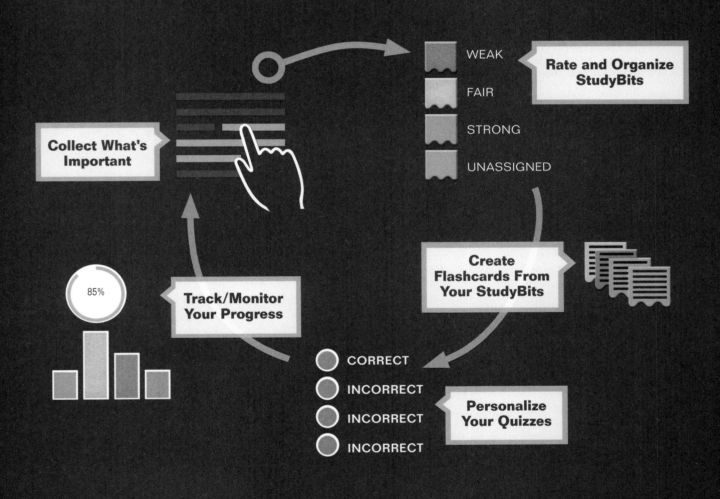

Rate and Organize
StudyBits

WEAK

FAIR

STRONG

UNASSIGNED

Collect What's
Important

Create
Flashcards From
Your StudyBits

Track/Monitor
Your Progress

85%

CORRECT

INCORRECT

INCORRECT

INCORRECT

Personalize
Your Quizzes

4LTR
PRESS

Access MKTG ONLINE at www.cengagebrain.com

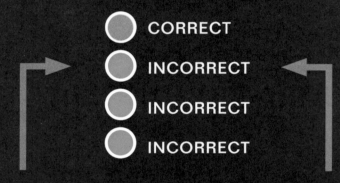

MKTG
ONLINE

PREPARE FOR TESTS ON THE STUDYBOARD!

CORRECT

INCORRECT

INCORRECT

INCORRECT

Personalize Quizzes from Your StudyBits

Take Practice Quizzes by Chapter

CHAPTER QUIZZES

▶ Chapter 1

Chapter 2

Chapter 3

Chapter 4

4LTR
PRESS

Access MKTG ONLINE at www.cengagebrain.com